OXFORD WORLD'S CLASSICS

===

W. B. Yeats
The Major Works

===

Edited with an Introduction and Notes by
EDWARD LARRISSY

OXFORD
UNIVERSITY PRESS

OXFORD
UNIVERSITY PRESS

Great Clarendon Street, Oxford OX2 6DP

Oxford University Press is a department of the University of Oxford.
It furthers the University's objective of excellence in research, scholarship,
and education by publishing worldwide in

Oxford New York

Athens Auckland Bangkok Bogotá Buenos Aires Cape Town
Chennai Dar es Salaam Delhi Florence Hong Kong Istanbul Karachi
Kolkata Kuala Lumpur Madrid Melbourne Mexico City Mumbai Nairobi
Paris São Paulo Shanghai Singapore Taipei Tokyo Toronto Warsaw

with associated companies in Berlin Ibadan

Oxford is a registered trade mark of Oxford University Press
in the UK and in certain other countries

British Library Cataloguing in Publication Data
Data available
ISBN 0–19–284283–8

3 5 7 9 10 8 6 4 2

Typeset by Jayvee, Trivandrum, India
Printed in Great Britain by
Clays Ltd, St Ives plc

W. B. YEATS

...don, ... the Metro-

... year his lifelong ... the occult began to take form when he helped to found ... Dublin Hermetic Society. In 1890 he joined the Hermetic Order of the Golden Dawn. At the same time he was a member of the Irish Republican Brotherhood, sharing a passion for Irish national liberation with Maud Gonne, the object of his unrequited love for many years. Irish mythology and folklore provided an important part of the subject-matter of his early work, and remained an inspiration to him throughout his life, although he never learnt the Irish language. Yeats was also a playwright and a founder-president of the Irish National Dramatic Society (1902), which was the basis of the Abbey Theatre, Dublin (1904), in which he was a producer-manager. After the establishment of the Irish Free State in 1922, Yeats became a senator. He won the Nobel Prize for literature in 1923. Yeats's early poetry is influenced by Romantic and Victorian models, but in the early years of the twentieth century he began to move towards what he saw as a clearer and more direct style. His later poems are regarded as among the greatest and most significant of the modern period. His occult researches remained at the centre of his thought, and are important for an understanding of many of his poems and plays. He claimed that his occult synthesis, *A Vision*, derived from communications of the spirit world with his wife, Georgie Hyde-Lees, whom he married in 1917. It exists in two different versions (1925 and 1937). Yeats died in France in 1939.

EDWARD LARRISSY is Professor of English Literature at the University of Leeds. He is the author of *William Blake* (1985), *Reading Twentieth-Century Poetry: The Language of Gender and Objects* (1990), and *Yeats the Poet: The Measures of Difference* (1994), and the editor of *Romanticism and Postmodernism* (1999).

OXFORD WORLD'S CLASSICS

*For over 100 years Oxford World's Classics have brought
readers closer to the world's great literature. Now with over 700
titles—from the 4,000-year-old myths of Mesopotamia to the
twentieth century's greatest novels—the series makes available
lesser-known as well as celebrated writing.*

*The pocket-sized hardbacks of the early years contained
introductions by Virginia Woolf, T. S. Eliot, Graham Greene,
and other literary figures which enriched the experience of reading.
Today the series is recognized for its fine scholarship and
reliability in texts that span world literature, drama and poetry,
religion, philosophy and politics. Each edition includes perceptive
commentary and essential background information to meet the
changing needs of readers.*

CONTENTS

Italics indicate a prose work

SHORTER POEMS AND LYRICS

From RESPONSIBILITIES (1914)

From THE WILD SWANS AT COOLE (1919)

INTRODUCTION

I

YEATS'S early work is usually seen as a late development of Romanticism: it would be quite surprising if it were not. He was born in 1865, only thirty-eight years after the death of his revered William Blake. He reached 15 years of age in 1880, when the reputations of Byron and Shelley, for example, were in the main still unchallenged and secure. But there are many different Romanticisms, and many ways of learning from them. Although Blake and Shelley are dominating influences on his work, his view of them was conditioned by the late nineteenth-century emphasis on lyric intensity and on the poetic characteristics required to achieve it: symbolism and musicality. It is hard to imagine the early Yeats even attempting to write something like the more abstract passages in Blake's Prophetic Books or the more philosophical ones in Shelley's *Prometheus Unbound*. And Yeats had recent and contemporary models to whom he could turn who would support his reading of Romanticism—the Pre-Raphaelites and, in particular, William Morris. It is not necessary, then, to assume the influence of French *symbolisme* on Yeats's earliest work, for instance on *The Wanderings of Oisin*, and indeed it is highly unlikely that this was an influence until he met Arthur Symons in the early 1890s, after the composition of *Oisin* and the poems which now come under the heading *Crossways*. Nevertheless, Symons, whose *The Symbolist Movement in Literature* (1899) was dedicated to Yeats, offered a more pondered theory and also new models, in the form of Verlaine and Mallarmé, in particular.

Verlaine's recommendation in his 'Art poétique' of suggestive musicality, and Mallarmé's in 'Crise de vers' of a technique of symbolic suggestion, are undoubted influences on the distilled intensity of Yeats's most truly symbolist volume *The Wind among the Reeds* (1899). It is, to say the least, unfortunate that this book, perhaps the one symbolist masterpiece in the English language, should have been for so long overshadowed by the anti-Romantic battles of Anglo-American modernism. A feature of these battles was the tendency to relegate Yeats's early 'Romantic' work in favour of the directness of the later work. Yet any dispassionate consideration of *The Wind among the Reeds* reveals a ruthless concentration of purpose and means, and a unique richness and complexity of effect.

Consider what is arguably one of the finest poems in the volume, 'The Song of Wandering Aengus'. The setting for the initial event is beside a stream in the twilight of dawn. Aengus is thus positioned both at a physical and a temporal boundary, and traditionally, both in Celtic and other folklores, boundaries could function like cracks or openings through which the supernatural could intervene. Since Aengus is fishing with 'a hazel wand', and hazel is a magical wood in Celtic tradition, he could be said to be asking for something magical to occur—something which will answer to the 'fire' of desire in his head. The fairy woman who then appears is that answer, the ideal woman of his dreams; and his subsequent lifelong pursuit of her is no more than what one should do with an ideal woman. When he finds her, in a land beyond time, he will bring together the alienated polarities of feminine and masculine, lunar and solar, plucking 'The silver apples of the moon, | The golden apples of the sun'. But these are also the cosmic polarities around which the whole universe is structured, the Night and Day of the world of time. The timeless principle of all things has thus been glimpsed through the initial twilight which divides night and day.

But the poem is far more than this symbolic scheme. It offers, for instance, an evocative picture of the uncertainty of twilight by bringing together in one impressionist image the flickering of the stars and the flickering of moths: 'when white moths were on the wing, | And moth-like stars were flickering out'. It picks up the word 'flickering' and makes music by echoing it with 'glimmering' and 'brightening'. Sounds, too, could be said to flicker: 'something rustled on the floor'. And the final stanza, with its reference to a magical orchard beyond the world, picks up the idea of flickering in the image of 'dappled grass', intensifying it musically by an internal rhyme with 'apples'. This reading should suggest that the idea of Yeats's early poetry as a repository of dim, misty words and emotions can be subject to severe qualification. Such a reaction often amounts to little more than a dislike of those features of style and diction which Yeats shares with other poets of the late nineteenth century. But much of his early poetry displays a comparable complexity.

Yeats's poetry, however, was even more systematically pondered than the above reading would suggest, and this also can be demonstrated on the basis of 'The Song of Wandering Aengus'. It was not merely the appreciation of a supernatural tale that led to the inclusion of that 'wand' in the poem, or of what amounts to a magical evocation, for Yeats did not see any essential difference between the symbols of poetry and those used in magical rituals: this is made absolutely clear in his essays on 'Magic' (pp. 344–50) and on 'The Symbolism of Poetry' (pp. 358–65).

The difference between the two uses of symbols is only one of purpose and intensity. Both in magical ritual and in poetry symbols allow us to evoke the 'great mind and great memory' (essay on 'Magic'), a concept that Yeats came to call *Anima Mundi* ('The Soul of the World'), and which bears a strong resemblance to Jung's 'Collective Unconscious', except that Yeats believed that his archetypal symbols possessed a real supernatural existence. From 1890 and for many years Yeats was a member of the Hermetic Order of the Golden Dawn, a secret society of magicians which included Aleister Crowley, the notorious practitioner of 'Sex Magick', and A. E. Waite, the designer of a Tarot pack which is still current. Yeats, then, was a magician, and it is not misleading to claim that his poems are magical, in the sense that they are intended to elicit in the minds of his readers a genuine contact with supernatural powers. Like magical rituals and invocations, they have to induce the right state of mind by the judicious use of symbols and the suggestive power of words.

Yeats's purpose in thus acting on the minds of his readers was also carefully pondered. It was, in fact, a nationalist purpose: to be precise, it was connected to the high value he placed on the Celtic temperament and its evocation: the latter would act as a powerful prompt to Irish lib-eration. If Yeats wanted to find Celtic magic he did not have far to look: the Druids were regarded by antiquarians such as Eugene O'Curry (1796–1862) as having practised a form of magic which was not essen-tially different from that of the Magi in the East. Yeats, taking the hint, believed that the outlines of magical belief and practice were everywhere the same, but that they had achieved a particularly developed form in Celtic Druidism. As he says in one of his last poems ('Under Ben Bul-ben'), 'And ancient Ireland knew it all'. Furthermore, he believed that the marginalization of the Celtic lands in the modern period had had at least one fortunate consequence, which was that the inhabitants of Celtic countries had remained far closer to the roots of magical thinking than those of industrialized countries. This belief, for which he is in part indebted to Ernest Renan and Matthew Arnold, is clearly expounded in his essay on 'The Celtic Element in Literature' (pp. 369–78). Yeats even thought, along with many other Celticists of the late nineteenth century, that the Celtic spirit would triumph in a new age that would dawn in the twentieth century.[1] So by bringing his readers' minds into contact with eternal powers, in the form in which they appeared in Celtic mythology,

---

[1] Marjorie Reeves and Warwick Gould, *Joachim of Fiore and the Myth of the Eternal Evangel* (Oxford, 1987), 202–29.

Yeats believed he was bringing the world in general closer to liberation from what he saw as the deadly materialism of progressive nineteenth-century thought. He also believed that he was creating sympathy abroad with the Irish cause, and, most of all, inspiring it with confidence at home—in fact, with the truest form of confidence there is, since he was feeding the spirit, where others could only offer the superficiality of what normally passes for political debate.

This is precisely the point he seeks to convey in his poem 'To Ireland in the Coming Times' (pp. 25-6), which is as much a political testament as a literary one. He compares himself with earlier nineteenth-century poets who had sought to create an Irish national poetry in English, and asserts that he should be regarded as the more patriotic precisely because of his magical endeavours:

> Nor may I less be counted one
> With Davis, Mangan, Ferguson,
> Because, to him who ponders well
> My rhymes more than their rhyming tell
> Of things discovered in the deep,
> Where only body's laid asleep.
> For the elemental creatures go
> About my table to and fro,
> That hurry from unmeasured mind . . .
> Ah, faeries, dancing under the moon,
> A Druid land, a Druid tune!

II

Yeats's poetic style changes in the early years of the twentieth century. A number of factors can be seen as contributing to an increasing direct-ness of language, and an increasing tendency to present himself, albeit with notable rhetorical artifice, as one who speaks directly to the reader out of a living context, sometimes with bitterness about Romantic dreams and even about the Irish people and Irish nationalism. Disillu-sion with the previous character of his relationship with Maud Gonne, the woman he loved, must be seen as a factor in this change. In the 1890s she had shared his millenarian hopes for the Celtic spirit and had even co-operated enthusiastically in his magical endeavours to bring about its renewal. Her revelation in 1898 that she had for long had a lover, Lucien Millevoye, was followed by her marriage to Major John MacBride in 1903. These were hard blows for Yeats, who had to be satisfied with a 'spiritual marriage' to her. The sense that he had become too passive and otherworldly, and that he must cultivate a 'masculine' spirit, found its aesthetic correlative in the belief that the poetry of the late nineteenth century, including his own, was decadent in a malign sense. His reading of Nietzsche contributed to this change of attitude. The new mood is struck in a poem such as 'Never Give all the Heart', from the volume *In the Seven Woods* (1904), and is memorably epitomized by a poem from the later volume *Responsibilities* (1914), 'A Coat'.

But there is another important fact to remember: Yeats was a play-wright, a founder member of the Irish Literary Theatre (1898), who for some years had been preoccupied with the problem of finding a supple and expressive medium for drama in verse. George Steiner derided the 'stained glass' quality of the plays, as if Yeats were some Victorian poet, inflicting on his audiences the sub-Shakespearian maunderings of peo-ple in picturesque costumes.[2] There may be something in this as regards the early plays, but it is obviously unfair about much of what Yeats wrote after 1916, when *At the Hawk's Well*, the first of the plays to be influ-enced by the Japanese Noh, was performed. The non-naturalistic assumptions which guided its writing, and even more strikingly, that of *The Only Jealousy of Emer* (pp. 270–81), are daring and innovative, with few characters, brief action, and the use of music and masks. Yeats developed the bold spareness he adopted in these experiments to good effect in plays that seem superficially more conventional, most notably *Purgatory* (pp. 334–40). He is rightly seen as a forerunner of Beckett's drama.

The tension between artifice and naturalness which sets in from the early years of the twentieth century continues throughout the rest of his work. It can be illuminated by reference to the drama, which can be seen both as requiring the sense of a living voice and as necessitating the adoption of a Mask. Yeats never ceases to believe in a supernatural realm inhabited by spirits and archetypal images, and these constitute a reposi-tory of eternally recurring moods or forms of life, which provide a lim-ited set of masks. In his great occult work *A Vision* (1925 and 1937: see pp. 422–42), there are only twenty-six masks which any human being can adopt in life, and they are handed down by a kind of supernatural stage-manager, the *Daimon*. Yet we have to make our way in the change-ableness of the world. Between these twin pressures Yeats creates the passionate and forceful rhetoric which characterizes so much of his mature work. The tension expresses itself in the subject-matter, as well as the style, of the poems. In 'Sailing to Byzantium' he yearns to be

---

[2] George Steiner, *The Death of Tragedy* (London, 1961), 318.

gathered into 'the artifice of eternity', dying into a condition like that of the sages in the gold mosaic of a church wall and thus transcending the pain of mortality. But in the very next poem in the volume (*The Tower*) he rages against the constraints of old age, longing to be able to express the youthful desires and energy which still animate him. The sages in their gold mosaic are the eternal images and symbols in yet another form; and indeed one cannot say that Yeats ceases to be a symbolist in many of his poems. But the mortal man's cry of anguish at mortality grows stronger in his later work, for instance in a poem such as 'The Spur':

> You think it horrible that lust and rage
> Should dance attendance upon my old age;
> They were not such a plague when I was young;
> What else have I to spur me into song?

III

It is not only against the Romanticism of the earlier work that poets and critics have reacted. One frequently encounters a distaste for what is called the 'rhetoric' of the later work, and in Ireland this has a political as well as an aesthetic meaning. The Northern Irish poet John Montague makes the aesthetic point in his poem, 'Tim', about an old farm horse who is not 'that legendary Pegasus', as a Yeatsian horse might be (and sometimes was). 'Tim' has a lesson for Montague, 'denying | rhetoric with your patience, | forcing me to drink | from the trough of reality.' But in 'Speech for an Ideal Irish Election', Montague refers to the 'Enlarged profile, gun and phrase' of the nationalist politician. Here he makes the link between the aesthetic and the political: between the rhetoric that is blind and the rhetoric that kills.

It was a link that Yeats himself was inclined to see in his own work: 'Did that play of mine send out | Certain men the English shot?' Yeats's question, about the influence on the Easter Rising of his nationalist play *Cathleen ni Houlihan*, was answered in the negative by Auden, when he asserted, in 'In Memory of W. B. Yeats', that 'poetry makes nothing happen'. In Ireland they are not so sure, and recent events will not have settled the matter in favour of Auden. Yet a profound irony attends any estimate of Yeats that emphasizes nationalist rhetoric, or even one that sees him, with Edward Said, as a 'poet of decolonization'.[3] To gauge the problem, it is not enough to state that Yeats came from an Anglo–Irish Protestant tra-

---

[3] Edward Said, 'Yeats and Decolonization', *Culture and Imperialism* (London, 1994), 278.

dition, for so did Emmet and Wolfe Tone and Parnell, as he constantly reminds us. Nevertheless, this is a good starting-point for reaching an understanding of Yeats's profound ambivalence about certain aspects of Irish nationalism. Part of this ambivalence is famously expressed in 'September 1913', during a period when he was tempted to despair of the possibility of an independent Ireland and was repelled by what he saw as the narrow philistinism and materialism of the Catholic middle class.

But there is more to this than temporary disillusionment; for Yeats is not only the author of the patriotic play *Cathleen ni Houlihan*, he is also the boy whose first songs were Orange rhymes, and whose dream was 'to die fighting the Fenians'. In the Introductory Rhymes to *Responsibilities* (1914) he proudly recalls his forebears who, in the Williamite wars, withstood 'James and his Irish'. He it is who, in the same volume, bestows on some of his compatriots the demeaning names 'Biddy' and 'Paudeen', the better to deride their priest-ridden venality. In 'Easter 1916', he is compelled by his continuing allegiance to celebrate the heroes of the Easter Rising, and moved by the kind of sacrifice for which he always had the deepest respect, but nevertheless finds it necessary, in the interests of truth, to remind us that he had always found these martyrs both irksome and comical. The portrait of Con Markievicz is particularly unsparing: 'That woman's days were spent | In ignorant good-will'. While she languished in prison, he wrote a poem lamenting her descent from lovely aristocrat to virulent demagogue: 'Blind and leader of the blind | Drinking the foul ditch where they lie' ('On a Political Prisoner'). As a Senator of the Irish Free State, he opposed Catholic-inspired measures to make divorce almost impossible, invoking Milton and Protestant liberty in a passionate and scornful peroration.

Yet Yeats, the former member of the Irish Republican Brotherhood, whose final poems remember not only Cuchulain but Patrick Pearse, is never one-sided. He is, after all, the poet of antinomies. But these antinomies take their form from one major antinomy: that which is involved in the hyphenated condition of being Anglo-Irish:

I had noticed that Irish Catholics among whom had been born so many political martyrs had not the good taste, the household courtesy and decency of the Protestant Ireland I had known, yet Protestant Ireland seemed to think of nothing but getting on in the world. I thought we might bring the halves together if we had a national literature that made Ireland beautiful in the memory, and yet had been freed from provincialism by an exacting criticism, a European pose.

The Anglo–Irish poet is better able than the Catholic one to perform this role of balancing measure and energy. Yet finding the balance is not a matter of achieving an ideal stasis, for 'wisdom is a butterfly, | And not a gloomy bird of prey'. It is a matter of trying out contrary positions, seeing the truth in each, like some shape-shifting Druid of Ancient Ireland, or like Blake in *Songs of Innocence and of Experience*. And from the songs of the Happy and Sad Shepherds to 'Vacillation' this is what Yeats does.

IV

Yet the experience of division, of 'antinomies', only increases the yearning for unity. Yeats's oft-repeated desire for 'Unity of Being' was paralleled in his early manhood by a desire for Unity of Culture. As I have suggested, Yeats saw a uniquely appropriate role for the Anglo–Irish poet in bringing this unity about. Nevertheless, the ideal implied an art that must remain in contact with the people. This contact was a two-way affair, whereby the artist would learn from folklore and ballad, but would also tour around Ireland with plays that were reminiscent of 'a mediaeval miracle play' in order that, in the end, 'the popular imagination' would be filled with Irish 'saints and heroes' (from the theatrical review *Samhain*, 1901). Yeats eventually despaired of the possibility of his kind of 'People's Theatre'. He was, of course, proud that he had been involved in creating anything remotely like it, as he had been in the case of the Irish Literary Theatre (later the Abbey Theatre). But the results convinced him that the objectivity and alienation of the modern world were so infectious that the imaginations both of playwrights and people were, on the whole, sullied. The experiment with a small-scale theatre influenced by the Noh must be seen as the movement towards a more aristocratic model of the arts, which were to become repositories of refinement and wisdom for the discerning few. Yet even this model still encompassed the organic life of the nation. In 'To a Wealthy Man . . .' (*Responsibilities*), Yeats asks, rhetorically, whether the Renaissance Duke Ercole d'Este of Ferrara consulted the critical taste of the onion-sellers in the market before he set about becoming a patron of the arts. Of course not. But the Duke was still intent on building a national tradition, as Yeats makes clear. And he remains wedded to the notion of an organic culture even after he asserts the commanding role of the aristocratic artist.

Turning from the social to the individual, Unity of Being has long been recognized as a central category in Yeats's thinking. Yet it has tended to be seen in broad terms, such as the union of thought and feeling, or body and soul. But Yeats's self-fashioning is not only an attempt to draw together aspects of experience, but also to find a public role that would connect with private experience, thus uniting thought and action. To take merely the activities of the 1890s: he sought a forum for his poetic ideas among a group of like-minded poets in the Rhymers' Club; he believed in magic, but he also joined a secret society of magicians; he wished for the independence of Ireland, so he joined the Irish Republican Brotherhood. His later membership of the Irish Senate is another example of this seeking for public expression. What one really has, then, is spheres of unified thought and action. And these spheres themselves are all connected in his thinking. Even his love for Maud Gonne can easily be connected with these overlapping spheres of public activity and private passion. She too is a fervent Irish patriot, so appropriately enough she becomes another in the long list of female personifications of Ireland, and is linked to the Irish poetic tradition, in which such personifications are legion, by acting the part of one of the most famous names in that list, Cathleen ni Houlihan, in the play of that title. But she also has to be brought into the circle of magicians, and is induced (quite willingly) to join the Order of the Golden Dawn. Part of the justification for this is the one referred to above, whereby the Celtic temperament is closely attuned to the world divined by magic.

This brings us back to the topic of magic and the occult sciences, which remains interwoven with Yeats's profoundest thoughts throughout his life, and should never be treated as an eccentricity to be discounted in a consideration of his poetry and criticism. To take one very telling example, Yeats's long experience as playwright and theatre-manager lies behind his development of the theory of the Mask, which holds that the artist can only find forceful and precise expression in the adoption of a willed and artificial persona. But there are more exotic sources of this theory than can be found in the costume-room. For they chiefly derive from Yeats's experiments with spiritualism and the occult sciences. It is well known that the concept of the Mask is closely related to that of the anti-self, as expounded in 'Anima Hominis' (pp. 410–15). The anti-self is very much what it sounds like: the image of a being that is opposite to the self. It is this very quality of being opposite that attracts the self, and leads it to try to adopt the semblance of the anti-self. This semblance is the Mask.

The idea of the anti-self was developed out of a number of seances which Yeats attended between 1909 and 1917. These seemed to indicate that his anti-self was not merely a collection of attributes opposite to his own, but a really existent spirit, namely that of the geographer Leo Africanus (c. 1485–c. 1554), a Moor of Spain educated in Morocco who had been forcibly converted to Catholicism in Rome, but had escaped to Tunis and renounced his conversion.[4] Many years ago Richard Ellmann described these seances and indicated their importance to Yeats.[5] But it is open to question whether the point has really been taken; whether, that is, it is widely enough understood that Yeats believed we walk haunted through our lives, and that the relationship with a ghost is the source of creativity. Of course, the spirit communications which led to the writing of *A Vision* are better known. But, while their message is of supreme importance to the understanding of Yeats, there is something less fundamental about them than the prior doctrine of the anti-self which, in any case, is incorporated into their thinking.

In recent years, however, there has been a most illuminating tendency to examine Yeats's occult interests in the light of his Anglo-Irish background. Most notably, R. F. Foster has pointed out the powerful strain of occultist enthusiasm among the Anglo-Irish, some of it connected to the pervasive Protestant institution of Freemasonry.[6] Not that Yeats was ever a Freemason. But the masonic connections of the Golden Dawn are well attested. The intersecting dark and light triangles of *A Vision* have their most obvious source in the Rosicrucian texts of Robert Fludd;[7] and Rosicrucianism was the main source for the speculations both of esoteric masonry and of the Golden Dawn. Since Yeats clearly believed that the magic and esoteric lore he knew were substantially the same as those known to the Druids, he was able to think of his Protestant inheritance as offering not only a system to vie with Catholicism, but one which had truer access to a perennial wisdom possessed by the ancient Celts.

But what can Yeats's 'hocus-pocus' mean to an agnostic and materialistic culture such as our own? Even to the religious his immaterialism can seem outmoded and naïve, as it must do to those, like the former bishop of Durham, who think that the orthodox idea of the Resurrection is of 'a conjuring trick with bones'. Of course, we can accept, as Yeats was sometimes inclined to do, the possibility that his ghostly instructors

---

[4] An edition of, and commentary upon, the automatic writing to which the seances gave rise is provided by Steve L. Adams and George Mills Harper (eds.), 'The Manuscript of "Leo Africanus" ', in Richard J. Finneran (ed.), *Yeats Annual No. 1* (London, 1982), 3–47.

[5] Richard Ellmann, *W. B. Yeats: The Man and the Masks*, 2nd edn. (London, 1979), 195–7.

[6] R. F. Foster, 'Protestant Magic: W. B. Yeats and the Spell of Irish History' (Chatterton Lecture, 1989), *Proceedings of the British Academy* 75 (1989), 243–66.

[7] Edward Larrissy, *Yeats the Poet: The Measures of Difference* (Hemel Hempstead, 1994), 144–7. Rosicrucianism in these islands was shaped by the work of Fludd (1574–1637). Some commentators on Yeats attempt to separate the Rosicrucian influence from that of Christianity and of the cabala (Jewish mystical writings). But Fludd was a Christian cabalist.

merely came to give him 'metaphors for poetry'. The point may seem somewhat weaker when we realize that those metaphors themselves have to do with the relationship between material existence and a world of really existent spirits, as in the concept of the anti-self. Yet we can, of course, treat the idea of that relationship precisely as one of the metaphors: a metaphor, that is, about images and their central import-ance in our lives; a metaphor in which spirit stands for image. We can attempt, then, to sidestep Yeats's assertions (for instance, in *Per Amica Silentia Lunae*: see pp. 410–22) that images are themselves of the same substance as spirits and inhabit the same world of *Anima Mundi*. This attempt can yield illuminating results, for while Yeats was talking about spirits he was, indeed, talking also about images, and he often did so in a way which left it open to the reader to remain agnostic about the spirits.

Another answer to the question would be less kind to the present moment: would question the assumption that much of what currently passes, at least in journals and newspapers, for consensus about the nature of reality should be accorded more respect than the cautious con-clusions reached by a man of Yeats's intelligence throughout a lifetime of learned speculation. But if this answer seems unpalatable, it may at least serve to introduce an important general point on similar lines. However much we may be in a position now to achieve a renewed sym-pathy with Yeats's problems and poetic modes, he is an unfashionable thinker: and the character of that unfashionableness may itself have value for us. For as with some of the other modernists, images of ancient aristocracy, heroism, and holiness are, in his work, allied with a con-temptuous critique of liberalism and conventional middle-class values. A radical right-wing thinker, such as Yeats, or his friend Ezra Pound, may help to open up the question of value by subverting, criticizing, and making strange the sinister utilitarianism and moral vacuity of the dom-inant tendencies of modern thought; may, indeed, help us to explore the question of the universality or relativity of values. It is unlikely that such help will become less necessary.

V

Speaking of fashion, how has Yeats's reputation fared? The question is interesting because it is not often asked, and because the answer is informa-tive about the state of literary culture at the present time. Towards the end of the twentieth century, over half a century since his death, the poet who has been elevated to the modernist trinity of Yeats, Eliot, and Pound is still the subject of a vast and, indeed, growing academic industry,

and among literary scholars there has been little disagreement with the
high estimate in which his work came to be held in the years after the First
World War. Furthermore, readers of poetry hold his work in the highest
esteem. Some of his poems are among the best-loved and most famous in
the English language. There has, however, been one curious, and prob-
ably transient, note of doubt. Among poets themselves, at least since about
1970, Yeats is less frequently seen as a possible model. How different
things were not so very long ago. In Britain he was a formative influence
on the poets who came to prominence in the 1950s and 1960s: on Thom
Gunn, on John Wain, even on the early Larkin and Hughes. In America
he haunted the work of Theodore Roethke, and was a palpable presence
in that of Allen Tate and the early John Berryman. Only in Ireland did
the disillusionment of the bards set in early, and there it was partly for
socio-historical reasons which themselves merit study. Of course, Yeats
had his followers there, in the shape of poets now little remembered, such
as F. R. Higgins or W. R. Rodgers, but for many this last Romantic and
would-be aristocrat was too remote from the realities of Ireland. Austin
Clarke sought to recover Gaelic measures and romance in a more authen-
tic form than he was able to find in Yeats's Celtic Twilight. And Patrick
Kavanagh asserted, by precept and example, that the Irish poet must find
the universal in the mundane clay of the Irish parish, or find it nowhere—
least of all in fairyland or Byzantium. Kavanagh is the most pervasive
Irish influence on the last generation of Irish poets, but they, like him,
went to England for models of a fidelity to experience they did not fully
recognize in Yeats. And so it is that, even in the case of a poet as sympa-
thetic to Yeats as Seamus Heaney, the comparisons one seeks with his
early work seem to come more readily from Hardy, or Edward Thomas,
and also from the more grittily Teutonic aspects of Ted Hughes.

   Implicit in these reactions is the reaction against symbolism and Roman-
ticism. One may, of course, ask whether there are many in the long list of
twentieth-century rebellions against Romanticism which have succeeded
in escaping from it. Arguably these poets merely exchange the idealism and
symbolism of post-Shelleyan Romanticism for the fidelity to experience of
a post-Wordsworthian variety. But the question is how they themselves
saw the matter, and there can be little doubt about the answer to that.

   But it is probable that the generation of poets now learning their craft
will be better able than the last to understand what Yeats was trying to
accomplish. As we have seen, in his middle and late periods he invests
much energy in a strong rhetorical voice, and often does so in the service
of contrary positions. To be always fine and forceful in utterance, but sel-
dom decided in conviction, is a curious state to inhabit. Yet perhaps it is

a state with which we can recover some sympathy in the postmodern world, where we doubt of any deep truth, but value the styles and masks a provisional truth may adopt. Certainly the work of a poet who can reasonably be called postmodern—John Ashbery—suggests a parallel at this rather general level. For Ashbery also is sententious, rhetorical, even florid, though his scepticism is far more corrosively profound than Yeats's. But if we really understood the legacy of Romanticism, instead of reworking the partial polemics of Eliot and Pound, we should perhaps not be surprised to find that the last Romantic was also the first postmodern. It is some years now since Frank Kermode made the essential point in *Romantic Image* of linking the discovery of subjective truth, in Wilde and Yeats, with the cultivation of style and mask.[8] He proceeded to show how the artifacts thus created prefigure the autonomy accorded to modernist works. If postmodernism is indebted to modernism for almost everything but the depth of its scepticism, we should not be surprised to find that it too, like modernism, is still indebted to Romanticism.

Of course, another side of being a last Romantic is to display frequent nostalgia for a lost organic society, or seek present rootedness in hallowed places, and Yeats does these things. Yet his aesthetic is inimical to mere mimesis, and the ambiguous syntax, remote imagery, and vacillation of many of his poems make such connections seem problematic. The condition of being Anglo-Irish is at the root of this divided enterprise, though it might be claimed that most Irish writing is conditioned by social fissuring and a consciousness of warring signs, and that this is the reason for the semiotic disruptions to which it is so challengingly prone. Here again the present generation, educated to perceive the divided inheritances of post-colonialism, may find it easier to understand Yeats's ambivalent attitudes and poses, and, to turn the accusation around, find them truer to experience than a naïve search for origins, or the belief that one can make an enduring art out of 'accurate perception', as some contemporary poets seem to believe.

VI

This volume aims to provide a comprehensive and representative selection of Yeats's writings in all kinds. No other book offers plays, criticism, and other types of writing alongside the poems in one volume. This mere fact makes it a uniquely valuable resource for the student and the general reader. It is obvious, however, that I have been more

[8] Frank Kermode, *Romantic Image* (London, 1957), 43–8.

generous in my representations of poems and plays than of other genres, which is because I believe that Yeats's reputation must continue to rest on his achievements as poet and playwright. The volume will be the more useful for reflecting this belief.

Within the sections allotted to each type of writing, this edition takes a broadly chronological approach. Thus, in the case of the shorter poems, we start with a selection from *Crossways*, which was the name given to a group of poems in *Poems* (1895), most of which had come from *The Wanderings of Oisin and Other Poems* (1889), and we finish with a selection of the poems to be found in *Last Poems and Two Plays* (1939). Yeats kept rewriting his poems, though, and this edition offers the last published versions in which his intention was expressed, which means that he has often revised them significantly. Nevertheless, in reading the poems in the order in which they were first published one can best judge the development of Yeats's poetic style. But other considerations, of course, played a vital part in the selections here. Thus, in the case of the plays it was essential to give examples of his early manner as well as of the switch to a style influenced by some acquaintance with the Japanese Noh theatre, here represented by *The Only Jealousy of Emer* (1919). There are other reasons for choosing this play, however, for it also belongs, in virtue of its subject-matter, to the Cuchulain cycle: that is, a group of plays which treat episodes in the life of Cuchulain, the champion warrior of ancient Ulster, who is the hero of a number of sagas in Old Irish. Of the plays printed here, *On Baile's Strand* (1904) and *The Death of Cuchulain* (1939) also belong to this group, and the great tragic tale of *Deirdre* (1907) derives from the same saga material. The figure of Cuchulain, who makes several appearances in the poetry, is central to Yeats's idea of the hero. These plays are essential reading for anyone wishing to arrive at a true estimate of that idea. The selection here also departs from chronology by following Yeats's practice, in his *Collected Plays*, of printing *On Baile's Strand* after *Deirdre* and before *The Only Jealousy of Emer*: this ordering allows an intelligible consecutive reading of all three.

In selecting critical essays I have chosen to give full representation to those well-known early essays in which Yeats expounds his idiosyncratic magical symbolism, and his indebtedness to Blake and Shelley. To Blake he owes a particular debt, and in the process of incurring it he became a serious Blake scholar, as the three-volume edition he prepared with Edwin Ellis makes clear. Yeats felt ambivalent about the propensity to 'measurement' associated with Blake's invented deity, Urizen, who represents a kind of God the Father with a taste for mathematics, and in view of the importance of 'measurement' in Yeats's work, it seemed illuminating to include part of the commentary on Blake's *Book of Urizen* from the edition. The essay on 'The Theatre' should be useful in a volume containing a selection of plays. And the late essay, 'A General Introduction for my Work', seemed indispensable in a selection such as this. The social commentary from *On the Boiler* remains too little known. The eugenic theories expounded there do not show Yeats in a favourable light, although similar ideas were much more common in all sections of the intelligentsia until after the Second World War, whether or not they had, like Yeats, flirted with fascism. However, a knowledge of Yeats's views on these matters is certainly relevant to an understanding of the play *Purgatory* and of some of the later poems: what, for instance, does he really mean when he refers, in 'Under Ben Bulben' (composed 1938), to 'Base-born products of base beds'? Yeats's politics were by no means uniformly illiberal, though, as the Senate Speeches on Divorce and on The Condition of Schools indicate (pp. 448–52). In the 1920s, when these speeches were made in the Senate of the newly established Irish Free State, in which the Catholic Church exercised a dominant influence on social policy, Yeats was cast in the role of the Anglo-Irish defender of a liberal, civilized Protestant tradition, and he relished the part. His sense of the value of that tradition gave him a nicely distanced eye about new enthusiasms, such as that for reviving the Irish language, a goal with which he nevertheless sympathized (p. 448).

I have chosen to group together certain writings I call 'Occult Speculation'. This is partly because I want to convey the fact that Yeats's beliefs in these matters were subject to evolution. The female *Daimon* in a memorable passage from the first version of *A Vision* (1925; pp. 428–30) is notably different from the more generally known stage-manager of the second version (1937). Furthermore, the discussions of the anti-self and the spirit world in *Per Amica Silentia Lunae* give a much clearer and more memorable conception of some of the essential co-ordinates of Yeats's occult thinking than are to be found in the more abstract handling of *A Vision*.

In the case of the autobiographical writings I have concentrated on recollections of three people who could be said to have modified Yeats's imaginative life, except in the case of the first passage, about his childhood days in Sligo, because of its revealing glimpse of a significantly Protestant context in which even the stable-boy sang Orange rhymes (p. 453). And in the case of the letters I have attempted to give a glimpse of Yeats's developing aesthetic thought, which is rendered the more trenchant and suggestive because of the relatively improvised character of their formulations.

ACKNOWLEDGEMENTS

I should like to acknowledge the great benefit conferred on me by the President and Fellows of St John's College, Oxford, in awarding me a Summer Scholarship in 1992 which provided me with much-needed time in which I was able to make use of the Bodleian Library and the English Faculty Library. I am also grateful to be able to acknowledge the warm encouragement offered by that most learned Yeatsian, Professor John Kelly, while I was there. He can, however, bear no responsibility for the errors I have committed, since, as far as I know, he has never seen a word of this edition, and in any case, I had made no decisions at that point.

I am indebted to the theoretical and practical labours of Richard J. Finneran, as all modern editors of Yeats should be. I have also found it useful to consider some of the decisions reached by Timothy Webb in his Penguin selection, *W. B. Yeats* (1991). And I have derived much profit from the commentaries of A. N. Jeffares.

I should also like to acknowledge the valuable advice offered by the readers for Oxford University Press, and the patient encouragement of my editor, Judith Luna.

CHRONOLOGY

1865 William Butler Yeats born (13 June) in Dublin, son of John Butler Yeats and Susan (née Pollexfen).

1866 Susan Mary (Lily) Yeats born.

1867 The family moves to London.

1868 Elizabeth Corbet (Lolly) Yeats born.

1871 Jack Butler Yeats born.

1884 Yeats enters the School of Art, Dublin.

1885 Yeats a founding member of the Dublin Hermetic Society. First poems published in *Dublin University Review*.

1887 The family returns to London. Yeats joins the Blavatsky Lodge of the Theosophical Society, and publishes his first poems in English magazines.

1888 Yeats joins esoteric section of Theosophical Society.

1889 Yeats publishes first book of poems, *The Wanderings of Oisin and other Poems*. Begins edition of Blake with Edwin Ellis. Edits *Fairy and Folk Tales of the Irish Peasantry*. Meets and falls in love with Maud Gonne.

1890 Joins the Hermetic Order of the Golden Dawn.

1891 Founding member of the Rhymers' Club, London-Irish Literary Society and National Literary Society in Dublin, with John O'Leary as president.

1892 *The Countess Kathleen and Various Legends and Lyrics*.

1893 *The Celtic Twilight*; and *The Works of William Blake*, 3 vols. (with Edwin Ellis).

1894 Meets Mrs Olivia Shakespear.

1895 *Poems* (his first collected edition). Edits *A Book of Irish Verse*.

1896 Meets Lady Gregory. Member of the Irish Republican Brotherhood.

1897 *The Secret Rose*.

1898 Plans Irish Literary Theatre with Edward Martyn and Lady Gregory.

1899 *The Wind among the Reeds*.

1900 Yeats's mother dies. He forms a new Order of the Golden Dawn after disagreements with Aleister Crowley and MacGregor Mathers.

1902 Becomes president of the Irish National Dramatic Society.

Cathleen ni Houlihan is performed in Dublin, with Maud Gonne in the title role.

1903   *In the Seven Woods* and *Ideas of Good and Evil*. Maud Gonne marries Major John MacBride.

1904   The Abbey Theatre, Dublin, opens. Yeats is producer-manager.

1905   *Stories of Red Hanrahan*.

1906   *Poems 1895–1905*.

1907   Yeats defies rioters at performance of J. M. Synge's *The Playboy of the Western World*. Tours Italy with Lady Gregory and her son Robert. His father departs for New York.

1908   *Collected Poems*, 8 vols. Visits Maud Gonne in Paris. Meets Ezra Pound.

1909   Death of J. M. Synge.

1910   Yeats receives a Civil List pension of £150 p.a.

1911   Meets his future wife, Georgie Hyde-Lees.

1913   Ezra Pound acts as Yeats's secretary.

1914   *Responsibilities*.

1915   Yeats refuses a knighthood.

1916   The Easter Rising. Maud Gonne's husband, Major John MacBride, is executed for his part in it. Yeats proposes to Maud Gonne and is refused.

1917   Yeats proposes to Maud Gonne's daughter, Iseult, and is refused. Marries Georgie Hyde-Lees (20 October). Shortly afterwards she begins to produce the automatic writing which provides the material for *A Vision*. *The Wild Swans at Coole* published.

1919   Anne Butler Yeats born (26 Feb.) in Dublin. Move to Ballylee. Winter spent in Oxford.

1920   American tour, accompanied by Mrs Yeats.

1921   Michael Butler Yeats born (22 Aug.). *Michael Robartes and the Dancer*.

1922   Irish Free State established. Irish Civil War as a result of Constitution accepting the partition of Ireland. Yeats made a senator of the new state.

1923   Yeats receives the Nobel Prize for literature, and visits Stockholm to receive it (Dec.), where he delivers his acceptance speech, *The Bounty of Sweden*.

1924   Work towards completion of the first version of *A Vision*. Visits Sicily (Nov.).

1926   First version of *A Vision* published Jan., dated 1925.

1927   Congestion of the lungs and influenza lead to collapse.

1928 Rapallo (Apr.). Declines to stand for re-election to Irish Senate because of ill-health. *The Tower*.

1929 Last visit to Ballylee in the summer. Collapse from Malta fever in Rapallo (Dec.).

1931 Receives D.Litt. from Oxford (May). Spends winter at Coole Park with Lady Gregory, who is dying.

1932 Death of Lady Gregory (May). Yeats helps to found Irish Academy of Letters.

1933 *The Winding Stair and Other Poems. Collected Poems.*

1934 Steinach rejuvenation operation. *Collected Plays*.

1935 Attacks of lung congestion. Collaborates with Shri Purohit Swami on translation of *Upanishads. A Full Moon in March* published.

1936 Seriously ill. Heart problems and nephritis. BBC broadcast on Modern Poetry. His edition of *The Oxford Book of Modern Verse* published.

1937 More BBC broadcasts. Revised version of *A Vision* published. *Essays 1931–1936*.

1938 Jan.–Mar. in the south of France. Last public appearance for Abbey Theatre performance of *Purgatory* (Aug.). *New Poems*.

1939 Dies 28 Jan. Buried Roquebrune, France.

1948 Yeats's body reinterred at Drumcliff churchyard, Sligo.

NOTE ON THE TEXT

In general, I have used the last published version in which Yeats expressed his intention. Thus, for the poems up to and including *The Winding Stair*, I print the versions in *Collected Poems* (1933), except that the texts of 'The Phases of the Moon', 'Leda and the Swan', and 'All Souls' Night' are those to be found in *A Vision* (1937). The texts of *A Full Moon in March* (1935), *New Poems* (1938), and *On the Boiler* (1939) provide the copy-texts for the selections from those volumes. The selection of *Last Poems* is taken from *Last Poems and Two Plays*, except that some are based on *London Mercury*, December 1938 ('Hound Voice'; 'John Kinsella's Lament for Mrs Mary Moore'; 'High Talk'); *London Mercury*, January 1939 ('Man and the Echo'; 'The Circus Animals' Desertion'; 'Politics'); and *London Mercury*, March 1939 ('The Statues'; 'News for the Delphic Oracle'; 'Long-legged Fly'; 'A Bronze Head').

The texts of the plays are as follows. From *Nine One-Act Plays* (1937): *Cathleen ni Houlihan, Deirdre, On Baile's Strand, The Words upon the Window-Pane*. From *The Collected Plays of W. B. Yeats* (1934): *The Only Jealousy of Emer, Calvary, The Cat and the Moon, The Resurrection*. From *Last Poems and Two Plays* (Dublin, 1939): *The Death of Cuchulain*. From *On the Boiler* (Dublin, 1939): *Purgatory*.

The extract from the edition of Blake edited by Yeats and Edwin Ellis (1893) comes from the edition itself. The ensuing essays, up to and including 'The Moods' and originally published in *Ideas of Good and Evil* (1903), are based on the texts in *Essays* (1924), as are the extracts from *Per Amica Silentia Lunae*. The story, 'The Adoration of the Magi', is in the text to be found in *Early Poems and Stories* (1925). For copyright reasons 'A General Introduction for my Work' is taken from *Explorations* (1962), and the texts of the letters from *The Collected Letters of W. B. Yeats*, vol. i: *1865–1895*, ed. John Kelly and Eric Domville (Oxford, 1986) for the first two printed; from the third volume of the same edition, *1901–1904*, ed. John Kelly and Ronald Schuchard (1994) for the next one; and from *The Letters of W. B. Yeats*, ed. Allan Wade (London, 1954) for the remainder. I am grateful to John Kelly for permission to copy the letters mentioned from *The Collected Letters*. The remainder are reprinted from *Letters of W. B. Yeats*, ed. Allan Wade (Rupert Hart-Davis, 1954), by permission of Oxford University Press as publisher of *The Collected Letters of W. B. Yeats* (General Editor John Kelly).

The selections from the two versions of *A Vision* come directly from the texts. The Senate Speeches come from *Seanad Éireann* (Proceedings of the Irish Senate), and the autobiographical writings from *The Autobiography of W. B. Yeats* (New York, 1938).

Note that, since this book is a selection of writings in various kinds, it cannot be assumed that any of the competing theories about how to compile a *Collected Poems* of Yeats has direct relevance to the selection of poems found here.

The degree sign (°) indicates a note at the end of the book.

SHORTER POEMS AND LYRICS

From Crossways (1889)°

'The stars are threshed, and the souls are threshed from their husks.'°
WILLIAM BLAKE

The Song of the Happy Shepherd

The woods of Arcady are dead,°
And over is their antique joy;
Of old the world on dreaming fed;
Grey Truth is now her painted toy;
Yet still she turns her restless head:
But O, sick children of the world,
Of all the many changing things
In dreary dancing past us whirled,
To the cracked tune that Chronos sings,°
Words alone are certain good.   10
Where are now the warring kings,
Word be-mockers?—By the Rood°
Where are now the warring kings?
An idle word is now their glory,
By the stammering schoolboy said,
Reading some entangled story:
The kings of the old time are dead;
The wandering earth herself may be
Only a sudden flaming word,
In clanging space a moment heard,   20
Troubling the endless reverie.

Then nowise worship dusty deeds,
Nor seek, for this is also sooth,
To hunger fiercely after truth,
Lest all thy toiling only breeds
New dreams, new dreams; there is no truth
Saving in thine own heart. Seek, then,
No learning from the starry men,
Who follow with the optic glass
The whirling ways of stars that pass—   30
Seek, then, for this is also sooth,

No word of theirs—the cold star-bane
Has cloven and rent their hearts in twain,
And dead is all their human truth.
Go gather by the humming sea
Some twisted, echo-harbouring shell,
And to its lips thy story tell,
And they thy comforters will be,
Rewarding in melodious guile°
Thy fretful words a little while,   40
Till they shall singing fade in ruth
And die a pearly brotherhood;
For words alone are certain good:
Sing, then, for this is also sooth.

I must be gone: there is a grave
Where daffodil and lily wave,
And I would please the hapless faun,
Buried under the sleepy ground,
With mirthful songs before the dawn.
His shouting days with mirth were crowned;   50
And still I dream he treads the lawn,
Walking ghostly in the dew,
Pierced by my glad singing through,
My songs of old earth's dreamy youth:
But ah! she dreams not now; dream thou!
For fair are poppies on the brow:
Dream, dream, for this is also sooth.

The Sad Shepherd

There was a man whom Sorrow named his friend,
And he, of his high comrade Sorrow dreaming,
Went walking with slow steps along the gleaming
And humming sands, where windy surges wend:
And he called loudly to the stars to bend
From their pale thrones and comfort him, but they
Among themselves laugh on and sing alway:
And then the man whom Sorrow named his friend
Cried out, *Dim sea, hear my most piteous story!*
The sea swept on and cried her old cry still,   10

Rolling along in dreams from hill to hill.
He fled the persecution of her glory
And, in a far-off, gentle valley stopping,
Cried all his story to the dewdrops glistening.
But naught they heard, for they are always listening,
The dewdrops, for the sound of their own dropping.
And then the man whom Sorrow named his friend
Sought once again the shore, and found a shell,
And thought, *I will my heavy story tell*
Till my own words, re-echoing, shall send 20
Their sadness through a hollow, pearly heart;
And my own tale again for me shall sing,
And my own whispering words be comforting,
And lo! my ancient burden may depart.
Then he sang softly nigh the pearly rim;
But the sad dweller by the sea-ways lone
Changed all he sang to inarticulate moan
Among her wildering whirls, forgetting him.

The Indian upon God

I passed along the water's edge below the humid trees,
My spirit rocked in evening light, the rushes round my knees,
My spirit rocked in sleep and sighs; and saw the moor-fowl pace
All dripping on a grassy slope, and saw them cease to chase
Each other round in circles, and heard the eldest speak:
Who holds the world between His bill and made us strong or weak
Is an undying moorfowl, and He lives beyond the sky.
The rains are from His dripping wing, the moonbeams from His eye.
I passed a little further on and heard a lotus talk:
Who made the world and ruleth it, He hangeth on a stalk, 10
For I am in His image made, and all this tinkling tide
Is but a sliding drop of rain between His petals wide.
A little way within the gloom a roebuck raised his eyes
Brimful of starlight, and he said: *The Stamper of the Skies,*
He is a gentle roebuck; for how else, I pray, could He
Conceive a thing so sad and soft, a gentle thing like me?
I passed a little further on and heard a peacock say:
Who made the grass and made the worms and made my feathers gay,

He is a monstrous peacock, and He waveth all the night
His languid tail above us, lit with myriad spots of light.   20

The Indian to his Love

The island dreams under the dawn
And great boughs drop tranquillity;
The peahens dance on a smooth lawn,
A parrot sways upon a tree,
Raging at his own image in the enamelled sea.

Here we will moor our lonely ship
And wander ever with woven hands,
Murmuring softly lip to lip,
Along the grass, along the sands,
Murmuring how far away are the unquiet lands: 10

How we alone of mortals are
Hid under quiet boughs apart,
While our love grows an Indian star,
A meteor of the burning heart,
One with the tide that gleams, the wings that gleam
    and dart,

The heavy boughs, the burnished dove
That moans and sighs a hundred days:
How when we die our shades will rove,
When eve has hushed the feathered ways,
With vapoury footsole by the water's drowsy blaze.   20

Ephemera

'Your eyes that once were never weary of mine
Are bowed in sorrow under pendulous lids,
Because our love is waning.'
                    And then she:
'Although our love is waning, let us stand
By the lone border of the lake once more,
Together in that hour of gentleness
When the poor tired child, Passion, falls asleep:

How far away the stars seem, and how far
Is our first kiss, and ah, how old my heart!'
Pensive they paced along the faded leaves,   10
While slowly he whose hand held hers replied:
'Passion has often worn our wandering hearts.'

The woods were round them, and the yellow leaves
Fell like faint meteors in the gloom, and once
A rabbit old and lame limped down the path;
Autumn was over him: and now they stood
On the lone border of the lake once more:
Turning, he saw that she had thrust dead leaves
Gathered in silence, dewy as her eyes,
In bosom and hair.
                            'Ah, do not mourn,' he said,   20
'That we are tired, for other loves await us;
Hate on and love through unrepining hours.
Before us lies eternity; our souls
Are love, and a continual farewell.'

The Madness of King Goll°

I sat on cushioned otter-skin:
My word was law from Ith to Emain,°
And shook at Invar Amargin°
The hearts of the world-troubling seamen,
And drove tumult and war away
From girl and boy and man and beast;
The fields grew fatter day by day,
The wild fowl of the air increased;
And every ancient Ollave said,°
While he bent down his fading head,   10
'He drives away the Northern cold.'
They will not hush, the leaves a-flutter round me,
     the beech leaves old.

I sat and mused and drank sweet wine;
A herdsman came from inland valleys,
Crying, the pirates drove his swine
To fill their dark-beaked hollow galleys.

I called my battle-breaking men
And my loud brazen battle-cars
From rolling vale and rivery glen;
And under the blinking of the stars   20
Fell on the pirates by the deep,
And hurled them in the gulph of sleep:
These hands won many a torque of gold.
They will not hush, the leaves a-flutter round me,
    the beech leaves old.

But slowly, as I shouting slew
And trampled in the bubbling mire,
In my most secret spirit grew
A whirling and a wandering fire:
I stood: keen stars above me shone,
Around me shone keen eyes of men: 30
I laughed aloud and hurried on
By rocky shore and rushy fen;
I laughed because birds fluttered by,
And starlight gleamed, and clouds flew high,
And rushes waved and waters rolled.
They will not hush, the leaves a-flutter round me,
    the beech leaves old.

And now I wander in the woods
When summer gluts the golden bees,
Or in autumnal solitudes
Arise the leopard-coloured trees;   40
Or when along the wintry strands
The cormorants shiver on their rocks;
I wander on, and wave my hands,
And sing, and shake my heavy locks.
The grey wolf knows me; by one ear
I lead along the woodland deer;
The hares run by me growing bold.
They will not hush, the leaves a-flutter round me,
    the beech leaves old.

I came upon a little town
That slumbered in the harvest moon,
And passed a-tiptoe up and down,   50

Murmuring, to a fitful tune,
How I have followed, night and day,
A tramping of tremendous feet,
And saw where this old tympan lay
Deserted on a doorway seat,
And bore it to the woods with me;
Of some inhuman misery
Our married voices wildly trolled.
They will not hush, the leaves a-flutter round me,
    the beech leaves old.   60

I sang how, when day's toil is done,
Orchil shakes out her long dark hair°
That hides away the dying sun
And sheds faint odours through the air:
When my hand passed from wire to wire
It quenched, with sound like falling dew,
The whirling and the wandering fire;
But lift a mournful ulalu,°
For the kind wires are torn and still,
And I must wander wood and hill   70
Through summer's heat and winter's cold.
They will not hush, the leaves a-flutter round me,
    the beech leaves old.

The Stolen Child

Where dips the rocky highland
Of Sleuth Wood in the lake,°
There lies a leafy island
Where flapping herons wake
The drowsy water-rats;
There we've hid our faery vats,
Full of berries
And of reddest stolen cherries.
Come away, O human child!
To the waters and the wild   10
With a faery, hand in hand,
For the world's more full of weeping than you
    can understand.

Where the wave of moonlight glosses
The dim grey sands with light,
Far off by furthest Rosses°
We foot it all the night,
Weaving olden dances,
Mingling hands and mingling glances
Till the moon has taken flight;
To and fro we leap   20
And chase the frothy bubbles,
While the world is full of troubles
And is anxious in its sleep.
Come away, O human child!
To the waters and the wild
With a faery, hand in hand,
For the world's more full of weeping than you
        can understand.

Where the wandering water gushes
From the hills above Glen-Car,°
In pools among the rushes   30
That scarce could bathe a star,
We seek for slumbering trout
And whispering in their ears
Give them unquiet dreams;
Leaning softly out
From ferns that drop their tears
Over the young streams.
Come away, O human child!
To the waters and the wild
With a faery, hand in hand,   40
For the world's more full of weeping than you
        can understand.

Away with us he's going,
The solemn-eyed:
He'll hear no more the lowing
Of the calves on the warm hillside
Or the kettle on the hob
Sing peace into his breast,
Or see the brown mice bob
Round and round the oatmeal-chest.

For he comes, the human child,   50
To the waters and the wild
With a faery, hand in hand,
From a world more full of weeping than he
*   can understand.*

Down by the Salley Gardens°

Down by the salley gardens my love and I did meet;
She passed the salley gardens with little snow-white feet.
She bid me take love easy, as the leaves grow on the tree;
But I, being young and foolish, with her would not agree.

In a field by the river my love and I did stand,
And on my leaning shoulder she laid her snow-white hand.
She bid me take life easy, as the grass grows on the weirs;
But I was young and foolish, and now am full of tears.

The Ballad of Father O'Hart

Good Father John O'Hart
In penal days rode out°
To a shoneen who had free lands°
And his own snipe and trout.

In trust took he John's lands;
Sleiveens were all his race;°
And he gave them as dowers to his daughters,
And they married beyond their place.

But Father John went up,
And Father John went down;   10
And he wore small holes in his shoes,
And he wore large holes in his gown.

All loved him, only the shoneen,
Whom the devils have by the hair,
From the wives, and the cats, and the children,
To the birds in the white of the air.

The birds, for he opened their cages
As he went up and down;
And he said with a smile, 'Have peace now';
And he went his way with a frown.   20

But if when anyone died
Came keeners hoarser than rooks,
He bade them give over their keening;°
For he was a man of books.

And these were the works of John,
When, weeping score by score,
People came into Coloony;°
For he'd died at ninety-four.

There was no human keening;
The birds from Knocknarea°   30
And the world round Knocknashee°
Came keening in that day.

The young birds and old birds
Came flying, heavy and sad;
Keening in from Tiraragh,°
Keening from Ballinafad;°

Keening from Inishmurray,°
Nor stayed for bite or sup;
This way were all reproved
Who dig old customs up.   40

From The Rose (1893)°

To the Rose upon the Rood of Time

Red Rose, proud Rose, sad Rose of all my days!
Come near me, while I sing the ancient ways:
Cuchulain battling with the bitter tide;°
The Druid, grey, wood-nurtured, quiet-eyed,

Who cast round Fergus dreams, and ruin untold;°
And thine own sadness, whereof stars, grown old
In dancing silver-sandalled on the sea,
Sing in their high and lonely melody.
Come near, that no more blinded by man's fate,
I find under the boughs of love and hate,   10
In all poor foolish things that live a day,
Eternal beauty wandering on her way.

Come near, come near, come near—Ah, leave me still
A little space for the rose-breath to fill!
Lest I no more hear common things that crave;
The weak worm hiding down in its small cave,
The field-mouse running by me in the grass,
And heavy mortal hopes that toil and pass;
But seek alone to hear the strange things said
By God to the bright hearts of those long dead,   20
And learn to chaunt a tongue men do not know.
Come near; I would, before my time to go,
Sing of old Eire and the ancient ways:
Red Rose, proud Rose, sad Rose of all my days.

Fergus and the Druid°

Fergus. This whole day have I followed in the rocks,
     And you have changed and flowed from shape to shape,
     First as a raven on whose ancient wings
     Scarcely a feather lingered, then you seemed
     A weasel moving on from stone to stone,
     And now at last you wear a human shape,
     A thin grey man half lost in gathering night.

Druid. What would you, king of the proud Red Branch
     kings?°

Fergus. This would I say, most wise of living souls:
     Young subtle Conchubar sat close by me   10
     When I gave judgment, and his words were wise,
     And what to me was burden without end,
     To him seemed easy, so I laid the crown
     Upon his head to cast away my sorrow.

Druid. What would you, king of the proud Red Branch
   kings?

Fergus. A king and proud! and that is my despair.
   I feast amid my people on the hill,
   And pace the woods, and drive my chariot-wheels
   In the white border of the murmuring sea;
   And still I feel the crown upon my head.   20

Druid. What would you, Fergus?

Fergus.   Be no more a king
   But learn the dreaming wisdom that is yours.

Druid. Look on my thin grey hair and hollow cheeks
   And on these hands that may not lift the sword,
   This body trembling like a wind-blown reed.
   No woman's loved me, no man sought my help.

Fergus. A king is but a foolish labourer
   Who wastes his blood to be another's dream.

Druid. Take, if you must, this little bag of dreams;
   Unloose the cord, and they will wrap you round.   30

Fergus. I see my life go drifting like a river
   From change to change; I have been many things—
   A green drop in the surge, a gleam of light
   Upon a sword, a fir-tree on a hill,
   An old slave grinding at a heavy quern,
   A king sitting upon a chair of gold—
   And all these things were wonderful and great;
   But now I have grown nothing, knowing all.
   Ah! Druid, Druid, how great webs of sorrow
   Lay hidden in the small slate-coloured thing!   40

Cuchulain's Fight with the Sea°

   A man came slowly from the setting sun,
   To Emer, raddling raiment in her dun,°
   And said, 'I am that swineherd whom you bid

Go watch the road between the wood and tide,
But now I have no need to watch it more.'

Then Emer cast the web upon the floor,
And raising arms all raddled with the dye,
Parted her lips with a loud sudden cry.

That swineherd stared upon her face and said,
'No man alive, no man among the dead,   10
Has won the gold his cars of battle bring.'

'But if your master comes home triumphing
Why must you blench and shake from foot to crown?'

Thereon he shook the more and cast him down
Upon the web-heaped floor, and cried his word:
'With him is one sweet-throated like a bird.'

'You dare me to my face,' and thereupon
She smote with raddled fist, and where her son
Herded the cattle came with stumbling feet,
And cried with angry voice, 'It is not meet   20
To idle life away, a common herd.'

'I have long waited, mother, for that word:
But wherefore now?'
                              'There is a man to die;
You have the heaviest arm under the sky.'

'Whether under its daylight or its stars
My father stands amid his battle-cars.'

'But you have grown to be the taller man.'

'Yet somewhere under starlight or the sun
My father stands.'
                              'Aged, worn out with wars
On foot, on horseback or in battle-cars.'   30

'I only ask what way my journey lies,
For He who made you bitter made you wise.'

'The Red Branch camp in a great company°
Between wood's rim and the horses of the sea.
Go there, and light a camp-fire at wood's rim;
But tell your name and lineage to him
Whose blade compels, and wait till they have found
Some feasting man that the same oath has bound.'

Among those feasting men Cuchulain dwelt,
And his young sweetheart close beside him knelt,   40
Stared on the mournful wonder of his eyes,
Even as Spring upon the ancient skies,
And pondered on the glory of his days;
And all around the harp-string told his praise,
And Conchubar, the Red Branch king of kings,°
With his own fingers touched the brazen strings.

At last Cuchulain spake, 'Some man has made
His evening fire amid the leafy shade.
I have often heard him singing to and fro,
I have often heard the sweet sound of his bow.   50
Seek out what man he is.'

                 One went and came.
'He bade me let all know he gives his name
At the sword-point, and waits till we have found
Some feasting man that the same oath has bound.'

Cuchulain cried, 'I am the only man
Of all this host so bound from childhood on.'

After short fighting in the leafy shade,
He spake to the young man, 'Is there no maid
Who loves you, no white arms to wrap you round,
Or do you long for the dim sleepy ground,   60
That you have come and dared me to my face?'

'The dooms of men are in God's hidden place.'

'Your head a while seemed like a woman's head
That I loved once.'
              Again the fighting sped,
But now the war-rage in Cuchulain woke,
And through that new blade's guard the old blade broke,

And pierced him.
　　　　　　　'Speak before your breath is done.'

'Cuchulain I, mighty Cuchulain's son.'

'I put you from your pain. I can no more.'

While day its burden on to evening bore,　　　　70
With head bowed on his knees Cuchulain stayed;
Then Conchubar sent that sweet-throated maid,
And she, to win him, his grey hair caressed;
In vain her arms, in vain her soft white breast.
Then Conchubar, the subtlest of all men,
Ranking his Druids round him ten by ten,
Spake thus: 'Cuchulain will dwell there and brood
For three days more in dreadful quietude,
And then arise, and raving slay us all.
Chaunt in his ear delusions magical,　　　　80
That he may fight the horses of the sea.'
The Druids took them to their mystery,
And chaunted for three days.
　　　　　　　Cuchulain stirred,
Stared on the horses of the sea, and heard
The cars of battle and his own name cried;
And fought with the invulnerable tide.

The Rose of the World

Who dreamed that beauty passes like a dream?
For these red lips, with all their mournful pride,
Mournful that no new wonder may betide,
Troy passed away in one high funeral gleam,°
And Usna's children died.°

We and the labouring world are passing by:
Amid men's souls, that waver and give place
Like the pale waters in their wintry race,
Under the passing stars, foam of the sky,
Lives on this lonely face.　　　　10

Bow down, archangels, in your dim abode:
Before you were, or any hearts to beat,
Weary and kind one lingered by His seat;
He made the world to be a grassy road
Before her wandering feet.

The Rose of Peace

If Michael, leader of God's host°
When Heaven and Hell are met,
Looked down on you from Heaven's door-post
He would his deeds forget.

Brooding no more upon God's wars
In his divine homestead,
He would go weave out of the stars
A chaplet for your head.

And all folk seeing him bow down,
And white stars tell your praise,
Would come at last to God's great town,   10
Led on by gentle ways;

And God would bid His warfare cease,
Saying all things were well;
And softly make a rosy peace,
A peace of Heaven with Hell.

The Rose of Battle°

Rose of all Roses, Rose of all the World!
The tall thought-woven sails, that flap unfurled
Above the tide of hours, trouble the air,
And God's bell buoyed to be the water's care;
While hushed from fear, or loud with hope, a band
With blown, spray-dabbled hair gather at hand.
Turn if you may from battles never done,

I call, as they go by me one by one,
Danger no refuge holds, and war no peace,
For him who hears love sing and never cease,   10
Beside her clean-swept hearth, her quiet shade:
But gather all for whom no love hath made
A woven silence, or but came to cast
A song into the air, and singing passed
To smile on the pale dawn; and gather you
Who have sought more than is in rain or dew,
Or in the sun and moon, or on the earth,
Or sighs amid the wandering, starry mirth,
Or comes in laughter from the sea's sad lips,
And wage God's battles in the long grey ships.   20
The sad, the lonely, the insatiable,
To these Old Night shall all her mystery tell;
God's bell has claimed them by the little cry
Of their sad hearts, that may not live nor die.

Rose of all Roses, Rose of all the World!
You, too, have come where the dim tides are hurled
Upon the wharves of sorrow, and heard ring
The bell that calls us on; the sweet far thing.
Beauty grown sad with its eternity
Made you of us, and of the dim grey sea.   30
Our long ships loose thought-woven sails and wait,
For God has bid them share an equal fate;
And when at last, defeated in His wars,
They have gone down under the same white stars,
We shall no longer hear the little cry
Of our sad hearts, that may not live nor die.

The Lake Isle of Innisfree°

I will arise and go now, and go to Innisfree,
And a small cabin build there, of clay and wattles
    made:
Nine bean-rows will I have there, a hive for the honey-
    bee,
And live alone in the bee-loud glade.

And I shall have some peace there, for peace comes
    dropping slow
Dropping from the veils of the morning to where the
    cricket sings;
There midnight's all a glimmer, and noon a purple glow,
And evening full of the linnet's wings.

I will arise and go now, for always night and day
I hear lake water lapping with low sounds by the
    shore;   10
While I stand on the roadway, or on the pavements
    grey,
I hear it in the deep heart's core.

The Pity of Love

A pity beyond all telling
Is hid in the heart of love:
The folk who are buying and selling,
The clouds on their journey above,
The cold wet winds ever blowing,
And the shadowy hazel grove
Where mouse-grey waters are flowing,
Threaten the head that I love.

The Sorrow of Love

The brawling of a sparrow in the eaves,
The brilliant moon and all the milky sky,
And all that famous harmony of leaves,
Had blotted out man's image and his cry.

A girl arose that had red mournful lips
And seemed the greatness of the world in tears,
Doomed like Odysseus and the labouring ships°
And proud as Priam murdered with his peers;°

Arose, and on the instant clamorous eaves,
A climbing moon upon an empty sky,   10

And all that lamentation of the leaves,
Could but compose man's image and his cry.

When You are Old°

When you are old and grey and full of sleep,
And nodding by the fire, take down this book,
And slowly read, and dream of the soft look
Your eyes had once, and of their shadows deep;

How many loved your moments of glad grace,
And loved your beauty with love false or true,
But one man loved the pilgrim soul in you,
And loved the sorrows of your changing face;

And bending down beside the glowing bars,
Murmur, a little sadly, how Love fled   10
And paced upon the mountains overhead
And hid his face amid a crowd of stars.

The White Birds

I would that we were, my beloved, white birds on the
        foam of the sea!
We tire of the flame of the meteor, before it can fade
        and flee;
And the flame of the blue star of twilight, hung
        low on the rim of the sky,
Has awaked in our hearts, my beloved, a sadness that
        may not die.

A weariness comes from those dreamers, dew-dabbled,
        the lily and rose;
Ah, dream not of them, my beloved, the flame of the
        meteor that goes,
Or the flame of the blue star that lingers hung low in
        the fall of the dew:
For I would we were changed to white birds on the
        wandering foam: I and you!

I am haunted by numberless islands, and many a
    Danaan shore,
Where Time would surely forget us, and Sorrow come
    near us no more;   10
Soon far from the rose and the lily and fret of the
    flames would we be,
Were we only white birds, my beloved, buoyed out on
    the foam of the sea!

Who Goes with Fergus?°

Who will go drive with Fergus now,
And pierce the deep wood's woven shade,
And dance upon the level shore?
Young man, lift up your russet brow,
And lift your tender eyelids, maid,
And brood on hopes and fear no more.

And no more turn aside and brood
Upon love's bitter mystery;
For Fergus rules the brazen cars,
And rules the shadows of the wood,   10
And the white breast of the dim sea
And all dishevelled wandering stars.

The Man who Dreamed of Faeryland

He stood among a crowd at Drumahair;°
His heart hung all upon a silken dress,
And he had known at last some tenderness,
Before earth took him to her stony care;
But when a man poured fish into a pile,
It seemed they raised their little silver heads,
And sang what gold morning or evening sheds
Upon a woven world-forgotten isle
Where people love beside the ravelled seas;
That Time can never mar a lover's vows   10

Under that woven changeless roof of boughs:
The singing shook him out of his new ease.

He wandered by the sands of Lissadell;°
His mind ran all on money cares and fears,
And he had known at last some prudent years
Before they heaped his grave under the hill;
But while he passed before a plashy place,
A lug-worm with its grey and muddy mouth
Sang that somewhere to north or west or south
There dwelt a gay, exulting, gentle race   20
Under the golden or the silver skies;
That if a dancer stayed his hungry foot
It seemed the sun and moon were in the fruit:
And at that singing he was no more wise.

He mused beside the well of Scanavin,°
He mused upon his mockers: without fail
His sudden vengeance were a country tale,
When earthy night had drunk his body in;
But one small knot-grass growing by the pool
Sang where—unnecessary cruel voice—   30
Old silence bids its chosen race rejoice,
Whatever ravelled waters rise and fall
Or stormy silver fret the gold of day,
And midnight there enfold them like a fleece
And lover there by lover be at peace.
The tale drove his fine angry mood away.

He slept under the hill of Lugnagall;°
And might have known at last unhaunted sleep
Under that cold and vapour-turbaned steep,
Now that the earth had taken man and all: 40
Did not the worms that spired about his bones
Proclaim with that unwearied, reedy cry
That God has laid His fingers on the sky,
That from those fingers glittering summer runs
Upon the dancer by the dreamless wave.
Why should those lovers that no lovers miss
Dream, until God burn Nature with a kiss?
The man has found no comfort in the grave.

The Two Trees

Beloved, gaze in thine own heart,
The holy tree is growing there;
From joy the holy branches start,
And all the trembling flowers they bear.
The changing colours of its fruit
Have dowered the stars with merry light;
The surety of its hidden root
Has planted quiet in the night;
The shaking of its leafy head
Has given the waves their melody,   10
And made my lips and music wed,
Murmuring a wizard song for thee.
There the Loves a circle go,
The flaming circle of our days,
Gyring, spiring to and fro
In those great ignorant leafy ways;
Remembering all that shaken hair
And how the wingèd sandals dart,
Thine eyes grow full of tender care:
Beloved, gaze in thine own heart.   20

Gaze no more in the bitter glass
The demons, with their subtle guile,
Lift up before us when they pass,
Or only gaze a little while;
For there a fatal image grows
That the stormy night receives,
Roots half hidden under snows,
Broken boughs and blackened leaves.
For all things turn to barrenness
In the dim glass the demons hold,   30
The glass of outer weariness,
Made when God slept in times of old.
There, through the broken branches, go
The ravens of unresting thought;
Flying, crying, to and fro,
Cruel claw and hungry throat,
Or else they stand and sniff the wind,
And shake their ragged wings; alas!

Thy tender eyes grow all unkind:
Gaze no more in the bitter glass.   40

To Ireland in the Coming Times

Know, that I would accounted be
True brother of a company
That sang, to sweeten Ireland's wrong,
Ballad and story, rann and song;°
Nor be I any less of them,
Because the red-rose-bordered hem
Of her, whose history began
Before God made the angelic clan,
Trails all about the written page.
When Time began to rant and rage   10
The measure of her flying feet
Made Ireland's heart begin to beat;
And Time bade all his candles flare
To light a measure here and there;
And may the thoughts of Ireland brood
Upon a measured quietude.

Nor may I less be counted one
With Davis, Mangan, Ferguson,°
Because, to him who ponders well,
My rhymes more than their rhyming tell   20
Of things discovered in the deep,
Where only body's laid asleep.
For the elemental creatures go
About my table to and fro,
That hurry from unmeasured mind
To rant and rage in flood and wind;
Yet he who treads in measured ways
May surely barter gaze for gaze.
Man ever journeys on with them
After the red-rose-bordered hem.   30
Ah, faeries, dancing under the moon,
A Druid land, a Druid tune!
While still I may, I write for you

The love I lived, the dream I knew.
From our birthday, until we die,
Is but the winking of an eye;
And we, our singing and our love,
What measurer Time has lit above,
And all benighted things that go
About my table to and fro,   40
Are passing on to where may be,
In truth's consuming ecstasy,
No place for love and dream at all;
For God goes by with white footfall.
I cast my heart into my rhymes,
That you, in the dim coming times,
May know how my heart went with them
After the red-rose-bordered hem.

From The Wind among the Reeds (1899)

The Hosting of the Sidhe°

The host is riding from Knocknarea°
And over the grave of Clooth-na-Bare;°
Caoilte tossing his burning hair,°
And Niamh calling *Away, come away:*°
Empty your heart of its mortal dream.
The winds awaken, the leaves whirl round,
Our cheeks are pale, our hair is unbound,
Our breasts are heaving, our eyes are agleam,
Our arms are waving, our lips are apart;
And if any gaze on our rushing band,   10
We come between him and the deed of his hand,
We come between him and the hope of his heart.
The host is rushing 'twixt night and day,
And where is there hope or deed as fair?
Caoilte tossing his burning hair,
And Niamh calling *Away, come away.*

The Everlasting Voices

O sweet everlasting Voices, be still;
Go to the guards of the heavenly fold
And bid them wander obeying your will,
Flame under flame, till Time be no more;
Have you not heard that our hearts are old,
That you call in birds, in wind on the hill,
In shaken boughs, in tide on the shore?
O sweet everlasting Voices, be still.

The Moods

Time drops in decay,
Like a candle burnt out,
And the mountains and woods
Have their day, have their day;
What one in the rout
Of the fire-born moods
Has fallen away?

The Lover Tells of the Rose in his Heart

All things uncomely and broken, all things worn out
and old,
The cry of a child by the roadway, the creak of a
lumbering cart,
The heavy steps of the ploughman, splashing the
wintry mould,
Are wronging your image that blossoms a rose in the
deeps of my heart.

The wrong of unshapely things is a wrong too great
to be told;
I hunger to build them anew and sit on a green knoll
apart,
With the earth and the sky and the water, re-made, like
a casket of gold

For my dreams of your image that blossoms a rose in
   the deeps of my heart.

The Host of the Air

O'Driscoll drove with a song
The wild duck and the drake
From the tall and the tufted reeds
Of the drear Hart Lake.°

And he saw how the reeds grew dark
At the coming of night-tide,
And dreamed of the long dim hair
Of Bridget his bride.

He heard while he sang and dreamed
A piper piping away,   10
And never was piping so sad,
And never was piping so gay.

And he saw young men and young girls
Who danced on a level place,
And Bridget his bride among them,
With a sad and a gay face.

The dancers crowded about him
And many a sweet thing said,
And a young man brought him red wine
And a young girl white bread.   20

But Bridget drew him by the sleeve
Away from the merry bands,
To old men playing at cards
With a twinkling of ancient hands.

The bread and the wine had a doom,
For these were the host of the air;
He sat and played in a dream
Of her long dim hair.

He played with the merry old men
And thought not of evil chance,   30
Until one bore Bridget his bride
Away from the merry dance.

He bore her away in his arms,
The handsomest young man there,
And his neck and his breast and his arms
Were drowned in her long dim hair.

O'Driscoll scattered the cards
And out of his dream awoke:
Old men and young men and young girls
Were gone like a drifting smoke;   40

But he heard high up in the air
A piper piping away,
And never was piping so sad,
And never was piping so gay.

The Song of Wandering Aengus°

I went out to the hazel wood,°
Because a fire was in my head,
And cut and peeled a hazel wand,
And hooked a berry to a thread;
And when white moths were on the wing,
And moth-like stars were flickering out,
I dropped the berry in a stream
And caught a little silver trout.

When I had laid it on the floor
I went to blow the fire aflame,   10
But something rustled on the floor,
And some one called me by my name:
It had become a glimmering girl
With apple blossom in her hair
Who called me by my name and ran
And faded through the brightening air.

Though I am old with wandering
Through hollow lands and hilly lands,
I will find out where she has gone,
And kiss her lips and take her hands;   20
And walk among long dappled grass,
And pluck till time and times are done
The silver apples of the moon,
The golden apples of the sun.

The Lover Mourns for the Loss of Love

Pale brows, still hands and dim hair,
I had a beautiful friend
And dreamed that the old despair
Would end in love in the end:
She looked in my heart one day
And saw your image was there;
She has gone weeping away.

He Reproves the Curlew

O curlew, cry no more in the air,
Or only to the water in the West;
Because your crying brings to my mind
Passion-dimmed eyes and long heavy hair
That was shaken out over my breast:
There is enough evil in the crying of wind.

He Remembers Forgotten Beauty

When my arms wrap you round I press
My heart upon the loveliness
That has long faded from the world;
The jewelled crowns that kings have hurled
In shadowy pools, when armies fled;

The love-tales wrought with silken thread
By dreaming ladies upon cloth
That has made fat the murderous moth;
The roses that of old time were
Woven by ladies in their hair,   10
The dew-cold lilies ladies bore
Through many a sacred corridor
Where such grey clouds of incense rose
That only God's eyes did not close:
For that pale breast and lingering hand
Come from a more dream-heavy land,
A more dream-heavy hour than this;
And when you sigh from kiss to kiss
I hear white Beauty sighing, too,
For hours when all must fade like dew,   20
But flame on flame, and deep on deep,
Throne over throne where in half sleep,
Their swords upon their iron knees,
Brood her high lonely mysteries.

The Cap and Bells

The jester walked in the garden:
The garden had fallen still;
He bade his soul rise upward
And stand on her window-sill.

It rose in a straight blue garment,
When owls began to call:
It had grown wise-tongued by thinking
Of a quiet and light footfall;

But the young queen would not listen;
She rose in her pale night-gown;   10
She drew in the heavy casement
And pushed the latches down.

He bade his heart go to her,
When the owls called out no more;

In a red and quivering garment
It sang to her through the door.

It had grown sweet-tongued by dreaming
Of a flutter of flower-like hair;
But she took up her fan from the table
And waved it off on the air.   20

'I have cap and bells,' he pondered,
'I will send them to her and die';
And when the morning whitened
He left them where she went by.

She laid them upon her bosom,
Under a cloud of her hair,
And her red lips sang them a love-song
Till stars grew out of the air.

She opened her door and her window,
And the heart and the soul came through,   30
To her right hand came the red one,
To her left hand came the blue.

They set up a noise like crickets,
A chattering wise and sweet,
And her hair was a folded flower
And the quiet of love in her feet.

The Valley of the Black Pig°

The dews drop slowly and dreams gather: unknown
          spears
Suddenly hurtle before my dream-awakened eyes,
And then the clash of fallen horsemen and the cries
Of unknown perishing armies beat about my ears.
We who still labour by the cromlech on the shore,
The grey cairn on the hill, when day sinks drowned in
          dew,
Being weary of the world's empires, bow down to you,
Master of the still stars and of the flaming door.

He Hears the Cry of the Sedge

I wander by the edge
Of this desolate lake
Where wind cries in the sedge:
Until the axle break
That keeps the stars in their round,
And hands hurl in the deep
The banners of East and West,
And the girdle of light is unbound,
Your breast will not lie by the breast
Of your beloved in sleep.   10

The Secret Rose

Far-off, most secret, and inviolate Rose,
Enfold me in my hour of hours; where those
Who sought thee in the Holy Sepulchre,°
Or in the wine-vat, dwell beyond the stir
And tumult of defeated dreams; and deep
Among pale eyelids, heavy with the sleep
Men have named beauty. Thy great leaves enfold
The ancient beards, the helms of ruby and gold
Of the crowned Magi; and the king whose eyes°
Saw the Pierced Hands and Rood of elder rise°   10
In Druid vapour and make the torches dim;
Till vain frenzy awoke and he died; and him
Who met Fand walking among flaming dew°
By a grey shore where the wind never blew,
And lost the world and Emer for a kiss;
And him who drove the gods out of their liss,°
And till a hundred morns had flowered red
Feasted, and wept the barrows of his dead;
And the proud dreaming king who flung the crown°
And sorrow away, and calling bard and clown   20
Dwelt among wine-stained wanderers in deep woods;
And him who sold tillage, and house, and goods,°
And sought through lands and islands numberless
    years,
Until he found, with laughter and with tears,

A woman of so shining loveliness
That men threshed corn at midnight by a tress,
A little stolen tress. I, too, await
The hour of thy great wind of love and hate.
When shall the stars be blown about the sky,
Like the sparks blown out of a smithy, and die?   30
Surely thine hour has come, thy great wind blows,
Far-off, most secret, and inviolate Rose?

The Poet Pleads with the Elemental Powers

The Powers whose name and shape no living creature
    knows
Have pulled the Immortal Rose;
And though the Seven Lights bowed in their dance and
    wept,°
The Polar Dragon slept,°
His heavy rings uncoiled from glimmering deep to deep:
When will he wake from sleep?

Great Powers of falling wave and wind and windy fire,
With your harmonious choir
Encircle her I love and sing her into peace,
That my old care may cease;   10
Unfold your flaming wings and cover out of sight
The nets of day and night.

Dim Powers of drowsy thought, let her no longer be
Like the pale cup of the sea,
When winds have gathered and sun and moon burned
    dim
Above its cloudy rim;
But let a gentle silence wrought with music flow
Whither her footsteps go.

He Wishes for the Cloths of Heaven

Had I the heavens' embroidered cloths,
Enwrought with golden and silver light,

The blue and the dim and the dark cloths
Of night and light and the half-light,
I would spread the cloths under your feet:
But I, being poor, have only my dreams;
I have spread my dreams under your feet;
Tread softly because you tread on my dreams.

He Thinks of his Past Greatness when a Part of the Constellations of Heaven°

I have drunk ale from the Country of the Young°
And weep because I know all things now:
I have been a hazel-tree, and they hung°
The Pilot Star and the Crooked Plough°
Among my leaves in times out of mind:
I became a rush that horses tread:
I became a man, a hater of the wind,
Knowing one, out of all things, alone, that his head
May not lie on the breast nor his lips on the hair
Of the woman that he loves, until he dies.   10
O beast of the wilderness, bird of the air,
Must I endure your amorous cries?

The Fiddler of Dooney°

When I play on my fiddle in Dooney,
Folk dance like a wave of the sea;
My cousin is priest in Kilvarnet,
My brother in Mocharabuiee.°

I passed my brother and cousin:
They read in their books of prayer;
I read in my book of songs
I bought at the Sligo fair.

When we come at the end of time
To Peter sitting in state,   10
He will smile on the three old spirits,
But call me first through the gate;

For the good are always the merry,
Save by an evil chance,
And the merry love the fiddle,
And the merry love to dance:

And when the folk there spy me,
They will all come up to me,
With 'Here is the fiddler of Dooney!'
And dance like a wave of the sea.   20

From In the Seven Woods (1904)

The Folly of being Comforted

One that is ever kind said yesterday:
'Your well-belovèd's hair has threads of grey,
And little shadows come about her eyes;
Time can but make it easier to be wise
Though now it seems impossible, and so
All that you need is patience.'
                                        Heart cries, 'No,
I have not a crumb of comfort, not a grain.
Time can but make her beauty over again:
Because of that great nobleness of hers
The fire that stirs about her, when she stirs,   10
Burns but more clearly. O she had not these ways
When all the wild summer was in her gaze.'

O heart! O heart! if she'd but turn her head,
You'd know the folly of being comforted.

Never Give all the Heart

Never give all the heart, for love
Will hardly seem worth thinking of
To passionate women if it seem

Certain, and they never dream
That it fades out from kiss to kiss;
For everything that's lovely is
But a brief, dreamy, kind delight.
O never give the heart outright,
For they, for all smooth lips can say,
Have given their hearts up to the play.   10
And who could play it well enough
If deaf and dumb and blind with love?
He that made this knows all the cost,
For he gave all his heart and lost.

Adam's Curse°

We sat together at one summer's end,
That beautiful mild woman, your close friend,
And you and I, and talked of poetry.
I said, 'A line will take us hours maybe;
Yet if it does not seem a moment's thought,
Our stitching and unstitching has been naught.
Better go down upon your marrow-bones
And scrub a kitchen pavement, or break stones
Like an old pauper, in all kinds of weather;
For to articulate sweet sounds together   10
Is to work harder than all these, and yet
Be thought an idler by the noisy set
Of bankers, schoolmasters, and clergymen
The martyrs call the world.'

                              And thereupon
That beautiful mild woman for whose sake
There's many a one shall find out all heartache
On finding that her voice is sweet and low
Replied, 'To be born woman is to know—
Although they do not talk of it at school—
That we must labour to be beautiful.'   20

I said, 'It's certain there is no fine thing
Since Adam's fall but needs much labouring.
There have been lovers who thought love should be

So much compounded of high courtesy
That they would sigh and quote with learned looks
Precedents out of beautiful old books;
Yet now it seems an idle trade enough.'

We sat grown quiet at the name of love;
We saw the last embers of daylight die,
And in the trembling blue-green of the sky   30
A moon, worn as if it had been a shell
Washed by time's waters as they rose and fell
About the stars and broke in days and years.

I had a thought for no one's but your ears:
That you were beautiful, and that I strove
To love you in the old high way of love;
That it had all seemed happy, and yet we'd grown
As weary-hearted as that hollow moon.

Red Hanrahan's Song about Ireland°

The old brown thorn-trees break in two high over
        Cummen Strand,°
Under a bitter black wind that blows from the left
        hand;
Our courage breaks like an old tree in a black wind and
        dies,
But we have hidden in our hearts the flame out of the
        eyes
Of Cathleen, the daughter of Houlihan.°

The wind has bundled up the clouds high over
        Knocknarea,
And thrown the thunder on the stones for all that
        Maeve can say.°
Angers that are like noisy clouds have set our hearts
        abeat;
But we have all bent low and low and kissed the quiet
        feet
Of Cathleen, the daughter of Houlihan.   10

The yellow pool has overflowed high up on Clooth-
    na-Bare,°
For the wet winds are blowing out of the clinging air;
Like heavy flooded waters our bodies and our blood;
But purer than a tall candle before the Holy Rood°
Is Cathleen, the daughter of Houlihan.

O do not Love Too Long

Sweetheart, do not love too long:
I loved long and long,
And grew to be out of fashion
Like an old song.

All through the years of our youth
Neither could have known
Their own thought from the other's,
We were so much at one.

But O, in a minute she changed—
O do not love too long,   10
Or you will grow out of fashion
Like an old song.

The Happy Townland

There's many a strong farmer
Whose heart would break in two,
If he could see the townland
That we are riding to;
Boughs have their fruit and blossom
At all times of the year;
Rivers are running over
With red beer and brown beer.
An old man plays the bagpipes
In a golden and silver wood;   10
Queens, their eyes blue like the ice,
Are dancing in a crowd.

The little fox he murmured,
'O what of the world's bane?'
The sun was laughing sweetly,
The moon plucked at my rein;
But the little red fox murmured,
'O do not pluck at his rein,
He is riding to the townland
That is the world's bane.'   20

When their hearts are so high
That they would come to blows,
They unhook their heavy swords
From golden and silver boughs;
But all that are killed in battle
Awaken to life again.
It is lucky that their story
Is not known among men,
For O, the strong farmers
That would let the spade lie,   30
Their hearts would be like a cup
That somebody had drunk dry.

The little fox he murmured,
'O what of the world's bane?'
The sun was laughing sweetly,
The moon plucked at my rein;
But the little red fox murmured,
'O do not pluck at his rein,
He is riding to the townland
That is the world's bane.'   40

Michael will unhook his trumpet
From a bough overhead,
And blow a little noise
When the supper has been spread.
Gabriel will come from the water°
With a fish-tail, and talk
Of wonders that have happened
On wet roads where men walk,
And lift up an old horn
Of hammered silver, and drink   50

Till he has fallen asleep
Upon the starry brink.

The little fox he murmured,
'O what of the world's bane?'
The sun was laughing sweetly,
The moon plucked at my rein;
But the little red fox murmured,
'O do not pluck at his rein,
He is riding to the townland
That is the world's bane.'   60

From The Green Helmet and Other Poems (1910)

A Woman Homer Sung°

If any man drew near
When I was young,
I thought, 'He holds her dear,'
And shook with hate and fear.
But O! 'twas bitter wrong
If he could pass her by
With an indifferent eye.

Whereon I wrote and wrought,
And now, being grey,
I dream that I have brought   10
To such a pitch my thought
That coming time can say,
'He shadowed in a glass
What thing her body was.'

For she had fiery blood
When I was young,
And trod so sweetly proud

As 'twere upon a cloud,
A woman Homer sung,
That life and letters seem   20
But an heroic dream.

No Second Troy°

Why should I blame her that she filled my days
With misery, or that she would of late
Have taught to ignorant men most violent ways,
Or hurled the little streets upon the great,
Had they but courage equal to desire?
What could have made her peaceful with a mind
That nobleness made simple as a fire,
With beauty like a tightened bow, a kind
That is not natural in an age like this,
Being high and solitary and most stern?   10
Why, what could she have done, being what
     she is?
Was there another Troy for her to burn?

Reconciliation

Some may have blamed you that you took away
The verses that could move them on the day
When, the ears being deafened, the sight of the
     eyes blind
With lightning, you went from me, and I could
     find
Nothing to make a song about but kings,
Helmets, and swords, and half-forgotten things
That were like memories of you—but now
We'll out, for the world lives as long ago;
And while we're in our laughing, weeping fit,
Hurl helmets, crowns, and swords into the pit.   10
But, dear, cling close to me; since you were gone,
My barren thoughts have chilled me to the bone.

The Fascination of What's Difficult

The fascination of what's difficult
Has dried the sap out of my veins, and rent
Spontaneous joy and natural content
Out of my heart. There's something ails our colt°
That must, as if it had not holy blood
Nor on Olympus leaped from cloud to cloud,°
Shiver under the lash, strain, sweat and jolt
As though it dragged road metal. My curse on plays
That have to be set up in fifty ways,
On the day's war with every knave and dolt,   10
Theatre business, management of men.
I swear before the dawn comes round again
I'll find the stable and pull out the bolt.

The Coming of Wisdom with Time

Though leaves are many, the root is one;
Through all the lying days of my youth
I swayed my leaves and flowers in the sun;
Now I may wither into the truth.

On Hearing that the Students of our New University have Joined the Agitation against Immoral Literature°

Where, where but here have Pride and Truth,
That long to give themselves for wage,
To shake their wicked sides at youth
Restraining reckless middle-age?

The Mask

'Put off that mask of burning gold
With emerald eyes.'
'O no, my dear, you make so bold

To find if hearts be wild and wise,
And yet not cold.'

'I would but find what's there to find,
Love or deceit.'
'It was the mask engaged your mind,
And after set your heart to beat,
Not what's behind.'   10

'But lest you are my enemy,
I must enquire.'
'O no, my dear, let all that be;
What matter, so there is but fire
In you, in me?'

Upon a House Shaken by the Land Agitation

How should the world be luckier if this house,°
Where passion and precision have been one
Time out of mind, became too ruinous
To breed the lidless eye that loves the sun?
And the sweet laughing eagle thoughts that grow
Where wings have memory of wings, and all
That comes of the best knit to the best? Although
Mean roof-trees were the sturdier for its fall,
How should their luck run high enough to reach
The gifts that govern men, and after these   10
To gradual Time's last gift, a written speech
Wrought of high laughter, loveliness and ease?

At the Abbey Theatre°
(Imitated from Ronsard)°

Dear Craoibhin Aoibhin, look into our case.°
When we are high and airy hundreds say
That if we hold that flight they'll leave the place,
While those same hundreds mock another day
Because we have made our art of common things,
So bitterly, you'd dream they longed to look

All their lives through into some drift of wings.
You've dandled them and fed them from the book
And know them to the bone; impart to us—
We'll keep the secret—a new trick to please.   10
Is there a bridle for this Proteus°
That turns and changes like his draughty seas?
Or is there none, most popular of men,
But when they mock us, that we mock again?

All Things can Tempt Me

All things can tempt me from this craft of verse:
One time it was a woman's face, or worse—
The seeming needs of my fool-driven land;
Now nothing but comes readier to the hand
Than this accustomed toil. When I was young,
I had not given a penny for a song
Did not the poet sing it with such airs
That one believed he had a sword upstairs;
Yet would be now, could I but have my wish,
Colder and dumber and deafer than a fish.   10

Brown Penny

I whispered, 'I am too young,'
And then, 'I am old enough';
Wherefore I threw a penny
To find out if I might love.
'Go and love, go and love, young man,
If the lady be young and fair.'
Ah, penny, brown penny, brown penny,
I am looped in the loops of her hair.

O love is the crooked thing,
There is nobody wise enough   10
To find out all that is in it,
For he would be thinking of love

Till the stars had run away
And the shadows eaten the moon.
Ah, penny, brown penny, brown penny,
One cannot begin it too soon.

From Responsibilities (1914)

'*In dreams begins responsibility.*'

Old Play°

'*How am I fallen from myself, for a long time now
I have not seen the Prince of Chang in my dreams.*'

KHOUNG-FOU-TSEU°

[*Introductory Rhymes*]

*Pardon, old fathers, if you still remain
Somewhere in ear-shot for the story's end,
Old Dublin merchant 'free of the ten and four'*°
*Or trading out of Galway into Spain;
Old country scholar, Robert Emmet's friend,*°
*A hundred-year-old memory to the poor;
Merchant and scholar who have left me blood
That has not passed through any huckster's loin,
Soldiers that gave, whatever die was cast:
A Butler or an Armstrong that withstood*°   10
*Beside the brackish waters of the Boyne
James and his Irish when the Dutchman crossed;*°
Old merchant skipper that leaped overboard°
*After a ragged hat in Biscay Bay;
You most of all, silent and fierce old man,*°
*Because the daily spectacle that stirred
My fancy, and set my boyish lips to say,
'Only the wasteful virtues earn the sun';
Pardon that for a barren passion's sake,
Although I have come close on forty-nine,*   20
*I have no child, I have nothing but a book,
Nothing but that to prove your blood and mine.*

January 1914

The Grey Rock°

Poets with whom I learned my trade,
Companions of the Cheshire Cheese,°
Here's an old story I've re-made,
Imagining 'twould better please
Your ears than stories now in fashion,
Though you may think I waste my breath
Pretending that there can be passion
That has more life in it than death,
And though at bottling of your wine
Old wholesome Goban had no say;°   10
The moral's yours because it's mine.

When cups went round at close of day—
Is not that how good stories run?—
The gods were sitting at the board
In their great house at Slievenamon.°
They sang a drowsy song, or snored,
For all were full of wine and meat.
The smoky torches made a glare
On metal Goban'd hammered at,
On old deep silver rolling there   20
Or on some still unemptied cup
That he, when frenzy stirred his thews,
Had hammcrcd out on mountain top
To hold the sacred stuff he brews
That only gods may buy of him.

Now from that juice that made them wise
All those had lifted up the dim
Imaginations of their eyes,
For one that was like woman made
Before their sleepy eyelids ran   30
And trembling with her passion said,
'Come out and dig for a dead man,
Who's burrowing somewhere in the ground,
And mock him to his face and then
Hollo him on with horse and hound,
For he is the worst of all dead men.'

We should be dazed and terror-struck,
If we but saw in dreams that room,
Those wine-drenched eyes, and curse our luck
That emptied all our days to come.   40
I knew a woman none could please,
Because she dreamed when but a child
Of men and women made like these;
And after, when her blood ran wild,
Had ravelled her own story out,
And said, 'In two or in three years
I needs must marry some poor lout,'
And having said it, burst in tears.

Since, tavern comrades, you have died,
Maybe your images have stood,   50
Mere bone and muscle thrown aside,
Before that roomful or as good.
You had to face your ends when young—
'Twas wine or women, or some curse—
But never made a poorer song
That you might have a heavier purse,
Nor gave loud service to a cause
That you might have a troop of friends.
You kept the Muses' sterner laws,
And unrepenting faced your ends,   60
And therefore earned the right—and yet
Dowson and Johnson most I praise—°
To troop with those the world's forgot,
And copy their proud steady gaze.

'The Danish troop was driven out
Between the dawn and dusk,' she said;
'Although the event was long in doubt,
Although the King of Ireland's dead
And half the kings, before sundown
All was accomplished.

                        'When this day   70
Murrough, the King of Ireland's son,°
Foot after foot was giving way,
He and his best troops back to back
Had perished there, but the Danes ran,

Stricken with panic from the attack,
The shouting of an unseen man;
And being thankful Murrough found,
Led by a footsole dipped in blood
That had made prints upon the ground,
Where by old thorn-trees that man stood;   80
And though when he gazed here and there,
He had but gazed on thorn-trees, spoke,
"Who is the friend that seems but air
And yet could give so fine a stroke?"
Thereon a young man met his eye,
Who said, "Because she held me in
Her love, and would not have me die,
Rock-nurtured Aoife took a pin,°
And pushing it into my shirt,
Promised that for a pin's sake,   90
No man should see to do me hurt;
But there it's gone; I will not take
The fortune that had been my shame
Seeing, King's son, what wounds you have."
'Twas roundly spoke, but when night came
He had betrayed me to his grave,
For he and the King's son were dead.
I'd promised him two hundred years,
And when for all I'd done or said—
And these immortal eyes shed tears—   100
He claimed his country's need was most,
I'd saved his life, yet for the sake
Of a new friend he has turned a ghost.
What does he care if my heart break?
I call for spade and horse and hound
That we may harry him.' Thereon
She cast herself upon the ground
And rent her clothes and made her moan:
'Why are they faithless when their might
Is from the holy shades that rove   110
The grey rock and the windy light?
Why should the faithfullest heart most love
The bitter sweetness of false faces?
Why must the lasting love what passes,
Why are the gods by men betrayed?'

But thereon every god stood up
With a slow smile and without sound,
And stretching forth his arm and cup
To where she moaned upon the ground,
Suddenly drenched her to the skin;　　　　　　120
And she with Goban's wine adrip,
No more remembering what had been,
Stared at the gods with laughing lip.

I have kept my faith, though faith was tried,
To that rock-born, rock-wandering foot,
And the world's altered since you died,
And I am in no good repute
With the loud host before the sea,
That think sword-strokes were better meant
Than lover's music—let that be,　　　　　　130
So that the wandering foot's content.

To a Wealthy Man who Promised a Second Subscription to the Dublin Municipal Gallery if it were Proved the People Wanted Pictures°

You gave, but will not give again
Until enough of Paudeen's pence
By Biddy's halfpennies have lain°
To be 'some sort of evidence,'
Before you'll put your guineas down,
That things it were a pride to give
Are what the blind and ignorant town
Imagines best to make it thrive.
What cared Duke Ercole, that bid°
His mummers to the market-place,　　　　　　10
What th'onion-sellers thought or did
So that his Plautus set the pace°
For the Italian comedies?
And Guidobaldo, when he made°
That grammar school of courtesies
Where wit and beauty learned their trade
 Upon Urbino's windy hill,
 Had sent no runners to and fro
 That he might learn the shepherds' will.

And when they drove out Cosimo,°   20
Indifferent how the rancour ran,
He gave the hours they had set free
To Michelozzo's latest plan
For the San Marco Library,°
Whence turbulent Italy should draw
Delight in Art whose end is peace,
In logic and in natural law
By sucking at the dugs of Greece.

Your open hand but shows our loss,
For he knew better how to live.   30
Let Paudeens play at pitch and toss,
Look up in the sun's eye and give
What the exultant heart calls good
That some new day may breed the best
Because you gave, not what they would,
But the right twigs for an eagle's nest!

    December 1912

September 1913°

What need you, being come to sense,
But fumble in a greasy till
And add the halfpence to the pence
And prayer to shivering prayer, until
You have dried the marrow from the bone;
For men were born to pray and save:
Romantic Ireland's dead and gone,
It's with O'Leary in the grave.°

Yet they were of a different kind,
The names that stilled your childish play,   10
They have gone about the world like wind,
But little time had they to pray
For whom the hangman's rope was spun,
And what, God help us, could they save?
Romantic Ireland's dead and gone,
It's with O'Leary in the grave.

Was it for this the wild geese spread°
The grey wing upon every tide;

For this that all that blood was shed,
For this Edward Fitzgerald died,°   20
And Robert Emmet and Wolfe Tone,°
All that delirium of the brave?
Romantic Ireland's dead and gone,
It's with O'Leary in the grave.

Yet could we turn the years again,
And call those exiles as they were
In all their loneliness and pain,
You'd cry, 'Some woman's yellow hair
Has maddened every mother's son':
They weighed so lightly what they gave.   30
But let them be, they're dead and gone,
They're with O'Leary in the grave.

To a Friend whose Work has Come to Nothing°

Now all the truth is out,
Be secret and take defeat
From any brazen throat,
For how can you compete,
Being honour bred, with one
Who, were it proved he lies,
Were neither shamed in his own
Nor in his neighbours' eyes?
Bred to a harder thing
Than Triumph, turn away   10
And like a laughing string
Whereon mad fingers play
Amid a place of stone,
Be secret and exult,
Because of all things known
That is most difficult.

Paudeen°

Indignant at the fumbling wits, the obscure spite
Of our old Paudeen in his shop, I stumbled blind

Among the stones and thorn-trees, under morning light;
Until a curlew cried and in the luminous wind
A curlew answered; and suddenly thereupon I thought
That on the lonely height where all are in God's eye,
There cannot be, confusion of our sound forgot,
A single soul that lacks a sweet crystalline cry.

To a Shade°

If you have revisited the town, thin Shade,
Whether to look upon your monument
(I wonder if the builder has been paid)
Or happier-thoughted when the day is spent
To drink of that salt breath out of the sea
When grey gulls flit about instead of men,
And the gaunt houses put on majesty:
Let these content you and be gone again;
For they are at their old tricks yet.
                              A man°
Of your own passionate serving kind who
        had brought   10
In his full hands what, had they only known,
Had given their children's children loftier
        thought,
Sweeter emotion, working in their veins
Like gentle blood, has been driven from
        the place,
And insult heaped upon him for his pains,
And for his open-handedness, disgrace;
Your enemy, an old foul mouth, had set°
The pack upon him.
                        Go, unquiet wanderer,
And gather the Glasnevin coverlet°
About your head till the dust stops your ear,   20
The time for you to taste of that salt breath
And listen at the corners has not come;
You had enough of sorrow before death—
Away, away! You are safer in the tomb.

        September 29, 1913

On Those that Hated 'The Playboy of the Western World,' 1907°

Once, when midnight smote the air,
Eunuchs ran through Hell and met
On every crowded street to stare
Upon great Juan riding by:°
Even like these to rail and sweat
Staring upon his sinewy thigh.

The Three Hermits

Three old hermits took the air
By a cold and desolate sea,
First was muttering a prayer,
Second rummaged for a flea;
On a windy stone, the third,
Giddy with his hundredth year,
Sang unnoticed like a bird:
'Though the Door of Death is near
And what waits behind the door,
Three times in a single day   10
I, though upright on the shore,
Fall asleep when I should pray.'
So the first, but now the second:
'We're but given what we have earned
When all thoughts and deeds are reckoned,
So it's plain to be discerned
That the shades of holy men
Who have failed, being weak of will,
Pass the Door of Birth again,
And are plagued by crowds, until   20
They've the passion to escape.'
Moaned the other, 'They are thrown
Into some most fearful shape.'
But the second mocked his moan:
'They are not changed to anything,
Having loved God once, but maybe
To a poet or a king
Or a witty lovely lady.'

While he'd rummaged rags and hair,
Caught and cracked his flea, the third,   30
Giddy with his hundredth year,
Sang unnoticed like a bird.

The Mountain Tomb

Pour wine and dance if manhood still have pride,
Bring roses if the rose be yet in bloom;
The cataract smokes upon the mountain side,
Our Father Rosicross is in his tomb.°

Pull down the blinds, bring fiddle and clarionet
That there be no foot silent in the room
Nor mouth from kissing, nor from wine unwet;
Our Father Rosicross is in his tomb.

In vain, in vain; the cataract still cries;
The everlasting taper lights the gloom;   10
All wisdom shut into his onyx eyes,
Our Father Rosicross sleeps in his tomb.

I

To a Child Dancing in the Wind

Dance there upon the shore;
What need have you to care
For wind or water's roar?
And tumble out your hair
That the salt drops have wet;
Being young you have not known
The fool's triumph, nor yet
Love lost as soon as won,
Nor the best labourer dead
And all the sheaves to bind.   10
What need have you to dread
The monstrous crying of wind?

II

Two Years Later

Has no one said those daring
Kind eyes should be more learn'd?
Or warned you how despairing
The moths are when they are burned?
I could have warned you; but you are young,
So we speak a different tongue.

O you will take whatever's offered
And dream that all the world's a friend,
Suffer as your mother suffered,
Be as broken in the end.   10
But I am old and you are young,
And I speak a barbarous tongue.

Fallen Majesty

Although crowds gathered once if she but showed
        her face,°
And even old men's eyes grew dim, this hand alone,
Like some last courtier at a gypsy camping-place
Babbling of fallen majesty, records what's gone.

The lineaments, a heart that laughter has made sweet,
These, these remain, but I record what's gone. A crowd
Will gather, and not know it walks the very street
Whereon a thing once walked that seemed a burning
        cloud.

Friends

Now must I these three praise—
Three women that have wrought°
What joy is in my days:
One because no thought,
Nor those unpassing cares,
No, not in these fifteen

Many-times-troubled years,
Could ever come between
Mind and delighted mind;
And one because her hand   10
Had strength that could unbind
What none can understand,
What none can have and thrive,
Youth's dreamy load, till she
So changed me that I live
Labouring in ecstasy.
And what of her that took
All till my youth was gone
With scarce a pitying look?
How could I praise that one?   20
When day begins to break
I count my good and bad,
Being wakeful for her sake,
Remembering what she had,
What eagle look still shows,
While up from my heart's root
So great a sweetness flows
I shake from head to foot.

The Cold Heaven

Suddenly I saw the cold and rook-delighting heaven
That seemed as though ice burned and was but the
        more ice,
And thereupon imagination and heart were driven
So wild that every casual thought of that and this
Vanished, and left but memories, that should be out
        of season
With the hot blood of youth, of love crossed long ago;
And I took all the blame out of all sense and reason,
Until I cried and trembled and rocked to and fro,
Riddled with light. Ah! when the ghost begins to
        quicken,
Confusion of the death-bed over, is it sent   10
Out naked on the roads, as the books say, and stricken
By the injustice of the skies for punishment?

That the Night Come

She lived in storm and strife,
Her soul had such desire
For what proud death may bring
That it could not endure
The common good of life,
But lived as 'twere a king
That packed his marriage day
With banneret and pennon,
Trumpet and kettledrum,
And the outrageous cannon,   10
To bundle time away
That the night come.

An Appointment

Being out of heart with government
I took a broken root to fling
Where the proud, wayward squirrel went,
Taking delight that he could spring;
And he, with that low whinnying sound
That is like laughter, sprang again
And so to the other tree at a bound.
Nor the tame will, nor timid brain,
Nor heavy knitting of the brow
Bred that fierce tooth and cleanly limb   10
And threw him up to laugh on the bough;
No government appointed him.

The Magi°

Now as at all times I can see in the mind's eye,
In their stiff, painted clothes, the pale unsatisfied ones
Appear and disappear in the blue depth of the sky
With all their ancient faces like rain-beaten stones,
And all their helms of silver hovering side by side,

And all their eyes still fixed, hoping to find once more,
Being by Calvary's turbulence unsatisfied,
The uncontrollable mystery on the bestial floor.

The Dolls

A doll in the doll-maker's house
Looks at the cradle and bawls:
'That is an insult to us.'
But the oldest of all the dolls,
Who had seen, being kept for show,
Generations of his sort,
Out-screams the whole shelf: 'Although
There's not a man can report
Evil of this place,
The man and the woman bring   10
Hither, to our disgrace,
A noisy and filthy thing.'
Hearing him groan and stretch
The doll-maker's wife is aware
Her husband has heard the wretch,
And crouched by the arm of his chair,
She murmurs into his ear,
Head upon shoulder leant:
'My dear, my dear, O dear,
It was an accident.'   20

A Coat

I made my song a coat
Covered with embroideries
Out of old mythologies
From heel to throat;
But the fools caught it,
Wore it in the world's eyes
As though they'd wrought it.
Song, let them take it,
For there's more enterprise
In walking naked.   10

From The Wild Swans at Coole (1919)

The Wild Swans at Coole°

The trees are in their autumn beauty,
The woodland paths are dry,
Under the October twilight the water
Mirrors a still sky;
Upon the brimming water among the stones
Are nine-and-fifty swans.

The nineteenth autumn has come upon me
Since I first made my count;
I saw, before I had well finished,
All suddenly mount   10
And scatter wheeling in great broken rings
Upon their clamorous wings.

I have looked upon those brilliant creatures,
And now my heart is sore.
All's changed since I, hearing at twilight,
The first time on this shore,
The bell-beat of their wings above my head,
Trod with a lighter tread.

Unwearied still, lover by lover,
They paddle in the cold   20
Companionable streams or climb the air;
Their hearts have not grown old;
Passion or conquest, wander where they will,
Attend upon them still.

But now they drift on the still water,
Mysterious, beautiful;
Among what rushes will they build,
By what lake's edge or pool
Delight men's eyes when I awake some day
To find they have flown away?   30

In Memory of Major Robert Gregory°

I

Now that we're almost settled in our house
I'll name the friends that cannot sup with us
Beside a fire of turf in th'ancient tower,
And having talked to some late hour
Climb up the narrow winding stair to bed:
Discoverers of forgotten truth
Or mere companions of my youth,
All, all are in my thoughts to-night being dead.

II

Always we'd have the new friend meet the old
And we are hurt if either friend seem cold,   10
And there is salt to lengthen out the smart
In the affections of our heart,
And quarrels are blown up upon that head;
But not a friend that I would bring
This night can set us quarrelling,
For all that come into my mind are dead.

III

Lionel Johnson comes the first to mind,°
That loved his learning better than mankind,
Though courteous to the worst; much falling he
Brooded upon sanctity   20
Till all his Greek and Latin learning seemed
A long blast upon the horn that brought
A little nearer to his thought
A measureless consummation that he dreamed.

IV

And that enquiring man John Synge comes next,°
That dying chose the living world for text
And never could have rested in the tomb
But that, long travelling, he had come
Towards nightfall upon certain set apart
In a most desolate stony place,   30
Towards nightfall upon a race
Passionate and simple like his heart.

V

And then I think of old George Pollexfen,°
In muscular youth well known to Mayo men°
For horsemanship at meets or at racecourses,
That could have shown how pure-bred horses
And solid men, for all their passion, live
But as the outrageous stars incline
By opposition, square and trine;°
Having grown sluggish and contemplative.   40

VI

They were my close companions many a year,
A portion of my mind and life, as it were,
And now their breathless faces seem to look
Out of some old picture-book;
I am accustomed to their lack of breath,
But not that my dear friend's dear son,
Our Sidney and our perfect man,°
Could share in that discourtesy of death.

VII

For all things the delighted eye now sees
Were loved by him; the old storm-broken trees   50
That cast their shadows upon road and bridge;
The tower set on the stream's edge;
The ford where drinking cattle make a stir
Nightly, and startled by that sound
The water-hen must change her ground;
He might have been your heartiest welcomer.

VIII

When with the Galway foxhounds he would ride
From Castle Taylor to the Roxborough side°
Or Esserkelly plain, few kept his pace;
At Mooneen he had leaped a place°   60
So perilous that half the astonished meet
Had shut their eyes; and where was it
He rode a race without a bit?
And yet his mind outran the horses' feet.

IX

We dreamed that a great painter had been born
To cold Clare rock and Galway rock and thorn,°
To that stern colour and that delicate line
That are our secret discipline
Wherein the gazing heart doubles her might.
Soldier, scholar, horseman, he,   70
And yet he had the intensity
To have published all to be a world's delight.

X

What other could so well have counselled us
In all lovely intricacies of a house
As he that practised or that understood
All work in metal or in wood,
In moulded plaster or in carven stone?
Soldier, scholar, horseman, he,
And all he did done perfectly
As though he had but that one trade alone.   80

XI

Some burn damp faggots, others may consume
The entire combustible world in one small room
As though dried straw, and if we turn about
The bare chimney is gone black out
Because the work had finished in that flare.
Soldier, scholar, horseman, he,
As 'twere all life's epitome.
What made us dream that he could comb grey hair?

XII

I had thought, seeing how bitter is that wind
That shakes the shutter, to have brought to mind   90
All those that manhood tried, or childhood loved
Or boyish intellect approved,
With some appropriate commentary on each;
Until imagination brought
A fitter welcome; but a thought
Of that late death took all my heart for speech.

An Irish Airman Foresees his Death

I know that I shall meet my fate
Somewhere among the clouds above;
Those that I fight I do not hate,
Those that I guard I do not love;
My country is Kiltartan Cross,°
My countrymen Kiltartan's poor,
No likely end could bring them loss
Or leave them happier than before.
Nor law, nor duty bade me fight,
Nor public men, nor cheering crowds,   10
A lonely impulse of delight
Drove to this tumult in the clouds;
I balanced all, brought all to mind,
The years to come seemed waste of breath,
A waste of breath the years behind
In balance with this life, this death.

Men Improve with the Years

I am worn out with dreams;
A weather-worn, marble triton°
Among the streams;
And all day long I look
Upon this lady's beauty
As though I had found in a book
A pictured beauty,
Pleased to have filled the eyes
Or the discerning ears,
Delighted to be but wise,   10
For men improve with the years;
And yet, and yet,
Is this my dream, or the truth?
O would that we had met
When I had my burning youth!
But I grow old among dreams,
A weather-worn, marble triton
Among the streams.

The Collar-bone of a Hare

Would I could cast a sail on the water
Where many a king has gone
And many a king's daughter,
And alight at the comely trees and the lawn,
The playing upon pipes and the dancing,
And learn that the best thing is
To change my loves while dancing
And pay but a kiss for a kiss.

I would find by the edge of that water
The collar-bone of a hare   10
Worn thin by the lapping of water,
And pierce it through with a gimlet and stare
At the old bitter world where they marry in churches,
And laugh over the untroubled water
At all who marry in churches,
Through the white thin bone of a hare.

Solomon to Sheba°

Sang Solomon to Sheba,
And kissed her dusky face,
'All day long from mid-day
We have talked in the one place,
All day long from shadowless noon
We have gone round and round
In the narrow theme of love
Like an old horse in a pound.'

To Solomon sang Sheba,
Planted on his knees,   10
'If you had broached a matter
That might the learned please,
You had before the sun had thrown
Our shadows on the ground
Discovered that my thoughts, not it,
Are but a narrow pound.'

Said Solomon to Sheba,
And kissed her Arab eyes,
'There's not a man or woman
Born under the skies   20
Dare match in learning with us two,
And all day long we have found
There's not a thing but love can make
The world a narrow pound.'

The Living Beauty

I bade, because the wick and oil are spent
And frozen are the channels of the blood,
My discontented heart to draw content
From beauty that is cast out of a mould
In bronze, or that in dazzling marble appears,
Appears, but when we have gone is gone again,
Being more indifferent to our solitude
Than 'twere an apparition. O heart, we are old;
The living beauty is for younger men:
We cannot pay its tribute of wild tears.   10

A Song

I thought no more was needed
Youth to prolong
Than dumb-bell and foil
To keep the body young.
O who could have foretold
That the heart grows old?

Though I have many words,
What woman's satisfied,
I am no longer faint
Because at her side?   10
O who could have foretold
That the heart grows old?

I have not lost desire
But the heart that I had;
I thought 'twould burn my body
Laid on the death-bed,
For who could have foretold
That the heart grows old?

The Scholars

Bald heads forgetful of their sins,
Old, learned, respectable bald heads
Edit and annotate the lines
That young men, tossing on their beds,
Rhymed out in love's despair
To flatter beauty's ignorant ear.

All shuffle there; all cough in ink;
All wear the carpet with their shoes;
All think what other people think;
All know the man their neighbour knows.   10
Lord, what would they say
Did their Catullus walk that way?°

On Woman

May God be praised for woman
That gives up all her mind,
A man may find in no man
A friendship of her kind
That covers all he has brought
As with her flesh and bone,
Nor quarrels with a thought
Because it is not her own.

Though pedantry denies,
It's plain the Bible means   10
That Solomon grew wise
While talking with his queens,°
Yet never could, although

They say he counted grass,
Count all the praises due
When Sheba was his lass,
When she the iron wrought, or
When from the smithy fire
It shuddered in the water:
Harshness of their desire   20
That made them stretch and yawn,
Pleasure that comes with sleep,
Shudder that made them one.
What else He give or keep
God grant me—no, not here,
For I am not so bold
To hope a thing so dear
Now I am growing old,
But when, if the tale's true,
The Pestle of the moon   30
That pounds up all anew
Brings me to birth again—°
To find what once I had
And know what once I have known,
Until I am driven mad,
Sleep driven from my bed,
By tenderness and care,
Pity, an aching head,
Gnashing of teeth, despair;
And all because of some one   40
Perverse creature of chance,
And live like Solomon
That Sheba led a dance.

The Fisherman

Although I can see him still,
The freckled man who goes
To a grey place on a hill
In grey Connemara clothes°
At dawn to cast his flies,
It's long since I began
To call up to the eyes

This wise and simple man.
All day I'd looked in the face
What I had hoped 'twould be   10
To write for my own race
And the reality;
The living men that I hate,
The dead man that I loved,
The craven man in his seat,
The insolent unreproved,
And no knave brought to book
Who has won a drunken cheer,
The witty man and his joke
Aimed at the commonest ear,   20
The clever man who cries
The catch-cries of the clown,
The beating down of the wise
And great Art beaten down.

Maybe a twelvemonth since
Suddenly I began,
In scorn of this audience,
Imagining a man,
And his sun-freckled face,
And grey Connemara cloth,   30
Climbing up to a place
Where stone is dark under froth,
And the down-turn of his wrist
When the flies drop in the stream;
A man who does not exist,
A man who is but a dream;
And cried, 'Before I am old
I shall have written him one
Poem maybe as cold
And passionate as the dawn.'   40

Her Praise

She is foremost of those that I would hear praised.
I have gone about the house, gone up and down

As a man does who has published a new book,
Or a young girl dressed out in her new gown,
And though I have turned the talk by hook or crook
Until her praise should be the uppermost theme,
A woman spoke of some new tale she had read,
A man confusedly in a half dream
As though some other name ran in his head.
She is foremost of those that I would hear praised.   10
I will talk no more of books or the long war
But walk by the dry thorn until I have found
Some beggar sheltering from the wind, and there
Manage the talk until her name come round.
If there be rags enough he will know her name
And be well pleased remembering it, for in the old
    days,
Though she had young men's praise and old men's
    blame,
Among the poor both old and young gave her praise.

A Thought from Propertius°

She might, so noble from head
To great shapely knees
The long flowing line,
Have walked to the altar
Through the holy images
At Pallas Athena's side,°
Or been fit spoil for a centaur
Drunk with the unmixed wine.

Broken Dreams

There is grey in your hair.
Young men no longer suddenly catch their breath
When you are passing;
But maybe some old gaffer mutters a blessing
Because it was your prayer

Recovered him upon the bed of death.
For your sole sake—that all heart's ache have known,
And given to others all heart's ache,
From meagre girlhood's putting on
Burdensome beauty—for your sole sake   10
Heaven has put away the stroke of her doom,
So great her portion in that peace you make
By merely walking in a room.

Your beauty can but leave among us
Vague memories, nothing but memories.
A young man when the old men are done talking
Will say to an old man, 'Tell me of that lady
The poet stubborn with his passion sang us
When age might well have chilled his blood.'

Vague memories, nothing but memories,   20
But in the grave all, all, shall be renewed.
The certainty that I shall see that lady
Leaning or standing or walking
In the first loveliness of womanhood,
And with the fervour of my youthful eyes,
Has set me muttering like a fool.

You are more beautiful than any one,
And yet your body had a flaw:
Your small hands were not beautiful,
And I am afraid that you will run   30
And paddle to the wrist
In that mysterious, always brimming lake
Where those that have obeyed the holy law
Paddle and are perfect. Leave unchanged
The hands that I have kissed,
For old sakes' sake.

The last stroke of midnight dies.
All day in the one chair
From dream to dream and rhyme to rhyme I have
     ranged
In rambling talk with an image of air: 40
Vague memories, nothing but memories.

The Balloon of the Mind

Hands, do what you're bid:
Bring the balloon of the mind
That bellies and drags in the wind
Into its narrow shed.

To a Squirrel at Kyle-na-No°

Come play with me;
Why should you run
Through the shaking tree
As though I'd a gun
To strike you dead?
When all I would do
Is to scratch your head
And let you go.

On being Asked for a War Poem

I think it better that in times like these
A poet's mouth be silent, for in truth
We have no gift to set a statesman right;
He has had enough of meddling who can please
A young girl in the indolence of her youth,
Or an old man upon a winter's night.

Ego Dominus Tuus°

Hic. On the grey sand beside the shallow stream°
     Under your old wind-beaten tower, where still°
     A lamp burns on beside the open book
     That Michael Robartes left, you walk in the moon°
     And though you have passed the best of life still trace,
     Enthralled by the unconquerable delusion,
     Magical shapes.

Ille.   By the help of an image
     I call to my own opposite, summon all

That I have handled least, least looked upon.

Hic. And I would find myself and not an image.   10

Ille. That is our modern hope and by its light
    We have lit upon the gentle, sensitive mind
    And lost the old nonchalance of the hand;
    Whether we have chosen chisel, pen or brush,
    We are but critics, or but half create,
    Timid, entangled, empty and abashed,
    Lacking the countenance of our friends.

Hic.   And yet
    The chief imagination of Christendom,
    Dante Alighieri, so utterly found himself
    That he has made that hollow face of his   20
    More plain to the mind's eye than any face
    But that of Christ.

Ille.   And did he find himself
    Or was the hunger that had made it hollow
    A hunger for the apple on the bough
    Most out of reach? and is that spectral image
    The man that Lapo and that Guido knew?°
    I think he fashioned from his opposite
    An image that might have been a stony face
    Staring upon a Bedouin's horse-hair roof
    From doored and windowed cliff, or half upturned   30
    Among the coarse grass and the camel-dung.
    He set his chisel to the hardest stone.
    Being mocked by Guido for his lecherous life,
    Derided and deriding, driven out
    To climb that stair and eat that bitter bread,
    He found the unpersuadable justice, he found
    The most exalted lady loved by a man.°

Hic. Yet surely there are men who have made their art
    Out of no tragic war, lovers of life,
    Impulsive men that look for happiness   40
    And sing when they have found it.

Ille.   No, not sing,
    For those that love the world serve it in action,
    Grow rich, popular and full of influence,
    And should they paint or write, still it is action:

The struggle of the fly in marmalade.
The rhetorician would deceive his neighbours,
The sentimentalist himself; while art
Is but a vision of reality.
What portion in the world can the artist have
Who has awakened from the common dream   50
But dissipation and despair?

Hic.   And yet
No one denies to Keats love of the world;°
Remember his deliberate happiness.

Ille. His art is happy, but who knows his mind?
I see a schoolboy when I think of him,
With face and nose pressed to a sweet-shop window,
For certainly he sank into his grave
His senses and his heart unsatisfied,
And made—being poor, ailing and ignorant,
Shut out from all the luxury of the world,   60
The coarse-bred son of a livery-stable keeper—
Luxuriant song.

Hic.   Why should you leave the lamp
Burning alone beside an open book,
And trace these characters upon the sands?
A style is found by sedentary toil
And by the imitation of great masters.

Ille. Because I seek an image, not a book.
Those men that in their writings are most wise
Own nothing but their blind, stupefied hearts.
I call to the mysterious one who yet   70
Shall walk the wet sands by the edge of the stream
And look most like me, being indeed my double,
And prove of all imaginable things
The most unlike, being my anti-self,
And standing by these characters disclose
All that I seek; and whisper it as though
He were afraid the birds, who cry aloud
Their momentary cries before it is dawn,
Would carry it away to blasphemous men.

The Phases of the Moon°

An old man cocked his ear upon a bridge;
He and his friend, their faces to the South,
Had trod the uneven road. Their boots were soiled,
Their Connemara cloth worn out of shape;°
They had kept a steady pace as though their beds,
Despite a dwindling and late risen moon,
Were distant still. An old man cocked his ear.

Aherne. What made that sound?

Robartes.   A rat or water-hen°
  Splashed, or an otter slid into the stream.
  We are on the bridge; that shadow is the tower,   10
  And the light proves that he is reading still.
  He has found, after the manner of his kind,
  Mere images; chosen this place to live in
  Because, it may be, of the candle-light
  From the far tower where Milton's Platonist°
  Sat late, or Shelley's visionary prince:°
  The lonely light that Samuel Palmer engraved,°
  An image of mysterious wisdom won by toil;
  And now he seeks in book or manuscript
  What he shall never find.

Aherne.   Why should not you   20
  Who know it all ring at his door, and speak
  Just truth enough to show that his whole life
  Will scarcely find for him a broken crust
  Of all those truths that are your daily bread;
  And when you have spoken take the roads again?

Robartes. He wrote of me in that extravagant style
  He had learned from Pater, and to round his tale°
  Said I was dead; and dead I choose to be.°

Aherne. Sing me the changes of the moon once more;
  True song, though speech: 'mine author sung it me.'   30

Robartes. Twenty-and-eight the phases of the moon,
  The full and the moon's dark and all the crescents,
  Twenty-and-eight, and yet but six-and-twenty
  The cradles that a man must needs be rocked in;
  For there's no human life at the full or the dark.

From the first crescent to the half, the dream
But summons to adventure, and the man
Is always happy like a bird or a beast;
But while the moon is rounding towards the full
He follows whatever whim's most difficult   40
Among whims not impossible, and though scarred,
As with the cat-o'-nine-tails of the mind,
His body moulded from within his body
Grows comelier. Eleven pass, and then
Athena takes Achilles by the hair,°
Hector is in the dust, Nietzsche is born,°
Because the hero's crescent is the twelfth.
And yet, twice born, twice buried, grow he must,
Before the full moon, helpless as a worm.
The thirteenth moon but sets the soul at war   50
In its own being, and when that war's begun
There is no muscle in the arm; and after,
Under the frenzy of the fourteenth moon,
The soul begins to tremble into stillness,
To die into the labyrinth of itself!

Aherne. Sing out the song; sing to the end, and sing
    The strange reward of all that discipline.

Robartes. All thought becomes an image and the soul
    Becomes a body: that body and that soul
    Too perfect at the full to lie in a cradle,   60
    Too lonely for the traffic of the world:
    Body and soul cast out and cast away
    Beyond the visible world.

Aherne.   All dreams of the soul
    End in a beautiful man's or woman's body.

Robartes. Have you not always known it?

Aherne.   The song will have it
    That those that we have loved got their long fingers
    From death, and wounds, or on Sinai's top,°
    Or from some bloody whip in their own hands.
    They ran from cradle to cradle till at last
    Their beauty dropped out of the loneliness   70
    Of body and soul.

Robartes.   The lover's heart knows that.

Aherne. It must be that the terror in their eyes
　Is memory or foreknowledge of the hour
　When all is fed with light and heaven is bare.

Robartes. When the moon's full those creatures of the
　　full
　Are met on the waste hills by country men
　Who shudder and hurry by: body and soul
　Estranged amid the strangeness of themselves,
　Caught up in contemplation, the mind's eye
　Fixed upon images that once were thought,　　　　　80
　For perfected, completed, and immovable
　Images can break the solitude
　Of lovely, satisfied, indifferent eyes.

　　And thereupon with aged, high-pitched voice
　　Aherne laughed, thinking of the man within,
　　His sleepless candle and laborious pen.

Robartes. And after that the crumbling of the moon:
　The soul remembering its loneliness
　Shudders in many cradles; all is changed.
　It would be the world's servant, and as it serves,　　90
　Choosing whatever task's most difficult
　Among tasks not impossible, it takes
　Upon the body and upon the soul
　The coarseness of the drudge.

Aherne.　　　　　　　　　　Before the full
　It sought itself and afterwards the world.

Robartes. Because you are forgotten, half out of life,
　And never wrote a book, your thought is clear.
　Reformer, merchant, statesman, learned man,
　Dutiful husband, honest wife by turn,
　Cradle upon cradle, and all in flight and all　　　　100
　Deformed, because there is no deformity
　But saves us from a dream.

Aherne.　　　　　　　　　　And what of those
　That the last servile crescent has set free?

Robartes. Because all dark, like those that are all light,
　They are cast beyond the verge, and in a cloud,

Crying to one another like the bats;
But having no desire they cannot tell
What's good or bad, or what it is to triumph
At the perfection of one's own obedience;
And yet they speak what's blown into the mind;   110
Deformed beyond deformity, unformed,
Insipid as the dough before it is baked,
They change their bodies at a word.

Aherne.   And then?

Robartes. When all the dough has been so kneaded up
     That it can take what form cook Nature fancies,
     The first thin crescent is wheeled round once more.

Aherne. But the escape; the song's not finished yet.

Robartes. Hunchback and Saint and Fool are the last
     crescents.
     The burning bow that once could shoot an arrow
     Out of the up and down, the wagon-wheel   120
     Of beauty's cruelty and wisdom's chatter—
     Out of that raving tide—is drawn betwixt
     Deformity of body and of mind.

Aherne. Were not our beds far off I'd ring the bell,
     Stand under the rough roof-timbers of the hall
     Beside the castle door, where all is stark
     Austerity, a place set out for wisdom
     That he will never find; I'd play a part;
     He would never know me after all these years
     But take me for some drunken country man;   130
     I'd stand and mutter there until he caught
     'Hunchback and Saint and Fool', and that they came
     Under the three last crescents of the moon,
     And then I'd stagger out. He'd crack his wits
     Day after day, yet never find the meaning.

And then he laughed to think that what seemed hard
Should be so simple—a bat rose from the hazels
And circled round him with its squeaky cry,
The light in the tower window was put out.

The Cat and the Moon

The cat went here and there
And the moon spun round like a top,
And the nearest kin of the moon,
The creeping cat, looked up.
Black Minnaloushe stared at the moon,
For, wander and wail as he would,
The pure cold light in the sky
Troubled his animal blood.
Minnaloushe runs in the grass
Lifting his delicate feet.   10
Do you dance, Minnaloushe, do you dance?
When two close kindred meet,
What better than call a dance?
Maybe the moon may learn,
Tired of that courtly fashion,
A new dance turn.
Minnaloushe creeps through the grass
From moonlit place to place,
The sacred moon overhead
Has taken a new phase.   20
Does Minnaloushe know that his pupils
Will pass from change to change,
And that from round to crescent,
From crescent to round they range?
Minnaloushe creeps through the grass
Alone, important and wise,
And lifts to the changing moon
His changing eyes.

The Double Vision of Michael Robartes°

I

On the grey rock of Cashel the mind's eye°
Has called up the cold spirits that are born
When the old moon is vanished from the sky
And the new still hides her horn.

Under blank eyes and fingers never still
The particular is pounded till it is man.

When had I my own will?
O not since life began.

Constrained, arraigned, baffled, bent and unbent
By these wire-jointed jaws and limbs of wood,   10
Themselves obedient,
Knowing not evil and good;
Obedient to some hidden magical breath.
They do not even feel, so abstract are they,
So dead beyond our death,
Triumph that we obey.

II

On the grey rock of Cashel I suddenly saw
A Sphinx with woman breast and lion paw,
A Buddha, hand at rest,
Hand lifted up that blest;   20

And right between these two a girl at play
That, it may be, had danced her life away,
For now being dead it seemed
That she of dancing dreamed.

Although I saw it all in the mind's eye
There can be nothing solider till I die;
I saw by the moon's light
Now at its fifteenth night.

One lashed her tail; her eyes lit by the moon
Gazed upon all things known, all things unknown,   30
In triumph of intellect
With motionless head erect.

That other's moonlit eyeballs never moved,
Being fixed on all things loved, all things unloved,
Yet little peace he had,
For those that love are sad.

O little did they care who danced between,
And little she by whom her dance was seen
So she had outdanced thought.
Body perfection brought,   40

For what but eye and ear silence the mind
With the minute particulars of mankind?

Mind moved yet seemed to stop
As 'twere a spinning-top.

In contemplation had those three so wrought
Upon a moment, and so stretched it out
That they, time overthrown,
Were dead yet flesh and bone.

III

I knew that I had seen, had seen at last
That girl my unremembering nights hold fast   50
Or else my dreams that fly
If I should rub an eye,

And yet in flying fling into my meat
A crazy juice that makes the pulses beat
As though I had been undone
By Homer's Paragon°

Who never gave the burning town a thought;
To such a pitch of folly I am brought,
Being caught between the pull
Of the dark moon and the full,   60

The commonness of thought and images
That have the frenzy of our western seas.
Thereon I made my moan,
And after kissed a stone,

And after that arranged it in a song
Seeing that I, ignorant for so long,
Had been rewarded thus
In Cormac's ruined house.°

From Michael Robartes and the Dancer (1921)

Michael Robartes and the Dancer°

He. Opinion is not worth a rush;
   In this altar-piece the knight,

Who grips his long spear so to push
That dragon through the fading light,
Loved the lady; and it's plain
The half-dead dragon was her thought,
That every morning rose again
And dug its claws and shrieked and fought.
Could the impossible come to pass
She would have time to turn her eyes,   10
Her lover thought, upon the glass
And on the instant would grow wise.

She. You mean they argued.

He.   Put it so;
But bear in mind your lover's wage
Is what your looking-glass can show,
And that he will turn green with rage
At all that is not pictured there.

She. May I not put myself to college?

He. Go pluck Athena by the hair;°
For what mere book can grant a knowledge   20
With an impassioned gravity
Appropriate to that beating breast,
That vigorous thigh, that dreaming eye?
And may the devil take the rest.

She. And must no beautiful woman be
Learned like a man?

He.   Paul Veronese°
And all his sacred company
Imagined bodies all their days
By the lagoon you love so much,°
For proud, soft, ceremonious proof   30
That all must come to sight and touch;
While Michael Angelo's Sistine roof,
His 'Morning' and his 'Night' disclose°
How sinew that has been pulled tight,
Or it may be loosened in repose,
Can rule by supernatural right
Yet be but sinew.

She.   I have heard said
There is great danger in the body.

He. Did God in portioning wine and bread
    Give man His thought or His mere body?   40

She. My wretched dragon is perplexed.

He. I have principles to prove me right.
    It follows from this Latin text
    That blest souls are not composite,
    And that all beautiful women may
    Live in uncomposite blessedness,
    And lead us to the like—if they
    Will banish every thought, unless
    The lineaments that please their view
    When the long looking-glass is full,   50
    Even from the foot-sole think it too.

She. They say such different things at school.

Solomon and the Witch°

And thus declared that Arab lady:
'Last night, where under the wild moon
On grassy mattress I had laid me,
Within my arms great Solomon,
I suddenly cried out in a strange tongue
Not his, not mine.'
            Who understood
Whatever has been said, sighed, sung,
Howled, miau-d, barked, brayed, belled, yelled,
    cried, crowed,
Thereon replied: 'A cockerel
Crew from a blossoming apple bough   10
Three hundred years before the Fall,
And never crew again till now,
And would not now but that he thought,
Chance being at one with Choice at last,
All that the brigand apple brought
And this foul world were dead at last.
He that crowed out eternity
Thought to have crowed it in again.
For though love has a spider's eye
To find out some appropriate pain—   20

Aye, though all passion's in the glance—
For every nerve, and tests a lover
With cruelties of Choice and Chance;
And when at last that murder's over
Maybe the bride-bed brings despair,
For each an imagined image brings
And finds a real image there;
Yet the world ends when these two things,
Though several, are a single light,
When oil and wick are burned in one;   30
Therefore a blessed moon last night
Gave Sheba to her Solomon.'

'Yet the world stays.'
                   'If that be so,
Your cockerel found us in the wrong
Although he thought it worth a crow.
Maybe an image is too strong
Or maybe is not strong enough.'

'The night has fallen; not a sound
In the forbidden sacred grove
Unless a petal hit the ground,   40
Nor any human sight within it
But the crushed grass where we have lain;
And the moon is wilder every minute.
O! Solomon! let us try again.'

Under Saturn°

Do not because this day I have grown saturnine
Imagine that lost love, inseparable from my thought
Because I have no other youth, can make me pine;
For how should I forget the wisdom that you brought,
The comfort that you made? Although my wits have gone
On a fantastic ride, my horse's flanks are spurred
By childish memories of an old cross Pollexfen,
And of a Middleton, whose name you never heard,
And of a red-haired Yeats whose looks, although he
    died°

Before my time, seem like a vivid memory.   10
You heard that labouring man who had served my
    people. He said
Upon the open road, near to the Sligo quay—
No, no, not said, but cried it out—'You have come
    again,
And surely after twenty years it was time to come.'
I am thinking of a child's vow sworn in vain
Never to leave that valley his fathers called their home.

    November 1919

Easter, 1916°

    I have met them at close of day
    Coming with vivid faces
    From counter or desk among grey
    Eighteenth-century houses.
    I have passed with a nod of the head
    Or polite meaningless words,
    Or have lingered awhile and said
    Polite meaningless words,
    And thought before I had done
    Of a mocking tale or a gibe   10
    To please a companion
    Around the fire at the club,
    Being certain that they and I
    But lived where motley is worn:
    All changed, changed utterly:
    A terrible beauty is born.

    That woman's days were spent°
    In ignorant good-will,
    Her nights in argument
    Until her voice grew shrill.   20
    What voice more sweet than hers
    When, young and beautiful,
    She rode to harriers?
    This man had kept a school
    And rode our wingèd horse;°
    This other his helper and friend°

Was coming into his force;
He might have won fame in the end,
So sensitive his nature seemed,
So daring and sweet his thought.
This other man I had dreamed°   30
A drunken, vainglorious lout.
He had done most bitter wrong
To some who are near my heart,
Yet I number him in the song;
He, too, has resigned his part
In the casual comedy;
He, too, has been changed in his turn,
Transformed utterly:
A terrible beauty is born.   40

Hearts with one purpose alone
Through summer and winter seem
Enchanted to a stone
To trouble the living stream.
The horse that comes from the road,
The rider, the birds that range
From cloud to tumbling cloud,
Minute by minute they change;
A shadow of cloud on the stream
Changes minute by minute;   50
A horse-hoof slides on the brim,
And a horse plashes within it;
The long-legged moor-hens dive,
And hens to moor-cocks call;
Minute by minute they live:
The stone's in the midst of all.

Too long a sacrifice
Can make a stone of the heart.
O when may it suffice?
That is Heaven's part, our part   60
To murmur name upon name,
As a mother names her child
When sleep at last has come
On limbs that had run wild.
What is it but nightfall?

No, no, not night but death;
Was it needless death after all?
For England may keep faith°
For all that is done and said.
We know their dream; enough   70
To know they dreamed and are dead;
And what if excess of love
Bewildered them till they died?
I write it out in a verse—
MacDonagh and MacBride
And Connolly and Pearse°
Now and in time to be,
Wherever green is worn,
Are changed, changed utterly:
A terrible beauty is born.   80

September 25, 1916

Sixteen Dead Men°

O but we talked at large before
The sixteen men were shot,
But who can talk of give and take,
What should be and what not
While those dead men are loitering there
To stir the boiling pot?

You say that we should still the land
Till Germany's overcome;°
But who is there to argue that
Now Pearse is deaf and dumb?°   10
And is their logic to outweigh
MacDonagh's bony thumb?°

How could you dream they'd listen
That have an ear alone
For those new comrades they have found,
Lord Edward and Wolfe Tone,°
Or meddle with our give and take
That converse bone to bone?

The Rose Tree

'O words are lightly spoken,'
Said Pearse to Connolly,°
'Maybe a breath of politic words
Has withered our Rose Tree;
Or maybe but a wind that blows
Across the bitter sea.'

'It needs to be but watered,'
James Connolly replied,
'To make the green come out again
And spread on every side,   10
And shake the blossom from the bud
To be the garden's pride.'

'But where can we draw water,'
Said Pearse to Connolly,
'When all the wells are parched away?
O plain as plain can be
There's nothing but our own red blood
Can make a right Rose Tree.'

On a Political Prisoner°

She that but little patience knew,
From childhood on, had now so much
A grey gull lost its fear and flew
Down to her cell and there alit,
And there endured her fingers' touch
And from her fingers ate its bit.

Did she in touching that lone wing
Recall the years before her mind
Became a bitter, an abstract thing,
Her thought some popular enmity: 10
Blind and leader of the blind
Drinking the foul ditch where they lie?

When long ago I saw her ride
Under Ben Bulben to the meet,°
The beauty of her country-side

With all youth's lonely wildness stirred,
She seemed to have grown clean and sweet
Like any rock-bred, sea-borne bird:

Sea-borne, or balanced on the air
When first it sprang out of the nest   20
Upon some lofty rock to stare
Upon the cloudy canopy,
While under its storm-beaten breast
Cried out the hollows of the sea.

Towards Break of Day

Was it the double of my dream
The woman that by me lay
Dreamed, or did we halve a dream
Under the first cold gleam of day?

I thought: 'There is a waterfall
Upon Ben Bulben side°
That all my childhood counted dear;
Were I to travel far and wide
I could not find a thing so dear.'
My memories had magnified   10
So many times childish delight.

I would have touched it like a child
But knew my finger could but have touched
Cold stone and water. I grew wild
Even accusing Heaven because
It had set down among its laws:
Nothing that we love over-much
Is ponderable to our touch.

I dreamed towards break of day,
The cold blown spray in my nostril.   20
But she that beside me lay
Had watched in bitterer sleep
The marvellous stag of Arthur,°
That lofty white stag, leap
From mountain steep to steep.

Demon and Beast

For certain minutes at the least
That crafty demon and that loud beast
That plague me day and night
Ran out of my sight;
Though I had long perned in the gyre,
Between my hatred and desire,
I saw my freedom won
And all laugh in the sun.

The glittering eyes in a death's head
Of old Luke Wadding's portrait said°   10
Welcome, and the Ormondes all°
Nodded upon the wall,
And even Strafford smiled as though°
It made him happier to know
I understood his plan.
Now that the loud beast ran
There was no portrait in the Gallery°
But beckoned to sweet company,
For all men's thoughts grew clear
Being dear as mine are dear.   20

But soon a tear-drop started up,
For aimless joy had made me stop
Beside the little lake°
To watch a white gull take
A bit of bread thrown up into the air;
Now gyring down and perning there°
He splashed where an absurd
Portly green-pated bird
Shook off the water from his back;
Being no more demoniac   30
A stupid happy creature
Could rouse my whole nature.

Yet I am certain as can be
That every natural victory
Belongs to beast or demon,
That never yet had freeman

Right mastery of natural things,
And that mere growing old, that brings
Chilled blood, this sweetness brought;
Yet have no dearer thought   40
Than that I may find out a way
To make it linger half a day.

O what a sweetness strayed
Through barren Thebaid,°
Or by the Mareotic sea°
When that exultant Anthony°
And twice a thousand more
Starved upon the shore
And withered to a bag of bones!
What had the Caesars but their thrones?   50

The Second Coming°

Turning and turning in the widening gyre°
The falcon cannot hear the falconer;
Things fall apart; the centre cannot hold;
Mere anarchy is loosed upon the world,
The blood-dimmed tide is loosed, and everywhere
The ceremony of innocence is drowned;
The best lack all conviction, while the worst
Are full of passionate intensity.

Surely some revelation is at hand;
Surely the Second Coming is at hand.   10
The Second Coming! Hardly are those words out
When a vast image out of *Spiritus Mundi*°
Troubles my sight: somewhere in sands of the desert
A shape with lion body and the head of a man,
A gaze blank and pitiless as the sun,
Is moving its slow thighs, while all about it
Reel shadows of the indignant desert birds.
The darkness drops again; but now I know
That twenty centuries of stony sleep
Were vexed to nightmare by a rocking cradle,   20

And what rough beast, its hour come round at last,
Slouches towards Bethlehem to be born?

A Prayer for my Daughter°

Once more the storm is howling, and half hid
Under this cradle-hood and coverlid
My child sleeps on. There is no obstacle
But Gregory's wood and one bare hill°
Whereby the haystack- and roof-levelling wind,
Bred on the Atlantic, can be stayed;
And for an hour I have walked and prayed
Because of the great gloom that is in my mind.

I have walked and prayed for this young child an hour
And heard the sea-wind scream upon the tower,   10
And under the arches of the bridge, and scream
In the elms above the flooded stream;
Imagining in excited reverie
That the future years had come,
Dancing to a frenzied drum,
Out of the murderous innocence of the sea.

May she be granted beauty and yet not
Beauty to make a stranger's eye distraught,
Or hers before a looking-glass, for such,
Being made beautiful overmuch,   20
Consider beauty a sufficient end,
Lose natural kindness and maybe
The heart-revealing intimacy
That chooses right, and never find a friend.

Helen being chosen found life flat and dull°
And later had much trouble from a fool,°
While that great Queen, that rose out of the spray,°
Being fatherless could have her way
Yet chose a bandy-leggèd smith for man.°
It's certain that fine women eat   30
A crazy salad with their meat
Whereby the Horn of Plenty is undone.°

In courtesy I'd have her chiefly learned;
Hearts are not had as a gift but hearts are earned
By those that are not entirely beautiful;
Yet many, that have played the fool
For beauty's very self, has charm made wise,
And many a poor man that has roved,
Loved and thought himself beloved,
From a glad kindness cannot take his eyes.   40

May she become a flourishing hidden tree
That all her thoughts may like the linnet be,
And have no business but dispensing round
Their magnanimities of sound,
Nor but in merriment begin a chase,
Nor but in merriment a quarrel.
O may she live like some green laurel
Rooted in one dear perpetual place.

My mind, because the minds that I have loved,
The sort of beauty that I have approved,   50
Prosper but little, has dried up of late,
Yet knows that to be choked with hate
May well be of all evil chances chief.
If there's no hatred in a mind
Assault and battery of the wind
Can never tear the linnet from the leaf.

An intellectual hatred is the worst,
So let her think opinions are accursed.
Have I not seen the loveliest woman born°
Out of the mouth of Plenty's horn,   60
Because of her opinionated mind
Barter that horn and every good
By quiet natures understood
For an old bellows full of angry wind?

Considering that, all hatred driven hence,
The soul recovers radical innocence
And learns at last that it is self-delighting,
Self-appeasing, self-affrighting,
And that its own sweet will is Heaven's will;

She can, though every face should scowl   70
And every windy quarter howl
Or every bellows burst, be happy still.

And may her bridegroom bring her to a house
Where all's accustomed, ceremonious;
For arrogance and hatred are the wares
Peddled in the thoroughfares.
How but in custom and in ceremony
Are innocence and beauty born?
Ceremony's a name for the rich horn,
And custom for the spreading laurel tree.   80

  June 1919

To be Carved on a Stone at Thoor Ballylee

I, the poet William Yeats,
With old mill boards and sea-green slates,
And smithy work from the Gort forge,°
Restored this tower for my wife George;°
And may these characters remain
When all is ruin once again.

From The Tower (1928)

Sailing to Byzantium°

I

That is no country for old men. The young°
In one another's arms, birds in the trees,
—Those dying generations—at their song,
The salmon-falls, the mackerel-crowded seas,
Fish, flesh, or fowl, commend all summer long
Whatever is begotten, born, and dies.
Caught in that sensual music all neglect
Monuments of unageing intellect.

II

An aged man is but a paltry thing,
A tattered coat upon a stick, unless   10
Soul clap its hands and sing, and louder sing°
For every tatter in its mortal dress,
Nor is there singing school but studying
Monuments of its own magnificence;
And therefore I have sailed the seas and come
To the holy city of Byzantium.

III

O sages standing in God's holy fire
As in the gold mosaic of a wall,°
Come from the holy fire, perne in a gyre,°
And be the singing-masters of my soul.   20
Consume my heart away; sick with desire
And fastened to a dying animal
It knows not what it is; and gather me
Into the artifice of eternity.

IV

Once out of nature I shall never take
My bodily form from any natural thing,
But such a form as Grecian goldsmiths make
Of hammered gold and gold enamelling
To keep a drowsy Emperor awake;
Or set upon a golden bough to sing°   30
To lords and ladies of Byzantium
Of what is past, or passing, or to come.

1927

The Tower

I

What shall I do with this absurdity—
O heart, O troubled heart—this caricature,
Decrepit age that has been tied to me
As to a dog's tail?
                    Never had I more

Excited, passionate, fantastical
Imagination, nor an ear and eye
That more expected the impossible—
No, not in boyhood when with rod and fly,
Or the humbler worm, I climbed Ben Bulben's back°
And had the livelong summer day to spend.   10
It seems that I must bid the Muse go pack,
Choose Plato and Plotinus for a friend°
Until imagination, ear and eye,
Can be content with argument and deal
In abstract things; or be derided by
A sort of battered kettle at the heel.

II

I pace upon the battlements and stare
On the foundations of a house, or where
Tree, like a sooty finger, starts from the earth;
And send imagination forth   20
Under the day's declining beam, and call
Images and memories
From ruin or from ancient trees,
For I would ask a question of them all.

Beyond that ridge lived Mrs French, and once
When every silver candlestick or sconce
Lit up the dark mahogany and the wine,
A serving-man, that could divine
That most respected lady's every wish,
Ran and with the garden shears   30
Clipped an insolent farmer's ears
And brought them in a little covered dish.

Some few remembered still when I was young
A peasant girl commended by a song,
Who'd lived somewhere upon that rocky place,
And praised the colour of her face,
And had the greater joy in praising her,
Remembering that, if walked she there,
Farmers jostled at the fair
So great a glory did the song confer.   40

And certain men, being maddened by those rhymes,
Or else by toasting her a score of times,
Rose from the table and declared it right
To test their fancy by their sight;
But they mistook the brightness of the moon
For the prosaic light of day—
Music had driven their wits astray—
And one was drowned in the great bog of Cloone.°

Strange, but the man who made the song was blind;°
Yet, now I have considered it, I find   50
That nothing strange; the tragedy began
With Homer that was a blind man,°
And Helen has all living hearts betrayed.°
O may the moon and sunlight seem
One inextricable beam,
For if I triumph I must make men mad.

And I myself created Hanrahan°
And drove him drunk or sober through the dawn
From somewhere in the neighbouring cottages.
Caught by an old man's juggleries   60
He stumbled, tumbled, fumbled to and fro
And had but broken knees for hire
And horrible splendour of desire;
I thought it all out twenty years ago:

Good fellows shuffled cards in an old bawn;
And when that ancient ruffian's turn was on
He so bewitched the cards under his thumb
That all but the one card became
A pack of hounds and not a pack of cards,
And that he changed into a hare.   70
Hanrahan rose in frenzy there
And followed up those baying creatures towards—

O towards I have forgotten what—enough!
I must recall a man that neither love
Nor music nor an enemy's clipped ear
Could, he was so harried, cheer;
A figure that has grown so fabulous

There's not a neighbour left to say
When he finished his dog's day:
An ancient bankrupt master of this house.   80

Before that ruin came, for centuries,
Rough men-at-arms, cross-gartered to the knees
Or shod in iron, climbed the narrow stairs,
And certain men-at-arms there were
Whose images, in the Great Memory stored,°
Come with loud cry and panting breast
To break upon a sleeper's rest
While their great wooden dice beat on the board.

As I would question all, come all who can;
Come old, necessitous, half-mounted man;   90
And bring beauty's blind rambling celebrant;
The red man the juggler sent
Through God-forsaken meadows; Mrs French,
Gifted with so fine an ear;
The man drowned in a bog's mire,
When mocking muses chose the country wench.

Did all old men and women, rich and poor,
Who trod upon these rocks or passed this door,
Whether in public or in secret rage
As I do now against old age?   100
But I have found an answer in those eyes
That are impatient to be gone;
Go therefore; but leave Hanrahan,
For I need all his mighty memories.

Old lecher with a love on every wind,
Bring up out of that deep considering mind
All that you have discovered in the grave,
For it is certain that you have
Reckoned up every unforeknown, unseeing
Plunge, lured by a softening eye,   110
Or by a touch or a sigh,
Into the labyrinth of another's being;

Does the imagination dwell the most
Upon a woman won or woman lost?

If on the lost, admit you turned aside
From a great labyrinth out of pride,
Cowardice, some silly over-subtle thought
Or anything called conscience once;
And that if memory recur, the sun's
Under eclipse and the day blotted out.   120

III

It is time that I wrote my will;
I choose upstanding men
That climb the streams until
The fountain leap, and at dawn
Drop their cast at the side
Of dripping stone; I declare
They shall inherit my pride,
The pride of people that were
Bound neither to Cause nor to State,
Neither to slaves that were spat on,   130
Nor to the tyrants that spat,
The people of Burke and of Grattan°
That gave, though free to refuse—
Pride, like that of the morn,
When the headlong light is loose,
Or that of the fabulous horn,
Or that of the sudden shower
When all streams are dry,
Or that of the hour
When the swan must fix his eye   140
Upon a fading gleam,
Float out upon a long
Last reach of glittering stream
And there sing his last song.
And I declare my faith:
I mock Plotinus' thought
And cry in Plato's teeth,
Death and life were not
Till man made up the whole,
Made lock, stock and barrel   150
Out of his bitter soul,
Aye, sun and moon and star, all,
And further add to that

That, being dead, we rise,
Dream and so create
Translunar Paradise.
I have prepared my peace
With learned Italian things
And the proud stones of Greece,
Poet's imaginings   160
And memories of love,
Memories of the words of women,
All those things whereof
Man makes a superhuman
Mirror-resembling dream.

As at the loophole there
The daws chatter and scream,
And drop twigs layer upon layer.
When they have mounted up,
The mother bird will rest   170
On their hollow top,
And so warm her wild nest.

I leave both faith and pride
To young upstanding men
Climbing the mountain side,
That under bursting dawn
They may drop a fly;
Being of that metal made
Till it was broken by
This sedentary trade.   180

Now shall I make my soul,
Compelling it to study
In a learned school
Till the wreck of body,
Slow decay of blood,
Testy delirium
Or dull decrepitude,
Or what worse evil come—
The death of friends, or death
Of every brilliant eye   190

That made a catch in the breath—
Seem but the clouds of the sky
When the horizon fades;
Or a bird's sleepy cry
Among the deepening shades.

1926

Meditations in Time of Civil War°

I

Ancestral Houses

Surely among a rich man's flowering lawns,
Amid the rustle of his planted hills,
Life overflows without ambitious pains;
And rains down life until the basin spills,
And mounts more dizzy high the more it rains
As though to choose whatever shape it wills
And never stoop to a mechanical
Or servile shape, at others' beck and call.

Mere dreams, mere dreams! Yet Homer had not
      sung
Had he not found it certain beyond dreams   10
That out of life's own self-delight had sprung
The abounding glittering jet; though now it seems
As if some marvellous empty sea-shell flung
Out of the obscure dark of the rich streams,
And not a fountain, were the symbol which
Shadows the inherited glory of the rich.

Some violent bitter man, some powerful man
Called architect and artist in, that they,
Bitter and violent men, might rear in stone
The sweetness that all longed for night and day, 20
The gentleness none there had ever known;
But when the master's buried mice can play,
And maybe the great-grandson of that house,
For all its bronze and marble, 's but a mouse.

O what if gardens where the peacock strays
With delicate feet upon old terraces,
Or else all Juno from an urn displays°
Before the indifferent garden deities;
O what if levelled lawns and gravelled ways
Where slippered Contemplation finds his ease   30
And Childhood a delight for every sense,
But take our greatness with our violence?

What if the glory of escutcheoned doors,
And buildings that a haughtier age designed,
The pacing to and fro on polished floors
Amid great chambers and long galleries, lined
With famous portraits of our ancestors;
What if those things the greatest of mankind
Consider most to magnify, or to bless,
But take our greatness with our bitterness?   40

II

My House

An ancient bridge, and a more ancient tower,
A farmhouse that is sheltered by its wall,
An acre of stony ground,
Where the symbolic rose can break in flower,
Old ragged elms, old thorns innumerable,
The sound of the rain or sound
Of every wind that blows;
The stilted water-hen
Crossing stream again
Scared by the splashing of a dozen cows;   10

A winding stair, a chamber arched with stone,
A grey stone fireplace with an open hearth,
A candle and written page.
Il Penseroso's Platonist toiled on°
In some like chamber, shadowing forth
How the daemonic rage
Imagined everything.
Benighted travellers
From markets and from fairs
Have seen his midnight candle glimmering.   20

Two men have founded here. A man-at-arms
Gathered a score of horse and spent his days
In this tumultuous spot,
Where through long wars and sudden night alarms
His dwindling score and he seemed castaways
Forgetting and forgot;
And I, that after me
My bodily heirs may find,
To exalt a lonely mind,
Befitting emblems of adversity.   30

III
My Table

Two heavy trestles, and a board
Where Sato's gift, a changeless sword,°
By pen and paper lies,
That it may moralise
My days out of their aimlessness.
A bit of an embroidered dress
Covers its wooden sheath.
Chaucer had not drawn breath
When it was forged. In Sato's house,
Curved like new moon, moon-luminous,   10
It lay five hundred years.
Yet if no change appears
No moon; only an aching heart
Conceives a changeless work of art.
Our learned men have urged
That when and where 'twas forged
A marvellous accomplishment,
In painting or in pottery, went
From father unto son
And through the centuries ran   20
And seemed unchanging like the sword.
Soul's beauty being most adored,
Men and their business took
The soul's unchanging look;
For the most rich inheritor,
Knowing that none could pass Heaven's door
That loved inferior art,

Had such an aching heart
That he, although a country's talk
For silken clothes and stately walk,   30
Had waking wits; it seemed
Juno's peacock screamed.

IV

My Descendants

Having inherited a vigorous mind
From my old fathers, I must nourish dreams
And leave a woman and a man behind
As vigorous of mind, and yet it seems
Life scarce can cast a fragrance on the wind,
Scarce spread a glory to the morning beams,
But the torn petals strew the garden plot;
And there's but common greenness after that.

And what if my descendants lose the flower
Through natural declension of the soul,   10
Through too much business with the passing hour,
Through too much play, or marriage with a fool?
May this laborious stair and this stark tower
Become a roofless ruin that the owl
May build in the cracked masonry and cry
Her desolation to the desolate sky.

The Primum Mobile that fashioned us°
Has made the very owls in circles move;
And I, that count myself most prosperous,
Seeing that love and friendship are enough,   20
For an old neighbour's friendship chose the house
And decked and altered it for a girl's love,
And know whatever flourish and decline
These stones remain their monument and mine.

V

The Road at my Door

An affable Irregular,°
A heavily-built Falstaffian man,°
Comes cracking jokes of civil war

As though to die by gunshot were
The finest play under the sun.

A brown Lieutenant and his men,
Half dressed in national uniform,°
Stand at my door, and I complain
Of the foul weather, hail and rain,
A pear tree broken by the storm.   10

I count those feathered balls of soot
The moor-hen guides upon the stream,
To silence the envy in my thought;
And turn towards my chamber, caught
In the cold snows of a dream.

VI

The Stare's Nest by my Window°

The bees build in the crevices
Of loosening masonry, and there
The mother birds bring grubs and flies.
My wall is loosening; honey-bees,
Come build in the empty house of the stare.

We are closed in, and the key is turned
On our uncertainty; somewhere
A man is killed, or a house burned,
Yet no clear fact to be discerned:
Come build in the empty house of the stare.   10

A barricade of stone or of wood;
Some fourteen days of civil war;
Last night they trundled down the road
That dead young soldier in his blood:
Come build in the empty house of the stare.

We had fed the heart on fantasies,
The heart's grown brutal from the fare;
More substance in our enmities
Than in our love; O honey-bees,
Come build in the empty house of the stare.   20

VII

*I see Phantoms of Hatred and of the Heart's
Fullness and of the Coming Emptiness*

I climb to the tower-top and lean upon broken stone,
A mist that is like blown snow is sweeping over all,
Valley, river, and elms, under the light of a moon
That seems unlike itself, that seems unchangeable,
A glittering sword out of the east. A puff of wind
And those white glimmering fragments of the mist
    sweep by.
Frenzies bewilder, reveries perturb the mind;
Monstrous familiar images swim to the mind's eye.

'Vengeance upon the murderers,' the cry goes up,
'Vengeance for Jacques Molay.' In cloud-pale rags, or
    in lace,°   10
The rage-driven, rage-tormented, and rage-hungry troop,
Trooper belabouring trooper, biting at arm or at face,
Plunges towards nothing, arms and fingers spreading
    wide
For the embrace of nothing; and I, my wits astray
Because of all that senseless tumult, all but cried
For vengeance on the murderers of Jacques Molay.

Their legs long, delicate and slender, aquamarine their
    eyes,
Magical unicorns bear ladies on their backs.
The ladies close their musing eyes. No prophecies,
Remembered out of Babylonian almanacs,°   20
Have closed the ladies' eyes, their minds are but a pool
Where even longing drowns under its own excess;
Nothing but stillness can remain when hearts are full
Of their own sweetness, bodies of their loveliness.

The cloud-pale unicorns, the eyes of aquamarine,
The quivering half-closed eyelids, the rags of cloud or of
    lace,
Or eyes that rage has brightened, arms it has made lean,
Give place to an indifferent multitude, give place
To brazen hawks. Nor self-delighting reverie,

Nor hate of what's to come, nor pity for what's gone,   30
Nothing but grip of claw, and the eye's complacency,
The innumerable clanging wings that have put out the
    moon.

I turn away and shut the door, and on the stair
Wonder how many times I could have proved my
    worth
In something that all others understand or share;
But O! ambitious heart, had such a proof drawn forth
A company of friends, a conscience set at ease,
It had but made us pine the more. The abstract joy,
The half-read wisdom of daemonic images,
Suffice the ageing man as once the growing boy.   40

  1923

Nineteen Hundred and Nineteen°

I

Many ingenious lovely things are gone
That seemed sheer miracle to the multitude,
Protected from the circle of the moon
That pitches common things about. There stood
Amid the ornamental bronze and stone
An ancient image made of olive wood—
And gone are Phidias' famous ivories°
And all the golden grasshoppers and bees.°

We too had many pretty toys when young;
A law indifferent to blame or praise,   10
To bribe or threat; habits that made old wrong
Melt down, as it were wax in the sun's rays;
Public opinion ripening for so long
We thought it would outlive all future days.
O what fine thought we had because we thought
That the worst rogues and rascals had died out.

All teeth were drawn, all ancient tricks unlearned,
And a great army but a showy thing;

What matter that no cannon had been turned
Into a ploughshare? Parliament and king   20
Thought that unless a little powder burned
The trumpeters might burst with trumpeting
And yet it lack all glory; and perchance
The guardsmen's drowsy chargers would not prance.

Now days are dragon-ridden, the nightmare
Rides upon sleep: a drunken soldiery
Can leave the mother, murdered at her door,
To crawl in her own blood, and go scot-free;
The night can sweat with terror as before
We pieced our thoughts into philosophy,   30
And planned to bring the world under a rule,
Who are but weasels fighting in a hole.

He who can read the signs nor sink unmanned
Into the half-deceit of some intoxicant
From shallow wits; who knows no work can stand,
Whether health, wealth or peace of mind were spent
On master-work of intellect or hand,
No honour leave its mighty monument,
Has but one comfort left: all triumph would
But break upon his ghostly solitude.   40

But is there any comfort to be found?
Man is in love and loves what vanishes,
What more is there to say? That country round
None dared admit, if such a thought were his,
Incendiary or bigot could be found
To burn that stump on the Acropolis,°
Or break in bits the famous ivories
Or traffic in the grasshoppers or bees.

II

When Loie Fuller's Chinese dancers enwound°
A shining web, a floating ribbon of cloth,   50
It seemed that a dragon of air
Had fallen among dancers, had whirled them round
Or hurried them off on its own furious path;
So the Platonic Year°
Whirls out new right and wrong,

Whirls in the old instead;
All men are dancers and their tread
Goes to the barbarous clangour of a gong.

III

Some moralist or mythological poet
Compares the solitary soul to a swan;   60
I am satisfied with that,
Satisfied if a troubled mirror show it,
Before that brief gleam of its life be gone,
An image of its state;
The wings half spread for flight,
The breast thrust out in pride
Whether to play, or to ride
Those winds that clamour of approaching night.

A man in his own secret meditation
Is lost amid the labyrinth that he has made   70
In art or politics;
Some Platonist affirms that in the station°
Where we should cast off body and trade
The ancient habit sticks,
And that if our works could
But vanish with our breath
That were a lucky death,
For triumph can but mar our solitude.

The swan has leaped into the desolate heaven:
That image can bring wildness, bring a rage   80
To end all things, to end
What my laborious life imagined, even
The half-imagined, the half-written page;
O but we dreamed to mend
Whatever mischief seemed
To afflict mankind, but now
That winds of winter blow
Learn that we were crack-pated when we dreamed.

IV

We, who seven years ago
Talked of honour and of truth,   90

Shriek with pleasure if we show
The weasel's twist, the weasel's tooth.

V

Come let us mock at the great
That had such burdens on the mind
And toiled so hard and late
To leave some monument behind,
Nor thought of the levelling wind.

Come let us mock at the wise;
With all those calendars whereon
They fixed old aching eyes,   100
They never saw how seasons run,
And now but gape at the sun.

Come let us mock at the good
That fancied goodness might be gay,
And sick of solitude
Might proclaim a holiday:
Wind shrieked—and where are they?

Mock mockers after that
That would not lift a hand maybe
To help good, wise or great   110
To bar that foul storm out, for we
Traffic in mockery.

VI

Violence upon the roads: violence of horses;
Some few have handsome riders, are garlanded
On delicate sensitive ear or tossing mane,
But wearied running round and round in their
          courses
All break and vanish, and evil gathers head:
Herodias' daughters have returned again,°
A sudden blast of dusty wind and after
Thunder of feet, tumult of images,   120
Their purpose in the labyrinth of the wind;
And should some crazy hand dare touch a daughter
All turn with amorous cries, or angry cries,

According to the wind, for all are blind.
But now wind drops, dust settles; thereupon
There lurches past, his great eyes without thought
Under the shadow of stupid straw-pale locks,
That insolent fiend Robert Artisson°
To whom the love-lorn Lady Kyteler brought
Bronzed peacock feathers, red combs of her cocks.   130

1919

The Wheel

Through winter-time we call on spring,
And through the spring on summer call,
And when abounding hedges ring
Declare that winter's best of all;
And after that there's nothing good
Because the spring-time has not come—
Nor know that what disturbs our blood
Is but its longing for the tomb.

A Prayer for my Son°

Bid a strong ghost stand at the head
That my Michael may sleep sound,
Nor cry, nor turn in the bed
Till his morning meal come round;
And may departing twilight keep
All dread afar till morning's back,
That his mother may not lack
Her fill of sleep.

Bid the ghost have sword in fist:
Some there are, for I avow   10
Such devilish things exist,
Who have planned his murder, for they know°
Of some most haughty deed or thought
That waits upon his future days,

And would through hatred of the bays
Bring that to nought.

Though You can fashion everything°
From nothing every day, and teach
The morning stars to sing,
You have lacked articulate speech   20
To tell Your simplest want, and known,
Wailing upon a woman's knee,
All of that worst ignominy
Of flesh and bone;

And when through all the town there ran
The servants of Your enemy,
A woman and a man,
Unless the Holy Writings lie,
Hurried through the smooth and rough
And through the fertile and waste,   30
Protecting, till the danger past,
With human love.°

Leda and the Swan°

A sudden blow: the great wings beating still
Above the staggering girl, her thighs caressed
By the dark webs, her nape caught in his bill,
He holds her helpless breast upon his breast.

How can those terrified vague fingers push
The feathered glory from her loosening thighs,
And how can body, laid in that white rush,
But feel the strange heart beating where it lies?

A shudder in the loins engenders there
The broken wall, the burning roof and tower   10
And Agamemnon dead.
                              Being so caught up,°
So mastered by the brute blood of the air,
Did she put on his knowledge with his power
Before the indifferent beak could let her drop?

On a Picture of a Black Centaur by
Edmund Dulac°

Your hooves have stamped at the black margin of the
    wood,
Even where horrible green parrots call and swing.
My works are all stamped down into the sultry mud.
I knew that horse-play, knew it for a murderous thing.
What wholesome sun has ripened is wholesome food
    to eat,
And that alone; yet I, being driven half insane
Because of some green wing, gathered old mummy
    wheat°
In the mad abstract dark and ground it grain by grain
And after baked it slowly in an oven; but now
I bring full-flavoured wine out of a barrel found   10
Where seven Ephesian topers slept and never knew°
When Alexander's empire passed, they slept so sound.°
Stretch out your limbs and sleep a long Saturnian sleep;°
I have loved you better than my soul for all my words,
And there is none so fit to keep a watch and keep
Unwearied eyes upon those horrible green birds.

Among School Children°

I

I walk through the long schoolroom questioning;
A kind old nun in a white hood replies;
The children learn to cipher and to sing,
To study reading-books and history,
To cut and sew, be neat in everything
In the best modern way—the children's eyes°
In momentary wonder stare upon
A sixty-year-old smiling public man.°

II

I dream of a Ledaean body, bent°
Above a sinking fire, a tale that she   10
Told of a harsh reproof, or trivial event

That changed some childish day to tragedy—
Told, and it seemed that our two natures blent
Into a sphere from youthful sympathy,
Or else, to alter Plato's parable,°
Into the yolk and white of the one shell.

III

And thinking of that fit of grief or rage
I look upon one child or t'other there
And wonder if she stood so at that age—
For even daughters of the swan can share   20
Something of every paddler's heritage—
And had that colour upon cheek or hair,
And thereupon my heart is driven wild:
She stands before me as a living child.

IV

Her present image floats into the mind—
Did Quattrocento finger fashion it°
Hollow of cheek as though it drank the wind
And took a mess of shadows for its meat?
And I though never of Ledaean kind
Had pretty plumage once—enough of that,   30
Better to smile on all that smile, and show
There is a comfortable kind of old scarecrow.

V

What youthful mother, a shape upon her lap
Honey of generation had betrayed,°
And that must sleep, shriek, struggle to escape
As recollection or the drug decide,
Would think her son, did she but see that shape
With sixty or more winters on its head,
A compensation for the pang of his birth,
Or the uncertainty of his setting forth?   40

VI

Plato thought nature but a spume that plays°
Upon a ghostly paradigm of things;
Solider Aristotle played the taws°
Upon the bottom of a king of kings;°

World-famous golden-thighed Pythagoras°
Fingered upon a fiddle-stick or strings
What a star sang and careless Muses heard:
Old clothes upon old sticks to scare a bird.

VII

Both nuns and mothers worship images,
But those the candles light are not as those   50
That animate a mother's reveries,
But keep a marble or a bronze repose.
And yet they too break hearts—O Presences
That passion, piety or affection knows,
And that all heavenly glory symbolise—
O self-born mockers of man's enterprise;

VIII

Labour is blossoming or dancing where
The body is not bruised to pleasure soul,
Nor beauty born out of its own despair,
Nor blear-eyed wisdom out of midnight oil.   60
O chestnut tree, great rooted blossomer,
Are you the leaf, the blossom or the bole?
O body swayed to music, O brightening glance,
How can we know the dancer from the dance?

Colonus' Praise°

(From 'Oedipus at Colonus')

Chorus. Come praise Colonus' horses, and come praise
    The wine-dark of the wood's intricacies,
    The nightingale that deafens daylight there,
    If daylight ever visit where,
    Unvisited by tempest or by sun,
    Immortal ladies tread the ground
    Dizzy with harmonious sound,
    Semele's lad a gay companion.°

    And yonder in the gymnasts' garden thrives
    The self-sown, self-begotten shape that gives   10

Athenian intellect its mastery,
Even the grey-leaved olive-tree
Miracle-bred out of the living stone;
Nor accident of peace nor war
Shall wither that old marvel, for
The great grey-eyed Athena stares thereon.°

Who comes into this country, and has come
Where golden crocus and narcissus bloom,
Where the Great Mother, mourning for her daughter°
And beauty-drunken by the water   20
Glittering among grey-leaved olive-trees,
Has plucked a flower and sung her loss;
Who finds abounding Cephisus°
Has found the loveliest spectacle there is.

Because this country has a pious mind
And so remembers that when all mankind
But trod the road, or splashed about the shore,
Poseidon gave it bit and oar,°
Every Colonus lad or lass discourses
Of that oar and of that bit;   30
Summer and winter, day and night,
Of horses and horses of the sea, white horses.

From A Man Young and Old

I

First Love

Though nurtured like the sailing moon
In beauty's murderous brood,
She walked awhile and blushed awhile
And on my pathway stood
Until I thought her body bore
A heart of flesh and blood.

But since I laid a hand thereon
And found a heart of stone
I have attempted many things
And not a thing is done,   10

For every hand is lunatic
That travels on the moon.

She smiled and that transfigured me
And left me but a lout,
Maundering here, and maundering there,
Emptier of thought
Than the heavenly circuit of its stars
When the moon sails out.

II

Human Dignity

Like the moon her kindness is,
If kindness I may call
What has no comprehension in't,
But is the same for all
As though my sorrow were a scene
Upon a painted wall.

So like a bit of stone I lie
Under a broken tree.
I could recover if I shrieked
My heart's agony   10
To passing bird, but I am dumb
From human dignity.

III

The Mermaid

A mermaid found a swimming lad,
Picked him for her own,
Pressed her body to his body,
Laughed; and plunging down
Forgot in cruel happiness
That even lovers drown.

All Souls' Night°

Epilogue to 'A Vision'

Midnight has come and the great Christ Church bell°
And many a lesser bell sound through the room;

And it is All Souls' Night.
And two long glasses brimmed with muscatel
Bubble upon the table. A ghost may come;
For it is a ghost's right,
His element is so fine
Being sharpened by his death,
To drink from the wine-breath
While our gross palates drink from the whole wine.   10

I need some mind that, if the cannon sound
From every quarter of the world, can stay
Wound in mind's pondering,
As mummies in the mummy-cloth are wound;
Because I have a marvellous thing to say,
A certain marvellous thing
None but the living mock,
Though not for sober ear;
It may be all that hear
Should laugh and weep an hour upon the clock.   20

Horton's the first I call. He loved strange thought°
And knew that sweet extremity of pride
That's called platonic love,
And that to such a pitch of passion wrought
Nothing could bring him, when his lady died,
Anodyne for his love.
Words were but wasted breath;
One dear hope had he:
The inclemency
Of that or the next winter would be death.   30

Two thoughts were so mixed up I could not tell
Whether of her or God he thought the most,
But think that his mind's eye,
When upward turned, on one sole image fell;
And that a slight companionable ghost,
Wild with divinity,
Had so lit up the whole
Immense miraculous house
The Bible promised us,
It seemed a gold-fish swimming in a bowl.   40

On Florence Emery I call the next,°
Who finding the first wrinkles on a face
Admired and beautiful,
And by foreknowledge of the future vexed;
Diminished beauty, multiplied commonplace;
Preferred to teach a school
Away from neighbour or friend,
Among dark skins, and there
Permit foul years to wear
Hidden from eyesight to the unnoticed end.°   50

Before that end much had she ravelled out
From a discourse in figurative speech
By some learned Indian
On the soul's journey. How it is whirled about
Wherever the orbit of the moon can reach,
Until it plunge into the sun;
And there, free and yet fast,
Being both Chance and Choice,
Forget its broken toys
And sink into its own delight at last.   60

I call MacGregor Mathers from his grave,°
For in my first hard spring-time we were friends,
Although of late estranged.
I thought him half a lunatic, half knave,
And told him so, but friendship never ends;
And what if mind seem changed,
And it seem changed with the mind,
When thoughts rise up unbid
On generous things that he did
And I grow half contented to be blind!   70

He had much industry at setting out,
Much boisterous courage, before loneliness
Had driven him crazed;
For meditations upon unknown thought
Make human intercourse grow less and less;
They are neither paid nor praised.
But he'd object to the host,
The glass because my glass;

A ghost-lover he was
And may have grown more arrogant being a ghost.   80

But names are nothing. What matter who it be,
So that his elements have grown so fine
The fume of muscatel
Can give his sharpened palate ecstasy
No living man can drink from the whole wine.
I have mummy truths to tell
Whereat the living mock,
Though not for sober ear,
For maybe all that hear
Should laugh and weep an hour upon the clock.   90

Such thought—such thought have I that hold it tight
Till meditation master all its parts,
Nothing can stay my glance
Until that glance run in the world's despite
To where the damned have howled away their hearts,
And where the blessed dance;
Such thought, that in it bound
I need no other thing,
Wound in mind's wandering
As mummies in the mummy-cloth are wound.   100

> *Oxford, Autumn* 1920

From The Winding Stair and Other Poems (1933)°

In Memory of Eva Gore-Booth and Con Markiewicz°

The light of evening, Lissadell,°
Great windows open to the south,
Two girls in silk kimonos, both
Beautiful, one a gazelle.
But a raving autumn shears

Blossom from the summer's wreath;
The older is condemned to death,
Pardoned, drags out lonely years
Conspiring among the ignorant.
I know not what the younger dreams—   10
Some vague Utopia—and she seems,
When withered old and skeleton-gaunt,
An image of such politics.
Many a time I think to seek
One or the other out and speak
Of that old Georgian mansion, mix
Pictures of the mind, recall
That table and the talk of youth,
Two girls in silk kimonos, both
Beautiful, one a gazelle.   20

Dear shadows, now you know it all,
All the folly of a fight
With a common wrong or right.
The innocent and the beautiful
Have no enemy but time;
Arise and bid me strike a match
And strike another till time catch;
Should the conflagration climb,
Run till all the sages know.
We the great gazebo built,°   30
They convicted us of guilt;
Bid me strike a match and blow.

October 1927

Death

Nor dread nor hope attend
A dying animal;
A man awaits his end
Dreading and hoping all;
Many times he died,
Many times rose again.
A great man in his pride°
Confronting murderous men
Casts derision upon

Supersession of breath;   10
He knows death to the bone—
Man has created death.

A Dialogue of Self and Soul

I

My Soul. I summon to the winding ancient stair;
    Set all your mind upon the steep ascent,
    Upon the broken, crumbling battlement,
    Upon the breathless starlit air,
    Upon the star that marks the hidden pole;
    Fix every wandering thought upon
    That quarter where all thought is done:
    Who can distinguish darkness from the soul?

My Self. The consecrated blade upon my knees
    Is Sato's ancient blade, still as it was,°   10
    Still razor-keen, still like a looking-glass
    Unspotted by the centuries;
    That flowering, silken, old embroidery, torn
    From some court-lady's dress and round
    The wooden scabbard bound and wound,
    Can, tattered, still protect, faded adorn.

My Soul. Why should the imagination of a man
    Long past his prime remember things that are
    Emblematical of love and war?
    Think of ancestral night that can,   20
    If but imagination scorn the earth
    And intellect its wandering
    To this and that and t'other thing,
    Deliver from the crime of death and birth.

My Self. Montashigi, third of his family, fashioned it°
    Five hundred years ago, about it lie
    Flowers from I know not what embroidery—
    Heart's purple—and all these I set
    For emblems of the day against the tower
    Emblematical of the night,   30
    And claim as by a soldier's right
    A charter to commit the crime once more.

My Soul. Such fullness in that quarter overflows
   And falls into the basin of the mind
   That man is stricken deaf and dumb and blind,
   For intellect no longer knows
   Is from the *Ought*, or *Knower* from the *Known*—
   That is to say, ascends to Heaven;
   Only the dead can be forgiven;
   But when I think of that my tongue's a stone.   40

II

My Self. A living man is blind and drinks his drop.
   What matter if the ditches are impure?
   What matter if I live it all once more?
   Endure that toil of growing up;
   The ignominy of boyhood; the distress
   Of boyhood changing into man;
   The unfinished man and his pain
   Brought face to face with his own clumsiness;

   The finished man among his enemies?—
   How in the name of Heaven can he escape   50
   That defiling and disfigured shape
   The mirror of malicious eyes
   Casts upon his eyes until at last
   He thinks that shape must be his shape?
   And what's the good of an escape
   If honour find him in the wintry blast?

   I am content to live it all again
   And yet again, if it be life to pitch
   Into the frog-spawn of a blind man's ditch,
   A blind man battering blind men;   60
   Or into that most fecund ditch of all,
   The folly that man does
   Or must suffer, if he woos
   A proud woman not kindred of his soul.

   I am content to follow to its source,
   Every event in action or in thought;
   Measure the lot; forgive myself the lot!
   When such as I cast out remorse

So great a sweetness flows into the breast
We must laugh and we must sing,   70
We are blest by everything,
Everything we look upon is blest.

Blood and the Moon°

I

Blessed be this place,
More blessed still this tower;
A bloody, arrogant power
Rose out of the race
Uttering, mastering it,
Rose like these walls from these
Storm-beaten cottages—
In mockery I have set
A powerful emblem up,
And sing it rhyme upon rhyme   10
In mockery of a time
Half dead at the top.

II

Alexandria's was a beacon tower, and Babylon's
An image of the moving heavens, a log-book of the
        sun's journey and the moon's;°
And Shelley had his towers, thought's crowned powers
        he called them once.°

I declare this tower is my symbol; I declare
This winding, gyring, spiring treadmill of a stair is my
        ancestral stair;
That Goldsmith and the Dean, Berkeley and Burke
        have travelled there.°

Swift beating on his breast in sibylline frenzy blind
Because the heart in his blood-sodden breast had
        dragged him down into mankind,   20
Goldsmith deliberately sipping at the honey-pot of his
        mind,

And haughtier-headed Burke that proved the State a
    tree,
That this unconquerable labyrinth of the birds, century after
    century,
Cast but dead leaves to mathematical equality;

And God-appointed Berkeley that proved all things a
    dream,°
That this pragmatical, preposterous pig of a world, its
    farrow that so solid seem,
Must vanish on the instant if the mind but change its
    theme;

Saeva Indignatio and the labourer's hire,°
The strength that gives our blood and state
    magnanimity of its own desire;
Everything that is not God consumed with intellectual
    fire.   30

III

The purity of the unclouded moon
Has flung its arrowy shaft upon the floor.
Seven centuries have passed and it is pure,
The blood of innocence has left no stain.
There, on blood-saturated ground, have stood
Soldier, assassin, executioner,
Whether for daily pittance or in blind fear
Or out of abstract hatred, and shed blood,
But could not cast a single jet thereon.
Odour of blood on the ancestral stair!   40
And we that have shed none must gather there
And clamour in drunken frenzy for the moon.

IV

Upon the dusty, glittering windows cling,
And seem to cling upon the moonlit skies,
Tortoiseshell butterflies, peacock butterflies,
A couple of night-moths are on the wing.
Is every modern nation like the tower,
Half dead at the top? No matter what I said,
For wisdom is the property of the dead,

A something incompatible with life; and power,   50
Like everything that has the stain of blood,
A property of the living; but no stain
Can come upon the visage of the moon
When it has looked in glory from a cloud.

Coole Park, 1929°

I meditate upon a swallow's flight,
Upon an aged woman and her house,
A sycamore and lime tree lost in night
Although that western cloud is luminous,
Great works constructed there in nature's spite
For scholars and for poets after us,
Thoughts long knitted into a single thought,
A dance-like glory that those walls begot.

There Hyde before he had beaten into prose°
That noble blade the Muses buckled on,   10
There one that ruffled in a manly pose
For all his timid heart, there that slow man,
That meditative man, John Synge, and those°
Impetuous men, Shaw Taylor and Hugh Lane°
Found pride established in humility,
A scene well set and excellent company.

They came like swallows and like swallows went,
And yet a woman's powerful character
Could keep a swallow to its first intent;
And half a dozen in formation there,   20
That seemed to whirl upon a compass-point,
Found certainty upon the dreaming air,
The intellectual sweetness of those lines
That cut through time or cross it withershins.

Here, traveller, scholar, poet, take your stand
When all those rooms and passages are gone,
When nettles wave upon a shapeless mound
And saplings root among the broken stone,
And dedicate—eyes bent upon the ground,

Back turned upon the brightness of the sun   30
And all the sensuality of the shade—
A moment's memory to that laurelled head.

Coole and Ballylee, 1931°

Under my window-ledge the waters race,
Otters below and moor-hens on the top,
Run for a mile undimmed in Heaven's face
Then darkening through 'dark' Raftery's 'cellar' drop,°
Run underground, rise in a rocky place
In Coole demesne, and there to finish up
Spread to a lake and drop into a hole.
What's water but the generated soul?

Upon the border of that lake's a wood
Now all dry sticks under a wintry sun,   10
And in a copse of beeches there I stood,
For Nature's pulled her tragic buskin on
And all the rant's a mirror of my mood:
At sudden thunder of the mounting swan
I turned about and looked where branches break
The glittering reaches of the flooded lake.

Another emblem there! That stormy white
But seems a concentration of the sky;
And, like the soul, it sails into the sight
And in the morning's gone, no man knows why;   20
And is so lovely that it sets to right
What knowledge or its lack had set awry,
So arrogantly pure, a child might think
It can be murdered with a spot of ink.

Sound of a stick upon the floor, a sound
From somebody that toils from chair to chair;
Beloved books that famous hands have bound,
Old marble heads, old pictures everywhere;
Great rooms where travelled men and children found
Content or joy; a last inheritor   30

Where none has reigned that lacked a name and fame
Or out of folly into folly came.

A spot whereon the founders lived and died
Seemed once more dear than life; ancestral trees,
Or gardens rich in memory glorified
Marriages, alliances and families,
And every bride's ambition satisfied.
Where fashion or mere fantasy decrees
Man shifts about—all that great glory spent—
Like some poor Arab tribesman and his tent.   40

We were the last romantics—chose for theme
Traditional sanctity and loveliness;
Whatever's written in what poets name
The book of the people; whatever most can bless
The mind of man or elevate a rhyme;
But all is changed, that high horse riderless,
Though mounted in that saddle Homer rode
Where the swan drifts upon a darkening flood.

For Anne Gregory°

'Never shall a young man,
Thrown into despair
By those great honey-coloured
Ramparts at your ear,
Love you for yourself alone
And not your yellow hair.'

'But I can get a hair-dye
And set such colour there,
Brown, or black, or carrot,
That young men in despair   10
May love me for myself alone
And not my yellow hair.'

'I heard an old religious man
But yesternight declare
That he had found a text to prove

That only God, my dear,
Could love you for yourself alone
And not your yellow hair.'

Swift's Epitaph°

Swift has sailed into his rest;
Savage indignation there
Cannot lacerate his breast.
Imitate him if you dare,
World-besotted traveller; he
Served human liberty.

At Algeciras—A Meditation upon Death°

The heron-billed pale cattle-birds
That feed on some foul parasite
Of the Moroccan flocks and herds
Cross the narrow Straits to light
In the rich midnight of the garden trees
Till the dawn break upon those mingled seas.

Often at evening when a boy
Would I carry to a friend—
Hoping more substantial joy
Did an older mind commend—   10
Not such as are in Newton's metaphor,°
But actual shells of Rosses' level shore.°

Greater glory in the sun,
An evening chill upon the air,
Bid imagination run
Much on the Great Questioner;°
What He can question, what if questioned I
Can with a fitting confidence reply.

November 1928

The Choice

The intellect of man is forced to choose
Perfection of the life, or of the work,
And if it take the second must refuse
A heavenly mansion, raging in the dark.
When all that story's finished, what's the news?
In luck or out the toil has left its mark:
That old perplexity an empty purse,
Or the day's vanity, the night's remorse.

Mohini Chatterjee°

I asked if I should pray,
But the Brahmin said,
'Pray for nothing, say
Every night in bed,
"I have been a king,
I have been a slave,
Nor is there anything,
Fool, rascal, knave,
That I have not been,
And yet upon my breast   10
A myriad heads have lain."'

That he might set at rest
A boy's turbulent days
Mohini Chatterjee
Spoke these, or words like these.
I add in commentary,
'Old lovers yet may have
All that time denied—
Grave is heaped on grave
That they be satisfied—   20
Over the blackened earth
The old troops parade,
Birth is heaped on birth
That such cannonade
May thunder time away,
Birth-hour and death-hour meet,

> Or, as great sages say,
> Men dance on deathless feet.'

1928

Byzantium°

The unpurged images of day recede;
The Emperor's drunken soldiery are abed;
Night resonance recedes, night-walkers' song
After great cathedral gong;°
A starlit or a moonlit dome disdains°
All that man is,
All mere complexities,
The fury and the mire of human veins.

Before me floats an image, man or shade,
Shade more than man, more image than a shade;   10
For Hades' bobbin bound in mummy-cloth
May unwind the winding path;°
A mouth that has no moisture and no breath
Breathless mouths may summon;
I hail the superhuman;
I call it death-in-life and life-in-death.

Miracle, bird or golden handiwork,
More miracle than bird or handiwork,
Planted on the star-lit golden bough,
Can like the cocks of Hades crow,   20
Or, by the moon embittered, scorn aloud
In glory of changeless metal
Common bird or petal
And all complexities of mire or blood.

At midnight on the Emperor's pavement flit
Flames that no faggot feeds, nor steel has lit,
Nor storm disturbs, flames begotten of flame,
Where blood-begotten spirits come
And all complexities of fury leave,

Dying into a dance,   30
An agony of trance,
An agony of flame that cannot singe a sleeve.

Astraddle on the dolphin's mire and blood,
Spirit after spirit! The smithies break the flood,°
The golden smithies of the Emperor!
Marbles of the dancing floor
Break bitter furies of complexity,
Those images that yet
Fresh images beget,
That dolphin-torn, that gong-tormented sea.   40

        1930

Vacillation

I

Between extremities
Man runs his course;
A brand, or flaming breath,
Comes to destroy
All those antinomies
Of day and night;
The body calls it death,
The heart remorse.
But if these be right
What is joy?   10

II

A tree there is that from its topmost bough°
Is half all glittering flame and half all green
Abounding foliage moistened with the dew;
And half is half and yet is all the scene;
And half and half consume what they renew,
And he that Attis' image hangs between°
That staring fury and the blind lush leaf
May know not what he knows, but knows not grief.

III

Get all the gold and silver that you can,
Satisfy ambition, or animate   20

The trivial days and ram them with the sun,
And yet upon these maxims meditate:
All women dote upon an idle man
Although their children need a rich estate;
No man has ever lived that had enough
Of children's gratitude or woman's love.

No longer in Lethean foliage caught°
Begin the preparation for your death
And from the fortieth winter by that thought
Test every work of intellect or faith,   30
And everything that your own hands have
    wrought,
And call those works extravagance of breath
That are not suited for such men as come
Proud, open-eyed and laughing to the tomb.

IV

My fiftieth year had come and gone,
I sat, a solitary man,
In a crowded London shop,
An open book and empty cup
On the marble table-top.

While on the shop and street I gazed   40
My body of a sudden blazed;
And twenty minutes more or less
It seemed, so great my happiness,
That I was blessèd and could bless.

V

Although the summer sunlight gild
Cloudy leafage of the sky,
Or wintry moonlight sink the field
In storm-scattered intricacy,
I cannot look thereon,
Responsibility so weighs me down.   50

Things said or done long years ago,
Or things I did not do or say
But thought that I might say or do,

Weigh me down, and not a day
But something is recalled,
My conscience or my vanity appalled.

VI

A rivery field spread out below,
An odour of the new-mown hay
In his nostrils, the great lord of Chou°
Cried, casting off the mountain snow,   60
'Let all things pass away.'

Wheels by milk-white asses drawn
Where Babylon or Nineveh°
Rose; some conqueror drew rein
And cried to battle-weary men,
'Let all things pass away.'

From man's blood-sodden heart are sprung
Those branches of the night and day
Where the gaudy moon is hung.
What's the meaning of all song?   70
'Let all things pass away.'

VII

The Soul. Seek out reality, leave things that seem.

The Heart. What, be a singer born and lack a theme?

The Soul. Isaiah's coal, what more can man desire?°

The Heart. Struck dumb in the simplicity of fire!

The Soul. Look on that fire, salvation walks within.

The Heart. What theme had Homer but original sin?

VIII

Must we part, Von Hügel, though much alike, for we°
Accept the miracles of the saints and honour sanctity?
The body of Saint Teresa lies undecayed in tomb,°   80
Bathed in miraculous oil, sweet odours from it come,
Healing from its lettered slab. Those self-same hands
    perchance
Eternalised the body of a modern saint that once

Had scooped out Pharaoh's mummy. I—though heart
    might find relief
Did I become a Christian man and choose for my belief
What seems most welcome in the tomb—play a
    predestined part.
Homer is my example and his unchristened heart.
The lion and the honeycomb, what has Scripture said?°
So get you gone, Von Hügel, though with blessings on
    your head.

    1932

Gratitude to the Unknown Instructors°

> What they undertook to do
> They brought to pass;
> All things hang like a drop of dew
> Upon a blade of grass.

From Words for Music Perhaps

I

Crazy Jane and the Bishop

Bring me to the blasted oak
That I, midnight upon the stroke,
(*All find safety in the tomb*.)
May call down curses on his head
Because of my dear Jack that's dead.
Coxcomb was the least he said:
The solid man and the coxcomb.

Nor was he Bishop when his ban
Banished Jack the Journeyman,
(*All find safety in the tomb*.)   10
Nor so much as parish priest,
Yet he, an old book in his fist,
Cried that we lived like beast and beast:
The solid man and the coxcomb.

The Bishop has a skin, God knows,
Wrinkled like the foot of a goose,
(*All find safety in the tomb.*)
Nor can he hide in holy black
The heron's hunch upon his back,
But a birch-tree stood my Jack: 20
The solid man and the coxcomb.

Jack had my virginity,
And bids me to the oak, for he
(*All find safety in the tomb.*)
Wanders out into the night
And there is shelter under it,
But should that other come, I spit:
The solid man and the coxcomb.

II

Crazy Jane Reproved

I care not what the sailors say:
All those dreadful thunder-stones,
All that storm that blots the day
Can but show that Heaven yawns;
Great Europa played the fool°
That changed a lover for a bull.
Fol de rol, fol de rol.

To round that shell's elaborate whorl,
Adorning every secret track
With the delicate mother-of-pearl,   10
Made the joints of Heaven crack:
So never hang your heart upon
A roaring, ranting journeyman.
Fol de rol, fol de rol.

III

Crazy Jane on the Day of Judgment

'Love is all
Unsatisfied

That cannot take the whole
Body and soul';
And that is what Jane said.

'Take the sour
If you take me,
I can scoff and lour
And scold for an hour,'
'That's certainly the case,' said he.   10

'Naked I lay,
The grass my bed;
Naked and hidden away,
That black day';
And that is what Jane said.

'What can be shown?
What true love be?
All could be known or shown
If Time were but gone.'
'That's certainly the case,' said he.   20

IV

Crazy Jane and Jack the Journeyman

I know, although when looks meet
I tremble to the bone,
The more I leave the door unlatched
The sooner love is gone,
For love is but a skein unwound
Between the dark and dawn.

A lonely ghost the ghost is
That to God shall come;
I—love's skein upon the ground,
My body in the tomb—   10
Shall leap into the light lost
In my mother's womb.

But were I left to lie alone
In an empty bed,

The skein so bound us ghost to ghost
When he turned his head
Passing on the road that night,
Mine would walk being dead.

V

Crazy Jane on God

That lover of a night
Came when he would,
Went in the dawning light
Whether I would or no;
Men come, men go;
All things remain in God.

Banners choke the sky;
Men–at–arms tread;
Armoured horses neigh
Where the great battle was   10
In the narrow pass:
All things remain in God.

Before their eyes a house
That from childhood stood
Uninhabited, ruinous,
Suddenly lit up
From door to top;
All things remain in God.

I had wild Jack for a lover;
Though like a road   20
That men pass over
My body makes no moan
But sings on:
All things remain in God.

VI

Crazy Jane Talks with the Bishop

I met the Bishop on the road
And much said he and I.

'Those breasts are flat and fallen now,
Those veins must soon be dry;
Live in a heavenly mansion,
Not in some foul sty.'

'Fair and foul are near of kin,
And fair needs foul,' I cried.
'My friends are gone, but that's a truth
Nor grave nor bed denied,   10
Learned in bodily lowliness
And in the heart's pride.

'A woman can be proud and stiff
When on love intent;
But Love has pitched his mansion in
The place of excrement;
For nothing can be sole or whole
That has not been rent.'

VIII
Girl's Song

I went out alone
To sing a song or two,
My fancy on a man,
And you know who.

Another came in sight
That on a stick relied
To hold himself upright;
I sat and cried.

And that was all my song—
When everything is told,   10
Saw I an old man young
Or young man old?

XV
Three Things

'O cruel Death, give three things back,'
Sang a bone upon the shore;

'A child found all a child can lack,
Whether of pleasure or of rest,
Upon the abundance of my breast':
A bone wave-whitened and dried in the wind.

'Three dear things that women know,'
Sang a bone upon the shore;
'A man if I but held him so
When my body was alive   10
Found all the pleasure that life gave':
A bone wave-whitened and dried in the wind.

'The third thing that I think of yet,'
Sang a bone upon the shore,
'Is that morning when I met
Face to face my rightful man
And did after stretch and yawn':
A bone wave-whitened and dried in the wind.

XVII

After Long Silence

Speech after long silence; it is right,
All other lovers being estranged or dead,
Unfriendly lamplight hid under its shade,
The curtains drawn upon unfriendly night,
That we descant and yet again descant
Upon the supreme theme of Art and Song:
Bodily decrepitude is wisdom; young
We loved each other and were ignorant.

XVIII

Mad as the Mist and Snow

Bolt and bar the shutter,
For the foul winds blow:
Our minds are at their best this night,
And I seem to know
That everything outside us is
Mad as the mist and snow.

Horace there by Homer stands,°
Plato stands below,
And here is Tully's open page.°
How many years ago   10
Were you and I unlettered lads
Mad as the mist and snow?

You ask what makes me sigh, old friend,
What makes me shudder so?
I shudder and I sigh to think
That even Cicero°
And many-minded Homer were
Mad as the mist and snow.

XIX

Those Dancing Days are Gone

Come, let me sing into your ear;
Those dancing days are gone,
All that silk and satin gear;
Crouch upon a stone,
Wrapping that foul body up
In as foul a rag:
I carry the sun in a golden cup,
The moon in a silver bag.

Curse as you may I sing it through;
What matter if the knave   10
That the most could pleasure you,
The children that he gave,
Are somewhere sleeping like a top
Under a marble flag?
I carry the sun in a golden cup,
The moon in a silver bag.

I thought it out this very day,
Noon upon the clock,
A man may put pretence away
Who leans upon a stick,   20
May sing, and sing until he drop,

Whether to maid or hag:
I carry the sun in a golden cup,
The moon in a silver bag.

XX

'I am of Ireland'°

'I am of Ireland,
And the Holy Land of Ireland,
And time runs on,' cried she.
'Come out of charity,
Come dance with me in Ireland.'

One man, one man alone
In that outlandish gear,
One solitary man
Of all that rambled there
Had turned his stately head.   10
'That is a long way off,
And time runs on,' he said,
'And the night grows rough.'

'I am of Ireland,
And the Holy Land of Ireland,
And time runs on,' cried she.
'Come out of charity
And dance with me in Ireland.'

'The fiddlers are all thumbs,
Or the fiddle-string accursed,   20
The drums and the kettledrums
And the trumpets all are burst,
And the trombone,' cried he,
'The trumpet and trombone,'
And cocked a malicious eye,
'But time runs on, runs on.'

'I am of Ireland,
And the Holy Land of Ireland,
And time runs on,' cried she.
'Come out of charity   30
And dance with me in Ireland.'

XXV

The Delphic Oracle upon Plotinus°

Behold that great Plotinus swim,
Buffeted by such seas;
Bland Rhadamanthus beckons him,°
But the Golden Race looks dim,°
Salt blood blocks his eyes.
Scattered on the level grass
Or winding through the grove
Plato there and Minos pass,°
There stately Pythagoras°
And all the choir of Love.   10

August 19, 1931

From A Woman Young and Old

I

Father and Child

She hears me strike the board and say
That she is under ban
Of all good men and women,
Being mentioned with a man
That has the worst of all bad names;
And thereupon replies
That his hair is beautiful,
Cold as the March wind his eyes.

II

Before the World was Made

If I make the lashes dark
And the eyes more bright
And the lips more scarlet,
Or ask if all be right

From mirror after mirror,
No vanity's displayed:
I'm looking for the face I had
Before the world was made.

What if I look upon a man
As though on my beloved,   10
And my blood be cold the while
And my heart unmoved?
Why should he think me cruel
Or that he is betrayed?
I'd have him love the thing that was
Before the world was made.

V

Consolation

O but there is wisdom
In what the sages said;
But stretch that body for a while
And lay down that head
Till I have told the sages
Where man is comforted.

How could passion run so deep
Had I never thought
That the crime of being born
Blackens all our lot?   10
But where the crime's committed
The crime can be forgot.

VII

Parting

He. Dear, I must be gone
     While night shuts the eyes
     Of the household spies;
     That song announces dawn.

She. No, night's bird and love's
     Bids all true lovers rest,

While his loud song reproves
The murderous stealth of day.

He. Daylight already flies
From mountain crest to crest.   10

She. That light is from the moon.

He. That bird . . .

She.   Let him sing on,
I offer to love's play
My dark declivities.

VIII

Her Vision in the Wood

Dry timber under that rich foliage,
At wine-dark midnight in the sacred wood,
Too old for a man's love I stood in rage
Imagining men. Imagining that I could
A greater with a lesser pang assuage
Or but to find if withered vein ran blood,
I tore my body that its wine might cover
Whatever could recall the lip of lover.

And after that I held my fingers up,
Stared at the wine-dark nail, or dark that ran   10
Down every withered finger from the top;
But the dark changed to red, and torches shone,
And deafening music shook the leaves; a troop
Shouldered a litter with a wounded man,
Or smote upon the string and to the sound
Sang of the beast that gave the fatal wound.

All stately women moving to a song
With loosened hair or foreheads grief-distraught,
It seemed a Quattrocento painter's throng,°
A thoughtless image of Mantegna's thought—°   20
Why should they think that are for ever young?
Till suddenly in grief's contagion caught,
I stared upon his blood-bedabbled breast
And sang my malediction with the rest.

That thing all blood and mire, that beast-torn wreck,
Half turned and fixed a glazing eye on mine,
And, though love's bitter-sweet had all come back,
Those bodies from a picture or a coin
Nor saw my body fall nor heard it shriek,
Nor knew, drunken with singing as with wine,   30
That they had brought no fabulous symbol there
But my heart's victim and its torturer.

IX

A Last Confession

What lively lad most pleasured me
Of all that with me lay?
I answer that I gave my soul
And loved in misery,
But had great pleasure with a lad
That I loved bodily.

Flinging from his arms I laughed
To think his passion such
He fancied that I gave a soul
Did but our bodies touch,   10
And laughed upon his breast to think
Beast gave beast as much.

I gave what other women gave
That stepped out of their clothes,
But when this soul, its body off,
Naked to naked goes,
He it has found shall find therein
What none other knows,

And give his own and take his own
And rule in his own right;   20
And though it loved in misery
Close and cling so tight,
There's not a bird of day that dare
Extinguish that delight.

XI

From the 'Antigone'°

Overcome—O bitter sweetness,
Inhabitant of the soft cheek of a girl—
The rich man and his affairs,
The fat flocks and the fields' fatness,
Mariners, rough harvesters;
Overcome Gods upon Parnassus;°

Overcome the Empyrean; hurl°
Heaven and Earth out of their places,
That in the same calamity
Brother and brother, friend and friend,°   10
Family and family,
City and city may contend,
By that great glory driven wild.

Pray I will and sing I must,
And yet I weep—Oedipus' child
Descends into the loveless dust.°

From A Full Moon in March (1935)

Parnell's Funeral°

I

Under the Great Comedian's tomb the crowd.°
A bundle of tempestuous cloud is blown
About the sky; where that is clear of cloud
Brightness remains; a brighter star shoots down;°
What shudders run through all that animal blood?
What is this sacrifice? Can someone there
Recall the Cretan barb that pierced a star?

Rich foliage that the starlight glittered through,
A frenzied crowd, and where the branches sprang

A beautiful seated boy; a sacred bow;   10
A woman, and an arrow on a string;
A pierced boy, image of a star laid low.
That woman, the Great Mother imaging,
Cut out his heart. Some master of design
Stamped boy and tree upon Sicilian coin.°

An age is the reversal of an age:
When strangers murdered Emmet, Fitzgerald, Tone,°
We lived like men that watch a painted stage.
What matter for the scene, the scene once gone:
It had not touched our lives. But popular rage,   20
Hysterica passio dragged this quarry down.°
None shared our guilt; nor did we play a part
Upon a painted stage when we devoured his heart.

Come, fix upon me that accusing eye.
I thirst for accusation. All that was sung,
All that was said in Ireland is a lie
Bred out of the contagion of the throng,
Saving the rhyme rats hear before they die.
Leave nothing but the nothings that belong
To this bare soul, let all men judge that can   30
Whether it be an animal or a man.

II

The rest I pass, one sentence I unsay.
Had de Valera eaten Parnell's heart°
No loose-lipped demagogue had won the day,
No civil rancour torn the land apart.

Had Cosgrave eaten Parnell's heart, the land's°
Imagination had been satisfied,
Or lacking that, government in such hands,
O'Higgins its sole statesman had not died.°

Had even O'Duffy—but I name no more—°   40
Their school a crowd, his master solitude;
Through Jonathan Swift's dark grove he passed,
        and there°
Plucked bitter wisdom that enriched his blood.

From Supernatural Songs

I

Ribh at the Tomb of Baile and Aillinn°

Because you have found me in the pitch-dark night
With open book you ask me what I do.
Mark and digest my tale, carry it afar
To those that never saw this tonsured head
Nor heard this voice that ninety years have cracked.
Of Baile and Aillinn you need not speak,
All know their tale, all know what leaf and twig,
What juncture of the apple and the yew,
Surmount their bones; but speak what none have heard.

The miracle that gave them such a death   10
Transfigured to pure substance what had once
Been bone and sinew; when such bodies join
There is no touching here, nor touching there,
Nor straining joy, but whole is joined to whole;
For the intercourse of angels is a light
Where for its moment both seem lost, consumed.

Here in the pitch-dark atmosphere above
The trembling of the apple and the yew,
Here on the anniversary of their death,
The anniversary of their first embrace,   20
Those lovers, purified by tragedy,
Hurry into each other's arms; these eyes,
By water, herb and solitary prayer
Made aquiline, are open to that light.
Though somewhat broken by the leaves, that light
Lies in a circle on the grass; therein
I turn the pages of my holy book.

III

Ribh in Ecstasy

What matter that you understood no word!
Doubtless I spoke or sang what I had heard

In broken sentences. My soul had found
All happiness in its own cause or ground.
Godhead on Godhead in sexual spasm begot
Godhead. Some shadow fell. My soul forgot
Those amorous cries that out of quiet come
And must the common round of day resume.

IV

There

There all the barrel-hoops are knit,
There all the serpent-tails are bit,
There all the gyres converge in one,
There all the planets drop in the Sun.

V

Ribh Considers Christian Love Insufficient

Why should I seek for love or study it?
It is of God and passes human wit;
I study hatred with great diligence,
For that's a passion in my own control,
A sort of besom that can clear the soul
Of everything that is not mind or sense.

Why do I hate man, woman or event?
That is a light my jealous soul has sent.
From terror and deception freed it can
Discover impurities, can show at last   10
How soul may walk when all such things are past,
How soul could walk before such things began.

Then my delivered soul herself shall learn
A darker knowledge and in hatred turn
From every thought of God mankind has had.
Thought is a garment and the soul's a bride
That cannot in that trash and tinsel hide:
Hatred of God may bring the soul to God.

At stroke of midnight soul cannot endure
A bodily or mental furniture.   20
What can she take until her Master give!
Where can she look until He make the show!
What can she know until He bid her know!
How can she live till in her blood He live!

IX

The Four Ages of Man

He with body waged a fight,
But body won; it walks upright.

Then he struggled with the heart;
Innocence and peace depart.

Then he struggled with the mind;
His proud heart he left behind.

Now his wars on God begin;
At stroke of midnight God shall win.

XII

Meru°

Civilisation is hooped together, brought
Under a rule, under the semblance of peace
By manifold illusion; but man's life is thought,
And he, despite his terror, cannot cease
Ravening through century after century,
Ravening, raging, and uprooting that he may come
Into the desolation of reality:
Egypt and Greece good–bye, and good-bye, Rome!
Hermits upon Mount Meru or Everest,
Caverned in night under the drifted snow,   10
Or where that snow and winter's dreadful blast
Beat down upon their naked bodies, know
That day brings round the night, that before dawn
His glory and his monuments are gone.

The Gyres°

The gyres! the gyres! Old Rocky Face look forth;°
Things thought too long can be no longer thought
For beauty dies of beauty, worth of worth,
And ancient lineaments are blotted out.
Irrational streams of blood are staining earth;
Empedocles has thrown all things about;°
Hector is dead and there's a light in Troy;°
We that look on but laugh in tragic joy.

What matter though numb nightmare ride on top
And blood and mire the sensitive body stain?   10
What matter? Heave no sigh, let no tear drop,
A greater, a more gracious time has gone;
For painted forms or boxes of make-up
In ancient tombs I sighed, but not again;
What matter? Out of Cavern comes a voice
And all it knows is that one word 'Rejoice.'

Conduct and work grow coarse, and coarse the soul,
What matter! Those that Rocky Face holds dear,
Lovers of horses and of women, shall
From marble of a broken sepulchre   20
Or dark betwixt the polecat and the owl,
Or any rich, dark nothing disinter
The workman, noble and saint, and all things run
On that unfashionable gyre again.

Lapis Lazuli
(*For Harry Clifton*)°

I have heard that hysterical women say
They are sick of the palette and fiddle-bow,
Of poets that are always gay,
For everybody knows or else should know

That if nothing drastic is done
Aeroplane and Zeppelin will come out,°
Pitch like King Billy bomb-balls in°
Until the town lie beaten flat.

All perform their tragic play,
There struts Hamlet, there is Lear,   10
That's Ophelia, that Cordelia;
Yet they, should the last scene be there
The great stage curtain about to drop,
If worthy their prominent part in the play,
Do not break up their lines to weep.
They know that Hamlet and Lear are gay;
Gaiety transfiguring all that dread.
All men have aimed at, found and lost;
Black out; Heaven blazing into the head:
Tragedy wrought to its uttermost.   20
Though Hamlet rambles and Lear rages,
And all the drop scenes drop at once°
Upon a hundred thousand stages,
It cannot grow by an inch or an ounce.

On their own feet they came, or on shipboard,
Camel-back, horse-back, ass-back, mule-back,
Old civilisations put to the sword.
Then they and their wisdom went to rack:
No handiwork of Callimachus°
Who handled marble as if it were bronze,   30
Made draperies that seemed to rise
When sea-wind swept the corner, stands;
His long lamp chimney shaped like the stem°
Of a slender palm, stood but a day;
All things fall and are built again
And those that build them again are gay.

Two Chinamen, behind them a third,
Are carved in Lapis Lazuli,   .
Over them flies a long-legged bird
A symbol of longevity;   40
The third, doubtless a serving-man
Carries a musical instrument.

Every discolouration of the stone,
Every accidental crack or dent
Seems a water-course or an avalanche,
Or lofty slope where it still snows
Though doubtless plum or cherry-branch
Sweetens the little half-way house
Those Chinamen climb towards, and I
Delight to imagine them seated there;   50
There, on the mountain and the sky,
On all the tragic scene they stare;
One asks for mournful melodies;
Accomplished fingers begin to play;
Their eyes mid many wrinkles, their eyes,
Their ancient, glittering eyes, are gay.

Imitated from the Japanese°

A most astonishing thing
Seventy years have I lived;

(Hurrah for the flowers of Spring
For Spring is here again.)

Seventy years have I lived
No ragged beggar man,
Seventy years have I lived,
Seventy years man and boy,
And never have I danced for joy.

The Lady's First Song

I turn round
Like a dumb beast in a show,
Neither know what I am
Nor where I go,
My language beaten
Into one name;
I am in love
And that is my shame.

What hurts the soul
My soul adores,   10
No better than a beast
Upon all fours.

The Lady's Second Song

What sort of man is coming
To lie between your feet?
What matter we are but women.
Wash; make your body sweet;
I have cupboards of dried fragrance
I can strew the sheet.
        The Lord have mercy upon us.

He shall love my soul as though
Body were not at all,
He shall love your body   10
Untroubled by the soul,
Love cram love's two divisions
Yet keep his substance whole.
        The Lord have mercy upon us.

Soul must learn a love that is
Proper to my breast,
Limbs a love in common
With every noble beast.
If soul may look and body touch
Which is the more blest?   20
        The Lord have mercy upon us.

The Lady's Third Song

When you and my true lover meet
And he plays tunes between your feet,
Speak no evil of the soul,
Nor think that body is the whole
For I that am his daylight lady
Know worse evil of the body;

But in honour split his love
Till either neither have enough,
That I may hear if we should kiss
A contrapuntal serpent hiss,   10
You, should hand explore a thigh,
All the labouring heavens sigh.

The Lover's Song

Bird sighs for the air,
Thought for I know not where,
For the womb the seed sighs.
Now sinks the same rest
On mind, on nest,
On straining thighs.

An Acre of Grass

Picture and book remain,
An acre of green grass
For air and exercise,
Now strength of body goes,
Midnight an old house
Where nothing stirs but a mouse.

My temptation is quiet.
Here at life's end
Neither loose imagination,
Nor the mill of the mind   10
Consuming its rag and bone,
Can make the truth known.

Grant me an old man's frenzy.
Myself must I remake
Till I am Timon and Lear°
Or that William Blake°
Who beat upon the wall
Till truth obeyed his call;

A mind Michael Angelo knew°
That can pierce the clouds   20
Or inspired by frenzy
Shake the dead in their shrouds,
Forgotten else by mankind
An old man's eagle mind.

What Then?

His chosen comrades thought at school
He must grow a famous man;
He thought the same and lived by rule,
All his twenties crammed with toil;
'What then?' sang Plato's ghost, 'what then?' °

Everything he wrote was read,
After certain years he won
Sufficient money for his need,
Friends that have been friends indeed;
'What then?' sang Plato's ghost, 'what then?'   10

All his happier dreams came true—
A small old house, wife, daughter, son,
Grounds where plum and cabbage grew,
Poets and Wits about him drew;
'What then?' sang Plato's ghost, 'what then?'

'The work is done,' grown old he thought,
'According to my boyish plan;
Let the fools rage, I swerved in nought,
Something to perfection brought;'
But louder sang that ghost 'What then?'   20

Beautiful Lofty Things

Beautiful lofty things; O'Leary's noble head;°
My father upon the Abbey stage, before him a raging
     crowd.°
'This Land of Saints,' and then as the applause died out,

'Of plaster Saints;' his beautiful mischievous head thrown
   back.
Standish O'Grady supporting himself between the tables°
Speaking to a drunken audience high nonsensical words;
Augusta Gregory seated at her great ormolu table
Her eightieth winter approaching; 'Yesterday he threatened
   my life,
I told him that nightly from six to seven I sat at this table
The blinds drawn up;' Maud Gonne at Howth station
   waiting a train,°   10
Pallas Athene in that straight back and arrogant head:°
All the Olympians; a thing never known again.°

A Crazed Girl

That crazed girl improvising her music,
Her poetry, dancing upon the shore,
Her soul in division from itself
Climbing, falling she knew not where,
Hiding amid the cargo of a steamship
Her knee-cap broken, that girl I declare
A beautiful lofty thing, or a thing
Heroically lost, heroically found.

No matter what disaster occurred
She stood in desperate music wound   10
Wound, wound, and she made in her triumph
Where the bales and the baskets lay
No common intelligible sound
But sang, 'O sea-starved hungry sea.'

The Curse of Cromwell°

You ask what I have found and far and wide I go,
Nothing but Cromwell's house and Cromwell's murderous
   crew,
The lovers and the dancers are beaten into the clay,°

And the tall men and the swordsmen and the horsemen
    where are they?
And there is an old beggar wandering in his pride
His fathers served their fathers before Christ was
    crucified.°
     O what of that, O what of that
     What is there left to say?

All neighbourly content and easy talk are gone
But there's no good complaining, for money's rant is on,   10
He that's mounting up must on his neighbour mount
And we and all the Muses are things of no account.
They have schooling of their own but I pass their schooling by,
What can they know that we know that know the time to die?
     O what of that, O what of that
     What is there left to say?

But there's another knowledge that my heart destroys
As the fox in the old fable destroyed the Spartan boy's°
Because it proves that things both can and cannot be;
That the swordsmen and the ladies can still keep company;   20
Can pay the poet for a verse and hear the fiddle sound
That I am still their servant though all are underground.
     O what of that, O what of that
     What is there left to say?

I came on a great house in the middle of the night°
Its open lighted doorway and its windows all alight,
And all my friends were there and made me welcome too;
But I woke in an old ruin that the winds howled through;
And when I pay attention I must out and walk
Among the dogs and horses that understand my talk.   30
     O what of that, O what of that
     What is there left to say?

The Ghost of Roger Casement°

    O what has made that sudden noise?
    What on the threshold stands?

It never crossed the sea because
John Bull and the sea are friends;°
But this is not the old sea
Nor this the old seashore.
What gave that roar of mockery,
That roar in the sea's roar?

The ghost of Roger Casement
Is beating on the door.   10

John Bull has stood for Parliament,
A dog must have his day,
The country thinks no end of him
For he knows how to say
At a beanfeast or a banquet,
That all must hang their trust
Upon the British Empire,
Upon the Church of Christ.

The ghost of Roger Casement
Is beating on the door.   20

John Bull has gone to India°
And all must pay him heed
For histories are there to prove
That none of another breed
Has had a like inheritance,
Or sucked such milk as he,
And there's no luck about a house
If it lack honesty.

The ghost of Roger Casement
Is beating on the door.   30

I poked about a village church
And found his family tomb
And copied out what I could read
In that religious gloom;
Found many a famous man there;
But fame and virtue rot.
Draw round beloved and bitter men,
Draw round and raise a shout;

The ghost of Roger Casement
Is beating on the door.   40

Come Gather Round Me Parnellites°

Come gather round me Parnellites
And praise our chosen man,
Stand upright on your legs awhile,
Stand upright while you can,
For soon we lie where he is laid
And he is underground;
Come fill up all those glasses
And pass the bottle round.

And here's a cogent reason
And I have many more,   10
He fought the might of England
And saved the Irish poor,
Whatever good a farmer's got
He brought it all to pass;
And here's another reason,
That Parnell loved a lass.

And here's a final reason,
He was of such a kind
Every man that sings a song
Keeps Parnell in his mind   20
For Parnell was a proud man,
No prouder trod the ground,
And a proud man's a lovely man
So pass the bottle round.

The Bishops and the Party
That tragic story made,
A husband that had sold his wife°
And after that betrayed;
But stories that live longest
Are sung above the glass,   30

And Parnell loved his country
And Parnell loved his lass.

Parnell°

Parnell came down the road, he said to a cheering man;
'Ireland shall get her freedom and you still break stone.'

The Spur

You think it horrible that lust and rage
Should dance attendance upon my old age;
They were not such a plague when I was young;
What else have I to spur me into song?

Those Images

What if I bade you leave
The cavern of the mind?
There's better exercise
In the sunlight and wind.

I never bade you go
To Moscow or to Rome,
Renounce that drudgery,
Call the Muses home.

Seek those images
That constitute the wild,   10
The lion and the virgin,
The harlot and the child.

Find in middle air
An eagle on the wing,
Recognise the five
That make the Muses sing.°

The Municipal Gallery Re-visited°

I

Around me the images of thirty years;
An ambush; pilgrims at the water-side;
Casement upon trial, half hidden by the bars,°
Guarded; Griffith staring in hysterical pride;°
Kevin O'Higgins' countenance that wears°
A gentle questioning look that cannot hide
A soul incapable of remorse or rest;
A revolutionary soldier kneeling to be blessed.

II

An Abbot or Archbishop with an upraised hand
Blessing the Tricolour. 'This is not' I say   10
'The dead Ireland of my youth, but an Ireland
The poets have imagined, terrible and gay.'
Before a woman's portrait suddenly I stand;
Beautiful and gentle in her Venetian way.
I met her all but fifty years ago
For twenty minutes in some studio.

III

Heart smitten with emotion I sink down
My heart recovering with covered eyes;
Wherever I had looked I had looked upon
My permanent or impermanent images;   20
Augusta Gregory's son; her sister's son,°
Hugh Lane, 'onlie begetter' of all these;°
Hazel Lavery living and dying, that tale°
As though some ballad singer had sung it all.

IV

Mancini's portrait of Augusta Gregory,°
'Greatest since Rembrandt,' according to John Synge;°
A great ebullient portrait certainly;
But where is the brush that could show anything
Of all that pride and that humility,
And I am in despair that time may bring   30
Approved patterns of women or of men
But not that selfsame excellence again.

V

My mediaeval knees lack health until they bend,
But in that woman, in that household where
Honour had lived so long, all lacking found.
Childless I thought 'my children may find here
Deep-rooted things,' but never foresaw its end,
And now that end has come I have not wept;
No fox can foul the lair the badger swept.

VI

(An image out of Spenser and the common tongue)°   40
John Synge, I and Augusta Gregory thought
All that we did, all that we said or sang
Must come from contact with the soil, from that
Contact everything Antaeus-like grew strong.°
We three alone in modern times had brought
Everything down to that sole test again,
Dream of the noble and the beggarman.

VII

And here's John Synge himself, that rooted man
'Forgetting human words,' a grave deep face.
You that would judge me do not judge alone   50
This book or that, come to this hallowed place
Where my friends' portraits hang and look thereon;
Ireland's history in their lineaments trace;
Think where man's glory most begins and ends
And say my glory was I had such friends.

From On the Boiler (1939)

Why should not Old Men be Mad?

Why should not old men be mad?
Some have known a likely lad
That had a sound fly fisher's wrist

Turn to a drunken journalist;
A girl that knew all Dante once°
Live to bear children to a dunce;
A Helen of social welfare dream°
Climb on a wagonette to scream.
Some think it a matter of course that chance
Should starve good men and bad advance,   10
That if their neighbours figured plain,
As though upon a lighted screen,
No single story would they find
Of an unbroken happy mind,
A finish worthy of the start.
Young men know nothing of this sort,
Observant old men know it well;
And when they know what old books tell
And that no better can be had,
Know why an old man should be mad.   20

Crazy Jane on the Mountain

I am tired of cursing the Bishop°
(Said Crazy Jane)
Nine books or nine hats
Would not make him a man.
I have found something worse
To meditate on.
A King had some beautiful cousins
But where are they gone?
Battered to death in a cellar
And he stuck to his throne.   10
Last night I lay on the mountain
(Said Crazy Jane)
There in a two-horsed carriage
That on two wheels ran
Great bladdered Emer sat,°
Her violent man
Cuchulain, sat at her side,°
Thereupon,
Propped upon my two knees,

I kissed a stone;   20
I lay stretched out in the dirt
And I cried tears down.

From Last Poems and Two Plays (1939)

Under Ben Bulben°

I

Swear by what the sages spoke
Round the Mareotic Lake°
That the Witch of Atlas knew,°
Spoke and set the cocks a–crow.

Swear by those horsemen, by those women,
Complexion and form prove superhuman,°
That pale, long visaged company
That airs in immortality
Completeness of their passions won;
Now they ride the wintry dawn   10
Where Ben Bulben sets the scene.

Here's the gist of what they mean.

II

Many times man lives and dies
Between his two eternities,
That of race and that of soul,
And ancient Ireland knew it all.
Whether man die in his bed
Or the rifle knocks him dead,
A brief parting from those dear
Is the worst man has to fear.   20
Though grave–diggers' toil is long,
Sharp their spades, their muscles strong,
They but thrust their buried men
Back in the human mind again.

III

You that Mitchel's prayer have heard
'Send war in our time, O Lord!'°
Know that when all words are said
And a man is fighting mad,
Something drops from eyes long blind
He completes his partial mind,   30
For an instant stands at ease,
Laughs aloud, his heart at peace,
Even the wisest man grows tense
With some sort of violence
Before he can accomplish fate,
Know his work or choose his mate.

IV

Poet and sculptor, do the work,
Nor let the modish painter shirk
What his great forefathers did,
Bring the soul of man to God,   40
Make him fill the cradles right.

Measurement began our might:
Forms a stark Egyptian thought,
Forms that gentler Phidias wrought.°
Michaelangelo left a proof
On the Sistine Chapel roof,
Where but half-awakened Adam°
Can disturb globe-trotting Madam
Till her bowels are in heat,
Proof that there's a purpose set   50
Before the secret working mind:
Profane perfection of mankind.

Quattro-cento put in paint,°
On backgrounds for a God or Saint,
Gardens where a soul's at ease;
Where everything that meets the eye,
Flowers and grass and cloudless sky,
Resemble forms that are or seem
When sleepers wake and yet still dream,

And when it's vanished still declare,   60
With only bed and bedstead there,
That heavens had opened.
                    Gyres run on;
When that greater dream had gone
Calvert and Wilson, Blake and Claude,°
Prepared a rest for the people of God,
Palmer's phrase, but after that °
Confusion fell upon our thought.

V

Irish poets, learn your trade,
Sing whatever is well made,
Scorn the sort now growing up   70
All out of shape from toe to top,
Their unremembering hearts and heads
Base-born products of base beds.
Sing the peasantry, and then
Hard-riding country gentlemen,
The holiness of monks, and after
Porter-drinkers' randy laughter;
Sing the lords and ladies gay
That were beaten into the clay
Through seven heroic centuries;   80
Cast your mind on other days
That we in coming days may be
Still the indomitable Irishry.

VI

Under bare Ben Bulben's head
In Drumcliffe churchyard Yeats is laid.°
An ancestor was rector there
Long years ago, a church stands near,
By the road an ancient cross.
No marble, no conventional phrase;
On limestone quarried near the spot   90
By his command these words are cut:

        Cast a cold eye
        On life, on death.
        Horseman pass by!

    September 4th 1938

The Black Tower

Say that the men of the old black tower
Though they but feed as the goatherd feeds,
Their money spent, their wine gone sour,
Lack nothing that a soldier needs,
That all are oath-bound men;
Those banners come not in.

There in the tomb stand the dead upright,°
But winds come up from the shore,
They shake when the winds roar,
Old bones upon the mountain shake.   10

Those banners come to bribe or threaten,
Or whisper that a man's a fool
Who, when his own right king's forgotten,
Cares what king sets up his rule.
If he died long ago
Why do you dread us so?

There in the tomb drops the faint moonlight,
But wind comes up from the shore,
They shake when the winds roar,
Old bones upon the mountain shake.   20

The tower's old cook that must climb and clamber
Catching small birds in the dew of the morn,
When we hale men lie stretched in slumber
Swears that he hears the king's great horn.
But he's a lying hound;
Stand we on guard oath-bound!

There in the tomb the dark grows blacker,
But wind comes up from the shore,
They shake when the winds roar,
Old bones upon the mountain shake   30

   January 21st 1939

Cuchulain Comforted°

A man that had six mortal wounds, a man°
Violent and famous, strode among the dead;
Eyes stared out of the branches and were gone.

Then certain Shrouds that muttered head to head
Came and were gone. He leant upon a tree
As though to meditate on wounds and blood.

A Shroud that seemed to have authority
Among those bird-like things came and let fall
A bundle of linen. Shrouds by two and three

Came creeping up because the man was still;   10
And thereupon that linen-carrier said:
'Your life can grow much sweeter if you will

'Obey our ancient rule and make a shroud.
Mainly because of what we only know
The rattle of those arms makes us afraid.

We thread the needles' eyes and all we do
All must together do.' That done, the man
Took up the nearest and began to sew.

'Now must we sing and sing the best we can
But first you must be told our character: 20
Convicted cowards all by kindred slain

Or driven from home and left to die in fear.'
They sang, but had nor human tunes nor words,
Though all was done in common as before

They had changed their throats and had the throats
        of birds.

    January 13*th* 1939

In Tara's Halls°

A man I praise that once in Tara's Halls
Said to the woman on his knees, 'Lie still,
My hundredth year is at an end. I think
That something is about to happen, I think
That the adventure of old age begins.
To many women I have said "lie still",
And given everything a woman needs,
A roof, good clothes, passion, love perhaps,
But never asked for love; should I ask that
I shall be old indeed'.
               Thereon the man   10
Went to the Sacred House and stood between
The golden plough and harrow and spoke aloud
That all attendants and the casual crowd might hear:
'God I have loved, but should I ask return
Of God or woman, the time were come to die.'
He bade, his hundred and first year at end,
Diggers and carpenters make grave and coffin;
Saw that the grave was deep, the coffin sound,
Summoned the generations of his house,
Lay in the coffin, stopped his breath and died.   20

The Statues

Pythagoras planned it. Why did the people stare?°
His numbers, though they moved or seemed to move
In marble or in bronze, lacked character.
But boys and girls pale from the imagined love
Of solitary beds, knew what they were,
That passion could bring character enough;
And pressed at midnight in some public place
Live lips upon a plummet-measured face.

No! Greater than Pythagoras, for the men
That with a mallet or a chisel modelled these   10
Calculations that look but casual flesh, put down

All Asiatic vague immensities,
And not the banks of oars that swam upon
The many-headed foam at Salamis.°
Europe put off that foam when Phidias°
Gave women dreams and dreams their looking-glass.

One image crossed the many-headed, sat
Under the tropic shade, grew round and slow,
No Hamlet thin from eating flies, a fat
Dreamer of the Middle Ages. Empty eyeballs knew   20
That knowledge increases unreality, that
Mirror on mirror mirrored is all the show.
When gong and conch declare the hour to bless
Grimalkin crawls to Buddha's emptiness.°

When Pearse summoned Cuchulain to his side,°
What stalked through the Post Office? What intellect,°
What calculation, number, measurement, replied?
We Irish, born into that ancient sect
But thrown upon this filthy modern tide
And by its formless, spawning, fury wrecked,   30
Climb to our proper dark, that we may trace
The lineaments of a plummet-measured face.

    April 9th 1938

News for the Delphic Oracle°

I

There all the golden codgers lay,°
There the silver dew,
And the great water sighed for love
And the wind sighed too.
Man-picker Niamh leant and sighed
By Oisin on the grass;°
There sighed amid his choir of love
Tall Pythagoras.°
Plotinus came and looked about,°
The salt flakes on his breast,   10

And having stretched and yawned awhile
Lay sighing like the rest.

II

Straddling each a dolphin's back°
And steadied by a fin
Those Innocents re-live their death,
Their wounds open again.
The ecstatic waters laugh because
Their cries are sweet and strange,
Through their ancestral patterns dance,
And the brute dolphins plunge   20
Until in some cliff-sheltered bay
Where wade the choir of love
Proffering its sacred laurel crowns,
They pitch their burdens off.

III

Slim adolescence that a nymph has stripped,
Peleus on Thetis stares,°
Her limbs are delicate as an eyelid,
Love has blinded him with tears;
But Thetis' belly listens.
Down the mountain walls   30
From where Pan's cavern is°
Intolerable music falls.
Foul goat-head, brutal arm appear,
Belly, shoulder, bum,
Flash fishlike; nymphs and satyrs
Copulate in the foam.

Long-legged Fly

That civilisation may not sink
Its great battle lost,
Quiet the dog, tether the pony
To a distant post.
Our master Caesar is in the tent°
Where the maps are spread,

His eyes fixed upon nothing,
A hand under his head.

Like a long-legged fly upon the stream
His mind moves upon silence.   10

That the topless towers be burnt°
And men recall that face,
Move most gently if move you must
In this lonely place.
She thinks, part woman, three parts a child,
That nobody looks; her feet
Practise a tinker shuffle
Picked up on the street.

Like a long-legged fly upon the stream
Her mind moves upon silence.   20

That girls at puberty may find
The first Adam in their thought,
Shut the door of the Pope's Chapel,
Keep those children out.
There on that scaffolding reclines
Michael Angelo.°
With no more sound than the mice make
His hand moves to and fro.

Like a long-legged fly upon the stream
His mind moves upon silence.   30

A Bronze Head°

Here at right of the entrance this bronze head,
Human, super-human, a bird's round eye,
Everything else withered and mummy-dead.
What great tomb-haunter sweeps the distant sky;
(Something may linger there though all else die;)
And finds there nothing to make its terror less
Hysterico-passio of its own emptiness?°

No dark tomb-haunter once; her form all full
As though with magnanimity of light
Yet a most gentle woman; who can tell   10
Which of her forms has shown her substance right,
Or may be substance can be composite,
Profound McTaggart thought so, and in a breath°
A mouthful hold the extreme of life and death.

But even at the starting-post, all sleek and new,
I saw the wildness in her and I thought
A vision of terror that it must live through
Had shattered her soul. Propinquity had brought
Imagination to that pitch where it casts out
All that is not itself. I had grown wild   20
And wandered murmuring everywhere 'my child, my
        child!'

Or else I thought her supernatural;
As though a sterner eye looked through her eye
On this foul world in its decline and fall;
On gangling stocks grown great, great stocks run dry,
Ancestral pearls all pitched into a sty,
Heroic reverie mocked by clown and knave,
And wondered what was left for massacre to save.

Hound Voice

Because we love bare hills and stunted trees
And were the last to choose the settled ground,
Its boredom of the desk or of the spade, because
So many years companioned by a hound,
Our voices carry; and though slumber bound,
Some few half wake and half renew their choice,
Give tongue, proclaim their hidden name—'hound voice.'

The women that I picked spoke sweet and low
And yet gave tongue. 'Hound Voices' were they all.
We picked each other from afar and knew   10
What hour of terror comes to test the soul,

And in that terror's name obeyed the call,
And understood, what none have understood,
Those images that waken in the blood.

Some day we shall get up before the dawn
And find our ancient hounds before the door,
And wide awake know that the hunt is on;
Stumbling upon the blood-dark track once more,
That stumbling to the kill beside the shore;
Then cleaning out and bandaging of wounds,   20
And chants of victory amid the encircling hounds.

John Kinsella's Lament for Mrs Mary Moore°

I

A bloody and a sudden end,
   Gunshot or a noose,
For death who takes what man would keep,
   Leaves what man would lose.
He might have had my sister
   My cousins by the score,
But nothing satisfied the fool
   But my dear Mary Moore,
None other knows what pleasures man
   At table or in bed.   10
What shall I do for pretty girls
   Now my old bawd is dead?

II

Though stiff to strike a bargain
   Like an old Jew man,
Her bargain struck we laughed and talked
   And emptied many a can;
And O! but she had stories
   Though not for the priest's ear,
To keep the soul of man alive
   Banish age and care,   20
And being old she put a skin
   On everything she said.°
What shall I do for pretty girls
   Now my old bawd is dead?

III

The priests have got a book that says
    But for Adam's sin
Eden's Garden would be there
    And I there within.
No expectation fails there
    No pleasing habit ends   30
No man grows old, no girl grows cold,
    But friends walk by friends.
Who quarrels over halfpennies
    That plucks the trees for bread?
What shall I do for pretty girls
    Now my old bawd is dead?

High Talk

Processions that lack high stilts have nothing that
    catches the eye.
What if my great-granddad had a pair that were
    twenty foot high,
And mine were but fifteen foot, no modern stalks
    upon higher,
Some rogue of the world stole them to patch up a
    fence or a fire.

Because piebald ponies, led bears, caged lions, make
    but poor shows,
Because children demand Daddy-long-legs upon his
    timber toes,
Because women in the upper stories demand a face at the pane
That patching old heels they may shriek, I take to
    chisel and plane.

Malachi Stilt-Jack am I, whatever I learned has run wild,
From collar to collar, from stilt to stilt, from father
    to child.   10
All metaphor, Malachi, stilts and all. A barnacle goose
Far up in the stretches of night; night splits and the
    dawn breaks loose;

I, through the terrible novelty of light, stalk on, stalk on;
Those great sea-horses bare their teeth and laugh at the dawn.

The Apparitions

Because there is safety in derision
I talked about an apparition,
I took no trouble to convince,
Or seem plausible to a man of sense,
Distrustful of that popular eye
Whether it be bold or sly.
Fifteen apparitions have I seen;
The worst a coat upon a coat-hanger.

I have found nothing half so good
As my long-planned half solitude,   10
Where I can sit up half the night
With some friend that has the wit
Not to allow his looks to tell
When I am unintelligible.
Fifteen apparitions have I seen;
The worst a coat upon a coat-hanger.

When a man grows old his joy
Grows more deep day after day,
His empty heart is full at length
But he has need of all that strength   20
Because of the increasing Night
That opens her mystery and fright.
Fifteen apparitions have I seen;
The worst a coat upon a coat-hanger.

Man and the Echo

MAN

In a cleft that's christened Alt°
Under broken stone I halt
At the bottom of a pit

That broad noon has never lit,
And shout a secret to the stone.
All that I have said and done,
Now that I am old and ill,
Turns into a question till
I lie awake night after night
And never get the answers right.   10
Did that play of mine send out°
Certain men the English shot?
Did words of mine put too great strain
On that woman's reeling brain?°
Could my spoken words have checked
That whereby a house lay wrecked?°
And all seems evil until I
Sleepless would lie down and die.

ECHO

Lie down and die.

MAN

              That were to shirk
The spiritual intellect's great work   20
And shirk it in vain. There is no release
In a bodkin or disease,
Nor can there be a work so great
As that which cleans man's dirty slate.
While man can still his body keep
Wine or love drug him to sleep,
Waking he thanks the Lord that he
Has body and its stupidity,
But body gone he sleeps no more
And till his intellect grows sure   30
That all's arranged in one clear view
Pursues the thoughts that I pursue,
Then stands in judgment on his soul,
And, all work done, dismisses all
Out of intellect and sight
And sinks at last into the night.

ECHO

Into the night.

MAN

O rocky voice

Shall we in that great night rejoice?
What do we know but that we face
One another in this place?　　　　　　　　　　40
But hush, for I have lost the theme,
Its joy or night seem but a dream;
Up there some hawk or owl has struck
Dropping out of sky or rock,
A stricken rabbit is crying out
And its cry distracts my thought.

The Circus Animals' Desertion

I

I sought a theme and sought for it in vain,
I sought it daily for six weeks or so.
Maybe at last being but a broken man
I must be satisfied with my heart, although
Winter and summer till old age began
My circus animals were all on show,
Those stilted boys, that burnished chariot,
Lion and woman and the Lord knows what.

II

What can I but enumerate old themes,
First that sea-rider Oisin led by the nose　　　　10
Through three enchanted islands, allegorical dreams,
Vain gaiety, vain battle, vain repose,
Themes of the embittered heart, or so it seems,
That might adorn old songs or courtly shows;
But what cared I that set him on to ride,
I, starved for the bosom of his fairy bride.°

And then a counter-truth filled out its play,
'The Countess Cathleen' was the name I gave it,
She, pity-crazed, had given her soul away
But masterful Heaven had intervened to save it.°　　　20
I thought my dear must her own soul destroy°

So did fanaticism and hate enslave it,
And this brought forth a dream and soon enough
This dream itself had all my thought and love.

And when the Fool and Blind Man stole the bread
Cuchulain fought the ungovernable sea;°
Heart mysteries there, and yet when all is said
It was the dream itself enchanted me:
Character isolated by a deed
To engross the present and dominate memory.   30
Players and painted stage took all my love
And not those things that they were emblems of.

III

Those masterful images because complete
Grew in pure mind but out of what began?
A mound of refuse or the sweepings of a street,
Old kettles, old bottles, and a broken can,
Old iron, old bones, old rags, that raving slut
Who keeps the till. Now that my ladder's gone
I must lie down where all the ladders start
In the foul rag and bone shop of the heart.   40

Politics

*'In our time the destiny of man presents its
meanings in political terms.'—Thomas Mann.°*

How can I, that girl standing there,
My attention fix
On Roman or on Russian
Or on Spanish politics,
Yet here's a travelled man that knows
What he talks about,
And there's a politician
That has both read and thought,
And maybe what they say is true
Of war and war's alarms,   10
But O that I were young again
And held her in my arms.

LONG POEMS

From The Wanderings of Oisin (1889)°

BOOK I

S. Patrick. You who are bent, and bald, and blind,°
 With a heavy heart and a wandering mind,
 Have known three centuries, poets sing,
 Of dalliance with a demon thing.

Oisin. Sad to remember, sick with years,
 The swift innumerable spears;
 The horsemen with their floating hair,
 And bowls of barley, honey, and wine,
 Those merry couples dancing in tune,
 And the white body that lay by mine;   10
 But the tale, though words be lighter than air,
 Must live to be old like the wandering moon.

 Caoilte, and Conan, and Finn were there,°
 When we followed a deer with our baying hounds,
 With Bran, Sceolan, and Lomair,°
 And passing the Firbolgs' burial-mounds,°
 Came to the cairn-heaped grassy hill
 Where passionate Maeve is stony-still;°
 And found on the dove-grey edge of the sea
 A pearl-pale, high-born lady, who rode   20
 On a horse with bridle of findrinny;°
 And like a sunset were her lips,
 A stormy sunset on doomed ships;
 A citron colour gloomed in her hair,
 But down to her feet white vesture flowed,
 And with the glimmering crimson glowed
 Of many a figured embroidery;
 And it was bound with a pearl-pale shell
 That wavered like the summer streams,
 As her soft bosom rose and fell.   30

S. Patrick. You are still wrecked among heathen dreams.

Oisin. 'Why do you wind no horn?' she said.
  'And every hero droop his head?
  The hornless deer is not more sad
  That many a peaceful moment had,
  More sleek than any granary mouse,
  In his own leafy forest house
  Among the waving fields of fern:
  The hunting of heroes should be glad.'

  'O pleasant woman,' answered Finn,   40
  'We think on Oscar's pencilled urn,
  And on the heroes lying slain
  On Gabhra's raven-covered plain;°
  But where are your noble kith and kin,
  And from what country do you ride?'

  'My father and my mother are
  Aengus and Edain, my own name°
  Niamh, and my country far°
  Beyond the tumbling of this tide.'

  'What dream came with you that you came   50
  Through bitter tide on foam-wet feet?
  Did your companion wander away
  From where the birds of Aengus wing?'°

  Thereon did she look haughty and sweet:
  'I have not yet, war-weary king,
  Been spoken of with any man;
  Yet now I choose, for these four feet
  Ran through the foam and ran to this
  That I might have your son to kiss.'

  'Were there no better than my son   60
  That you through all that foam should run?'

  'I loved no man, though kings besought,
  Until the Danaan poets brought°
  Rhyme that rhymed upon Oisin's name,
  And now I am dizzy with the thought
  Of all that wisdom and the fame

Of battles broken by his hands,
Of stories builded by his words
That are like coloured Asian birds
At evening in their rainless lands.'   70

O Patrick, by your brazen bell,
There was no limb of mine but fell
Into a desperate gulph of love!
'You only will I wed,' I cried,
'And I will make a thousand songs,
And set your name all names above,
And captives bound with leathern thongs
Shall kneel and praise you, one by one,
At evening in my western dun.'

'O Oisin, mount by me and ride   80
To shores by the wash of the tremulous tide,
Where men have heaped no burial-mounds,
And the days pass by like a wayward tune,
Where broken faith has never been known,
And the blushes of first love never have flown;
And there I will give you a hundred hounds;
No mightier creatures bay at the moon;
And a hundred robes of murmuring silk,
And a hundred calves and a hundred sheep
Whose long wool whiter than sea-froth flows,   90
And a hundred spears and a hundred bows,
And oil and wine and honey and milk,
And always never-anxious sleep;
While a hundred youths, mighty of limb,
But knowing nor tumult nor hate nor strife,
And a hundred ladies, merry as birds,
Who when they dance to a fitful measure
Have a speed like the speed of the salmon herds,
Shall follow your horn and obey your whim,
And you shall know the Danaan leisure;   100
And Niamh be with you for a wife,'
Then she sighed gently, 'It grows late.
Music and love and sleep await,
Where I would be when the white moon climbs,
The red sun falls and the world grows dim.'

And then I mounted and she bound me
With her triumphing arms around me,
And whispering to herself enwound me;
But when the horse had felt my weight,
He shook himself and neighed three times: 110
Caoilte, Conan, and Finn came near,
And wept, and raised their lamenting hands,
And bid me stay, with many a tear;
But we rode out from the human lands.
In what far kingdom do you go,
Ah, Fenians, with the shield and bow?
Or are you phantoms white as snow,
Whose lips had life's most prosperous glow?
O you, with whom in sloping valleys,
Or down the dewy forest alleys,   120
I chased at morn the flying deer,
With whom I hurled the hurrying spear,
And heard the foemen's bucklers rattle,
And broke the heaving ranks of battle!
And Bran, Sceolan, and Lomair,
Where are you with your long rough hair?
You go not where the red deer feeds,
Nor tear the foemen from their steeds.

            .   .   .   .   .

And now, still sad, we came to where
A beautiful young man dreamed within
A house of wattles, clay, and skin;
One hand upheld his beardless chin,   250
And one a sceptre flashing out
Wild flames of red and gold and blue,
Like to a merry wandering rout
Of dancers leaping in the air;
And men and ladies knelt them there
And showed their eyes with teardrops dim,
And with low murmurs prayed to him,
And kissed the sceptre with red lips,
And touched it with their finger-tips.

He held that flashing sceptre up.   260
'Joy drowns the twilight in the dew,
And fills with stars night's purple cup,

And wakes the sluggard seeds of corn,
And stirs the young kid's budding horn,
And makes the infant ferns unwrap,
And for the peewit paints his cap,
And rolls along the unwieldy sun,
And makes the little planets run:
And if joy were not on the earth,
There were an end of change and birth, 270
And Earth and Heaven and Hell would die,
And in some gloomy barrow lie
Folded like a frozen fly;
Then mock at Death and Time with glances
And wavering arms and wandering dances.

'Men's hearts of old were drops of flame
That from the saffron morning came,
Or drops of silver joy that fell
Out of the moon's pale twisted shell;
But now hearts cry that hearts are slaves, 280
And toss and turn in narrow caves;
But here there is nor law nor rule,
Nor have hands held a weary tool;
And here there is nor Change nor Death,
But only kind and merry breath,
For joy is God and God is joy.'
With one long glance for girl and boy
And the pale blossom of the moon,
He fell into a Druid swoon.

．　．　．　．　．　．

BOOK III

Fled foam underneath us, and round us, a wandering
and milky smoke,
High as the saddle-girth, covering away from our
glances the tide;
And those that fled, and that followed, from the foam-
pale distance broke;
The immortal desire of Immortals we saw in their
faces, and sighed.

I mused on the chase with the Fenians, and Bran,
    Sceolan, Lomair,
And never a song sang Niamh, and over my finger-tips
Came now the sliding of tears and sweeping of mist-
    cold hair,
And now the warmth of sighs, and after the quiver of lips.

Were we days long or hours long in riding, when,
    rolled in a grisly peace,
An isle lay level before us, with dripping hazel and oak?   10
And we stood on a sea's edge we saw not; for whiter
    than new-washed fleece
Fled foam underneath us, and round us, a wandering
    and milky smoke.

And we rode on the plains of the sea's edge; the sea's
    edge barren and grey,
Grey sand on the green of the grasses and over the
    dripping trees,
Dripping and doubling landward, as though they would
    hasten away,
Like an army of old men longing for rest from the
    moan of the seas.

But the trees grew taller and closer, immense in their
    wrinkling bark;
Dropping; a murmurous dropping; old silence and that
    one sound;
For no live creatures lived there, no weasels moved in
    the dark:
Long sighs arose in our spirits, beneath us bubbled the
    ground.   20

And the ears of the horse went sinking away in the
    hollow night,
For, as drift from a sailor slow drowning the gleams of
    the world and the sun,
Ceased on our hands and our faces, on hazel and oak
    leaf, the light,
And the stars were blotted above us, and the whole of
    the world was one.

Till the horse gave a whinny; for, cumbrous with stems
    of the hazel and oak,
A valley flowed down from his hoofs, and there in the
    long grass lay,
Under the starlight and shadow, a monstrous
    slumbering folk,
Their naked and gleaming bodies poured out and
    heaped in the way.

And by them were arrow and war-axe, arrow and
    shield and blade;
And dew-blanched horns, in whose hollow a child of
    three years old   30
Could sleep on a couch of rushes, and all inwrought
    and inlaid,
And more comely than man can make them with
    bronze and silver and gold.

And each of the huge white creatures was huger than
    fourscore men;
The tops of their ears were feathered, their hands were
    the claws of birds,
And, shaking the plumes of the grasses and the leaves
    of the mural glen,
The breathing came from those bodies, long warless,
    grown whiter than curds.

The wood was so spacious above them, that He who
    has stars for His flocks
Could fondle the leaves with His fingers, nor go from
    His dew-cumbered skies;
So long were they sleeping, the owls had builded their
    nests in their locks,
Filling the fibrous dimness with long generations of
    eyes.   40

And over the limbs and the valley the slow owls
    wandered and came,
Now in a place of star-fire, and now in a shadow-place wide;
And the chief of the huge white creatures, his knees in
    the soft star-flame,

Lay loose in a place of shadow: we drew the reins by
    his side.

Golden the nails of his bird-claws, flung loosely along
    the dim ground;
In one was a branch soft-shining with bells more many
    than sighs
In midst of an old man's bosom; owls ruffling and
    pacing around
Sidled their bodies against him, filling the shade with
    their eyes.

And my gaze was thronged with the sleepers; no, not
    since the world began,
In realms where the handsome were many, nor in
    glamours by demons flung,   50
Have faces alive with such beauty been known to the
    salt eye of man,
Yet weary with passions that faded when the sevenfold
    seas were young.

And I gazed on the bell-branch, sleep's forebear, far
    sung by the Sennachies.°
I saw how those slumberers, grown weary, there
    camping in grasses deep,
Of wars with the wide world and pacing the shores of
    the wandering seas,
Laid hands on the bell-branch and swayed it, and fed
    of unhuman sleep.

Snatching the horn of Niamh, I blew a long lingering
    note.
Came sound from those monstrous sleepers, a sound like
    the stirring of flies.
He, shaking the fold of his lips, and heaving the pillar
    of his throat,
Watched me with mournful wonder out of the wells of
    his eyes.   60

I cried, 'Come out of the shadow, king of the nails of
    gold!

And tell of your goodly household and the goodly
    works of your hands,
That we may muse in the starlight and talk of the
    battles of old;
Your questioner, Oisin, is worthy, he comes from the
    Fenian lands.'

Half open his eyes were, and held me, dull with the
    smoke of their dreams;
His lips moved slowly in answer, no answer out of
    them came;
Then he swayed in his fingers the bell-branch, slow
    dropping a sound in faint streams
Softer than snow-flakes in April and piercing the
    marrow like flame.

Wrapt in the wave of that music, with weariness more
    than of earth,
The moil of my centuries filled me; and gone like a
    sea-covered stone   70
Were the memories of the whole of my sorrow and the
    memories of the whole of my mirth,
And a softness came from the starlight and filled me
    full to the bone.

In the roots of the grasses, the sorrels, I laid my body as low;
And the pearl-pale Niamh lay by me, her brow on the
    midst of my breast;
And the horse was gone in the distance, and years after
    years 'gan flow;
Square leaves of the ivy moved over us, binding us
    down to our rest.

And, man of the many white croziers, a century there
    I forgot
How the fetlocks drip blood in the battle, when the
    fallen on fallen lie rolled;
How the falconer follows the falcon in the weeds of
    the heron's plot,
And the name of the demon whose hammer made
    Conchubar's sword-blade of old.   80

And, man of the many white croziers, a century there
 I forgot
That the spear-shaft is made out of ashwood, the shield
 out of osier and hide;
How the hammers spring on the anvil, on the spear-
 head's burning spot;
How the slow, blue-eyed oxen of Finn low sadly at
 evening tide.

But in dreams, mild man of the croziers, driving the
 dust with their throngs,
Moved round me, of seamen or landsmen, all who are
 winter tales;
Came by me the kings of the Red Branch, with roaring
 of laughter and songs,
Or moved as they moved once, love-making or piercing
 the tempest with sails.

Came Blanid, Mac Nessa, tall Fergus who feastward of
 old time slunk,°
Cook Barach, the traitor; and warward, the spittle on
 his beard never dry,°   90
Dark Balor, as old as a forest, car-borne, his mighty head sunk°
Helpless, men lifting the lids of his weary and death-
 making eye.

And by me, in soft red raiment, the Fenians moved in
 loud streams,
And Grania, walking and smiling, sewed with her
 needle of bone.°
So lived I and lived not, so wrought I and wrought not,
 with creatures of dreams,
In a long iron sleep, as a fish in the water goes dumb as
 a stone.

At times our slumber was lightened. When the sun was
 on silver or gold;
When brushed with the wings of the owls, in the
 dimness they love going by;
When a glow-worm was green on a grass-leaf, lured
 from his lair in the mould;

Half wakening, we lifted our eyelids, and gazed on the
     grass with a sigh.   100

So watched I when, man of the croziers, at the heel of a
     century fell,
Weak, in the midst of the meadow, from his miles in
     the midst of the air,
A starling like them that forgathered 'neath a moon
     waking white as a shell
When the Fenians made foray at morning with Bran,
     Sceolan, Lomair.

I awoke: the strange horse without summons out of the
     distance ran,
Thrusting his nose to my shoulder; he knew in his
     bosom deep
That once more moved in my bosom the ancient
     sadness of man,
And that I would leave the Immortals, their dimness,
     their dews dropping sleep.

O, had you seen beautiful Niamh grow white as the
     waters are white,
Lord of the croziers, you even had lifted your hands
     and wept: 110
But, the bird in my fingers, I mounted, remembering
     alone that delight
Of twilight and slumber were gone, and that hoofs
     impatiently stept.

I cried, 'O Niamh! O white one! if only a twelve-
     houred day,
I must gaze on the beard of Finn, and move where the
     old men and young
In the Fenians' dwellings of wattle lean on the
     chessboards and play,
Ah, sweet to me now were even bald Conan's slanderous
     tongue!

'Like me were some galley forsaken far off in Meridian
     isle,°

Remembering its long-oared companions, sails turning
    to threadbare rags;
No more to crawl on the seas with long oars mile after
    mile,
But to be amid shooting of flies and flowering of rushes
    and flags.'   120

Their motionless eyeballs of spirits grown mild with
    mysterious thought,
Watched her those seamless faces from the valley's
    glimmering girth;
As she murmured, 'O wandering Oisin, the strength
    of the bell-branch is naught,
For there moves alive in your fingers the fluttering
    sadness of earth.

'Then go through the lands in the saddle and see what
    the mortals do,
And softly come to your Niamh over the tops of the tide;
But weep for your Niamh, O Oisin, weep; for if only
    your shoe
Brush lightly as haymouse earth's pebbles, you will
    come no more to my side.

'O flaming lion of the world, O when will you turn to
    your rest?'
I saw from a distant saddle; from the earth she made
    her moan: 130
'I would die like a small withered leaf in the autumn,
    for breast unto breast
We shall mingle no more, nor our gazes empty their
    sweetness lone

'In the isles of the farthest seas where only the spirits
    come.
Were the winds less soft than the breath of a pigeon
    who sleeps on her nest,
Nor lost in the star-fires and odours the sound of the
    sea's vague drum?
O flaming lion of the world, O when will you turn to
    your rest?'

The wailing grew distant; I rode by the woods of the
    wrinkling bark,
Where ever is murmurous dropping, old silence and
    that one sound;
For no live creatures live there, no weasels move in the
    dark;
In a reverie forgetful of all things, over the bubbling
    ground.   140

And I rode by the plains of the sea's edge, where all is
    barren and grey,
Grey sand on the green of the grasses and over the
    dripping trees,
Dripping and doubling landward, as though they
    would hasten away,
Like an army of old men longing for rest from the
    moan of the seas.

And the winds made the sands on the sea's edge turning
    and turning go,
As my mind made the names of the Fenians. Far from
    the hazel and oak,
I rode away on the surges, where, high as the saddle-bow,
Fled foam underneath me, and round me, a wandering
    and milky smoke.

Long fled the foam-flakes around me, the winds fled
    out of the vast,
Snatching the bird in secret; nor knew I, embosomed
    apart,   150
When they froze the cloth on my body like armour
    riveted fast,
For Remembrance, lifting her leanness, keened in the
    gates of my heart.

Till, fattening the winds of the morning, an odour of
    new-mown hay
Came, and my forehead fell low, and my tears like
    berries fell down;
Later a sound came, half lost in the sound of a shore
    far away,

From the great grass-barnacle calling, and later the
    shore-weeds brown.

If I were as I once was, the strong hoofs crushing the
    sand and the shells,
Coming out of the sea as the dawn comes, a chaunt of
    love on my lips,
Not coughing, my head on my knees, and praying, and
    wroth with the bells,
I would leave no saint's head on his body from Rachlin to
    Bera of ships.°   160

Making way from the kindling surges, I rode on a
    bridle-path
Much wondering to see upon all hands, of wattles and
    woodwork made,
Your bell-mounted churches, and guardless the sacred
    cairn and the rath,°
And a small and a feeble populace stooping with
    mattock and spade,

Or weeding or ploughing with faces a-shining with
    much-toil wet;
While in this place and that place, with bodies
    unglorious, their chieftains stood,
Awaiting in patience the straw-death, croziered one,
    caught in your net:
Went the laughter of scorn from my mouth like the
    roaring of wind in a wood.

And before I went by them so huge and so speedy with
    eyes so bright,
Came after the hard gaze of youth, or an old man lifted
    his head: 170
And I rode and I rode, and I cried out, 'The Fenians
    hunt wolves in the night,
So sleep thee by daytime,' A voice cried, 'The Fenians
    a long time are dead.'

A whitebeard stood hushed on the pathway, the flesh
    of his face as dried grass,

And in folds round his eyes and his mouth, he sad as a
    child without milk;
And the dreams of the islands were gone, and I knew
    how men sorrow and pass,
And their hound, and their horse, and their love, and
    their eyes that glimmer like silk.

And wrapping my face in my hair, I murmured, 'In
    old age they ceased';
And my tears were larger than berries, and I
    murmured, 'Where white clouds lie spread
On Crevroe or broad Knockfefin, with many of old they feast°
On the floors of the gods.' He cried, 'No, the gods a
    long time are dead.'   180

And lonely and longing for Niamh, I shivered and
    turned me about,
The heart in me longing to leap like a grasshopper into
    her heart;
I turned and rode to the westward, and followed the
    sea's old shout
Till I saw where Maeve lies sleeping till starlight and
    midnight part.°

And there at the foot of the mountain, two carried a
    sack full of sand,
They bore it with staggering and sweating, but fell
    with their burden at length.
Leaning down from the gem-studded saddle, I flung it
    five yards with my hand,
With a sob for men waxing so weakly, a sob for the
    Fenians' old strength.

The rest you have heard of, O croziered man; how,
    when divided the girth,
I fell on the path, and the horse went away like a
    summer fly;   190
And my years three hundred fell on me, and I rose, and
    walked on the earth,
A creeping old man, full of sleep, with the spittle on
    his beard never dry.

How the men of the sand-sack showed me a church
    with its belfry in air;
Sorry place, where for swing of the war-axe in my dim
    eyes the crozier gleams;
What place have Caoilte and Conan, and Bran, Sceolan,
    Lomair?
Speak, you too are old with your memories, an old man
    surrounded with dreams.

S. Patrick. Where the flesh of the footsole clingeth on
    the burning stones is their place;
Where the demons whip them with wires on the
    burning stones of wide Hell,
Watching the blessèd ones move far off, and the
    smile on God's face,
Between them a gateway of brass, and the howl of the
    angels who fell.   200

Oisin. Put the staff in my hands; for I go to the Fenians,
    O cleric, to chaunt
The war-songs that roused them of old; they will rise,
    making clouds with their breath,
Innumerable, singing, exultant; the clay underneath
    them shall pant,
And demons be broken in pieces, and trampled
    beneath them in death.

And demons afraid in their darkness; deep horror of
    eyes and of wings,
Afraid, their ears on the earth laid, shall listen and
    rise up and weep;
Hearing the shaking of shields and the quiver of
    stretched bowstrings,
Hearing Hell loud with a murmur, as shouting and
    mocking we sweep.

We will tear out the flaming stones, and batter the
    gateway of brass
And enter, and none sayeth 'No' when there enters
    the strongly armed guest;   210
Make clean as a broom cleans, and march on as oxen
    move over young grass;

Then feast, making converse of wars, and of old
    wounds, and turn to our rest.

S. Patrick. On the flaming stones, without refuge, the
    limbs of the Fenians are tost;
None war on the masters of Hell, who could break
    up the world in their rage;
But kneel and wear out the flags and pray for your
    soul that is lost
Through the demon love of its youth and its godless
    and passionate age.

Oisin. Ah me! to be shaken with coughing and broken
    with old age and pain,
Without laughter, a show unto children, alone with
    remembrance and fear;
All emptied of purple hours as a beggar's cloak in
    the rain,
As a hay-cock out on the flood, or a wolf sucked
    under a weir.   220

It were sad to gaze on the blessèd and no man I loved
    of old there;
I throw down the chain of small stones! when life in
    my body has ceased,
I will go to Caoilte, and Conan, and Bran, Sceolan,
    Lomair,
And dwell in the house of the Fenians, be they in
    flames or at feast.

Baile and Aillinn (1903)

ARGUMENT. *Baile and Aillinn were lovers, but Aengus, the Master of Love,
wishing them to be happy in his own land among the dead, told to each a story
of the other's death, so that their hearts were broken and they died.*°

    I hardly hear the curlew cry,
    Nor the grey rush when the wind is high,
    Before my thoughts begin to run
    On the heir of Ulad, Buan's son,°

Baile, who had the honey mouth;
And that mild woman of the south,
Aillinn, who was King Lugaid's heir.°
Their love was never drowned in care
Of this or that thing, nor grew cold
Because their bodies had grown old.   10
Being forbid to marry on earth,
They blossomed to immortal mirth.

About the time when Christ was born,
When the long wars for the White Horn°
And the Brown Bull had not yet come,
Young Baile Honey-Mouth, whom some
Called rather Baile Little-Land,
Rode out of Emain with a band°
Of harpers and young men; and they
Imagined, as they struck the way   20
To many-pastured Muirthemne,°
That all things fell out happily,
And there, for all that fools had said,
Baile and Aillinn would be wed.

They found an old man running there:
He had ragged long grass-coloured hair;
He had knees that stuck out of his hose;
He had puddle-water in his shoes;
He had half a cloak to keep him dry,
Although he had a squirrel's eye.   30

O wandering birds and rushy beds,
You put such folly in our heads
With all this crying in the wind;
No common love is to our mind,
And our poor Kate or Nan is less
Than any whose unhappiness
Awoke the harp-strings long ago.
Yet they that know all things but know
That all this life can give us is
A child's laughter, a woman's kiss.   40
Who was it put so great a scorn
In the grey reeds that night and morn

Are trodden and broken by the herds,
And in the light bodies of birds
The north wind tumbles to and fro
And pinches among hail and snow?

That runner said: 'I am from the south;
I run to Baile Honey-Mouth,
To tell him how the girl Aillinn
Rode from the country of her kin,   50
And old and young men rode with her:
For all that country had been astir
If anybody half as fair
Had chosen a husband anywhere
But where it could see her every day.
When they had ridden a little way
An old man caught the horse's head
With: "You must home again, and wed
With somebody in your own land."
A young man cried and kissed her hand,   60
"O lady, wed with one of us";
And when no face grew piteous
For any gentle thing she spake,
She fell and died of the heart-break.'

Because a lover's heart's worn out,
Being tumbled and blown about
By its own blind imagining,
And will believe that anything
That is bad enough to be true, is true,
Baile's heart was broken in two;   70
And he, being laid upon green boughs,
Was carried to the goodly house
Where the Hound of Ulad sat before°
The brazen pillars of his door,
His face bowed low to weep the end
Of the harper's daughter and her friend.
For although years had passed away
He always wept them on that day,
For on that day they had been betrayed;
And now that Honey-Mouth is laid   80
Under a cairn of sleepy stone

Before his eyes, he has tears for none,
Although he is carrying stone, but two
For whom the cairn's but heaped anew.

We hold, because our memory is
So full of that thing and of this,
That out of sight is out of mind.
But the grey rush under the wind
And the grey bird with crooked bill
Have such long memories that they still   90
Remember Deirdre and her man;
And when we walk with Kate or Nan
About the windy water-side,
Our hearts can hear the voices chide.
How could we be so soon content,
Who know the way that Naoise went?
And they have news of Deirdre's eyes,
Who being lovely was so wise—
Ah! wise, my heart knows well how wise.

Now had that old gaunt crafty one,   100
Gathering his cloak about him, run
Where Aillinn rode with waiting-maids,
Who amid leafy lights and shades
Dreamed of the hands that would unlace
Their bodices in some dim place
When they had come to the marriage-bed,
And harpers, pacing with high head
As though their music were enough
To make the savage heart of love
Grow gentle without sorrowing,   110
Imagining and pondering
Heaven knows what calamity;

'Another's hurried off,' cried he,
'From heat and cold and wind and wave;
They have heaped the stones above his grave
In Muirthemne, and over it
In changeless Ogham letters writ—°
Baile, that was of Rury's seed.°
But the gods long ago decreed

No waiting-maid should ever spread   120
Baile and Aillinn's marriage-bed,
For they should clip and clip again
Where wild bees hive on the Great Plain.
Therefore it is but little news
That put this hurry in my shoes.'

Then seeing that he scarce had spoke
Before her love-worn heart had broke,
He ran and laughed until he came
To that high hill the herdsmen name
The Hill Seat of Leighin, because°   130
Some god or king had made the laws
That held the land together there,
In old times among the clouds of the air.

That old man climbed; the day grew dim;
Two swans came flying up to him,
Linked by a gold chain each to each,
And with low murmuring laughing speech
Alighted on the windy grass.
They knew him: his changed body was
Tall, proud and ruddy, and light wings   140
Were hovering over the harp-strings
That Edain, Midhir's wife, had wove°
In the hid place, being crazed by love.

What shall I call them? fish that swim,
Scale rubbing scale where light is dim
By a broad water-lily leaf;
Or mice in the one wheaten sheaf
Forgotten at the threshing-place;
Or birds lost in the one clear space
Of morning light in a dim sky;   150
Or, it may be, the eyelids of one eye,
Or the door-pillars of one house,
Or two sweet blossoming apple-boughs
That have one shadow on the ground;
Or the two strings that made one sound
Where that wise harper's finger ran.
For this young girl and this young man

Have happiness without an end,
Because they have made so good a friend.

They know all wonders, for they pass   160
The towery gates of Gorias,
And Findrias and Falias,
And long-forgotten Murias,°
Among the giant kings whose hoard,
Cauldron and spear and stone and sword,°
Was robbed before earth gave the wheat;
Wandering from broken street to street
They come where some huge watcher is,
And tremble with their love and kiss.

They know undying things, for they   170
Wander where earth withers away,
Though nothing troubles the great streams
But light from the pale stars, and gleams
From the holy orchards, where there is none
But fruit that is of precious stone,
Or apples of the sun and moon.

What were our praise to them? They eat
Quiet's wild heart, like daily meat;
Who when night thickens are afloat
On dappled skins in a glass boat,   180
Far out under a windless sky;
While over them birds of Aengus fly,
And over the tiller and the prow,
And waving white wings to and fro
Awaken wanderings of light air
To stir their coverlet and their hair.

And poets found, old writers say,
A yew tree where his body lay;
But a wild apple hid the grass
With its sweet blossom where hers was;   190
And being in good heart, because
A better time had come again
After the deaths of many men,
And that long fighting at the ford,°

They wrote on tablets of thin board,
Made of the apple and the yew,
All the love stories that they knew.

Let rush and bird cry out their fill
Of the harper's daughter if they will,
Beloved, I am not afraid of her.   200
She is not wiser nor lovelier,
And you are more high of heart than she,
For all her wanderings over-sea;
But I'd have bird and rush forget
Those other two; for never yet
Has lover lived, but longed to wive
Like them that are no more alive.

PLAYS

Cathleen ni Houlihan (1902)°

PERSONS IN THE PLAY

Peter Gillane

*Michael Gillane, his son, going to
be married*

*Patrick Gillane, a lad of twelve,
Michael's brother*

Bridget Gillane, Peter's wife

Delia Cahel, engaged to Michael

The Poor Old Woman

Neighbours

*Interior of a cottage close to Killala, in 1798.° Bridget is standing at a
table undoing a parcel. Peter is sitting at one side of the fire, Patrick at
the other.*

Peter. What is that sound I hear?

Patrick. I don't hear anything. [*He listens.*] I hear it now. It's like
cheering. [*He goes to the window and looks out.*] I wonder what
they are cheering about. I don't see anybody.

Peter. It might be a hurling.

Patrick. There's no hurling to-day. It must be down in the town the
cheering is.

Bridget. I suppose the boys must be having some sport of their own.
Come over here, Peter, and look at Michael's wedding clothes.

Peter [*shifts his chair to table*]. Those are grand clothes, indeed.   10

Bridget. You hadn't clothes like that when you married me, and no
coat to put on of a Sunday more than any other day.

Peter. That is true, indeed. We never thought a son of our own
would be wearing a suit of that sort for his wedding, or have so
good a place to bring a wife to.

Patrick [*who is still at the window*]. There's an old woman coming
down the road. I don't know is it here she is coming.

Bridget. It will be a neighbour coming to hear about Michael's wed-
ding. Can you see who it is?

Patrick. I think it is a stranger, but she's not coming to the house.   20
She's turned into the gap that goes down where Maurteen and
his sons are shearing sheep. [*He turns towards Bridget.*] Do you
remember what Winny of the Cross Roads was saying the other

night about the strange woman that goes through the country whatever time there's war or trouble coming?

Bridget. Don't be bothering us about Winny's talk, but go and open the door for your brother. I hear him coming up the path.

Peter. I hope he has brought Delia's fortune with him safe, for fear the people might go back on the bargain and I after making it. Trouble enough I had making it.   30

[*Patrick opens the door and Michael comes in.*]

Bridget. What kept you, Michael? We were looking out for you this long time.

Michael. I went round by the priest's house to bid him be ready to marry us to-morrow.

Bridget. Did he say anything?

Michael. He said it was a very nice match, and that he was never better pleased to marry any two in his parish than myself and Delia Cahel.

Peter. Have you got the fortune, Michael?

Michael. Here it is.   40

[*Michael puts bag on table and goes over and leans against chimney-jamb. Bridget, who has been all this time examining the clothes, pulling the seams and trying the lining of the pockets, etc., puts the clothes on the dresser.*]

Peter [*getting up and taking the bag in his hand and turning out the money*]. Yes, I made the bargain well for you, Michael. Old John Cahel would sooner have kept a share of this a while longer. 'Let me keep the half of it until the first boy is born,' says he. 'You will not,' says I. 'Whether there is or is not a boy, the whole hundred pounds must be in Michael's hands before he brings your daughter to the house.' The wife spoke to him then, and he gave in at the end.

Bridget. You seem well pleased to be handling the money, Peter.

Peter. Indeed, I wish I had had the luck to get a hundred pounds, or twenty pounds itself, with the wife I married.   50

Bridget. Well, if I didn't bring much I didn't get much. What had you the day I married you but a flock of hens and you feeding them, and a few lambs and you driving them to the market at Ballina?° [*She is vexed and bangs a jug on the dresser.*] If I brought no fortune I worked it out in my bones, laying down the baby, Michael that is standing there now, on a stook of straw, while I dug the potatoes, and never asking big dresses or anything but to be working.

Peter. That is true, indeed. [*He pats her arm.*

Bridget. Leave me alone now till I ready the house for the woman 60
that is to come into it.

Peter. You are the best woman in Ireland, but money is good, too. [*He begins handling the money again and sits down.*] I never thought to see so much money within my four walls. We can do great things now we have it. We can take the ten acres of land we have the chance of since Jamsie Dempsey died, and stock it. We will go to the fair at Ballina to buy the stock. Did Delia ask any of the money for her own use, Michael?

Michael. She did not, indeed. She did not seem to take much notice of it, or to look at it at all. 70

Bridget. That's no wonder. Why would she look at it when she had yourself to look at, a fine, strong young man? It is proud she must be to get you; a good steady boy that will make use of the money, and not be running through it or spending it on drink like another.

Peter. It's likely Michael himself was not thinking much of the fortune either, but of what sort the girl was to look at.

Michael [*coming over towards the table*]. Well, you would like a nice comely girl to be beside you, and to go walking with you. The fortune only lasts for a while, but the woman will be there always. 80

Patrick [*turning round from the window*]. They are cheering again down in the town. Maybe they are landing horses from Enniscrone.° They do be cheering when the horses take the water well.

Michael. There are no horses in it. Where would they be going and no fair at hand? Go down to the town, Patrick, and see what is going on.

Patrick [*opens the door to go out, but stops for a moment on the threshold*]. Will Delia remember, do you think, to bring the greyhound pup she promised me when she would be coming to the house?

Michael. She will surely.

[*Patrick goes out, leaving the door open.*

Peter. It will be Patrick's turn next to be looking for a fortune, but he   90
won't find it so easy to get it and he with no place of his own.

Bridget. I do be thinking sometimes, now things are going so well
with us, and the Cahels such a good back to us in the district, and
Delia's own uncle a priest, we might be put in the way of making
Patrick a priest some day, and he so good at his books.

Peter. Time enough, time enough. You have always your head full
of plans, Bridget.

Bridget. We will be well able to give him learning, and not to send
him tramping the country like a poor scholar that lives on char-
ity.   100

Michael. They're not done cheering yet.

[*He goes over to the door and stands there for a moment, putting
up his hand to shade his eyes.*]

Bridget. Do you see anything?

Michael. I see an old woman coming up the path.

Bridget. Who is it, I wonder? It must be the strange woman Patrick
saw a while ago.

Michael. I don't think it's one of the neighbours anyway, but she has
her cloak over her face.

Bridget. It might be some poor woman heard we were making ready
for the wedding and came to look for her share.

Peter. I may as well put the money out of sight. There is no use leav-   110
ing it out for every stranger to look at.

[*He goes over to a large box in the corner, opens it and puts the
bag in and fumbles at the lock.*]

Michael. There she is, father! [*An Old Woman passes the window
slowly. She looks at Michael as she passes.*] I'd sooner a stranger not
to come to the house the night before my wedding.

Bridget. Open the door, Michael; don't keep the poor woman wait-
ing.

[*The Old Woman comes in. Michael stands aside to make way
for her.*]

Old Woman. God save all here!

Peter. God save you kindly!

Old Woman. You have good shelter here.

Peter. You are welcome to whatever shelter we have.   120

Bridget. Sit down there by the fire and welcome.

Old Woman [*warming her hands*]. There is a hard wind outside.

> [*Michael watches her curiously from the door. Peter comes over to the table.*]

Peter. Have you travelled far to-day?

Old Woman. I have travelled far, very far; there are few have travelled so far as myself, and there's many a one that doesn't make me welcome. There was one that had strong sons I thought were friends of mine, but they were shearing their sheep, and they wouldn't listen to me.

Peter. It's a pity indeed for any person to have no place of their own.

Old Woman. That's true for you indeed, and it's long I'm on the   130
roads since I first went wandering.

Bridget. It is a wonder you are not worn out with so much wandering.

Old Woman. Sometimes my feet are tired and my hands are quiet, but there is no quiet in my heart. When the people see me quiet, they think old age has come on me and that all the stir has gone out of me. But when the trouble is on me I must be talking to my friends.

Bridget. What was it put you wandering?

Old Woman. Too many strangers in the house.°   140

Bridget. Indeed you look as if you'd had your share of trouble.

Old Woman. I have had trouble indeed.

Bridget. What was it put the trouble on you?

Old Woman. My land that was taken from me.

Peter. Was it much land they took from you?

Old Woman. My four beautiful green fields.°

Peter. [*aside to Bridget*]. Do you think could she be the widow Casey that was put out of her holding at Kilglass° a while ago?

Bridget. She is not. I saw the widow Casey one time at the market in Ballina, a stout fresh woman.   150

Peter [*to Old Woman*]. Did you hear a noise of cheering, and you coming up the hill?

Old Woman. I thought I heard the noise I used to hear when my friends came to visit me.

> [*She begins singing half to herself.*]

> I will go cry with the woman,
> For yellow-haired Donough is dead,°
> With a hempen rope for a neckcloth,
> And a white cloth on his head,——

Michael [*coming from the door*]. What is it that you are singing, ma'am?   160

Old Woman. Singing I am about a man I knew one time, yellow-haired Donough that was hanged in Galway.

> [*She goes on singing, much louder.*]

> I am come to cry with you, woman,
> My hair is unwound and unbound;
> I remember him ploughing his field,
> Turning up the red side of the ground,
> And building his barn on the hill
> With the good mortared stone;
> O! we'd have pulled down the gallows
> Had it happened in Enniscrone!   170

Michael. What was it brought him to his death?

Old Woman. He died for love of me: many a man has died for love of me.

Peter [*aside to Bridget*]. Her trouble has put her wits astray.

Michael. Is it long since that song was made? Is it long since he got his death?

Old Woman. Not long, not long. But there were others that died for love of me a long time ago.

Michael. Were they neighbours of your own, ma'am?

Old Woman. Come here beside me and I'll tell you about them.   180
[*Michael sits down beside her on the hearth.*] There was a red man of the O'Donnells from the north, and a man of the O'Sullivans from the south, and there was one Brian that lost his life at Clontarf° by the sea, and there were a great many in the west, some that died hundreds of years ago, and there are some that will die to-morrow.

Michael. Is it in the west that men will die to-morrow?

Old Woman. Come nearer, nearer to me.

Bridget. Is she right, do you think? Or is she a woman from beyond
the world?   190

Peter. She doesn't know well what she's talking about, with the
want and the trouble she has gone through.

Bridget. The poor thing, we should treat her well.

Peter. Give her a drink of milk and a bit of the oaten cake.

Bridget. Maybe we should give her something along with that, to
bring her on her way. A few pence or a shilling itself, and we with
so much money in the house.

Peter. Indeed I'd not begrudge it to her if we had it to spare, but if
we go running through what we have, we'll soon have to break
the hundred pounds, and that would be a pity.   200

Bridget. Shame on you, Peter. Give her the shilling and your bless-
ing with it, or our own luck will go from us.

  [*Peter goes to the box and takes out a shilling.*]

Bridget [*to the Old Woman*]. Will you have a drink of milk,
ma'am?

Old Woman. It is not food or drink that I want.

Peter [*offering the shilling*]. Here is something for you.

Old Woman. This is not what I want. It is not silver I want.

Peter. What is it you would be asking for?

Old Woman. If anyone would give me help he must give me himself,
he must give me all.   210

  [*Peter goes over to the table staring at the shilling in his hand in
  a bewildered way, and stands whispering to Bridget.*]

Michael. Have you no one to care you in your age, ma'am?

Old Woman. I have not. With all the lovers that brought me their
love I never set out the bed for any.

Michael. Are you lonely going the roads, ma'am?

Old Woman. I have my thoughts and I have my hopes.

Michael. What hopes have you to hold to?

Old Woman. The hope of getting my beautiful fields back again; the
hope of putting the strangers out of my house.

Michael. What way will you do that, ma'am?

Old Woman. I have good friends that will help me. They are gather-   220
ing to help me now. I am not afraid. If they are put down to-day
they will get the upper hand to-morrow. [*She gets up.*] I must be
going to meet my friends. They are coming to help me and I must
be there to welcome them. I must call the neighbours together to
welcome them.

Michael. I will go with you.

Bridget. It is not her friends you have to go and welcome, Michael;
it is the girl coming into the house you have to welcome. You
have plenty to do; it is food and drink you have to bring to the
house. The woman that is coming home is not coming with   230
empty hands; you would not have an empty house before her.
[*To the Old Woman.*] Maybe you don't know, ma'am that my son
is going to be married to-morrow.

Old Woman. It is not a man going to his marriage that I look to for
help.

Peter [*to Bridget*]. Who is she, do you think, at all?

Bridget. You did not tell us your name yet, ma'am.

Old Woman. Some call me the Poor Old Woman,° and there are
some that call me Cathleen, the daughter of Houlihan.

Peter. I think I knew some one of that name, once. Who was it, I   240
wonder? It must have been some one I knew when I was a boy.
No, no; I remember, I heard it in a song.

Old Woman [*who is standing in the doorway*]. They are wondering
that there were songs made for me; there have been many songs
made for me, I heard one on the wind this morning.

[*Sings*]

Do not make a great keening°
When the graves have been dug to-morrow.
Do not call the white-scarfed riders°
To the burying that shall be to-morrow.

Do not spread food to call strangers   250
To the wakes that shall be to-morrow;
Do not give money for prayers
For the dead that shall die to-morrow. . . .

They will have no need of prayers, they will have no need of
prayers.

Michael. I do not know what that song means, but tell me something I can do for you.

Peter. Come over to me, Michael.

Michael. Hush, father, listen to her.

Old Woman. It is a hard service they take that help me. Many that 260 are red-cheeked now will be pale-cheeked; many that have been free to walk the hills and the bogs and the rushes will be sent to walk hard streets in far countries; many a good plan will be broken; many that have gathered money will not stay to spend it; many a child will be born and there will be no father at its christening to give it a name. They that have red cheeks will have pale cheeks for my sake, and for all that, they will think they are well paid.   *[She goes out; her voice is heard outside singing.*

> They shall be remembered for ever,
> They shall be alive for ever,   270
> They shall be speaking for ever,
> The people shall hear them for ever.

Bridget [to Peter]. Look at him, Peter; he has the look of a man that has got the touch.° *[Raising her voice.]* Look here, Michael, at the wedding clothes. Such grand clothes as these are! You have a right to fit them on now; it would be a pity to-morrow if they did not fit. The boys would be laughing at you. Take them, Michael, and go into the room and fit them on.

[She puts them on his arm.]

Michael. What wedding are you talking of? What clothes will I be wearing to-morrow?   280

Bridget. These are the clothes you are going to wear when you marry Delia Cahel to-morrow.

Michael. I had forgotten that.

[He looks at the clothes and turns towards the inner room, but stops at the sound of cheering outside.]

Peter. There is the shouting come to our own door. What is it has happened?

[Neighbours come crowding in, Patrick and Delia with them.]

Patrick. There are ships in the Bay; the French are landing at Killala!

[*Peter takes his pipe from his mouth and his hat off, and stands up. The clothes slip from Michael's arm.*]

Delia. Michael! [*He takes no notice.*] Michael! [*He turns towards her.*] Why do you look at me like a stranger?

    [*She drops his arm. Bridget goes over towards her.*]

Patrick. The boys are all hurrying down the hillside to join the 290 French.

Delia. Michael won't be going to join the French.

Bridget [*to Peter*]. Tell him not to go, Peter.

Peter. It's no use. He doesn't hear a word we're saying.

Bridget. Try and coax him over to the fire.

Delia. Michael, Michael! You won't leave me! You won't join the French, and we going to be married!

    [*She puts her arms about him, he turns towards her as if about to yield.*]

    Old Woman's voice outside.

They shall be speaking for ever,

The people shall hear them for ever.

    [*Michael breaks away from Delia, stands for a second at the door, then rushes out, following the Old Woman's voice. Bridget takes Delia, who is crying silently, into her arms.*]

Peter [*to Patrick, laying a hand on his arm*]. Did you see an old 300 woman going down the path?

Patrick. I did not, but I saw a young girl, and she had the walk of a queen.

               THE END

Deirdre (1907)°

TO
MRS. PATRICK CAMPBELL°
who in the generosity of her genius has played my
Deirdre in Dublin and London with the Abbey
Company, as well as with her own people, and
IN MEMORY OF
ROBERT GREGORY
who designed the beautiful scene she played it in.

PERSONS IN THE PLAY

Musicians
Fergus,° an old man
Naoise (pronounced Neesh-e), a
   young king
Deirdre, his queen

A Dark-faced Messenger
Conchubar (pronounced Conohar),
   the old King of Uladh,° who is
   still strong and vigorous
A Dark-faced Executioner

A Guest-house in a wood. It is a rough house of timber; through the doors and some of the windows one can see the great spaces of the wood, the sky dimming, night closing in. But a window to the left shows the thick leaves of a coppice; the landscape suggests silence and loneliness. There is a door to right and left, and through the side windows one can see anybody who approaches either door, a moment before he enters. In the centre, a part of the house is curtained off; the curtains are drawn. There are unlighted torches in brackets on the walls. There is, at one side, a small table with a chessboard and chessmen upon it. At the other side of the room there is a brazier with a fire; two women, with musical instruments beside them, crouch about the brazier: they are comely women of about forty. Another woman, who carries a stringed instrument, enters hurriedly; she speaks, at first standing in the doorway.

First Musician. I have a story right, my wanderers,
  That has so mixed with fable in our songs
  That all seemed fabulous. We are come, by chance,
  Into King Conchubar's country, and this house
  Is an old guest-house built for travellers
  From the seashore to Conchubar's royal house,
  And there are certain hills among these woods
  And there Queen Deirdre grew.

Second Musician.   That famous queen
   Who has been wandering with her lover Naoise
   Somewhere beyond the edges of the world?   10

First Musician [*going nearer to the brazier*]. Some dozen years ago,
    King Conchubar found
   A house upon a hillside in this wood,
   And there a child with an old witch to nurse her,
   And nobody to say if she were human,
   Or of the gods, or anything at all
   Of who she was or why she was hidden there,
   But that she'd too much beauty for good luck.
   He went up thither daily, till at last
   She put on womanhood, and he lost peace,
   And Deirdre's tale began. The King was old.
   A month or so before the marriage-day,   20
   A young man, in the laughing scorn of his youth,
   Naoise, the son of Usna, climbed up there,
   And having wooed, or, as some say, been wooed,
   Carried her off.

Second Musician.   The tale were well enough
   Had it a finish.

First Musician.   Hush! I have more to tell;
   But gather close about that I may whisper
   The secrets of a king.

Second Musician.   There's none to hear!

First Musician. I have been to Conchubar's house and
    followed up
   A crowd of servants going out and in
   With loads upon their heads: embroideries   30
   To hang upon the walls, or new-mown rushes
   To strew upon the floors, and came at length
   To a great room.

Second Musician.   Be silent; there are steps!

   [*Enter Fergus, an old man, who moves about from door to window
   excitedly through what follows.*]

Fergus. I thought to find a message from the King.
   You are musicians by these instruments,
   And if as seems—for you are comely women—
   You can praise love, you'll have the best of luck,

For there'll be two, before the night is in,
That bargained for their love, and paid for it   40
All that men value. You have but the time
To weigh a happy music with a sad,
To find what is most pleasing to a lover,
Before the son of Usna and his queen
Have passed this threshold.

First Musician.   Deirdre and her man!

Fergus. I was to have found a message in this house,
    And ran to meet it. Is there no messenger
    From Conchubar to Fergus, son of Rogh?

First Musician. Are Deirdre and her lover tired of life?

Fergus. You are not of this country, or you'd know   50
    That they are in my charge and all forgiven.

First Musician. We have no country but the roads of the world.

Fergus. Then you should know that all things change in the world,
    And hatred turns to love and love to hate,
    And even kings forgive.

First Musician.   An old man's love
    Who casts no second line is hard to cure;
    His jealousy is like his love.

Fergus.   And that's but true.
    You have learned something in your wanderings.
    He was so hard to cure that the whole court,
    But I alone, thought it impossible;   60
    Yet after I had urged it at all seasons,
    I had my way, and all's forgiven now;
    And you shall speak the welcome and the joy
    That I lack tongue for.

First Musician.   Yet old men are jealous.

Fergus [*going to door*]. I am Conchubar's near friend, and that
        weighed somewhat,
    And it was policy to pardon them.
    The need of some young, famous, popular man
    To lead the troops, the murmur of the crowd,
    And his own natural impulse, urged him to it.
    They have been wandering half a dozen years.   70

First Musician. And yet old men are jealous.

Fergus [*coming from door*].   Sing the more sweetly
  Because, though age is arid as a bone,
  This man has flowered. I've need of music, too;
  If this grey head would suffer no reproach,
  I'd dance and sing—

> [*Dark-faced men with strange, barbaric dress and arms begin to
> pass by the doors and windows. They pass one by one and in
> silence.*]

                              and dance till the hour ran out,
  Because I have accomplished this good deed.

First Musician. Look there—there at the window, those dark men,
  With murderous and outlandish-looking arms—
  They've been about the house all day.

Fergus [*looking after them*].   What are you?
  Where do you come from, who is it sent you here?   80

First Musician. They will not answer you.

Fergus.   They do not hear.

First Musician. Forgive my open speech, but to these eyes
  That have seen many lands they are such men
  As kings will gather for a murderous task
  That neither bribes, commands, nor promises
  Can bring their people to.

Fergus.   And that is why
  You harped upon an old man's jealousy.
  A trifle sets you quaking. Conchubar's fame
  Brings merchandise on every wind that blows.
  They may have brought him Libyan dragon-skin,   90
  Or the ivory of the fierce unicorn.

First Musician. If these be merchants, I have seen the goods
  They have brought to Conchubar, and understood
  His murderous purpose.

Fergus.   Murderous, you say?
  Why, what new gossip of the roads is this?
  But I'll not hear.

First Musician.   It may be life or death.
  There is a room in Conchubar's house, and there——

Fergus. Be silent, or I'll drive you from the door.

There's many a one that would do more than that,
And make it prison, or death, or banishment   100
To slander the High King.
    [*Suddenly restraining himself and speaking gently.*]
                  He is my friend;
I have his oath, and I am well content.
I have known his mind as if it were my own
These many years, and there is none alive
Shall buzz against him, and I there to stop it.
I know myself, and him, and your wild thought
Fed on extravagant poetry, and lit
By such a dazzle of old fabulous tales
That common things are lost, and all that's strange
Is true because 'twere pity if it were not.   110
            [*Going to the door again.*]
Quick! quick! your instruments! they are coming now.
I hear the hoofs a-clatter. Begin that song!
But what is it to be? I'd have them hear
A music foaming up out of the house
Like wine out of a cup. Come now, a verse
Of some old time not worth remembering,
And all the lovelier because a bubble.
Begin, begin, of some old king and queen,
Of Lugaidh Redstripe or another; no, not him,°
He and his lady perished wretchedly.   120
        First Musician [*singing*]
       'Why is it', Queen Edain said,°
         If I do but climb the stair . . .

Fergus. Ah! that is better. . . . They are alighted now.
  Shake all your cockscombs, children; these are lovers.
                    [*Fergus goes out.*

          First Musician
       'Why is it', Queen Edain said,
         'If I do but climb the stair
       To the tower overhead,
         When the winds are calling there,
       Or the gannets calling out
         In waste places of the sky,   130
       There's so much to think about
         That I cry, that I cry?'

Second Musician

But her goodman answered her:
  'Love would be a thing of naught
Had not all his limbs a stir
  Born out of immoderate thought;
Were he anything by half,
  Were his measure running dry.
Lovers, if they may not laugh,
  Have to cry, have to cry.'   140

[*Deirdre, Naoise, and Fergus have been seen for a moment
through the windows, but now they have entered.*]

The Three Musicians [*together*]

But is Edain worth a song
  Now the hunt begins anew?
Praise the beautiful and strong;
  Praise the redness of the yew;
Praise the blossoming apple-stem.
  But our silence had been wise.
What is all our praise to them
  That have one another's eyes?

Deirdre. Silence your music, though I thank you for it;
  But the wind's blown upon my hair, and I   150
  Must set the jewels on my neck and head
  For one that's coming.

Naoise.   Your colour has all gone
  As 'twere with fear, and there's no cause for that.

Deirdre. These women have the raddle that they use°
  To make them brave and confident, although
  Dread, toil, or cold may chill the blood o' their cheeks.
  You'll help me, women. It is my husband's will
  I show my trust in one that may be here
  Before the mind can call the colour up.
  My husband took these rubies from a king   160
  Of Surracha that was so murderous°
  He seemed all glittering dragon. Now wearing them
  Myself wars on myself, for I myself—
  That do my husband's will, yet fear to do it—
  Grow dragonish to myself.

[*The women have gathered about her. Naoise has stood looking at her, but Fergus brings him to the chess-table.*]

Naoise. No messenger!
It's strange that there is none to welcome us.

Fergus. King Conchubar has sent no messenger
That he may come himself.

Naoise. And being himself,
Being High King, he cannot break his faith.
I have his word and I must take that word,   170
Or prove myself unworthy of my nurture
Under a great man's roof.

Fergus. We'll play at chess
Till the King comes. It is but natural
That she should doubt him, for her house has been
The hole of the badger and the den of the fox.

Naoise. If I had not King Conchubar's word I'd think
That chess-board ominous.

Fergus. How can a board
That has been lying there these many years
Be lucky or unlucky?

Naoise. It is the board
Where Lugaidh Redstripe and that wife of his,   180
Who had a seamew's body half the year,
Played at the chess upon the night they died.

Fergus. I can remember now, a tale of treachery,
A broken promise and a journey's end—
But it were best forgot.

[*Deirdre has been standing with the women about her. They have been helping her to put on her jewels and to put the pigment on her cheeks and arrange her hair. She has gradually grown attentive to what Fergus is saying.*]

Naoise. If the tale's true,
When it was plain that they had been betrayed,
They moved the men and waited for the end
As it were bedtime, and had so quiet minds
They hardly winked their eyes when the sword flashed.

Fergus. She never could have played so, being a woman,   190
If she had not the cold sea's blood in her.

Deirdre. The gods turn clouds and casual accidents
   Into omens.

Naoise.   It would but ill become us,
   Now that King Conchubar has pledged his word,
   Should we be startled by a cloud or a shadow.

Deirdre. There's none to welcome us.

Naoise.   Being his guest,
   Words that would wrong him can but wrong ourselves.

Deirdre. An empty house upon the journey's end!
   Is that the way a king that means no mischief
   Honours a guest?

Fergus.   He is but making ready   200
   A welcome in his house, arranging where
   The moorhen and the mallard go, and where
   The speckled heathcock on a golden dish.

Deirdre. Had he no messenger?

Naoise.   Such words and fears
   Wrong this old man who's pledged his word to us.
   We must not speak or think as women do,
   That when the house is all a–bed sit up
   Marking among the ashes with a stick
   Till they are terrified.—Being what we are
   We must meet all things with an equal mind.   210
   [*To Fergus.*] Come, let us look if there's a messenger
   From Conchubar. We cannot see from this
   Because we are blinded by the leaves and twigs,
   But it may be the wood will thin again.
   It is but kind that when the lips we love
   Speak words that are unfitting for kings' ears
   Our ears be deaf.

Fergus.   But now I had to threaten
   These wanderers because they would have weighed
   Some crazy fantasy of their own brain
   Or gossip of the road with Conchubar's word.   220
   If I had thought so little of mankind
   I never could have moved him to this pardon.
   I have believed the best of every man,
   And find that to believe it is enough
   To make a bad man show him at his best,

Or even a good man swing his lantern higher.

> [*Naoise and Fergus go out. The last words are spoken as they go through the door. One can see them through part of what follows, either through door or window. They move about, talking or looking along the road towards Conchubar's house.*

First Musician. If anything lies heavy on your heart,
Speak freely of it, knowing it is certain
That you will never see my face again.

Deirdre. You've been in love?

First Musician.   If you would speak of love,   230
Speak freely. There is nothing in the world
That has been friendly to us but the kisses
That were upon our lips, and when we are old
Their memory will be all the life we have.

Deirdre. There was a man that loved me. He was old;
I could not love him. Now I can but fear.
He has made promises, and brought me home;
But though I turn it over in my thoughts,
I cannot tell if they are sound and wholesome,
Or hackles on the hook.

First Musician.   I have heard he loved you   240
As some old miser loves the dragon-stone
He hides among the cobwebs near the roof.

Deirdre. You mean that when a man who has loved like that
Is after crossed, love drowns in its own flood,
And that love drowned and floating is but hate;
And that a king who hates sleeps ill at night
Till he has killed; and that, though the day laughs,
We shall be dead at cock-crow.

First Musician.   You've not my thought.
When I lost one I loved distractedly,
I blamed my crafty rival and not him,
And fancied, till my passion had run out,   250
That could I carry him away with me,
And tell him all my love, I'd keep him yet.

Deirdre. Ah! now I catch your meaning, that this king
Will murder Naoise, and keep me alive.

First Musician. 'Tis you that put that meaning upon words
Spoken at random.

Deirdre.   Wanderers like you,
 Who have their wit alone to keep their lives,
 Speak nothing that is bitter to the ear
 At random; if they hint at it at all   260
 Their eyes and ears have gathered it so lately
 That it is crying out in them for speech.

First Musician. We have little that is certain.

Deirdre.   Certain or not,
 Speak it out quickly, I beseech you to it;
 I never have met any of your kind
 But that I gave them money, food, and fire.

First Musician. There are strange, miracle-working, wicked
      stones,
 Men tear out of the heart and the hot brain
 Of Libyan dragons.

Deirdre.   The hot Istain stone,
 And the cold stone of Fanes, that have power°   270
 To stir even those at enmity to love.

First Musician. They have so great an influence, if but sewn
 In the embroideries that curtain in
 The bridal bed.

Deirdre.   O Mover of the stars
 That made this delicate house of ivory,
 And made my soul its mistress, keep it safe!

First Musician. I have seen a bridal bed, so curtained in,
 So decked for miracle in Conchubar's house,
 And learned that a bride's coming.

Deirdre.   And I the bride?
 Here is worse treachery than the seamew suffered,   280
 For she but died and mixed into the dust
 Of her dear comrade, but I am to live
 And lie in the one bed with him I hate.
 Where is Naoise? I was not alone like this
 When Conchubar first chose me for his wife;
 I cried in sleeping or waking and he came,
 But now there is worse need.

Naoise [*entering with Fergus*].   Why have you called?
 I was but standing there, without the door.

Deirdre. I have heard terrible mysterious things, 290
    Magical horrors and the spells of wizards.

Fergus. Why, that's no wonder. You have been listening
    To singers of the roads that gather up
    The stories of the world.

Deirdre.   But I have one
    To make the stories of the world but nothing.

Naoise. Be silent if it is against the King
    Whose guest you are.

Fergus.   No, let her speak it out.
    I know the High King's heart as it were my own,
    And can refute a slander, but already
    I have warned these women that it may be death. 300

Naoise. I will not weigh the gossip of the roads
    With the King's word. I ask your pardon for her:
    She has the heart of the wild birds that fear
    The net of the fowler or the wicker cage.

Deirdre. Am I to see the fowler and the cage
    And speak no word at all?

Naoise.   You would have known,
    Had they not bred you in that mountainous place,
    That when we give a word and take a word
    Sorrow is put away, past wrong forgotten.

Deirdre. Though death may come of it?

Naoise.   Though death may come. 310

Deirdre. When first we came into this empty house
    You had foreknowledge of our death, and even
    When speaking of the paleness of my cheek
    Your own cheek blanched.

Naoise.   Listen to this old man.
    He can remember all the promises
    We trusted to.

Deirdre.   You speak from the lips out,
    And I am pleading for your life and mine.

Naoise. Listen to this old man, for many think
    He has a golden tongue.

Deirdre.   Then I will say

What it were best to carry to the grave.   320
Look at my face where the leaf raddled it
And at these rubies on my hair and breast.
It was for him, to stir him to desire,
I put on beauty; yes, for Conchubar.

Naoise. What frenzy put these words into your mouth?

Deirdre. No frenzy, for what need is there for frenzy
To change what shifts with every change of the wind,
Or else there is no truth in men's old sayings?
Was I not born a woman?

Naoise.   You're mocking me.

Deirdre. And is there mockery in this face and eyes,   330
Or in this body, in these limbs that brought
So many mischiefs? Look at me and say
If that that shakes my limbs be mockery.

Naoise. What woman is there that a man can trust
But at the moment when he kisses her
At the first midnight?

Deirdre.   Were it not most strange
That women should put evil in men's hearts
And lack it in themselves? And yet I think
That being half good I might change round again
Were we aboard our ship and on the sea.   340

Naoise. We'll to the horses and take ship again.

Fergus. Fool, she but seeks to rouse your jealousy
With crafty words.

Deirdre.   Were we not born to wander?
These jewels have been reaped by the innocent sword
Upon a mountain, and a mountain bred me;
But who can tell what change can come to love
Among the valleys? I speak no falsehood now.
Away to windy summits, and there mock
The night-jar and the valley-keeping bird!

Fergus. Men blamed you that you stirred a quarrel up   350
That has brought death to many. I have made peace,
Poured water on the fire, but if you fly
King Conchubar may think that he is mocked
And the house blaze again: and in what quarter,

If Conchubar were the treacherous man you think,
Would you find safety now that you have come
Into the very middle of his power,
Under his very eyes?

Deirdre.   Under his eyes
And in the very middle of his power!
Then there is but one way to make all safe,   360
I'll spoil this beauty that brought misery
And houseless wandering on the man I loved.
These wanderers will show me how to do it;
To clip this hair to baldness, blacken my skin
With walnut juice, and tear my face with briars.
O that the creatures of the woods had torn
My body with their claws!

Fergus.   What, wilder yet!

Deirdre [*to Naoise*]. Whatever were to happen to my face
I'd be myself, and there's not any way
But this to bring all trouble to an end.   370

Naoise. Leave the gods' handiwork unblotched, and wait
For their decision, our decision is past.

    [*A Dark-faced Messenger comes to the threshold.*]

Fergus. Peace, peace; the messenger is at the door;
He stands upon the threshold; he stands there;
He stands, King Conchubar's purpose on his lips.

Messenger. Supper is on the table. Conchubar
Is waiting for his guests.

Fergus.   All's well again!
All's well! All's well! You cried your doubts so loud
That I had almost doubted.

Naoise.   We doubted him,
And he the while but busy in his house   380
For the more welcome.

Deirdre.   The message is not finished.

Fergus. Come quickly. Conchubar will laugh, that I——
Although I held out boldly in my speech—
That I, even I——

Deirdre.   Wait, wait! He is not done.

Messenger. Deirdre and Fergus, son of Rogh, are summoned;
    But not the traitor that bore off the Queen.
    It is enough that the King pardon her,
    And call her to his table and his bed.

Naoise. So, then, it's treachery.

Fergus.   I'll not believe it.

Naoise. Lead on and I will follow at your heels   390
    That I may challenge him before his court
    To match me there, or match me in some place
    Where none can come between us but our swords,
    For I have found no truth on any tongue
    That's not of iron.

Messenger.   I am Conchubar's man,
    I am content to serve an iron tongue:
    That Tongue commands that Fergus, son of Rogh,
    And Deirdre come this night into his house,
    And none but they.   [*He goes, followed by Naoise.*

Fergus.   Some rogue, some enemy,
    Has bribed him to embroil us with the King;   400
    I know that he has lied because I know
    King Conchubar's mind as if it were my own,
    But I'll find out the truth.

        [*He is about to follow Naoise, but Deirdre stops him.*]

Deirdre.   No, no, old man.
    You thought the best, and the worst came of it;
    We listened to the counsel of the wise,
    And so turned fools. But ride and bring your friends.
    Go, and go quickly. Conchubar has not seen me;
    It may be that his passion is asleep,
    And that we may escape.

Fergus.   But I'll go first,
    And follow up that Libyan heel, and send   410
    Such words to Conchubar that he may know
    At how great peril he lays hands upon you.

                [*Naoise enters.*]

Naoise. The Libyan, knowing that a servant's life
    Is safe from hands like mine, but turned and mocked.

Fergus. I'll call my friends, and call the reaping-hooks.°

And carry you in safety to the ships.
My name has still some power. I will protect,
Or, if that is impossible, revenge.

[*Goes out by other door.*

Naoise [*who is calm, like a man who has passed beyond life*].
    The crib has fallen and the birds are in it;°
    There is not one of the great oaks about us   420
    But shades a hundred men.

Deirdre.   Let's out and die,
    Or break away, if the chance favour us.

Naoise. They would but drag you from me, stained with blood.
    Their barbarous weapons would but mar that beauty,
    And I would have you die as a queen should—
    In a death–chamber. You are in my charge.
    We will wait here, and when they come upon us,
    I'll hold them from the doors, and when that's over,
    Give you a cleanly death with this grey edge.

Deirdre. I will stay here; but you go out and fight.   430
    Our way of life has brought no friends to us,
    And if we do not buy them leaving it,
    We shall be ever friendless.

Naoise.   What do they say?
    That Lugaidh Redstripe and that wife of his
    Sat at this chess-board, waiting for their end.
    They knew that there was nothing that could save them,
    And so played chess as they had any night
    For years, and waited for the stroke of sword.
    I never heard a death so out of reach
    Of common hearts, a high and comely end.   440
    What need have I, that gave up all for love,
    To die like an old king out of a fable,
    Fighting and passionate? What need is there
    For all that ostentation at my setting?
    I have loved truly and betrayed no man.
    I need no lightning at the end, no beating
    In a vain fury at the cage's door.
    [*To Musicians.*] Had you been here when that man and his queen
    Played at so high a game, could you have found
    An ancient poem for the praise of it?   450

It should have set out plainly that those two,
Because no man and woman have loved better,
Might sit on there contentedly, and weigh
The joy comes after. I have heard the seamew
Sat there, with all the colour in her cheeks,
As though she'd say: 'There's nothing happening
But that a king and queen are playing chess.'

Deirdre. He's in the right, though I have not been born
Of the cold, haughty waves, my veins being hot,
And though I have loved better than that queen,   460
I'll have as quiet fingers on the board.
O, singing women, set it down in a book,
That love is all we need, even though it is
But the last drops we gather up like this;
And though the drops are all we have known of life,
For we have been most friendless—praise us for it,
And praise the double sunset, for naught's lacking
But a good end to the long, cloudy day.

Naoise. Light torches there and drive the shadows out,
For day's grey end comes up.

> [*A Musician lights a torch in the fire and then crosses before the chess-players, and slowly lights the torches in the sconces. The light is almost gone from the wood, but there is a clear evening light in the sky, increasing the sense of solitude and loneliness.*]

Deirdre.   Make no sad music.   470
What is it but a king and queen at chess?
They need a music that can mix itself
Into imagination, but not break
The steady thinking that the hard game needs.

> [*During the chess, the Musicians sing this song*]

> Love is an immoderate thing
>   And can never be content
> Till it dip an ageing wing
>   Where some laughing element
> Leaps and Time's old lanthorn dims.
>   What's the merit in love-play,   480
> In the tumult of the limbs
>   That dies out before 'tis day,
> Heart on heart, or mouth on mouth,

   All that mingling of our breath,
   When love-longing is but drouth
    For the things come after death?

[*During the last verses Deirdre rises from the board and kneels
 at Naoise's feet.*]

Deirdre. I cannot go on playing like that woman
 That had but the cold blood of the sea in her veins.

Naoise. It is your move. Take up your man again.

Deirdre. Do you remember that first night in the woods   490
 We lay all night on leaves, and looking up,
 When the first grey of the dawn awoke the birds,
 Saw leaves above us? You thought that I still slept,
 And bending down to kiss me on the eyes,
 Found they were open. Bend and kiss me now,
 For it may be the last before our death.
 And when that's over, we'll be different;
 Imperishable things, a cloud or a fire.
 And I know nothing but this body, nothing
 But that old vehement, bewildering kiss.   500

    [*Conchubar comes to the door.*]

First Musician. Children, beware!

Naoise [*laughing*].   He has taken up my challenge;
 Whether I am a ghost or living man
 When day has broken, I'll forget the rest,
 And say that there is kingly stuff in him.

  [*Turns to fetch spear and shield, and then sees that Conchubar
 has gone.*]

First Musician. He came to spy upon you, not to fight.

Naoise. A prudent hunter, therefore, but no king.
 He'd find if what has fallen in the pit
 Were worth the hunting, but has come too near,
 And I turn hunter. You're not man, but beast.
 Go scurry in the bushes, now, beast, beast,   510
 For now it's topsy-turvy. I upon you.

    [*He rushes out after Conchubar.*

Deirdre. You have a knife there, thrust into your girdle.
 I'd have you give it me.

First Musician.   No, but I dare not.

Deirdre. No, but you must.

First Musician.   If harm should come to you,
   They'd know I gave it.

Deirdre [*snatching knife*]. There is no mark on this
   To make it different from any other
   Out of a common forge.

              [*Goes to the door and looks out.*]

First Musician.   You have taken it,
   I did not give it you; but there are times
   When such a thing is all the friend one has.

Deirdre. The leaves hide all, and there's no way to find   520
   What path to follow. Why is there no sound?

              [*She goes from door to window.*]

First Musician. Where would you go?

Deirdre.   To strike a blow for Naoise,
   If Conchubar call the Libyans to his aid.
   But why is there no clash? They have met by this!

First Musician. Listen. I am called wise. If Conchubar win,
   You have a woman's wile that can do much,
   Even with men in pride of victory.
   He is in love and old. What were one knife
   Among a hundred?

Deirdre [*going towards them*]. Women, if I die,
   If Naoise die this night, how will you praise?   530
   What words seek out? for that will stand to you;
   For being but dead we shall have many friends.
   All through your wanderings, the doors of kings
   Shall be thrown wider open, the poor man's hearth
   Heaped with new turf, because you are wearing this

              [*Gives Musician a bracelet.*]

   To show that you have Deirdre's story right.

First Musician. Have you not been paid servants in love's house
   To sweep the ashes out and keep the doors?
   And though you have suffered all for mere love's sake
   You'd live your lives again.

Deirdre.   Even this last hour.   540

              [*Conchubar enters with dark-faced men.*]

Conchubar. One woman and two men; that is the quarrel
  That knows no mending. Bring in the man she chose
  Because of his beauty and the strength of his youth.

  [*The dark-faced men drag in Naoise entangled in a net.*]

Naoise. I have been taken like a bird or a fish.

Conchubar. He cried 'Beast, beast!' and in a blind-beast rage
  He ran at me and fell into the nets,
  But we were careful for your sake, and took him
  With all the comeliness that woke desire
  Unbroken in him. I being old and lenient,
  I would not hurt a hair upon his head.   550

Deirdre. What do you say? Have you forgiven him?

Naoise. He is but mocking us. What's left to say
  Now that the seven years' hunt is at an end?

Deirdre. He never doubted you until I made him,
  And therefore all the blame for what he says
  Should fall on me.

Conchubar.   But his young blood is hot,
  And if we're of one mind, he shall go free,
  And I ask nothing for it, or, if something,
  Nothing I could not take. There is no king
  In the wide world that, being so greatly wronged,   560
  Could copy me, and give all vengeance up.
  Although her marriage-day had all but come,
  You carried her away; but I'll show mercy.
  Because you had the insolent strength of youth
  You carried her away; but I've had time
  To think it out through all these seven years.
  I will show mercy.

Naoise.   You have many words.

Conchubar. I will not make a bargain; I but ask
  What is already mine.

  [*Deirdre moves slowly towards Conchubar while he is speaking,
  her eyes fixed upon him.*]

                You may go free
  If Deirdre will but walk into my house   570
  Before the people's eyes, that they may know,
  When I have put the crown upon her head,

I have not taken her by force and guile.
The doors are open, and the floors are strewed
And in the bridal chamber curtains sewn
With all enchantments that give happiness
By races that are germane to the sun,
And nearest him, and have no blood in their veins—
For when they're wounded the wound drips with wine—
Nor speech but singing. At the bridal door   580
Two fair king's daughters carry in their hands
The crown and robe.

Deirdre.   O no! Not that, not that!
Ask any other thing but that one thing.
Leave me with Naoise. We will go away
Into some country at the ends of the earth.
We'll trouble you no more; and there is no one
That will not praise you if you pardon us.
'He is good, he is good', they'll say to one another;
'There's nobody like him, for he forgave
Deirdre and Naoise.'

Conchubar.   Do you think that I   590
Shall let you go again, after seven years
Of longing and of planning here and there,
And trafficking with merchants for the stones
That make all sure, and watching my own face°
That none might read it?

Deirdre [*to Naoise*].   It's better to go with him.
Why should you die when one can bear it all?
My life is over; it's better to obey.
Why should you die? I will not live long, Naoise.
I'd not have you believe I'd long stay living;
O no, no, no! You will go far away.   600
You will forget me. Speak, speak, Naoise, speak,
And say that it is better that I go.
I will not ask it. Do not speak a word,
For I will take it all upon myself.
Conchubar, I will go.

Naoise.   And do you think
That, were I given life at such a price,
I would not cast it from me? O my eagle!

Why do you beat vain wings upon the rock
When hollow night's above?

Deirdre.   It's better, Naoise.
It may be hard for you, but you'll forget.   610
For what am I, to be remembered always?
And there are other women. There was one,
The daughter of the King of Leodas;°
I could not sleep because of her. Speak to him;
Tell it out plain, and make him understand.
And if it be he thinks I shall stay living,
Say that I will not.

Naoise.   Would I had lost life
Among those Scottish kings that sought it of me°
Because you were my wife, or that the worst
Had taken you before this bargaining!   620
O eagle! If you were to do this thing,
And buy my life of Conchubar with your body,
Love's law being broken, I would stand alone
Upon the eternal summits, and call out,
And you could never come there, being banished.

Deirdre [*kneeling to Conchubar*]. I would obey, but cannot.
    Pardon us.
I know that you are good. I have heard you praised
For giving gifts; and you will pardon us,
Although I cannot go into your house.
It was my fault. I only should be punished.   630

            [*Unseen by Deirdre, Naoise is gagged.*]

The very moment these eyes fell on him,
I told him; I held out my hands to him;
How could he refuse? At first he would not—
I am not lying—he remembered you.
What do I say? My hands?—No, no, my lips—
For I had pressed my lips upon his lips—
I swear it is not false—my breast to his;

        [*Conchubar motions; Naoise, unseen by Deirdre, is taken
        behind the curtain.*]

Until I woke the passion that's in all,
And how could he resist? I had my beauty.

You may have need of him, a brave, strong man,   640
Who is not foolish at the council-board,
Nor does he quarrel by the candle-light
And give hard blows to dogs. A cup of wine
Moves him to mirth, not madness.

[*She stands up.*]
                                        What am I saying?
You may have need of him, for you have none
Who is so good a sword, or so well loved
Among the common people. You may need him,
And what king knows when the hour of need may come?
You dream that you have men enough. You laugh.
Yes; you are laughing to yourself. You say,   650
'I am Conchubar—I have no need of him.'
You will cry out for him some day and say,
'If Naoise were but living'——[*she misses Naoise*].
                                        Where is he?
Where have you sent him? Where is the son of Usna?
Where is he, O, where is he?

[*She staggers over to the Musicians. The Executioner has come
out with a sword on which there is blood; Conchubar points to it.
The Musicians give a wail.*]

Conchubar. The traitor who has carried off my wife
No longer lives. Come to my house now, Deirdre,
For he that called himself your husband's dead.

Deirdre. O, do not touch me. Let me go to him.   [*Pause.*
King Conchubar is right. My husband's dead.   660
A single woman is of no account,
Lacking array of servants, linen cupboards,
The bacon hanging—and King Conchubar's house
All ready, too—I'll to King Conchubar's house.
It is but wisdom to do willingly
What has to be.

Conchubar.   But why are you so calm?
I thought that you would curse me and cry out,
And fall upon the ground and tear your hair.

Deirdre [*laughing*]. You know too much of women to think so;
Though, if I were less worthy of desire,   670
I would pretend as much; but, being myself,
It is enough that you were master here.

Although we are so delicately made,
There's something brutal in us, and we are won
By those who can shed blood. It was some woman
That taught you how to woo: but do not touch me:
I shall do all you bid me, but not yet,
Because I have to do what's customary.
We lay the dead out, folding up the hands,
Closing the eyes, and stretching out the feet,   680
And push a pillow underneath the head,
Till all's in order; and all this I'll do
For Naoise, son of Usna.

Conchubar.   It is not fitting.
You are not now a wanderer, but a queen,
And there are plenty that can do these things.

Deirdre [*motioning Conchubar away*]. No, no. Not yet. I cannot be
      your queen
Till the past's finished, and its debts are paid.
When a man dies, and there are debts unpaid,
He wanders by the debtor's bed and cries,
'There's so much owing.'

Conchubar.   You are deceiving me.   690
You long to look upon his face again.
Why should I give you now to a dead man
That took you from a living?

                    [*He makes a step towards her.*]

Deirdre.   In good time.
You'll stir me to more passion than he could,
And yet, if you are wise, you'll grant me this:
That I go look upon him that was once
So strong and comely and held his head so high
That women envied me. For I will see him
All blood-bedabbled and his beauty gone.
It's better, when you're beside me in your strength,   700
That the mind's eye should call up the soiled body,
And not the shape I loved. Look at him, women.
He heard me pleading to be given up,
Although my lover was still living, and yet
He doubts my purpose. I will have you tell him
How changeable all women are; how soon

Even the best of lovers is forgot
When his day's finished.

Conchubar.   No; but I will trust
The strength that you have praised, and not your purpose.

Deirdre [*almost with a caress*]. It is so small a gift and you will
          grant it   710
Because it is the first that I have asked.
He has refused. There is no sap in him;
Nothing but empty veins. I thought as much.
He has refused me the first thing I have asked—
Me, me, his wife. I understand him now;
I know the sort of life I'll have with him;
But he must drag me to his house by force.
If he refuses [*she laughs*], he shall be mocked of all.
They'll say to one another, 'Look at him
That is so jealous that he lured a man   720
From over sea, and murdered him, and yet
He trembled at the thought of a dead face!'

                    [*She has her hand upon the curtain.*]

Conchubar. How do I know that you have not some knife,
And go to die upon his body?

Deirdre.   Have me searched,
If you would make so little of your queen.
It may be that I have a knife hid here
Under my dress. Bid one of these dark slaves
To search me for it.   [*Pause.*

Conchubar.   Go to your farewells, Queen.

Deirdre. Now strike the wire, and sing to it a while,
Knowing that all is happy, and that you know   730
Within what bride-bed I shall lie this night,
And by what man, and lie close up to him,
For the bed's narrow, and there outsleep the cock-crow.

                              [*She goes behind the curtain.*

First Musician. They are gone, they are gone. The proud may lie by
          the proud.

Second Musician. Though we were bidden to sing, cry nothing loud.

First Musician. They are gone, they are gone.

Second Musician.   Whispering were enough.

First Musician. Into the secret wilderness of their love.

Second Musician. A high, grey cairn. What more is to be said?

First Musician. Eagles have gone into their cloudy bed.

> [*Shouting outside. Fergus enters. Many men with scythes and sickles and torches gather about the doors. The house is lit with the glare of their torches.*]

Fergus. Where's Naoise, son of Usna, and his queen?   740
I and a thousand reaping-hooks and scythes
Demand him of you.

Conchubar.   You have come too late.
I have accomplished all. Deirdre is mine;
She is my queen, and no man now can rob me.
I had to climb the topmost bough, and pull
This apple among the winds. Open the curtain
That Fergus learn my triumph from her lips.

> [*The curtain is drawn back. The Musicians begin to keen with low voices.*]

No, no; I'll not believe it. She is not dead—
She cannot have escaped a second time!

Fergus. King, she is dead; but lay no hand upon her.   750
What's this but empty cage and tangled wire,
Now the bird's gone? But I'll not have you touch it.

Conchubar. You are all traitors, all against me—all.
And she has deceived me for a second time;
And every common man can keep his wife,
But not the King.

> [*Loud shouting outside:* 'Death to Conchubar!' 'Where is Naoise?' *etc. The dark-faced men gather round Conchubar and draw their swords; but he motions them away.*]

                    I have no need of weapons,
There's not a traitor that dare stop my way.
Howl, if you will; but I, being King, did right
In choosing her most fitting to be Queen,
And letting no boy lover take the sway.   760

THE END

On Baile's Strand (1904)°

TO
WILLIAM FAY°
because of the beautiful fantasy of his playing in the
character of the Fool

PERSONS IN THE PLAY

A Fool
A Blind Man
Cuchulain, *King of Muirthemne*°
Conchubar, *High King of Ulad*°
A Young Man, *son of Cuchulain*
Kings and Singing Women

A great hall at Dundealgan,° *not 'Cuchulain's great ancient house' but
an assembly house nearer to the sea. A big door at the back, and through
the door misty light as of sea-mist. There are many chairs and one long
bench. One of these chairs, which is towards the front of the stage, is big-
ger than the others. Somewhere at the back there is a table with flagons
of ale upon it and drinking-horns. There is a small door at one side of the
hall. A Fool and Blind Man, both ragged, and their features made
grotesque and extravagant by masks, come in through the door at the
back. The Blind Man leans upon a staff.*

Fool. What a clever man you are though you are blind! There's
nobody with two eyes in his head that is as clever as you are. Who
but you could have thought that the henwife sleeps every day a
little at noon? I would never be able to steal anything if you didn't
tell me where to look for it. And what a good cook you are! You
take the fowl out of my hands after I have stolen it and plucked it,
and you put it into the big pot at the fire there, and I can go out
and run races with the witches at the edge of the waves and get an
appetite, and when I've got it, there's the hen waiting inside for
me, done to the turn.

Blind Man [*who is feeling about with his stick*]. Done to the turn.

Fool [*putting his arm round Blind Man's neck*]. Come now, I'll have a
leg and you'll have a leg, and we'll draw lots for the wish-bone.
I'll be praising you, I'll be praising you while we're eating it, for

10

your good plans and for your good cooking. There's nobody in the world like you, Blind Man. Come, come. Wait a minute. I shouldn't have closed the door. There are some that look for me, and I wouldn't like them not to find me. Don't tell it to anybody, Blind Man. There are some that follow me. Boann° herself out of the river and Fand° out of the deep sea. Witches they are, and they come by in the wind, and they cry, 'Give a kiss, Fool, give a kiss', that's what they cry. That's wide enough. All the witches can come in now. I wouldn't have them beat at the door and say, 'Where is the Fool? Why has he put a lock on the door?' Maybe they'll hear the bubbling of the pot and come in and sit on the ground. But we won't give them any of the fowl. Let them go back to the sea, let them go back to the sea.

Blind Man [*feeling legs of big chair with his hands*]. Ah! [*Then, in a louder voice as he feels the back of it.*] Ah—ah—

Fool. Why do you say 'Ah-ah'?

Blind Man. I know the big chair. It is to-day the High King Conchubar is coming. They have brought out his chair. He is going to be Cuchulain's master in earnest from this day out. It is that he's coming for.

Fool. He must be a great man to be Cuchulain's master.

Blind Man. So he is. He is a great man. He is over all the rest of the kings of Ireland.

Fool. Cuchulain's master! I thought Cuchulain could do anything he liked.

Blind Man. So he did, so he did. But he ran too wild, and Conchubar is coming to-day to put an oath upon him that will stop his rambling and make him as biddable as a house-dog and keep him always at his hand. He will sit in this chair and put the oath upon him.

Fool. How will he do that?

Blind Man. You have no wits to understand such things. [*The Blind Man has got into the chair.*] He will sit up in this chair and he'll say: 'Take the oath, Cuchulain. I bid you take the oath. Do as I tell you. What are your wits compared with mine, and what are your riches compared with mine? And what sons have you to pay your debts and to put a stone over you when you die? Take the oath, I tell you. Take a strong oath.'

Fool [*crumpling himself up and whining*]. I will not. I'll take no oath. I want my dinner.

Blind Man. Hush, hush! It is not done yet.

Fool. You said it was done to a turn.

Blind Man. Did I, now? Well, it might be done, and not done. The wings might be white, but the legs might be red. The flesh might stick hard to the bones and not come away in the teeth. But, believe me, Fool, it will be well done before you put your teeth   60
in it.

Fool. My teeth are growing long with the hunger.

Blind Man. I'll tell you a story—the kings have story-tellers while they are waiting for their dinner—I will tell you a story with a fight in it, a story with a champion in it, and a ship and a queen's son that has his mind set on killing somebody that you and I know.

Fool. Who is that? Who is he coming to kill?

Blind Man. Wait, now, till you hear. When you were stealing the fowl, I was lying in a hole in the sand, and I heard three men   70
coming with a shuffling sort of noise. They were wounded and groaning.

Fool. Go on. Tell me about the fight.

Blind Man. There had been a fight, a great fight, a tremendous great fight. A young man had landed on the shore, the guardians of the shore had asked his name, and he had refused to tell it, and he had killed one, and others had run away.

Fool. That's enough. Come on now to the fowl. I wish it was bigger. I wish it was as big as a goose.

Blind Man. Hush! I haven't told you all. I know who that young   80
man° is. I heard the men who were running away say he had red hair, that he had come from Aoife's country,° that he was coming to kill Cuchulain.

Fool. Nobody can do that.

[*To a tune*]

Cuchulain has killed kings,
Kings and sons of kings,
Dragons out of the water,
And witches out of the air,

Banachas and Bonachas and people of the woods.°

Blind Man. Hush! hush! 90

Fool [*still singing*].

>Witches that steal the milk,
>Fomor that steal the children,°
>Hags that have heads like hares,
>Hares that have claws like witches,
>All riding a-cock-horse

[*Spoken*]

Out of the very bottom of the bitter black North.

Blind Man. Hush, I say!

Fool. Does Cuchulain know that he is coming to kill him?

Blind Man. How would he know that with his head in the clouds? He doesn't care for common fighting. Why would he put himself 100 out, and nobody in it but that young man? Now if it were a white fawn that might turn into a queen before morning—

Fool. Come to the fowl. I wish it was as big as a pig; a fowl with goose grease and pig's crackling.

Blind Man. No hurry, no hurry. I know whose son it is. I wouldn't tell anybody else, but I will tell you,—a secret is better to you than your dinner. You like being told secrets.

Fool. Tell me the secret.

Blind Man. That young man is Aoife's son. I am sure it is Aoife's son, it flows in upon me that it is Aoife's son. You have often 110 heard me talking of Aoife, the great woman-fighter Cuchulain got the mastery over in the North?

Fool. I know, I know. She is one of those cross queens that live in hungry Scotland.

Blind Man. I am sure it is her son. I was in Aoife's country for a long time.

Fool. That was before you were blinded for putting a curse upon the wind.

Blind Man. There was a boy in her house that had her own red colour on him, and everybody said he was to be brought up to kill 120 Cuchulain, that she hated Cuchulain. She used to put a helmet on a pillar-stone and call it Cuchulain and set him casting at it. There is a step outside—Cuchulain's step.

[*Cuchulain passes by in the mist outside the big door.*]

Fool. Where is Cuchulain going?

Blind Man. He is going to meet Conchubar that has bidden him to take the oath.

Fool. Ah, an oath, Blind Man. How can I remember so many things at once? Who is going to take an oath?

Blind Man. Cuchulain is going to take an oath to Conchubar who is High King.   130

Fool. What a mix-up you make of everything, Blind Man! You were telling me one story, and now you are telling me another story. . . . How can I get the hang of it at the end if you mix everything at the beginning? Wait till I settle it out. There now, there's Cuchulain [*he points to one foot*], and there is the young man [*he points to the other foot*] that is coming to kill him, and Cuchulain doesn't know. But where's Conchubar? [*Takes bag from side.*] That's Conchubar with all his riches—Cuchulain, young man, Conchubar.—And where's Aoife? [*Throws up cap.*] There is Aoife, high up on the mountains in high hungry Scotland.   140 Maybe it is not true after all. Maybe it was your own making up. It's many a time you cheated me before with your lies. Come to the cooking-pot, my stomach is pinched and rusty. Would you have it to be creaking like a gate?

Blind Man. I tell you it's true. And more than that is true. If you listen to what I say, you'll forget your stomach.

Fool. I won't.

Blind Man. Listen. I know who the young man's father is, but I won't say. I would be afraid to say. Ah, Fool, you would forget everything if you could know who the young man's father is.   150

Fool. Who is it? Tell me now quick, or I'll shake you. Come, out with it, or I'll shake you.

[*A murmur of voices in the distance.*]

Blind Man. Wait, wait. There's somebody coming. . . . It is Cuchulain is coming. He's coming back with the High King. Go and ask Cuchulain. He'll tell you. It's little you'll care about the cooking-pot when you have asked Cuchulain that . . .

[*Blind Man goes out by side door.*

Fool. I'll ask him. Cuchulain will know. He was in Aoife's country.

[*Goes up stage.*] I'll ask him. [*Turns and goes down stage.*] But, no,
I won't ask him, I would be afraid. [*Going up again.*] Yes, I will
ask him. What harm in asking? The Blind Man said I was to ask 160
him. [*Going down.*] No, no, I'll not ask him. He might kill me. I
have but killed hens and geese and pigs. He has killed kings.
[*Goes up again almost to big door.*] Who says I'm afraid? I'm not
afraid. I'm no coward. I'll ask him. No, no, Cuchulain, I'm not
going to ask you.

> He has killed kings,
> Kings and the sons of kings,
> Dragons out of the water,
> And witches out of the air,

Banachas and Bonachas and people of the woods.   170

> [*Fool goes out by side door, the last words being heard outside.
> Cuchulain and Conchubar enter through the big door at the
> back. While they are still outside, Cuchulain's voice is heard
> raised in anger. He is a dark man, something over forty years of
> age. Conchubar is much older and carries a long staff, elabo-
> rately carved or with an elaborate gold handle.*]

Cuchulain. Because I have killed men without your bidding
  And have rewarded others at my own pleasure,
  Because of half a score of trifling things,
  You'd lay this oath upon me, and now——and now
  You add another pebble to the heap,
  And I must be your man, well-nigh your bondsman,
  Because a youngster out of Aoife's country
  Has found the shore ill-guarded.

Conchubar.   He came to land
  While you were somewhere out of sight and hearing,
  Hunting or dancing with your wild companions.   180

Cuchulain. He can be driven out. I'll not be bound.
  I'll dance or hunt, or quarrel or make love,
  Wherever and whenever I've a mind to.
  If time had not put water in your blood,
  You never would have thought it.

Conchubar.   I would leave
  A strong and settled country to my children.

Cuchulain. And I must be obedient in all things;
  Give up my will to yours; go where you please;

Come when you call; sit at the council-board
Among the unshapely bodies of old men;   190
I whose mere name has kept this country safe,
I that in early days have driven out
Maeve of Cruachan and the northern pirates,°
The hundred kings of Sorcha, and the kings°
Out of the Garden in the East of the World.
Must I, that held you on the throne when all
Had pulled you from it, swear obedience
As if I were some cattle-raising king?
Are my shins speckled with the heat of the fire,
Or have my hands no skill but to make figures   200
Upon the ashes with a stick? Am I
So slack and idle that I need a whip
Before I serve you?

Conchubar.   No, no whip, Cuchulain,
But every day my children come and say:
'This man is growing harder to endure.
How can we be at safety with this man
That nobody can buy or bid or bind?
We shall be at his mercy when you are gone;
He burns the earth as if he were a fire,
And time can never touch him.'

Cuchulain.   And so the tale   210
Grows finer yet; and I am to obey
Whatever child you set upon the throne,
As if it were yourself!

Conchubar.   Most certainly.
I am High King, my son shall be High King;
And you for all the wildness of your blood,
And though your father came out of the sun,
Are but a little king and weigh but light
In anything that touches government,
If put into the balance with my children.

Cuchulain. It's well that we should speak our minds out plainly,   220
For when we die we shall be spoken of
In many countries. We in our young days
Have seen the heavens like a burning cloud
Brooding upon the world, and being more
Than men can be now that cloud's lifted up,

We should be the more truthful. Conchubar,
I do not like your children—they have no pith,
No marrow in their bones, and will lie soft
Where you and I lie hard.

Conchubar.   You rail at them
Because you have no children of your own.   230

Cuchulain. I think myself most lucky that I leave
No pallid ghost or mockery of a man
To drift and mutter in the corridors
Where I have laughed and sung.

Conchubar.   That is not true,
For all your boasting of the truth between us;
For there is no man having house and lands,
That have been in the one family, called
By that one family's name for centuries,
But is made miserable if he know
They are to pass into a stranger's keeping,   240
As yours will pass.

Cuchulain.   The most of men feel that,
But you and I leave names upon the harp.

Conchubar. You play with arguments as lawyers do,
And put no heart in them. I know your thoughts,
For we have slept under the one cloak and drunk
From the one wine-cup. I know you to the bone,
I have heard you cry, aye, in your very sleep,
'I have no son', and with such bitterness
That I have gone upon my knees and prayed
That it might be amended.

Cuchulain.   For you thought   250
That I should be as biddable as others
Had I their reason for it; but that's not true;
For I would need a weightier argument
Than one that marred me in the copying,
As I have that clean hawk out of the air
That, as men say, begot this body of mine°
Upon a mortal woman.

Conchubar.   Now as ever
You mock at every reasonable hope,

And would have nothing, or impossible things.
What eye has ever looked upon the child   260
Would satisfy a mind like that?

Cuchulain.   I would leave
My house and name to none that would not face
Even myself in battle.

Conchubar.   Being swift of foot,
And making light of every common chance,
You should have overtaken on the hills
Some daughter of the air, or on the shore
A daughter of the Country-under-Wave.°

Cuchulain. I am not blasphemous.

Conchubar.   Yet you despise
Our queens, and would not call a child your own,
If one of them had borne him.

Cuchulain.   I have not said it.   270

Conchubar. Ah! I remember I have heard you boast,
When the ale was in your blood, that there was one
In Scotland, where you had learnt the trade of war,
That had a stone-pale cheek and red-brown hair;
And that although you had loved other women,
You'd sooner that fierce woman of the camp
Bore you a son than any queen among them.

Cuchulain. You call her a 'fierce woman of the camp',
For, having lived among the spinning-wheels,
You'd have no woman near that would not say,   280
'Ah! how wise!' 'What will you have for supper?'
'What shall I wear that I may please you, sir?'
And keep that humming through the day and night
For ever. A fierce woman of the camp!
But I am getting angry about nothing.
You have never seen her. Ah! Conchubar, had you seen her
With that high, laughing, turbulent head of hers
Thrown backward, and the bowstring at her ear,
Or sitting at the fire with those grave eyes
Full of good counsel as it were with wine,   290
Or when love ran through all the lineaments
Of her wild body—although she had no child,
None other had all beauty, queen or lover,

Or was so fitted to give birth to kings.

Conchubar. There's nothing I can say but drifts you farther
From the one weighty matter. That very woman—
For I know well that you are praising Aoife—
Now hates you and will leave no subtlety
Unknotted that might run into a noose
About your throat, no army in idleness   300
That might bring ruin on this land you serve.

Cuchulain. No wonder in that, no wonder at all in that.
I never have known love but as a kiss
In the mid-battle, and a difficult truce
Of oil and water, candles and dark night,
Hillside and hollow, the hot-footed sun
And the cold, sliding, slippery-footed moon—
A brief forgiveness between opposites
That have been hatreds for three times the age
Of this long-'stablished ground.

Conchubar.   Listen to me.   310
Aoife makes war on us, and every day
Our enemies grow greater and beat the walls
More bitterly, and you within the walls
Are every day more turbulent; and yet,
When I would speak about these things, your fancy
Runs as it were a swallow on the wind.

> [*Outside the door in the blue light of the sea-mist are many old
> and young Kings; amongst them are three Women, two of whom
> carry a bowl of fire. The third, in what follows, puts from time
> to time fragrant herbs into the fire so that it flickers up into
> brighter flame.*]

Look at the door and what men gather there—
Old counsellors that steer the land with me,
And younger kings, the dancers and harp-players
That follow in your tumults, and all these   320
Are held there by the one anxiety.
Will you be bound into obedience
And so make this land safe for them and theirs?
You are but half a king and I but half;
I need your might of hand and burning heart,
And you my wisdom.

Cuchulain [*going near to door*]. Nestlings of a high nest,
    Hawks that have followed me into the air
    And looked upon the sun, we'll out of this
    And sail upon the wind once more. This king
    Would have me take an oath to do his will,   330
    And having listened to his tune from morning,
    I will no more of it. Run to the stable
    And set the horses to the chariot-pole,
    And send a messenger to the harp-players.
    We'll find a level place among the woods,
    And dance awhile.

A Young King.   Cuchulain, take the oath.
    There is none here that would not have you take it.

Cuchulain. You'd have me take it? Are you of one mind?

The Kings. All, all, all, all!

A Young King.   Do what the High King bids you.   340

Conchubar. There is not one but dreads this turbulence
    Now that they're settled men.

Cuchulain.   Are you so changed,
    Or have I grown more dangerous of late?
    But that's not it. I understand it all.
    It's you that have changed. You've wives and children now,
    And for that reason cannot follow one
    That lives like a bird's flight from tree to tree.—
    It's time the years put water in my blood
    And drowned the wildness of it, for all's changed,
    But that unchanged.—I'll take what oath you will: 350
    The moon, the sun, the water, light, or air,
    I do not care how binding.

Conchubar.   On this fire
    That has been lighted from your hearth and mine;
    The older men shall be my witnesses,
    The younger, yours. The holders of the fire
    Shall purify the thresholds of the house
    With waving fire, and shut the outer door,
    According to the custom; and sing rhyme
    That has come down from the old law-makers
    To blow the witches out. Considering   360
    That the wild will of man could be oath-bound,

But that a woman's could not, they bid us sing
Against the will of woman at its wildest
In the Shape-Changers that run upon the wind.°

> [*Conchubar has gone on to his throne.*

The Women. [*They sing in a very low voice after the first few words
so that the others all but drown their words.*]

May this fire have driven out
The Shape-Changers that can put
Ruin on a great king's house
Until all be ruinous.
Names whereby a man has known
The threshold and the hearthstone,   370
Gather on the wind and drive
The women none can kiss and thrive,
For they are but whirling wind,
Out of memory and mind.
They would make a prince decay
With light images of clay
Planted in the running wave;
Or, for many shapes they have,
They would change them into hounds
Until he had died of his wounds,   380
Though the change were but a whim;
Or they'd hurl a spell at him,
That he follow with desire
Bodies that can never tire
Or grow kind, for they anoint
All their bodies, joint by joint,
With a miracle-working juice
That is made out of the grease
Of the ungoverned unicorn.
But the man is thrice forlorn,   390
Emptied, ruined, wracked, and lost,
That they follow, for at most
They will give him kiss for kiss
While they murmur, 'After this
Hatred may be sweet to the taste'.
Those wild hands that have embraced
All his body can but shove
At the burning wheel of love

Till the side of hate comes up.
Therefore in this ancient cup　　　　　　　　　　400
May the sword-blades drink their fill
Of the home-brew there, until
They will have for masters none
But the threshold and hearthstone.

Cuchulain [*speaking, while they are singing*]. I'll take and keep this
　　　oath, and from this day
I shall be what you please, my chicks, my nestlings.
Yet I had thought you were of those that praised
Whatever life could make the pulse run quickly,
Even though it were brief, and that you held
That a free gift was better than a forced.——　　　410
But that's all over.——I will keep it, too;
I never gave a gift and took it again.
If the wild horse should break the chariot-pole,
It would be punished. Should that be in the oath?

　　　[*Two of the Women, still singing, crouch in front of him holding
　　　the bowl over their heads. He spreads his hands over the flame.*]

I swear to be obedient in all things
To Conchubar, and to uphold his children.

Conchubar. We are one being, as these flames are one:
I give my wisdom, and I take your strength.
Now thrust the swords into the flame, and pray
That they may serve the threshold and the hearthstone　　　420
With faithful service.

　　　[*The Kings kneel in a semicircle before the two Women and
　　　Cuchulain, who thrusts his sword into the flame. They all put
　　　the points of their swords into the flame. The third Woman is at
　　　the back near the big door.*]

Cuchulain.　　　　　　　　　O pure, glittering ones
That should be more than wife or friend or mistress,
Give us the enduring will, the unquenchable hope,
The friendliness of the sword!——

　　　[*The song grows louder, and the last words ring out clearly.
　　　There is a loud knocking at the door, and a cry of* 'Open!
　　　open!']

Conchubar. Some king that has been loitering on the way.
Open the door, for I would have all know

That the oath's finished and Cuchulain bound,
And that the swords are drinking up the flame.

   [*The door is opened by the third Woman, and a Young
   Man with a drawn sword enters.*]

Young Man. I am of Aoife's country.

   [*The Kings rush towards him. Cuchulain throws himself between.*]

Cuchulain.   Put up your swords.
He is but one. Aoife is far away.   430

Young Man. I have come alone into the midst of you
To weigh this sword against Cuchulain's sword.

Conchubar. And are you noble? for if of common seed,
You cannot weigh your sword against his sword
But in mixed battle.

Young Man.   I am under bonds
To tell my name to no man; but it's noble.

Conchubar. But I would know your name and not your bonds.
You cannot speak in the Assembly House,
If you are not noble.

First Old King.   Answer the High King!

Young Man. I will give no other proof than the hawk gives   440
That it's no sparrow!

     [*He is silent for a moment, then speaks to all.*]

                 Yet look upon me, kings.
I, too, am of that ancient seed, and carry
The signs about this body and in these bones.

Cuchulain. To have shown the hawk's grey feather is enough,
And you speak highly, too. Give me that helmet.
I'd thought they had grown weary sending champions.
That sword and belt will do. This fighting's welcome.
The High King there has promised me his wisdom;
But the hawk's sleepy till its well-beloved
Cries out amid the acorns, or it has seen   450
Its enemy like a speck upon the sun.
What's wisdom to the hawk, when that clear eye
Is burning nearer up in the high air?

    [*Looks hard at Young Man; then comes down steps and grasps
    Young Man by shoulder.*]

Hither into the light.
[*To Conchubar.*]   The very tint
Of her that I was speaking of but now.
Not a pin's difference.
[*To Young Man.*]   You are from the North,
Where there are many that have that tint of hair—
Red-brown, the light red-brown. Come nearer, boy,
For I would have another look at you.
There's more likeness—a pale, a stone-pale cheek.   460
What brought you, boy? Have you no fear of death?

Young Man. Whether I live or die is in the gods' hands.

Cuchulain. That is all words, all words; a young man's talk.
I am their plough, their harrow, their very strength:
For he that's in the sun begot this body°
Upon a mortal woman, and I have heard tell
It seemed as if he had outrun the moon
That he must follow always through waste heaven,
He loved so happily. He'll be but slow
To break a tree that was so sweetly planted.   470
Let's see that arm. I'll see it if I choose.
That arm had a good father and a good mother,
But it is not like this.

Young Man.   You are mocking me;
You think I am not worthy to be fought.
But I'll not wrangle but with this talkative knife.

Cuchulain. Put up your sword; I am not mocking you.
I'd have you for my friend, but if it's not
Because you have a hot heart and a cold eye,
I cannot tell the reason.
[*To Conchubar.*]   He has got her fierceness,
And nobody is as fierce as those pale women.   480
But I will keep him with me, Conchubar,
That he may set my memory upon her
When the day's fading.—You will stop with us,
And we will hunt the deer and the wild bulls;
And, when we have grown weary, light our fires
Between the wood and water, or on some mountain
Where the Shape-Changers of the morning come.
The High King there would make a mock of me
Because I did not take a wife among them.

Why do you hang your head? It's a good life: 490
The head grows prouder in the light of the dawn,
And friendship thickens in the murmuring dark
Where the spare hazels meet the wool-white foam.
But I can see there's no more need for words
And that you'll be my friend from this day out.

Conchubar. He has come hither not in his own name
But in Queen Aoife's, and has challenged us
In challenging the foremost man of us all.

Cuchulain. Well, well, what matter?

Conchubar.   You think it does not matter,
And that a fancy lighter than the air, 500
A whim of the moment, has more matter in it.
For having none that shall reign after you,
You cannot think as I do, who would leave
A throne too high for insult.

Cuchulain.   Let your children
Re-mortar their inheritance, as we have,
And put more muscle on.—I'll give you gifts,
But I'd have something too—that arm-ring, boy.
We'll have this quarrel out when you are older.

Young Man. There is no man I'd sooner have my friend
Than you, whose name has gone about the world 510
As if it had been the wind; but Aoife'd say
I had turned coward.

Cuchulain.   I will give you gifts
That Aoife'll know, and all her people know,
To have come from me.   [*Showing cloak*.

                                    My father gave me this.
He came to try me, rising up at dawn
Out of the cold dark of the rich sea.
He challenged me to battle, but before
My sword had touched his sword, told me his name,
Gave me this cloak, and vanished. It was woven
By women of the Country-under-Wave 520
Out of the fleeces of the sea. O! tell her
I was afraid, or tell her what you will.
No; tell her that I heard a raven croak
On the north side of the house, and was afraid.

Conchubar. Some witch of the air has troubled Cuchulain's mind.

Cuchulain. No witchcraft. His head is like a woman's head
    I had a fancy for.

Conchubar.   A witch of the air
    Can make a leaf confound us with memories.
    They run upon the wind and hurl the spells
    That make us nothing, out of the invisible wind.   530
    They have gone to school to learn the trick of it.

Cuchulain. No, no—there's nothing out of common here;
    The winds are innocent.—That arm-ring, boy.

A King. If I've your leave I'll take this challenge up.

Another King. No, give it me, High King, for this wild Aoife
    Has carried off my slaves.

Another King.   No, give it me,
    For she has harried me in house and herd.

Another King. I claim this fight.

Other Kings [*together*].   And I! And I! And I!

Cuchulain. Back! back! Put up your swords! Put up your swords!
    There's none alive that shall accept a challenge   540
    I have refused. Laegaire, put up your sword!°

Young Man. No, let them come. If they've a mind for it,
    I'll try it out with any two together.

Cuchulain. That's spoken as I'd have spoken it at your age.
    But you are in my house. Whatever man
    Would fight with you shall fight it out with me.
    They're dumb, they're dumb. How many of you would meet

                                        [*Draws sword.*

    This mutterer, this old whistler, this sand-piper,
    This edge that's greyer than the tide, this mouse
    That's gnawing at the timbers of the world,   550
    This, this—Boy, I would meet them all in arms
    If I'd a son like you. He would avenge me
    When I have withstood for the last time the men
    Whose fathers, brothers, sons, and friends I have killed
    Upholding Conchubar, when the four provinces
    Have gathered with the ravens over them.
    But I'd need no avenger. You and I

Would scatter them like water from a dish.

Young Man. We'll stand by one another from this out.
   Here is the ring.

Cuchulain.   No, turn and turn about.   560
   But my turn's first because I am the older.

                              [*Spreading out cloak.*

Nine queens out of the Country-under-Wave
Have woven it with the fleeces of the sea
And they were long embroidering at it.—Boy,
If I had fought my father, he'd have killed me,
As certainly as if I had a son
And fought with him, I should be deadly to him;
For the old fiery fountains are far off
And every day there is less heat o' the blood.

Conchubar [*in a loud voice*]. No more of this. I will not have this   570
   friendship.
   Cuchulain is my man, and I forbid it.
   He shall not go unfought, for I myself—

Cuchulain. I will not have it.

Conchubar.   You lay commands on me?

Cuchulain [*seizing Conchubar*]. You shall not stir, High King. I'll
   hold you there.

Conchubar. Witchcraft has maddened you.

The Kings [*shouting*].   Yes, witchcraft! witchcraft!

First Old King. Some witch has worked upon your mind, Cuchulain.
   The head of that young man seemed like a woman's
   You'd had a fancy for. Then of a sudden
   You laid your hands on the High King himself!

Cuchulain. And laid my hands on the High King himself?   580

Conchubar. Some witch is floating in the air above us.

Cuchulain. Yes, witchcraft! witchcraft! Witches of the air!
   [*To Young Man.*] Why did you? Who was it set you to this work?
   Out, out! I say, for now it's sword on sword!

Young Man. But . . . but I did not.

Cuchulain.   Out, I say, out, out!

   [*Young Man goes out followed by Cuchulain. The Kings follow*

them out with confused cries, and words one can hardly hear
because of the noise. Some cry, 'Quicker, quicker!' 'Why are
you so long at the door?' 'We'll be too late!' 'Have they
begun to fight?' 'Can you see if they are fighting?' *and so on.*
Their voices drown each other. The three Women are left
alone.]

First Woman. I have seen, I have seen!

Second Woman.   What do you cry aloud?

First Woman. The Ever-living have shown me what's to come.°

Third Woman. How? Where?

First Woman.   -   In the ashes of the bowl.

Second Woman. While you were holding it between your hands?

Third Woman. Speak quickly!

First Woman.   I have seen Cuchulain's roof-tree   590
Leap into fire, and the walls split and blacken.

Second Woman. Cuchulain has gone out to die.

Third Woman.   O! O!

Second Woman. Who could have thought that one so great as he
Should meet his end at this unnoted sword!

First Woman. Life drifts between a fool and a blind man
To the end, and nobody can know his end.

Second Woman. Come, look upon the quenching of this greatness.

[*The other two go to the door, but they stop for a moment upon*
the threshold and wail.]

First Woman. No crying out, for there'll be need of cries
And rending of the hair when it's all finished.

[*The Women go out. There is the sound of clashing swords from*
time to time during what follows.
[*Enter the Fool, dragging the Blind Man.*]

Fool. You have eaten it, you have eaten it! You have left me nothing   600
but the bones.

[*He throws Blind Man down by big chair.*]

Blind Man. O, that I should have to endure such a plague! O, I ache
all over! O, I am pulled to pieces! This is the way you pay me all
the good I have done you.

Fool. You have eaten it! You have told me lies. I might have known

you had eaten it when I saw your slow, sleepy walk. Lie there till
the kings come. O, I will tell Conchubar and Cuchulain and all
the kings about you!

Blind Man. What would have happened to you but for me, and you
without your wits? If I did not take care of you, what would you   610
do for food and warmth?

Fool. You take care of me? You stay safe, and send me into every
kind of danger. You sent me down the cliff for gulls' eggs while
you warmed your blind eyes in the sun; and then you ate all that
were good for food. You left me the eggs that were neither egg
nor bird. [*Blind Man tries to rise; Fool makes him lie down again.*]
Keep quiet now, till I shut the door. There is some noise out-
side—a high vexing noise, so that I can't be listening to myself.
[*Shuts the big door.*] Why can't they be quiet? why can't they be
quiet? [*Blind Man tries to get away.*] Ah! you would get away,   620
would you? [*Follows Blind Man and brings him back.*] Lie there!
lie there! No, you won't get away! Lie there till the kings come.
I'll tell them all about you. I will tell it all. How you sit warming
yourself, when you have made me light a fire of sticks, while I sit
blowing it with my mouth. Do you not always make me take the
windy side of the bush when it blows, and the rainy side when it
rains?

Blind Man. O, good Fool! listen to me. Think of the care I have
taken of you. I have brought you to many a warm hearth, where
there was a good welcome for you, but you would not stay there;   630
you were always wandering about.

Fool. The last time you brought me in, it was not I who wandered
away, but you that got put out because you took the crubeen° out
of the pot when nobody was looking. Keep quiet, now!

Cuchulain [*rushing in*]. Witchcraft! There is no witchcraft on the
earth, or among the witches of the air, that these hands cannot
break.

Fool. Listen to me, Cuchulain. I left him turning the fowl at the fire.
He ate it all, though I had stolen it. He left me nothing but the
feathers.   640

Cuchulain. Fill me a horn of ale!

Blind Man. I gave him what he likes best. You do not know how vain
this Fool is. He likes nothing so well as a feather.

Fool. He left me nothing but the bones and feathers. Nothing but the feathers, though I had stolen it.

Cuchulain. Give me that horn. Quarrels here, too! [*Drinks*.] What is there between you two that is worth a quarrel? Out with it!

Blind Man. Where would he be but for me? I must be always thinking—thinking to get food for the two of us, and when we've got it, if the moon is at the full or the tide on the turn, he'll leave the   650
rabbit in the snare till it is full of maggots, or let the trout slip back through his hands into the stream.

[*The Fool has begun singing while the Blind Man is speaking.*]

Fool [*singing*].

> When you were an acorn on the tree-top,
>   Then was I an eagle-cock;
> Now that you are a withered old block,
>   Still am I an eagle-cock.

Blind Man. Listen to him, now. That's the sort of talk I have to put up with day out, day in.

[*The Fool is putting the feathers into his hair. Cuchulain takes a handful of feathers out of a heap the Fool has on the bench beside him, and out of the Fool's hair, and begins to wipe the blood from his sword with them.*]

Fool. He has taken my feathers to wipe his sword. It is blood that he is wiping from his sword.   660

Cuchulain [*goes up to door at back and throws away feathers*].

They are standing about his body. They will not awaken him, for all his witchcraft.

Blind Man. It is that young champion that he has killed. He that came out of Aoife's country.

Cuchulain. He thought to have saved himself with witchcraft.

Fool. That Blind Man there said he would kill you. He came from Aoife's country to kill you. That Blind Man said they had taught him every kind of weapon that he might do it. But I always knew that you would kill him.

Cuchulain [*to the Blind Man*]. You knew him, then?

Blind Man. I saw him, when I had my eyes, in Aoife's country.   670

Cuchulain. You were in Aoife's country?

Blind Man. I knew him and his mother there.

Cuchulain. He was about to speak of her when he died.

Blind Man. He was a queen's son.

Cuchulain. What queen? what queen? [*Seizes Blind Man, who is now sitting upon the bench*.] Was it Scathach?°
There were many queens. All the rulers there were queens.

Blind Man. No, not Scathach.

Cuchulain. It was Uathach,° then? Speak! speak!   680

Blind Man. I cannot speak; you are clutching me too tightly. [*Cuchulain lets him go*.] I cannot remember who it was. I am not certain. It was some queen.

Fool. He said a while ago that the young man was Aoife's son.

Cuchulain. She? No, no! She had no son when I was there.

Fool. That Blind Man there said that she owned him for her son.

Cuchulain. I had rather he had been some other woman's son. What father had he? A soldier out of Alba?° She was an amorous woman—a proud, pale, amorous woman.

Blind Man. None knew whose son he was.   690

Cuchulain. None knew! Did you know, old listener at doors?

Blind Man. No, no; I knew nothing.

Fool. He said a while ago that he heard Aoife boast that she'd never but the one lover, and he the only man that had overcome her in battle.   [*Pause*.

Blind Man. Somebody is trembling, Fool! The bench is shaking. Why are you trembling? Is Cuchulain going to hurt us? It was not I who told you, Cuchulain.

Fool. It is Cuchulain who is trembling. It is Cuchulain who is shaking the bench.   700

Blind Man. It is his own son he has slain.

Cuchulain. 'Twas they that did it, the pale windy people.
Where? where? where? My sword against the thunder!
But no, for they have always been my friends;
And though they love to blow a smoking coal
Till it's all flame, the wars they blow aflame
Are full of glory, and heart-uplifting pride,
And not like this. The wars they love awaken

Old fingers and the sleepy strings of harps.
Who did it then? Are you afraid? Speak out!   710
For I have put you under my protection,
And will reward you well. Dubthach the Chafer?
He'd an old grudge. No, for he is with Maeve.°
Laegaire did it! Why do you not speak?
What is this house? [*Pause.*] Now I remember all.

> [*Comes before Conchubar's chair, and strikes out with his
> sword, as if Conchubar was sitting upon it.*]

'Twas you who did it—you who sat up there
With your old rod of kingship, like a magpie
Nursing a stolen spoon. No, not a magpie,
A maggot that is eating up the earth!
Yes, but a magpie, for he's flown away.   720
Where did he fly to?

Blind Man.   He is outside the door.

Cuchulain. Outside the door?

Blind Man.   Between the door and the sea.

Cuchulain. Conchubar, Conchubar! the sword into your heart!

> [*He rushes out. Pause. Fool creeps up to the big door and looks
> after him.*

Fool. He is going up to King Conchubar. They are all about the
young man. No, no, he is standing still. There is a great wave
going to break, and he is looking at it. Ah! now he is running
down to the sea, but he is holding up his sword as if he were going
into a fight. [*Pause.*] Well struck! well struck!

Blind Man. What is he doing now?

Fool. O! he is fighting the waves!   730

Blind Man. He sees King Conchubar's crown on every one of them.

Fool. There, he has struck at a big one! He has struck the crown off
it; he has made the foam fly. There again, another big one!

Blind Man. Where are the kings? What are the kings doing?

Fool. They are shouting and running down to the shore, and the
people are running out of the houses. They are all running.

Blind Man. You say they are running out of the houses? There will
be nobody left in the houses. Listen, Fool!

Fool. There, he is down! He is up again. He is going out in the deep water. There is a big wave. It has gone over him. I cannot see him   740
now. He has killed kings and giants, but the waves have mastered him, the waves have mastered him!

Blind Man. Come here, Fool!

Fool. The waves have mastered him.

Blind Man. Come here!

Fool. The waves have mastered him.

Blind Man. Come here, I say.

Fool [*coming towards him, but looking backwards towards the door*]. What is it?

Blind Man. There will be nobody in the houses. Come this way; come quickly! The ovens will be full. We will put our hands into   750
the ovens.   [*They go out.*

THE END

The Only Jealousy of Emer (1919)°

PERSONS IN THE PLAY

Three Musicians (*their faces made up to resemble masks*)
The Ghost of Cuchulain (*wearing a mask*)
The Figure of Cuchulain (*wearing a mask*)
Emer
Eithne Inguba° } (*masked, or their faces made up to resemble masks*)
Woman of the Sidhe (*wearing a mask*)°

Enter Musicians, who are dressed and made up as in 'At the Hawk's Well'. They have the same musical instruments, which can either be already upon the stage or be brought in by the First Musician before he stands in the centre with the cloth between his hands, or by a player when the cloth has been unfolded. The stage as before can be against the wall of any room, and the same black cloth can be used as in 'At the Hawk's Well'.

[*Song for the folding and unfolding of the cloth*]

First Musician.
    A woman's beauty is like a white
    Frail bird, like a white sea-bird alone
    At daybreak after stormy night
    Between two furrows upon the ploughed land:
    A sudden storm, and it was thrown
    Between dark furrows upon the ploughed land.
    How many centuries spent
    The sedentary soul
    In toils of measurement
    Beyond eagle or mole,
    Beyond hearing or seeing,
    Or Archimedes' guess,
    To raise into being
    That loveliness?°

    A strange, unserviceable thing,
    A fragile, exquisite, pale shell,
    That the vast troubled waters bring

To the loud sands before day has broken.
The storm arose and suddenly fell
Amid the dark before day had broken.   20
What death? what discipline?
What bonds no man could unbind,
Being imagined within
The labyrinth of the mind,
What pursuing or fleeing,
What wounds, what bloody press,
Dragged into being
This loveliness?

> [*When the cloth is folded again the Musicians take their place
> against the wall. The folding of the cloth shows on one side of the
> stage the curtained bed or litter on which lies a man in his grave-
> clothes. He wears an heroic mask. Another man with exactly
> similar clothes and mask crouches near the front. Emer is sitting
> beside the bed.*]

First Musician [*speaking*]. I call before the eyes a roof
With cross-beams darkened by smoke;   30
A fisher's net hangs from a beam,
A long oar lies against the wall.
I call up a poor fisher's house;
A man lies dead or swooning,
That amorous man,
That amorous, violent man, renowned Cuchulain,
Queen Emer at his side.
At her own bidding all the rest have gone;
But now one comes on hesitating feet,
Young Eithne Inguba, Cuchulain's mistress.   40
She stands a moment in the open door.
Beyond the open door the bitter sea,
The shining, bitter sea, is crying out,
[*singing*] White shell, white wing!
I will not choose for my friend
A frail, unserviceable thing
That drifts and dreams, and but knows
That waters are without end
And that wind blows.

Emer [*speaking*]. Come hither, come sit down beside the bed;   50
You need not be afraid, for I myself

Sent for you, Eithne Inguba.

Eithne Inguba.   No, Madam,
　I have too deeply wronged you to sit there.

Emer. Of all the people in the world we two,
　And we alone, may watch together here,
　Because we have loved him best.

Eithne Inguba.   And is he dead?

Emer. Although they have dressed him out in his grave-clothes
　And stretched his limbs, Cuchulain is not dead;
　The very heavens when that day's at hand,
　So that his death may not lack ceremony,   60
　Will throw out fires, and the earth grow red with blood.
　There shall not be a scullion but foreknows it
　Like the world's end.

Eithne Inguba.   How did he come to this?

Emer. Towards noon in the assembly of the kings
　He met with one who seemed a while most dear.
　The kings stood round; some quarrel was blown up;
　He drove him out and killed him on the shore
　At Baile's tree, and he who was so killed
　Was his own son begot on some wild woman
　When he was young, or so I have heard it said;   70
　And thereupon, knowing what man he had killed,
　And being mad with sorrow, he ran out;
　And after, to his middle in the foam,
　With shield before him and with sword in hand,
　He fought the deathless sea. The kings looked on°
　And not a king dared stretch an arm, or even
　Dared call his name, but all stood wondering
　In that dumb stupor like cattle in a gale,
　Until at last, as though he had fixed his eyes
　On a new enemy, he waded out   80
　Until the water had swept over him;
　But the waves washed his senseless image up
　And laid it at this door.

Eithne Inguba.   How pale he looks!

Emer. He is not dead.

Eithne Inguba.   You have not kissed his lips
　Nor laid his head upon your breast.

Emer.   It may be
    An image has been put into his place,
    A sea-borne log bewitched into his likeness,
    Or some stark horseman grown too old to ride
    Among the troops of Manannan, Son of the Sea,°
    Now that his joints are stiff.

Eithne Inguba.   Cry out his name.   90
    All that are taken from our sight, they say,
    Loiter amid the scenery of their lives
    For certain hours or days, and should he hear
    He might, being angry, drive the changeling out.

Emer. It is hard to make them hear amid their darkness,
    And it is long since I could call him home;
    I am but his wife, but if you cry aloud
    With the sweet voice that is so dear to him
    He cannot help but listen.

Eithne Inguba.   He loves me best,
    Being his newest love, but in the end   100
    Will love the woman best who loved him first
    And loved him through the years when love seemed lost.

Emer. I have that hope, the hope that some day somewhere
    We'll sit together at the hearth again.

Eithne Inguba. Women like me, the violent hour passed over,
    Are flung into some corner like old nut-shells.
    Cuchulain, listen.

Emer.   No, not yet, for first
    I'll cover up his face to hide the sea;
    And throw new logs upon the hearth and stir
    The half-burnt logs until they break in flame.   110
    Old Manannan's unbridled horses come°
    Out of the sea, and on their backs his horsemen;
    But all the enchantments of the dreaming foam
    Dread the hearth-fire.

> [*She pulls the curtains of the bed so as to hide the sick man's face,
> that the actor may change his mask unseen. She goes to one
> side of the platform and moves her hand as though putting logs
> on a fire and stirring it into a blaze. While she makes these
> movements the Musicians play, marking the movements with
> drum and flute perhaps.*

Having finished she stands beside the imaginary fire at a distance from
Cuchulain and Eithne Inguba.]

                              Call on Cuchulain now.

Eithne Inguba. Can you not hear my voice?

Emer.   Bend over him;
   Call out dear secrets till you have touched his heart,
   If he lies there; and if he is not there,
   Till you have made him jealous.

Eithne Inguba.   Cuchulain, listen.

Emer. Those words sound timidly; to be afraid
   Because his wife is but three paces off,   120
   When there is so great need, were but to prove
   The man that chose you made but a poor choice:
   We're but two women struggling with the sea.

Eithne Inguba. O my beloved, pardon me, that I
   Have been ashamed. I thrust my shame away.
   I have never sent a message or called out,
   Scarce had a longing for your company
   But you have known and come; and if indeed
   You are lying there, stretch out your arms and speak;
   Open your mouth and speak, for to this hour   130
   My company has made you talkative.
   What ails your tongue, or what has closed your ears?
   Our passion had not chilled when we were parted
   On the pale shore under the breaking dawn.
   He cannot speak: or else his ears are closed
   And no sound reaches him.

Emer.   Then kiss that image;
   The pressure of your mouth upon his mouth
   May reach him where he is.

Eithne Inguba [*starting back*]. It is no man.
   I felt some evil thing that dried my heart
   When my lips touched it.

Emer.   No, his body stirs;   140
   The pressure of your mouth has called him home;
   He has thrown the changeling out.

Eithne Inguba [*going further off*].   Look at that arm;
   That arm is withered to the very socket.

Emer [*going up to the bed*]. What do you come for; and from where?

Figure of Cuchulain.   I have come
  From Manannan's court upon a bridleless horse.

Emer. What one among the Sidhe has dared to lie°
  Upon Cuchulain's bed and take his image?

Figure of Cuchulain. I am named Bricriu—not the man—that
    Bricriu,°
  Maker of discord among gods and men,
  Called Bricriu of the Sidhe.

Emer.   Come for what purpose?   150

Figure of Cuchulain [*sitting up parting curtain and showing its distorted
    face, as Eithne Inguba goes out*]. I show my face, and everything
  he loves
  Must fly away.

Emer.   You people of the wind
  Are full of lying speech and mockery:
  I have not fled your face.

Figure of Cuchulain.   You are not loved.

Emer. And therefore have no dread to meet your eyes
  And to demand him of you.

Figure of Cuchulain.   For that I have come.
  You have but to pay the price and he is free.

Emer. Do the Sidhe bargain?

Figure of Cuchulain.   When they would free a captive
  They take in ransom a less valued thing.
  The fisher, when some knowledgeable man   160
  Restores to him his wife, or son, or daughter,
  Knows he must lose a boat or net, or it may be
  The cow that gives his children milk; and some
  Have offered their own lives. I do not ask
  Your life, or any valuable thing;
  You spoke but now of the mere chance that some day
  You'd be the apple of his eye again
  When old and ailing, but renounce that chance
  And he shall live again.

Emer.   I do not question
  But you have brought ill-luck on all he loves;   170

And now, because I am thrown beyond your power
Unless your words are lies, you come to bargain.

Figure of Cuchulain. You loved your mastery, when but newly
married.
And I love mine for all my withered arm;
You have but to put yourself into that power
And he shall live again.

Emer.   No, never, never.

Figure of Cuchulain. You dare not be accursed, yet he has dared.

Emer. I have but two joyous thoughts, two things I prize,
A hope, a memory, and now you claim that hope.

Figure of Cuchulain. He'll never sit beside you at the hearth   180
Or make old bones, but die of wounds and toil
On some far shore or mountain, a strange woman
Beside his mattress.

Emer.   You ask for my one hope
That you may bring your curse on all about him.

Figure of Cuchulain. You've watched his loves and you have not
been jealous,
Knowing that he would tire, but do those tire
That love the Sidhe? Come closer to the bed
That I may touch your eyes and give them sight.

   [*He touches her eyes with his left hand, the right being withered.*]

Emer [*seeing the crouching Ghost of Cuchulain*]. My husband is
there.

Figure of Cuchulain. I have dissolved the dark
That hid him from your eyes, but not that other   190
That's hidden you from his.

Emer.   O husband, husband!

Figure of Cuchulain. He cannot hear—being shut off, a phantom
That can neither touch, nor hear, nor see;
The longing and the cries have drawn him hither.
He heard no sound, heard no articulate sound;
They could but banish rest, and make him dream,
And in that dream, as do all dreaming shades
Before they are accustomed to their freedom,
He has taken his familiar form; and yet

He crouches there not knowing where he is   200
    Or at whose side he is crouched.

> [*A Woman of the Sidhe has entered and stands a little inside the
> door.*]

Emer.   Who is this woman?

Figure of Cuchulain. She has hurried from the Country-under-Wave
    And dreamed herself into that shape that he
    May glitter in her basket; for the Sidhe
    Are dexterous fishers and they fish for men
    With dreams upon the hook.

Emer.   And so that woman
    Has hid herself in this disguise and made
    Herself into a lie.

Figure of Cuchulain. A dream is body;
    The dead move ever towards a dreamless youth
    And when they dream no more return no more;   210
    And those more holy shades that never lived
    But visit you in dreams.

Emer.   I know her sort.
    They find our men asleep, weary with war,
    Lap them in cloudy hair or kiss their lips;
    Our men awake in ignorance of it all
    But when we take them in our arms at night
    We cannot break their solitude.

> [*She draws a knife from her girdle.*]

Figure of Cuchulain.   No knife
    Can wound that body of air. Be silent; listen;
    I have not given you eyes and ears for nothing.

> [*The Woman of the Sidhe moves round the crouching Ghost of
> Cuchulain at front of stage in a dance that grows gradually
> quicker, as he slowly awakes. At moments she may drop her hair
> upon his head, but she does not kiss him. She is accompanied by
> string and flute and drum. Her mask and clothes must suggest
> gold or bronze or brass or silver, so that she seems more an idol
> than a human being. This suggestion may be repeated in her
> movements. Her hair, too, must keep the metallic suggestion.*]

Ghost of Cuchulain. Who is it stands before me there   220
    Shedding such light from limb and hair

As when the moon, complete at last
With every labouring crescent past,
And lonely with extreme delight,
Flings out upon the fifteenth night?°

Woman of the Sidhe. Because I long I am not complete.
What pulled your hands about your feet,
Pulled down your head upon your knees,
And hid your face?

Ghost of Cuchulain.   Old memories:
A woman in her happy youth   230
Before her man had broken troth,
Dead men and women. Memories
Have pulled my head upon my knees.

Woman of the Sidhe. Could you that have loved many a woman
That did not reach beyond the human,
Lacking a day to be complete,
Love one that, though her heart can beat,
Lacks it but by an hour or so?

Ghost of Cuchulain. I know you now, for long ago
I met you on a cloudy hill   240
Beside old thorn-trees and a well.
A woman danced and a hawk flew,°
I held out arms and hands; but you,
That now seem friendly, fled away,
Half woman and half bird of prey.

Woman of the Sidhe. Hold out your arms and hands again;
You were not so dumbfounded when
I was that bird of prey, and yet
I am all woman now.

Ghost of Cuchulain.   I am not
The young and passionate man I was,   250
And though that brilliant light surpass
All crescent forms, my memories
Weigh down my hands, abash my eyes.

Woman of the Sidhe. Then kiss my mouth. Though memory
Be beauty's bitterest enemy
I have no dread, for at my kiss
Memory on the moment vanishes:
Nothing but beauty can remain.

Ghost of Cuchulain. And shall I never know again
   Intricacies of blind remorse?   260

Woman of the Sidhe. Time shall seem to stay his course;
   When your mouth and my mouth meet
   All my round shall be complete
   Imagining all its circles run;
   And there shall be oblivion
   Even to quench Cuchulain's drouth,
   Even to still that heart.

Ghost of Cuchulain.   Your mouth!

        [*They are about to kiss, he turns away*.]

   O Emer, Emer!

Woman of the Sidhe. So then it is she
   Made you impure with memory.

Ghost of Cuchulain. O Emer, Emer, there we stand;   270
   Side by side and hand in hand
   Tread the threshold of the house
   As when our parents married us.

Woman of the Sidhe. Being among the dead you love her
   That valued every slut above her
   While you still lived.

Ghost of Cuchulain.   O my lost Emer!

Woman of the Sidhe. And there is not a loose-tongued schemer
   But could draw you, if not dead,
   From her table and her bed.
   But what could make you fit to wive   280
   With flesh and blood, being born to live
   Where no one speaks of broken troth,
   For all have washed out of their eyes
   Wind-blown dirt of their memories
   To improve their sight?

Ghost of Cuchulain.   Your mouth, your mouth!

      [*She goes out followed by Ghost of Cuchulain*.

Figure of Cuchulain. Cry out that you renounce his love; make haste
   And cry that you renounce his love for ever.

Emer. No, never will I give that cry.

Figure of Cuchulain.   Fool, fool!

I am Fand's enemy come to thwart her will,
And you stand gaping there. There is still time.   290
Hear how the horses trample on the shore,
Hear how they trample! She has mounted up.
Cuchulain's not beside her in the chariot.
There is still a moment left; cry out, cry out!
Renounce him, and her power is at an end.
Cuchulain's foot is on the chariot-step.
Cry—

Emer.   I renounce Cuchulain's love for ever.

> [*The Figure of Cuchulain sinks back upon the bed, half-draw-*
> *ing the curtain. Eithne Inguba comes in and kneels by bed.*]

Eithne Inguba. Come to me, my beloved, it is I.
I, Eithne Inguba. Look! He is there.
He has come back and moved upon the bed.   300
And it is I that won him from the sea,
That brought him back to life.

Emer.   Cuchulain wakes.

> [*The figure turns round. It once more wears the heroic mask.*]

Cuchulain. Your arms, your arms! O Eithne Inguba,
I have been in some strange place and am afraid.

> [*The First Musician comes to the front of stage, the others from*
> *each side, and unfold the cloth singing.*]
> [*Song for the unfolding and folding of the cloth*]

The Musicians.
Why does your heart beat thus?
Plain to be understood,
I have met in a man's house
A statue of solitude,
Moving there and walking;
Its strange heart beating fast   310
For all our talking.
O still that heart at last.

O bitter reward
Of many a tragic tomb!
And we though astonished are dumb
Or give but a sigh and a word,
A passing word.

Although the door be shut
And all seem well enough,
Although wide world hold not   320
A man but will give you his love
The moment he has looked at you,
He that has loved the best
May turn from a statue
His too human breast.

O bitter reward
Of many a tragic tomb!
And we though astonished are dumb
Or give but a sigh and a word,
A passing word.   330

What makes your heart so beat?
What man is at your side?
When beauty is complete
Your own thought will have died
And danger not be diminished;
Dimmed at three-quarter light,
When moon's round is finished
The stars are out of sight.

O bitter reward
Of many a tragic tomb!
And we though astonished are dumb   340
Or give but a sigh and a word,
A passing word.

[*When the cloth is folded again the stage is bare.*

THE END

Calvary (1920)

PERSONS IN THE PLAY

Three Musicians (*their faces made up to resemble masks*)
Christ (*wearing a mask*)
Lazarus (*wearing a mask*)
Judas (*wearing a mask*)
Three Roman Soldiers (*their faces masked or made up to resemble masks*)

At the beginning of the play the First Musician comes to the front of the bare place, round three sides of which the audience are seated, with a folded cloth hanging from his joined hands. Two other Musicians come, as in the preceding play, one from either side, and unfold the cloth so that it shuts out the stage, and then fold it again, singing and moving rhythmically. They do the same at the end of the play, which enables the players to leave the stage unseen.

[*Song for the folding and unfolding of the cloth*]

First Musician.
  Motionless under the moon-beam,
  Up to his feathers in the stream;
  Although fish leap, the white heron
  Shivers in a dumbfounded dream.

Second Musician.
  God has not died for the white heron.°

Third Musician.
  Although half famished he'll not dare
  Dip or do anything but stare
  Upon the glittering image of a heron,
  That now is lost and now is there.

Second Musician.
  God has not died for the white heron.

First Musician.
  But that the full is shortly gone
  And after that is crescent moon,
  It's certain that the moon-crazed heron
  Would be but fishes' diet soon.°

Second Musician.
    God has not died for the white heron.

    [*The three Musicians are now seated by the drum, flute, and zither at the back of stage.*]

First Musician. The road to Calvary, and I beside it
    Upon an ancient stone. Good Friday's come,
    The day whereon Christ dreams His passion through.
    He climbs up hither but as a dreamer climbs.
    The cross that but exists because He dreams it   20
    Shortens His breath and wears away His strength.
    And now He stands amid a mocking crowd,
    Heavily breathing.

    [*A player with the mask of Christ and carrying a cross has entered and now stands leaning upon the cross.*]

                Those that are behind
    Climb on the shoulders of the men in front
    To shout their mockery: 'Work a miracle',
    Cries one, 'and save yourself'; another cries,
    'Call on your father now before your bones
    Have been picked bare by the great desert birds';
    Another cries, 'Call out with a loud voice
    And tell him that his son is cast away   30
    Amid the mockery of his enemies'.

                 [*Singing*]

            O, but the mockers' cry
            Makes my heart afraid,
            As though a flute of bone
            Taken from a heron's thigh,
            A heron crazed by the moon,
            Were cleverly, softly played.

                 [*Speaking*]

    Who is this from whom the crowd has shrunk,
    As though he had some look that terrified?
    He has a deathly face, and yet he moves   40
    Like a young foal that sees the hunt go by
    And races in the field.

        [*A player with the mask of Lazarus has entered.*]°

Lazarus.   He raised me up.
    I am the man that died and was raised up;

I am called Lazarus.

Christic.   Seeing that you died,
Lay in the tomb four days and were raised up,
You will not mock at me.

Lazarus.   For four whole days
I had been dead and I was lying still
In an old comfortable mountain cavern
When you came climbing there with a great crowd
And dragged me to the light.

Christ.   I called your name: 50
'Lazarus, come out', I said, and you came out
Bound up in cloths, your face bound in a cloth.

Lazarus. You took my death, give me your death instead.

Christ. I gave you life.

Lazarus.   But death is what I ask.
Alive I never could escape your love,
And when I sickened towards my death I thought,
'I'll to the desert, or chuckle in a corner,
Mere ghost, a solitary thing.' I died
And saw no more until I saw you stand
In the opening of the tomb; 'Come out!' you called;   60
You dragged me to the light as boys drag out
A rabbit when they have dug its hole away;
And now with all the shouting at your heels
You travel towards the death I am denied.
And that is why I have hurried to this road
And claimed your death.

Christ.   But I have conquered death,
And all the dead shall be raised up again.

Lazarus. Then what I heard is true. I thought to die
When my allotted years ran out again;
And that, being gone, you could not hinder it;   70
But now you will blind with light the solitude
That death has made; you will disturb that corner
Where I had thought I might lie safe for ever.

Christ. I do my Father's will.

Lazarus.   And not your own;
And I was free four days, four days being dead.

Climb up to Calvary, but turn your eyes
From Lazarus that cannot find a tomb
Although he search all height and depth: make way,
Make way for Lazarus that must go search
Among the desert places where there is nothing   80
But howling wind and solitary birds.   [*He goes out.*

First Musician. The crowd shrinks backward from the face that
        seems
    Death-stricken and death-hungry still; and now
    Martha, and those three Marys, and the rest°
    That live but in His love are gathered round Him.
    He holds His right arm out, and on His arm
    Their lips are pressed and their tears fall; and now
    They cast them on the ground before His dirty
    Blood-dabbled feet and clean them with their hair.

                    [*Sings*]

                Take but His love away,   90
                Their love becomes a feather
                Of eagle, swan or gull,
                Or a drowned heron's feather
                Tossed hither and thither
                Upon the bitter spray
                And the moon at the full.°

Christ. I felt their hair upon my feet a moment
    And then they fled away—why have they fled?
    Why has the street grown empty of a sudden
    As though all fled in terror?

Judas [*who has just entered*].   I am Judas   100
    That sold you for the thirty pieces of silver.

Christ. You were beside me every day, and saw
    The dead raised up and blind men given their sight,
    And all that I have said and taught you have known,
    Yet doubt that I am God.

Judas.   I have not doubted;
    I knew it from the first moment that I saw you;
    I had no need of miracles to prove it.

Christ. And yet you have betrayed me.

Judas.   I have betrayed you

Because you seemed all-powerful.

Christ.   My Father
Even now, if I were but to whisper it,   110
Would break the world in His miraculous fury
To set me free.

Judas.   And is there not one man
In the wide world that is not in your power?

Christ. My Father put all men into my hands.

Judas. That was the very thought that drove me wild.
I could not bear to think you had but to whistle
And I must do; but after that I thought,
'Whatever man betrays Him will be free';
And life grew bearable again. And now
Is there a secret left I do not know,   120
Knowing that if a man betrays a God
He is the stronger of the two?

Christ.   But if
'Twere the commandment of that God Himself,
That God were still the stronger.

Judas.   When I planned it
There was no live thing near me but a heron
So full of itself that it seemed terrified.

Christ. But my betrayal was decreed that hour
When the foundations of the world were laid.

Judas. It was decreed that somebody betray you—
I'd thought of that—but not that I should do it,   130
I the man Judas, born on such a day,
In such a village, such and such his parents;
Nor that I'd go with my old coat upon me
To the High Priest, and chuckle to myself
As people chuckle when alone, and do it
For thirty pieces and no more, no less,
And neither with a nod nor a sent message,
But with a kiss upon your cheek. I did it,
I, Judas, and no other man, and now
You cannot even save me.

Christ.   Begone from me.   140

                [*Three Roman Soldiers have entered.*]

First Roman Soldier. He has been chosen to hold up the cross.

[*During what follows, Judas holds up the cross while Christ
stands with His arms stretched out upon it.*]

Second Roman Soldier. We'll keep the rest away; they are too persis-
tent;
They are always wanting something.

Third Roman Soldier.   Die in peace.
There's no one here but Judas and ourselves.

Christ. And who are you that ask your God for nothing?

Third Roman Soldier. We are the gamblers, and when you are dead
We'll settle who is to have that cloak of yours
By throwing dice.

Second Roman Soldier. Our dice were carved
Out of an old sheep's thigh at Ephesus.

First Roman Soldier. Although but one of us can win the cloak   150
That will not make us quarrel; what does it matter?
One day one loses and the next day wins.

Second Roman Soldier. Whatever happens is the best, we say,
So that it's unexpected.

Third Roman Soldier.   Had you sent
A crier through the world you had not found
More comfortable companions for a death-bed
Than three old gamblers that have asked for nothing.

First Roman Soldier. They say you're good and that you made the
world,
But it's no matter.

Second Roman Soldier. Come now; let us dance
The dance of the dice-throwers, for it may be   160
He cannot live much longer and has not seen it.

Third Roman Soldier. If he were but the God of dice he'd know it,
But he is not that God.

First Roman Soldier.   One thing is plain,
To know that he has nothing that we need
Must be a comfort to him.

Second Roman Soldier.   In the dance
We quarrel for a while, but settle it
By throwing dice, and after that, being friends,

Join hand to hand and wheel about the cross.

                                                    [*They dance.*

Christ. My Father, why hast Thou forsaken Me?

            [*Song for the folding and unfolding of the cloth*]

First Musician.
    Lonely the sea-bird lies at her rest,   170
    Blown like a dawn-blenched parcel of spray
    Upon the wind, or follows her prey
    Under a great wave's hollowing crest.

Second Musician.
    God has not appeared to the birds.

Third Musician.
    The ger-eagle has chosen his part
    In blue deep of the upper air
    Where one-eyed day can meet his stare;
    He is content with his savage heart.

Second Musician.
    God has not appeared to the birds.

First Musician.
    But where have last year's cygnets gone?   180
    The lake is empty; why do they fling
    White wing out beside white wing?
    What can a swan need but a swan?

Second Musician.
    God has not appeared to the birds.

                              THE END

The Cat and the Moon (1926)

TO

JOHN MASEFIELD

PERSONS IN THE PLAY

A Blind Beggar
A Lame Beggar
Three Musicians

SCENE.—*The scene is any bare place before a wall against which stands a patterned screen, or hangs a patterned curtain suggesting Saint Colman's Well.° Three Musicians are sitting close to the wall, with zither, drum and flute. Their faces are made up to resemble masks.*

First Musician [*singing*].

> The cat went here and there
> And the moon spun round like a top,
> And the nearest kin of the moon,
> The creeping cat, looked up.
> Black Minnaloushe stared at the moon,
> For, wander and wail as he would,
> The pure cold light in the sky
> Troubled his animal blood.

[*Two beggars enter—a blind man with a lame man on his back. They wear grotesque masks. The Blind Beggar is counting the paces.*]

Blind Beggar. One thousand and six, one thousand and seven, one thousand and nine. Look well now, for we should be in sight of the holy well of Saint Colman. The beggar at the cross-roads said it was one thousand paces from where he stood and a few paces over. Look well now, can you see the big ash-tree that's above it?

Lame Beggar [*getting down*]. No, not yet.

Blind Beggar. Then we must have taken a wrong turn; flighty you always were, and maybe before the day is over, you will have me drowned in Kiltartan River or maybe in the sea itself.

Lame Beggar. I have brought you the right way, but you are a lazy man, Blind Man, and you make very short strides.

10

Blind Beggar. It's great daring you have, and how could I make a   20
long stride and you on my back from the peep o' day?

Lame Beggar. And maybe the beggar of the cross-roads was only
making it up when he said a thousand paces and a few paces
more. You and I, being beggars, know the way of beggars, and
maybe he never paced it at all, being a lazy man.

Blind Beggar. Get up. It's too much talk you have.

Lame Beggar [*getting up*]. But as I was saying, he being a lazy man—
O, O, O, stop pinching the calf of my leg and I'll not say another
word till I'm spoken to.

> [*They go round the stage once, moving to drum-taps, and as
> they move the following song is sung.*]

First Musician [*singing*]

> Minnaloushe runs in the grass   30
> Lifting his delicate feet.
> Do you dance, Minnaloushe, do you dance?
> When two close kindred meet
> What better than call a dance?
> Maybe the moon may learn,
> Tired of that courtly fashion,
> A new dance turn.

Blind Beggar. Do you see the big ash-tree?

Lame Beggar. I do then, and the wall under it, and the flat stone, and
the things upon the stone; and here is a good dry place to kneel in.   40

Blind Beggar. You may get down so. [*Lame Beggar gets down.*] I
begin to have it in my mind that I am a great fool, and it was you
who egged me on with your flighty talk.

Lame Beggar. How should you be a great fool to ask the saint to give
you back your two eyes?

Blind Beggar. There is many gives money to a blind man and would
give nothing but a curse to a whole man, and if it was not for one
thing—but no matter anyway.

Lame Beggar. If I speak out all that's in my mind you won't take a
blow at me at all?   50

Blind Beggar. I will not this time.

Lame Beggar. Then I'll tell you why you are not a great fool. When
you go out to pick up a chicken, or maybe a stray goose on the
road, or a cabbage from a neighbour's garden, I have to go riding

on your back; and if I want a goose, or a chicken, or a cabbage, I must have your two legs under me.

Blind Beggar. That's true now, and if we were whole men and went different ways, there'd be as much again between us.

Lame Beggar. And your own goods keep going from you because you are blind. 60

Blind Beggar. Rogues and thieves ye all are, but there are some I may have my eyes on yet.

Lame Beggar. Because there's no one to see a man slipping in at the door, or throwing a leg over the wall of a yard, you are a bitter temptation to many a poor man, and I say it's not right, it's not right at all. There are poor men that because you are blind will be delayed in Purgatory.

Blind Beggar. Though you are a rogue, Lame Man, maybe you are in the right.

Lame Beggar. And maybe we'll see the blessed saint this day, for 70 there's an odd one sees him, and maybe that will be a grander thing than having my two legs, though legs are a grand thing.

Blind Beggar. You're getting flighty again, Lame Man; what could be better for you than to have your two legs?

Lame Beggar. Do you think now will the saint put an ear on him at all, and we without an Ave or a Pater-noster to put before the prayer or after the prayer?

Blind Beggar. Wise though you are and flighty though you are, and you throwing eyes to the right of you and eyes to the left of you, there's many a thing you don't know about the heart of man. 80

Lame Beggar. But it stands to reason that he'd be put out and he maybe with a great liking for the Latin.

Blind Beggar. I have it in mind that the saint will be better pleased at us not knowing a prayer at all, and that we had best say what we want in plain language. What pleasure can he have in all that holy company kneeling at his well on holidays and Sundays, and they as innocent maybe as himself?

Lame Beggar. That's a strange thing to say, and do you say it as I or another might say it, or as a blind man?

Blind Beggar. I say it as a blind man, I say it because since I went 90 blind in the tenth year of my age, I have been hearing and remembering the knowledges of the world.

Lame Beggar. And you who are a blind man say that a saint, and he living in a pure well of water, would soonest be talking with a sinful man.

Blind Beggar. Do you mind what the beggar told you about the holy man in the big house at Laban?°

Lame Beggar. Nothing stays in my head, Blind Man.

Blind Beggar. What does he do but go knocking about the roads with an old lecher from the county of Mayo,° and he a woman-hater from the day of his birth! And what do they talk of by candle-light and by daylight? The old lecher does be telling over all the sins he committed, or maybe never committed at all, and the man of Laban does be trying to head him off and quiet him down that he may quit telling them. 100

Lame Beggar. Maybe it is converting him he is.

Blind Beggar. If you were a blind man you wouldn't say a foolish thing the like of that. He wouldn't have him different, no, not if he was to get all Ireland. If he was different, what would they find to talk about, will you answer me that now? 110

Lame Beggar. We have great wisdom between us, that's certain.

Blind Beggar. Now the Church says that it is a good thought, and a sweet thought, and a comfortable thought, that every man may have a saint to look after him, and I, being blind, give it out to all the world that the bigger the sinner the better pleased is the saint. I am sure and certain that Saint Colman would not have us two different from what we are.

Lame Beggar. I'll not give in to that, for, as I was saying, he has a great liking maybe for the Latin.

Blind Beggar. Is it contradicting me you are? Are you in reach of my arm? [*swinging stick*]. 120

Lame Beggar. I'm not, Blind Man, you couldn't touch me at all; but as I was saying—

First Musician [*speaking*]. Will you be cured or will you be blessed?

Lame Beggar. Lord save us, that is the saint's voice and we not on our knees.   [*They kneel.*

Blind Beggar. Is he standing before us, Lame Man?

Lame Beggar. I cannot see him at all. It is in the ash-tree he is, or up in the air.

First Musician. Will you be cured or will you be blessed?   130

Lame Beggar. There he is again.

Blind Beggar. I'll be cured of my blindness.

First Musician. I am a saint and lonely. Will you become blessed and stay blind and we will be together always?

Blind Beggar. No, no, your Reverence, if I have to choose, I'll have the sight of my two eyes, for those that have their sight are always stealing my things and telling me lies, and some maybe that are near me. So don't take it bad of me, Holy Man, that I ask the sight of my two eyes.

Lame Beggar. No one robs him and no one tells him lies, it's all in his   140
head, it is. He's had his tongue on me all day because he thinks I stole a sheep of his.

Blind Beggar. It was the feel of his sheepskin coat put it into my head, but my sheep was black, they say, and he tells me, Holy Man, that his sheepskin is of the most lovely white wool so that it is a joy to be looking at it.

First Musician. Lame Man, will you be cured or will you be blessed?

Lame Beggar. What would it be like to be blessed?

First Musician. You would be of the kin of the blessed saints and of the martyrs.   150

Lame Beggar. Is it true now that they have a book and that they write the names of the blessed in that book?

First Musician. Many a time I have seen the book, and your name would be in it.

Lame Beggar. It would be a grand thing to have two legs under me, but I have it in my mind that it would be a grander thing to have my name in that book.

First Musician. It would be a grander thing.

Lame Beggar. I will stay lame, Holy Man, and I will be blessed.

First Musician. In the name of the Father, the Son and the Holy   160
Spirit I give this Blind Man sight and I make this Lame Man blessed.

Blind Beggar. I see it all now, the blue sky and the big ash-tree and the well and the flat stone,—all as I have heard the people say— and the things the praying people put on the stone, the beads and the candles and the leaves torn out of prayer-books, and the hair-pins and the buttons. It is a great sight and a blessed sight, but I don't see yourself, Holy Man—is it up in the big tree you are?

Lame Beggar. Why, there he is in front of you and he laughing out of his wrinkled face.   170

Blind Beggar. Where, where?

Lame Beggar. Why, there, between you and the ash-tree.

Blind Beggar. There's nobody there—you're at your lies again.

Lame Beggar. I am blessed, and that is why I can see the holy saint.

Blind Beggar. But if I don't see the saint, there's something else I can see.

Lame Beggar. The blue sky and green leaves are a great sight, and a strange sight to one that has been long blind.

Blind Beggar. There is a stranger sight than that, and that is the skin of my own black sheep on your back.   180

Lame Beggar. Haven't I been telling you from the peep o' day that my sheepskin is that white it would dazzle you?

Blind Beggar. Are you so swept with the words that you've never thought that when I had my own two eyes, I'd see what colour was on it?

Lame Beggar [*very dejected*]. I never thought of that.

Blind Beggar. Are you that flighty?

Lame Beggar. I am that flighty. [*Cheering up.*] But am I not blessed, and it's a sin to speak against the blessed?

Blind Beggar. Well, I'll speak against the blessed, and I'll tell you   190 something more that I'll do. All the while you were telling me how, if I had my two eyes, I could pick up a chicken here and a goose there, while my neighbours were in bed, do you know what I was thinking?

Lame Beggar. Some wicked blind man's thought.

Blind Beggar. It was, and it's not gone from me yet. I was saying to myself, I have a long arm and a strong arm and a very weighty arm, and when I get my own two eyes I shall know where to hit.

Lame Beggar. Don't lay a hand on me. Forty years we've been knocking about the roads together, and I wouldn't have you   200 bring your soul into mortal peril.

Blind Beggar. I have been saying to myself, I shall know where to hit and how to hit and who to hit.

Lame Beggar. Do you not know that I am blessed? Would you be as bad as Caesar and as Herod and Nero and the other wicked emperors of antiquity?

Blind Beggar. Where'll I hit him, for the love of God, where'll I hit him?

> [*Blind Beggar beats Lame Beggar. The beating takes the form of a dance and is accompanied on drum and flute. The Blind Beggar goes out.*]

Lame Beggar. That is a soul lost, Holy Man.

First Musician. Maybe so. 210

Lame Beggar. I'd better be going, Holy Man, for he'll rouse the whole country against me.

First Musician. He'll do that.

Lame Beggar. And I have it in my mind not to even myself again with the martyrs, and the holy confessors, till I am more used to being blessed.

First Musician. Bend down your back.

Lame Beggar. What for, Holy Man?

First Musician. That I may get up on it.

Lame Beggar. But my lame legs would never bear the weight of you. 220

First Musician. I'm up now.

Lame Beggar. I don't feel you at all.

First Musician. I don't weigh more than a grasshopper.

Lame Beggar. You do not.

First Musician. Are you happy?

Lame Beggar. I would be if I was right sure I was blessed.

First Musician. Haven't you got me for a friend?

Lame Beggar. I have so.

First Musician. Then you're blessed.

Lame Beggar. Will you see that they put my name in the book? 230

First Musician. I will then.

Lame Beggar. Let us be going, Holy Man.

First Musician. But you must bless the road.

Lame Beggar. I haven't the right words.

First Musician. What do you want words for? Bow to what is before you, bow to what is behind you, bow to what is to the left of you, bow to what is to the right of you.

> [*The Lame Beggar begins to bow.*

First Musician. That's no good.

Lame Beggar. No good, Holy Man?

First Musician. No good at all. You must dance.   240

Lame Beggar. But how can I dance? Ain't I a lame man?

First Musician. Aren't you blessed?

Lame Beggar. Maybe so.

First Musician. Aren't you a miracle?

Lame Beggar. I am, Holy Man.

First Musician. Then dance, and that'll be a miracle.

> [*The Lame Beggar begins to dance, at first clumsily, moving about with his stick, then he throws away the stick and dances more and more quickly. Perhaps whenever he strikes the ground strongly with his lame foot the cymbals clash. He goes out dancing, after which follows the First Musician's song.*]

First Musician [*singing*].

> Minnaloushe creeps through the grass
> From moonlight place to place.
> The sacred moon overhead
> Has taken a new phase.   250
> Does Minnaloushe know that his pupils
> Will pass from change to change,
> And that from round to crescent,
> From crescent to round they range?
> Minnaloushe creeps through the grass
> Alone, important and wise,
> And lifts to the changing moon
> His changing eyes.

THE END

The Resurrection (1931)°

TO

JUNZO SATO°

PERSONS IN THE PLAY

The Hebrew	*The Syrian*
The Greek	*Christ*
Three Musicians	

*Before I had finished this play I saw that its subject-matter might make
it unsuited for the public stage in England or in Ireland. I had begun it
with an ordinary stage scene in the mind's eye, curtained walls, a win-
dow and door at back, a curtained door at left. I now changed the stage
directions and wrote songs for the unfolding and folding of the curtain
that it might be played in a studio or a drawing-room like my dance
plays, or at the Peacock Theatre° before a specially chosen audience. If
it is played at the Peacock Theatre the Musicians may sing the opening
and closing songs, as they pull apart or pull together the proscenium cur-
tain; the whole stage may be hung with curtains with an opening at the
left. While the play is in progress the Musicians will sit towards the right
of the audience, if at the Peacock, on the step which separates the stage
from the audience, or one on either side of the proscenium.*

[*Song for the unfolding and folding of the curtain*]

I

I saw a staring virgin stand
Where holy Dionysus died,°
And tear the heart out of his side,
And lay the heart upon her hand
And bear that beating heart away;
And then did all the Muses sing
Of Magnus Annus at the spring,
As though God's death were but a play.°

II

Another Troy must rise and set,
Another lineage feed the crow,

10

Another Argo's painted prow
Drive to a flashier bauble yet.°
The Roman Empire stood appalled:
It dropped the reins of peace and war
When that fierce virgin and her Star°
Out of the fabulous darkness called.

[*The Hebrew is discovered alone upon the stage; he has a sword or spear. The Musicians make faint drum-taps, or sound a rattle; the Greek enters through the audience from the left.*]

The Hebrew. Did you find out what the noise was?

The Greek. Yes, I asked a Rabbi.

The Hebrew. Were you not afraid?

The Greek. How could he know that I am called a Christian? I wore   20
the cap I brought from Alexandria. He said the followers of
Dionysus were parading the streets with rattles and drums; that
such a thing had never happened in this city before; that the
Roman authorities were afraid to interfere. The followers of
Dionysus have been out among the fields tearing a goat to pieces
and drinking its blood, and are now wandering through the
streets like a pack of wolves. The mob was so terrified of their
frenzy that it left them alone, or, as seemed more likely, so busy
hunting Christians it had time for nothing else. I turned to go,   30
but he called me back and asked where I lived. When I said out-
side the gates, he asked if it was true that the dead had broken out
of the cemeteries.

The Hebrew. We can keep the mob off for some minutes, long
enough for the Eleven° to escape over the roofs. I shall defend the
narrow stair between this and the street until I am killed, then
you will take my place. Why is not the Syrian here?

The Greek. I met him at the door and sent him on a message; he will
be back before long.

The Hebrew. The three of us will be few enough for the work in   40
hand.

The Greek [*glancing towards the opening at the left*]. What are they
doing now?

The Hebrew. While you were down below, James brought a loaf out
of a bag, and Nathanael° found a skin of wine. They put them on
the table. It was a long time since they had eaten anything. Then

they began to speak in low voices, and John spoke of the last time they had eaten in that room.

The Greek. They were thirteen then.°

The Hebrew. He said that Jesus divided bread and wine amongst   50
them. When John had spoken they sat still, nobody eating or drinking. If you stand here you will see them. That is Peter close to the window. He has been quite motionless for a long time, his head upon his breast.

The Greek. Is it true that when the soldier asked him if he were a follower of Jesus he denied it?

The Hebrew. Yes, it is true. James told me. Peter told the others what he had done. But when the moment came they were all afraid. I must not blame. I might have been no braver. What are we all but dogs who have lost their master?   60

The Greek. Yet you and I if the mob come will die rather than let it up that stair.

The Hebrew. Ah! That is different. I am going to draw that curtain; they must not hear what I am going to say. [*He draws curtain.*]

The Greek. I know what is in your mind.

The Hebrew. They are afraid because they do not know what to think. When Jesus was taken they could no longer believe him the Messiah. We can find consolation, but for the Eleven it was always complete light or complete darkness.

The Greek. Because they are so much older.   70

The Hebrew. No, no. You have only to look into their faces to see they were intended to be saints. They are unfitted for anything else. What makes you laugh?

The Greek. Something I can see through the window. There, where I am pointing. There, at the end of the street. [*They stand together looking out over the heads of the audience.*]

The Hebrew. I cannot see anything.

The Greek. The hill.

The Hebrew. That is Calvary.

The Greek. And the three crosses on the top of it. [*He laughs again.*]

The Hebrew. Be quiet. You do not know what you are doing. You   80
have gone out of your mind. You are laughing at Calvary.

The Greek. No, no. I am laughing because they thought they were nailing the hands of a living man upon the Cross, and all the time there was nothing there but a phantom.

The Hebrew. I saw him buried.

The Greek. We Greeks understand these things. No god has ever been buried; no god has ever suffered. Christ only seemed to be born, only seemed to eat, seemed to sleep, seemed to walk, seemed to die. I did not mean to tell you until I had proof. 90

The Hebrew. Proof?

The Greek. I shall have proof before nightfall.

The Hebrew. You talk wildly, but a masterless dog can bay the moon.

The Greek. No Jew can understand these things.

The Hebrew. It is you who do not understand. It is I and those men in there, perhaps, who begin to understand at last. He was nothing more than a man, the best man who ever lived. Nobody before him had so pitied human misery. He preached the coming of the Messiah because he thought the Messiah would take it 100 all upon himself. Then some day when he was very tired, after a long journey perhaps, he thought that he himself was the Messiah. He thought it because of all destinies it seemed the most terrible.

The Greek. How could a man think himself the Messiah?

The Hebrew. It was always foretold that he would be born of a woman.

The Greek. To say that a god can be born of a woman, carried in her womb, fed upon her breast, washed as children are washed, is the most terrible blasphemy. 110

The Hebrew. If the Messiah were not born of a woman he could not take away the sins of man. Every sin starts a stream of suffering, but the Messiah takes it all away.

The Greek. Every man's sins are his property. Nobody else has a right to them.

The Hebrew. The Messiah is able to exhaust human suffering as though it were all gathered together in the spot of a burning-glass.

The Greek. That makes me shudder. The utmost possible suffering
as an object of worship! You are morbid because your nation has   120
no statues.

The Hebrew. What I have described is what I thought until three
days ago.

The Greek. I say that there is nothing in the tomb.

The Hebrew. I saw him carried up the mountain and the tomb shut
upon him.

The Greek. I have sent the Syrian to the tomb to prove that there is
nothing there.

The Hebrew. You knew the danger we were all in and yet you weak-
ened our guard?   130

The Greek. I have risked the apostles' lives and our own. What I
have sent the Syrian to find out is more important.

The Hebrew. None of us are in our right mind to-day. I have got
something in my own head that shocks me.

The Greek. Something you do not want to speak about?

The Hebrew. I am glad that he was not the Messiah; we might all
have been deceived to our lives' end, or learnt the truth too late.
One had to sacrifice everything that the divine suffering might,
as it were, descend into one's mind and soul and make them pure.
[*A sound of rattles and drums, at first in short bursts that come
between sentences, but gradually growing continuous.*] One had to   140
give up all worldly knowledge, all ambition, do nothing of one's
own will. Only the divine could have any reality. God had to take
complete possession. It must be a terrible thing when one is old,
and the tomb round the corner, to think of all the ambitions one
has put aside; to think, perhaps, a great deal about women. I want
to marry and have children.

The Greek [*who is standing facing the audience, and looking out over
their heads*]. It is the worshippers of Dionysus. They are under
the window now. There is a group of women who carry upon
their shoulders a bier with an image of the dead god upon it.
No, they are not women. They are men dressed as women. I   150
have seen something like it in Alexandria. They are all silent, as
if something were going to happen. My God! What a spectacle!
In Alexandria a few men paint their lips vermilion. They
imitate women that they may attain in worship a woman's

self-abandonment. No great harm comes of it—but here! Come
and look for yourself.

The Hebrew. I will not look at such madmen.

The Greek. Though the music has stopped some men are still dan-
cing, and some of the dancers have gashed themselves with
knives, imagining themselves, I suppose, at once the god and the   160
Titans that murdered him.° A little further off a man and woman
are coupling in the middle of the street. She thinks the surrender
to some man the dance threw into her arms may bring her god
back to life. All are from the foreign quarter, to judge by face and
costume, and are the most ignorant and excitable class of Asiatic
Greeks, the dregs of the population. Such people suffer terribly
and seek forgetfulness in monstrous ceremonies. Ah, that is what
they were waiting for. The crowd has parted to make way for a
singer. It is a girl. No, not a girl; a boy from the theatre. I know
him. He acts girls' parts. He is dressed as a girl, but his finger-   170
nails are gilded and his wig is made of gilded cords. He looks like
a statue out of some temple. I remember something of the kind in
Alexandria. Three days after the full moon, a full moon in
March, they sing the death of the god and pray for his resurrec-
tion.

> [*One of the Musicians sings the following song*]
>
> > Astrea's holy child!°
> > A rattle in the wood
> > Where a Titan strode!
> > His rattle drew the child
> > Into that solitude.   180

Barrum Barrum Barrum [*Drum-taps accompany and follow the
words*].

> > We wandering women,
> > Wives for all that come,
> > Tried to draw him home;
> > And every wandering woman
> > Beat upon a drum.

Barrum Barrum Barrum [*Drum-taps as before*].

> > But the murderous Titans
> > Where the woods grow dim
> > Stood and waited him.   190
> > The great hands of those Titans

Tore limb from limb.
Barrum Barrum Barrum [*Drum-taps as before*].

On virgin Astrea
That can succour all
Wandering women call;
Call out to Astrea
That the moon stood at the full.
Barrum Barrum Barrum [*Drum-taps as before*].

The Greek. I cannot think all that self-surrender and self-abasement   200
is Greek, despite the Greek name of its god. When the goddess
came to Achilles in the battle° she did not interfere with his soul,
she took him by his yellow hair. Lucretius° thinks that the gods
appear in the visions of the day and night but are indifferent to
human fate; that, however, is the exaggeration of a Roman
rhetorician. They can be discovered by contemplation, in their
faces a high keen joy like the cry of a bat, and the man who lives
heroically gives them the only earthly body that they covet. He,
as it were, copies their gestures and their acts. What seems their
indifference is but their eternal possession of themselves. Man,   210
too, remains separate. He does not surrender his soul. He keeps
his privacy.

[*Drum-taps to represent knocking at the door*]

The Hebrew. There is someone at the door, but I dare not open with
that crowd in the street.

The Greek. You need not be afraid. The crowd has begun to move
away. [*The Hebrew goes down into the audience towards the left*.] I
deduce from our great philosophers that a god can overwhelm
man with disaster, take health and wealth away, but man keeps
his privacy. If that is the Syrian he may bring such confirmation
that mankind will never forget his words.   220

The Hebrew [*from amongst the audience*]. It is the Syrian. There is
something wrong. He is ill or drunk. [*He helps the Syrian on to the
stage*.]

The Syrian. I am like a drunken man. I can hardly stand upon my
feet. Something incredible has happened. I have run all the way.

The Hebrew. Well?

The Syrian. I must tell the Eleven at once. Are they still in there?
Everybody must be told.

The Hebrew. What is it? Get your breath and speak.

The Syrian. I was on my way to the tomb. I met the Galilean
women, Mary the mother of Jesus, Mary the mother of James,　230
and the other women. The younger women were pale with
excitement and began to speak all together. I did not know what
they were saying; but Mary the mother of James said that they
had been to the tomb at daybreak and found that it was empty.

The Greek. Ah!

The Hebrew. The tomb cannot be empty. I will not believe it.

The Syrian. At the door stood a man all shining, and cried out that
Christ had arisen. [*Faint drum-taps and the faint sound of a rattle.*]
As they came down the mountain a man stood suddenly at their
side; that man was Christ himself. They stooped down and　240
kissed his feet. Now stand out of my way that I may tell Peter and
James and John.

The Hebrew [*standing before the curtained entrance of the inner room*].
I will not stand out of the way.

The Syrian. Did you hear what I said? Our master has arisen.

The Hebrew. I will not have the Eleven disturbed for the dreams of
women.

The Greek. The women were not dreaming. They told you the
truth, and yet this man is in the right. He is in charge here. We
must all be convinced before we speak to the Eleven.

The Syrian. The Eleven will be able to judge better than we.　250

The Greek. Though we are so much younger we know more of the
world than they do.

The Hebrew. If you told your story they would no more believe
it than I do, but Peter's misery would be increased. I know
him longer than you do and I know what would happen. Peter
would remember that the women did not flinch; that not one
amongst them denied her master; that the dream proved their
love and faith. Then he would remember that he had lacked both,
and imagine that John was looking at him. He would turn away
and bury his head in his hands.　260

The Greek. I said that we must all be convinced, but there is another
reason why you must not tell them anything. Somebody else is
coming. I am certain that Jesus never had a human body; that he

is a phantom and can pass through that wall; that he will so pass; that he will pass through this room; that he himself will speak to the apostles.

The Syrian. He is no phantom. We put a great stone over the mouth° of the tomb, and the women say that it has been rolled back.

The Hebrew. The Romans heard yesterday that some of our people   270 planned to steal the body, and to put abroad a story that Christ had arisen; and so escape the shame of our defeat. They probably stole it in the night.

The Syrian. The Romans put sentries at the tomb. The women found the sentries asleep. Christ had put them asleep that they might not see him move the stone.

The Greek. A hand without bones, without sinews, cannot move a stone.

The Syrian. What matter if it contradicts all human knowledge?— another Argo seeks another fleece, another Troy° is sacked.   280

The Greek. Why are you laughing?

The Syrian. What is human knowledge?

The Greek. The knowledge that keeps the road from here to Persia free from robbers, that has built the beautiful humane cities, that has made the modern world, that stands between us and the barbarian.

The Syrian. But what if there is something it cannot explain, something more important than anything else?

The Greek. You talk as if you wanted the barbarian back.

The Syrian. What if there is always something that lies outside   290 knowledge, outside order? What if at the moment when knowledge and order seem complete that something appears?

                                      [*He has begun to laugh.*

The Hebrew. Stop laughing.

The Syrian. What if the irrational return? What if the circle begin again?

The Hebrew. Stop! He laughed when he saw Calvary through the window, and now you laugh.

The Greek. He too has lost control of himself.

The Hebrew. Stop, I tell you. [*Drums and rattles*.]

The Syrian. But I am not laughing. It is the people out there who are   300
laughing.

The Hebrew. No, they are shaking rattles and beating drums.

The Syrian. I thought they were laughing. How horrible!

The Greek [*looking out over heads of audience*]. The worshippers of
Dionysus are coming this way again. They have hidden their
image of the dead god, and have begun their lunatic cry, 'God has
arisen! God has arisen!'

> [*The Musicians who have been saying* 'God has arisen!' *fall
> silent*.]

They will cry 'God has arisen!' through all the streets of the city.
They can make their god live and die at their pleasure; but why
are they silent? They are dancing silently. They are coming   310
nearer and nearer dancing all the while, using some kind of
ancient step unlike anything I have seen in Alexandria. They are
almost under the window now.

The Hebrew. They have come back to mock us, because their god
arises every year, whereas our god is dead for ever.

The Greek. How they roll their painted eyes as the dance grows
quicker and quicker! They are under the window. Why are they
all suddenly motionless? Why are all those unseeing eyes turned
upon this house? Is there anything strange about this house?

The Hebrew. Somebody has come into the room.   320

The Greek. Where?

The Hebrew. I do not know; but I thought I heard a step.

The Greek. I knew that he would come.

The Hebrew. There is no one here. I shut the door at the foot of the
steps.

The Greek. The curtain over there is moving.

The Hebrew. No, it is quite still, and besides there is nothing behind
it but a blank wall.

The Greek. Look, look!

The Hebrew. Yes, it has begun to move. [*During what follows he backs*   330
in terror towards the left-hand corner of the stage.]

The Greek. There is someone coming through it.

[*The figure of Christ wearing a recognisable but stylistic mask enters through the curtain. The Syrian slowly draws back the curtain that shuts off the inner room where the apostles are. The three young men are towards the left of the stage, the figure of Christ is at the back towards the right.*

The Greek. It is the phantom of our master. Why are you afraid? He has been crucified and buried, but only in semblance, and is among us once more. [*The Hebrew kneels.*] There is nothing here but a phantom, it has no flesh and blood. Because I know the truth I am not afraid. Look, I will touch it. It may be hard under my hand like a statue—I have heard of such things—or my hand may pass through it—but there is no flesh and blood. [*He goes slowly up to the figure and passes his hand over its side.*] The heart of a phantom is beating! The heart of a phantom is beating! [*He* 340 *screams. The figure of Christ crosses the stage and passes into the inner room.*]

The Syrian. He is standing in the midst of them. Some are afraid. He looks at Peter and James and John. He smiles. He has parted the clothes at his side. He shows them his side. There is a great wound there. Thomas has put his hand into the wound.° He has put his hand where the heart is.

The Greek. O Athens, Alexandria, Rome, something has come to destroy you. The heart of a phantom is beating. Man has begun to die. Your words are clear at last, O Heraclitus. God and man die each other's life, live each other's death.°

[*The Musicians rise, one or more singing the following words. If the performance is in a private room or studio, they unfold and fold a curtain as in my dance plays; if at the Peacock Theatre, they draw the proscenium curtain across.*]

I

In pity for man's darkening thought 350
He walked that room and issued thence
In Galilean turbulence;
The Babylonian starlight brought
A fabulous, formless darkness in;
Odour of blood when Christ was slain
Made all Platonic tolerance vain
And vain all Doric discipline.°

II

Everything that man esteems
Endures a moment or a day:
Love's pleasure drives his love away,   360
The painter's brush consumes his dreams;
The herald's cry, the soldier's tread
Exhaust his glory and his might:
Whatever flames upon the night
Man's own resinous heart has fed.

THE END

The Words upon the Window-Pane (1934)°

PERSONS IN THE PLAY

Dr Trench	*Cornelius Patterson*
Miss Mackenna	*Abraham Johnson*
John Corbet	*Mrs Mallet*
Mrs Henderson	

A lodging-house room, an armchair, a little table in front of it, chairs on either side. A fireplace and window. A kettle on the hob and some tea-things on a dresser. A door to back and towards the right. Through the door one can see an entrance hall. The sound of a knocker. Miss Mackenna passes through and then she re-enters hall together with John Corbet, a man of twenty-two or twenty-three, and Dr Trench, a man of between sixty and seventy.

Dr Trench [*in hall*]. May I introduce John Corbet, one of the Corbets of Ballymoney,° but at present a Cambridge student? This is Miss Mackenna, our energetic secretary. [*They come into room, take off their coats.*]

Miss Mackenna. I thought it better to let you in myself. This country is still sufficiently medieval to make spiritualism an undesirable theme for gossip. Give me your coats and hats, I will put them in my own room. It is just across the hall. Better sit down, your watches must be fast. Mrs Henderson is lying down, as she always does before a séance. We won't begin for ten minutes yet.

[*She goes out with hats and coats.*

Dr Trench. Miss Mackenna does all the real work of the Dublin   10
Spiritualists' Association. She did all the correspondence with Mrs Henderson, and persuaded the landlady to let her this big room and a small room upstairs. We are a poor society and could not guarantee anything in advance. Mrs Henderson has come from London at her own risk. She was born in Dublin and wants to spread the movement here. She lives very economically and

does not expect a great deal. We all give what we can. A poor woman with the soul of an apostle.

John Corbet. Have there been many séances?

Dr Trench. Only three so far.   20

John Corbet. I hope she will not mind my scepticism. I have looked into Myers' *Human Personality*° and a wild book by Conan Doyle,° but am unconvinced.

Dr Trench. We all have to find the truth for ourselves. Lord Dunraven,° then Lord Adare, introduced my father to the famous David Home.° My father often told me that he saw David Home floating in the air in broad daylight, but I did not believe a word of it. I had to investigate for myself, and I was very hard to convince. Mrs Piper, an American trance medium, not unlike Mrs Henderson, convinced me.   30

John Corbet. A state of somnambulism and voices coming through her lips that purport to be those of dead persons?

Dr Trench. Exactly: quite the best kind of mediumship if you want to establish the identity of a spirit. But do not expect too much. There has been a hostile influence.

John Corbet. You mean an evil spirit?

Dr Trench. The poet Blake said that he never knew a bad man that had not something very good about him. I say a hostile influence, an influence that disturbed the last séance very seriously. I cannot tell you what happened, for I have not been at any of Mrs   40
Henderson's séances. Trance mediumship has nothing new to show me—I told the young people when they made me their President that I would probably stay at home, that I could get more out of Emanuel Swedenborg° than out of any séance. [*A knock.*] That is probably old Cornelius Patterson; he thinks they race horses and whippets in the other world, and is, so they tell me, so anxious to find out if he is right that he is always punctual. Miss Mackenna will keep him to herself for some minutes. He gives her tips for Harold's Cross.°

   [*Miss Mackenna crosses to hall door and admits Cornelius Patterson. She brings him to her room across the hall.*]

John Corbet [*who has been wandering about*]. This is a wonderful   50
room for a lodging-house.

Dr Trench. It was a private house until about fifty years ago. It was not so near the town in those days, and there are large stables at the back. Quite a number of notable people lived here. Grattan° was born upstairs—no, not Grattan, Curran° perhaps—I forget— but I do know that this house in the early part of the eighteenth century belonged to friends of Jonathan Swift,° or rather of Stella. Swift chaffed her in the *Journal to Stella*° because of cer- tain small sums of money she lost at cards probably in this very room. That was before Vanessa° appeared upon the scene. It was   60 a country house in those days, surrounded by trees and gardens. Somebody cut some lines from a poem of hers upon the window- pane°—tradition says Stella herself. [*A knock.*] Here they are, but you will hardly make them out in this light. [*They stand in the window. Corbet stoops down to see better. Miss Mackenna and Abra- ham Johnson enter and stand near door.*]

Abraham Johnson. Where is Mrs Henderson?

Miss Mackenna. She is upstairs; she always rests before a séance.

Abraham Johnson. I must see her before the séance. I know exactly what to do to get rid of this evil influence.

Miss Mackenna. If you go up to see her there will be no séance at all. She says it is dangerous even to think, much less to speak of, an   70 evil influence.

Abraham Johnson. Then I shall speak to the President.

Miss Mackenna. Better talk the whole thing over first in my room. Mrs Henderson says that there must be perfect harmony.

Abraham Johnson. Something must be done. The last séance was completely spoiled. [*A knock.*]

Miss Mackenna. That may be Mrs Mallet; she is a very experienced spiritualist. Come to my room, old Patterson and some others are there already. [*She brings him to the other room and later crosses to hall door to admit Mrs Mallet.*]

John Corbet. I know those lines well—they are part of a poem Stella   80 wrote for Swift's fifty-fourth birthday.° Only three poems of hers—and some lines she added to a poem of Swift's have come down to us, but they are enough to prove her a better poet than Swift. Even those few words on the window make me think of a seventeenth-century poet, Donne° or Crashaw.° [*He quotes*]

> 'You taught how I might youth prolong
> By knowing what is right and wrong,

How from my heart to bring supplies
Of lustre to my fading eyes.'°

How strange that a celibate scholar, well on in life, should keep   90
the love of two such women! He met Vanessa in London at the
height of his political power. She followed him to Dublin. She
loved him for nine years, perhaps died of love, but Stella loved
him all her life.

Dr Trench. I have shown that writing to several persons and you are
the first who has recognised the lines.

John Corbet. I am writing an essay on Swift and Stella for my doc-
torate at Cambridge. I hope to prove that in Swift's day men of
intellect reached the height of their power—the greatest position
they ever attained in society and the State, that everything great   100
in Ireland and in our character, in what remains of our architec-
ture, comes from that day; that we have kept its seal longer than
England.

Dr Trench. A tragic life: Bolingbroke, Harley, Ormonde,° all those
great Ministers that were his friends, banished and broken.

John Corbet. I do not think you can explain him in that way—his
tragedy had deeper foundations, his ideal order was the Roman
Senate, his ideal men Brutus and Cato.° Such an order and such
men had seemed possible once more, but the movement passed
and he foresaw the ruin to come, Democracy, Rousseau,° the   110
French Revolution; that is why he hated the common run of
men—'I hate lawyers, I hate doctors,' he said, 'though I love
Dr So-and-so and Judge So-and so'—that is why he wrote *Gul-
liver*, that is why he wore out his brain, that is why he felt *saeva
indignatio*,° that is why he sleeps under the greatest epitaph in
history. You remember how it goes? It is almost finer in English
than in Latin: 'He has gone where fierce indignation can lacerate
his heart no more.'

[*Abraham Johnson comes in, followed by Mrs Mallet and Cor-
nelius Patterson.*]

Abraham Johnson. Something must be done, Dr Trench, to drive
away the influence that has destroyed our séances. I have come   120
here week after week at considerable expense. I am from Belfast.
I am by profession a minister of the Gospel, I do a great deal of
work among the poor and ignorant. I produce considerable effect
by singing and preaching, but I know that my effect should be

much greater than it is. My hope is that I shall be able to communicate with the great Evangelist Sankey. I want to ask him to stand invisible beside me when I speak or sing, and lay his hands upon my head and give me such a portion of his power that my work may be blessed as the work of Moody and Sankey was blessed.   130

Mrs Mallet. What Mr Johnson says about the hostile influence is quite true. The last two séances were completely spoilt. I am thinking of starting a tea-shop in Folkestone. I followed Mrs Henderson to Dublin to get my husband's advice, but two spirits kept talking and would not let any other spirit say a word.

Dr Trench. Did the spirits say the same thing and go through the same drama at both séances?

Mrs Mallet. Yes—just as if they were characters in some kind of horrible play.

Dr Trench. That is what I was afraid of.   140

Mrs Mallet. My husband was drowned at sea ten years ago, but constantly speaks to me through Mrs Henderson as if he were still alive. He advises me about everything I do, and I am utterly lost if I cannot question him.

Cornelius Patterson. I never did like the Heaven they talk about in churches: but when somebody told me that Mrs Mallet's husband ate and drank and went about with his favourite dog, I said to myself, 'That is the place for Corney Patterson'. I came here to find out if it was true, and I declare to God I have not heard one word about it.   150

Abraham Johnson. I ask you, Dr Trench, as President of the Dublin Spiritualists' Association, to permit me to read the ritual of exorcism appointed for such occasions. After the last séance I copied it out of an old book in the library of Belfast University. I have it here.

                              [*He takes paper out of his pocket.*

Dr Trench. The spirits are people like ourselves, we treat them as our guests and protect them from discourtesy and violence, and every exorcism is a curse or a threatened curse. We do not admit that there are evil spirits. Some spirits are earth-bound°—they think they are still living and go over and over some action of   160
their past lives, just as we go over and over some painful thought,

except that where they are thought is reality. For instance, when a spirit which has died a violent death comes to a medium for the first time, it re-lives all the pains of death.

Mrs Mallet. When my husband came for the first time the medium gasped and struggled as if she was drowning. It was terrible to watch.

Dr Trench. Sometimes a spirit re-lives° not the pain of death but some passionate or tragic moment of life. Swedenborg° describes this and gives the reason for it. There is an incident of the kind in 170 the *Odyssey*, and many in Eastern literature; the murderer repeats his murder, the robber his robbery, the lover his sere-nade, the soldier hears the trumpet once again. If I were a Catholic I would say that such spirits were in Purgatory. In vain do we write *requiescat in pace* upon the tomb, for they must suf-fer, and we in our turn must suffer until God gives peace. Such spirits do not often come to séances unless those séances are held in houses where those spirits lived, or where the event took place. This spirit which speaks those incomprehensible words and does not answer when spoken to is of such a nature. The more patient 180 we are, the more quickly will it pass out of its passion and its remorse.

Abraham Johnson. I am still convinced that the spirit which dis-turbed the last séance is evil. If I may not exorcise it I will cer-tainly pray for protection.

Dr Trench. Mrs Henderson's control, Lulu, is able and experienced and can protect both medium and sitters, but it may help Lulu if you pray that the spirit find rest.

> [*Abraham Johnson sits down and prays silently, moving his lips. Mrs Henderson comes in with Miss Mackenna and others. Miss Mackenna shuts the door.*]

Dr Trench. Mrs Henderson, may I introduce to you Mr Corbet, a young man from Cambridge and a sceptic, who hopes that you 190 will be able to convince him?

Mrs Henderson. We were all sceptics once. He must not expect too much from a first séance. He must persevere. [*She sits in the arm-chair and the others begin to seat themselves. Miss Mackenna goes to John Corbet and they remain standing.*]

Miss Mackenna. I am glad that you are a sceptic.

John Corbet. I thought you were a spiritualist.

Miss Mackenna. I have seen a good many séances, and sometimes think it is all coincidence and thought-transference. [*She says this in a low voice.*] Then at other times I think as Dr Trench does, and then I feel like Job—you know the quotation°—the hair of my head stands up. A spirit passes before my face. 200

Mrs Mallet. Turn the key, Dr Trench, we don't want anybody blundering in here. [*Dr Trench locks door.*] Come and sit here, Miss Mackenna.

Miss Mackenna. No, I am going to sit beside Mr Corbet.

[*Corbet and Miss Mackenna sit down.*]

John Corbet. You feel like Job to-night?

Miss Mackenna. I feel that something is going to happen, that is why I am glad that you are a sceptic.

John Corbet. You feel safer?

Miss Mackenna. Yes, safer.

Mrs Henderson. I am glad to meet all my dear friends again and to 210 welcome Mr Corbet amongst us. As he is a stranger I must explain that we do not call up spirits, we make the right conditions and they come. I do not know who is going to come; sometimes there are a great many and the guides choose between them. The guides try to send somebody for everybody but do not always succeed. If you want to speak to some dear friend who has passed over, do not be discouraged. If your friend cannot come this time, maybe he can next time. My control is a dear little girl called Lulu who died when she was five or six years old. She describes the spirits present and tells us what spirit wants to 220 speak. Miss Mackenna, a verse of a hymn, please, the same we had last time, and will everyone join in the singing.

[*They sing the following lines from Hymn 564,° Dublin Church Hymnal.*]

Sun of my soul, Thou Saviour dear,
It is not night if Thou be near:
O may no earth-born cloud arise
To hide Thee from Thy servant's eyes.'

[*Mrs Henderson is leaning back in her chair asleep.*]

Miss Mackenna [*to John Corbet*]. She always snores like that when she is going off.

Mrs Henderson [*in a child's voice*]. That bad man, that bad old man in the corner, they have let him come back. Lulu is going to scream. O.... O.... [*in a man's voice*]. How dare you write to her? How dare you ask if we were married? How dare you question her?

Dr Trench. A soul in its agony—it cannot see us or hear us.

Mrs Henderson [*upright and rigid, only her lips moving, and still in a man's voice*]. You sit crouching there. Did you not hear what I   270 said? How dared you question her? I found you an ignorant little girl without intellect, without moral ambition. How many times did I not stay away from great men's houses, how many times forsake the Lord Treasurer,° how many times neglect the business of the State that we might read Plutarch° together?

[*Abraham Johnson half rises. Dr Trench motions him to remain seated.*]

Dr Trench. Silence!

Abraham Johnson. But, Dr Trench . . .

Dr Trench. Hush—we can do nothing.

Mrs Henderson [*speaking as before*]. I taught you to think in every situation of life not as Hester Vanhomrigh° would think in that sit-   280 uation, but as Cato or Brutus° would, and now you behave like some common slut with her ear against the keyhole.

John Corbet [*to Miss Mackenna*]. It is Swift, Jonathan Swift, talking to the woman he called Vanessa. She was christened Hester Vanhomrigh.

Mrs Henderson [*in Vanessa's voice*]. I questioned her, Jonathan, because I love. Why have you let me spend hours in your company if you did not want me to love you? [*In Swift's voice.*] When I re-built Rome in your mind it was as though I walked its streets. [*In Vanessa's voice*]. Was that all, Jonathan? Was I nothing but a   290 painter's canvas? [*In Swift's voice.*] My God, do you think it was easy? I was a man of strong passions and I had sworn never to marry. [*In Vanessa's voice.*] If you and she are not married, why should we not marry like other men and women? I loved you from the first moment when you came to my mother's house and began to teach me. I thought it would be enough to look at you, to speak to you, to hear you speak. I followed you to Ireland five years ago and I can bear it no longer. It is not enough to look, to

speak, to hear. Jonathan, Jonathan, I am a woman, the women
Brutus and Cato loved were not different. [*In Swift's voice.*] I   300
have something in my blood that no child must inherit. I have
constant attacks of dizziness;° I pretend they come from a surfeit
of fruit when I was a child. I had them in London. . . . There was
a great doctor there, Dr Arbuthnot,° I told him of those attacks of
dizziness, I told him of worse things. It was he who explained.
There is a line of Dryden's°. . . . [*In Vanessa's voice.*] O, I know—
'Great wits are sure to madness near allied'. If you had children,
Jonathan, my blood would make them healthy. I will take your
hand, I will lay it upon my heart—upon the Vanhomrigh blood
that has been healthy for generations. [*Mrs Henderson slowly*   310
raises her left hand.] That is the first time you have touched my
body, Jonathan. [*Mrs Henderson stands up and remains rigid. In*
Swift's voice.] What do I care if it be healthy? What do I care if it
could make mine healthy? Am I to add another to the healthy ras-
caldom and knavery of the world? [*In Vanessa's voice.*] Look at
me, Jonathan. Your arrogant intellect separates us. Give me both
your hands. I will put them upon my breast. [*Mrs Henderson*
raises her right hand to the level of her left and then raises both to her
breast.] O, it is white—white as the gambler's dice—white ivory
dice. Think of the uncertainty. Perhaps a mad child—perhaps a
rascal—Perhaps a knave—perhaps not, Jonathan. The dice of   320
the intellect are loaded, but I am the common ivory dice. [*Her*
hands are stretched out as though drawing somebody towards her.] It
is not my hands that draw you back. My hands are weak, they
could not draw you back if you did not love as I love. You said
that you have strong passions; that is true, Jonathan—no man in
Ireland is so passionate. That is why you need me, that is why you
need children, nobody has greater need. You are growing old. An
old man without children is very solitary. Even his friends, men
as old as he, turn away, they turn towards the young, their chil-
dren or their children's children. They cannot endure an old   330
man like themselves. [*Mrs Henderson moves away from the chair,*
her movements gradually growing convulsive.] You are not too old
for the dice, Jonathan, but a few years if you turn away will make
you an old miserable childless man. [*In Swift's voice.*] O God,
hear the prayer of Jonathan Swift, that afflicted man, and grant
that he may leave to posterity nothing but his intellect that came
to him from Heaven. [*In Vanessa's voice.*] Can you face solitude
with that mind, Jonathan? [*Mrs Henderson goes to the door, finds*

that it is closed.] Dice, white ivory dice. [*In Swift's voice.*] My
God, I am left alone with my enemy. Who locked the door, who 340
locked me in with my enemy? [*Mrs Henderson beats upon the door,
sinks to the floor and then speaks as Lulu.*] Bad old man! Do not let
him come back. Bad old man does not know he is dead. Lulu can-
not find fathers, mothers, sons that have passed over. Power
almost gone. [*Mrs Mallet leads Mrs Henderson, who seems very
exhausted, back to her chair. She is still asleep. She speaks again as
Lulu.*] Another verse of hymn. Everybody sing. Hymn will bring
good influence.

[*They sing*]

'If some poor wandering child of Thine°
Have spurned to-day the voice divine,
Now, Lord, the gracious work begin;   350
Let him no more lie down in sin.'

[*During the hymn Mrs Henderson has been murmuring
'Stella', but the singing has almost drowned her voice. The
singers draw one another's attention to the fact that she is speak-
ing. The singing stops.*]

Dr Trench. I thought she was speaking.

Mrs Mallet. I saw her lips move.

Dr Trench. She would be more comfortable with a cushion, but we
might wake her.

Mrs Mallet. Nothing can wake her out of a trance like that until she
wakes up herself. [*She brings a cushion and she and Dr Trench put
Mrs Henderson into a more comfortable position.*]

Mrs Henderson [*in Swift's voice*]. Stella.

Miss Mackenna [*to John Corbet*]. Did you hear that? She said
'Stella'.   360

John Corbet. Vanessa has gone, Stella has taken her place.

Miss Mackenna. Did you notice the change while we were singing?
The new influence in the room?

John Corbet. I thought I did, but it must have been fancy.

Mrs Mallet. Hush!

Mrs Henderson [*in Swift's voice*]. Have I wronged you, beloved
Stella? Are you unhappy? You have no children, you have no
lover, you have no husband. A cross and ageing man for friend—

nothing but that. But no, do not answer—you have answered
already in that poem you wrote for my last birthday. With what 370
scorn you speak of the common lot of women 'with no adorn-
ment but a face—'°

> 'Before the thirtieth year of life
> A maid forlorn or hated wife.'

It is the thought of the great Chrysostom° who wrote in a famous
passage that women loved according to the soul, loved as saints
can love, keep their beauty longer, have greater happiness than
women loved according to the flesh. That thought has comforted
me, but it is a terrible thing to be responsible for another's happi-
ness. There are moments when I doubt, when I think Chrysos- 380
tom may have been wrong. But now I have your poem to drive
doubt away. You have addressed me in these noble words:

> 'You taught how I might youth prolong°
> By knowing what is right and wrong;
> How from my heart to bring supplies
> Of lustre to my fading eyes;
> How soon a beauteous mind repairs
> The loss of chang'd or falling hairs;
> How wit and virtue from within
> Can spread a smoothness o'er the skin.' 390

John Corbet. The words upon the window-pane!

Mrs Henderson [*in Swift's voice*]. Then, because you understand
that I am afraid of solitude, afraid of outliving my friends—and
myself—you comfort me in that last verse—you overpraise my
moral nature when you attribute to it a rich mantle, but O how
touching those words which describe your love:

> 'Late dying, may you cast a shred
> Of that rich mantle o'er my head;
> To bear with dignity my sorrow,
> One day alone, then die to-morrow.' 400

Yes, you will close my eyes, Stella. O, you will live long after me,
dear Stella, for you are still a young woman, but you will close my
eyes. [*Mrs Henderson sinks back in chair and speaks as Lulu.*] Bad
old man gone. Power all used up. Lulu can do no more Good-
bye, friends. [*Mrs Henderson, speaking in her own voice.*] Go away,
go away! [*She wakes.*] I saw him a moment ago, has he spoilt the
séance again?

Mrs Mallet. Yes, Mrs Henderson, my husband came, but he was driven away.

Dr Trench. Mrs Henderson is very tired. We must leave her to rest. 410 [*To Mrs Henderson.*] You did your best and nobody can do more than that. [*He takes out money.*]

Mrs Henderson. No. . . . No. . . . I cannot take any money, not after a séance like that.

Dr Trench. Of course you must take it, Mrs Henderson. [*He puts money on table, and Mrs Henderson gives a furtive glance to see how much it is. She does the same as each sitter lays down his or her money.*]

Mrs Mallet. A bad séance is just as exhausting as a good séance, and you must be paid.

Mrs Henderson. No. . . . No. . . . Please don't. It is very wrong to take money for such a failure.

[*Mrs Mallet lays down money.*

Cornelius Patterson. A jockey is paid whether he wins or not. [*He* 420 *lays down money.*]

Miss Mackenna. That spirit rather thrilled me. [*She lays down money.*]

Mrs Henderson. If you insist, I must take it.

Abraham Johnson. I shall pray for you to-night. I shall ask God to bless and protect your séances. [*He lays down money.*]

[*All go out except John Corbet and Mrs Henderson.*

John Corbet. I know you are tired, Mrs Henderson, but I must speak to you. I have been deeply moved by what I have heard. This is my contribution to prove that I am satisfied, completely satisfied. [*He puts a note on the table.*]

Mrs Henderson. A pound note—nobody ever gives me more than ten shillings, and yet the séance was a failure.

John Corbet [*sitting down near Mrs Henderson*]. When I say I am sat- 430 isfied I do not mean that I am convinced it was the work of spir- its. I prefer to think that you created it all, that you are an accomplished actress and scholar. In my essay for my Cambridge doctorate I examine all the explanations of Swift's celibacy offered by his biographers and prove that the explanation you selected was the only plausible one. But there is something I

must ask you. Swift was the chief representative of the intellect
of his epoch, that arrogant intellect free at last from superstition.
He foresaw its collapse. He foresaw Democracy, he must have
dreaded the future. Did he refuse to beget children because of   440
that dread? Was Swift mad? Or was it the intellect itself that was
mad?

Mrs Henderson. Who are you talking of, sir?

John Corbet. Swift, of course.

Mrs Henderson. Swift? I do not know anybody called Swift.

John Corbet. Jonathan Swift, whose spirit seemed to be present
to-night.

Mrs Henderson. What? That dirty old man?

John Corbet. He was neither old nor dirty when Stella and Vanessa
loved him.   450

Mrs Henderson. I saw him very clearly just as I woke up. His clothes
were dirty, his face covered with boils. Some disease had made
one of his eyes swell up, it stood out from his face like a hen's egg.

John Corbet. He looked like that in his old age. Stella had been dead
a long time. His brain had gone, his friends had deserted him.
The man appointed to take care of him beat him to keep him
quiet.

Mrs Henderson. Now they are old, now they are young. They
change all in a moment as their thought changes. It is sometimes
a terrible thing to be out of the body, God help us all.   460

Dr Trench [*at doorway*]. Come along, Corbet, Mrs Henderson is
tired out.

John Corbet. Good-bye, Mrs Henderson. [*He goes out with Dr
Trench. All the sitters except Miss Mackenna, who has returned to
her room, pass along the passage on their way to the front door. Mrs
Henderson counts the money, finds her purse, which is in a vase on the
mantelpiece, and puts the money in it.*]

Mrs Henderson. How tired I am! I'd be the better of a cup of tea. [*She
finds the teapot and puts kettle on fire, and then as she crouches down
by the hearth suddenly lifts up her hands and counting her fingers,
speaks in Swift's voice.*] Five great Ministers that were my friends
are gone, ten great Ministers that were my friends are gone. I
have not fingers enough to count the great Ministers that were

my friends and that are gone. [*She wakes with a start and speaks in her own voice.*] Where did I put that tea-caddy? Ah! there it is. And there should be a cup and saucer. [*She finds the saucer.*] But where's the cup? [*She moves aimlessly about the stage and then, letting the saucer fall and break, speaks in Swift's voice.*] Perish the day on which I was born!° 470

THE END

The Death of Cuchulain (1939)°

[*A bare stage of any period. A very old man looking like something
out of mythology.*]

Old Man. I have been asked to produce a play called 'The Death of
Cuchulain'. It is the last of a series° of plays which has for theme
his life and death. I have been selected because I am out of fash-
ion and out of date like the antiquated romantic stuff the thing is
made of. I am so old that I have forgotten the name of my father
and mother, unless indeed I am, as I affirm, the son of Talma,°
and he was so old that his friends and acquaintances still read
Virgil and Homer. When they told me I could have my own way,
I wrote certain guiding principles on a bit of newspaper. I
wanted an audience of fifty or a hundred, and if there are more I   10
beg them not to shuffle their feet or talk when the actors are
speaking. I am sure that as I am producing a play for people I like
it is not probable in this vile age, that they will be more in num-
ber than those who listened to the first performance of Milton's
Comus.° On the present occasion they must know the old epics°
and Mr Yeats' plays about them; such people however poor have
libraries of their own. If there are more than a hundred I won't be
able to escape people who are educating themselves out of the
book societies and the like, sciolists all, pickpockets and opinion-
ated bitches. Why pickpockets? I will explain that, I will make it   20
all quite clear.

[*Drum and pipe behind the scene, then silence.*]

That's from the musicians; I asked them to do that if I was getting
excited. If you were as old you would find it easy to get excited.
Before the night ends you will meet the music. There is a singer,
a piper and a drummer. I have picked them up here and there
about the streets, and I will teach them, if I live, the music of the
beggarman, Homer's music. I promise a dance. I wanted a dance
because where there are no words there is less to spoil. Emer
must dance, there must be severed heads—I am old, I belong to
mythology—severed heads for her to dance before. I had   30
thought to have had those heads carved, but no, if the dancer can

dance properly no wood-carving can look as well as a parallelo-
gram of painted wood. But I was at my wit's end to find a good
dancer; I could have got such a dancer once, but she has gone; the
tragi-comedian dancer, the tragic dancer, upon the same neck
love and loathing, life and death. I spit three times. I spit upon
the dancers painted by Degas.° I spit upon their short bodices,
their stiff stays, their toes whereon they spin like peg-tops, above
all upon that chambermaid face. They might have looked time-
less, Rameses the Great,° but not the chambermaid, that old   40
maid history. I spit ! I spit ! I spit !

> [*The stage is darkened, the curtain falls. Pipe and drum
> begin and continue, until the curtain rises on a bare stage.
> Half a minute later Eithne Inguba enters.*]

Eithne. Cuchulain! Cuchulain!

> [*Cuchulain enters from back*]

Eithne.   I am Emer's messenger,
  I am your wife's messenger, she has bid me say
  You must not linger here in sloth for Maeve
  With all those Connacht ruffians at her back
  Burns barns and houses up at Emain Macha:°
  Your house at Muirthemne already burns.°
  No matter what's the odds, no matter though
  Your death may come of it, ride out and fight.
  The scene is set and you must out and fight.   50

Cuchulain. You have told me nothing. I am already armed
  I have sent a messenger to gather men,
  And wait for his return. What have you there?

Eithne. I have nothing.

Cuchulain.   There is something in your hand.

Eithne. No.

Cuchulain. Have you a letter in your hand?

Eithne. I do not know how it got into my hand.
  I am straight from Emer. We were in some place.
  She spoke. She saw.

Cuchulain.   This letter is from Emer,
  It tells a different story. I am not to move
  Until to-morrow morning, for, if now,   60
  I must face odds no man can face and live.

To–morrow morning Conall Caernach comes°
With a great host.

Eithne.   I do not understand.
Who can have put that letter in my hand?

Cuchulain. And there is something more to make it certain
I shall not stir till morning; you are sent
To be my bedfellow, but have no fear,
All that is written but I much prefer
Your own unwritten words. I am for the fight
I and my handful are set upon the fight,   70
We have faced great odds before, a straw decided.

     [*The Morrigu enters and stands between them.*]

Eithne. I know that somebody or something is there
Yet nobody that I can see.

Cuchulain.   There is nobody.

Eithne. Who among the gods of the air and upper air
Has a bird's head?

Cuchulain.   Morrigu is headed like a crow.

Eithne [*dazed*]. Morrigu, war goddess, stands between.
Her black wing touched me upon the shoulder, and now
All is intelligible.

               [*Morrigu goes out.*

          Maeve put me in a trance,
Though when Cuchulain slept with her as a boy
She seemed as pretty as a bird, she has changed,   80
She has an eye in the middle of her forehead.

Cuchulain. A woman that has an eye in the middle of her forehead!
A woman that is headed like a crow!
But she that put those words into your mouth
Had nothing monstrous; you put them there yourself,
You need a younger man, a friendlier man,
But fearing what my violence might do
Thought out these words to send me to my death,
And were in such excitement you forgot
The letter in your hand.

Eithne.   Now that I wake   90
I say that Maeve did nothing out of reason;
What mouth could you believe if not my mouth?

Cuchulain. When I went mad at my son's death and drew°
   My sword against the sea, it was my wife
   That brought me back.°

Eithne.   Better women than I
   Have served you well, but 'twas to me you turned.

Cuchulain. You thought that if you changed I'd kill you for it
   When everything sublunary must change,
   And if I have not changed that goes to prove
   That I am monstrous.

Eithne.   You're not the man I loved,   100
   That violent man forgave no treachery.
   If thinking what you think you can forgive
   It is because you are about to die.

Cuchulain. Spoken too loudly and too near the door;
   Speak low if you would speak about my death,
   Or not in that strange voice exulting in it.
   Who knows what ears listen behind the door?

Eithne. Some that would not forgive a traitor, some
   That have the passion necessary to life,
   Some not about to die. When you are gone   110
   I shall denounce myself to all your cooks.
   Scullions, armourers, bed-makers, and messengers,
   Until they hammer me with a ladle, cut me with a knife,
   Impale me upon a spit, put me to death
   By what foul way best please their fancy,
   So that my shade can stand among the shades
   And greet your shade and prove it is no traitor.

Cuchulain. Women have spoken so, plotting a man's death.

                [Enter a servant]

Servant. Your great horse is bitted. All wait the word.

Cuchulain. I come to give it, but must ask a question.   120
   This woman wild with grief, declares that she
   Out of pure treachery has told me lies
   That should have brought my death. What can I do?
   How can I save her from her own wild words?

Servant. Is her confession true?

Cuchulain.   I make the truth!
   I say she brings a message from my wife.

Servant. What if I make her swallow poppy juice?

Cuchulain. What herbs seem suitable, but protect her life
  As if it were your own, and should I not return
  Give her to Conall Caernach because the women   130
  Have called him a good lover.

Eithne.   I might have peace that know
  The Morrigu, the woman like a crow
  Stands to my defence and cannot lie,
  But that Cuchulain is about to die.

  [*Pipe and drum. The stage grows dark for a moment. When it
  lights up again, it is empty. Cuchulain enters wounded. He tries
  to fasten himself to a pillar-stone with his belt. Aoife, an erect
  white-haired woman enters.*]

Aoife. Am I recognised, Cuchulain?

Cuchulain.   You fought with a sword,
  It seemed that we should kill each other, then
  Your body wearied and I took your sword.

Aoife. But look again, Cuchulain! Look again!

Cuchulain. Your hair is white.

Aoife.   That time was long ago
  And now it is my time. I have come to kill you.   140

Cuchulain. Where am I? Why am I here?

Aoife.   You asked their leave,
  When certain that you had six mortal wounds,
  To drink out of the pool.

Cuchulain.   I have put my belt
  About this stone and want to fasten it
  And die upon my feet, but am too weak.
  Fasten this belt.

              [*She helps him to do so*]

                  And now I know your name,
  Aoife, the mother of my son. We met
  At the Hawk's Well under the withered trees.
  I killed him upon Baile's Strand, that is why°
  Maeve parted ranks that she might let you through.   150
  You have a right to kill me.

Aoife.   Though I have,

Her army did not part to let me through.
The grey of Macha, that great horse of yours°
Killed in the battle, came out of the pool
As though it were alive, and went three times
In a great circle round you and that stone,
Then leaped into the pool and not a man
Of all that terrified army dare approach;
But I approach.

Cuchulain.   Because you have the right.

Aoife. But I am an old woman now, and that   160
  Your strength may not start up when the time comes
  I wind my veil about this ancient stone
  And fasten you to it.

Cuchulain.   But do not spoil your veil.
  Your veils are beautiful, some with threads of gold.

Aoife. I am too old to care for such things now.

              [*She has wound the veil about him*]

Cuchulain. There was no reason so to spoil your veil
  I am weak from loss of blood.

Aoife.   I was afraid,
  But now that I have wound you in the veil,
  I am not afraid. But how did my son fight?

Cuchulain. Age makes more skilful but not better men.   170

Aoife. I have been told you did not know his name,
  And wanted, because he had a look of me,
  To be his friend, but Conchubar forbade it.

Cuchulain. Forbade it and commanded me to fight;
  That very day I had sworn to do his will,
  Yet refused him, and spoke about a look;
  But somebody spoke of witchcraft and I said
  Witchcraft had made the look, and fought and killed him.
  Then I went mad, I fought against the sea.

Aoife. I seemed invulnerable; you took my sword,   180
  You threw me on the ground and left me there.
  I searched the mountain for your sleeping place
  And laid my virgin body at your side,
  And yet because you had left me, hated you.
  And thought that I would kill you in your sleep

And yet begot a son that night between
Two black thorn trees.

Cuchulain.   I cannot understand.

Aoife. Because about to die!
                              Somebody comes.
Some countryman; and when he finds you here
And none to protect him, will be terrified.   190
I will keep out of his sight for I have things
That I must ask questions on before I kill you.

> [*She goes, the Blind Man of Baile's Strand comes in. He moves
> his stick about until he finds the standing stone; he lays his stick
> down, stoops and touches Cuchulain's feet. He feels the legs.*]

Blind Man. Ah! Ah!

Cuchulain.   I think you are a blind old man.

Blind Man. A blind old beggar man. What is your name?

Cuchulain. Cuchulain.

Blind Man.   They say that you are weak with wounds.
I stood between a Fool and the sea at Baile's Strand
When you went mad. What's bound about your hands
So that they cannot move? Some womanish stuff.
I have been fumbling with my stick since dawn
And then heard many voices. I began to beg.   200
Somebody said that I was in Maeve's tent,
And somebody else, a big man by his voice,
That if I brought Cuchulain's head in a bag
I would be given twelve pennies; I had the bag
To carry what I get at kitchen doors,
Somebody told me how to find the place;
I thought it would have taken till the night
But this has been my lucky day.

Cuchulain.   Twelve pennies!

Blind Man. I would not promise anything until the woman,
The great queen Maeve herself, repeated the words.   210

Cuchulain. Twelve pennies! What better reason for killing a man?
You have a knife, but have you sharpened it?

Blind Man. I keep it sharp because it cuts my food.

> [*He lays bag on ground and begins feeling Cuchulain's body, his
> hands mounting upward.*]

Cuchulain. I think that you know everything Blind Man.
   My mother or my nurse said that the blind
   Know everything.

Blind Man.   No, but they have good sense.
   How could I have got twelve pennies for your head
   If I had not good sense?

Cuchulain.   There floats out there
   The shape that I shall take when I am dead,
   My soul's first shape, a soft feathery shape,   220
   And is not that a strange shape for a soul
   Of a great fighting man?

Blind Man.   Your shoulder is there,
   This is your neck. Ah! Ah! Are you ready Cuchulain?

Cuchulain. I say, it is about to sing.

                    [*The stage darkens*]

Blind Man.   Ah! Ah!
   [*Music of pipe and drum, the curtain falls. The music ceases as
   the curtain rises upon a bare stage. There is nobody upon the
   stage except a woman with a crow's head. She is the Morrigu.
   She stands towards the back. She holds a black parallelogram,
   the size of a man's head. There are six other parallelograms
   near the back cloth.*]

Morrigu. The dead can hear me and to the dead I speak.
   This head is great Cuchulain's, those other six
   Gave him six mortal wounds; this man came first,
   Youth lingered though the years ran on, that season
   A woman loves the best. Maeve's latest lover,
   This man, had given him the second wound,   230
   He had possessed her once; these were her sons,
   Two valiant men that gave the third and fourth;
   These other men were men of no account,
   They saw that he was weakening and crept in.
   One gave him the sixth wound and one the fifth;
   Conall avenged him. I arranged the dance.

   [*Emer enters. The Morrigu places the head of Cuchulain upon
   the ground and goes out. Emer runs in and begins to dance. She
   so moves that she seems to rage against the heads of those that
   had wounded Cuchulain, perhaps makes movements as though
   to strike them, going three times round the circle of the heads.*

She then moves towards the head of Cuchulain, it may, if need
be, be raised above the others on a pedestal. She moves as if in
adoration or in triumph. She is about to prostrate herself before
it. Perhaps does so. Then rises, looking up as though listening;
she seems to hesitate between the head and what she hears. Then
she stands motionless. There is silence and in the silence a few
faint bird notes. The stage darkens slowly. Then comes loud
music, but now it is quite different. It is the music of some Irish
Fair of our day. The stage brightens. Emer and the head are
gone. There is none there but the three musicians. They are in
ragged street singers' clothing; two of them begin to play the pipe
and drum. They cease. The street singer begins to sing.]

Singer. The harlot sang to the beggarman.
 I meet them face to face
 Conall, Cuchulain, Usna's boys,°
 All that most ancient race;   240
 Maeve had three in an hour they say.
 I adore those clever eyes,
 Those muscular bodies, but can get
 No grip upon their thighs.°
 I meet those long pale faces
 Hear their great horses, then°
 Recall what centuries have passed
 Since they were living men.
 That there are still some living
 That do my limbs unclothe,   250
 But that the flesh my flesh has gripped
 I both adore and loathe.

                    [*Pipe and drum music*]
Singer. Are those things that men adore and loathe
 Their sole reality?
 What stood in the Post Office°
 With Pearse and Connolly?°
 What comes out of the mountain
 Where men first shed their blood,
 Who thought Cuchulain till it seemed
 He stood where they had stood?   260

 No body like his body
 Has modern woman borne.

But an old man looking back on life
Imagines it in scorn.
A statue's there to mark the place
By Oliver Sheppard done,°
So ends the tale that the harlot
Sang to the beggarman.

[*Music from pipe and drum*

THE CURTAIN FALLS

Purgatory° (1939)

[*A ruined house and a bare tree in the background.*]

Boy. Half-door, hall door
  Hither and thither day and night
  Hill or hollow, shouldering this pack
  Hearing you talk.

Old Man.   Study that house
  I think about its jokes and stories;
  I try to remember what the butler
  Said to a drunken gamekeeper
  In mid-October, but I cannot,
  If I cannot, none living can.
  Where are the jokes and stories of a house,   10
  Its threshold gone to patch a pig-sty?

Boy. So you have come this path before?

Old Man. The moonlight falls upon the path,
  The shadow of a cloud upon the house
  And that's symbolical; study that tree,
  What is it like?
Boy.   A silly old man.

Old Man. It's like—no matter what it's like.
  I saw it a year ago stripped bare as now,
  So I chose a better trade.

  I saw it fifty years ago   20
  Before the thunderbolt had riven it,
  Green leaves, ripe leaves, leaves thick as butter,
  Fat, greasy life. Stand there and look,
  Because there is somebody in that house.

      [*The Boy puts down pack and stands in the doorway*]
Boy. There's nobody here.
Old Man.   There's somebody there.
Boy. The floor is gone, the windows gone,
  And where there should be roof there's sky,
  And here's a bit of an egg-shell thrown
  Out of a jackdaw's nest.

Old Man.   But there are some
   That do not care what's gone, what's left;   30
   The souls in Purgatory that come back
   To habitations and familiar spots.

Boy. Your wits are out again.

Old Man.   Re-live
   Their transgressions, and that not once
   But many times; they know at last
   The consequence of those transgressions
   Whether upon others or upon themselves;
   Upon others, others may bring help,
   For when the consequence is at an end
   The dream must end; upon themselves   40
   There is no help but in themselves
   And in the mercy of God.

Boy.   I have had enough!
   Talk to the jackdaws, if talk you must.

Old Man. Stop! Sit there upon that stone.
   That is the house where I was born.

Boy. The big old house that was burnt down?

Old Man. My mother that was your grand-dam owned it,
   This scenery and this countryside,
   Kennel and stable, horse and hound—

   She had a horse at the Curragh, and there met°   50
   My father, a groom in a training stable;
   Looked at him and married him.
   Her mother never spoke to her again,
   And she did right.

Boy.   What's right and wrong?
   My grand-dad got the girl and the money.

Old Man. Looked at him and married him,
   And he squandered everything she had.

   She never knew the worst, because
   She died in giving birth to me,
   But now she knows it all, being dead.   60

   Great people lived and died in this house;
   Magistrates, colonels, members of Parliament,

Captains and Governors, and long ago
Men that had fought at Aughrim and the Boyne.°
Some that had gone on government work
To London or to India came home to die,
Or came from London every spring
To look at the May-blossom in the park.
They had loved the trees that he cut down
To pay what he had lost at cards   70
Or spent on horses, drink and women;
Had loved the house, had loved all
The intricate passages of the house,
But he killed the house; to kill a house
Where great men grew up, married, died,
I here declare a capital offence.

Boy. My God, but you had luck! Grand clothes,
And maybe a grand horse to ride.

Old Man. That he might keep me upon his level
He never sent me to school, but some   80
Half-loved me for my half of her:
A gamekeeper's wife taught me to read,
A Catholic curate taught me Latin.
There were old books and books made fine
By eighteenth century French binding, books
Modern and ancient, books by the ton.

Boy. What education have you given me?

Old Man. I gave the education that befits
A bastard that a pedlar got
Upon a tinker's daughter in a ditch.   90
When I had come to sixteen years old
My father burned down the house when drunk.

Boy. But that is my age, sixteen years old.
At the Puck Fair.°

Old Man.   And everything was burnt;
Books, library, all were burnt.

Boy. Is what I have heard upon the road the truth,
That you killed him in the burning house?

Old Man. There's nobody here but our two selves?

Boy. Nobody, Father.

Old Man.   I stuck him with a knife,
   That knife that cuts my dinner now,   100
   And after that I left him in the fire;
   They dragged him out, somebody saw
   The knife-wound but could not be certain
   Because the body was all black and charred.
   Then some that were his drunken friends
   Swore they would put me upon trial,
   Spoke of quarrels, a threat I had made.
   The gamekeeper gave me some old clothes,
   I ran away, worked here and there
   Till I became a pedlar on the roads,   110
   No good trade, but good enough
   Because I am my father's son,
   Because of what I did or may do.
   Listen to the hoof beats! Listen, listen!

Boy. I cannot hear a sound.

Old Man.   Beat! Beat!
   This night is the anniversary
   Of my mother's wedding night,
   Or of the night wherein I was begotten.
   My father is riding from the public house
   A whiskey bottle under his arm.   120

       [*A window is lit showing a young girl.*]

   Look at the window; she stands there
   Listening, the servants are all in bed,
   She is alone, he has stayed late
   Bragging and drinking in the public house.

Boy. There's nothing but an empty gap in the wall.
   You have made it up. No, you are mad!
   You are getting madder every day.

Old Man. It's louder now because he rides
   Upon a gravelled avenue
   All grass to-day. The hoof beat stops,   130
   He has gone to the other side of the house
   Gone to the stable, put the horse up.
   She has gone down to open the door.
   This night she is no better than her man
   And does not mind that he is half drunk,

She is mad about him. They mount the stairs
She brings him into her own chamber.
And that is the marriage chamber now.
The window is dimly lit again.
Do not let him touch you! It is not true   140
That drunken men cannot beget
And if he touch he must beget
And you must bear his murderer.
Deaf! Both deaf! If I should throw
A stick or stone they would not hear;
And that's a proof my wits are out.
But there's a problem: she must live
Through everything in exact detail,
Driven to it by remorse, and yet
Can she renew the sexual act   150
And find no pleasure in it, and if not,
If pleasure and remorse must both be there
Which is the greater?
                              I lack schooling.
Go fetch Tertullian; he and I°
Will ravel all that problem out
Whilst those two lie upon the mattress
Begetting me.
                    Come back! Come back!
And so you thought to slip away,
My bag of money between your fingers,
And that I could not talk and see!   160
You have been rummaging in the pack.

        [*The light in the window has faded out.*]

Boy. You never gave me my right share.

Old Man. And had I given it, young as you are
    You would have spent it upon drink.

Boy. What if I did? I had a right
    To get it and spend it as I chose.

Old Man. Give me that bag and no more words.

Boy. I will not.

Old Man.   I will break your fingers.

[*They struggle for the bag. In the struggle it drops, scattering the money. The Old Man staggers but does not fall. They stand looking at each other. Window is lit up, a man is seen pouring whiskey into a glass.*]

Boy. What if I killed you? You killed my grand-dad,
    Because you were young and he was old;   170
    Now I am young and you are old.

Old Man [*Staring at window*]. Better looking, those sixteen years—

Boy. What are you muttering?

Old Man. Younger—and yet
    She should have known he was not her kind.

Boy. What are you saying? Out with it!

        [*Old Man points to window*]

My God! The window is lit up
And somebody stands there, although
The floorboards are all burnt away.

Old Man. The window is lit up because my father   180
    Has come to find a glass for his whiskey.
    He leans there like some tired beast.

Boy. A dead, living, murdered man.

Old Man. Then the bride-sleep fell upon Adam:
    Where did I read those words?
                   And yet
There's nothing leaning in the window
But the impression upon my mother's mind,
Being dead she is alone in her remorse.

Boy. A body that was a bundle of old bones
    Before I was born. Horrible! Horrible! [*He covers his eyes.*   190

Old Man. That beast there would know nothing, being nothing,
    It I should kill a man under the window,
    He would not even turn his head.

        [*He stabs the Boy*]

My father and my son on the same jack-knife!
That finishes—there—there—there—

    [*He stabs again and again. The window grows dark.*]

'Hush-a-bye baby, thy father's a knight,
Thy mother a lady, lovely and bright.'

No, that is something that I read in a book,
And if I sing, it must be to my mother,
And I lack rhyme.

[*The stage has grown dark except where the tree stands in white
light.*]

                Study that tree.
It stands there like a purified soul,   200
All cold, sweet, glistening light.
Dear mother, the window is dark again
But you are in the light because
I finished all that consequence.
I killed that lad because he had grown up,
He would have struck a woman's fancy,
Begot, and passed pollution on.
I am a wretched foul old man
And therefore harmless. When I have stuck
This old jack-knife into a sod   210
And pulled it out all bright again,
And picked up all the money that he dropped
I'll to a distant place, and there
Tell my old jokes among new men.

[*He cleans the knife and begins to pick up money.*]

Hoof beats! Dear God
How quickly it returns—beat—beat—
Her mind cannot hold up that dream.
Twice a murderer and all for nothing,
And she must animate that dead night
Not once but many times!

                O God   220
Release my mother's soul from its dream!
Mankind can do no more. Appease
The misery of the living and the remorse of the dead.

                THE END

PROSE

Essays and Commentary

from the Commentary on Blake's The First Book of Urizen°

PREFACE

This is the story of one of the eternal states or moods° of man, which are from everlasting. The individual enters these Moods and passes on, leaving them in the Universal Bosom, as travellers leave in space the lands through which they go. The name of the Mood is Urizen.

PROLOGUE

Urizen is seen in vision as the primeval priest, or spiritual father, assuming power among the spirits or imaginative moods of Great Eternity, an unimaginative mood by contrast, or rather he desires to be so in order to be a separate self—self-contemplating—and dominate other moods. The Eternals therefore gave him a place in the region of selfishness, of personality, of experience, the North, the iron land that the senses create in the mind, for the land of the South, from which he first came, is mind-created, not merely mind-analyzed. It is in the bosom of God, and no selfishness is allowed there, no personality that is not merely a means of brotherhood.°

CHAPTER I

1. Separated from the imaginative, Urizen ceased to give light. He became a shadow. (Shadow means cloud or liquid, and has the qualities of blood, the dark region of sensuous action.) He became like a void, a vacuum, like nature that is not conscious life; that is, not anything except the potency of unfertilized maternity. (What is not conscious life is nothing to itself). He was Urizen, with no other eternal attributes left than that of potency. And this was hidden.

2. Eternals propagate by division, and by their masculine portions, or States, acting on their feminine portions, or Spaces. Division is the first step of paternal action. Urizen divided and measured, he fertilized, as well as he could, his void. The void entered into, such is the eternal law, becomes a womb. Compare 'Milton,'° p. 43, 1. 37. It was ninefold, and the number in itself was a promise of offspring. Change, but not light, appeared. In dark desire of fatherhood, yet with no creative imagination, Urizen struggled in desolate loneliness, for the senses, inhabitants of the North, are not Human company.

from Magic

I

I believe in the practice and philosophy of what we have agreed to call magic,° in what I must call the evocation of spirits, though I do not know what they are, in the power of creating magical illusions, in the visions of truth in the depths of the mind when the eyes are closed; and I believe in three doctrines, which have, as I think, been handed down from early times, and been the foundations of nearly all magical practices. These doctrines are—

(1) That the borders of our mind are ever shifting, and that many minds can flow into one another, as it were, and create or reveal a single mind, a single energy.

(2) That the borders of our memories are as shifting, and that our memories are a part of one great memory, the memory of Nature herself.

(3) That this great mind and great memory can be evoked by symbols.

I often think I would put this belief in magic from me if I could, for I have come to see or to imagine, in men and women, in houses, in handicrafts, in nearly all sights and sounds, a certain evil, a certain ugliness, that comes from the slow perishing through the centuries of a quality of mind that made this belief and its evidences common over the world.

II

Some ten or twelve years ago, a man with whom I have since quarrelled for sound reasons, a very singular man who had given his life to studies other men despised, asked me and an acquaintance, who is now dead, to witness a magical work. He lived a little way from London, and on the way my acquaintance told me that he did not believe in magic, but that a novel of Bulwer Lytton's had taken such a hold upon his imagination that he was going to give much of his time and all his thought to magic. He longed to believe in it, and had studied, though not learnedly, geomancy, astrology, chiromancy, and much cabalistic symbolism, and yet doubted if the soul outlived the body. He awaited the magical work full of scepticism. He expected nothing more than an air of romance, an illusion as of the stage, that might capture the consenting imagination for an hour. The evoker of spirits and his beautiful wife received us in a little house, on the edge of some kind of garden or park belonging to an eccentric rich man, whose curiosities he arranged and dusted, and he made his evocation in a long room that had a raised place on the floor at one end, a kind of dais, but was furnished meagrely and cheaply. I sat with my acquaintance in the middle of the room, and the evoker of spirits on the dais, and his wife between us and him. He held a wooden mace in his hand, and turning to a tablet of many-coloured squares, with a number on each of the squares, that stood near him on a chair, he repeated a form of words. Almost at once my imagination began to move of itself and to bring before me vivid images that, though never too vivid to be imagination, as I had always understood it, had yet a motion of their own, a life I could not change or shape. . . .

III

Then I asked to have some past life of mine revealed, and a new evocation was made before the tablet full of little squares. I cannot remember so well who saw this or that detail, for now I was interested in little but the vision itself. I had come to a conclusion about the method. I knew that the vision may be in part common to several people.

A man in chain armour passed through a castle door, and the seeress noticed with surprise the bareness and rudeness of castle rooms. There was nothing of the magnificence or the pageantry she had expected. The man came to a large hall and to a little chapel opening out of it, where a ceremony was taking place. There were six girls dressed in white, who took from the altar some yellow object—I thought it was gold, for though, like my acquaintance, I was told not to see, I could not help seeing. Somebody else thought that it was yellow flowers, and I think the girls, though I cannot remember clearly, laid it between the man's hands. He went out for a time, and as he passed through the great hall one of us, I forget whom, noticed that he passed over two gravestones. Then the vision became broken, but presently he stood in a monk's habit among men-at-arms in the middle of a village reading from a parchment. He was calling villagers about him, and presently he and they and the men-at-arms took ship for some long voyage. The vision became broken again, and when we could see clearly they had come to what seemed the Holy Land. They had begun some kind of sacred labour among palm-trees. The common men among them stood idle, but the gentlemen carried large stones, bringing them from certain directions, from the cardinal points I think, with a ceremonious formality. The evoker of spirits said they must be making some masonic house. His mind, like the minds of so many students of these hidden things, was always running on masonry and discovering it in strange places.

We broke the vision that we might have supper, breaking it with some form of words which I forget. When supper had ended the seeress cried out that while we had been eating they had been building, and that they had built not a masonic house but a great stone cross. . . .

VI

I once saw a young Irish woman, fresh from a convent school, cast into a profound trance, though not by a method known to any hypnotist. In her waking state she thought the apple of Eve was the kind of apple you can buy at the greengrocer's, but in her trance she saw the Tree of Life° with ever-sighing souls moving in its branches instead of sap, and among its leaves all the fowls of the air, and on its highest bough one white fowl wearing a crown. When I went home I took from the shelf a translation of *The Book of Concealed Mystery*,[1] an old Jewish book, and cutting the pages came upon this passage, which I cannot think I had ever read: 'The Tree, . . . is the Tree of the Knowledge of Good and of Evil . . . in its branches the birds lodge and build their nests, the souls and the angels have their place.'

I once saw a young Church of Ireland man, a bank clerk in the west of Ireland, thrown in a like trance. I have no doubt that he, too, was quite certain that the apple of Eve was a greengrocer's apple, and yet he saw the tree and heard the souls sighing through its branches, and saw apples with human faces, and laying his ear to an apple heard a sound as of fighting hosts within. Presently he strayed from the tree and came to the edge of Eden, and there he found himself not by the wilderness he had learned of at the Sunday-school, but upon the summit of a great mountain, of a mountain 'two miles high.' The whole summit, in contradiction to all that would have seemed probable to his waking mind, was a great walled garden. Some years afterwards I found a mediaeval diagram, which pictured Eden as a walled garden upon a high mountain.

Where did these intricate symbols come from? Neither I nor the one or two people present or the seers had ever seen, I am convinced, the description in *The Book of Concealed Mystery*, or the mediaeval diagram. Remember that the images appeared in a moment perfect in all their complexity. If one can imagine that the seers or that I myself or another had indeed read of these images and forgotten it, that the supernatural artist's knowledge of what was in our buried memories accounted for these visions, there are numberless other visions to account for. One cannot go on believing in improbable knowledge for ever. For instance,

---

[1] Translated by Mathers in *The Kabbalah Unveiled*.

I find in my diary that on December 27, 1897, a seer, to whom I had
given a certain old Irish symbol, saw Brigit,° the goddess, holding out 'a
glittering and wriggling serpent,' and yet I feel certain that neither I nor
he knew anything of her association with the serpent until *Carmina
Gadelica*° was published a few months ago. And an old Irish woman who
can neither read nor write has described to me a woman dressed like
Dian, with helmet, and short skirt and sandals, and what seemed to be
buskins. Why, too, among all the countless stories of visions that I have
gathered in Ireland, or that a friend has gathered for me, are there none
that mix the dress of different periods? The seers when they are but
speaking from tradition will mix everything together, and speak of Finn
mac Cool° going to the Assizes at Cork. Almost every one who has ever
busied himself with such matters has come, in trance or dream, upon
some new and strange symbol or event, which he has afterwards found
in some work he had never read or heard of. Examples like this are as yet
too little classified, too little analysed, to convince the stranger, but some
of them are proof enough for those they have happened to, proof that
there is a memory of nature that reveals events and symbols of distant
centuries. Mystics of many countries and many centuries have spoken of
this memory; and the honest men and charlatans, who keep the magical
traditions which will some day be studied as a part of folk-lore, base most
that is of importance in their claims upon this memory. I have read of it
in *Paracelsus*° and in some Indian book that describes the people of past
days as still living within it, 'Thinking the thought and doing the deed.'
And I have found it in the prophetic books of William Blake,° who calls
its images 'the bright sculptures of Los's Hall';° and says that all events,
'all love stories,' renew themselves from those images. It is perhaps well
that so few believe in it, for if many did many would go out of parlia-
ments and universities and libraries and run into the wilderness to so
waste the body, and to so hush the unquiet mind that, still living, they
might pass the doors the dead pass daily; for who among the wise would
trouble himself with making laws or in writing history or in weighing the
earth if the things of eternity seemed ready to hand?

VII

I find in my diary of magical events for 1899 that I awoke at 3 a.m. out of
a nightmare, and imagined one symbol to prevent its recurrence, and
imagined another, a simple geometrical form, which calls up dreams of
luxuriant vegetable life, that I might have pleasant dreams, I imagined it
faintly, being very sleepy, and went to sleep. I had confused dreams
which seemed to have no relation with the symbol. I awoke about eight,

having for the time forgotten both nightmare and symbol. Presently I dozed off again and began half to dream and half to see, as one does between sleep and waking, enormous flowers and grapes. I awoke and recognised that what I had dreamed or seen was the kind of thing appropriate to the symbol before I remembered having used it. I find another record, though made some time after the event, of having imagined over the head of a person, who was a little of a seer, a combined symbol of elemental air and elemental water. This person, who did not know what symbol I was using, saw a pigeon flying with a lobster in his bill. I find that on December 13, 1898, I used a certain star-shaped symbol with a seeress, getting her to look at it intently before she began seeing. She saw a rough stone house, and in the middle of the house the skull of a horse. I find that I had used the same symbol a few days before with a seer, and that he had seen a rough stone house, and in the middle of the house something under a cloth marked with the Hammer of Thor.° He had lifted the cloth and discovered a skeleton of gold with teeth of diamonds, and eyes of some unknown dim precious stones. I had made a note to this last vision, pointing out that we had been using a Solar symbol a little earlier. Solar symbols often call up visions of gold and precious stones. I do not give these examples to prove my arguments, but to illustrate them. I know that my examples will awaken in all who have not met the like, or who are not on other grounds inclined towards my arguments, a most natural incredulity. It was long before I myself would admit an inherent power in symbols, for it long seemed to me that one could account for everything by the power of one imagination over another, or by telepathy, as 'The Society for Psychical Research'° would say. The symbol seemed powerful, I thought, merely because we thought it powerful, and we would do just as well without it. In those days I used symbols made with some ingenuity instead of merely imagining them. I used to give them to the person I was experimenting with, and tell him to hold them to his forehead without looking at them; and sometimes I made a mistake. I learned from these mistakes that if I did not myself imagine the symbol, in which case he would have a mixed vision, it was the symbol I gave by mistake[1] that produced the vision. Then I met with a seer who could say to me, 'I have a vision of a square pond, but I can see your thought, and you expect me to see an oblong pond,' or, 'The symbol you are imagining has made me see a woman holding a crystal,

---

[1] I forgot that my 'subconsciousness' would know clairvoyantly what symbol I had really given and would respond to the associations of that symbol. I am, however, certain that the main symbols (symbolic roots, as it were) draw upon associations which are beyond the reach of the individual 'subconsciousness'. 1924.

but it was a moonlight sea I should have seen.' I discovered that the symbol hardly ever failed to call up its typical scene, its typical event, its typical person, but that I could practically never call up, no matter how vividly I imagined it, the particular scene, the particular event, the particular person I had in my own mind, and that when I could, the two visions rose side by side.

I cannot now think symbols less than the greatest of all powers whether they are used consciously by the masters of magic, or half unconsciously by their successors, the poet, the musician and the artist. At first I tried to distinguish between symbols and symbols, between what I called inherent symbols and arbitrary symbols, but the distinction has come to mean little or nothing. Whether their power has arisen out of themselves, or whether it has an arbitrary origin, matters little, for they act, as I believe, because the great memory° associates them with certain events and moods and persons. Whatever the passions of man have gathered about, becomes a symbol in the great memory, and in the hands of him who has the secret it is a worker of wonders, a caller-up of angels or of devils. The symbols are of all kinds, for everything in heaven or earth has its association, momentous or trivial, in the great memory, and one never knows what forgotten events may have plunged it, like the toadstool and the ragweed, into the great passions. Knowledgeable men and women in Ireland sometimes distinguish between the simples that work cures by some medical property in the herb, and those that do their work by magic. Such magical simples as the husk of the flax, water out of the fork of an elm-tree, do their work, as I think, by awaking in the depths of the mind where it mingles with the great mind, and is enlarged by the great memory, some curative energy, some hypnotic command. They are not what we call faith cures, for they have been much used and successfully, the traditions of all lands affirm, over children and over animals, and to me they seem the only medicine that could have been committed safely to ancient hands. To pluck the wrong leaf would have been to go uncured, but, if one had eaten it, one might have been poisoned.

VIII

I have now described the belief in magic which has set me all but unwilling among those lean and fierce minds who are at war with their time, who cannot accept the days as they pass, simply and gladly; and I look at what I have written with some alarm, for I have told more of the ancient secret than many among my fellow-students think it right to tell. I have come to believe so many strange things because of experience, that I see little reason to doubt the truth of many things that are beyond my experience; and it may be that there are beings who watch over that ancient secret, as all tradition affirms, and resent, and perhaps avenge, too fluent speech. They say in the Aran Islands° that if you speak over-much of the things of Faery your tongue becomes like a stone, and it seems to me, though doubtless naturalistic reason would call it Auto-suggestion or the like, that I have often felt my tongue become just so heavy and clumsy. More than once, too, as I wrote this very essay I have become uneasy, and have torn up some paragraph, not for any literary reason, but because some incident or some symbol that would perhaps have meant nothing to the reader, seemed, I know not why, to belong to hidden things. Yet I must write or be of no account to any cause, good or evil; I must commit what merchandise of wisdom I have to this ship of written speech, and after all, I have many a time watched it put out to sea with not less alarm when all the speech was rhyme. We who write, we who bear witness, must often hear our hearts cry out against us, com-plaining because of their hidden things, and I know not but he who speaks of wisdom may not sometimes, in the change that is coming upon the world, have to fear the anger of the people of Faery, whose country is the heart of the world—'The Land of the Living Heart.' Who can keep always to the little pathway between speech and silence, where one meets none but discreet revelations? And surely, at whatever risk, we must cry out that imagination is always seeking to remake the world according to the impulses and the patterns in that great Mind, and that great Memory? Can there be anything so important as to cry out that what we call romance, poetry, intellectual beauty, is the only signal that the supreme Enchanter, or some one in His councils, is speaking of what has been, and shall be again, in the consummation of time?

1901

from The Philosophy of Shelley's Poetry

. . . As Shelley° sailed along those great rivers and saw or imagined the cave that associated itself with rivers in his mind, he saw half-ruined towers upon the hilltops, and once at any rate a tower is used to symbol-ise a meaning that is the contrary to the meaning symbolised by caves. Cythna's lover° is brought through the cave where there is a polluted fountain to a high tower, for being man's far-seeing mind, when the world has cast him out he must to the 'towers of thought's crowned powers'; nor is it possible for Shelley to have forgotten this first imprisonment when he made men imprison Lionel° in a tower for a like offence; and because I know how hard it is to forget a symbolical meaning, once one has found it, I believe Shelley had more than a romantic scene in his mind when he made Prince Athanase° follow his mysterious studies in a lighted tower above the sea, and when he made the old hermit watch over Laon in his sickness in a half-ruined tower, wherein the sea, here doubtless as to Cythna, 'the one mind,' threw 'spangled sands' and 'rarest sea shells.' The tower, important in Maeterlinck,° as in Shelley, is, like the sea, and rivers, and caves with fountains, a very ancient symbol, and would perhaps, as years went by, have grown more important in his poetry. The contrast between it and the cave in *Laon and Cythna* suggests a contrast between the mind looking outward upon men and things and the mind looking inward upon itself, which may or may not have been in Shelley's mind, but certainly helps, with one knows not how many other dim meanings, to give the poem mystery and shadow. It is only by ancient symbols, by symbols that have numberless meanings beside the one or two the writer lays an emphasis upon, or the half-score he knows of, that any highly subjective art can escape from the barrenness and shallowness of a too conscious arrangement, into the abundance and depth of nature. The poet of essences and pure ideas must seek in the half-lights that glimmer from symbol to symbol as if to the ends of the earth, all that the epic and dramatic poet finds of mystery and shadow in the accidental circumstances of life. . . .

In ancient times, it seems to me that Blake, who for all his protest was glad to be alive, and ever spoke of his gladness, would have worshipped in some chapel of the Sun, but that Shelley, who hated life because he sought 'more in life than any understood,' would have wandered, lost in a ceaseless reverie, in some chapel of the Star of infinite desire.

I think too that as he knelt before an altar, where a thin flame burnt in a lamp made of green agate, a single vision would have come to him again and again, a vision of a boat drifting down a broad river between high hills where there were caves and towers, and following the light of one Star; and that voices would have told him how there is for every man some one scene, some one adventure, some one picture that is the image of his secret life, for wisdom first speaks in images, and that this one image, if he would but brood over it his life long, would lead his soul, disentangled from unmeaning circumstance and the ebb and flow of the world, into that far household, where the undying gods await all whose souls have become simple as flame, whose bodies have become quiet as an agate lamp.

But he was born in a day when the old wisdom had vanished and was content merely to write verses, and often with little thought of more than verses.

1900

William Blake and the Imagination

There have been men who loved the future like a mistress, and the future mixed her breath into their breath and shook her hair about them, and hid them from the understanding of their times. William Blake was one of these men, and if he spoke confusedly and obscurely it was because he spoke of things for whose speaking he could find no models in the world he knew. He announced the religion of art, of which no man dreamed in the world he knew; and he understood it more perfectly than the thousands of subtle spirits who have received its baptism in the world we know, because, in the beginning of important things—in the beginning of love, in the beginning of the day, in the beginning of any work—there is a moment when we understand more perfectly than we understand again until all is finished. In his time educated people believed that they amused themselves with books of imagination, but that they 'made their souls' by listening to sermons and by doing or by not doing certain things. When they had to explain why serious people like themselves honoured the great poets greatly they were hard put to it for lack of good reasons. In our time we are agreed that we 'make our souls' out of some one of the great poets of ancient times, or out of Shelley or Wordsworth, or Goethe or Balzac, or Flaubert, or Count Tolstoy,° in the books he wrote before he became a prophet and fell into a lesser order, or out of Mr Whistler's pictures,° while we amuse ourselves, or, at best, make a poorer sort of soul, by listening to sermons or by doing or by not doing certain things. We write of great writers, even of writers whose beauty would once have seemed an unholy beauty, with rapt sentences like those our fathers kept for the beatitudes and mysteries of the Church; and no matter what we believe with our lips, we believe with our hearts that beautiful things, as Browning said in his one prose essay° that was not in verse, have 'lain burningly on the Divine hand,' and that when time has begun to wither, the Divine hand will fall heavily on bad taste and vulgarity. When no man believed these things William Blake° believed them, and began that preaching against the Philistines, which is as the preaching of the Middle Ages against the Saracen.

He had learned from Jacob Boehme° and from old alchemist writers that imagination was the first emanation of divinity, 'the body of God,' 'the Divine members,' and he drew the deduction, which they did not draw, that the imaginative arts were therefore the greatest of Divine revelations, and that the sympathy with all living things, sinful and righteous alike, which the imaginative arts awaken, is that forgiveness of sins commanded by Christ. The reason, and by the reason he meant deduction from the observations of the senses, binds us to mortality because it binds us to the senses, and divides us from each other by showing us our clashing interests; but imagination divides us from mortality by the immortality of beauty, and binds us to each other by opening the secret doors of all hearts. He cried again and again that everything that lives is holy, and that nothing is unholy except things that do not live—lethargies, and cruelties, and timidities, and that denial of imagination which is the root they grew from in old times. Passions, because most living, are most holy—and this was a scandalous paradox in his time—and man shall enter eternity borne upon their wings.

And he understood this so literally that certain drawings to *Vala*,° had he carried them beyond the first faint pencillings, the first faint washes of colour, would have been a pretty scandal to his time and to our time. The sensations of this 'foolish body,' this 'phantom of the earth and water,' were in themselves but half-living things, 'vegetative' things, but passion that 'eternal glory' made them a part of the body of God.

This philosophy kept him more simply a poet than any poet of his time, for it made him content to express every beautiful feeling that came into his head without troubling about its utility or chaining it to any utility. Sometimes one feels, even when one is reading poets of a better time—Tennyson° or Wordsworth,° let us say—that they have troubled the energy and simplicity of their imaginative passions by asking whether they were for the helping or for the hindrance of the world, instead of believing that all beautiful things have 'lain burningly on the Divine hand.' But when one reads Blake, it is as though the spray of an inexhaustible fountain of beauty was blown into our faces, and not merely when one reads the *Songs of Innocence*,° or the lyrics he wished to call 'The Ideas of Good and Evil,'° but when one reads those 'Prophetic Works'° in which he spoke confusedly and obscurely because he spoke of things for whose speaking he could find no models in the world about him. He was a symbolist who had to invent his symbols; and his counties of England, with their correspondence to tribes of Israel, and his mountains and rivers, with their correspondence to parts of a man's body, are arbitrary as some of the symbolism in the *Axël* of the symbolist Villiers de l'Isle-Adam° is arbitrary, while they mix incongruous things as *Axël* does not. He was a man crying out for a mythology, and trying to make one because he could not find one to his hand. Had he been a Catholic of Dante's° time he would have been well content with Mary and the angels; or had he been a scholar of our time he would have taken his symbols where Wagner took his, from Norse mythology;° or have followed, with the help of Professor Rhys,° that pathway into Welsh mythology which he found in 'Jerusalem;' or have gone to Ireland and chosen for his symbols the sacred mountains, along whose sides the peasant still sees enchanted fires, and the divinities which have not faded from the belief, if they have faded from the prayers of simple hearts; and have spoken without mixing incongruous things because he spoke of things that had been long steeped in emotion; and have been less obscure because a traditional mythology stood on the threshold of his meaning and on the margin of his sacred darkness. If 'Enitharmon' had been named Freia, or Gwydeon, or Danu,° and made live in Ancient Norway, or Ancient Wales, or Ancient Ireland, we would have forgotten that her maker was a mystic; and the hymn of her harping, that is in *Vala*,° would but have reminded us of many ancient hymns.

> The joy of woman is the death of her most beloved,
> Who dies for love of her,
> In torments of fierce jealousy and pangs of adoration.
> The lovers' night bears on my song,
> And the nine spheres rejoice beneath my powerful control.
> They sing unwearied to the notes of my immortal hand.
> The solemn, silent moon
> Reverberates the long harmony sounding upon my limbs.
> The birds and beasts rejoice and play,
> And every one seeks for his mate to prove his inmost joy.
> Furious and terrible they sport and rend the nether deep.
> The deep lifts up his rugged head,
> And lost in infinite hovering wings vanishes with a cry.
> The fading cry is ever dying,
> The living voice is ever living in its inmost joy.

1897

Symbolism in Painting

In England, which has made great Symbolic Art, most people dislike an art if they are told it is symbolic, for they confuse symbol and allegory. Even Johnson's Dictionary° sees no great difference, for it calls a Symbol 'That which comprehends in its figure a representation of something else'; and an Allegory, 'A figurative discourse, in which something other is intended than is contained in the words literally taken.' It is only a very modern Dictionary that calls a Symbol 'the sign or representation of any moral thing by the images or properties of natural things,' which, though an imperfect definition, is not unlike 'The things below are as the things above' of the Emerald Tablet of Hermes!° *The Faerie Queene* and *The Pilgrim's Progress*° have been so important in England that Allegory has overtopped Symbolism, and for a time has overwhelmed it in its own downfall. William Blake was perhaps the first modern to insist on a difference; and the other day, when I sat for my portrait to a German Symbolist in Paris, whose talk was all of his love for Symbolism and his hatred for Allegory, his definitions were the same as William Blake's, of whom he knew nothing. William Blake has written, 'Vision or imagination'—meaning symbolism by these words—'is a representation of what actually exists, really or unchangeably. Fable or Allegory is formed by the daughters of Memory.' The German insisted with many determined gestures, that Symbolism said things which could not be said so perfectly in any other way, and needed but a right instinct for its understanding; while Allegory said things which could be said as well, or better, in another way, and needed a right knowledge for its understanding. The one thing gave dumb things voices, and bodiless things bodies; while the other read a meaning—which had never lacked its voice or its body—into something heard or seen, and loved less for the meaning than for its own sake. The only symbols he cared for were the shapes and motions of the body; ears hidden by the hair, to make one think of a mind busy with inner voices; and a head so bent that back and neck made the one curve, as in Blake's 'Vision of Bloodthirstiness,'° to call up an emotion of bodily strength; and he would not put even a lily, or a rose, or a poppy into a picture to express purity, or love, or sleep, because he thought such emblems were allegorical, and had their meaning by a traditional and not by a natural right. I said that the rose, and the lily, and the poppy were so married, by their colour and their odour and their use, to love and purity and sleep, or to other symbols of love and purity and sleep, and had been so long a part of the imagination of the world, that a symbolist might use them to help out his meaning without becoming an allegorist. I think I quoted the lily in the hand of the angel in Rossetti's 'Annunciation,' and the lily in the jar in his 'Childhood of Mary, Virgin,'° and thought they made the more important symbols, the women's bodies, and the angels' bodies, and the clear morning light, take that place, in the great procession of Christian symbols, where they can alone have all their meaning and all their beauty.

It is hard to say where Allegory and Symbolism melt into one another, but it is not hard to say where either comes to its perfection; and though one may doubt whether Allegory or Symbolism is the greater in the horns of Michael Angelo's 'Moses,'° one need not doubt that its symbolism has helped to awaken the modern imagination; while Tintoretto's 'Origin of the Milky Way,'° which is Allegory without any Symbolism, is, apart from its fine painting, but a moment's amusement for our fancy. A hundred generations might write out what seemed the meaning of the one, and they would write different meanings, for no symbol tells all its meaning to any generation; but when you have said, 'That woman there is Juno, and the milk out of her breast is making the Milky Way,' you have told the meaning of the other, and the fine painting, which has added so much irrelevant beauty, has not told it better.

All Art that is not mere story-telling, or mere portraiture, is symbolic, and has the purpose of those symbolic talismans which mediaeval magicians made with complex colours and forms, and bade their patients ponder over daily, and guard with holy secrecy; for it entangles, in complex colours and forms, a part of the Divine Essence. A person or a landscape that is a part of a story or a portrait, evokes but so much emotion as the story or the portrait can permit without loosening the bonds that make it a story or a portrait; but if you liberate a person or a landscape from the bonds of motives and their actions, causes and their effects, and from all bonds but the bonds of your love, it will change under your eyes, and become a symbol of an infinite emotion, a perfected emotion, a part of the Divine Essence; for we love nothing but the perfect, and our dreams make all things perfect, that we may love them. Religious and visionary people, monks and nuns, and medicine-men and opium-eaters, see symbols in their trances; for religious and visionary thought is thought about perfection and the way to perfection; and symbols are the only things free enough from all bonds to speak of perfection.

Wagner's dramas, Keats' odes, Blake's pictures and poems, Calvert's pictures, Rossetti's pictures, Villiers de l'Isle-Adam's plays, and the black-and-white art of Mr Beardsley and Mr Ricketts, and the lithographs of Mr Shannon, and the pictures of Mr Whistler, and the plays of M. Maeterlinck, and the poetry of Verlaine, in our own day, but differ from the religious art of Giotto° and his disciples in having accepted all symbolisms, the symbolism of the ancient shepherds and star-gazers, that symbolism of bodily beauty which seemed a wicked thing to Fra Angelico,° the symbolism in day and night, and winter and summer, spring and autumn, once so great a part of an older religion than Christianity; and in having accepted all the Divine Intellect, its anger and its pity, its waking and its sleep, its love and its lust, for the substance of their art. A Keats or a Calvert is as much a symbolist as a Blake° or a Wagner; but he is a fragmentary symbolist, for while he evokes in his persons and his landscapes an infinite emotion, a perfected emotion, a part of the Divine Essence, he does not set his symbols in the great procession as Blake would have him, 'in a certain order, suited' to his 'imaginative energy.' If you paint a beautiful woman and fill her face, as Rossetti filled so many faces, with an infinite love, a perfected love, 'one's eyes meet no mortal thing when they meet the light of her peaceful eyes,' as Michael Angelo said of Vittoria Colonna;° but one's thoughts stray to mortal things, and ask, maybe, 'Has her lover gone from her, or is he coming?' or 'What predestinated unhappiness has made the shadow in her eyes?' If you paint the same face, and set a winged rose or a rose of gold somewhere about her, one's thoughts are of her immortal sisters, Piety and Jealousy, and of her mother, Ancestral Beauty, and of her high kinsmen, the Holy Orders, whose swords make a continual music before her face. The systematic mystic is not the greatest of artists, because his imagination is too great to be bounded by a picture or a song, and because only imperfection in a mirror of perfection, or perfection in a mirror of imperfection, delights our frailty. There is indeed a systematic mystic in every poet or painter who, like Rossetti, delights in a traditional Symbolism, or, like Wagner, delights in a personal Symbolism; and such men often fall into trances, or have waking dreams. Their thought wanders from the woman who is Love herself, to her sisters and her forebears, and to all the great procession; and so august a beauty moves before the mind, that they forget the things which move before the eyes. William Blake,° who was the chanticleer of the new dawn, has written: 'If the spectator could enter into one of these images of his imagination, approaching them in the fiery chariot of his contemplative thought, if ... he could make a friend and companion of one of these images of wonder, which always entreat him to leave mortal things (as he must know), then would he arise from the grave, then would he meet the Lord in the air, and then he would be happy.' And again, 'The world of imagination is the world of Eternity. It is the Divine bosom into which we shall all go after the death of the vegetated body. The world of imagination is infinite and eternal, whereas the world of generation or vegetation is finite and temporal. There exist in that eternal world the eternal realities of everything which we see reflected in the vegetable glass of nature.'

Every visionary knows that the mind's eye soon comes to see a capricious and variable world, which the will cannot shape or change, though it can call it up and banish it again. I closed my eyes a moment ago, and a company of people in blue robes swept by me in a blinding light, and had gone before I had done more than see little roses embroidered on the hems of their robes, and confused, blossoming apple-boughs some-where beyond them, and recognised one of the company by his square, black, curling beard.[1] I have often seen him; and one night a year ago I asked him questions which he answered by showing me flowers and pre-cious stones, of whose meaning I had no knowledge, and he seemed too perfected a soul for any knowledge that cannot be spoken in symbol or metaphor.

Are he and his blue-robed companions, and their like, 'the Eternal realities' of which we are the reflection 'in the vegetable glass of nature,' or a momentary dream? To answer is to take sides in the only contro-versy in which it is greatly worth taking sides, and in the only contro-versy which may never be decided.

1898

The Symbolism of Poetry

I

'Symbolism, as seen in the writers of our day, would have no value if it were not seen also, under one disguise or another, in every great imaginative writer,' writes Mr Arthur Symons° in *The Symbolist Movement in Literature*, a subtle book which I cannot praise as I would, because it has been dedicated to me; and he goes on to show how many profound writers have in the last few years sought for a philosophy of poetry in the doctrine of symbolism, and how even in countries where it is almost scandalous to seek for any philosophy of poetry, new writers are following them in their search. We do not know what the writers of ancient times talked of among themselves, and one bull is all that remains of Shakespeare's talk, who was on the edge of modern times; and the journalist is convinced, it seems, that they talked of wine and women and politics, but never about their art, or never quite seriously about their art. He is certain that no one, who had a philosophy of his art or a theory of how he should write, has ever made a work of art, that people have no imagination who do not write without forethought and afterthought as he writes his own articles. He says this with enthusiasm,

---

[1] I did not mean that this particular vision had the intensity either of a dream or of those pictures that pass before us between sleep and waking. I had learned, and my fellow-students had learned, as described in *The Trembling of the Veil*, to set free imagination when we would, that it might follow its own law and impulse.   1924.

because he has heard it at so many comfortable dinner-tables, where some one had mentioned through carelessness, or foolish zeal, a book whose difficulty had offended indolence, or a man who had not forgotten that beauty is an accusation. Those formulas and generalisations, in which a hidden sergeant has drilled the ideas of journalists and through them the ideas of all but all the modern world, have created in their turn a forgetfulness like that of soldiers in battle, so that journalists and their readers have forgotten, among many like events, that Wagner° spent seven years arranging and explaining his ideas before he began his most characteristic music; that opera, and with it modern music, arose from certain talks at the house of one Giovanni Bardi° of Florence; and that the Pleiade° laid the foundations of modern French literature with a pamphlet. Goethe° has said, 'a poet needs all philosophy, but he must keep it out of his work,' though that is not always necessary; and almost certainly no great art, outside England, where journalists are more powerful and ideas less plentiful than elsewhere, has arisen without a great criticism, for its herald or its interpreter and protector, and it may be for this reason that great art, now that vulgarity has armed itself and multiplied itself, is perhaps dead in England.

All writers, all artists of any kind, in so far as they have had any philosophical or critical power, perhaps just in so far as they have been deliberate artists at all, have had some philosophy, some criticism of their art; and it has often been this philosophy, or this criticism, that has evoked their most startling inspiration, calling into outer life some portion of the divine life, or of the buried reality, which could alone extinguish in the emotions what their philosophy or their criticism would extinguish in the intellect. They have sought for no new thing, it may be, but only to understand and to copy the pure inspiration of early times, but because the divine life wars upon our outer life, and must needs change its weapons and its movements as we change ours, inspiration has come to them in beautiful startling shapes. The scientific movement brought with it a literature, which was always tending to lose itself in externalities of all kinds, in opinion, in declamation, in picturesque writing, in word-painting, or in what Mr Symons has called an attempt 'to build in brick and mortar inside the covers of a book'; and now writers have begun to dwell upon the element of evocation, of suggestion, upon what we call the symbolism in great writers.

II

In 'Symbolism in Painting,' I tried to describe the element of symbolism that is in pictures and sculpture, and described a little the symbolism in poetry, but did not describe at all the continuous indefinable symbolism which is the substance of all style.

There are no lines with more melancholy beauty than these by Burns—

> The white moon is setting behind the white wave,
> And Time is setting with me, O!°

and these lines are perfectly symbolical. Take from them the whiteness of the moon and of the wave, whose relation to the setting of Time is too subtle for the intellect, and you take from them their beauty. But, when all are together, moon and wave and whiteness and setting Time and the last melancholy cry, they evoke an emotion which cannot be evoked by any other arrangement of colours and sounds and forms. We may call this metaphorical writing, but it is better to call it symbolical writing, because metaphors are not profound enough to be moving, when they are not symbols, and when they are symbols they are the most perfect of all, because the most subtle, outside of pure sound, and through them one can best find out what symbols are. If one begins the reverie with any beautiful lines that one can remember, one finds they are like those by Burns. Begin with this line by Blake—

> The gay fishes on the wave when the moon sucks up the dew;°

or these lines by Nash—

> Brightness falls from the air,
> Queens have died young and fair,
> Dust hath closed Helen's eye;°

or these lines by Shakespeare—

> Timon hath made his everlasting mansion
> Upon the beached verge of the salt flood;
> Who once a day with his embossed froth
> The turbulent surge shall cover;°

or take some line that is quite simple, that gets its beauty from its place in a story, and see how it flickers with the light of the many symbols that have given the story its beauty, as a sword-blade may flicker with the light of burning towers.

All sounds, all colours, all forms, either because of their pre-ordained energies or because of long association, evoke indefinable and yet precise emotions, or, as I prefer to think, call down among us certain disembodied powers, whose footsteps over our hearts we call emotions; and when sound, and colour, and form are in a musical relation, a beautiful relation to one another, they become as it were one sound, one colour, one form, and evoke an emotion that is made out of their distinct evocations and yet is one emotion. The same relation exists between all portions of every work of art, whether it be an epic or a song, and the more perfect it is, and the more various and numerous the elements that have flowed into its perfection, the more powerful will be the emotion, the power, the god it calls among us. Because an emotion does not exist, or does not become perceptible and active among us, till it has found its expression, in colour or in sound or in form, or in all of these, and because no two modulations or arrangements of these evoke the same emotion, poets and painters and musicians, and in a less degree because their effects are momentary, day and night and cloud and shadow, are continually making and un-making mankind. It is indeed only those things which seem useless or very feeble that have any power, and all those things that seem useful or strong, armies, moving wheels, modes of architecture, modes of government, speculations of the reason, would have been a little different if some mind long ago had not given itself to some emotion, as a woman gives herself to her lover, and shaped sounds or colours or forms, or all of these, into a musical relation, that their emotion might live in other minds. A little lyric evokes an emotion, and this emotion gathers others about it and melts into their being in the making of some great epic; and at last, needing an always less delicate body, or symbol, as it grows more powerful, it flows out, with all it has gathered, among the blind instincts of daily life, where it moves a power within powers, as one sees ring within ring in the stem of an old tree. This is maybe what Arthur O'Shaughnessy[n] meant when he made his poets say they had built Nineveh with their sighing; and I am certainly never certain, when I hear of some war, or of some religious excitement or of some new manufacture, or of anything else that fills the ear of the world, that it has not all happened because of something that a boy piped in Thessaly. I remember once telling a seer to ask one among the gods who, as she believed, were standing about her in their symbolic bodies, what would come of a charming but seeming trivial labour of a friend, and the form answering, 'the devastation of peoples and the overwhelming of cities.' I doubt indeed if the crude circumstance of the world, which seems to create all our emotions, does more than reflect, as in multiplying mirrors, the emotions that have come to solitary men in moments of poetical contemplation; or that love itself would be more than an animal hunger but for the poet and his shadow the priest, for unless we believe that outer things are the reality, we must believe that the gross is the shadow of the subtle, that things are wise before they become foolish, and secret before they cry out in the market-place. Solitary men in moments of contemplation receive, as I think, the creative impulse from the lowest of the Nine Hierarchies,° and so make and unmake mankind, and even the world itself, for does not 'the eye altering alter all'?°

> Our towns are copied fragments from our breast;
> And all man's Babylons strive but to impart
> The grandeurs of his Babylonian heart.°

III

The purpose of rhythm, it has always seemed to me, is to prolong the moment of contemplation, the moment when we are both asleep and awake, which is the one moment of creation, by hushing us with an alluring monotony, while it holds us waking by variety, to keep us in that state of perhaps real trance, in which the mind liberated from the pressure of the will is unfolded in symbols. If certain sensitive persons listen persistently to the ticking of a watch, or gaze persistently on the monotonous flashing of a light, they fall into the hypnotic trance; and rhythm is but the ticking of a watch made softer, that one must needs listen, and various, that one may not be swept beyond memory or grow weary of listening; while the patterns of the artist are but the monotonous flash woven to take the eyes in a subtler enchantment. I have heard in meditation voices that were forgotten the moment they had spoken; and I have been swept, when in more profound meditation, beyond all memory but of those things that came from beyond the threshold of waking life. I was writing once at a very symbolical and abstract poem, when my pen fell on the ground; and as I stooped to pick it up, I remembered some phantastic adventure that yet did not seem phantastic, and then another like adventure, and when I asked myself when these things had happened, I found that I was remembering my dreams for many nights. I tried to remember what I had done the day before, and then what I had done that morning; but all my waking life had perished from me, and it was only after a struggle that I came to remember it again, and as I did so that more powerful and startling life perished in its turn. Had my pen not fallen on the ground and so made me turn from the images that I was weaving into verse, I would never have known that meditation had become trance, for I would have been like one who does not know that he is passing through a wood because his eyes are on the pathway. So I think that in the making and in the understanding of a work of art, and the more easily if it is full of patterns and symbols and music, we are lured to the threshold of sleep, and it may be far beyond it, without knowing that we have ever set our feet upon the steps of horn or of ivory.

IV

Besides emotional symbols, symbols that evoke emotions alone,—and in this sense all alluring or hateful things are symbols, although their relations with one another are too subtle to delight us fully, away from rhythm and pattern,—there are intellectual symbols, symbols that evoke ideas alone, or ideas mingled with emotions; and outside the very definite traditions of mysticism and the less definite criticism of certain modern poets, these alone are called symbols. Most things belong to one or another kind, according to the way we speak of them and the companions we give them, for symbols, associated with ideas that are more than fragments of the shadows thrown upon the intellect by the emotions they evoke, are the playthings of the allegorist or the pedant, and soon pass away. If I say 'white' or 'purple' in an ordinary line of poetry, they evoke emotions so exclusively that I cannot say why they move me; but if I bring them into the same sentence with such obvious intellectual symbols as a cross or a crown of thorns, I think of purity and sovereignty. Furthermore, innumerable meanings, which are held to 'white' or to 'purple' by bonds of subtle suggestion, and alike in the emotions and in the intellect, move visibly through my mind, and move invisibly beyond the threshold of sleep, casting lights and shadows of an indefinable wisdom on what had seemed before, it may be, but sterility and noisy violence. It is the intellect that decides where the reader shall ponder over the procession of the symbols, and if the symbols are merely emotional, he gazes from amid the accidents and destinies of the world; but if the symbols are intellectual too, he becomes himself a part of pure intellect, and he is himself mingled with the procession. If I watch a rushy pool in the moonlight, my emotion at its beauty is mixed with memories of the man that I have seen ploughing by its margin, or of the lovers I saw there a night ago; but if I look at the moon herself and remember any of her ancient names and meanings, I move among divine people, and things that have shaken off our mortality, the tower of ivory, the queen of waters, the shining stag among enchanted woods, the white hare sitting upon the hilltop, the fool of faery with his shining cup full of dreams, and it may be 'make a friend of one of these images of wonder,' and 'meet the Lord in the air.' So, too, if one is moved by Shakespeare, who is content with emotional symbols that he may come the nearer to our sympathy, one is mixed with the whole spectacle of the world; while if one is moved by Dante, or by the myth of Demeter,° one is mixed into the shadow of God or of a goddess. So too one is furthest from symbols when one is busy doing this or that, but the soul moves among symbols and unfolds in symbols when trance, or madness, or deep meditation has withdrawn it from every impulse but its own. 'I then saw,' wrote Gérard de Nerval° of his madness, 'vaguely drifting into form, plastic images of antiquity, which outlined themselves, became definite, and seemed to represent symbols of which I only seized the idea with difficulty.' In an earlier time he would have been of that multitude, whose souls' austerity withdrew, even more perfectly than madness could withdraw his soul, from hope and memory, from desire and regret, that they might reveal those processions of symbols that men bow to before altars, and woo with incense and offerings. But being of our time, he has been like Maeterlinck, like Villiers de l'Isle Adam in *Axël*,° like all who are preoccupied with intellectual symbols in our time, a foreshadower of the new sacred book, of which all the arts, as somebody has said, are beginning to dream. How can the arts overcome the slow dying of men's hearts that we call the progress of the world, and lay their hands upon men's heart-strings again, without becoming the garment of religion as in old times?

V

If people were to accept the theory that poetry moves us because of its symbolism, what change should one look for in the manner of our poetry? A return to the way of our fathers, a casting out of descriptions of nature for the sake of nature, of the moral law for the sake of the moral law, a casting out of all anecdotes and of that brooding over scientific opinion that so often extinguished the central flame in Tennyson, and of that vehemence that would make us do or not do certain things; or, in other words, we should come to understand that the beryl stone was enchanted by our fathers that it might unfold the pictures in its heart, and not to mirror our own excited faces, or the boughs waving outside the window. With this change of substance, this return to imagination, this understanding that the laws of art, which are the hidden laws of the world, can alone bind the imagination, would come a change of style, and we would cast out of serious poetry those energetic rhythms, as of a man running, which are the invention of the will with its eyes always on something to be done or undone; and we would seek out those wavering, meditative, organic rhythms, which are the embodiment of the imagination, that neither desires nor hates, because it has done with time, and only wishes to gaze upon some reality, some beauty; nor would it be any longer possible for anybody to deny the importance of form, in all its kinds, for although you can expound an opinion, or describe a thing when your words are not quite well chosen, you cannot give a body to something that moves beyond the senses, unless your words are as subtle, as complex, as full of mysterious life, as the body of a flower or of a woman. The form of sincere poetry, unlike the form of the popular poetry, may indeed be sometimes obscure, or ungrammatical as in some of the best of the Songs of Innocence and Experience,° but it must have the perfections that escape analysis, the subtleties that have a new meaning every day, and it must have all this whether it be but a little song made out of a moment of dreamy indolence, or some great epic made out of the dreams of one poet and of a hundred generations whose hands were never weary of the sword.

1900

The Theatre

I

I remember, some years ago, advising a distinguished, though too little recognised, writer of poetical plays to write a play as unlike ordinary plays as possible, that it might be judged with a fresh mind, and to put it on the stage in some little suburban hall, where a little audience would pay its expenses. I said that he should follow it the year after, at the same time of the year, with another play, and so on from year to year; and that the people who read books, and do not go to the theatre, would gradually find out about him. I suggested that he should begin with a pastoral play, because nobody would expect from a pastoral play the succession of nervous tremors which the plays of commerce, like the novels of commerce, have substituted for the purification that comes with pity and terror to the imagination and intellect. He followed my advice in part, and had a small but perfect success, filling his small theatre for twice the number of performances he had announced; but instead of being content with the praise of his equals, and waiting to win their praise another year, he hired immediately a well-known London theatre, and put his pastoral play and a new play before a meagre and unintelligent audience. I still remember his pastoral play with delight, because, if not always of a high excellence, it was always poetical; but I remember it at the small theatre, where my pleasure was magnified by the pleasure of those about me, and not at the big theatre, where it made me uncomfortable, as an unwelcome guest always makes one uncomfortable.

Why should we thrust our works, which we have written with imaginative sincerity and filled with spiritual desire, before those quite excellent people who think that Rossetti's° women are 'guys,' that Rodin's° women are 'ugly,' and that Ibsen° is 'immoral,' and who only

Mrs Henderson [*in a child's voice*]. Lulu so glad to see all her friends.

Mrs Mallet. And we are glad you have come, Lulu. 230

Mrs Henderson [*in a child's voice*]. Lulu glad to see new friend.

Miss Mackenna [*to John Corbet*]. She is speaking to you.

John Corbet. Thank you, Lulu.

Mrs Henderson [*in a child's voice*]. You mustn't laugh at the way I talk.

John Corbet. I am not laughing, Lulu.

Mrs Henderson [*in a child's voice*]. Nobody must laugh. Lulu does her best but can't say big long words. Lulu sees a tall man here, lots of hair on face [*Mrs Henderson passes her hands over her cheeks and chin*], not much on the top of his head [*Mrs Henderson passes* 240 *her hand over the top of her head*], red necktie, and such a funny sort of pin.

Mrs Mallet. Yes. . . . Yes. . . .

Mrs Henderson [*in a child's voice*]. Pin like a horseshoe.

Mrs Mallet. It's my husband.

Mr Henderson [*in a child's voice*]. He has a message.

Mrs Mallet. Yes.

Mrs Henderson [*in a child's voice*]. Lulu cannot hear. He is too far off. He has come near. Lulu can hear now. He says . . . he says, 'Drive that man away!' He is pointing to somebody in the corner, that 250 corner over there. He says it is the bad man who spoilt everything last time. If they won't drive him away, Lulu will scream.

Miss Mackenna. That horrible spirit again.

Abraham Johnson. Last time he monopolised the séance.

Mrs Mallet. He would not let anybody speak but himself.

Mrs Henderson [*in a child's voice*]. They have driven that bad man away. Lulu sees a young lady.

Mrs Mallet. Is not my husband here?

Mrs Henderson [*in the child's voice*]. Man with funny pin gone away. Young lady here—Lulu thinks she must be at a fancy dress 260 party, such funny clothes, hair all in curls—all bent down on floor near that old man with glasses.

Dr Trench. No, I do not recognize her.

want to be left at peace to enjoy the works so many clever men have made especially to suit them? We must make a theatre for ourselves and our friends, and for a few simple people who understand from sheer simplicity what we understand from scholarship and thought. We have planned the Irish Literary Theatre° with this hospitable emotion, and, that the right people may find out about us, we hope to act a play or two in the spring of every year; and that the right people may escape the stupefying memory of the theatre of commerce which clings even to them, our plays will be for the most part remote, spiritual, and ideal.

A common opinion is that the poetic drama has come to an end, because modern poets have no dramatic power; and Mr Binyon° seems to accept this opinion when he says: 'It has been too often assumed that it is the manager who bars the way to poetic plays. But it is much more probable that the poets have failed the managers. If poets mean to serve the stage, their dramas must be dramatic.' I find it easier to believe that audiences, who have learned, as I think, from the life of crowded cities to live upon the surface of life, and actors and managers, who study to please them, have changed, than that imagination, which is the voice of what is eternal in man, has changed. The arts are but one Art; and why should all intense painting and all intense poetry have become not merely unintelligible but hateful to the greater number of men and women, and intense drama move them to pleasure? The audiences of Sophocles° and of Shakespeare and of Calderon° were not unlike the audiences I have heard listening in Irish cabins to songs in Gaelic about 'an old poet telling his sins,' and about 'the five young men who were drowned last year,' and about 'the lovers that were drowned going to America,' or to some tale of Oisin and his three hundred years in Tir nan Oge.° Mr Bridges' *Return of Ulysses*,° one of the most beautiful and, as I think, dramatic of modern plays, might have some success in the Aran Islands,° if the Gaelic League would translate it into Gaelic, but I am quite certain that it would have no success in the Strand.

Blake has said that all Art is a labour to bring again the Golden Age,° and all culture is certainly a labour to bring again the simplicity of the first ages, with knowledge of good and evil added to it. The drama has need of cities that it may find men in sufficient numbers, and cities destroy the emotions to which it appeals, and therefore the days of the drama are brief and come but seldom. It has one day when the emotions of cities still remember the emotions of sailors and husbandmen and shepherds and users of the spear and the bow; as the houses and furniture and earthen vessels of cities, before the coming of machinery, remember the rocks and the woods and the hillside; and it has another day, now beginning, when thought and scholarship discover their desire. In the first day, it is the Art of the people; and in the second day, like the dramas acted of old times in the hidden places of temples, it is the preparation of a Priesthood. It may be, though the world is not old enough to show us any example, that this Priesthood will spread their Religion everywhere, and make their Art the Art of the people.

When the first day of the drama had passed by, actors found that an always larger number of people were more easily moved through the eyes than through the ears. The emotion that comes with the music of words is exhausting, like all intellectual emotions, and few people like exhausting emotions; and therefore actors began to speak as if they were reading something out of the newspapers. They forgot the noble art of oratory, and gave all their thought to the poor art of acting, that is content with the sympathy of our nerves; until at last those who love poetry found it better to read alone in their rooms what they had once delighted to hear sitting friend by friend, lover by beloved. I once asked Mr William Morris° if he had thought of writing a play, and he answered that he had, but would not write one, because actors did not know how to speak poetry with the half-chant men spoke it with in old times. Mr Swinburne's *Locrine*° was acted a month ago, and it was not badly acted, but nobody could tell whether it was fit for the stage or not, for not one rhythm, not one cry of passion, was spoken with a musical emphasis, and verse spoken without a musical emphasis seems but an artificial and cumbersome way of saying what might be said naturally and simply in prose.

As audiences and actors changed, managers learned to substitute meretricious landscapes, painted upon wood and canvas, for the descriptions of poetry, until the painted scenery, which had in Greece been a charming explanation of what was least important in the story, became as important as the story. It needed some imagination, some gift for day-dreams, to see the horses and the fields and flowers of Colonus° as one listened to the elders gathered about Oedipus, or to see 'the pendent bed and procreant cradle' of the 'martlet' as one listened to Duncan° before the castle of Macbeth; but it needs no imagination to admire a painting of one of the more obvious effects of nature painted by somebody who understands how to show everything to the most hurried glance. At the same time the managers made the costumes of the actors more and more magnificent, that the mind might sleep in peace, while the eye took pleasure in the magnificence of velvet and silk and in the physical beauty of women. These changes gradually perfected the theatre of commerce, the masterpiece of that movement towards externality in life and thought and Art, against which the criticism of our day is learning to protest.

Even if poetry were spoken as poetry, it would still seem out of place in many of its highest moments upon a stage, where the superficial appearances of nature are so closely copied; for poetry is founded upon convention, and becomes incredible the moment painting or gesture remind us that people do not speak verse when they meet upon the highway. The theatre of Art, when it comes to exist, must therefore discover grave and decorative gestures, such as delighted Rossetti and Madox Brown,° and grave and decorative scenery, that will be forgotten the moment an actor has said 'It is dawn,' or 'It is raining,' or 'The wind is shaking the trees'; and dresses of so little irrelevant magnificence that the mortal actors and actresses may change without much labour into the immortal people of romance. The theatre began in ritual, and it cannot come to its greatness again without recalling words to their ancient sovereignty.

It will take a generation, and perhaps generations, to restore the theatre of Art; for one must get one's actors, and perhaps one's scenery, from the theatre of commerce, until new actors and new painters have come to help one; and until many failures and imperfect successes have made a new tradition, and perfected in detail the ideal that is beginning to float before our eyes. If one could call one's painters and one's actors from where one would, how easy it would be! I know some painters,[1] who have never painted scenery, who could paint the scenery I want, but they have their own work to do; and in Ireland I have heard a red-haired orator[2] repeat some bad political verses with a voice that went through one like flame, and made them seem the most beautiful verses in the world; but he has no practical knowledge of the stage, and probably despises it.

May 1899

II

Dionysius, the Areopagite,° wrote that 'He has set the borders of the nations according to His angels.' It is these angels, each one the genius of some race about to be unfolded, that are the founders of intellectual traditions; and as lovers understand in their first glance all that is to befall them, and as poets and musicians see the whole work in its first impulse, so races prophesy at their awakening whatever the generations that are to prolong their traditions shall accomplish in detail. It is only at

---

[1] I had Charles Ricketts in my mind. 1924.°   [2] J. F. Taylor.°

the awakening—as in ancient Greece, or in Elizabethan England, or in contemporary Scandinavia—that great numbers of men understand that a right understanding of life and of destiny is more important than amusement. In London, where all the intellectual traditions gather to die, men hate a play if they are told it is literature, for they will not endure a spiritual superiority; but in Athens, where so many intellectual traditions were born, Euripides° once changed hostility to enthusiasm by asking his playgoers whether it was his business to teach them, or their business to teach him. New races understand instinctively, because the future cries in their ears, that the old revelations are insufficient, and that all life is revelation beginning in miracle and enthusiasm, and dying out as it unfolds itself in what we have mistaken for progress. It is one of our illusions, as I think, that education, the softening of manners, the perfecting of law—countless images of a fading light—can create nobleness and beauty, and that life moves slowly and evenly towards some perfection. Progress is miracle, and it is sudden, because miracles are the work of an all-powerful energy, and nature in herself has no power except to die and to forget. If one studies one's own mind, one comes to think with Blake, that 'every time less than a pulsation of the artery is equal to six thousand years, for in this period the poet's work is done; and all the great events of time start forth and are conceived in such a period, within a pulsation of the artery.'°

February 1900

The Celtic Element in Literature

I

Ernest Renan described what he held to be Celtic characteristics in *The Poetry of the Celtic Races*.° I must repeat the well-known sentences: 'No race communed so intimately as the Celtic race with the lower creation, or believed it to have so big a share of moral life.' The Celtic race had 'a realistic naturalism,' 'a love of nature for herself, a vivid feeling for her magic, commingled with the melancholy a man knows when he is face to face with her, and thinks he hears her communing with him about his origin and his destiny.' 'It has worn itself out in mistaking dreams for realities,' and 'compared with the classical imagination the Celtic imagination is indeed the infinite contrasted with the finite.' 'Its history is one long lament, it still recalls its exiles, its flights across the seas.' 'If at times it seems to be cheerful, its tear is not slow to glisten behind the smile. Its songs of joy end as elegies; there is nothing to equal the delightful sadness of its national melodies.' Matthew Arnold, in *The Study of Celtic Literature*,° has accepted this passion for nature, this imaginativeness, this melancholy, as Celtic characteristics, but has described them more elaborately. The Celtic passion for nature comes almost more from a sense of her 'mystery' than of her 'beauty,' and it adds 'charm and magic' to nature, and the Celtic imaginativeness and melancholy are alike 'a passionate, turbulent, indomitable reaction against the despotism of fact.' The Celt is not melancholy, as Faust or Werther° are melancholy, from 'a perfectly definite motive,' but because of something about him 'unaccountable, defiant and titanic.' How well one knows these sentences, better even than Renan's, and how well one knows the passages of prose and verse which he uses to prove that wherever English literature has the qualities these sentences describe, it has them from a Celtic source. Though I do not think any of us who write about Ireland have built any argument upon them, it is well to consider them a little, and see where they are helpful and where they are hurtful. If we do not, we may go mad some day, and the enemy root up our rose-garden and plant a cabbage-garden instead. Perhaps we must restate a little, Renan's and Arnold's argument.

II

Once every people in the world believed that trees were divine, and could take a human or grotesque shape and dance among the shadows; and that deer, and ravens and foxes, and wolves and bears, and clouds and pools, almost all things under the sun and moon, and the sun and moon, were not less divine and changeable. They saw in the rainbow the still bent bow of a god thrown down in his negligence; they heard in the thunder the sound of his beaten water-jar, or the tumult of his chariot wheels; and when a sudden flight of wild ducks, or of crows, passed over their heads, they thought they were gazing at the dead hastening to their rest; while they dreamed of so great a mystery in little things that they believed the waving of a hand, or of a sacred bough, enough to trouble far-off hearts, or hood the moon with darkness. All old literatures are full of these or of like imaginations, and all the poets of races, who have not lost this way of looking at things, could have said of themselves, as the poet of the *Kalevala*° said of himself, 'I have learned my songs from the music of many birds, and from the music of many waters.' When a mother in the *Kalevala* weeps for a daughter, who was drowned flying from an old suitor, she weeps so greatly that her tears become three rivers, and cast up three rocks, on which grow three birch-trees, where three cuckoos sit and sing, the one 'love, love,' the one 'suitor, suitor,' the one 'consolation, consolation.' And the makers of the Sagas made the squirrel run up and down the sacred ash-tree carrying words of hatred from the eagle to the worm, and from the worm to the eagle; although they had less of the old way than the makers of the *Kalevala*, for they lived in a more crowded and complicated world, and were learning the abstract meditation which lures men from visible beauty, and were unlearning, it may be, the impassioned meditation which brings men beyond the edge of trance and makes trees, and beasts, and dead things talk with human voices.

The old Irish and the old Welsh, though they had less of the old way than the makers of the *Kalevala*, had more of it than the makers of the Sagas, and it is this that distinguishes the examples Matthew Arnold quotes of their 'natural magic,' of their sense of 'the mystery' more than of 'the beauty' of nature. When Matthew Arnold wrote it was not easy to know as much as we know now of folk song and folk belief, and I do not think he understood that our 'natural magic' is but the ancient religion of the world, the ancient worship of nature and that troubled ecstasy before her, that certainty of all beautiful places being haunted, which it brought into men's minds. The ancient religion is in that passage of the *Mabinogion*° about the making of 'Flower Aspect.' Gwydion and Math made her° 'by charms and illusions' 'out of flowers.' 'They took the blossoms of the oak, and the blossoms of the broom, and the blossoms of the meadow-sweet, and produced from them a maiden the fairest and most graceful that man ever saw; and they baptized her, and called her Flower Aspect'; and one finds it in the not less beautiful passage about the burning Tree,° that has half its beauty from calling up a fancy of leaves so living and beautiful, they can be of no less living and beautiful a thing than flame: 'They saw a tall tree by the side of the river, one half of which was in flames from the root to the top, and the other half was green and in full leaf.' And one finds it very certainly in the quotations he makes from English poets to prove a Celtic influence in English poetry; in Keats's 'magic casements opening on the foam of perilous seas in faery lands forlorn';° in his 'moving waters at their priest-like task of pure ablution round earth's human shore';° in Shakespeare's 'floor of heaven,' 'inlaid with patens of bright gold'; and in his Dido standing 'on the wild sea banks,' 'a willow in her hand,' and waving it in the ritual of the old worship of nature and the spirits of nature, to wave 'her love to come again to Carthage.'° And his other examples have the delight and wonder of devout worshippers among the haunts of their divinities. Is there not such delight and wonder in the description of Olwen° in the *Mabino-gion*—'More yellow was her hair than the flower of the broom, and her skin was whiter than the foam of the wave, and fairer were her hands and her fingers than the blossoms of the wood-anemone amidst the spray of the meadow fountains'? And is there not such delight and wonder in—

> Meet we on hill, in dale, forest, or mead,
> By paved fountain or by rushy brook,
> Or on the beached margent of the sea?°

If men had never dreamed that fair women could be made out of flowers, or rise up out of meadow fountains and paved fountains, neither passage could have been written. Certainly the descriptions of nature made in what Matthew Arnold calls 'the faithful way,' or in what he calls 'the Greek way,' would have lost nothing if all the meadow fountains or paved fountains were but what they seemed. When Keats wrote, in the Greek way, which adds lightness and brightness to nature—

> What little town by river or sea-shore
> Or mountain built with quiet citadel,
> Is emptied of its folk, this pious morn;°

when Shakespeare wrote in the Greek way—

> I know a bank where the wild thyme blows,
> Where oxlips and the nodding violet grows;°

when Virgil wrote in the Greek way—

> Muscosi fontes et somno mollior herba,

and

> Pallentes violas et summa papavera carpens
> Narcissum et florem jungit bene olentis anethi;°

they looked at nature without ecstasy, but with the affection a man feels for the garden where he has walked daily and thought pleasant thoughts. They looked at nature in the modern way, the way of people who are poetical, but are more interested in one another than in a nature which has faded to be but friendly and pleasant, the way of people who have forgotten the ancient religion.

III

Men who lived in a world where anything might flow and change, and become any other thing; and among great gods whose passions were in the flaming sunset, and in the thunder and the thunder-shower, had not our thought of weight and measure. They worshipped nature and the abundance of nature, and had always, as it seems, for a supreme ritual that tumultuous dance among the hills or in the depths of the woods, where unearthly ecstasy fell upon the dancers, until they seemed the gods or the godlike beasts, and felt their souls overtopping the moon; and, as some think, imagined for the first time in the world the blessed country of the gods and of the happy dead. They had imaginative passions because they did not live within our own strait limits, and were nearer to ancient chaos, every man's desire, and had immortal models about them. The hare that ran by among the dew might have sat upon his haunches when the first man was made, and the poor bunch of rushes under their feet might have been a goddess laughing among the stars; and with but a little magic, a little waving of the hands, a little murmuring of the lips, they too could become a hare or a bunch of rushes, and know immortal love and immortal hatred.

All folk literature, and all literature that keeps the folk tradition, delights in unbounded and immortal things. The *Kalevala* delights in the seven hundred years that Luonoton wanders in the depths of the sea with Wäinämöinen in her womb, and the Mahomedan king in the Song of Roland°, pondering upon the greatness of Charlemagne, repeats over and over, 'He is three hundred years old, when will he be weary of war?' Cuchulain in the Irish folk tale had the passion of victory, and he overcame all men, and died warring upon the waves, because they alone had the strength to overcome him. The lover in the Irish folk song bids his beloved come with him into the woods, and see the salmon leap in the rivers, and hear the cuckoo sing, because death will never find them in the heart of the woods. Oisin,° new come from his three hundred years of faeryland, and of the love that is in faeryland, bids Saint Patrick cease his prayers a while and listen to the blackbird, because it is the blackbird of Derrycarn that Finn brought from Norway, three hundred years before, and set its nest upon the oak-tree with his own hands. Surely if one goes far enough into the woods, one will find there all that one is seeking? Who knows how many centuries the birds of the woods have been singing?

All folk literature has indeed a passion whose like is not in modern literature and music and art, except where it has come by some straight or crooked way out of ancient times. Love was held to be a fatal sickness in ancient Ireland, and there is a love-poem in *The Songs of Connacht*° that is like a death cry: 'My love, O she is my love, the woman who is most for destroying me, dearer is she for making me ill than the woman who would be for making me well. She is my treasure, O she is my treasure, the woman of the grey eyes . . . a woman who would not lay a hand under my head. . . . She is my love, O she is my love, the woman who left no strength in me; a woman who would not breathe a sigh after me, a woman who would not raise a stone at my tomb. . . . She is my secret love, O she is my secret love. A woman who tells me nothing, . . . a woman who does not remember me to be out. . . . She is my choice, O she is my choice, the woman who would not look back at me, the woman who would not make peace with me. . . . She is my desire, O she is my desire: a woman dearest to me under the sun, a woman who would not pay me heed, if I were to sit by her side. It is she ruined my heart and left a sigh for ever in me.' There is another song that ends, 'The Erne shall be in strong flood, the hills shall be torn down, and the sea shall have red waves, and blood shall be spilled, and every mountain valley and every moor shall be on high, before you shall perish, my little black rose.' Nor do the old Irish weigh and measure their hatred. The nurse of O'Sullivan Bere° in the folk song prays that the bed of his betrayer may be the red hearth-stone of hell for ever. And an Elizabethan Irish poet cries: 'Three things are waiting for my death. The devil, who is waiting for my soul and cares nothing for my body or my wealth; the worms, who are waiting for my body but care nothing for my soul or my wealth; my children, who are waiting for my wealth and care nothing for my body or my soul. O Christ, hang all three in the one noose.' Such love and hatred seek no mortal thing but their own infinity, and such love and hatred soon become love and hatred of the idea. The lover who loves so passionately can soon sing to his beloved like the lover in the poem by 'A.E.,' 'A vast desire awakes and grows into forgetfulness of thee.'°

When an early Irish poet calls the Irishman famous for much loving, and a proverb, a friend[1] has heard in the Highlands of Scotland, talks of the lovelessness of the Irishman, they may say but the same thing, for if your passion is but great enough it leads you to a country where there are many cloisters. The hater who hates with too good a heart soon comes also to hate the idea only; and from this idealism in love and hatred comes, as I think, a certain power of saying and forgetting things, especially a power of saying and forgetting things in politics, which others do not say and forget. The ancient farmers and herdsmen were full of love and hatred, and made their friends gods, and their enemies the enemies of gods, and those who keep their tradition are not less mythological. From this 'mistaking dreams,' which are perhaps essences, for 'real-

---

[1] William Sharp,° who probably invented the proverb, but, invented or not, it remains true.   1924

ities,' which are perhaps accidents, from this 'passionate, turbulent reaction against the despotism of fact,' comes, it may be, that melancholy which made all ancient peoples delight in tales that end in death and parting, as modern peoples delight in tales that end in marriage bells; and made all ancient peoples, who like the old Irish had a nature more lyrical than dramatic, delight in wild and beautiful lamentations. Life was so weighed down by the emptiness of the great forests and by the mystery of all things, and by the greatness of its own desires, and, as I think, by the loneliness of much beauty; and seemed so little and so fragile and so brief, that nothing could be more sweet in the memory than a tale that ended in death and parting, and than a wild and beautiful lamentation. Men did not mourn merely because their beloved was married to another, or because learning was bitter in the mouth, for such mourning believes that life might be happy were it different, and is therefore the less mourning; but because they had been born and must die with their great thirst unslaked. And so it is that all the august sorrowful persons of literature, Cassandra and Helen and Deirdre, and Lear and Tristan, have come out of legends and are indeed but the images of the primitive imagination mirrored in the little looking-glass of the modern and classic imagination. This is that 'melancholy a man knows when he is face to face' with nature, and thinks 'he hears her communing with him about' the mournfulness of being born and of dying; and how can it do otherwise than call into his mind 'its exiles, its flights across the seas,' that it may stir the ever-smouldering ashes? No Gaelic poetry is so popular in Gaelic-speaking places as the lamentations of Oisin, old and miserable, remembering the companions and the loves of his youth, and his three hundred years in faeryland, and his faery love: all dreams withering in the winds of time lament in his lamentations: 'The clouds are long above me this night; last night was a long night to me; although I find this day long, yesterday was still longer. Every day that comes to me is long. . . . No one in this great world is like me—a poor old man dragging stones. The clouds are long above me this night. I am the last man of the Fianna, the great Oisin, the son of Finn, listening to the sound of bells. The clouds are long above me this night.' Matthew Arnold quotes the lamentation of Llywarch Hen° as a type of the Celtic melancholy, but I prefer to quote it as a type of the primitive melancholy: 'O my crutch, is it not autumn when the fern is red and the water flag yellow? Have I not hated that which I love? . . . Behold, old age, which makes sport of me, from the hair of my head and my teeth, to my eyes which women loved. The four things I have all my life most hated fall upon me together—coughing and old age, sickness and sorrow. I am old, I am alone, shapeliness and warmth are gone from me, the couch of honour shall be no more mine; I am miserable, I am bent on my crutch. How evil was the lot allotted to Llywarch, the night he was brought forth! Sorrows without end and no deliverance from his burden.' An Elizabethan writer describes extravagant sorrow by calling it 'to weep Irish'; and Oisin and Llywarch Hen are, I think, a little nearer even to us modern Irish than they are to most people. That is why our poetry and much of our thought is melancholy. 'The same man,' writes Dr Hyde in the beautiful prose which he first writes in Gaelic, 'who will to-day be dancing, sporting, drinking, and shouting, will be soliloquising by himself to-morrow, heavy and sick and sad in his own lonely little hut, making a croon over departed hopes, lost life, the vanity of this world, and the coming of death.'

IV

Matthew Arnold asks how much of the Celt must one imagine in the ideal man of genius. I prefer to say, how much of the ancient hunters and fishers and of the ecstatic dancers among hills and woods must one imagine in the ideal man of genius. Certainly a thirst for unbounded emotion and a wild melancholy are troublesome things in the world, and do not make its life more easy or orderly, but it may be the arts are founded on the life beyond the world, and that they must cry in the ears of our penury until the world has been consumed and become a vision. Certainly, as Samuel Palmer° wrote, 'Excess is the vivifying spirit of the finest art, and we must always seek to make excess more abundantly excessive.' Matthew Arnold has said that if he were asked 'where English got its turn for melancholy and its turn for natural magic,' he 'would answer with little doubt that it got much of its melancholy from a Celtic source, with no doubt at all that from a Celtic source it got nearly all its natural magic.'

I will put this differently and say that literature dwindles to a mere chronicle of circumstance, or passionless phantasies, and passionless meditations, unless it is constantly flooded with the passions and beliefs of ancient times,[1] and that of all the fountains of the passions and beliefs of ancient times in Europe, the Sclavonic, the Finnish, the Scandinavian, and the Celtic, the Celtic alone has been for centuries close to the main river of European literature. It has again and again brought 'the vivifying spirit' 'of excess' into the arts of Europe. Ernest Renan has told

---

[1] I should have added as an alternative that the supernatural may at any moment create new myths, but I was timid.   1924

how the visions of Purgatory seen by pilgrims to Lough Derg°—once visions of the pagan underworld, as the boat made out of a hollow tree that bore the pilgrim to the holy island were alone enough to prove—gave European thought new symbols of a more abundant penitence; and had so great an influence that he has written, 'It cannot be doubted for a moment that to the number of poetical themes Europe owes to the genius of the Celt is to be added the framework of the divine comedy.'°

A little later the legends of Arthur and his table, and of the Holy Grail, once it seems the cauldron° of an Irish god, changed the literature of Europe, and it maybe changed, as it were, the very roots of man's emotions by their influence on the spirit of chivalry and on the spirit of romance; and later still Shakespeare found his Mab, and probably his Puck,° and one knows not how much else of his faery kingdom, in Celtic legend; while at the beginning of our own day Sir Walter Scott° gave Highland legends and Highland excitability so great a mastery over all romance that they seem romance itself.

In our own time Scandinavian tradition, because of the imagination of Richard Wagner and of William Morris° and of the earlier and, as I think, greater Heinrich Ibsen, has created a new romance, and through the imagination of Richard Wagner, become all but the most passionate element in the arts of the modern world. There is indeed but one other element as passionate, the still unfaded legends of Arthur and of the Holy Grail; and now a new fountain of legends, and, as I think, a more abundant fountain than any in Europe, is being opened, the fountain of Gaelic legends: the tale of Deirdre,° who alone among women who have set men mad had equal loveliness and wisdom; the tale of the Sons of Tuireann,° with its unintelligible mysteries, an old Grail Quest as I think; the tale of the four children changed into four swans, and lamenting over many waters; the tale of the love of Cuchulain for an immortal goddess, and his coming home to a mortal woman in the end;° the tale of his many battles at the ford with that dear friend he kissed before the battles, and over whose dead body he wept when he had killed him; the tale of his death and of the lamentations of Emer; the tale of the flight of Grainne with Diarmuid,° strangest of all tales of the fickleness of woman, and the tale of the coming of Oisin° out of faeryland, and of his memories and lamentations. 'The Celtic movement,' as I understand it, is principally the opening of this fountain, and none can measure of how great importance it may be to coming times, for every new fountain of legends is a new intoxication for the imagination of the world. It comes at a time when the imagination of the world is as ready, as it was at the coming of the tales of Arthur and of the Grail, for a new intoxication.

The reaction against the rationalism of the eighteenth century has mingled with a reaction against the materialism of the nineteenth century, and the symbolical movement, which has come to perfection in Germany in Wagner, in England in the Pre-Raphaelites,° in France in Villiers de l'Isle-Adam,° and Mallarmé,° and in Maeterlinck,° and has stirred the imagination of Ibsen° and D'Annunzio,° is certainly the only movement that is saying new things. The arts by brooding upon their own intensity have become religious, and are seeking, as I think Verhaeren° has said, to create a sacred book. They must, as religious thought has always done, utter themselves through legends; and the Sclavonic and Finnish legends tell of strange woods and seas, and the Scandinavian legends are held by a great master, and tell also of strange woods and seas, and the Welsh legends are held by almost as many great masters as the Greek legends, while the Irish legends move among known woods and seas, and have so much of a new beauty, that they may well give the opening century its most memorable symbols.

1897

I could have written this essay with much more precision and have much better illustrated my meaning if I had waited until Lady Gregory had finished her book of legends, *Cuchulain of Muirthemne*,° a book to set beside the *Morte d' Arthur*° and the *Mabinogion*.

1902

The Moods

Literature differs from explanatory and scientific writing in being wrought about a mood, or a community of moods, as the body is wrought about an invisible soul; and if it uses argument, theory, erudition, observation, and seems to grow hot in assertion or denial, it does so merely to make us partakers at the banquet of the moods. It seems to me that these moods are the labourers and messengers of the Ruler of All, the gods of ancient days still dwelling on their secret Olympus, the angels of more modern days ascending and descending upon their shining ladder; and that argument, theory, erudition, observation, are merely what Blake called 'little devils who fight for themselves,' illusions of our visible passing life, who must be made serve the moods, or we have no part in eternity. Everything that can be seen, touched, measured, explained, understood, argued over, is to the imaginative artist nothing more than a means, for he belongs to the invisible life, and delivers its ever new and ever ancient revelation. We hear much of his need for the restraints of reason, but the only restraint he can obey is the mysterious instinct that has made him an artist, and that teaches him to discover immortal moods in mortal desires, an undecaying hope in our trivial ambitions, a divine love in sexual passion.

1895

A General Introduction for my Work°

I. THE FIRST PRINCIPLE

A poet writes always of his personal life, in his finest work out of its tragedy, whatever it be, remorse, lost love, or mere loneliness; he never speaks directly as to someone at the breakfast table, there is always a phantasmagoria. Dante and Milton had mythologies, Shakespeare the characters of English history or of traditional romance; even when the poet seems most himself, when he is Raleigh and gives potentates the lie, or Shelley 'a nerve o'er which do creep the else unfelt oppressions of this earth,' or Byron when 'the soul wears out the breast' as 'the sword outwears its sheath,' he is never the bundle of accident and incoherence that sits down to breakfast; he has been reborn as an idea, something intended, complete. A novelist might describe his accidence, his incoherence, he must not; he is more type than man, more passion than type. He is Lear, Romeo, Oedipus, Tiresias;° he has stepped out of a play, and even the woman he loves is Rosalind,° Cleopatra,° never The Dark Lady.° He is part of his own phantasmagoria and we adore him because nature has grown intelligible, and by so doing a part of our creative power. 'When mind is lost in the light of the Self,' says the Prashna Upanishad, 'it dreams no more; still in the body it is lost in happiness.' 'A wise man seeks in Self,' says the Chandogya Upanishad,° 'those that are alive and those that are dead and gets what the world cannot give.' The world knows nothing because it has made nothing, we know everything because we have made everything.

II. SUBJECT-MATTER

It was through the old Fenian leader John O'Leary° I found my theme. His long imprisonment, his longer banishment, his magnificent head, his scholarship, his pride, his integrity, all that aristocratic dream nourished amid little shops and little farms, had drawn around him a group of young men; I was but eighteen or nineteen and had already,

under the influence of *The Faerie Queene* and *The Sad Shepherd*,° written
a pastoral play, and under that of Shelley's *Prometheus Unbound*° two
plays, one staged somewhere in the Caucasus, the other in a crater of the
moon; and I knew myself to be vague and incoherent. He gave me the
poems of Thomas Davis,° said they were not good poetry but had
changed his life when a young man, spoke of other poets associated with
Davis and *The Nation*° newspaper, probably lent me their books. I saw
even more clearly than O'Leary that they were not good poetry. I read
nothing but romantic literature; hated that dry eighteenth-century
rhetoric; but they had one quality I admired and admire: they were not
separated individual men; they spoke or tried to speak out of a people to
a people; behind them stretched the generations. I knew, though but
now and then as young men know things, that I must turn from that
modern literature Jonathan Swift compared to the web a spider draws
out of its bowels; I hated and still hate with an ever growing hatred the
literature of the point of view. I wanted, if my ignorance permitted, to
get back to Homer, to those that fed at his table. I wanted to cry as all men
cried, to laugh as all men laughed, and the Young Ireland poets when not
writing mere politics had the same want, but they did not know that the
common and its befitting language is the research of a lifetime and when
found may lack popular recognition. Then somebody, not O'Leary, told
me of Standish O'Grady° and his interpretation of Irish legends.
O'Leary had sent me to O'Curry,° but his unarranged and uninter-
preted history defeated my boyish indolence.

A generation before *The Nation* newspaper was founded the Royal
Irish Academy had begun the study of ancient Irish literature. That
study was as much a gift from the Protestant aristocracy which had cre-
ated the Parliament as *The Nation* and its school, though Davis and
Mitchel° were Protestants; was a gift from the Catholic middle classes
who were to create the Irish Free State. The Academy persuaded the
English Government to finance an ordnance survey on a large scale;
scholars, including that great scholar O'Donovan,° were sent from village
to village recording names and their legends. Perhaps it was the last
moment when such work could be well done, the memory of the people
was still intact, the collectors themselves had perhaps heard or seen the
banshee; the Royal Irish Academy and its public with equal enthusiasm
welcomed Pagan and Christian; thought the Round Towers a commem-
oration of Persian fire-worship. There was little orthodoxy to take alarm;
the Catholics were crushed and cowed; an honoured great-uncle of
mine—his portrait by some forgotten master hangs upon my bedroom
wall—a Church of Ireland rector, would upon occasion boast that you

could not ask a question he could not answer with a perfectly appropriate blasphemy or indecency. When several counties had been surveyed but nothing published, the Government, afraid of rousing dangerous patriotic emotion, withdrew support; large manuscript volumes remain containing much picturesque correspondence between scholars.

When modern Irish literature began, O'Grady's influence predominated. He could delight us with an extravagance we were too critical to share; a day will come, he said, when Slieve-na-mon° will be more famous than Olympus; yet he was no Nationalist as we understood the word, but in rebellion, as he was fond of explaining, against the House of Commons, not against the King. His cousin, that great scholar Hayes O'Grady,° would not join our non-political Irish Literary Society because he considered it a Fenian body, but boasted that although he had lived in England for forty years he had never made an English friend. He worked at the British Museum compiling their Gaelic catalogue and translating our heroic tales in an eighteenth-century frenzy; his heroine 'fractured her heart,' his hero 'ascended to the apex of the eminence' and there 'vibrated his javelin,' and afterwards took ship upon 'colossal ocean's superficies.' Both O'Gradys considered themselves as representing the old Irish land-owning aristocracy; both probably, Standish O'Grady certainly, thought that England, because decadent and democratic, had betrayed their order. It was another member of that order, Lady Gregory, who was to do for the heroic legends in *Gods and Fighting Men* and in *Cuchulain of Muirthemne*° what Lady Charlotte Guest's *Mabinogion*° had done with less beauty and style for those of Wales. Standish O'Grady had much modern sentiment, his style, like that of John Mitchel forty years before, shaped by Carlyle;° she formed her style upon the Anglo-Irish dialect of her neighbourhood, an old vivid speech with a partly Tudor vocabulary, a syntax partly moulded by men who still thought in Gaelic.

I had heard in Sligo cottages or from pilots at Rosses Point° endless stories of apparitions, whether of the recent dead or of the people of history and legend, of that Queen Maeve whose reputed cairn stands on the mountain over the bay.° Then at the British Museum I read stories Irish writers of the 'forties and 'fifties had written of such apparitions, but they enraged me more than pleased because they turned the country visions into a joke. But when I went from cottage to cottage with Lady Gregory and watched her hand recording that great collection she has called *Visions and Beliefs*° I escaped disfiguring humour.

Behind all Irish history hangs a great tapestry, even Christianity had to accept it and be itself pictured there. Nobody looking at its dim folds can say where Christianity begins and Druidism ends; 'There is one perfect among the birds, one perfect among the fish, and one among men that is perfect.' I can only explain by that suggestion of recent scholars— Professor Burkitt° of Cambridge commended it to my attention—that St Patrick came to Ireland not in the fifth century but towards the end of the second. The great controversies had not begun; Easter was still the first full moon after the Equinox. Upon that day the world had been created, the Ark rested upon Ararat, Moses led the Israelites out of Egypt; the umbilical cord which united Christianity to the ancient world had not yet been cut, Christ was still the half-brother of Dionysus.° A man just tonsured by the Druids could learn from the nearest Christian neighbour to sign himself with the Cross without sense of incongruity, nor would his children acquire that sense. The organised clans weakened Church organisation, they could accept the monk but not the bishop.

A modern man, *The Golden Bough°* and *Human Personality°* in his head, finds much that is congenial in St Patrick's Creed as recorded in his Confessions, and nothing to reject except the word 'soon' in the statement that Christ will soon judge the quick and the dead. He can repeat it, believe it even, without a thought of the historic Christ, or ancient Judea, or of anything subject to historical conjecture and shifting evidence; I repeat it and think of 'the Self' in the Upanishads. Into this tradition, oral and written, went in later years fragments of Neo-Platonism,° cabbalistic words—I have heard the words 'tetragrammaton agla'° in Doneraile°—the floating debris of mediaeval thought, but nothing that did not please the solitary mind. Even the religious equivalent for Baroque and Rococo could not come to us as thought, perhaps because Gaelic is incapable of abstraction. It came as cruelty. That tapestry filled the scene at the birth of modern Irish literature, it is there in the Synge of *The Well of the Saints*,° in James Stephens,° and in Lady Gregory throughout, in all of George Russell° that did not come from the Upanishads, and in all but my later poetry.

Sometimes I am told in commendation, if the newspaper is Irish, in condemnation if English, that my movement perished under the firing squads of 1916; sometimes that those firing squads made our realistic movement possible. If that statement is true, and it is only so in part, for romance was everywhere receding, it is because in the imagination of Pearse° and his fellow soldiers the Sacrifice of the Mass had found the Red Branch° in the tapestry; they went out to die calling upon Cuchulain:—

> Fall, Hercules, from Heaven in tempests hurled
> To cleanse the beastly stable of this world.°

In one sense the poets of 1916 were not of what the newspapers call my school. The Gaelic League, made timid by a modern popularisation of Catholicism sprung from the aspidistra and not from the root of Jesse,° dreaded intellectual daring and stuck to dictionary and grammar. Pearse and MacDonagh° and others among the executed men would have done, or attempted, in Gaelic what we did or attempted in English.

Our mythology, our legends, differ from those of other European countries because down to the end of the seventeenth century they had the attention, perhaps the unquestioned belief, of peasant and noble alike; Homer belongs to sedentary men, even to-day our ancient queens, our mediaeval soldiers and lovers, can make a pedlar shudder. I can put my own thought, despair perhaps from the study of present circumstance in the light of ancient philosophy, into the mouth of rambling poets of the seventeenth century, or even of some imagined ballad singer of to-day, and the deeper my thought the more credible, the more peasant-like, are ballad singer and rambling poet. Some modern poets contend that jazz and music-hall songs are the folk art of our time, that we should mould our art upon them; we Irish poets, modern men also, reject every folk art that does not go back to Olympus. Give me time and a little youth and I will prove that even 'Johnny, I hardly knew ye' goes back.

Mr Arnold Toynbee in an annex to the second volume of *The Study of History*° describes the birth and decay of what he calls the Far Western Christian culture; it lost at the Synod of Whitby its chance of mastering Europe, suffered final ecclesiastical defeat in the twelfth century with 'the thoroughgoing incorporation of the Irish Christendom into the Roman Church. In the political and literary spheres' it lasted unbroken till the seventeenth century. He then insists that if 'Jewish Zionism and Irish Nationalism succeed in achieving their aims, then Jewry and Irishry will each fit into its own tiny niche . . . among sixty or seventy national communities', find life somewhat easier, but cease to be 'the relic of an independent society . . . the romance of Ancient Ireland has at last come to an end . . . Modern Ireland has made up her mind, in our generation, to find her level as a willing inmate in our workaday Western world.'

If Irish literature goes on as my generation planned it, it may do something to keep the 'Irishry' living, nor will the work of the realists hinder, nor the figures they imagine, nor those described in memoirs of the revolution. These last especially, like certain great political predecessors, Parnell, Swift, Lord Edward,° have stepped back into the tapestry. It may be indeed that certain characteristics of the 'Irishry' must grow in importance. When Lady Gregory asked me to annotate her *Visions and Beliefs*° I began, that I might understand what she had taken down in Galway, an investigation of contemporary spiritualism. For several years I frequented those mediums who in various poor parts of London instruct artisans or their wives for a few pence upon their relations to their dead, to their employers, and to their children; then I compared what she had heard in Galway, or I in London, with the visions of Swedenborg,° and, after my inadequate notes had been published, with Indian belief. If Lady Gregory had not said when we passed an old man in the woods, 'That man may know the secret of the ages,' I might never have talked with Shri Purohit Swāmi nor made him translate his Master's travels in Tibet, nor helped him translate the Upanishads. I think I now know why the gamekeeper at Coole heard the footsteps of a deer on the edge of the lake where no deer had passed for a hundred years, and why a certain cracked old priest said that nobody had been to hell or heaven in his time, meaning thereby that the Rath had got them all; that the dead stayed where they had lived, or near it, sought no abstract region of blessing or punishment but retreated, as it were, into the hidden character of their neighbourhood. I am convinced that in two or three generations it will become generally known that the mechanical theory has no reality, that the natural and supernatural are knit together, that to escape a dangerous fanaticism we must study a new science; at that moment Europeans may find something attractive in a Christ posed against a background not of Judaism but of Druidism, not shut off in dead history, but flowing, concrete, phenomenal.

I was born into this faith, have lived in it, and shall die in it; my Christ, a legitimate deduction from the Creed of St Patrick° as I think, is that Unity of Being Dante compared to a perfectly proportioned human body,° Blake's 'Imagination,' what the Upanishads have named 'Self': nor is this unity distant and therefore intellectually understandable, but imminent, differing from man to man and age to age, taking upon itself pain and ugliness, 'eye of newt, and toe of frog.'

Subconscious preoccupation with this theme brought me *A Vision*, its harsh geometry an incomplete interpretation. The 'Irishry' have preserved their ancient 'deposit' through wars which, during the sixteenth and seventeenth centuries, became wars of extermination; no people, Lecky said at the opening of his *Ireland in the Eighteenth Century*,° have undergone greater persecution, nor did that persecution altogether cease up to our own day. No people hate as we do in whom that past is always alive, there are moments when hatred poisons my life and I accuse myself of effeminacy because I have not given it adequate expression. It is not enough to have put it into the mouth of a rambling peasant poet. Then I remind myself that though mine is the first English marriage I know of in the direct line, all my family names are English, and that I owe my soul to Shakespeare, to Spenser and to Blake, perhaps to William Morris, and to the English language in which I think, speak, and write, that everything I love has come to me through English; my hatred tortures me with love, my love with hate. I am like the Tibetan monk who dreams at his initiation that he is eaten by a wild beast and learns on waking that he himself is eater and eaten. This is Irish hatred and solitude, the hatred of human life that made Swift write *Gulliver* and the epitaph upon his tomb,° that can still make us wag between extremes and doubt our sanity.

Again and again I am asked why I do not write in Gaelic. Some four or five years ago I was invited to dinner by a London society and found myself among London journalists, Indian students, and foreign political refugees. An Indian paper says it was a dinner in my honour; I hope not; I have forgotten, though I have a clear memory of my own angry mind. I should have spoken as men are expected to speak at public dinners; I should have paid and been paid conventional compliments; then they would speak of the refugees; from that on all would be lively and topical, foreign tyranny would be arraigned, England seem even to those confused Indians the protector of liberty; I grew angrier and angrier; Wordsworth, that typical Englishman, had published his famous sonnet to François Dominique Toussaint, a Santo Domingo Negro:—

> There's not a breathing of the common wind
> That will forget thee°

in the year when Emmet° conspired and died, and he remembered that rebellion as little as the half hanging and the pitch cap that preceded it by half a dozen years. That there might be no topical speeches I denounced the oppression of the people of India; being a man of letters, not a politician, I told how they had been forced to learn everything, even their own Sanskrit, through the vehicle of English till the first discoverer of wisdom had become bywords for vague abstract facility. I begged the Indian writers present to remember that no man can think or write with music and vigour except in his mother tongue. I turned a friendly audience hostile, yet when I think of that scene I am unrepentant and angry.

I could no more have written in Gaelic than can those Indians write in English; Gaelic is my national language, but it is not my mother tongue.

III. STYLE AND ATTITUDE

Style is almost unconscious. I know what I have tried to do, little what I have done. Contemporary lyric poems, even those that moved me—*The Stream's Secret, Dolores*°—seemed too long, but an Irish preference for a swift current might be mere indolence, yet Burns may have felt the same when he read Thomson and Cowper.° The English mind is meditative, rich, deliberate; it may remember the Thames valley. I planned to write short lyrics or poetic drama where every speech would be short and concentrated, knit by dramatic tension, and I did so with more confidence because young English poets were at that time writing out of emotion at the moment of crisis, though their old slow-moving meditation returned almost at once. Then, and in this English poetry has followed my lead, I tried to make the language of poetry coincide with that of passionate, normal speech. I wanted to write in whatever language comes most naturally when we soliloquise, as I do all day long, upon the events of our own lives or of any life where we can see ourselves for the moment. I sometimes compare myself with the mad old slum women I hear denouncing and remembering; 'How dare you,' I heard one say of some imaginary suitor, 'and you without health or a home!' If I spoke my thoughts aloud they might be as angry and as wild. It was a long time before I had made a language to my liking; I began to make it when I discovered some twenty years ago that I must seek, not as Wordsworth thought, words in common use, but a powerful and passionate syntax, and a complete coincidence between period and stanza. Because I need a passionate syntax for passionate subject-matter I compel myself to accept those traditional metres that have developed with the language. Ezra Pound, Turner, Lawrence° wrote admirable free verse, I could not. I would lose myself, become joyless like those mad old women. The translators of the Bible, Sir Thomas Browne,° certain translators from the Greek when translators still bothered about rhythm, created a form midway between prose and verse that seems natural to impersonal meditation; but all that is personal soon rots; it must be packed in ice or salt. Once when I was in delirium from pneumonia I dictated a letter to George Moore° telling him to eat salt because it was a symbol of eternity; the delirium passed, I had no memory of that letter, but I must have meant what I now mean. If I wrote of personal love or sorrow in free verse, or in any rhythm that left it unchanged, amid all its accidence, I would be full of self-contempt because of my egotism and indiscretion, and foresee the boredom of my reader. I must choose a traditional stanza, even what I alter must seem traditional. I commit my emotion to

shepherds, herdsmen, camel-drivers, learned men, Milton's or Shel-
ley's Platonist, that tower Palmer drew.° Talk to me of originality and I
will turn on you with rage. I am a crowd, I am a lonely man, I am noth-
ing. Ancient salt is best packing. The heroes of Shakespeare convey to us
through their looks, or through the metaphorical patterns of their
speech, the sudden enlargement of their vision, their ecstasy at the
approach of death: 'She should have died hereafter,' 'Of many thousand
kisses, the poor last,' 'Absent thee from felicity awhile.' They have
become God or Mother Goddess, the pelican, 'My baby at my breast,'
but all must be cold; no actress has ever sobbed when she played Cleo-
patra, even the shallow brain of a producer has never thought of such a
thing. The supernatural is present, cold winds blow across our hands,
upon our faces, the thermometer falls, and because of that cold we are
hated by journalists and groundlings. There may be in this or that detail
painful tragedy, but in the whole work none. I have heard Lady Gregory
say, rejecting some play in the modern manner sent to the Abbey
Theatre, 'Tragedy must be a joy to the man who dies.' Nor is it any
different with lyrics, songs, narrative poems; neither scholars nor the
populace have sung or read anything generation after generation
because of its pain. The maid of honour whose tragedy they sing must be
lifted out of history with timeless pattern, she is one of the four Maries,
the rhythm is old and familiar, imagination must dance, must be carried
beyond feeling into the aboriginal ice. Is ice the correct word? I once
boasted, copying the phrase from a letter of my father's, that I would
write a poem 'cold and passionate as the dawn.'

When I wrote in blank verse I was dissatisfied; my vaguely mediaeval
Countess Cathleen° fitted the measure, but our Heroic Age went better,
or so I fancied, in the ballad metre of *The Green Helmet*°. There was
something in what I felt about Deirdre, about Cuchulain, that rejected
the Renaissance and its characteristic metres, and this was a principal
reason why I created in dance plays the form that varies blank verse with
lyric metres. When I speak blank verse and analyse my feelings, I stand
at a moment of history when instinct, its traditional songs and dances, its
general agreement, is of the past. I have been cast up out of the whale's
belly though I still remember the sound and sway that came from
beyond its ribs, and, like the Queen in Paul Fort's ballad,° I smell of the
fish of the sea. The contrapuntal structure of the verse, to employ a term
adopted by Robert Bridges,° combines the past and present. If I repeat
the first line of *Paradise Lost* so as to emphasise its five feet I am among
the folk singers—'Of mán's first dísobédience ánd the frúit,' but speak it
as I should I cross it with another emphasis, that of passionate prose—

'Of mán's fírst disobédience and the frúit,' or 'Of mán's fírst dísobedi-
ence and the frúit'; the folk song is still there, but a ghostly voice, an
unvariable possibility, an unconscious norm. What moves me and my
hearer is a vivid speech that has no laws except that it must not exorcise
the ghostly voice. I am awake and asleep, at my moment of revelation,
self-possessed in self-surrender; there is no rhyme, no echo of the beaten
drum, the dancing foot, that would overset my balance. When I was a
boy I wrote a poem upon dancing that had one good line: 'They snatch
with their hands at the sleep of the skies.' If I sat down and thought for a
year I would discover that but for certain syllabic limitations, a rejection
or acceptance of certain elisions, I must wake or sleep.

The Countess Cathleen could speak a blank verse which I had loos-
ened, almost put out of joint, for her need, because I thought of her as
mediaeval and thereby connected her with the general European move-
ment. For Deirdre and Cuchulain and all the other figures of Irish
legend are still in the whale's belly.

IV. WHITHER?

The young English poets reject dream and personal emotion; they
have thought out opinions that join them to this or that political party;
they employ an intricate psychology, action in character, not as in the
ballads character in action, and all consider that they have a right to the
same close attention that men pay to the mathematician and the meta-
physician. One of the more distinguished has just explained that man
has hitherto slept but must now awake. They are determined to express
the factory, the metropolis, that they may be modern. Young men teach-
ing school in some picturesque cathedral town, or settled for life in Capri
or in Sicily, defend their type of metaphor by saying that it comes natu-
rally to a man who travels to his work by Tube. I am indebted to a man
of this school who went through my work at my request, crossing out all
conventional metaphors, but they seem to me to have rejected also those
dream associations which were the whole art of Mallarmé.° He had
topped a previous wave. As they express not what the Upanishads call
'that ancient Self' but individual intellect, they have the right to choose
the man in the Tube because of his objective importance. They attempt
to kill the whale, push the Renaissance higher yet, outthink Leonardo;
their verse kills the folk ghost and yet would remain verse. I am joined to
the 'Irishry' and I expect a counter-Renaissance. No doubt it is part of
the game to push that Renaissance; I make no complaint; I am accus-
tomed to the geometrical arrangement of history in *A Vision*, but I go
deeper than 'custom' for my convictions. When I stand upon O'Connell

Bridge° in the half-light and notice that discordant architecture, all
those electric signs, where modern heterogeneity has taken physical
form, a vague hatred comes up out of my own dark and I am certain that
wherever in Europe there are minds strong enough to lead others the
same vague hatred rises; in four or five or in less generations this hatred
will have issued in violence and imposed some kind of rule of kindred. I
cannot know the nature of that rule, for its opposite fills the light; all I
can do to bring it nearer is to intensify my hatred. I am no Nationalist,
except in Ireland for passing reasons; State and Nation are the work of
intellect, and when you consider what comes before and after them they
are, as Victor Hugo said of something or other, not worth the blade of
grass God gives for the nest of the linnet.

1937

from On the Boiler°

To-morrow's Revolution

I

When I was in my 'teens I admired my father above all men; from him I
learnt to admire Balzac° and to set certain passages in Shakespeare above
all else in literature, but when I was twenty-three or twenty-four I read
Ruskin's 'Unto This Last'° of which I do not remember a word, and we
began to quarrel, for he was John Stuart Mill's° disciple. Once he threw
me against a picture with such violence that I broke the glass with the
back of my head. But it was not only with my father that I quarrelled, nor
were economics the only theme. There was no dominant opinion I could
accept. Then finding out that I (having no clear case—my opponent's
case had been clarifying itself for centuries) had become both boor and
bore I invented a patter, allowing myself an easy man's insincerity, and
for honesty's sake a little malice, and now it seems that I can talk nothing
else. But I think I have succeeded, and that none of my friends know that
I am a fanatic. My reader may say that it was all natural, that every gen-
eration is against its predecessor, but that conflict is superficial, an exalt-
ation of the individual life that had little importance before modern
journalism; that other war, where opposites die each other's life, live

each other's death, is a slow-moving thing. We who are the opposites of our times should for the most part work at our art and for good manners' sake be silent. What matter if our art or science lack hearty acquiescence, seem narrow and traditional? Horne built the smallest church in London, went to Italy and became the foremost authority upon Botticelli.° Ricketts° made pictures that suggest Delacroix° by their colour and remind us by their theatrical composition that Talma° once invoked the thunderbolt; Synge fled to the Aran Islands to escape 'the squalor of the poor and the nullity of the rich', and found among forgotten people a mirror for his bitterness. I gave certain years to writing plays in Shakespearean blank verse about Irish kings for whom nobody cared a farthing. After all, Asiatic conquerors before battle invoked their ancestors, and a few years ago a Japanese admiral thanked his for guiding the torpedoes.

II

But now I must, if I can, put away my patter, speak to the young men before the ox treads on my tongue. Here is my text; I take it from 'The Anatomy of Melancholy.'°

'So many different ways are we plagued and punished for our fathers' defaults: in so much that, as Fernelius truly saith, "it is the greatest part of our felicity to be well born, and it were happy for human kind, if only such parents as are sound of body and mind should be suffered to marry." An husbandman will sow none but the best and choicest seed upon his land; he will not rear a bull or an horse except he be right shapen in all parts, or permit him to cover a mare, except he be well assured of his breed; we make choice of the best rams for our sheep, rear the neatest kine, and keep the best dogs, *quanto id diligentius in procreandis liberis observandum!* And how careful then should we be in begetting our children! In former times some countries have been so chary in this behalf, so stern, that, if a child were crooked or deformed in mind or body, they made him away; so did the Indians of old by the relation of Curtius°, and many other well-governed commonwealths, according to the discipline of those times. Heretofore in Scotland, saith Hect. Boethius°, if any were visited with the falling sickness, madness, gout, leprosy, or any such dangerous diseases, which was likely to be propagated from the father to the son, he was instantly gelded: a woman kept from all company of men; and if by chance, having some such disease, she were found to be with child, she and her brood were buried alive: and this was done for the common good, lest the whole nation should be injured or corrupted. A severe doom, you will say, and not to be used among Christians, yet more to be looked into than it is. For now by our too much facility in this kind, in giving way for all to marry that will, too much liberty and indulgence in tolerating all sorts, there is a vast confusion of hereditary diseases, no family secure, no man almost free from some grievous infirmity or other. When no choice is had, but still the eldest must marry, as so many stallions of the race; or if rich, be they fools or dizzards, lame or maimed, inable, intemperate, dissolute, exhaust through riot, as he said, *jure haereditario sapere jubentur*, they must be wise and able by inheritance; it comes to pass that our generation is corrupt, we have many weak persons, both in body and mind, many feral diseases raging amongst us, crazed families, *parentes peremptores*; our fathers bad, and we are like to be worse.'[1]

III

Though well-known specialists are convinced that the principal European nations are degenerating in body and in mind, their evidence remains almost unknown because a politician and newspaper that gave it adequate exposition would lose, the one his constituency, the other its circulation. That upon which success in life in the main depends may be called co-ordination or a capacity for sustained purpose[2] and this capacity, this innate intelligence or mother-wit, can be measured, in children especially, with great accuracy. The curious and elaborate tests are unlike school examinations because they eliminate, or almost eliminate, the child's acquired knowledge. This mother-wit is not everything and may have been the same in Bluebeard° and St Augustine; Gray's 'Milton'° remained for lack of acquired knowledge 'mute, inglorious'; but it outweighs everything else by, let us say, six to one, and is hereditary like the speed of a dog or a horse. Take a pair of twins and educate one in wealth, the other in poverty, test from time to time; their mother-wit will be the same. Pick a group of slum children, examine for mother-wit, move half the children to some other neighbourhood where they have better food, light and air, and after several months or years re-examine. Except for the increase which comes with age—it increases until we are seventeen and declines after thirty-five—there will be little

---

[1] 'The Anatomy of Melancholy', by Robert Burton, edited by the Rev. A. R. Shilleto, M.A., published by G. Bell & Sons, London, 1912. Part. I, Sect. 2, Mem. I, Subs. vi.

[2] I have deduced this rough definition of intelligence from the general nature of the 'intelligence tests' and from 'The Measurement of Intelligence' by Lewis M. Terman° (pages 44–47). I am indebted to the Secretary of the Eugenics Society for a long typed extract from this book. I am, indeed, indebted to his patience and courtesy for much of my information.

or no difference.[1] Furthermore, if you arrange an ascending scale from
the unemployed to skilled labour, from skilled labour to shopkeepers
and clerks, from shopkeepers and clerks to professional men,[2] there is
not only an increase of mother-wit but of the size of the body and its free-
dom from constitutional defects.[3] Intelligence and bodily vigour are not
in themselves connected, but those who in their mating have sought
intelligence have sought vigour also. As intelligence and freedom from
bodily defect increase, wealth increases in exact measure until enough
for the necessities of life is reached—fixed by Cattell at £140 a year—
and after that, with many exceptions, for men have other goals. There
are exceptions throughout; clever men are born among dunces, dunces
among clever men, and here and there a dunce earns much money, but
in every country the statistics work out the same average.

But this ascending scale has another character which may, or must,
turn all politics upside down; the families grow smaller as we ascend;
among the unemployed they average between four and five, among the
professional classes between two and three; among the unemployed
there are still families of twelve and thirteen, but when we reach skilled
labour families of six have come to an end, and this is true of all Western
Europe, Catholic and Protestant alike. Since about 1900 the better
stocks have not been replacing their numbers, while the stupider and

---

[1] A test of this kind with three hundred Glasgow children was summarised by Shep-
hard Dawson° in an address to the British Association in 1934. On re-examination eight-
een months after removal to better surroundings they did show 'a just appreciable
improvement'. Cattell° considers this seeming 'improvement' the result of tests which did
not sufficiently exclude acquired knowledge. Shephard Dawson, a cautious man, while
considering it encouraging to philanthropists, says that it was so small that those who ini-
tiate 'social welfare schemes may have to rely on the formation of habits that have to be
learned, rather than on any improvement in intelligence'. Cattell, with later and fuller
information from his own exhaustive investigations in Devonshire and in the town of
Leicester, would say not 'may' but 'must'.

[2] A well-known authority writes in answer to a question of mine: 'We have no statistics
for the leisured classes, owing to the difficulty of getting them into groups for examin-
ation'. It is a pity, for I want to know what happens to the plant when it gets from under the
stone.

[3] The physical degeneration is the most easy to measure. In England since 1873 the
average stature has declined about two inches, chest measurement about two inches and
weight about twenty pounds. In almost all European countries, especially those where
Catholicism encourages large families among the poor, there has been an equal or greater
decline. Military standards have been lowered almost everywhere; Spain has lowered hers
four times in the last forty years. Holland seems the one exception, and there, presumably
because the poor have reduced the size of their families, the average stature has risen with
astonishing rapidity. I summarise from Cattell's *Psychology and Social Progress*, pp. 102
and 112.

less healthy have been more than replacing theirs. Unless there is a change in the public mind every rank above the lowest must degenerate, and, as inferior men push up into its gaps, degenerate more and more quickly. The results are already visible in the degeneration of literature, newspapers, amusements (there was once a stock company playing Shakespeare in every considerable town), and, I am convinced, in benefactions like that of Lord Nuffield,° a self-made man, to Oxford, which must gradually substitute applied science for ancient wisdom. Not that it will matter much what they teach. Mr Bernard Shaw,° contemplating the impressive English school system, has remarked that his old nurse was right when she said that you couldn't make a silk purse out of a sow's ear.[1] Then, too, think of the growing cohesiveness, the growing frenzy, everybody thinking like everybody else, pre-occupation of all sorts with 'the youthful chimpanzee'. Any notable eighteenth century orator contrasts with Lloyd George,° as an orator of the great period in Greece and Rome with the Emperor Julian° among his troops in Gaul.

IV

The United States organised their troops sent to Europe in the Great War by tests of mother-wit, 'intelligence tests', and yet differ little from other democratic nations in their daily practice; and the new-formed democratic parliaments of India will doubtless destroy, if they can, the caste system that has saved Indian intellect. The Fascist countries know that civilisation has reached a crisis, and found their eloquence upon that knowledge, but from dread of attack or because they must feed their uneducatable masses, put quantity before quality; any hale man can dig or march. They offer bounties for the seventh, eighth, or ninth baby, and accelerate degeneration. In Russia, where the most intelligent families restrict their numbers as elsewhere, the stupidest man can earn a bounty by going to bed. Government there has the necessary authority, but as it thinks the social problem economic and not eugenic and ethnic—what was Karl Marx° but Macaulay° with his heels in the air?—it is the least likely to act. One nation has solved the problem in its chief city; in Stockholm all families are small; but the greater the intelligence the larger the family. Plato's Republic° with machines instead of slaves may dawn there, but like the other Scandinavian countries Sweden has spent on education far more than the great nations can afford with their

---

[1] I recommend to my readers Cattell's 'Fight for the National Intelligence', a book recommended by Lord Horder° and Leonard Darwin°. I have taken most of the facts in this section, and some of the arguments and metaphors that follow, from this book.

imperial responsibilities and ambitions, their always increasing social services and public works. That increase, too, can be calculated mathematically. But even if all Europe becomes sufficiently educated to follow the Swedish example, can it, or can Sweden itself, escape violence? If some financial re-organisation such as Major Douglas° plans, and that better organisation of agriculture and industry which many economists expect, enable everybody without effort to procure all necessities of life and so remove the last check upon the multiplication of the uneducatable masses, it will become the duty of the educated classes to seize and control one or more of those necessities. The drilled and docile masses may submit, but a prolonged civil war seems more likely, with the victory of the skilful, riding their machines as did the feudal knights their armoured horses. During the Great War Germany had four hundred submarine commanders, and sixty per cent. of the damage done was the work of twenty-four men. The danger is that there will be no war, that the skilled will attempt nothing, that the European civilisation, like those older civilisations that saw the triumph of their gangrel stocks, will accept decay. When I was writing 'A Vision'° I had constantly the word 'terror' impressed upon me, and once the old Stoic prophecy of earthquake, fire and flood at the end of an age, but this I did not take literally. It was because of that indefinable impression that I made Michael Robartes° say in 'A Vision': 'Dear predatory birds, prepare for war, prepare your children and all that you can reach . . . test art, morality, custom, thought, by Thermopylae,° make rich and poor act so to one another that they can stand together there. Love war because of its horror, that belief may be changed, civilisation renewed. We desire belief and lack it. Belief comes from shock and is not desired.'

V

The American intelligence tests put the Irish immigrant lowest in the scale, the English, the German and the Swede highest. Skilled men leave the industrial countries attracted by higher wages; what Irish go there are unskilled men driven by necessity, those that succeed are the few who, as a successful Irish-American lawyer said to me, escape from toil before it has killed them. These immigrants are our unemployed, and balance those that go to posts all over the British Empire as doctors, lawyers, soldiers, civil servants, or drift away drawn to the lights of London. In the opinion of most sociologists the level of mother-wit in all West-European countries is still much the same. But we are threatened as they are, already we have almost twice as many madmen as England for every hundred thousand. Sooner or later we must limit the families of the unintelligent classes, and if our government cannot send them doctor and clinic it must, till it get tired of it, send monk and confession box. We cannot go back as some dreamers would have us, to the old way of big families everywhere, even if the intelligent classes would consent, because that old way worked through lack of science and consequent great mortality among the children of those least fitted for modern civilisation.

Some of the inferiority of our emigrants in the United States and in Scotland may depend upon difference of historical phase. The tests usually employed are appropriate to a civilisation dominated by towns, by their objectivity and curiosity. Some of the tests are rectilinear mazes of increasing difficulty. The child marks with a pointer the way in, the way out at the other side, avoiding if he can turnings that lead nowhere. Probably he thinks of neighbouring streets where every turn is a right angle; an Achill child having no such image would probably fail through lack of attention. Other tests consist of fitting certain objects into pictures, but pictures are almost or wholly unknown in our remote districts. A Canadian artist told me that she once lodged with French-Canadian farmers and, noticing the thought they gave in planting a tree to the composition of the landscape, she gave the farmer's wife a picture. When she returned a year later the farmer's wife said, 'I made this apron out of that bit of canvas, but it took hours of scrubbing to get the dirt off.'[1] Then, we Irish are nearer than the English to the Mythic Age. Once, coming up from Cork, I got into talk with a fellow traveller and learned that he lived in County Cork, and as there was nothing noticeable about his accent I assumed that he was a Cork man. Presently he said: 'We have passed through three climates since we started; first our breath congealed on the glass, and then it ceased to do so, and now it congeals again'. I said: 'You are English?' He said, 'Yes, but how did you find out?' I said, 'No Irishman would have made that observation'. I forget what more I said, but it may have been that we are not disinterested observers, being much taken up with our own thoughts and emotions. The English are an objective people; they have no longer a sense of tragedy in their theatre; pity, which is fed by observation instead of experience, has taken its place; their poets are psychological, looking at their own minds from without. Ninette de Valois,° herself a Dublin

---

[1] Since I wrote this passage a friend has described to me Mayo boys and girls looking at a film or magazine page for the first time. It takes some little time before they understand that black and white splashes or black lines can represent natural objects. If it is a magazine page, some one will presently say 'That is a horse', or, 'That is a man'.

woman, protested the other day because somebody had called the theatre the province of the Jews and the Irish. 'The Irish', she said, 'are adaptable immigrants, the bigger and emptier a country the better it pleases them. When England fills up, they will disappear; they will lunch in bed instead of merely breakfasting there, they will be scared off by the Matriculation papers.'

Private Thoughts

(Should be skipped by Politicians and Journalists)

I

I am philosophical, not scientific, which means that observed facts do not mean much until I can make them part of my experience. Now that I am old and live in the past I often think of those ancestors of whom I have some detailed information. Such and such a diner-out and a charming man never did anything; such and such lost the never very great family fortune in some wild-cat scheme; such and such, perhaps deliberately for he was a strange, deep man, married into a family known for harsh dominating strength of character. Then, as my mood deepens, I discover all these men in my single mind, think that I myself have gone through the same vicissitudes, that I am going through them all at this very moment, and wonder if the balance has come right; then I go beyond those minds and my single mind and discover that I have been describing everybody's struggle, and the gyres turn in my thoughts. Vico° was the first modern philosopher to discover in his own mind, and in the European past, all human destiny. 'We can know nothing', he said, 'that we have not made.' Swift, too, Vico's contemporary, in his first political essay saw history as a personal experience, so too did Hegel in his 'Philosophy of History';[o1] Balzac in his letter to the Duchesse de Castris, and here and there in 'La Peau de chagrin' and 'Catherine de Medici'.°

---

[1] Hegel's historical dialectic is, I am persuaded, false, and its falsehood has led to the rancid ill-temper of the typical Communist and his incitements or condonations of murder. When the spring vegetables are over they have not been refuted, nor have they suffered in honour or reputation. Hegel in his more popular writings seems to misrepresent his own thought. Mind cannot be the ultimate reality seeing that in his 'Logic'° both mind and matter have their ground in spirit. To Hegel, as to the ancient Indian Sages, spirit is that which has value in itself.

When I allow my meditation to expand until the mind of my family merges into everybody's mind, I discover there, not only what Vico and Balzac found, but my own particular amusements and interests. First, no man can do the same thing twice if he has to put much mind into it, as every painter knows. Just when some school of painting has become popular, reproductions in every print-shop window, millionaires out-bidding one another, everybody's affection stirred, painters wear out their nerves establishing something else, and this something else must be the other side of the penny—for Heraclitus° was in the right. Oppos-ites are everywhere face to face, dying each other's life, living each other's death. When a man loves a girl it should be because her face and character offer what he lacks, the more profound his nature the more should he realise his lack and the greater be the difference. It is as though he wanted to take his own death into his arms and beget a stronger life upon that death. We should count men and women who pick, as it were, the dam or sire of a Derby winner from between the shafts of a cab, among persons of genius, for this genius makes all other kinds possible.

Our present civilisation began about the first Crusade, reached its mid-point in the Italian Renaissance; just when that point was passing Castiglione recorded in his 'Courtier'° what was said in the Court of Urbino somewhere about the first decade of the sixteenth century. These admirable conversationalists knew that the old spontaneous life had gone, and what a man must do to retain unity of being, mother-wit expressed in its perfection; he must know so many foreign tongues, know how to dance and sing, talk well, walk well, and be always in love. Elsewhere Titian° was painting great figures of the old, simple gener-ations; a little later came Van Dyke° and his sensitive fashionable faces where the impulse of life was fading. Somebody has written, 'There can be no wisdom without leisure', and those rich men of leisure still kept war and government for perquisites, and all else was done under their patronage. A City Father of a defeated Spanish town said that he could not understand it because their commander was not less well born than his opponent. They were at times great architects, they travelled every-where, read the classic authorities and designed buildings that still stir our admiration. When Bishop Berkeley° was asked to help to design the façade of Speaker Connolly's° fine house at Celbridge, he refused because too many country gentlemen were already at the task. Mean-while a famous event happened with much notoriety; Sir William Tem-ple and certain of his distinguished friends had affirmed the genuineness of the letters of Phalaris and the coarse, arrogant Bentley° had proved them in the wrong; culture, unity of being, no longer sufficed, and the specialists were already there. Swift, when little more than a boy, satirised what 'Gulliver' would satirise:

> 'But what does our proud ignorance Learning call?
>   We oddly Plato's paradox make good,
> Our knowledge is but mere remembrance all;
>   Remembrance is our treasure and our food;
> Nature's fair table-book, our tender souls,
> We scrawl all o'er with old and empty rules,
>   Stale memorandums of the schools:
>   For Learning's mighty treasures look
>   In that deep grave a book;
>   Think that she there does all her treasures hide,
> And that her troubled ghost still haunts there since she dy'd.
> Confine her walks to colleges and schools;
>   Her priest, her train, and followers show
>   As if they all were spectres too!
>   They purchase knowledge at th' expense
>   Of common breeding, common sense,
>   And grow at once scholars and fools;
>
>   Affect ill-manner'd pedantry,
> Rudeness, ill-nature, incivility,
>   And, sick with dregs of knowledge grown,
>   Which greedily they swallow down
> Still cast it up, and nauseate company'.°

II

The leisured men had still a characteristic work to do. During the eighteenth century they bred cattle instead of men, turning the fence-jumping, climbing, muscular cow and sheep of antiquity into fat and slothful butcher's meat. And now, their great task done, as it seems, they live the life of pleasure, taking what comes, marrying what's there, but now and again married by some reigning beauty, daughter of a barmaid man-picker who had doubled her own mettle with that of a man whose name she had forgotten or never known.

The specialist's job is anybody's job, seeing that for the most part he is made, not born. My best-informed relative says: 'Because Ireland is a backward country everybody is unique and knows that if he tumbles down somebody will pick him up. But an Englishman must be terrified, for there is a man exactly like him at every street corner.' A poet in an old Irish poem, travelling from great house to great house on his poet's business, meets a woman poet and asks for a child because a child of theirs would be a great poet. Parted, they died of love. The hero Finn,° wishing for a son not less strong of body, stood on the top of a hill and said he would marry the first woman that reached him. According to the tale, two thousand started level; but why should Jones of Twickenham bother?[1]

We cannot do the same thing twice, and the new thing must employ a new set of nerves or muscles. When a civilisation ends, task having led to task until everybody was bored, the whole turns bottom upwards, Nietzsche's 'transvaluation of all values'.° As we approach the phoenix' nest the old classes, with their power of co-ordinating events, evaporate, the mere multitude is everywhere with its empty photographic eyes. Yet we who have hated the age are joyous and happy. The new discipline wherever enforced or thought will recall forgotten beautiful faces. Whenever we or our forefathers have been most Christian—not the Christ of Byzantine mosaic but the soft, domesticated Christ of the painter's brush—perhaps even when we have felt ourselves abounding and yielding like the too friendly man who blabs all his secrets, we have been haunted by those faces dark with mystery, cast up by that other power that has ever more and more wrestled with ours, each living the other's death, dying the other's life. A woman's face, though she be lost or childless, may foretell a transformation of the people, be a more dire or beneficent omen than those trumpets heard by Etruscan seers in middle air.

III

But if I would escape from patter I must touch upon things too deep for my intellect and my knowledge, and besides I want to make my readers understand that explanations of the world lie one inside another, each complete in itself, like those perforated Chinese ivory balls. The mathematician Poincaré,° according to Henry Adams,° described space as the creation of our ancestors, meaning, I conclude, that mind split itself into mind and space. Space was to antiquity mind's inseparable 'other', coincident with objects, the table not the place it occupies. During the seventeenth century it was separated from mind and objects alike, and thought of as a nothing yet a reality, the place not the table, with material objects separated from taste, smell, sound, from all the

---

[1] In a fragment from some early version of 'The Courting of Emer', Emer° is chosen for the strength and volume of her bladder. This strength and volume were certainly considered signs of vigour. A woman of divine origin was murdered by jealous rivals because she made the deepest hole in the snow with her urine.

mathematician could not measure for its sole inhabitant, and this new matter and space men were told, had preceded mind and would live after. Nature or reality as known to poets and tramps has no moment, no impression, no perception like another, everything is unique, and nothing unique is measurable.

A line, whether made with rule and plummet or with a compass, must start somewhere. How convenient if men were but those dots, all exactly alike, all pushable, arrangeable, or, as Blake said, all intermeasurable by one another. Two and two must make four, though no two things are alike. A time had come when man must have certainty, and man knows what he has made. Man has made mathematics, but God reality. Instead of hierarchical society, where all men are different, came democracy; instead of a science which had re-discovered Anima Mundi,° its experiments and observations confirming the speculations of Henry More,° came materialism: all that whiggish world Swift stared on till he became a raging man. The ancient foundations had scarcely dispersed when Swift's young acquaintance Berkeley destroyed the new, for all that would listen, created modern philosophy and established for ever the subjectivity of space.[1] No educated man to-day accepts the objective matter and space of popular science, and yet deductions made by those who believed in both dominate the world, make possible the stimulation and condonation of revolutionary massacre and the multiplication of murderous weapons by substituting for the old humanity with its unique irreplaceable individuals something that can be chopped and measured like a piece of cheese; compel denial of the immortality of the soul by hiding from the mass of the people that the grave diggers have no place to bury us but in the human mind.

When I began to grow old I could no longer spend all my time amid masterpieces and in trying to make the like. I gave part of every day to mere entertainment, and it seemed when I was ill that great genius was 'mad as the mist and snow'.° Already in mid-Renaissance the world was weary of wisdom, science began to appear in the elaborate perspectives of its painters, in their sense of weight and tangibility; man was looking for some block where he could lay his head. But better than that, with Jacob's dream threatening,° get rid of man himself. Civilisation slept in the masses, wisdom in science. Is it criminal to sleep? I do not know; I do not say it.

---

[1] For a modern re-statement, see Boyce Gibbons' translation from Husserl's 'Ideas', pp. 128, 129, and elsewhere.

IV

Among those our civilisation must reject, or leave unrewarded at some level below that co-ordination that modern civilisation finds essential, exist precious faculties. When I was seven or eight I used to run about with a little negro girl, the only person at Rosses Point° who could find a plover's nest, and I have noticed that clairvoyance, prevision, and allied gifts, rare among the educated classes, are common among peasants. Among those peasants there is much of Asia, where Hegel has said every civilisation begins. Yet we must hold to what we have that the next civilisation may be born, not from a virgin's womb, nor a tomb without a body, not from a void, but of our own rich experience. These gifts must return, not in the mediumistic sleep dreaming or dreamless, but when we are wide awake. Eugenical and psychical research are the revolutionary movements with that element of novelty and sensation which sooner or later stir men to action. It may be, or it must be, that the best bred from the best shall claim again their ancient omens. And the serving-women 'shrank in their rejoicing before the eyes of the child', and 'the hour seemed awful to them' as they brought the child to its mother:

> 'And she said: "Now one of the earthly on the eyes of my
> child has gazed
> Nor shrunk before their glory, nor stayed her love amazed:
> I behold thee as Sigmund beholdeth—and I was the home of
> thine heart—
> Woe's me for the day when thou wert not, and the hour when
> we shall part".'°

. . .

Folk Tradition

'Dust hath Closed Helen's Eye'

I

I have been lately to a little group of houses, not many enough to be called a village, in the barony of Kiltartan in County Galway, whose name, Ballylee, is known through all the west of Ireland. There is the old square castle,[1] Ballylee, inhabited by a farmer and his wife, and a cottage where their daughter and their son-in-law live, and a little mill with an old miller, and old ash-trees throwing green shadows upon a little river and great stepping-stones. I went there two or three times last year to talk to the miller about Biddy Early, a wise woman that lived in Clare some years ago, and about her saying, 'There is a cure for all evil between the two mill-wheels of Ballylee', and to find out from him or another whether she meant the moss between the running waters or some other herb. I have been there this summer, and I shall be there again before it is autumn, because Mary Hynes, a beautiful woman whose name is still a wonder by turf fires, died there sixty years ago; for our feet would linger where beauty has lived its life of sorrow to make us understand that it is not of the world. An old man brought me a little way from the mill and the castle, and down a long, narrow boreen that was nearly lost in brambles and sloe bushes, and he said, 'That is the little old foundation of the house, but the most of it is taken for building walls, and the goats have ate those bushes that are growing over it till they've got cranky, and they won't grow any more. They say she was the handsomest girl in Ireland, her skin was like dribbled snow'—he meant driven snow, perhaps,—'and she had blushes in her cheeks. She had five handsome brothers, but all are gone now!' I talked to him about a poem in Irish, Raftery,° a famous poet, made about her, and how it said, 'there is a strong cellar in Ballylee'. He said the strong cellar was the great hole where the river sank underground, and he brought me to a deep pool, where an otter hurried away under a grey boulder, and told me that many fish came up out of the dark water at early morning 'to taste the fresh water coming down from the hills'.

[1] Ballylee Castle, or Thoor-Ballylee, as I have named it to escape from the too magnificent word 'castle', is now my property, and I spend my summers or some part of them there. (1924.)

I first heard of the poem from an old woman who lives about two miles farther up the river, and who remembers Raftery and Mary Hynes. She says, 'I never saw anybody so handsome as she was, and I never will till I die,' and that he was nearly blind, and had 'no way of living but to go round and to mark some house to go to, and then all the neighbours would gather to hear. If you treated him well he'd praise you, but if you did not, he'd fault you in Irish. He was the greatest poet in Ireland, and he'd make a song about that bush if he chanced to stand under it. There was a bush he stood under from the rain, and he made verses praising it, and then when the water came through he made verses dispraising it.' She sang the poem to a friend and to myself in Irish, and every word was audible and expressive, as the words in a song were always, as I think, before music grew too proud to be the garment of words, flowing and changing with the flowing and changing of their energies. The poem is not as natural as the best Irish poetry of the last century, for the thoughts are arranged in a too obviously traditional form, so the old poor half-blind man who made it has to speak as if he were a rich farmer offering the best of everything to the woman he loves, but it has naïve and tender phrases. The friend that was with me° has made some of the translation, but some of it has been made by the country people themselves. I think it has more of the simplicity of the Irish verses than one finds in most translations.

> Going to Mass by the will of God,
> The day came wet and the wind rose;
> I met Mary Hynes at the cross of Kiltartan,
> And I fell in love with her then and there.

> I spoke to her kind and mannerly,
> As by report was her own way;
> And she said, 'Raftery, my mind is easy,
> You may come to-day to Ballylee.'

> When I heard her offer I did not linger,
> When her talk went to my heart my heart rose.
> We had only to go across the three fields,
> We had daylight with us to Ballylee.

> The table was laid with glasses and a quart measure,
> She had fair hair, and she sitting beside me;
> And she said, 'Drink, Raftery, and a hundred
>   welcomes,
> There is a strong cellar in Ballylee.'

O star of light and O sun in harvest,
O amber hair, O my share of the world,
Will you come with me upon Sunday
Till we agree together before all the people?

I would not grudge you a song every Sunday
    evening,
Punch on the table, or wine if you would drink it,
But, O King of Glory, dry the roads before me,
Till I find the way to Ballylee.

There is sweet air on the side of the hill
When you are looking down upon Ballylee;
When you are walking in the valley picking nuts
    and blackberries,
There is music of the birds in it and music of the
    Sidhe.

What is the worth of greatness till you have the
    light
Of the flower of the branch that is by your side?
There is no god to deny it or to try and hide it,
She is the sun in the heavens who wounded my heart.

There was no part of Ireland I did not travel,
From the rivers to the tops of the mountains,
To the edge of Lough Greine whose mouth is
    hidden,
And I saw no beauty but was behind hers.

Her hair was shining, and her brows were shining
    too;
Her face was like herself, her mouth pleasant and
    sweet.
She is the pride, and I give her the branch,
She is the shining flower of Ballylee.

It is Mary Hynes, the calm and easy woman,
Has beauty in her mind and in her face.
If a hundred clerks were gathered together,
They could not write down a half of her ways.

An old weaver, whose son is supposed to go away among the Sidhe (the faeries) at night, says, 'Mary Hynes was the most beautiful thing ever made. My mother used to tell me about her, for she'd be at every hurling, and wherever she was she was dressed in white. As many as eleven men asked her in marriage in one day, but she wouldn't have any of them. There was a lot of men up beyond Kilbecanty° one night sitting together drinking, and talking of her, and one of them got up and set out to go to Ballylee and see her; but Cloon Bog was open then, and when he came to it he fell into the water, and they found him dead there in the morning. She died of the fever that was before the famine.' Another old man says he was only a child when he saw her, but he remembered that 'the strongest man that was among us, one John Madden, got his death of the head of her, cold he got crossing rivers in the night-time to get to Ballylee'. This is perhaps the man the other remembered, for tradition gives the one thing many shapes. There is an old woman who remembers her, at Derrybrien° among the Echtge hills,° a vast desolate place, which has changed little since the old poem said, 'the stag upon the cold summit of Echtge hears the cry of the wolves', but still mindful of many poems and of the dignity of ancient speech. She says, 'The sun and the moon never shone on anybody so handsome, and her skin was so white that it looked blue, and she had two little blushes on her cheeks.' And an old wrinkled woman who lives close by Ballylee, and has told me many tales of the Sidhe, says, 'I often saw Mary Hynes, she was handsome indeed. She had two bunches of curls beside her cheeks, and they were the colour of silver. I saw Mary Molloy that was drowned in the river beyond, and Mary Guthrie that was in Ardrahan,° but she took the sway of them both, a very comely creature. I was at her wake too—she had seen too much of the world. She was a kind creature. One day I was coming home through that field beyond, and I was tired, and who should come out but the Poisin Glegeal (the shining flower), and she gave me a glass of new milk.' This old woman meant no more than some beautiful bright colour by the colour of silver, for though I knew an old man—he is dead now—who thought she might know 'the cure for all the evils in the world', that the Sidhe knew, she has seen too little gold to know its colour. But a man by the shore at Kinvara,° who is too young to remember Mary Hynes, says, 'Everybody says there is no one at all to be seen now so handsome; it is said she had beautiful hair, the colour of gold. She was poor, but her clothes every day were the same as Sunday, she had such neatness. And if she went to any kind of a meeting, they would all be killing one another for a sight of her, and there was a great many in love with her, but she died young. It is said that no one that has a song made about them will ever live long.'

Those who are much admired are, it is held, taken by the Sidhe, who can use ungoverned feeling for their own ends, so that a father, as an old herb doctor told me once, may give his child into their hands, or a husband his wife. The admired and desired are only safe if one says 'God bless them' when one's eyes are upon them. The old woman that sang the song thinks, too, that Mary Hynes was 'taken', as the phrase is, 'for they have taken many that are not handsome, and why would they not take her? And people came from all parts to look at her, and maybe there were some that did not say "God bless her." ' An old man who lives by the sea at Duras° has as little doubt that she was taken, 'for there are some living yet can remember her coming to the pattern[1] there beyond, and she was said to be the handsomest girl in Ireland'. She died young because the gods loved her, for the Sidhe are the gods, and it may be that the old saying, which we forget to understand literally, meant her manner of death in old times. These poor countrymen and countrywomen in their beliefs, and in their emotions, are many years nearer to that old Greek world, that set beauty beside the fountain of things, than are our men of learning. She 'had seen too much of the world'; but these old men and women, when they tell of her, blame another and not her, and though they can be hard, they grow gentle as the old men of Troy grew gentle when Helen passed by on the walls.

The poet who helped her to so much fame has himself a great fame throughout the West of Ireland. Some think that Raftery was half blind, and say, 'I saw Raftery, a dark man, but he had sight enough to see her,' or the like, but some think he was wholly blind, as he may have been at the end of his life. Fable makes all things perfect in their kind, and her blind people must never look on the world and the sun. I asked a man I met one day, when I was looking for a pool *na mna Sidhe*° where women of faery have been seen, how Raftery could have admired Mary Hynes so much if he had been altogether blind? He said, 'I think Raftery was altogether blind, but those that are blind have a way of seeing things, and have the power to know more, and to feel more, and to do more, and to guess more than those that have their sight, and a certain wit and a certain wisdom is given to them.' Everybody, indeed, will tell you that he was very wise, for was he not only blind but a poet? The weaver, whose words about Mary Hynes I have already given, says, 'His poetry was the gift of the Almighty, for there are three things that are the gift of the Almighty—poetry and dancing and principles. That is why in the old times an ignorant man coming down from the hillside would be better behaved and have better learning than a man with education you'd meet now, for they got it from God'; and a man at Coole says, 'When he put

---

[1] A 'pattern', or 'patron', is a festival in honour of a saint.

his finger to one part of his head, everything would come to him as if it was written in a book'; and an old pensioner at Kiltartan says, 'He was standing under a bush one time, and he talked to it, and it answered him back in Irish. Some say it was the bush that spoke, but it must have been an enchanted voice in it, and it gave him the knowledge of all the things of the world. The bush withered up afterwards, and it is to be seen on the roadside now between this and Rahasine.' There is a poem of his about a bush, which I have never seen, and it may have come out of the cauldron of fable in this shape.

A friend of mine met a man once who had been with him when he died, but the people say that he died alone, and one Maurteen Gillane told Dr Hyde that all night long a light was seen streaming up to heaven from the roof of the house where he lay, and 'that was the angels who were with him'; and all night long there was a great light in the hovel, 'and that was the angels who were waking him. They gave that honour to him because he was so good a poet, and sang such religious songs.' It may be that in a few years Fable, who changes mortalities to immortalities in her cauldron, will have changed Mary Hynes and Raftery to perfect symbols of the sorrow of beauty and of the magnificence and penury of dreams.

1900

II

When I was in a northern town a while ago I had a long talk with a man who had lived in a neighbouring country district when he was a boy. He told me that when a very beautiful girl was born in a family that had not been noted for good looks, her beauty was thought to have come from the Sidhe, and to bring misfortune with it. He went over the names of several beautiful girls that he had known, and said that beauty had never brought happiness to anybody. It was a thing, he said, to be proud of and afraid of. I wish I had written out his words at the time, for they were more picturesque than my memory of them.

1902

'And Fair, Fierce Women'

One day a woman that I know came face to face with heroic beauty, that highest beauty which Blake says changes least from youth to age, a beauty which has been fading out of the arts, since that decadence we call progress set voluptuous beauty in its place. She was standing at the window, looking over to Knocknarea where Queen Maive is thought to be buried,° when she saw, as she has told me, 'the finest woman you ever saw travelling right across from the mountain and straight to her'. The woman had a sword by her side and a dagger lifted up in her hand, and was dressed in white, with bare arms and feet. She looked 'very strong, but not wicked', that is, not cruel. The old woman had seen the Irish giant, and 'though he was a fine man', he was nothing to this woman, 'for he was round, and could not have stepped out so soldierly'; 'she was like Mrs——' a stately lady of the neighbourhood, 'but she had no stomach on her, and was slight and broad in the shoulders, and was handsomer than any one you ever saw; she looked about thirty'. The old woman covered her eyes with her hands, and when she uncovered them the apparition had vanished. The neighbours were 'wild with her', she told me, because she did not wait to find out if there was a message, for they were sure it was Queen Maive, who often shows herself to the pilots. I asked the old woman if she had seen others like Queen Maive, and she said, 'Some of them have their hair down, but they look quite different, like the sleepy-looking ladies one sees in the papers. Those with their hair up are like this one. The others have long white dresses, but those with their hair up have short dresses, so that you can see their legs right up to the calf.' After some careful questioning I found that they wore what might very well be a kind of buskin; she went on, 'They are fine and dashing looking, like the men one sees riding their horses in twos and threes on the slopes of the mountains with their swords swinging.' She repeated over and over, 'There is no such race living now, none so finely proportioned,' or the like, and then said, 'The present Queen [1] is a nice, pleasant-looking woman, but she is not like her. What makes me think so little of the ladies is that I see none as they be,' meaning as the spirits, 'When I think of her and of the ladies now, they are like little children running about without knowing how to put their clothes on right. Is it the ladies? Why, I would not call them women at all.' The other day a friend of mine questioned an old woman in a Galway workhouse about Queen Maive, and was told that 'Queen Maive was handsome, and overcame all her enemies with a hazel stick, for the hazel is blessed, and the best weapon that can be got. You might walk the world with it,' but she grew 'very disagreeable in the end—oh very disagreeable. Best not to be talking about it. Best leave it between the book and the hearer.' My friend thought the old woman had got some scandal about Fergus son of Roy° and Maive in her head.

---

[1] Queen Victoria.

And I myself met once with a young man in the Burren Hills° who remembered an old poet who made his poems in Irish and had met when he was young, the young man said, one who called herself Maive, and said she was a queen 'among them', and asked him if he would have money or pleasure. He said he would have pleasure, and she gave him her love for a time, and then went from him, and ever after he was very mournful. The young man had often heard him sing the poem of lamentation that he made, but could only remember that it was 'very mournful', and that he called her 'beauty of all beauties'.

1902

Aristotle of the Books

The friend who can get the wood-cutter to talk more readily than he will to anybody else went lately to see his old wife. She lives in a cottage not far from the edge of the woods, and is as full of old talk as her husband. This time she began to talk of Goban,° the legendary mason, and his wisdom, but said presently, 'Aristotle of the Books, too, was very wise, and he had a great deal of experience, but did not the bees get the better of him in the end? He wanted to know how they packed the comb, and he wasted the better part of a fortnight watching them, and he could not see them doing it. Then he made a hive with a glass cover on it and put it over them, and he thought to see. But when he went and put his eyes to the glass, they had it all covered with wax so that it was as black as the pot; and he was as blind as before. He said he was never rightly kilt till then. They had him that time surely!'

1902

Occult Speculation

from Per Amica Silentia Lunae°

from Anima Hominis

III

When I think of any great poetical writer of the past (a realist is an historian and obscures the cleavage by the record of his eyes) I comprehend, if I know the lineaments of his life, that the work is the man's flight from his entire horoscope, his blind struggle in the network of the stars. William Morris,° a happy, busy, most irascible man, described dim colour and pensive emotion, following, beyond any man of his time, an indolent muse; while Savage Landor topped us all in calm nobility when the pen was in his hand, as in the daily violence of his passion when he had laid it down. He had in his *Imaginary Conversations*° reminded us, as it were, that the Venus de Milo is a stone, and yet he wrote when the copies did not come from the printer as soon as he expected: 'I have . . . had the resolution to tear in pieces all my sketches and projects and to forswear all future undertakings. I have tried to sleep away my time and pass two-thirds of the twenty-four hours in bed. I may speak of myself as a dead man.' I imagine Keats to have been born with that thirst for luxury common to many at the outsetting of the Romantic Movement, and not able, like wealthy Beckford,° to slake it with beautiful and strange objects. It drove him to imaginary delights; ignorant, poor, and in poor health, and not perfectly well-bred, he knew himself driven from tangible luxury; meeting Shelley, he was resentful and suspicious because he, as Leigh Hunt recalls, 'being a little too sensitive on the score of his origin, felt inclined to see in every man of birth his natural enemy.'

IV

Some thirty years ago I read a prose allegory by Simeon Solomon,° long out of print and unprocurable, and remember or seem to remember a sentence, 'a hollow image of fulfilled desire.' All happy art seems to me that hollow image, but when its lineaments express also the poverty or the exasperation that set its maker to the work, we call it tragic art. Keats but gave us his dream of luxury; but while reading Dante we never long escape the conflict, partly because the verses are at moments a mirror of his history, and yet more because that history is so clear and simple that it has the quality of art. I am no Dante scholar, and I but read him in Shadwell° or in Dante Rossetti,° but I am always persuaded that he celebrated the most pure lady° poet ever sung and the Divine Justice, not merely because death took that lady and Florence banished her singer, but because he had to struggle in his own heart with his unjust anger and his lust; while unlike those of the great poets, who are at peace with the world and at war with themselves, he fought a double war. 'Always,' says Boccaccio,° 'both in youth and maturity he found room among his virtues for lechery'; or as Matthew Arnold preferred to change the phrase, 'his conduct was exceeding irregular.' Guido Cavalcanti,° as Rossetti translates him, finds 'too much baseness' in his friend:

> And still thy speech of me, heartfelt and kind,
> Hath made me treasure up thy poetry;
> But now I dare not, for thy abject life,
> Make manifest that I approve thy rhymes.

And when Dante meets Beatrice in Eden, does she not reproach him because, when she had taken her presence away, he followed in spite of warning dreams, false images, and now, to save him in his own despite, she has 'visited . . . the Portals of the Dead,' and chosen Virgil for his courier? While Gino da Pistoia° complains that in his *Commedia* his 'lovely heresies . . . beat the right down and let the wrong go free':

> Therefore his vain decrees, wherein he lied,
> Must be like empty nutshells flung aside;
> Yet through the rash false witness set to grow,
> French and Italian vengeance on such pride
> May fall like Anthony on Cicero.

Dante himself sings to Giovanni Guirino° 'at the approach of death':

> The King, by whose rich grave his servants be
> With plenty beyond measure set to dwell,
> Ordains that I my bitter wrath dispel,
> And lift mine eyes to the great Consistory.

V

We make out of the quarrel with others, rhetoric, but of the quarrel with ourselves, poetry. Unlike the rhetoricians, who get a confident voice from remembering the crowd they have won or may win, we sing amid our uncertainty; and, smitten even in the presence of the most high beauty by the knowledge of our solitude, our rhythm shudders. I think, too, that no fine poet, no matter how disordered his life, has ever, even in his mere life, had pleasure for his end. Johnson and Dowson,° friends of my youth, were dissipated men, the one a drunkard, the other a drunkard and mad about women, and yet they had the gravity of men who had found life out and were awakening from the dream; and both, one in life and art and one in art and less in life, had a continual preoccupation with religion. Nor has any poet I have read of or heard of or met with been a sentimentalist. The other self, the anti-self or the antithetical self, as one may choose to name it, comes but to those who are no longer deceived, whose passion is reality. The sentimentalists are practical men who believe in money, in position, in a marriage bell, and whose understanding of happiness is to be so busy whether at work or at play, that all is forgotten but the momentary aim. They find their pleasure in a cup that is filled from Lethe's wharf, and for the awakening, for the vision, for the revelation of reality, tradition offers us a different word—ecstasy. An old artist wrote to me of his wanderings by the quays of New York, and how he found there a woman nursing a sick child, and drew her story from her. She spoke, too, of other children who had died: a long tragic story. 'I wanted to paint her,' he wrote, 'if I denied myself any of the pain I could not believe in my own ecstasy.' We must not make a false faith by hiding from our thoughts the causes of doubt, for faith is the highest achievement of the human intellect, the only gift man can make to God, and therefore it must be offered in sincerity. Neither must we create, by hiding ugliness, a false beauty as our offering to the world. He only can create the greatest imaginable beauty who has endured all imaginable pangs, for only when we have seen and foreseen what we dread shall we be rewarded by that dazzling unforeseen wing-footed wanderer. We could not find him if he were not in some sense of our being and yet of our being but as water with fire, a noise with silence. He is of all things not impossible the most difficult, for that only which comes easily can never be a portion of our being, 'Soon got, soon gone,' as the proverb says. I shall find the dark grow luminous, the void fruitful when I understand I have nothing, that the ringers in the tower have appointed for the hymen of the soul a passing bell.

The last knowledge has often come most quickly to turbulent men, and for a season brought new turbulence. When life puts away her conjuring tricks one by one, those that deceive us longest may well be the wine-cup and the sensual kiss, for our Chambers of Commerce and of Commons have not the divine architecture of the body, nor has their frenzy been ripened by the sun. The poet, because he may not stand within the sacred house but lives amid the whirlwinds that beset its threshold, may find his pardon.

VI

I think the Christian saint and hero, instead of being merely dissatisfied, make deliberate sacrifice. I remember reading once an autobiography of a man who had made a daring journey in disguise to Russian exiles in Siberia, and his telling how, very timid as a child, he schooled himself by wandering at night through dangerous streets. Saint and hero cannot be content to pass at moments to that hollow image and after become their heterogeneous selves, but would always, if they could, resemble the antithetical self. There is a shadow of type on type, for in all great poetical styles there is saint or hero, but when it is all over Dante can return to his chambering and Shakespeare to his 'pottle pot.' They sought no impossible perfection but when they handled paper or parchment. So too will saint or hero, because he works in his own flesh and blood and not in paper or parchment, have more deliberate understanding of that other flesh and blood.

Some years ago I began to believe that our culture, with its doctrine of sincerity and self-realisation, made us gentle and passive, and that the Middle Ages and the Renaissance were right to found theirs upon the imitation of Christ or of some classic hero. St Francis and Cæsar Borgia° made themselves over-mastering, creative persons by turning from the mirror to meditation upon a mask. When I had this thought I could see nothing else in life. I could not write the play I had planned, for all became allegorical, and though I tore up hundreds of pages in my endeavour to escape from allegory, my imagination became sterile for nearly five years and I only escaped at last when I had mocked in a comedy my own thought. I was always thinking of the element of imitation in style and in life, and of the life beyond heroic imitation. I find in an old diary: 'I think all happiness depends on the energy to assume the mask of some other life, on a re-birth as something not one's self, something created in a moment and perpetually renewed; in playing a game like that of a child where one loses the infinite pain of self-realisation, in a grotesque or solemn painted face put on that one may hide from the terror of judgement. . . . Perhaps all the sins and energies of the world are but the world's flight from an infinite blinding beam'; and again at an earlier date: 'If we cannot imagine ourselves as different from what we are, and try to assume that second self, we cannot impose a discipline upon ourselves though we may accept one from others. Active virtue, as distinguished from the passive acceptance of a code, is therefore theatrical, consciously dramatic, the wearing of a mask. . . .Wordsworth, great poet though he be, is so often flat and heavy partly because his moral sense, being a discipline he had not created, a mere obedience, has no theatrical element. This increases his popularity with the better kind of journalists and politicians who have written books.'

VII

I thought the hero found hanging upon some oak of Dodona an ancient mask, where perhaps there lingered something of Egypt, and that he changed it to his fancy, touching it a little here and there, gilding the eyebrows or putting a gilt line where the cheekbone comes; that when at last he looked out of its eyes he knew another's breath came and went within his breath upon the carven lips, and that his eyes were upon the instant fixed upon a visionary world: how else could the god have come to us in the forest? The good, unlearned books say that He who keeps the distant stars within His fold comes without intermediary, but Plutarch's° precepts and the experience of old women in Soho, ministering their witchcraft to servant girls at a shilling a piece, will have it that a strange living man may win for Daemon°[1] an illustrious dead man; but now I add another thought: the Daemon comes not as like to like but seeking its own opposite, for man and Daemon feed the hunger in one another's hearts. Because the ghost is simple, the man heterogeneous and confused, they are but knit together when the man has found a mask whose lineaments permit the expression of all the man most lacks, and it may be dreads, and of that only.

The more insatiable in all desire, the more resolute to refuse deception or an easy victory, the more close will be the bond, the more violent and definite the antipathy.

VIII

I think that all religious men have believed that there is a hand not ours in the events of life, and that, as somebody says in *Wilhelm Meister*,° accident is destiny; and I think it was Heraclitus° who said: the Daemon is our destiny. When I think of life as a struggle with the Daemon who would ever set us to the hardest work among those not impossible, I understand why there is a deep enmity between a man and his destiny,

---

[1] I could not distinguish at the time between the permanent Daemon and the impermanent, who may be 'an illustrious dead man,' though I knew the distinction was there. I shall deal with the matter in *A Vision*.   February 1924

and why a man loves nothing but his destiny. In an Anglo-Saxon poem a certain man is called, as though to call him something that summed up all heroism, 'Doom eager.'° I am persuaded that the Daemon delivers and deceives us, and that he wove that netting from the stars and threw the net from his shoulder. Then my imagination runs from Daemon to sweetheart, and I divine an analogy that evades the intellect. I remember that Greek antiquity has bid us look for the principal stars, that govern enemy and sweetheart alike, among those that are about to set, in the Seventh House as the astrologers say; and that it may be 'sexual love,' which is 'founded upon spiritual hate,' is an image of the warfare of man and Daemon; and I even wonder if there may not be some secret communion, some whispering in the dark between Daemon and sweetheart. I remember how often women when in love, grow superstitious, and believe that they can bring their lovers good luck; and I remember an old Irish story of three young men who went seeking for help in battle into the house of the gods at Slieve-na-mon.° 'You must first be married,' some god told them, 'because a man's good or evil luck comes to him through a woman.'

I sometimes fence for half an hour at the day's end, and when I close my eyes upon the pillow I see a foil playing before me the button to my face. We meet always in the deep of the mind, whatever our work, wherever our reverie carries us, that other Will.

IX

The poet finds and makes his mask in disappointment, the hero in defeat. The desire that is satisfied is not a great desire, nor has the shoulder used all its might that an unbreakable gate has never strained. The saint alone is not deceived, neither thrusting with his shoulder nor holding out unsatisfied hands. He would climb without wandering to the antithetical self of the world, the Indian narrowing his thought in meditation or driving it away in contemplation, the Christian copying Christ, the antithetical self of the classic world. For a hero loves the world till it breaks him, and the poet till it has broken faith; but while the world was yet debonair, the saint has turned away, and because he renounced Experience itself, he will wear his mask as he finds it. The poet or the hero, no matter upon what bark they found their mask, so teeming their fancy, somewhat change its lineaments, but the saint, whose life is but a round of customary duty, needs nothing the whole world does not need, and day by day he scourges in his body the Roman and Christian conquerors; Alexander and Caesar are famished in his cell.

from Anima Mundi°

VI

. . . All souls have a vehicle or body, and when one has said that, with More° and the Platonists one has escaped from the abstract schools who seek always the power of some church or institution, and found oneself with great poetry, and superstition which is but popular poetry, in a pleasant dangerous world. Beauty is indeed but bodily life in some ideal condition. The vehicle of the human soul is what used to be called the animal spirits, and Henry More quotes from Hippocrates° this sentence: 'The mind of man is . . . not nourished from meats and drinks from the belly, but by a clear luminous substance that redounds by separation from the blood.' These animal spirits fill up all parts of the body and make up the body of air, as certain writers of the seventeenth century have called it.[1] The soul has a plastic power, and can after death, or during life, should the vehicle leave the body for a while, mould it to any shape it will by an act of imagination, though the more unlike to the habitual that shape is, the greater the effort. To living and dead alike, the purity and abundance of the animal spirits are a chief power. The soul can mould from these an apparition clothed as if in life, and make it visible by showing it to our mind's eye, or by building into its substance certain particles drawn from the body of a medium till it is as visible and tangible as any other object. To help that building the ancients offered sheaves of corn, fragrant gum, and the odour of fruit and flowers, and the blood of victims. The half materialised vehicle slowly exudes from the skin in dull luminous drops or condenses from a luminous cloud, the light fading as weight and density increase. The witch, going beyond the medium, offered to the slowly animating phantom certain drops of her blood. The vehicle once separate from the living man or woman may be moulded by the souls of others as readily as by its own soul, and even it seems by the souls of the living. It becomes a part for a while of that stream of images which I have compared to reflections upon water. But how does it follow that souls who never have handled the modelling tool or the brush, make perfect images? Those materialisations who imprint their powerful faces

---

[1] This passage, I think, correctly represents the thought of Henry More, but it would, I now believe, have corresponded better with facts if I had described this 'clear luminous substance' as a sense-material envelope, moulded upon 'the body of air,' or true 'vehicle'; and if I had confined to it the words 'animal spirits.' It must, however, be looked upon as surviving, for a time, the death of the physical body. The spirits do not get from it the material from which their forms are made, but their forms take light from it as one candle takes light from another.　1924

upon paraffin wax, leave there sculpture that would have taken a good artist, making and imagining, many hours. How did it follow that an ignorant woman could, as Henry More believed, project her vehicle in so good a likeness of a hare, that horse and hound and huntsman followed with the bugle blowing? Is not the problem the same as of those finely articulated scenes and patterns that come out of the dark, seemingly completed in the winking of an eye, as we are lying half asleep, and of all those elaborate images that drift in moments of inspiration or evocation before the mind's eye? Our animal spirits or vehicles are but as it were a condensation of the vehicle of *Anima Mundi*, and give substance to its images in the faint materialisation of our common thought, or more grossly when a ghost is our visitor. It should be no great feat, once those images have dipped into our vehicle, to take their portraits in the photographic camera. Henry More will have it that a hen scared by a hawk when the cock is treading, hatches out a hawk-headed chicken (I am no stickler for the fact), because before the soul of the unborn bird can give the shape 'the deeply impassioned fancy of the mother' called from the general cistern of form a completing image. 'The soul of the world,' he runs on, 'interposes and insinuates into all generations of things while the matter is fluid and yielding, which would induce a man to believe that she may not stand idle in the transformation of the vehicle of the daemons, but assist the fancies and desires, and so help to clothe them and to utter them according to their own pleasures; or it may be sometimes against their wills, as the unwieldiness of the mother's fancy forces upon her a monstrous birth.' Though images appear to flow and drift, it may be that we but change in our relation to them, now losing, now finding with the shifting of our minds; and certainly Henry More speaks by the book, in claiming that those images may be hard to the right touch as 'pillars of crystal' and as solidly coloured as our own to the right eyes. Shelley, a good Platonist, seems in his earliest work to set this general soul in the place of God, an opinion, one may find from More's friend Cudworth° now affirmed, now combated by classic authority; but More would steady us with a definition. The general soul as apart from its vehicle is 'a substance incorporeal but without sense and animadversion pervading the whole matter of the universe and exercising a plastic power therein, according to the sundry predispositions and occasions, in the parts it works upon, raising such phenomena in the world, by directing the parts of the matter and their motion as cannot be resolved into mere mechanical powers.' I must assume that 'sense and animadversion,' perception and direction, are always faculties of individual soul, and that, as Blake said, 'God only acts or is in existing beings or men.'°

VII

The old theological conception of the individual soul as bodiless or abstract led to what Henry More calls 'contradictory debate' as to how many angels 'could dance booted and spurred upon the point of a needle,' and made it possible for rationalist physiology to persuade us that our thought has no corporeal existence but in the molecules of the brain. Shelley was of opinion that the 'thoughts which are called real or external objects' differed but in regularity of occurrence from 'hallucinations, dreams and ideas of madmen,' and noticed that he had dreamed, therefore lessening the difference, 'three several times between intervals of two or more years the same precise dream.' If all our mental images no less than apparitions (and I see no reason to distinguish) are forms existing in the general vehicle of *Anima Mundi*, and mirrored in our particular vehicle, many crooked things are made straight. I am persuaded that a logical process, or a series of related images, has body and period, and I think of *Anima Mundi* as a great pool or garden where it moves through its allotted growth like a great water plant or fragrantly branches in the air. Indeed as Spenser's Garden of Adonis:°

> There is the first seminary
> Of all things that are born to live and die
> According to their kynds.

The soul by changes of 'vital congruity,' More says, draws to it a certain thought, and this thought draws by its association the sequence of many thoughts, endowing them with a life in the vehicle meted out according to the intensity of the first perception. A seed is set growing, and this growth may go on apart from the power, apart even from the knowledge of the soul. If I wish to 'transfer' a thought I may think, let us say, of Cinderella's slipper, and my subject may see an old woman coming out of a chimney; or going to sleep I may wish to wake at seven o'clock and, though I never think of it again, I shall wake upon the instant. The thought has completed itself, certain acts of logic, turns, and knots in the stem have been accomplished out of sight and out of reach as it were. We are always starting these parasitic vegetables and letting them coil beyond our knowledge, and may become, like that lady in Balzac who, after a life of sanctity, plans upon her deathbed to fly with her renounced lover. After death a dream, a desire she had perhaps ceased to believe in, perhaps ceased almost to remember, must have recurred again and again with its anguish and its happiness. We can only refuse to start the wandering sequence or, if start it does, hold it in the intellectual light where time gallops, and so keep it from slipping down into the sluggish vehicle. The toil of the living is to free themselves from an endless sequence of objects, and that of the dead to free themselves from an endless sequence of thoughts. One sequence begets another, and these have power because of all those things we do, not for their own sake but for an imagined good.

VIII

Spiritism, whether of folk-lore or of the séance room, the visions of Swedenborg,° and the speculation of the Platonists and Japanese plays, will have it that we may see at certain roads and in certain houses old murders acted over again, and in certain fields dead huntsmen riding with horse and hound, or ancient armies fighting above bones or ashes. We carry to *Anima Mundi* our memory, and that memory is for a time our external world; and all passionate moments recur again and again, for passion desires its own recurrence more than any event, and whatever there is of corresponding complacency or remorse is our beginning of judgement; nor de we remember only the events of life, for thoughts bred of longing and of fear, all those parasitic vegetables that have slipped through our fingers, come again like a rope's end to smite us upon the face; and as Cornelius Agrippa° writes: 'We may dream ourselves to be consumed in flame and persecuted by daemons,' and certain spirits have complained that they would be hard put to it to arouse those who died, believing they could not awake till a trumpet shrilled. A ghost in a Japanese play is set afire by a fantastic scruple, and though a Buddhist priest explains that the fire would go out of itself if the ghost but ceased to believe in it, it cannot cease to believe. Cornelius Agrippa called such dreaming souls hobgoblins, and when Hamlet refused the bare bodkin because of what dreams may come, it was from no mere literary fancy. The soul can indeed, it appears, change these objects built about us by the memory, as it may change its shape; but the greater the change, the greater the effort and the sooner the return to the habitual images. Doubtless in either case the effort is often beyond its power. Years ago I was present when a woman consulted Madame Blavatsky° for a friend who saw her newly-dead husband nightly as a decaying corpse and smelt the odour of the grave. 'When he was dying,' said Madame Blavatsky, 'he thought the grave the end, and now that he is dead cannot throw off that imagination.' A Brahmin once told an actress friend of mine that he disliked acting, because if a man died playing Hamlet, he would be Hamlet in eternity. Yet after a time the soul partly frees itself and becomes 'the shape changer' of the legends, and can cast, like the mediæval magician, what illusions it would. There is an Irish countryman in one of Lady Gregory's books who had eaten with a stranger on the road, and some while later vomited, to discover he had but eaten chopped-up grass. One thinks, too, of the spirits that show themselves in the images of wild creatures.

IX

The dead, as the passionate necessity wears out, come into a measure of freedom and may turn the impulse of events, started while living, in some new direction, but they cannot originate except through the living. Then gradually they perceive, although they are still but living in their memories, harmonies, symbols, and patterns, as though all were being refashioned by an artist, and they are moved by emotions, sweet for no imagined good but in themselves, like those of children dancing in a ring; and I do not doubt that they make love in that union which Swedenborg has said is of the whole body and seems from far off an incandescence. Hitherto shade has communicated with shade in moments of common memory that recur like the figures of a dance in terror or in joy, but now they run together like to like, and their Covens and Fleets have rhythm and pattern. This running together and running of all to a centre and yet without loss of identity, has been prepared for by their exploration of their moral life, of its beneficiaries and its victims, and even of all its untrodden paths, and all their thoughts have moulded the vehicle and become event and circumstance. . . .

XII

The dead living in their memories, are, I am persuaded, the source of all that we call instinct, and it is their love and their desire, all unknowing, that make us drive beyond our reason, or in defiance of our interest it may be; and it is the dream martens that, all unknowing, are mastermasons to the living martens building about church windows their elaborate nests; and in their turn, the phantoms are stung to a keener delight from a concord between their luminous pure vehicle and our strong senses. It were to reproach the power or the beneficence of God, to believe those children of Alexander, who died wretchedly, could not throw an urnful to the heap, nor Caesarion[o1] murdered in childhood, whom Cleopatra bore to Caesar, nor the brief-lived younger Pericles Aspasia bore[o]—being so nobly born.

XIII

Because even the most wise dead can but arrange their memories as we arrange pieces upon a chess-board and obey remembered words alone,

[1] I have no better authority for Caesarion than Landor's play.[o]

he who would turn magician is forbidden by the Zoroastrian° oracle to change 'barbarous words' of invocation. Communication with *Anima Mundi* is through the association of thoughts or images or objects; and the famous dead and those of whom but a faint memory lingers, can still—and it is for no other end, that all unknowing, we value posthumous fame—tread the corridor and take the empty chair. A glove and a name can call their bearer; the shadows come to our elbow amid their old undisturbed habitations, and 'materialisation' itself is easier, it may be, among walls, or by rocks and trees, that bring before their memory some moment of emotion while they had still animate bodies.

Certainly the mother returns from the grave, and with arms that may be visible and solid, for a hurried moment, can comfort a neglected child or set the cradle rocking: and in all ages men have known and affirmed that when the soul is troubled, those that are a shade and a song live there

> And move like winds of light on dark and stormy air.

. . .

XVII

Each Daemon is drawn to whatever man or, if its nature is more general, to whatever nation it most differs from, and it shapes into its own image the antithetical dream of man or nation. The Jews had already shown by the precious metals, by the ostentatious wealth of Solomon's temple, the passion that has made them the money-lenders of the modern world. If they had not been rapacious, lustful, narrow and persecuting beyond the people of their time, the incarnation had been impossible; but it was an intellectual impulse from the Condition of Fire that shaped their antithetical self into that of the classic world. So always it is an impulse from some Daemon that gives to our vague, unsatisfied desire, beauty, a meaning and a form all can accept.

XVIII

Only in rapid and subtle thought, or in faint accents heard in the quiet of the mind, can the thought of the spirit come to us but little changed; for a mind, that grasps objects simultaneously according to the degree of its liberation, does not think the same thought with the mind that sees objects one after another. The purpose of most religious teaching, of the insistence upon the submission to God's will above all, is to make certain of the passivity of the vehicle where it is most pure and most tenuous. When we are passive where the vehicle is coarse, we become mediumistic, and the spirits who mould themselves in that coarse vehicle can only rarely and with great difficulty speak their own thoughts and keep their own memory. They are subject to a kind of drunkenness and are stupefied, old writers said, as if with honey, and readily mistake our memory for their own, and believe themselves whom and what we please. We bewilder and overmaster them, for once they are among the perceptions of successive objects, our reason, being but an instrument created and sharpened by those objects, is stronger than their intellect, and they can but repeat with brief glimpses from another state, our knowledge and our words. . . .

from A Vision (1925)°

Book I

Part I

3. The Great Wheel°

I

ANTITHETICAL AND PRIMARY°

The diagram of the Great Wheel shows a series of numbers and symbols which represent the Lunar phases; and all possible human types can be classified under one or other of these twenty-eight phases. Their number is that of the Arabic Mansions of the Moon° but they are used merely as a method of classification and for simplicity of classification their symbols are composed in an entirely arbitrary way. As the lunar circle narrows to a crescent and as the crescent narrows to a still narrower crescent, the Moon approaches the Sun, falls as it were under his influence; and for this reason the Sun and Moon in diagram 1 are considered to be imposed one upon another.

They may be coloured gold and silver respectively. The first phase is therefore full Sun as it were, and the 15th Phase full Moon, while Phases 8 and 22 are half Sun and half Moon. In Book II is described the geometrical foundation of this symbolism and of the other characters of the wheel. When one uses the phases, in popular exposition or for certain symbolic purposes, one considers full Sun as merely the night when there is no moon, and in representing any phase visibly one makes the part which is not lunar dark. The Sun is objective man and the Moon subjective man, or more properly the Sun is *primary* man and the Moon *anti-*

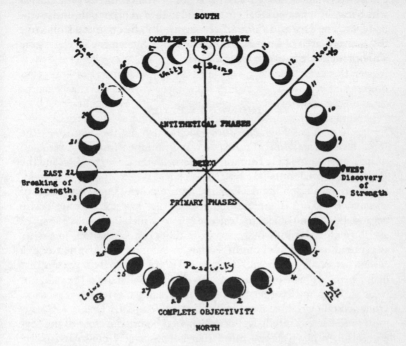

thetical man — terms that will be explained later. Objective and Subjective are not used in their metaphysical but in their colloquial sense. Murray's dictionary° describes the colloquial use of the word 'objective' thus. All that 'is presented to consciousness as opposed to consciousness of self, that is the object of perception or thought, the non-ego.' And again, objective when used in describing works of art means 'dealing with or laying stress upon that which is external to the mind, treating of outward things and events rather than inward thought', 'treating a subject so as to exhibit the actual facts, not coloured by the opinions or feelings of the writer.' The volume of Murray's dictionary containing letter S is not yet published, but as 'subjective' is the contrary to 'objective' it needs no further definition. Under the Sun's light we see things as they are, and go about our day's work, while under that of the Moon, we see things dimly, mysteriously, all is sleep and dream. All men are characterised upon a first analysis by the proportion in which these two characters or *Tinctures*,° the objective or *primary*, the subjective or *antithetical*, are combined. Man is said to have a series of embodiments (any one of which may be repeated) that correspond to the twenty-eight fundamental types. The *First* and *Fifteenth*, being wholly objective and subjective respectively, are not human embodiments, as human life is impossible without the strife between the *Tinctures*.

II
THE FOUR FACULTIES

Incarnate man has *Four Faculties* which constitute the *Tinctures*—the *Will*, the *Creative Mind*, the *Body of Fate*, and the *Mask*. The *Will* and *Mask* are predominately Lunar or *antithetical*, the *Creative Mind* and the *Body of Fate* predominately Solar or *primary*. When thought of in isolation, they take upon themselves the nature now of one phase, now of another. By *Will** is understood feeling that has not become desire because there is no object to desire; a bias by which the soul is classified and its phase fixed but which as yet is without result in action; an energy as yet uninfluenced by thought, action, or emotion; the first matter of a certain personality—choice. If a man's *Will* is at say Phase 17 we say that he is a man of Phase 17, and so on. By *Mask* is understood the image of what we wish to become, or of that to which we give our reverence. Under certain circumstances it is called the *Image*. By *Creative Mind* is meant intellect, as intellect was understood before the close of the seventeenth century—all the mind that is consciously constructive. By *Body of Fate* is understood the physical and mental environment, the changing human body, the stream of Phenomena as this affects a particular individual, all that is forced upon us from without, Time as it affects sensation. The *Will* when represented in the diagram is always opposite the *Mask*, the *Creative Mind* always opposite the *Body of Fate*.

The *Will* looks into a painted picture. The *Creative Mind* looks into a photograph, but both look into something which is the opposite of themselves. The picture is that which is chosen, while the photograph is heterogeneous. The photograph is fated, because by fate is understood that which comes from without, whereas the *Mask* is predestined, *Destiny* being that which comes to us from within. We best express the het-

---

* I have changed the 'creative genius' of the Documents into *Creative Mind* to avoid confusion between 'genius' and *Daimon*; and 'Ego' into *Will* for 'Ego' suggests the total man who is all *Four Faculties*. *Will* or self-will was the only word I could find not for man but Man's root. If Blake had not given 'selfhood' a special meaning it might have served my turn.   *September* 1925

erogeneousness of the photograph if we call it a photograph of a crowded street, which the *Creative Mind*—when not under the influence of the *Mask*—contemplates coldly; while the picture contains but few objects and the contemplating *Will* is impassioned and solitary.

All *Four Faculties* influence each other and the object of the diagram of the Wheel is to show when and in what proportions. When the *Will* predominates, and there is strong desire, the *Mask* or *Image* is sensuous, but when *Creative Mind* predominates it is abstract. When the *Mask* predominates it is idealised, when *Body of Fate* predominates it is concrete, and so on. An object is sensuous if I relate it to myself, '*my* fire, *my* chair,' etc., but it is concrete if I say '*a* chair, *a* fire,' and abstract if I but speak of it as the representative of a class—'*the* chair, *the* fire,' etc.

III
THE PLACE OF THE FOUR FACULTIES ON THE WHEEL

A man whose *Will* is at Phase 17 will have his *Creative Mind* at Phase 13 and his *Mask* at Phase 3 and his *Body of Fate* at Phase 27;° while a man whose *Will* is at Phase 3 would have all these positions exactly reversed. When *Will* is at Phase 15, *Creative Mind* is there also. On the other hand, when *Will* is at Phase 22, *Will* and *Body of Fate* are superimposed, while *Creative Mind* and *Mask* are superimposed at Phase 8. The points on diagram 1 marked *Head*, *Heart*, *Loins* and *Fall* mark where the four faculties are at equal distances from one another and that in part is why they are also represented by cardinal signs. They have also another significance which will be explained later.

Will and *Mask* are opposite in *Tincture*, *Creative Mind* and *Body of Fate* are opposite in *Tincture*. The one has the *primary* in the exact strength of the *antithetical* in the other, and vice versa. The *primary* and *antithetical* define the inclination of the *Will*, and through the *Will* affect the other three; this may be called the difference in quality. A *Will* at Phase 18 would have the exact amount of *antithetical* inclination that a *Will* at Phase 4 would have of *primary*. On the other hand, a *Will* at Phase 18 and *Creative Mind* at Phase 12 are exactly the same in the proportions of their *Tinctures*, have exactly the same quality of *Tincture* but move in opposite directions—one is going from Phase 1 to Phase 28 and the other from Phase 28 to Phase 1. It is therefore necessary to consider both direction and quality.

The relations between *Will* and *Mask*, *Creative Mind* and *Body of Fate* are called *oppositions*, and upon some occasions *contrasts*, while those between *Will* and *Creative Mind*, *Mask* and *Body of Fate* are called—for reasons which will appear later—*discords*.

Between Phase 12 and Phase 13, and between Phase 4 and Phase 5 in diagram 1 occurs what is called 'the *opening* of the *tinctures*,' and between Phase 18 and Phase 19, and between Phase 4 and Phase 5 what is called 'the closing.' This means that between Phase 12 and Phase 13 each Tincture divides into two, and closes up again between Phase 18 and Phase 19. Between Phase 26 and Phase 27 the Tinctures become one *Tincture*, and between Phase 4 and Phase 5 become two again. The *antithetical* before Phase 15 becomes the *primary* after Phase 15, and vice versa—that is to say, the thoughts and emotions that are in nature *antithetical* before Phase 15 are in nature *primary* after Phase 15; the man who before Phase 15 is harsh in his judgment of himself will turn that harshness to others after Phase 15.

The geometrical reasons both for this interchange and for the closing and opening of the *Tinctures* are discussed in Book II.

IV
DRAMA OF THE FACULTIES AND OF THE TINCTURES, ETC.

One can describe *antithetical* man by comparing him to the *Commedia del Arte* or improvised drama of Italy. The stage manager having chosen his actor, the *Will*, chooses for this actor, that he may display him the better, a scenario, *Body of Fate*, which offers to his *Creative Mind* the greatest possible difficulty that it can face without despair, and in which he must play a rôle and wear a *Mask* as unlike as possible to his natural character (or *Will*) and leaves him to improvise, through *Creative Mind*, the dialogue and the details of the plot. He must discover a being which only exists with extreme effort, when his muscles are as it were all taut and all his energies active, and for that reason the *Mask* is described as 'A form created by passion to unite us to ourselves.' Much of what follows will be a definition or description of this deeper being, which may become the unity described by Dante in the Convito.°

For *Primary* Man one must go to the Decline of the *Commedia del Arte*° for an example. The *Will* is weak and cannot create a rôle, and so, if it transform itself, does so after an accepted pattern, some traditional clown or pantaloon. It has perhaps no object but to move the crowd, and if it 'gags' it is that there may be plenty of topical allusions. In the *primary* phases Man must cease to desire *Mask* and *Image* by ceasing from self-expression, and substitute a motive of service for that of self-expression. Instead of the created *Mask* he has an imitative *Mask*; and when he recognises this, his *Mask* may become an image of mankind. The author of 'The Imitation of Christ'° was certainly a man of a late *primary* phase. It is said that the *antithetical Mask* is free, and the *primary Mask* enforced; and the free *Mask* is personality, a union of qualities, while the enforced mask is character, a union of quantities, and of their limitations—that is to say, of those limitations which give strength precisely because they are enforced. Personality, no matter how habitual, is a constantly renewed choice, and varies from an individual charm, in the more *antithetical* phases, to a hard objective dramatisation, which differs from character mainly because it is a dramatisation, in phases where the *antithetical Tincture* holds its predominance with difficulty.

Antithetical men are, like Landor°, violent in themselves because they hate all that impedes their personality, but are in their intellect (*Creative Mind*) gentle, but *primary* men whose hatreds are impersonal are violent in their intellect but gentle in themselves as doubtless Robespierre° was gentle.

The *Mask* before Phase 15 is described as 'a revelation' because through it the being obtains knowledge of itself, sees itself in personality; while after Phase 15 it is a 'concealment,' for the being grows incoherent, vague and broken, as its intellect (*Creative Mind*) is more and more concerned with objects that have no relation to its unity but a relation to the unity of Society or of material things, known through the *Body of Fate*, and adopts a personality which it more and more casts outward, more and more dramatises. It is now a dissolving violent phantom which would grip itself and hold itself together. The being of *Antithetical Man* is described as full of rage before Phase 12, against all in the world that hinders its expression, but after Phase 12 the rage is a knife turned against itself. After Phase 15, but before Phase 19, the being is full of phantasy, a continual escape from, and yet acknowledgment of all that allures in the world, a continual playing with all that must engulf it. The *primary* is that which serves, the *antithetical* is that which creates.

At Phase 8 is the 'Discovery of Strength,' an embodiment in sensuality, for the imitation that held it to the norm of the race has ceased and the personality with its own norm has not begun. *Primary* and *antithetical* are equal and fight for mastery; and when this fight is ended through the conviction of weakness and the preparation for rage, the *Mask* becomes once more voluntary. At Phase 22 is the 'Breaking of Strength,' for here the being makes its last attempt to impose its personality upon the world, before the *Mask* becomes enforced once more and Character is once more born.

To these two phases, perhaps to all phases, the being may return up to four times before it can pass on. It is claimed, however, that four times is the utmost possible. By being is understood that which divides into *Four Faculties*, by individual the *Will* analysed in relation to itself, by personality the *Will* analysed in relation to the *Mask*. It is because of the antithesis between *Will* and *Mask* that subjective natures are called *antithetical*, while those in whom individuality and *Creative Mind* predominate, and who are content with things as they find them, are called *primary*. Personality is strongest near Phase 15, individuality near Phase 22 and Phase 8.

XI

THE DAIMON, THE SEXES, UNITY OF BEING, NATURAL AND SUPERNATURAL UNITY

The *Will* and the *Creative Mind* are in the light, but the *Body of Fate* working through accident, in dark, while *Mask*, or *Image*, is a form selected instinctively for those emotional associations which come out of the dark, and this form is itself set before us by accident, or swims up from the dark portion of the mind. But there is another mind, or another part of our mind in this darkness, that is yet to its own perceptions in the light; and we in our turn are dark to that mind. These two minds (one always light* and one always dark, when considered by one mind alone), make up man and *Daimon*, the *Will* of the man being the *Mask* of the *Daimon*, the *Creative Mind* of the man being the *Body of Fate* of the *Daimon* and so on. The Wheel is in this way reversed, as St Peter at his crucifixion reversed° by the position of his body the position of the crucified Christ: 'Demon est Deus Inversus.'° Man's *Daimon* has therefore her energy° and bias, in man's *Mask*, and her constructive power in man's fate, and man and *Daimon* face each other in a perpetual conflict or embrace. This relation (the *Daimon* being of the opposite sex to that of man) may create a passion like that of sexual love. The relation of man and woman, in so far as it is passionate, reproduces the relation of man and *Daimon*, and becomes an element where man and *Daimon* sport, pursue one another, and do one another good or evil. This does not mean, however, that the men and women of opposite phases love one another, for a man generally chooses a woman whose *Mask* falls between his *Mask* and his *Body of Fate*, or just outside one or other; but that every man is, in the right of his sex, a wheel, or group of *Four Faculties*, and that every woman is, in the right of her sex, a wheel which reverses the masculine wheel. In so far as man and woman are swayed by their sex they interact as man and *Daimon* interact, though at other moments

---

* Light and dark are not used in this section as in the description of the phases, but as it were cross that light and dark at right angles. See diagrams in Sec. XVII, Book II.
September 1925

their phases may be side by side. The *Daimon* carries on her conflict, or friendship with a man, not only through the events of life, but in the mind itself, for she is in possession of the entire dark of the mind. The things we dream, or that come suddenly into our heads, are therefore her *Creative Mind* (our *Creative Mind* is her *Body of Fate*) through which her energy, or bias, finds expression; one can therefore, if one will, think of man as *Will* and *Creative Mind* alone, perpetually face to face with another being who is also but *Will* and *Creative Mind*, though these appear to man as the object of desire, or beauty, and as fate in all its forms. If man seeks to live wholly in the light, the *Daimon* will seek to quench that light in what is to man wholly darkness, and there is conflict and *Mask* and *Body of Fate* become evil; when however in *antithetical* man the *Daimonic* mind is permitted to flow through the events of his life (the *Daimonic Creative Mind*) and so to animate his *Creative Mind*, without putting out its light, there is Unity of Being. A man becomes passionate and this passion makes the *Daimonic* thought luminous with its peculiar light—this is the object of the *Daimon*—and she so creates a very personal form of heroism or of poetry. The *Daimon* herself is now passionless and has a form of thought, which has no need of premise and deduction, nor of any language, for it apprehends the truth by a faculty which is analogous to sight, and hearing, and taste, and touch, and smell, though without organs. He who attains Unity of Being is some man, who, while struggling with his fate and his destiny until every energy of his being has been roused, is content that he should so struggle with no final conquest. For him fate and freedom are not to be distinguished; he is no longer bitter, he may even love tragedy like those 'who love the gods and withstand them'; such men are able to bring all that happens, as well as all that they desire, into an emotional or intellectual synthesis and so to possess not the Vision of Good only but that of Evil. They are described as coming after death into dark and into light, whereas *primary* men, who do not receive revelation by conflict, are in dark or in light. In the *Convito* Dante speaks of his exile, and the gregariousness it thrust upon him, as a great misfortune for such as he; and yet as poet he must have accepted, not only that exile, but his grief for the death of Beatrice as that which made him *Daimonic*, not a writer of poetry alone like Guido Cavalcanti.° Intellectual creation accompanies or follows in *antithetical* man, the struggle of the being to overthrow its fate and this is symbolised by placing the *Creative Mind* in the phase opposite to that of the *Body of Fate*. Unity of Being becomes possible at Phase 12, and ceases to be possible at Phase 18, but is rare before Phase 13 and after Phase 17, and is most common at Phase 17. When man is in his most *antithetical* phases the *Daimon* is most *primary*; man pursues, loves, or hates, or both loves and hates—a form of passion, an *antithetical* image is imposed upon the *Daimonic* thought—but in man's most *primary* phases the *Daimon* is at her most *antithetical*. Man is now pursued with hatred, or with love; must receive an alien terror or joy; and it is to this final acceptance of the *Image* that we apply the phrases 'Unity with God,' 'Unity with Nature.' Unity with God is possible after Phase 26, though almost impossible before Phase 27 which is called 'The Saint,' while Unity with Nature may take place after Phase 1, and in its turn becomes impossible after Phase 4. But for the possibility of this union man in his *primary* phases would sink into a mechanical objectivity, become wholly automatic. At Phase 26, however, he can escape from that which he apprehends through the organs of sense, by submission to that which he can apprehend by the mind's eye and ear, its palate and its touch. When he is content to be pursued, to be ignored, to be hated even by that he so apprehends, he becomes the object not of hatred but of love, for the *Daimonic* mind, being now *antithetical*, has passed from thought to passion. *Antithetical* man pursuing, or hungry, with a passion like that of the beasts, may be exalted with a passion first discovered and expressed by finer minds than his; and the *Daimon* so pursuing, so hungry, is also so exalted, and we have therefore the right to describe our union with it, as union with Nature, or with God. When Phase 1 has been passed, the union is with nature.

According to the Solar symbolism, which is explained in Book II, two are not in light and two in dark, but all four in light as contrasted to *Four Principles* that are solar and entirely dark.

from A Vision (*1937*)

Introduction to 'A Vision'

'This way of publishing introductions to books, that are God knows when to come out, is either wholly new, or so long in practice that my small reading cannot trace it.'—Swift

I

The other day Lady Gregory said to me: 'You are a much better educated man than you were ten years ago and much more powerful in argument'. And I put *The Tower* and *The Winding Stair* into evidence to show that my poetry has gained in self-possession and power. I owe this change to an incredible experience.

II

On the afternoon of October 24th 1917, four days after my marriage, my wife surprised me by attempting automatic writing. What came in disjointed sentences, in almost illegible writing, was so exciting, sometimes so profound, that I persuaded her to give an hour or two day after day to the unknown writer, and after some half-dozen such hours offered to spend what remained of life explaining and piecing together those scattered sentences. 'No,' was the answer, 'we have come to give you metaphors for poetry.' The unknown writer took his theme at first from my just published *Per Amica Silentia Lunae*. I had made a distinction between the perfection that is from a man's combat with himself and that which is from a combat with circumstance, and upon this simple distinction he built up an elaborate classification of men according to their more or less complete expression of one type or the other. He supported his classification by a series of geometrical symbols and put these symbols in an order that answered the question in my essay as to whether some prophet could not prick upon the calendar the birth of a Napoleon or a Christ. A system of symbolism, strange to my wife and to myself, certainly awaited expression, and when I asked how long that would take I was told years. Sometimes when my mind strays back to those first days I remember that Browning's Paracelsus° did not obtain the secret until he had written his spiritual history at the bidding of his Byzantine teacher, that before initiation Wilhelm Meister° read his own history written by another, and I compare my *Per Amica* to those histories.

III

When the automatic writing began we were in a hotel on the edge of Ashdown Forest,° but soon returned to Ireland and spent much of 1918 at Glendalough,° at Rosses Point,° at Coole Park, at a house near it, at Thoor Ballylee, always more or less solitary, my wife bored and fatigued by her almost daily task and I thinking and talking of little else. Early in 1919 the communicator of the moment—they were constantly changed—said they would soon change the method from the written to the spoken word as that would fatigue her less, but the change did not come for some months. I was on a lecturing tour in America to earn a roof for Thoor Ballylee when it came. We had one of those little sleeping compartments in a train, with two berths, and were somewhere in Southern California. My wife, who had been asleep for some minutes, began to talk in her sleep, and from that on almost all communications came in that way. My teachers did not seem to speak out of her sleep but as if from above it, as though it were a tide upon which they floated. A chance word spoken before she fell asleep would sometimes start a dream that broke in upon the communications, as if from below, to trouble or overwhelm, as when she dreamed she was a cat lapping milk or a cat curled up asleep and therefore dumb. The cat returned night after night, and once when I tried to drive it away by making the sound one makes when playing at being a dog to amuse a child, she awoke trembling, and the shock was so violent that I never dared repeat it. It was plain therefore that, though the communicators' critical powers were awake, hers slept, or that she was aware of the idea the sound suggested but not of the sound.

IV

Whenever I received a certain signal (I will explain what it was later), I would get pencil and paper ready. After they had entranced my wife suddenly when sitting in a chair, I suggested that she must always be lying down before they put her to sleep. They seemed ignorant of our surroundings and might have done so at some inconvenient time or place; once when they had given their signal in a restaurant they explained that because we had spoken of a garden they had thought we were in it. Except at the start of a new topic, when they would speak or write a dozen sentences unquestioned, I had always to question, and every question to rise out of a previous answer and to deal with their chosen topic. My questions must be accurately worded, and, because they said their thought was swifter than ours, asked without delay or hesitation. I was constantly reproved for vague or confused questions, yet I could do no better, because, though it was plain from the first that their exposition was based upon a single geometrical conception, they kept me from mastering that conception. They shifted ground whenever my interest was at its height, whenever it seemed that the next day must reveal what, as I soon discovered, they were determined to withhold until all was upon paper. November 1917 had been given to an exposition of the twenty-eight typical incarnations or phases and to the movements of their *Four Faculties*,° and then on December 6th a cone or gyre had been drawn and related to the soul's judgment after death; and then just as I was about to discover that incarnations and judgment alike implied cones or gyres, one within the other, turning in opposite directions, two such cones were drawn and related neither to judgment nor to incarnations but to European history. They drew their first symbolical map of that history, and marked upon it the principal years of crisis, early in July 1918, some days before the publication of the first German edition of Spengler's *Decline of the West*,° which, though founded upon a different philosophy, gives the same years of crisis and draws the same general conclusions, and then returned to the soul's judgment. I believe that they so changed their theme because, had I grasped their central idea, I would have lacked the patience and the curiosity to follow their application of it, preferring some hasty application of my own. They once told me not to speak of any part of the system, except of the incarnations which were almost fully expounded, because if I did the people I talked to would talk to other people, and the communicators would mistake that misunderstanding for their own thought.

V

For the same reason they asked me not to read philosophy until their exposition was complete, and this increased my difficulties. Apart from two or three of the principal Platonic Dialogues I knew no philosophy. Arguments with my father, whose convictions had been formed by John Stuart Mill's attack upon Sir William Hamilton,° had destroyed my confidence and driven me from speculation to the direct experience of the Mystics. I had once known Blake as thoroughly as his unfinished confused Prophetic Books permitted, and I had read Swedenborg° and Boehme,°and my initiation into the 'Hermetic Students'° had filled my head with Cabalistic imagery,° but there was nothing in Blake, Swedenborg, Boehme or the Cabala to help me now. They encouraged me, however, to read history in relation to their historical logic, and biography in relation to their twenty-eight typical incarnations, that I might give concrete expression to their abstract thought. I read with an excitement I had not known since I was a boy with all knowledge before me, and made continual discoveries, and if my mind returned too soon to their unmixed abstraction they would say, 'We are starved'.

VI

Because they must, as they explained, soon finish, others whom they named Frustrators attempted to confuse us or waste time. Who these Frustrators were or why they acted so was never adequately explained, nor will be unless I can finish 'The Soul in Judgment' (Book III of this work), but they were always ingenious and sometimes cruel. The automatic script would deteriorate, grow sentimental or confused, and when I pointed this out the communicator would say, 'From such and such an hour, on such and such a day, all is frustration'. I would spread out the script and he would cross all out back to the answer that began it, but had I not divined frustration he would have said nothing. Was he

constrained by a drama which was part of conditions that made commu-
nication possible, was that drama itself part of the communication, had
my question to be asked before his mind cleared? Only once did he break
the rule and without waiting for a question declare some three or four
days' work frustration. A predecessor of his had described the geomet-
rical symbolism as created for my assistance and had seemed to dislike it,
another had complained that I used it to make their thought mechanical,
and a Frustrator doubtless played upon my weakness when he described
a geometrical model of the soul's state after death which could be turned
upon a lathe. The sudden indignant interruption suggested a mind
under a dream constraint which it could throw off if desire were strong
enough, as we can sometimes throw off a nightmare. It was part of their
purpose to affirm that all the gains of man come from conflict with the
opposite of his true being. Was communication itself such a conflict?
One said, as though it rested with me to decide what part I should play
in their dream, 'Remember we will deceive you if we can'. Upon the
other hand they seem like living men, are interested in all that interests
living men, as when at Oxford, where we spent our winters, one asked
upon hearing an owl hoot in the garden, if he might be silent for a while.
'Sounds like that', he said, 'give us great pleasure.' But some frustrations
found us helpless. Some six months before the communications came to
an end, a communicator announced that he was about to explain a new
branch of the philosophy and seemed to add, 'But please do not write
anything down, for when all is finished I will dictate a summary'. He
spoke almost nightly for I think three months, and at last I said, 'Let me
make notes, I cannot keep it all in my head'. He was disturbed to find that
I had written nothing down, and when I told him of the voice, said it was
frustration and that he could not summarise. I had already noticed that
if their thought was interrupted they had to find some appropriate
moment before they could take it up again, and that though they could
sometimes foretell physical events they could not foretell those
moments. Later still a frustration, if the communicator did not dream
what he said, took, as will be seen, a more cruel form.

VII

The automatic writing and the speech during sleep were illustrated or
accompanied by strange phenomena. While we were staying at a village
near Oxford we met two or three nights in succession what seemed a
sudden warm breath coming up from the ground at the same corner of
the road. One night when I was about to tell my wife some story of a
Russian mystic, without remembering that it might make her misun-

derstand an event in her own life, a sudden flash of light fell between us and a chair or table was violently struck. Then too there was much whistling, generally as a warning that some communicator would come when my wife was asleep. At first I was inclined to think that these whistlings were made by my wife without her knowing it, and once, when I heard the whistle and she did not, she felt a breath passing through her lips as though she had whistled. I had to give up this explanation when servants at the other end of the house were disturbed by a 'whistling ghost', and so much so that I asked the communicators to choose some other sign. Sweet smells were the most constant phenomena, now that of incense, now that of violets or roses or some other flower, and as perceptible to some half-dozen of our friends as to ourselves, though upon one occasion when my wife smelt hyacinth a friend smelt eau-de-cologne. A smell of roses filled the whole house when my son was born and was perceived there by the doctor and my wife and myself, and I have no doubt, though I did not question them, by the nurse and servants. Such smells came most often to my wife and myself when we passed through a door or were in some small enclosed place, but sometimes would form themselves in my pocket or even in the palms of my hands. When I took my hands out of my pocket on our way to Glastonbury they were strongly scented, and when I held them out for my wife to smell she said, 'May-flower, the Glastonbury thorn perhaps'.° I seldom knew why such smells came, nor why one sort rather than another, but sometimes they approved something said. When I spoke of a Chinese poem in which some old official described his coming retirement to a village inhabited by old men devoted to the classics, the air filled suddenly with the smell of violets, and that night some communicator explained that in such a place a man could escape those 'knots' of passion that prevent Unity of Being and must be expiated between lives or in another life. (Have I not found just such a village here in Rapallo? for, though Ezra Pound° is not old, we discuss Guido Cavalcanti and only quarrel a little.)

Sometimes if I had been ill some astringent smell like that of resinous wood filled the room, and sometimes, though rarely, a bad smell. These were often warnings: a smell of cat's excrement announced some being that had to be expelled, the smell of an extinguished candle that the communicators were 'starved'. A little after my son's birth I came home to confront my wife with the statement 'Michael is ill'. A smell of burnt feathers had announced what she and the doctor had hidden. When regular communication was near its end and my work of study and arrangement begun, I was told that henceforth the Frustrators would attack my health and that of my children, and one afternoon, knowing from the smell of burnt feathers that one of my children would be ill within three hours, I felt before I could recover self-control the mediaeval helpless horror at witchcraft. I can discover no apparent difference between a natural and a supernatural smell, except that the natural smell comes and goes gradually while the other is suddenly there and then as suddenly gone. But there were other phenomena. Sometimes they commented on my thoughts by the ringing of a little bell heard by my wife alone, and once my wife and I heard at the same hour in the afternoon, she at Ballylee and I at Coole, the sound of a little pipe, three or four notes, and once I heard a burst of music in the middle of the night; and when regular communications through script and sleep had come to an end, the communicators occasionally spoke—sometimes a word, sometimes a whole sentence. I was dictating to my wife, perhaps, and a voice would object to a sentence, and I could no more say where the voice came from than I could of the whistling, though confident that it came through my wife's personality. Once a Japanese who had dined with my wife and myself talked of Tolstoi's philosophy, which fascinates so many educated Japanese, and I put my objections vehemently. 'It is madness for the East', I said, 'which must face the West in arms', and much more of the same sort, and was, after he had gone, accusing myself of exaggerated and fantastic speech when I heard these words in a loud clear voice: 'You have said what we wanted to have said'. My wife, who was writing a letter at the other end of the room, had heard nothing, but found she had written those words in the letter, where they had no meaning. Sometimes my wife saw apparitions: before the birth of our son a great black bird, persons in clothes of the late sixteenth century and of the late seventeenth. There were still stranger phenomena that I prefer to remain silent about for the present because they seemed so incredible that they need a long story and much discussion.

VIII

Exposition in sleep came to an end in 1920, and I began an exhaustive study of some fifty copy-books of automatic script, and of a much smaller number of books recording what had come in sleep. Probably as many words had been spoken in sleep as had been written, but I could only summarise and much had been lost through frustration. I had already a small concordance in a large manuscript book, but now made a much larger, arranged like a card index. And then, though I had mastered nothing but the twenty-eight phases and the historical scheme, I was told that I must write, that I must seize the moment between ripe and rotten—there was a metaphor of apples about to fall and just fallen. They showed when I began that they assisted or approved, for they sent sign after sign. Sometimes if I stopped writing and drew one hand over another my hands smelt of violets or roses, sometimes the truth I sought would come to me in a dream, or I would feel myself stopped—but this has occurred to me since boyhood—when forming some sentence, whether in my mind or upon paper. When in 1926 the English translation of Spengler's book° came out, some weeks after *A Vision*, I found that not only were dates that I had been given the same as his but whole metaphors and symbols that had seemed my work alone. Both he and I had symbolised a difference between Greek and Roman thought by comparing the blank or painted eyes of Greek statues with the pierced eyeballs of the Roman statues, both had described as an illustration of Roman character the naturalistic portrait heads screwed on to stock bodies, both had found the same meaning in the round bird-like eyes of Byzantine sculpture, though he or his translator had preferred 'staring at infinity' to my 'staring at miracle'. I knew of no common source, no link between him and me, unless through

> The elemental things that go
> About my table to and fro.°

. . .

XIV

Some will associate the story I have just told with that popular spiritualism which has not dared to define itself, to go like all great spiritual movements through a tragedy of separation and rejection, which instead of asking whether it is not something almost incredible, because altogether new or forgotten, clings to all that is vague and obvious in popular Christianity; and hate me for that association. But Muses resemble women who creep out at night and give themselves to unknown sailors and return to talk of Chinese porcelain—porcelain is best made, a Japanese critic has said, where the conditions of life are hard—or of the Ninth Symphony—virginity renews itself like the moon—except that the Muses sometimes form in those low haunts their most lasting attachments.

XV

Some will ask whether I believe in the actual existence of my circuits of sun and moon. Those that include, now all recorded time in one circuit, now what Blake called 'the pulsaters of an artery', are plainly symbolical, but what of those that fixed, like a butterfly upon a pin, to our central date, the first day of our Era, divide actual history into periods of equal length?

To such a question I can but answer that if sometimes, overwhelmed by miracle as all men must be when in the midst of it, I have taken such periods literally, my reason has soon recovered; and now that the system stands out clearly in my imagination I regard them as stylistic arrangements of experience comparable to the cubes in the drawing of Wyndham Lewis° and to the ovoids in the sculpture of Brancusi.° They have helped me to hold in a single thought reality and justice.

November 23rd 1928, and later

from Book IV: The Great Year of the Ancients

XI

At the opening of Book V is a diagram where every date was fixed by my instructors.° They have adopted a system of cones not used elsewhere in this exposition. If one ignores the black numbers° it is simple enough. It shows the gyre of religion expanding as that of secular life contracts, until at the eleventh century the movements are reversed. *Mask* and *Body of Fate* are religion, *Will* and *Creative Mind* secular life. My instructors have inserted the black numbers because it enables them to bring into a straight line four periods corresponding to the *Four Faculties* that are in Flinders Petrie's sense of the word 'contemporaneous'. If we push this line of *Faculties* down from its starting-point at the birth of Christ (Year 1, and Phase 1 in the red letters),° to the eleventh century, with *Will* on the left red line, *Body of Fate* on the left black line, *Mask* on the next and so on; then push it upward, changing the order of the *Faculties* to that on the diagram, every moment of the era reveals itself as constituted by four interacting periods. If we keep the straight line passing through the *Four Faculties* of the same length as the bases of the triangles we can mark upon it the twenty-eight phases, putting Phase 1 at the left hand, and the line will show what the position of the *Faculties* would be upon an ordinary double cone which completed its movement in the two thousand years of the era. My instructors scrawled a figure with a line so marked once or twice upon the margin of the automatic script while writing of something else, and left me to guess its relevance. When one examines the line so divided one discovers that at the present moment, although we are passing into Phase 23 on the cone of civilisation, we are between Phases 25 and 26 on the cone of the era. I consider that a conflict between religious and secular thought, because it governs all that is most interior and spiritual in myself, must be the projector of the era, and I find it upon this slow-moving cone. Its *Four Faculties* so

THE HISTORICAL CONES°

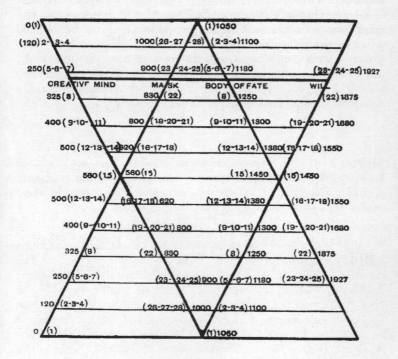

The numbers in brackets refer to phases, and the other numbers to dates AD. The line cutting the cones a little below 250, 900, 1180 and 1927 shows four historical *Faculties* related to the present moment. May 1925.

found are four periods of time eternally co-existent, four co-existent
acts; as seen in time we explain their effect by saying that the spirits of
the three periods that seem to us past are present among us, though
unseen.

When our historical era approaches Phase 1, or the beginning of a new
era, the *antithetical* East will beget upon the *primary* West and the child
or era so born will be *antithetical*. The *primary* child or era is predom-
inantly western, but because begotten upon the East, eastern in body,
and if I am right in thinking that my instructors imply not only the sym-
bolical but the geographical East, Asiatic. Only when that body begins to
wither can the Western Church predominate visibly.

. . .

XVI

My instructors certainly expect neither a 'primitive state' nor a return to
barbarism as primitivism and barbarism are ordinarily understood; *anti-
thetical* revelation is an intellectual influx neither from beyond mankind
nor born of a virgin, but begotten from our spirit and history.

XVII

At the birth of Christ took place, and at the coming *antithetical* influx
will take place, a change equivalent to the *interchange of the tinctures*. The
cone shaped like an ace of diamonds—in the historical diagram the cone
is folded upon itself—is Solar, religious and vital; those shaped like an
hour-glass Lunar, political and secular; but *Body of Fate* and *Mask* are in
the Solar cones during a *primary* dispensation, and in the Lunar during
an *antithetical*, while *Will* and *Creative Mind* occupy the opposing cones.
Mask and *Body of Fate* are symbolic woman, *Will* and *Creative Mind*
symbolic man; the man and woman of Blake's *Mental Traveller*.° Before
the birth of Christ religion and vitality were polytheistic, *antithetical*,
and to this the philosophers opposed their *primary*, secular thought.
Plato thinks all things into Unity and is the 'First Christian'. At the birth
of Christ religious life becomes *primary*, secular life *antithetical*—man
gives to Caesar the things that are Caesar's. A *primary* dispensation look-
ing beyond itself towards a transcendent power is dogmatic, levelling,
unifying, feminine, humane, peace its means and end; an *antithetical*
dispensation obeys imminent power, is expressive, hierarchical, mult-
iple, masculine, harsh, surgical. The approaching *antithetical* influx and
that particular *antithetical* dispensation for which the intellectual prepa-
ration has begun will reach its complete systematisation at that moment
when, as I have already shown, the Great Year° comes to its intellectual

climax. Something of what I have said it must be, the myth declares, for it must reverse our era and resume past eras in itself; what else it must be no man can say, for always at the critical moment the *Thirteenth Cone,*° the sphere, the unique intervenes.

> Somewhere in sands of the desert
> A shape with lion body and the head of a man,
> A gaze blank and pitiless as the sun,
> Is moving its slow thighs, while all about it
> Reel shadows of the indignant desert birds.°

. . .

from Book V: Dove or Swan

. . . I have not the knowledge (it may be that no man has the knowledge) to trace the rise of the Byzantine State° through Phases 9, 10 and 11. My diagram tells me that a hundred and sixty years brought that State to its 15th Phase, but I that know nothing but the arts and of these little, cannot revise the series of dates 'approximately correct' but given, it may be, for suggestion only. With a desire for simplicity of statement I would have preferred to find in the middle, not at the end, of the fifth century Phase 12, for that was, so far as the known evidence carries us, the moment when Byzantium became Byzantine and substituted for formal Roman magnificence, with its glorification of physical power, an architecture that suggests the Sacred City in the Apocalypse of St John. I think if I could be given a month of Antiquity and leave to spend it where I chose, I would spend it in Byzantium a little before Justinian° opened St Sophia° and closed the Academy of Plato.° I think I could find in some little wine-shop some philosophical worker in mosaic who could answer all my questions, the supernatural descending nearer to him than to Plotinus° even, for the pride of his delicate skill would make what was an instrument of power to princes and clerics, a murderous madness in the mob, show as a lovely flexible presence like that of a perfect human body.

I think that in early Byzantium, maybe never before or since in recorded history, religious, aesthetic and practical life were one, that architect and artificers—though not, it may be, poets, for language had been the instrument of controversy and must have grown abstract—spoke to the multitude and the few alike. The painter, the mosaic worker, the worker in gold and silver, the illuminator of sacred books, were almost impersonal, almost perhaps without the consciousness of individual design, absorbed in their subject-matter and that the vision of a whole people. They could copy out of old Gospel books those pictures that seemed as sacred as the text, and yet weave all into a vast design, the work of many that seemed the work of one, that made building, picture, pattern, metal-work of rail and lamp, seem but a single image; and this vision, this proclamation of their invisible master, had the Greek nobility, Satan always the still half-divine Serpent, never the horned scare-crow of the didactic Middle Ages.

. . .

Fiction

The Adoration of the Magi °

I was sitting reading late into the night a little after my last meeting with
Aherne,° when I heard a light knocking on my front door; and found
upon the doorstep three very old men with stout sticks in their hands,
who said they had been told I would be up and about, and that they were
to tell me important things. I brought them into my study, and when the
peacock curtains had closed behind us, I set their chairs for them close to
the fire, for I saw that the frost was on their great-coats of frieze and upon
the long beards that flowed almost to their waists. They took off their
great-coats, and leaned over the fire warming their hands, and I saw that
their clothes had much of the country of our time, but a little also, as it
seemed to me, of the town life of a more courtly time. When they had
warmed themselves—and they warmed themselves, I thought, less
because of the cold of the night than because of a pleasure in warmth for
the sake of warmth—they turned towards me, so that the light of the
lamp fell full upon their weather-beaten faces, and told the story I am
about to tell. Now one talked and now another, and they often inter-
rupted one another, with a desire, like that of countrymen, when they
tell a story, to leave no detail untold. When they had finished they made
me take notes of whatever conversation they had quoted, so that I might
have the exact words, and got up to go, and when I asked them where
they were going, and what they were doing, and by what names I should
call them, they would tell me nothing, except that they had been com-
manded to travel over Ireland continually, and upon foot and at night,
that they might live close to the stones and the trees and at the hours
when the immortals are awake.

I have let some years go by before writing out this story, for I am
always in dread of the illusions which come of that inquietude of the veil
of the Temple, which M. Mallarmé considers a characteristic of our
times;° and only write it now because I have grown to believe that there
is no dangerous idea which does not become less dangerous when writ-
ten out in sincere and careful English.

The three old men were three brothers, who had lived in one of the
western islands from their early manhood, and had cared all their lives
for nothing except for those classical writers and old Gaelic writers who

expounded an heroic and simple life. Night after night in winter, Gaelic story-tellers would chant old poems to them over the poteen; and night after night in summer, when the Gaelic story-tellers were at work in the fields or away at the fishing, they would read to one another Virgil and Homer, for they would not enjoy in solitude, but as the ancients enjoyed. At last a man, who told them he was Michael Robartes,° came to them in a fishing-boat, like St Brandan° drawn by some vision and called by some voice; and told them of the coming again of the gods and the ancient things; and their hearts, which had never endured the body and pressure of our time, but only of distant times, found nothing unlikely in anything he told them, but accepted all simply and were happy. Years passed, and one day, when the oldest of the old men, who had travelled in his youth and thought sometimes of other lands, looked out on the grey waters, on which the people see the dim outline of the Islands of the Young°—the Happy Islands where the Gaelic heroes live the lives of Homer's Phæacians°—a voice came out of the air over the waters and told him of the death of Michael Robartes. While they were still mourning, the next oldest of the old men fell asleep whilst he was reading out the Fifth Eclogue of Virgil,° and a strange voice spoke through him, and bid them set out for Paris, where a dying woman would give them secret names and thereby so transform the world that another Leda would open her knees to the swan, another Achilles° beleaguer Troy.

They left their island, and were at first troubled at all they saw in the world, and came to Paris, and there the youngest met a person in a dream, who told him they were to wander about at hazard until those who had been guiding their footsteps had brought them to a street and a house, whose likeness was shown him in the dream. They wandered hither and thither for many days, until one morning they came into some narrow and shabby streets, on the south of the Seine, where women with pale faces and untidy hair looked at them out of the windows; and just as they were about to turn back because Wisdom could not have alighted in so foolish a neighbourhood, they came to the street and the house of the dream. The oldest of the old men, who still remembered some of the modern languages he had known in his youth, went up to the door and knocked, and when he had knocked, the next in age to him said it was not a good house, and could not be the house they were looking for, and urged him to ask for somebody who could not be there and go away. The door was opened by an old over-dressed woman, who said, 'O you are her three kinsmen from Ireland. She has been expecting you all day.' The old men looked at one another and followed her upstairs, passing doors from which pale and untidy women thrust out their heads, and into a room where a beautiful woman lay asleep, another woman sitting by her.

The old woman said: 'Yes, they have come at last; now she will be able to die in peace,' and went out.

'We have been deceived by devils,' said one of the old men, 'for the immortals would not speak through a woman like this.'

'Yes,' said another, 'we have been deceived by devils, and we must go away quickly.'

'Yes,' said the third, 'we have been deceived by devils, but let us kneel down for a little, for we are by the deathbed of one that has been beautiful.' They knelt down, and the woman sitting by the bed whispered, and as though overcome with fear, and with lowered head, 'At the moment when you knocked she was suddenly convulsed and cried out as I have heard a woman in child-birth and fell backward as though in a swoon.' Then they watched for a little the face upon the pillow and wondered at its look, as of unquenchable desire, and at the porcelain-like refinement of the vessel in which so malevolent a flame had burned.

Suddenly the second oldest of them crowed like a cock, till the room seemed to shake with the crowing. The woman in the bed still slept on in her death-like sleep, but the woman who sat by her head crossed herself and grew pale, and the youngest of the old men cried out: 'A devil has gone into him, and we must begone or it will go into us also.' Before they could rise from their knees, a resonant chanting voice came from the lips that had crowed and said:

'I am not a devil, but I am Hermes the Shepherd of the Dead,° I run upon the errands of the gods, and you have heard my sign. The woman who lies there has given birth, and that which she bore has the likeness of a unicorn and is most unlike man of all living things, being cold, hard and virginal. It seemed to be born dancing; and was gone from the room wellnigh upon the instant, for it is of the nature of the unicorn to understand the shortness of life. She does not know it has gone for she fell into a stupor while it danced, but bend down your ears that you may learn the names that it must obey.' Neither of the other two old men spoke, but doubtless looked at the speaker with perplexity, for the voice began again: 'When the Immortals would overthrow the things that are to-day and bring the things that were yesterday, they have no one to help them, but one whom the things that are to-day have cast out. Bow down and very low, for they have chosen this woman in whose heart all follies have gathered, and in whose body all desires have awaked; this woman who has been driven out of Time and has lain upon the bosom of Eternity.'

The voice ended with a sigh, and immediately the old man awoke out of sleep, and said: 'Has a voice spoken through me, as it did when I fell asleep over my Virgil, or have I only been asleep?'

The oldest of them said: 'A voice has spoken through you. Where has your soul been while the voice was speaking through you?'

'I do not know where my soul has been, but I dreamed I was under the roof of a manger, and I looked down and I saw an ox and an ass; and I saw a red cock perching on the hay-rack; and a woman hugging a child; and three old men in chain armour kneeling with their heads bowed very low in front of the woman and the child. While I was looking the cock crowed and a man with wings on his heels swept up through the air, and as he passed me, cried out: "Foolish old men, you had once all the wisdom of the stars." I do not understand my dream or what it would have us do, but you who have heard the voice out of the wisdom of my sleep know what we have to do.'

Then the oldest of the old men told him they were to take the parchments they had brought with them out of their pockets and spread them on the ground. When they had spread them on the ground, they took out of their pockets their pens, made of three feathers, which had fallen from the wing of the old eagle that is believed to have talked of wisdom with St Patrick.

'He meant, I think,' said the youngest, as he put their ink-bottles by the side of the rolls of parchment, 'that when people are good the world likes them and takes possession of them, and so eternity comes through people who are not good or who have been forgotten. Perhaps Christianity was good and the world liked it, so now it is going away and the immortals are beginning to awake.'

'What you say has no wisdom,' said the oldest, 'because if there are many immortals, there cannot be only one immortal.'

'Yet it seems,' said the youngest, 'that the names we are to take down are the names of one, so it must be that he can take many forms.'

Then the woman on the bed moved as in a dream, and held out her arms as though to clasp the being that had left her, and murmured names of endearment and yet strange names, 'Harsh sweetness', 'Dear bitterness', 'O solitude', 'O terror', and after lay still for awhile. Then her voice changed, and she, no longer afraid and happy but seeming like any dying woman, murmured a name so faintly that the woman who sat by the bed bent down and put her ear close to her mouth.

The oldest of the old men said in French: 'There must have been yet one name which she had not given us, for she murmured a name while the spirit was going out of the body,' and the woman said, 'She was merely murmuring over the name of a symbolist painter she was fond of.

He used to go to something he called the Black Mass, and it was he who taught her to see visions and to hear voices.'

This is all the old men told me, and when I think of their speech and of their silence, of their coming and of their going, I am almost persuaded that had I followed them out of the house, I would have found no footsteps on the snow. They may, for all I or any man can say, have been themselves immortals: immortal demons, come to put an untrue story into my mind for some purpose I do not understand. Whatever they were, I have turned into a pathway which will lead me from them and from the Order of the Alchemical Rose.° I no longer live an elaborate and haughty life, but seek to lose myself among the prayers and the sorrows of the multitude. I pray best in poor chapels, where frieze coats brush against me as I kneel, and when I pray against the demons I repeat a prayer which was made I know not how many centuries ago to help some poor Gaelic man or woman who had suffered with a suffering like mine.

> *Seacht b-páidreacha fó seacht*
> *Chuir Muire faoi n-a Mac,*
> *Chuir Brighid faoi n-a brat,*
> *Chuir Dia faoi n-a neart,*
> *Eidir sinn 'san Sluagh Sidhe,*
> *Eidir sinn 'san Sluagh Gaoith.*

> Seven paters seven times,
> Send Mary by her Son,
> Send Bridget by her mantle,
> Send God by His strength,
> Between us and the faery host,
> Between us and the demons of the air.

Senate Speeches°

The Irish Language,° 14 November 1923

Mr Yeats: I wish to make a very emphatic protest against the histrionics which have crept into the whole Gaelic movement. People pretend to know a thing that they do not know and which they have not the smallest intention of ever learning. It seems to me to be discreditable and undesirable. I hope this will not be taken as being unsympathetic to the Gaelic movement. In the Abbey Theatre, on Monday night, a play in Irish was produced, and the theatre was packed with an enthusiastic audience. They knew Irish, and they were able to understand the language of the play, but I think this method of histrionics, and going through a childish performance of something we do not know, and which we do not intend to learn, will ultimately lead to a reaction against the language. I wish to say that I wish to see the country Irish speaking.

From the Debate on Divorce,° 11 June 1925

Mr Yeats: I should have said I do not intend to speak merely to the House. I have no doubt whatever, if circumstances were a little different, a very easy solution would be found for this whole difficulty. I judge from conversations that I have had with various persons that many would welcome a very simple solution, namely, that the Catholic members should remain absent when a Bill of Divorce was brought before the House that concerned Protestants and non-Catholics only, and that it would be left to the Protestant members, or some Committee appointed by those Protestant members, to be dealt with. I think it would be the first instinct of the members of both Houses to adopt some such solution and it is obvious, I think, that from every point of view of national policy and national reputation that that would be a wise policy to adopt. It is perhaps the deepest political passion with this nation that North and South will be united into one nation.

If it ever comes that North and South unite the North will not give up any liberty which she already possesses under its Constitution. You will then have to grant to another people what you refuse to grant to those within your borders. If you show that this country, Southern Ireland, is going to be governed by Catholic ideas and by Catholic ideas alone, you will never get the North. You will create an impassable barrier between South and North, and you will go on evermore with Catholic legislation and the North will, gradually, come to assimilate its divorce and other laws to those of England. You will put a wedge into the midst of this nation. I do not think this House has ever made a more serious decision than the decision which, I believe, it is about to make on this question. You will not get the North if you impose on the minority what the minority consider to be oppressive legislation. I have no doubt whatever that in the next few years the minority will make it perfectly plain that it does consider it exceedingly oppressive legislation to deprive it of rights which it has held since the 17th century. These rights were won by the labours of John Milton° and other great men, and won after strife, which is a famous part of the history of the Protestant people.

There is a reason why this country did not act upon what was its first impulse, and why this House and the Dáil did not act on their first impulse. Some of you may probably know that when the Committee was set up to draw up the Constitution of the Free State, they were urged to incorporate in the Constitution the indissolubility of marriage and they refused to do so. That was the expression of the political mind of Ireland. You are now urged to act on the advice of men who do not express the political mind, but who express the religious mind. I admit it must be exceedingly difficult for members of this House to resist the pressure that has been brought upon them. In the long warfare of this country with England the Catholic clergy took the side of the people, and owing to that they possess here an influence that they do not possess anywhere else in Europe. It is difficult for you, and I am sure it is difficult for Senator Mrs Wyse-Power, stalwart fighter as she is—

Mrs Wyse-Power: I do not see why my name should be mentioned.

An Cathaoirleach:° It is not in order to refer in this way to members of this House.

Mr Yeats: I am sure it is difficult for members of this House to resist the advice of their Archbishop, Most Rev Dr Byrne.

Mr Fitzgerald: I think this is becoming very heated.

Mr Yeats: I mean it to be heated. . . .

. . . I have said that this is a tolerant country, yet, remembering that we have in our principal streets certain monuments, I feel it necessary to say that it would be wiser if I had said this country is hesitant.

I have no doubt whatever that, when the iceberg melts it will become an exceedingly tolerant country. The monuments are rather local. I am thinking of O'Connell, Parnell, and Nelson.° You never have any trouble about O'Connell,° not the least. It was said about O'Connell, in his own day, that you could not throw a stick over a workhouse wall without hitting one of his children, but he believed in the indissolubility of marriage, and when he died his heart was very properly preserved in Rome. I am not quite sure whether it was in bronze or marble, but it is there, and I have no doubt the art was atrocious as was the art of the period in which it was made. We had a good deal of trouble about Parnell when he married a woman who became thereby Mrs Parnell.

An Cathaoirleach: Do you not think we might leave the dead alone?

Mr Yeats: I am passing on. I will not dwell long on them. When that happened, I can remember the Irish Catholic Bishops coming out with a declaration that he had thereby doubled his offence. That is, fundamentally, the difference between us. In the opinion of every Irish Protestant gentleman in this country he did what was essential as a man of honour. Now you are going to make that essential act impossible, and thereby interfere deeply with the conscience of the minority. I am anxious to draw the attention of the Bishop of Meath to Nelson. There is a proposal to remove Nelson because he interferes with the traffic.° Now, I would suggest to the Protestant Bishop of Meath that he should advocate the removal of Nelson on strictly moral grounds. We will then have the whole thing out, and discover whether the English people who teach the history of Nelson to their children, and hold it before the country as a moral one, or the Bishop of Meath represent, on the whole, public opinion. The Bishop of Meath would not, like his predecessors in Ireland eighty years ago, have given Nelson a Pillar. He would have preferred to give him the gallows, because Nelson should have been either hanged or transported. I think I have not greatly wronged the dead in suggesting that we have in our midst three very salutary objects of meditation which may, perhaps, make us a little more tolerant.

I wish to close rather more seriously; this is a matter of very great seriousness. I think it is tragic that within three years of this country gaining its independence we should be discussing a measure which a minority of this nation considers to be grossly oppressive. I am proud to consider myself a typical man of that minority. We are no petty people. We are one of the great stocks of Europe. There is no more famous stock in Europe. We are the people of Burke; we are the people of Grattan; we are the people of Swift, the people of Emmet,° the people of Parnell. We have created the most of the modern literature of this country. We have created the best of its political intelligence. Yet I do not altogether regret what has happened. I shall be able to find out, if not I, my children will be able to find out whether we have lost our stamina or not. You have defined our position for us and you have given us a popular following. If we have not lost our stamina then your victory will be very brief, and your defeat final. . . .

The State of School Education, 24 March 1926.
School Attendance Bill

I am not asking anything extravagant. I think we ought to do whatever is done by other countries of the same wealth as this nation in order to ensure the welfare of our children. We should consider, for instance, that there are at present some arrangements, not I think always very wise, as to the feeding of school-children in the towns. There are none in the country, and judging by my own countryside, where I live during the summer months, it is needed. Children will start early in the morning. They will be the greater portion of the day in school and they will have no adequate meals. They come away hungry, and it seems, if not very necessary, at least very desirable that they should have food. Then, of course, many other countries, perhaps not richer than this, have found means of seeing that children are properly clothed and that they have proper books. These are all difficult questions but they are desirable things.

I have no desire to speak on the question of the curriculum. It is being considered by a Commission at this moment. I wish that the Government had introduced a comprehensive educational measure dealing with all the details before asking us to compel children, by law, to go into the schools. Whether it is good for the children or not depends not only on the building but on the nature of the system under which they are taught. I am sure for a child to spend all day in school with a stupid, ill-trained man under an ill-taught system, is less good for that child than that the child should be running through the fields and learning nothing. I should like to draw the attention of the Government to one nation which has reformed its educational system in the most suggestive and profound way; that is Italy. It has not produced a system unique to Italy. It has simply gathered together the results of experiments all over the world. They are now teaching a system of education adapted to an agricultural nation like this or Italy, a system of education that will not turn out clerks only, but will turn out efficient men and women who can manage in the fields to do all the work of the nation. This system has been tried in Ireland. There are some schools carrying it out. There is one large primary school managed by nuns in the South of Ireland which has adopted practically the entire Italian system and which is carrying it out with great effect, has found that it is applicable, and that its teachers do not need special training to carry it out. The Italian Minister who adopted that policy was warned by everyone that it would not be possible to get this elaborate system carried out by partly educated people. It has been proved possible and of great benefit to the children.

In order to permit myself to give an intelligent vote—at one time I thought it would be a silent one—on this question I dislike doing more than making a suggestion. I have come here with two clear principles in mind. One is that we ought to be able to give the child of the poor as good an education as we give to the child of the rich. Of course the rich man's child remains longer at school. I have consulted teachers and people accustomed to the latest methods of education, and they are all clear that there is no reason why the education of the children of the poor should not be as good, while it lasts, as the education of the children of the rich. I would like to suggest another principle, that the child itself must be the end in education, and in anything that you want to do with the child. It is a curious thing how many times the education of Europe has drifted into error. The fact is forgotten that for two or three centuries people thought that their various religious systems were more important than the child. In the modern world the tendency is to think of the nation; that it is more important than the child. In Japan, I understand, the child is sacrificed to patriotism. I have seen education unified in America, so that the child is sacrificed to that of unified Americanism, and the human mind is codified. We are bound to go through the same passion ourselves. There is a tendency to subordinate the child to the idea of the nation. I suggest that whether we teach either Irish history, Anglo–Irish literature or Gaelic, we should always see that the child is the object and not any of our special perquisites.

Autobiographical Writings

from Reveries over Childhood and Youth

II
[*Childhood Days in Sligo*]

. . . There was a large garden behind the house° full of apple trees, with flower-beds and grass-plots in the centre, and two figure-heads of ships, one among the strawberry plants under a wall covered with fruit trees and one among the flowers. The one among the flowers was a white lady in flowing robes, while the other, a stalwart man in uniform, had been taken from a three-masted ship of my grandfather's called *The Russia*, and there was a belief among the servants that the stalwart man represented the Tsar and had been presented by the Tsar himself. The avenue, or as they say in England the drive, that went from the hall door through a clump of big trees to an insignificant gate and a road bordered by broken and dirty cottages, was but two or three hundred yards, and I often thought it should have been made to wind more, for I judged people's social importance mainly by the length of their avenues. This idea may have come from the stable-boy, for he was my principal friend. He had a book of Orange rhymes, and the days when we read them together in the hay-loft gave me the pleasure of rhyme for the first time. Later on I can remember being told, when there was a rumour of a Fenian rising, that rifles had been served out to the Orangemen; and presently, when I had begun to dream of my future life, I thought I would like to die fighting the Fenians. I was to build a very fast and beautiful ship and to have under my command a company of young men who were always to be in training like athletes and so become as brave and handsome as the young men in the story-books, and there was to be a big battle on the sea-shore near Rosses and I was to be killed. . . .

XXVIII
[*John O'Leary*]

I had very little money and one day the toll-taker at the metal bridge over the Liffey and a gossip of his laughed when I refused the halfpenny and said, 'No, I will go round by O'Connell Bridge'. When I called for the first time at a house in Leinster Road several middle-aged women were playing cards and suggested my taking a hand and gave me a glass of sherry.

The sherry went to my head and I was impoverished for days by the loss of sixpence. My hostess was Ellen O'Leary,° who kept house for her brother John O'Leary,° the Fenian, the handsomest old man I had ever seen. He had been condemned to twenty years' penal servitude but had been set free after five on condition that he did not return to Ireland for fifteen years. He had said to the Government, 'I will not return if Germany makes war on you, but I will return if France does'. He and his old sister lived exactly opposite the Orange leader for whom he had a great respect. His sister stirred my affection at first for no better reason than her likeness of face and figure to the matron of my London school, a friendly person, but when I came to know her I found sister and brother alike were of Plutarch's people. She told me of her brother's life, of the foundation of the Fenian movement, and of the arrests that followed (I believe that her own sweetheart had somehow fallen among the wreckage), of sentences of death pronounced upon false evidence amid a public panic, and told it all without bitterness. No fanaticism could thrive amid such gentleness. She never found it hard to believe that an opponent had as high a motive as her own and needed upon her difficult road no spur of hate.

Her brother seemed very unlike on a first hearing, for he had some violent oaths, 'Good God in Heaven' being one of them; and if he disliked anything one said or did, he spoke all his thought, but in a little one heard his justice match her charity. 'Never has there been a cause so bad', he would say, 'that it has not been defended by good men for good reasons.' Nor would he overvalue any man because they shared opinions; and when he lent me the poems of Davis and the Young Irelanders,° of whom I had known nothing, he did not, although the poems of Davis had made him a patriot, claim that they were very good poetry.

He had the moral genius that moves all young people and moves them the more if they are repelled by those who have strict opinions and yet have lived commonplace lives. I had begun, as would any other of my training, to say violent and paradoxical things to shock provincial sobriety, and Dowden's° ironical calm had come to seem but a professional pose. But here was something as spontaneous as the life of an artist. Sometimes he would say things that would have sounded well in some heroic Elizabethan play. It became my delight to rouse him to these outbursts for I was the poet in the presence of his theme. Once when I was defending an Irish politician who had made a great outcry because he was treated as a common felon, by showing that he did it for the cause's sake, he said, 'There are things that a man must not do to save a nation'. He would speak a sentence like that in ignorance of its passionate value, and would forget it the moment after. . . .

XXIX

From these debates, from O'Leary's conversation, and from the Irish books he lent or gave me has come all I have set my hand to since. I had begun to know a great deal about the Irish poets who had written in English. I read with excitement books I should find unreadable to-day, and found romance in lives that had neither wit nor adventure. I did not deceive myself, I knew how often they wrote a cold and abstract language, and yet I who had never wanted to see the houses where Keats and Shelley lived would ask everybody what sort of place Inchedony° was, because Callanan° had named after it a bad poem in the manner of *Childe Harold*.° Walking home from a debate, I remember saying to some college student, 'Ireland cannot put from her the habits learned from her old military civilization and from a church that prays in Latin. Those popular poets have not touched her heart, her poetry when it comes will be distinguished and lonely.' O'Leary had once said to me, 'Neither Ireland nor England knows the good from the bad in any art, but Ireland unlike England does not hate the good when it is pointed out to her'. I began to plot and scheme how one might seal with the right image the soft wax before it began to harden. I had noticed that Irish Catholics among whom had been born so many political martyrs had not the good taste, the household courtesy and decency of the Protestant Ireland I had known, yet Protestant Ireland seemed to think of nothing but getting on in the world. I thought we might bring the halves together if we had a national literature that made Ireland beautiful in the memory, and yet had been freed from provincialism by an exacting criticism, a European pose.

from The Trembling of the Veil°

Book I, Four Years: 1887–1891

VIII

[*Oscar Wilde*]

My first meeting with Oscar Wilde° was an astonishment. I never before heard a man talking with perfect sentences, as if he had written them all over night with labour and yet all spontaneous. There was present that night at Henley's,° by right of propinquity or of accident, a man full of the secret spite of dullness, who interrupted from time to time, and always to check or disorder thought; and I noticed with what mastery he was foiled and thrown. I noticed, too, that the impression of artificiality

that I think all Wilde's listeners have recorded came from the perfect
rounding of the sentences and from the deliberation that made it pos-
sible. That very impression helped him, as the effect of metre, or of the
antithetical prose of the seventeenth century, which is itself a true metre,
helped its writers, for he could pass without incongruity from some
unforeseen, swift stroke of wit to elaborate reverie. I heard him say a few
nights later: 'Give me *The Winter's Tale*, "Daffodils that come before the
swallow dare" but not *King Lear*. What is *King Lear* but poor life stag-
gering in the fog?' and the slow, carefully modulated cadence sounded
natural to my ears. That first night he praised Walter Pater's *Studies in
the History of the Renaissance*:° 'It is my golden book; I never travel any-
where without it; but it is the very flower of decadence: the last trumpet
should have sounded the moment it was written.' 'But,' said the dull
man, 'would you not have given us time to read it?' 'Oh no,' was the
retort, 'there would have been plenty of time afterwards—in either
world.' I think he seemed to us, baffled as we were by youth, or by infir-
mity, a triumphant figure, and to some of us a figure from another age, an
audacious Italian fifteenth-century figure. A few weeks before I had
heard one of my father's friends, an official in a publishing firm that had
employed both Wilde and Henley as editors, blaming Henley who was
'no use except under control' and praising Wilde, 'so indolent but such a
genius'; and now the firm became the topic of our talk. 'How often do you
go to the office?' said Henley. 'I used to go three times a week,' said
Wilde, 'for an hour a day but I have since struck off one of the days.' 'My
God,' said Henley, 'I went five times a week for five hours a day and when
I wanted to strike off a day they had a special committee meeting.' 'Fur-
thermore,' was Wilde's answer, 'I never answered their letters. I have
known men come to London full of bright prospects and seen them
complete wrecks in a few months through a habit of answering letters.'
He too knew how to keep our elders in their place, and his method was
plainly the more successful, for Henley had been dismissed. 'No he is not
an aesthete,' Henley commented later, being somewhat embarrassed by
Wilde's pre-Raphaelite entanglement; 'one soon finds that he is a scholar
and a gentleman.' And when I dined with Wilde a few days afterwards he
began at once, 'I had to strain every nerve to equal that man at all'; and I
was too loyal to speak my thought: 'You and not he said all the brilliant
things.' He like the rest of us had felt the strain of an intensity that
seemed to hold life at the point of drama. He had said on that first meet-
ing 'The basis of literary friendship is mixing the poisoned bowl'; and for
a few weeks Henley and he became close friends till, the astonishment of
their meeting over, diversity of character and ambition pushed them

apart, and, with half the cavern helping, Henley began mixing the poisoned bowl for Wilde. Yet Henley never wholly lost that first admiration, for after Wilde's downfall he said to me: 'Why did he do it? I told my lads to attack him and yet we might have fought under his banner.'. . .

Book V, 'The Stirring of the Bones', IV

IV

[Maud Gonne]

She [Maud Gonne°] was the first who spoke publicly or semi-publicly of the withdrawal of the Irish Members° as a practical policy for our time, so far as I know, but others may have been considering it. A nation in crisis becomes almost like a single mind, or rather like those minds I have described that become channels for parallel streams of thought, each stream taking the colour of the mind it flows through. These streams are not set moving, as I think, through conversation or publication, but through 'telepathic contact' at some depth below that of normal consciousness; and it is only years afterwards, when future events have shown the theme's importance, that we discover that they are different expressions of a common theme. That self-moving, self-creating nation necessitated an Irish centre of policy, and I planned a premature impossible peace between those two devouring heads because I was sedentary and thoughtful; but Maud Gonne was not sedentary, and I noticed that before some great event she did not think but became exceedingly superstitious. Are not such as she aware, at moments of great crisis, of some power beyond their own minds; or are they like some good portrait painter of my father's generation and only think when the model is under their eye? Once upon the eve of some demonstration, I found her with many caged larks and finches which she was about to set free for the luck's sake.

I abandoned my plans on discovering that our young men, not yet educated by Mr Birrell's university,° would certainly shout down every one they disagreed with, and that their finance was so extravagant that we must content ourselves with a foundation stone and an iron rail to protect it, for there could never be a statue; while she carried out every plan she made.

Her power over crowds was at its height, and some portion of the power came because she could still, even when pushing an abstract principle to what seemed to me an absurdity, keep her own mind free, and so when men and women did her bidding they did it not only because she was beautiful, but because that beauty suggested joy and freedom. Besides there was an element in her beauty that moved minds full of old Gaelic stories and poems, for she looked as though she lived in an ancient civilisation where all superiorities whether of the mind or the body were a part of public ceremonial, were in some way the crowd's creation, as the entrance of the Pope into St. Peter's is the crowd's creation. Her beauty, backed by her great stature, could instantly affect an assembly and not as often with our stage beauties because obvious and florid, for it was incredibly distinguished, and if—as must be that it might seem that assembly's very self, fused, unified, and solitary—her face, like the face of some Greek statue, showed little thought, her whole body seemed a master work of long labouring thought, as though a Scopas° had measured and calculated, consorted with Egyptian sages, and mathematicians out of Babylon, that he might outface even Artemisia's° sepulchral image with a living norm.

But in that ancient civilisation abstract thought scarce existed, while she but rose partially and for a moment out of raging abstraction; and for that reason, as I have known another woman do, she hated her own beauty, not its effect upon others, but its image in the mirror. Beauty is from the antithetical self, and a woman can scarce but hate it, for not only does it demand a painful daily service, but it calls for the denial or the dissolution of the self.

> How many centuries spent
> The sedentary soul,
> In toil of measurement
> Beyond eagle or mole
> Beyond hearing and seeing
> Or Archimedes' guess,
> To raise into being
> That loveliness?°

Letters

To Ernest Rhys,° [early February 1892]

3 Blenheim Road | Bedford Park | Chiswick. W

My dear Rhys

I return the poem. I like some of the stazas very much—especially the 6th & 7th of part one & the 1st of the third part also the last stanza of all. 'From the ancient house of Hendra'° is a genuine phrase of romance. I like the whole poem but not so well as others of yours I think. It is just a little perhaps too entirely a back-ground. It wants foreground—a central incident or some explanation why the house of Hendra should be more haunted° than all others. At the same time it is very interesting. I wish you would tell us even though it were but in a foot note who or what Hendra was. Its vagueness seems to me to take from the poems apparent antiquity & primeval quality & authenticity as a translation. I dont know about the Welsh but the Irish bards any way, always were explicit rather than suggestive in dealing with the supernatural. I was coming from such & such a town & staid in the house of such & such a person when I saw such & such a spirit dressed in such & such a cloak—is their method. They surround the vague with the definite. They would, to use Blakes expression, always hide Wisdom 'in a silver rod & Love in a golden bowl.'°

I enclose the poem you asked for. Please give my best regards to Mrs Rhys—

Yours very sncy
W. B. Yeats

To Katharine Tynan,° 2 March 1892

3 Blenheim Road | Bedford Park | Chiswick. | London. W

My dear Katey

First to answer your questions about the collection of 'Irish Love Songs'° of which by the by I heard from Unwins reader with great satisfaction for no one could do it so well as you. You should I think include a fair number from Davis.° He is very Irish & I find he grows upon me partly because of his great sincerity. His 'Plea for Love' is I think the best of all. You might also use 'The Marriage' 'Loves Longings' 'The Boatman of Kinsale' & 'Maire Bhan A Storr'. You should I think get

Sigerson or some one of that kind to give you phonetic equivalents the gaelic spelling he adopts is his own. 'Eogan' for instance should be written as it is pronounced 'Owen'. Do not forget ⟨among poetry other than Davis⟩[1] to include 'Kathleen O More' a marvellous lyric ⟨usually⟩ attributed to Reynolds. I think that 'the girl of the fine flown hair' in Walshes 'Irish Songs'° is good to[o]. There was a little thing by Hyde° in our ballad book 'Have you been on the mountain & seen there my love' which might go in. You might perhaps give from Oisin 'to an Isle in the Water' and an 'old song resung'° for they are more obviously Irish than my recent attempts at love poetry of which I enclose one or two things. I could have been of much greater help to you a while ago but I have not been reading the Irish ballads very recently & so cannot advise you so well there. By the by would not 'The Fairy Song' in the 'Rhymers Book'° do for your purpose It is extremely Irish & has been greatly liked—It is a love poem of a kind. You will be able to chose at any rate what you want of mine from Oisin, The R' book & the MS I send.

But enough of this matter. Blake is getting through the press. About two thirds & that the most trouble some part is gone to press & most of it is already in proof. I am also correcting 'The Countess Kathleen' for the press & getting ready a quantity of lyrics & ballads to go with it. It will be infinitely my best book. I have had rather a bad autumn with poor health & poorer spirits or I had made it better than it is. Health & spirits are I suppose mixed up in some queer way—not quite as the materialists say but in some fashion. I shall be back in Dublin again very soon now & look forward much to seeing you. I am always more at home in Dublin than any other where. My sisters send you greetings & ask when you will be in London as they enjoy your visits so greatly.

Yours always
W. B. Yeats

The following lyrics may perhaps help you to select something for your book. The first was written some months ago the second the other day.

When you are old.°

When you are old and grey and full of sleep
   And nodding by the fire, take down this book;
   And slowly read and dream of the soft look
Your eyes had once, and of their shaddows deep;

How many loved your moments of glad grace
   And loved your beauty with love false or true
   But one man loved the pilgrim soul in you,

[1] These angle brackets enclose text that has been cancelled by Yeats.

And loved the sorrows of your changing face;
And bending down beside the glowing bars
   Murmur, a little sad, "from us fled Love;
   He paced upon the mountains far above
And hid his face amid a crowd of stars".

        When you are sad.°
When you are sad
   The mother of the stars weeps too
And all her starlight is with sorrow mad
   And tears of fire fall gently in the dew.

When you are sad
   The mother of the wind mourns too
And her old wind that no mirth ever had
   Wanders & wails before my heart most true.

When you are sad
   The mother of the wave sighs too
And her dim wave bids men be no more glad
   And then the whole world's trouble weep with you.

I don't know whether these poems may not be too literary for your purpose. A book such as you are doing should be Irish before all else. People will go to English poetry for 'literary poetry' but will look to a book like your collection for a new flavour as of fresh turned mould. Davis, Fergusson, Allingham Mangan & Moore° should be your mainstay & every poem that shows English influence in any marked way should be rejected. No poetry has a right to live merely because it is good. It must be *the best of its kind*. The best Irish poets are this & every writer of imagination who is true to him self absolutely, may be so. I forgot to say in my letter that I would if I were you include Lovers 'Whistling Thief' & Walsh's 'Mo Craobhin Cno' & 'Mairgréad ni Chealleadh' (quite love poem enough) also 'A love ballad' by Mangan (it is in Gills 3rd collection & is from the Irish).

To George Russell (AE),° 14 May 1903

               18, Woburn Buildings, | W. C.

My dear Russell,

   I send you 'Ideas of Good and Evil'° a book which will I think have an interest. The only review that has been as yet is as enthusiastic as one could have wished. The book is only one half of the orange for I only got a grip on the other half very lately. I am no longer in much sympathy with an essay like the Autumn of the Body, not that I think that essay untrue. But I think I mistook for a permanent phase of the world what was only a preparation. The close of the last century was full of a strange desire to get out of form to get to some kind of disembodied beauty and now it seems to me the contrary impulse has come. I feel about me and in me an impulse to create form, to carry the realisation of beauty as far as possible. The Greeks said that the Dionysisic enthusiasm preceeded the Apollonic° and that the Dionysisic was sad and desirious, but that the Apollonic was joyful and self sufficient. Long ago I used to define to myself these two influences as the transfiguration on the mountain and the incarnation,° only the Transfiguration comes before the Incarnation in the natural order. I would like to know what you think of the book, and if you could make your Hermitists read it I have a notion that it would do them a world of good. I have not yet been through your poems° for the truth is I had to ransack all my books to find your two published volumes, and now that I have got one at any rate and I think the two I am up to my ears in the preparation of lectures. I shall have leisure however after next Tuesday, when I return from Manchester and will let you know at once then.

Yrs sny
W. B. Yeats

To J. B. Yeats, 23 February 1910

Abbey Theatre

My dear Father,

I have just finished dictating a first sketch of my lecture in London, it is on the dialect drama with Synge as the principal figure. All three lectures have worked themselves out as a plea for uniting literature once more to personality, the personality of the writer in lyric poetry or with imaginative personalities in drama. The only ground on which I differ from you is that I look upon character and personality as different things or perhaps different forms of the same thing. Juliet has personality, her Nurse has character. I look upon personality as the individual form of our passions (Dowson's° in his poetry or Byron in *Manfred*° or Forbes-Robertson° in a romantic part have all personality but we do not necessarily know much about their characters). Character belongs I think to Comedy, but all that's rather a long story and is connected with a whole mass of definitions.

I probably get the distinction from the stage, where we say a man is a 'character actor' meaning that he builds up a part out of observation, or we say that he is 'an emotional actor' meaning that he builds it up out of himself, and in this last case—we always add, if he is not common-place—that he has personality. Of course Shakespeare has both because he is always a tragic comedian.

In the process of writing my third lecture I found it led up to the thought of your letter which I am going to quote at the end. It has made me realize with some surprise how fully my philosophy of life has been inherited from you in all but its details and applications. What I want you to tell me

[*The rest of this letter is missing.*]

To Lady Gregory, [*11 May 1916*]

Royal Societies Club | St James's Street. S.W.
My dear Lady Gregory,

The Dublin tragedy° has been a great sorrow and anxiety. Cosgrave,° who I saw a few months ago in connection with the Municipal Gallery project and found our best supporter, has got many years' imprison-ment and to-day I see that an old friend Henry Dixon°—unless there are two of the name—who began with me the whole work of the literary movement has been shot in a barrack yard without trial of any kind. I have little doubt there have been many miscarriages of justice. The wife of a Belgian Minister of War told me a few days ago that three British officers had told her that the command of the British army in France should be made over to the French generals, and that French generals have told her that they await with great anxiety the result of the coming German attack on the English lines because of the incompetence of the English Higher Command as a whole. Haig however they believed in—he was recommended by the French for the post. I see therefore no rea-son to believe that the delicate instrument of Justice is being worked with precision in Dublin. I am trying to write a poem° on the men exe-cuted—'terrible beauty has been born again.' If the English Conserva-tive party had made a declaration that they did not intend to rescind the Home Rule Bill° there would have been no Rebellion. I had no idea that any public event could so deeply move me—and I am very despondent about the future. At the moment I feel that all the work of years has been overturned, all the bringing together of classes, all the freeing of Irish lit-erature and criticism from politics. Maud Gonne reminds me that she

saw the ruined houses about O'Connell Street and the wounded and
dying lying about the streets, in the first few days of the war. I perfectly
remember the vision and my making light of it and saying that if a true
vision at all it could only have a symbolised meaning. This is the only let-
ter I have had from her since she knew of the Rebellion. I have sent her
the papers every day. I do not yet know what she feels about her hus-
band's death. Her letter was written before she heard of it. Her main
thought seems to be 'tragic dignity has returned to Ireland.' She had
been told by two members of the Irish Party that 'Home Rule was
betrayed.' She thinks now that the sacrifice has made it safe. She is com-
ing to London if she can get a passport, but I doubt her getting one.
Indeed I shall be glad if she does not come yet—it is better for her to go
on nursing the French wounded till the trials are over. How strange that
old Count Plunkett and his wife and his three sons should all be drawn
into the net.

I sent on to you yesterday the proof sheets I had finished and fastened
up at the start of the Rebellion. I sent a letter with them giving an expla-
nation of what I want you to do. I have been able to do little work lately
and that chiefly on *Player Queen*° which always needs new touches in its
one bad place—first half of second act.

Yours
W. B. Yeats

To H. J. C. Grierson,° 21 February [1926]

82 Merrion Square

My dear Prof Grierson:

I have long put off writing to thank you for *The Background of English
Literature*° but my procrastination has not meant any lack of liking. I
have had your book at my bed side for weeks and have read it very
constantly. I am particularly indebted to you for your essay on Byron.
My own verse has more and more adopted—seemingly without any will
of mine—the syntax and vocabulary of common personal speech. The
passages you quote—that beginning 'our life is a false nature' down to
almost the end of the quotation where it becomes too elaborate with
'couch the mind'° and a great part of the long passage about Haidée°—I
got a queer sort of half dream prevision of the passage the day before
your book came with a reiteration of the words 'broad moon'—are
perfect personal speech. The over childish or over pretty or feminine
element in some good Wordsworth and in much poetry up to our date

comes from the lack of natural momentum in the syntax. This momentum underlies almost every Elizabethan and Jacobean lyric and is far more important than simplicity of vocabulary. If Wordsworth had found it he could have carried any amount of elaborate English. Byron, unlike the Elizabethans though he always tries for it, constantly allows it to die out in some mind-created construction, but is I think the one great English poet—though one can hardly call him great except in purpose and manhood—who sought it constantly. Blunt, though mostly an infuriating amateur, has it here and there in some Elizabethan sounding sonnet and is then very great. Perhaps in our world only an amateur can seek it at all—unless he keep to the surface like Kipling—or somebody like myself who seeks it with an intense unnatural labour that reduces composition to four or five lines a day. In a less artificial age it would come with our baby talk. The amateur has the necessary ease of soul but only succeeds a few times in his life.

I have been reading your Donne again—I have just spelt him 'done,' that is because I have been writing the material version of a chorus for a version of *Oedipus* intended for the stage and my faculties have gone to the deuce—especially that intoxicating 'St Lucies Day'° which I consider always an expression of passion and proof that he was the Countess of Bedford's lover. I have used the arrangement of the rhymes in the stanzas for a poem of my own, just finished. I have the Blake illustration to Gray° open on a little table which makes a kind of lectern between two book shelves. My large picture books take their turn there and yours has been there for the last month. The pictures grow in beauty with familiarity.

You may have noticed that we have had riots in the theatre again. I was with you when word reached me of the *Playboy* row. This time we had a packed theatre,° and had a packed theatre every day while the play was running, indeed numbers could not get in. The riot was soon over and displayed one curious effect of fine acting. When the Republicans rushed the stage a man caught up a girl, who had been playing a consumptive invalid, and folded her in a cloak as a preliminary to carrying her from the stage—she was not the actress in his eyes but the consumptive girl.

The theatre has now a great following. Indeed all things of the kind are going well with us—minds have been suddenly liberated from hereditary political passion and are looking for other interests. I feel constantly if I were but twenty years old and not over sixty all I ever wanted to do could be done easily. One never tires of life and at the last must die of thirst with the cup at one's lip.

Yours ever
W. B. Yeats

To Olivia Shakespear°

March 4 [*On envelope*: 'I forgot to post this. So sorry. March 12.']
[*Postmark Mar* 13, 1926]

82 Merrion Square

My dear Olivia,

I am so sorry about your teeth—I suppose you will get this in the nursing home—however the worst trial will be over. I know that one of the things I dread most is gas—'laughing gas' is I believe its lying name and that liar Southey called it 'a brave gas.'

I do not think Carmichael° or any other spirit spends his thought on such things as the preference for a tub rather than a tin or a fixed bath. When they come to us they take up old thoughts and interests. I had once to stay silent for some minutes as the spirit was listening to the hoot of an owl. 'Those sounds,' he said, 'give us intense pleasure.' When you are well again I want you to read the part of my book called 'The Gates of Pluto'°—it is overloaded with detail and not as bold in thought as it should have been but does I think reconcile spiritual fact with credible philosophy.

Why not send the embarrassing book to Harry Tucker° anonymously? He would be charmed to get it and at once attribute the gift to some old friend—you cannot tell how deeply touched he would be. He would hide it away and read it like his prayer book.

A Vision reminds me of the stones I used to drop as a child into a certain very deep well. The splash is very far off and very faint. Not a review except one by AE°—either the publisher has sold the review copies or the editors have—and no response of any kind except from a very learned doctor in the North of England who sends me profound and curious extracts from ancient philosophies on the subject of gyres. A few men here are reading me, so I may found an Irish heresy.

Yours affectionately
W. B. Yeats

To Sean O'Casey,° 20 April 1928

82 Merrion Square

My dear Casey°

. . . I had looked forward with great hope and excitement to reading your play,° and not merely because of my admiration for your work, for I bore in mind that the Abbey owed its recent prosperity to you. If you had not brought us your plays just at that moment I doubt if it would now exist. I read the first act with admiration, I thought it was the best first act you had written, and told a friend that you had surpassed yourself. The next night I read the second and third acts, and to-night I have read the fourth. I am sad and discouraged; you have no subject. You were interested in the Irish Civil War, and at every moment of those plays wrote out of your own amusement with life or your sense of its tragedy; you were excited, and we all caught your excitement; you were exasperated almost beyond endurance by what you had seen or heard, as a man is by what happens under his window, and you moved us as Swift moved his contemporaries.

But you are not interested in the great war; you never stood on its battlefields or walked its hospitals, and so write out of your opinions. You illustrate those opinions by a series of almost unrelated scenes, as you might in a leading article; there is no dominating character, no dominating action, neither psychological unity nor unity of action; and your great power of the past has been the creation of some unique character who dominated all about him and was himself a main impulse in some action that filled the play from beginning to end.

The mere greatness of the world war has thwarted you; it has refused to become mere background, and obtrudes itself upon the stage as so much dead wood that will not burn with the dramatic fire. Dramatic action is a fire that must burn up everything but itself; there should be no room in a play for anything that does not belong to it; the whole history of the world must be reduced to wallpaper in front of which the characters must pose and speak.

Among the things that dramatic action must burn up are the author's opinions; while he is writing he has no business to know anything that is not a portion of that action. Do you suppose for one moment that Shakespeare educated Hamlet and King Lear by telling them what he thought and believed? As I see it, Hamlet and Lear educated Shakespeare, and I have no doubt that in the process of that education he found out that he was an altogether different man to what he thought himself, and had altogether different beliefs. A dramatist can help his characters to educate him by thinking and studying everything that gives them the language they are groping for through his hands and eyes, but the control must be theirs, and that is why the ancient philosophers thought a poet or dramatist Daimon-possessed.

This is a hateful letter to write, or rather to dictate—I am dictating to my wife—and all the more so, because I cannot advise you to amend the play. It is all too abstract, after the first act; the second act is an interesting technical experiment, but it is too long for the material; and after that there is nothing. I can imagine how you have toiled over this play. A good scenario writes itself, it puts words into the mouths of all its characters while we sleep, but a bad scenario exacts the most miserable toil. I see nothing for it but a new theme, something you have found and no newspaper writer has ever found. What business have we with anything but the unique?

Put the dogmatism of this letter down to splenetic age and forgive it.

W.B.Y.

To Lady Gregory, 7 April 1930

Via Americhe 12–8

Dear Lady Gregory,

I had meant to write this with my own hand, but I have begun to work again and that uses up all my writing energy for the day. I begin in bed immediately after breakfast and work for about an hour.

We are on a mountain top about five miles from Rapallo in a hotel with large woody grounds about it and views over miles of mountain and sea; a most lovely place. I will never say again that I do not believe in climate, for after two or three days here I found myself almost normal again. We are staying another week and have been here a week. Just outside the gate of the hotel grounds there is a small restaurant and hotel which was once the lodging, or rather tenement house, where Nietzsche lived for some months and boasted to his friends of having found a place where there were eight walks. When we are not lost in mountain clouds it is brilliant sunlight and blue sea which melts imperceptibly into the sky. When I am not reading detective stories I am reading Swift, the *Diary to Stella*,° and his correspondence with Pope and Bolingbroke;° these men fascinate me, in Bolingbroke the last pose and in Swift the last passion of the Renaissance, in Pope, whom I dislike, an imitation both of pose and passion.

Masefield and his family, Siegfried Sassoon° and a friend, arrive in Rapallo in a few days, and I am hoping the mountain will not deter them. Ezra Pound arrived the other day, his first visit since I got ill—fear of infection—and being warned by his wife tried to be very peaceable but couldn't help being very litigious about Confucius who I consider should have worn an Eighteenth Century wig and preached in St. Paul's, and he thinks the perfect man.

Yours affectionately
W. B. Yeats

To Olivia Shakespear, 9 March [*1933*]

Riversdale°

My dear Olivia,

I shall be in London on April 10. I had meant to go rather sooner as my gardener says I should not miss the garden in April. You can apply much of the Swami thought to our life if you translate it. 'Act and remain apart from action.'

During the last few days I have been in conflict with certain people in the government about the Abbey. I had to risk its future: only yesterday did I get the decision I wished.. I watch myself with interest. I found that once I had a clear idea, and knew I was not acting from temper, I did not seem to be personally involved. I looked on as if some stranger was doing it all. I had an hour's interview with De Valera.° I had never met him before and I was impressed by his simplicity and honesty though we differed throughout. It was a curious experience, each recognised the other's point of view so completely. I had gone there full of suspicion but my suspicion vanished at once. You must not believe what you read in the English papers. They decide moral questions in the interest of their parties and express their decisions with a complacency that rouses other nations to fury. Here I think we are generally troubled about right and wrong, we don't decide easily. The hungry man is nearer to the Saint than the full man. 'A hair divides the false and true'—one should never be satisfied in any controversy until one has found the hair—one is liable to think it must look like a ship's cable.

I wish I could put the Swami's lectures° into the Cuala series° but I cannot. My sister's books° are like an old family magazine. A few hundred people buy them all and expect a common theme Only once did I put a book into the series that was not Irish—Ezra's Noh plays—and I had to write a long introduction to annex Japan to Ireland.

I have finished my essay on *Louis Lambert*.° How one loves Balzac's audience—great ladies, diplomatists, everybody who goes to grand opera, and ourselves. Then think of Tolstoy's—all the bores, not a poor sinner amongst them.

At the club the other day I spent an hour reading Comte de Tilly° but when I went back for another read it had gone. I like the love affairs but I would [like] more detail, they are too abstract. That affair in the carriage which was so unsatisfactory. One feels that neither the Persian nor the pedantic Indian amorist should have omitted from his work, travelling by carriage.

The Comte de Tilly should have been able to refer to precedents, or to create one, to find perhaps a new rhythm.

Joyce and D. H. Lawrence have however almost restored to us the Eastern simplicity. Neither perfectly, for D. H. Lawrence romanticises his material, with such words as 'essential fire,' 'darkness' etc, and Joyce never escapes from his Catholic sense of sin. Rabelais seems to escape from it by his vast energy. Yet why not take Swedenborg literally and think we attain, in a partial contact, what the spirits know throughout their being. He somewhere describes two spirits meeting, and as they touch they become a single conflagration. His vision may be true, Newton's cannot be. When I saw at Mrs. Crandon's objects moved and words spoken from some aerial centre, where there was nothing human, I rejected England and France and accepted Europe. Europe belongs to Dante and the witches' sabbath, not to Newton.

Yours affectionately
W. B. Yeats

To Ethel Mannin,° 11 December [1936]

Riversdale
My dear:
Of course I don't hate the people of England, considering all I owe to Shakespeare, Blake, Morris—they are the one people I cannot hate. I remember old John O'Leary, the Fenian leader, saying 'I think the English have finer native characters than we have, but we cannot become English.' I hate certain characteristics of modern England, characteristics that come because of government in the interests of a financial policy the people so little understand, or like, that they have to be tricked into supporting it. If an angel were to stand before me and say the policy is right and only through tricking the people can it be carried through, I would say 'Because you are an angel I must believe what you say. But what am I to do? Certain things drive me mad and I lose control of my tongue.'

> You think it horrible that Lust and Rage
> Should dance attendance upon my old age;
> They were not such a plague when I was young;
> What else have I to spur me into song?°

All through the Abyssinian war° my sympathy was with the Abyssinians, but those feelings were chilled by my knowledge that the English Government was using those feelings to help an Imperial policy I distrusted. To the wife of a Cabinet Minister who had discoursed to him on England's noble attitude, the monk Shree Purohit Swami said 'There cannot be two swords in one scabbard' and said no more.

Yes, I have a pension not given for poverty, though I was poor enough, but for 'intellectual services' or some such phrase. It was given at a time when Ireland was represented in parliament and voted out of the taxes of both countries. It is not voted annually, my surrender of it would not leave a vacancy for anybody else. When it was offered first I refused it (though my income was less than £200 a year). The second time it was offered it was explained to me that it implied no political bargain. I said 'Am I free to join an Irish insurrection?' The answer was 'Yes, perfectly.' I consider that I have earned that pension by services done to the people, not to government, and I accept it from the people. It has helped to set me free from the one thing I have always dreaded, that some day I might have to think of the prejudices or convictions of others before I wrote my own.

I am alarmed at the growing moral cowardice of the world, as the old security disappears—people run in packs that they may get courage from one another and even sit at home and shiver. You and I, my dear, were as it were put naked into the midst of armed men and women and we have both found arms and kept our independence. Dr McCartan° (Irish revolutionary agent to America during the Irish-English war, travelling to and fro as a sailor before the mast) invited members of the Executive Council and other notables to dinner here the other day, and spoke in his speech of 'the attack on Mr Yeats which has lasted for fifty years.' For twenty years I never even sent my books for review in to the Irish newspapers, an ignorant form of Catholicism is my enemy. At this moment as a reflection from civil war in Spain this Catholicism is more inflamed than ever before—but that is another story. Forgive me, I cannot recall ever having written so much in self-defence.

Yours affectionately
W. B. Yeats

As a young man I used to repeat to myself Blake's lines°

> 'And he his seventy disciples sent
> Against religion and government'

I hate more than you do, for my hatred can have no expression in action. I am a forerunner of that horde that will some day come down the mountains.

To Dorothy Wellesley,° 21 December [1936]

Riversdale

My dear Dorothy:

My wife has heard from the maker of the bust. She is in New York (expropriated from Majorca) and asks leave to exhibit it there in February. We have asked her after that to send it to London. We should do that in any case, as it will need negociation with the Irish Government to escape a heavy duty. It can be sent to you for inspection. But all that can wait.

Gogarty° once described the wit and phantasy of a friend of his called Tancred (who was, he declared, a descendant of the Crusader of that name). I knew him once, he had just been received into the Catholic Church. The ceremony over, some priest asked what had led him to the truth, and Tancred said 'I was in the Brompton Oratory and I saw on a tablet 'Pray for the soul of Elinor de Vaux,' and I thought the name so beautiful that I wanted to gain the privilege of praying for her.'

Turner writes to me 'They will some day be grateful for your discovery of Lady Dorothy.' A very strange man would have liked to do so ten years ago. Did you see in the papers about two years ago that a writer wrote a book which he meant 'as a serious work of art,' but which was alleged to contain obscene passages. He sent it to a publisher—the publisher reported him to the police, and he got six months. He had no talent but his case made some stir, and there was much indignation against the publisher. That man, I have just heard, had a cult of royalty—and had selected you—whom he imagined probably as somewhere near the throne—for boundless admiration. I cannot remember his name.

I thought the ex-King's broadcast moving, restrained and dignified, and from what I hear, the Archbishop's was the reverse.

My Anthology continues to sell, and the critics get more and more angry. When I excluded Wilfred Owen,° whom I consider unworthy of the poets' corner of a country newspaper, I did not know I was excluding a revered sandwich-board man of the revolution, and that somebody has put his worst and most famous poem in a glass-case in the British Museum—however, if I had known it, I would have excluded him just the same. He is all blood, dirt and sucked sugar-stick (look at the selection in *Faber's Anthology*—he calls poets 'bards,' a girl a 'maid,' and talks about 'Titanic wars'). There is every excuse for him, but none for those who like him.

I had a black fortnight, the result of nervous strain writing the Casement poem° you have seen, and another that you have not—beating the paste-board men—and some other odds and ends. I got sleepy and tired, and spent my day in bed and thought of my soul. Then I noticed that every time I thought of my soul I used some second-hand phrase, and knew by that that I was thinking of my soul from ambition and vanity. I said to myself 'Your job is to avoid deep places and to die blaspheming,' and I got well at once, went to the theatre at night, and by day took the bus to Dublin.

The B.B.C. have asked me to rehearse one of the programmes I suggest early in March. Will I find you then?

What makes your work so good is the masculine element allied to much feminine charm—your lines have the magnificent swing of your boyish body. I wish I could be a girl of nineteen for certain hours that I might feel it even more acutely. But, O my dear, do force yourself to write, it should become as natural to you as the movement of your limbs. When I cannot do anything else I take up some old fragment and try to add to it and perfect it—there are always so many fragments—I have just turned out a thing of joy, just such a fragment. Once more I am starting on another.

Yours with all affection,
W. B. Yeats

Have you noticed that the Greek androgynous statue is always the woman in man, never the man in woman? It was made for men who loved men first.

To Ethel Mannin, 9 October [?1938]

Riversdale

My dear Ethel,

I have read your novel° with very deep interest. All reading is slow with me because my eyes tire. I read a few pages and then sit idle for many minutes. I vexed George Moore by taking six weeks over his *Esther Waters,*° a book I greatly admired. When I had finished your book I re-read an essay on 'the idea of death' in the poetry of Rilke° and compared your thought with Rilke's and with the same thought as it is in what I call my 'private philosophy' (The *Vision* is my 'public philosophy'). My 'private philosophy' is the material dealing with individual mind which came to me with that on which the mainly historical *Vision* is based. I have not published it because I only half understand it. Your admirable and vivid book is the first book in England on the subject and is a very great stimulant to understanding. According to Rilke a man's death is born with him and if his life is successful and he escapes mere 'mass death' his nature is completed by his final union with it. Rilke gives Hamlet's death as an example. In my own philosophy the sensuous image is changed from time to time at predestined moments called *Initiationary Moments* (your hero takes ship for Bordeaux, he goes to the Fair, he goes to Russia and so on). One sensuous image leads to another because they are never analysed. At *The Critical Moment* they are dissolved by analysis and we enter by free will pure unified experience. When all the sensuous images are dissolved we meet true death. Franz will follow the idea of liberty through a series of *initiationary* movements—(1) Spain, and then somewhere else, but will never I think analyse the meaning of 'liberty' nor the particular sensuous image that seems to express it, and so will never meet true death. This idea of death suggests to me Blake's design (among those he did for Blair's *Grave*° I think) of the soul and body embracing. All men with subjective natures move towards a possible ecstasy, all with objective natures towards a possible wisdom. A German philosopher has said that men in Italian portraits seem to wait an accidental death from the blow of a dagger, whereas the men painted by Rembrandt have death already in their faces. Painters of the Zen school of Japanese Buddhism have the idea of the concordance of achievement and death, and connect both with what they call 'poverty.' To explain poverty they point to those paintings where they have suggested peace and loneliness by some single object or by a few strokes of the brush.

Is all this too abstract for your dear concrete soul?

Yours affectionately
W. B. Yeats

Yeats's Notes to his Poems

THE SPELLING OF GAELIC NAMES

In this edition of my poems I have adopted Lady Gregory's spelling of Gaelic names, with, I think, two exceptions. The 'd' of 'Edain' ran too well in my verse for me to adopt her perhaps more correct 'Etain,' and for some reason unknown to me I have always preferred 'Aengus' to her 'Angus.' In her *Gods and Fighting Men* and *Cuchulain of Muirthemne* she went as close to the Gaelic spelling as she could without making the names unpronounceable to the average reader.—1933

CROSSWAYS. THE ROSE

Many of the poems in *Crossways*, certainly those upon Indian subjects or upon shepherds and fauns, must have been written before I was twenty, for from the moment when I began *The Wanderings of Oisin*, which I did at that age, I believe, my subject-matter became Irish. Every time I have reprinted them I have considered the leaving out of most, and then remembered an old school friend who has some of them by heart, for no better reason, as I think, than that they remind him of his own youth. The little Indian dramatic scene was meant to be the first scene of a play about a man loved by two women, who had the one soul between them, the one woman waking when the other slept, and knowing but daylight as the other only night. It came into my head when I saw a man at Rosses Point carrying two salmon. 'One man with two souls,' I said, and added, 'O no, two people with one soul.' I am now once more in *A Vision* busy with that thought, the antitheses of day and of night and of moon and of sun. *The Rose* was part of my second book, *The Countess Cathleen and Various Legends and Lyrics*, 1892, and I notice upon reading these poems for the first time for several years that the quality symbolized as The Rose differs from the Intellectual Beauty of Shelley and of Spenser in that I have imagined it as suffering with man and not as something pursued and seen from afar. It must have been a thought of my generation, for I remember the mystical painter Horton, whose work had little of his personal charm and real strangeness, writing me these words, 'I met your beloved in Russell Square, and she was weeping,' by which he meant that he had seen a vision of my neglected soul.—1925

THE HOSTING OF THE SIDHE

The gods of ancient Ireland, the Tuatha de Danaan, or the Tribes of the goddess Danu, or the Sidhe, from Aes Sidhe, or Sluagh Sidhe, the people of the Faery Hills, as these words are usually explained, still ride the country as of old. Sidhe is also Gaelic for wind, and certainly the Sidhe have much to do with the wind. They journey in whirling wind, the winds that were called the dance of the daughters of Herodias in the Middle Ages, Herodias doubtless taking the place of some old goddess. When old country people see the leaves whirling on the road they bless themselves, because they believe the Sidhe to be passing by. Knocknarea is in Sligo, and the country people say that Maeve, still a great queen of the western Sidhe, is buried in the cairn of stones upon it. I have written of Clooth-na-Bare in *The Celtic Twilight*. She 'went all over the world, seeking a lake deep enough to drown her faery life, of which she had grown weary, leaping from hill to hill, and setting up a cairn of stones wherever her feet lighted, until, at last, she found the deepest water in the world in little Lough Ia, on the top of the bird mountain, in Sligo.' I forget, now, where I heard this story, but it may have been from a priest at Collooney. Clooth-na-Bare is evidently a corruption of Cailleac Bare, the old woman of Bare, who, under the names Bare, and Berah, and Beri, and Verah, and Dera, and Dhira, appears in the legends of many places.—1899–1906.

THE HOST OF THE AIR

This poem is founded on an old Gaelic ballad that was sung and translated for me by a woman at Ballisodare in County Sligo; but in the ballad the husband found the keeners keening his wife when he got to his house.—1899.

HE MOURNS FOR THE CHANGE THAT HAS COME UPON HIM AND HIS BELOVED AND LONGS FOR THE END OF THE WORLD

My deer and hound are properly related to the deer and hound that flicker in and out of the various tellings of the Arthurian legends, leading different knights upon adventures, and to the hounds and to the hornless deer at the beginning of, I think, all tellings of Oisin's journey to the country of the young. The hound is certainly related to the Hounds of Annwoyn or of Hades, who are white, and have red ears, and were heard, and are, perhaps, still heard by Welsh peasants, following some flying thing in the night winds; and is probably related to the hounds that Irish country people believe will awake and seize the souls of the dead if you lament them too loudly or too soon. An old woman told a friend and myself that she saw what she thought were white birds, flying over an enchanted place, but found, when she got near, that they had dogs' heads; and I do not doubt that my hound and these dog-headed birds are of the same family. I got my hound and deer out of a last-century Gaelic poem about Oisin's journey to the country of the young. After the hunting of the hornless deer, that leads him to the seashore, and while he is riding over the sea with Niamh, he sees amid the waters—I have not the Gaelic poem by me, and describe it from memory—a young man following a girl who has a golden apple, and afterwards a hound with one red ear following a deer with no horns. This hound and this deer seem plain images of the desire of the man 'which is for the woman,' and 'the desire of the woman which is for the desire of the man,' and of all desires that are as these. I have read them in this way in *The Wanderings of Oisin*, and have made my lover sigh because he has seen in their faces 'the immortal desire of Immortals.'

The man in my poem who has a hazel wand may have been Aengus, Master of Love; and I have made the boar without bristles come out of the West, because the place of sunset was in Ireland, as in other countries, a place of symbolic darkness and death.—1899.

THE CAP AND BELLS

I dreamed this story exactly as I have written it, and dreamed another long dream after it, trying to make out its meaning, and whether I was to write it in prose or verse. The first dream was more a vision than a dream, for it was beautiful and coherent, and gave me the sense of illumination and exaltation that one gets from visions, while the second dream was confused and meaningless. The poem has always meant a great deal to me, though, as is the way with symbolic poems, it has not always meant quite the same thing. Blake would have said, 'The authors are in eternity,' and I am quite sure they can only be questioned in dreams.—1899.

THE VALLEY OF THE BLACK PIG

All over Ireland there are prophecies of the coming rout of the enemies of Ireland, in a certain Valley of the Black Pig, and these prophecies are, no doubt, now, as they were in the Fenian days, a political force, I have heard of one man who would not give any money to the Land League, because the Battle could not be until the close of the century; but, as a rule, periods of trouble bring prophecies of its near coming. A few years before my time, an old man who lived at Lissadell, in Sligo, used to fall down in a fit and rave out descriptions of the Battle; and a man in Sligo has told me that it will be so great a battle that the horses shall go up to their fetlocks in blood, and that their girths, when it is over, will rot from their bellies for lack of a hand to unbuckle them. If one reads Rhys' *Celtic Heathendom* by the light of Frazer's *Golden Bough*, and puts together what one finds there about the boar that killed Diarmuid, and other old Celtic boars and sows, one sees that the battle is mythological, and that the Pig it is named from must be a type of cold and winter doing battle with the summer, or of death battling with life.—1899–1906.

THE SECRET ROSE

I find that I have unintentionally changed the old story of Conchubar's death. He did not see the Crucifixion in a vision but was told of it. He had been struck by a ball made out of the dried brains of an enemy and hurled out of a sling; and this ball had been left in his head, and his head had been mended, the *Book of Leinster* says, with thread of gold because his hair was like gold. Keeting, a writer of the time of Elizabeth, says: 'In that state did he remain seven years, until the Friday on which Christ was crucified, according to some historians; and when he saw the unusual changes of the creation and the eclipse of the sun and the moon at its full, he asked of Bucrach, a Leinster Druid, who was along with him, what was it that brought that unusual change upon the planets of Heaven and Earth. 'Jesus Christ, the Son of God,' said the Druid, 'who is now being crucified by the Jews.' 'That is a pity,' said Conchubar; 'were I in his presence I would kill those who were putting him to death.' And with that he brought out his sword, and rushed at a woody grove which was convenient to him, and began to cut and fell it; and what he said was, that if he were among the Jews, that was the usage he would give them, and from the excessiveness of his fury which seized upon him, the ball started out of his head, and some of the brain came after it, and in that way he died. The wood of Lanshraigh, in Feara Rois, is the name by which that shrubby wood is called.'

I have imagined Cuchulain meeting Fand 'walking among flaming dew,' because, I think, of something in Mr Standish O'Grady's books.

I have founded the man 'who drove the gods out of their liss,' or fort, upon something I have read about Caoilte after the battle of Gabhra, when almost all his companions were killed, driving the gods out of their liss, either at Osraighe, now Ossory, or at Eas Ruaidh, now Asseroe, a waterfall at Ballyshannon, where Ilbreac, one of the children of the goddess Danu, had a liss. But maybe I only read it in Mr Standish O'Grady, who has a fine imagination, for I find no such story in Lady Gregory's book.

I have founded 'the proud dreaming king' upon Fergus, the son of Roigh, but when I wrote my poem here, and in the song in my early book, 'Who will drive with Fergus now?' I only knew him in Mr Standish O'Grady, and my imagination dealt more freely with what I did know than I would approve of to-day.

I have founded 'him who sold tillage, and house, and goods,' upon something in 'The Red Pony,' a folk-tale in Mr Larminie's *West Irish Folk Tales*. A young man 'saw a light before him on the high-road. When he came as far, there was an open box on the road, and a light coming up out of it. He took up the box. There was a lock of hair in it. Presently he had to go to become the servant of a king for his living. There were eleven boys. When they were going out into the stable at ten o'clock, each of them took a light but he. He took no candle at all with him. Each of them went into his own stable. When he went into his stable he opened the box. He left it in a hole in the wall. The light was great. It was twice as much as in the other stables.' The king hears of it, and makes him show him the box. The king says, 'You must go and bring me the woman to whom the hair belongs.' In the end, the young man, and not the king, marries the woman.—1899–1906.

RESPONSIBILITIES, INTRODUCTORY RHYMES

'Free of the ten and four' is an error I cannot now correct, without more rewriting than I have a mind for. Some merchant in Villon, I forget the reference, was 'free of the ten and four.' Irish merchants exempted from certain duties by the Irish Parliament were, unless memory deceives me again—I cannot remember my authority—'free of the eight and six.'—1914.

POEMS BEGINNING WITH THAT 'TO A WEALTHY MAN'
AND ENDING WITH THAT 'TO A SHADE'

In the thirty years or so during which I have been reading Irish newspapers, three public controversies have stirred my imagination. The first was the Parnell controversy. There were reasons to justify a man's joining either party, but there were none to justify, on one side or on the other, lying accusations forgetful of past service, a frenzy of detraction. And another was the dispute over *The Playboy*. There may have been reasons for opposing as for supporting that violent, laughing thing, though I can see the one side only, but there cannot have been any for the lies, for the unscrupulous rhetoric spread against it in Ireland, and from Ireland to America. The third prepared for the Corporation's refusal of a building for Sir Hugh Lane's famous collection of pictures. . . .

[*Note.*—I leave out two long paragraphs which have been published in earlier editions of these poems. There is no need now to defend Sir Hugh Lane's pictures against Dublin newspapers. The trustees of the London National Gallery, through his leaving a codicil to his will unwitnessed, have claimed the pictures for London, and propose to build a wing to the Tate Gallery to contain them. Some that were hostile are now contrite, and doing what they can, or letting others do unhindered what they can, to persuade Parliament to such action as may restore the collection to Ireland.—Jan. 1917.]

These controversies, political, literary, and artistic, have showed that neither religion nor politics can of itself create minds with enough receptivity to become wise, or just and generous enough to make a nation. Other cities have been as stupid—Samuel Butler laughs at shocked Montreal for hiding the Discobolus in a lumber-room—but Dublin is the capital of a nation, and an ancient race has nowhere else to look for an education. Goethe in *Wilhelm Meister* describes a saintly and naturally gracious woman, who, getting into a quarrel over some trumpery detail of religious observance, grows—she and all her little religious community—angry and vindictive. In Ireland I am constantly reminded of that fable of the futility of all discipline that is not of the whole being. Religious Ireland—and the pious Protestants of my childhood were signal examples—thinks of divine things as a round of duties separated from life and not as an element that may be discovered in all circumstance and emotion, while political Ireland sees the good citizen but as a man who holds to certain opinions and not as a man of good will. Against all this we have but a few educated men and the remnants of an old traditional culture among the poor. Both were stronger forty years ago, before the rise of our new middle class which made its first public display during the nine years of the Parnellite split, showing how base at moments of excitement are minds without culture.—1914.

Lady Gregory in her Life of Sir Hugh Lane assumes that the poem which begins 'Now all the truth is out', was addressed to him. It was not; it was addressed to herself.—1922.

THE DOLLS

The fable for this poem came into my head while I was giving some lectures in Dublin. I had noticed once again how all thought among us is frozen into 'something other than human life.' After I had made the poem, I looked up one day into the blue of the sky, and suddenly imagined, as if lost in the blue of the sky, stiff figures in procession. I remembered that they were the habitual image suggested by blue sky, and looking for a second fable called them 'The Magi', complementary forms of those enraged dolls.—1914.

THE PHASES OF THE MOON

THE DOUBLE VISION OF MICHAEL ROBARTES

MICHAEL ROBARTES AND THE DANCER

Years ago I wrote three stories in which occur the names of Michael Robartes and Owen Aherne. I now consider that I used the actual names of two friends, and that one of these friends, Michael Robartes, has but lately returned from Mesopotamia, where he has partly found and partly thought out much philosophy. I consider that Aherne and Robartes, men to whose namesakes I had attributed a turbulent life or death, have quarrelled with me. They take their place in a phantasmagoria in which I endeavour to explain my philosophy of life and death. To some extent I wrote these poems as a text for exposition.—1922.

SAILING TO BYZANTIUM

(Stanza IV)

I have read somewhere that in the Emperor's palace at Byzantium was a tree made of gold and silver, and artificial birds that sang.

THE TOWER

The persons mentioned are associated by legend, story and tradition with the neighbourhood of Thoor Ballylee or Ballylee Castle, where the poem was written. Mrs French lived at Peterswell in the eighteenth century and was related to Sir Jonah Barrington, who described the incident of the ears and the trouble that came of it. The peasant beauty and the blind poet are Mary Hynes and Raftery, and the incident of the man drowned in Cloone Bog is recorded in my *Celtic Twilight*. Hanrahan's pursuit of the phantom hare and hounds is from my *Stories of Red Hanrahan*. The ghosts have been seen at their game of dice in what is now my bedroom, and the old bankrupt man lived about a hundred years ago. According to one legend he could only leave the Castle upon a Sunday because of his creditors, and according to another he hid in the secret passage.

In the passage about the Swan in Part III I have unconsciously echoed one of the loveliest lyrics of our time—Mr Sturge Moore's 'Dying Swan.' I often recited it during an American lecturing tour, which explains the theft.

THE DYING SWAN

O silver-throated Swan
Struck, struck! A golden dart
Clean through thy breast has gone
Home to thy heart.
Thrill, thrill, O silver throat!
O silver trumpet, pour
Love for defiance back
On him who smote!
And brim, brim o'er
With love; and ruby-dye thy track
Down thy last living reach
Of river, sail the golden light—
Enter the sun's heart—even teach,
O wondrous-gifted Pain, teach thou
The god to love, let him learn how.

When I wrote the lines about Plato and Plotinus I forgot that it is some-
thing in our own eyes that makes us see them as all transcendence. Has
not Plotinus written: 'Let every soul recall, then, at the outset the truth
that soul is the author of all living things, that it has breathed the life into
them all, whatever is nourished by earth and sea, all the creatures of the
air, the divine stars in the sky; it is the maker of the sun; itself formed and
ordered this vast heaven and conducts all that rhythmic motion—and it
is a principle distinct from all these to which it gives law and movement
and life, and it must of necessity be more honourable than they, for they
gather or dissolve as soul brings them life or abandons them, but soul,
since it never can abandon itself, is of eternal being'?—1928.

MEDITATIONS IN TIME OF CIVIL WAR

These poems were written at Thoor Ballylee in 1922, during the civil
war. Before they were finished the Republicans blew up our 'ancient
bridge' one midnight. They forbade us to leave the house, but were
otherwise polite, even saying at last 'Good-night, thank you,' as though
we had given them the bridge.

The sixth poem is called 'The Stare's Nest by My Window.' In the
west of Ireland we call a starling a stare, and during the civil war one built
in a hole in the masonry by my bedroom window.

In the second stanza of the seventh poem occur the words,
'Vengeance on the murderers of Jacques Molay.' A cry for vengeance
because of the murder of the Grand Master of the Templars seems to me
fit symbol for those who labour from hatred, and so for sterility in vari-

ous kinds. It is said to have been incorporated in the ritual of certain Masonic societies of the eighteenth century, and to have fed class-hatred.

I suppose that I must have put hawks into the fourth stanza because I have a ring with a hawk and a butterfly upon it, to symbolize the straight road of logic, and so of mechanism, and the crooked road of intuition: 'For wisdom is a butterfly and not a gloomy bird of prey.'—1928.

NINETEEN HUNDRED AND NINETEEN
(Sixth poem)

The country people see at times certain apparitions whom they name now 'fallen angels,' now 'ancient inhabitants of the country,' and describe as riding at whiles 'with flowers upon the heads of the horses.' I have assumed in the sixth poem that these horsemen, now that the times worsen, give way to worse. My last symbol, Robert Artisson, was an evil spirit much run after in Kilkenny at the start of the fourteenth century. Are not those who travel in the whirling dust also in the Platonic Year?

AMONG SCHOOL CHILDREN
(Stanza V)

I have taken the 'honey of generation' from Porphyry's essay on 'The Cave of the Nymphs,' but find no warrant in Porphyry for considering it the 'drug' that destroys the 'recollection' of pre-natal freedom. He blamed a cup of oblivion given in the zodiacal sign of Cancer.

THE WINDING STAIR AND OTHER POEMS

'I am of Ireland' is developed from three or four lines of an Irish fourteenth-century dance song somebody repeated to me a few years ago. 'The sun in a golden cup' in the poem that precedes it, though not 'The moon in a silver bag,' is a quotation from somewhere in Mr Ezra Pound's 'Cantos.' In this book and elsewhere, I have used towers, and one tower in particular, as symbols and have compared their winding stairs to the philosophical gyres, but it is hardly necessary to interpret what comes from the main track of thought and expression. Shelley uses towers constantly as symbols, and there are gyres in Swedenborg, and in Thomas Aquinas and certain classical authors. Part of the symbolism of 'Blood and the Moon' was suggested by the fact that Thoor Ballylee has a waste room at the top and that butterflies come in through the loop-holes and die against the window-panes. The 'learned astrologer' in 'Chosen' was Macrobius, and the particular passage was found for me by Dr Sturm, that too little known poet and mystic. It is from Macrobius's comment upon 'Scipio's Dream' (Lib. I. Cap. XII. Sec. 5): '... when the sun is in Aquarius, we sacrifice to the Shades, for it is in the sign inimical to human life; and from thence, the meeting-place of Zodiac and Milky Way, the descending soul by its defluction is drawn out of the spherical, the sole divine form, into the cone.' In 'The Mother of God' the words 'A fallen flare through the hollow of an ear' are, I am told, obscure. I had in my memory Byzantine mosaic pictures of the Annunciation, which show a line drawn from a star to the ear of the Virgin. She received the Word through the ear, a star fell, and a star was born.

When *The Winding Stair* was published separately by Macmillan & Co. it was introduced by the following dedication:

Dear Dulac,

I saw my *Hawk's Well* played by students of our Schools of Dancing and of Acting a couple of years ago in a little theatre called 'The Peacock,' which shares a roof with the Abbey Theatre. Watching Cuchulain in his lovely mask and costume, that ragged old masked man who seems hundreds of years old, that Guardian of the Well, with your great golden wings and dancing to your music, I had one of those moments of excitement that are the dramatist's reward and decided there and then to dedicate to you my next book of verse.

'A Woman Young and Old' was written before the publication of *The Tower*, but left out for some reason I cannot recall. I think that I was roused to write 'Death' and 'Blood and the Moon' by the assassination of Kevin O'Higgins, the finest intellect in Irish public life, and, I think I may add, to some extent, my friend. 'A Dialogue of Self and Soul' was written in the spring of 1928 during a long illness, indeed finished the day before a Cannes doctor told me to stop writing. Then in the spring of 1929 life returned as an impression of the uncontrollable energy and daring of the great creators; it seemed that but for journalism and criticism, all that evasion and explanation, the world would be torn in pieces. I wrote 'Mad as the Mist and Snow,' a mechanical little song, and after that almost all that group of poems called in memory of those exultant weeks 'Words for Music Perhaps.' Then ill again, I warmed myself back into life with 'Byzantium' and 'Veronica's Napkin,' looking for a theme that might befit my years. Since then I have added a few poems to 'Words for Music Perhaps,' but always keeping the mood and plan of the first poems.

1933

THE WANDERINGS OF OISIN

The poem is founded upon the Middle Irish dialogues of S. Patrick and Oisin and a certain Gaelic poem of the last century. The events it describes, like the events in most of the poems in this volume, are supposed to have taken place rather in the indefinite period, made up of many periods, described by the folk-tales, than in any particular century; it therefore, like the later Fenian stories themselves, mixes much that is mediaeval with much that is ancient. The Gaelic poems do not make Oisin go to more than one island, but a story in *Silva Gadelica* describes 'four paradises,' an island to the north, an island to the west, an island to the south, and Adam's paradise in the east.—1912.

NOTES

3 *Crossways*. This was never the name of a separate published volume. The title first appears in *Poems* (1895). The poems are a selection from *The Wanderings of Oisin and Other Poems* (1889) and *The Countess Kathleen and Various Legends and Lyrics* (1892). The word 'Crossways' refers to the various 'pathways' of the Tree of Life (a conception the Golden Dawn borrowed from the Jewish mystical writings in the cabbala) and also to Christ's cross, because the principle of Eternal Beauty has to suffer amid the contraries of Life.

Epigraph: '*The stars are threshed . . . husks.*' A misquotation of a line from William Blake's *Vala* (later called *The Four Zoas*). The line is given as 'And all the Nations were threshed out, and the stars threshed from their husks' in vol. iii of *The Works of William Blake*, ed. Edwin John Ellis and William Butler Yeats (London, 1893), *Four Zoas*, IX. 648.

The Song of the Happy Shepherd

l. 1. *Arcady*. Arcadia, a mountainous region of southern Greece, idealized in the pastoral tradition as a peaceful land inhabited by shepherds who have few cares.

l. 9. *Chronos*. Greek word for 'Time'. It became associated with Kronos, the name of one of the Titans, who was called Saturn by the Romans.

l. 12. *Rood*. The cross on which Christ was crucified.

4 l. 39. *Rewarding*. 'Rewording', found in some other editions, makes for a more interesting reading; but there is much support for 'Rewarding', and it seems to represent Yeats's final intentions.

7 *The Madness of King Goll*. In a note of 1887 Yeats explains that Goll 'or Gall' lived in the third century AD. He became deranged in the course of a battle. The version of the story Yeats knew had been influenced by the tale of *Suibhne Geilt* ('Mad Sweeney') which is known through the twelfth-century MS *Buile Shuibhne* ('The Frenzy of Sweeney'). This has been translated by Seamus Heaney as *Sweeney Astray* (1984).

l. 2. *Ith*. Possibly Magh Itha ('The Plain of Corn') in Co. Donegal, said to be named after Ith, an ancient invader of Ireland.   *Emain*. Emain Macha, capital of the Ulster of the heroic sagas.

l. 3. *Invar Amargin*. 'Amergin's Estuary': the mouth of the River Avoca in Co. Wicklow.

l. 9. *Ollave*. Member of the highest order of learned poets in ancient Ireland.

9 l. 62. *Orchil*. A demon sorceress.

9 l. 68. *ulalu*. Cry of mourning.

The Stolen Child

l. 2. *Sleuth Wood*. On the south of Lough Gill, south-east of Sligo, and more commonly known as Slish Wood.

10 l. 15. *Rosses*. Rosses Point, a seaside village on a small headland north-west of Sligo.

l. 29. *Glen-Car*. Glencar, a valley containing a lough, north-east of Sligo and not far from Drumcliff.

11 *Down by the Salley Gardens*. A 'salley' is a willow. This poem is influenced by a ballad Yeats heard sung in the village of Ballysodare, Co. Sligo.

The Ballad of Father O'Hart

l. 2. *penal days*. The Penal Laws were punitive and oppressive laws imposed upon Irish Catholics, in blatant contravention of the terms of the Treaty of Limerick (1691), from the late seventeenth to the early nineteenth century. They were the main cause of the descent of large sections of the Irish people into a condition of poverty unparalleled elsewhere in Europe.

l. 3. *shoneen*. Someone who affected English ways, from Irish *Seon*, which is the convention for English 'John': *seoinín* (with diminutive ending), pronounced *shoneen*, therefore means 'a little English John' or 'a little John Bull'. (The Irish for John is *Seán*, pronounced *Shawn*.)

l. 6. *Sleiveens*. Sly people.

12 ll. 22–3. *keeners . . . keening*. 'Keening' was ritual lamentation at a funeral. It involved wailing, crying, and the recitation of verses. One might hire professional keeners.

l. 27. *Coloony*. Collooney, a village in Co. Sligo.

l. 30. *Knocknarea*. A mountain in Co. Sligo.

l. 31. *Knocknashee*. A hill in Co. Sligo.

l. 35. *Tiraragh*. A barony in Co. Sligo.

l. 36. *Ballinafad*. A village in Co. Sligo.

l. 37. *Inishmurray*. An island off the coast of Co. Sligo.

The Rose. An important symbol in Yeats's work. In Irish poetry *Róisín* was a name sometimes given to a girl who personified Ireland, as in the traditional poem 'Mo Róisín Dubh' ('My Little Dark Rose') of which 'My Dark Rosaleen', by the Irish poet James Clarence Mangan (1803–49), is a free translation. The Rose was also central to the symbolism of the Hermetic Order of the Golden Dawn, a secret magical and occult society of which Yeats became an initiate in 1890. The Rosicrucian doctrines expounded in the Order centred on a mystic marriage of Rose and Cross. The Cross, recalled in the *Crossways* group of poems, represented the world of time and of contraries; the Rose, the flowering of that world through the intervention of the infinite. The Rose had feminine connotations, the Cross masculine. 'Intellectual Beauty' was another definition, borrowed from Shelley, which Yeats offered of the Rose. But it also symbolized the woman Yeats loved, Maud Gonne (1866–1953), who, though the daughter of a British army colonel, became active in the Irish nationalist movement.

To The Rose upon the Rood of Time

l. 3. *Cuchulain*. The central figure of the heroic cycle of tales centred on legendary events in Iron-Age Ulster, and her capital, Emain Macha. The best-known of these tales is the epic *Táin Bó Cuailgne* ('The Cattle Raid of Cooley'), usually known simply as 'the *Táin*'. Cuchulain was the champion warrior of the king of Ulster, Conchubar.

ll. 4–5. *Druid . . . Fergus*. See notes to 'Fergus and the Druid', below.

13 *Fergus and the Druid*. Fergus mac Roich was king of Ulster, but, persuaded by his wife Ness, he abdicated in favour of his stepson and her son, Conchubar. But Yeats is drawing here, and in 'Who Goes with Fergus?' (p. 22), on a version by the Irish poet Sir Samuel Ferguson (1810–86), 'The Abdication of Fergus Mac Roy'. In this Fergus gives up the throne 'that he might live at peace hunting in the woods'. Druids were, in brief, the priesthood of ancient Celtic societies (thus of Britain and Gaul, as well as Ireland). More precisely, they seem to have comprised the functions of magician, shaman, and professor of tribal lore. There are indications that ancient Celtic religion had pantheistic features and that these are related to the ability of certain magical beings, including Druids, to enter into different forms of life. Yeats's knowledge of these ideas is particularly evident in Fergus's first and last speeches.

l. 8. *Red Branch*. Emblem of the kings of Ulster and thus of their warriors.

14 *Cuchulain's Fight with the Sea*. For Cuchulain, see note to 'To the Rose upon the Rood of Time', above.

l. 2. *Emer*. Cuchulain's wife.   *raddling*. To dye red.   *dun*. Celtic word for fortress.

16 l. 33. *Red Branch*. See note to 'Fergus and the Druid', l. 8.

l. 45. *Conchubar*. See note to 'Fergus and the Druid', above.

The Rose of the World

17 l. 4. *Troy*. In Greek legend the Greeks sacked Troy after a lengthy siege because the Trojan prince, Paris, had abducted a Greek queen, Helen.

l. 5. *Usna*. (More correctly, Usnach.) Usnach had three sons, one of whom, Naoise (or Naisi), fell in love with Deirdre. Unfortunately, Conchubar wanted her for his wife. Deirdre and the sons of Usnach fled to Scotland. Tempted back to Ireland, Naoise and his brothers were killed by Conchubar's men. Deirdre committed suicide. For fuller information see notes to Yeats's play *Deirdre*, pp. 221–45.

The Rose of Peace

18 l. 1. *Michael*. Archangel and leader of the armies of heaven which defeated Satan.

The Rose of Battle. The original title was 'They went forth to the Battle but they always fell.' This is a slight misquotation of a phrase from one of the 'Ossian' poems of James Macpherson (1736–96), whose works did so much to encourage fascination with the Celtic in the Romantic period and later. Matthew Arnold (1822–88) quotes the phrase in his lectures *On Celtic Literature* to illustrate a truth about the temperament of the Celt.

19 *The Lake Isle of Innisfree*. Innishfree (*Inis Fraoigh*, 'Island of Heather') near the southern shore of Lough Gill, Co. Sligo.

The Sorrow of Love

20 l. 7. *Odysseus*. The hero of Homer's *Odyssey*. One of the Greeks who laid siege to Troy. After the city's fall he was doomed to wander the seas for ten years before being able to return to his home, the Greek island of Ithaca.

l. 8. *Priam*. King of Troy, killed during its fall.

21 *When You are Old*. A free imitation—not a translation—of 'Quand vous serez bien vieille', one of the *Sonnets pour Hélène* by Pierre de Ronsard (1524–85).

22 *Who Goes with Fergus?* For Fergus, see note to p. 13, 'Fergus and the Druid'.

The Man who Dreamed of Faeryland

l. 1. *Drumahair*. Dromahair, a village south-east of Lough Gill, in Co. Leitrim.

23 l. 13. *Lissadell*. Area near the sea on the northern shore of Drumcliff Bay, Co. Sligo. Lissadell House was the home of the Gore-Booth family, from which came Yeats's friends Constance (1868–1927) and Eva (1870–1926).

l. 25. *Scanavin*. In Co. Sligo.

l. 37. *Lugnagall*. Townland at the entrance to the valley of Glencar, Co. Sligo.

To Ireland in the Coming Times

25 l. 4. *rann*. Irish: a stanza

l. 18. *Davis, Mangan, Ferguson*. Thomas Davis (1814–45), Irish political leader and writer; James Clarence Mangan (1803–49), Irish poet; Sir Samuel Ferguson (1810–86), Irish poet.

The Wind among the Reeds

26 *The Hosting of the Sidhe*. 'Sidhe' (pronounced *Shee*, and sometimes Anglicized thus) is often translated 'fairies'; and that is acceptable, especially given that Yeats himself will use such locutions as 'Faery' and 'Faeryland' (e.g. in 'The Man who Dreamed of Faeryland', p. 22) when it is clear that

he is talking of the home of the Sidhe. Nevertheless, it must be remembered that they are really the ancient Irish gods and are usually (when visible) of at least human size.

l. 1. *Knocknarea.* Mountain in Co. Sligo. A cairn at its summit is thought to be the burial place of Queen Maeve (Medhbh), who in the *Táin* is queen of Connacht and adversary of the Ulstermen (see note to p. 12, 'To the Rose upon the Rood of Time'). Maeve is also associated with the Sidhe.

l. 2. *Clooth-na-Bare.* Region of Lough Ia in Co. Sligo. In his own note (see p. 480) Yeats explains that 'Clooth-na-Bare is evidently a corruption of Cailleac Bare, the old woman of Bare, who . . . appears in the legends of many places.' She is one of the Sidhe, but from the same note we learn that she had tired of their immortality.

l. 3. *Caoilte* (Pron. 'keeltya'.) One of the companions of Finn (modern Irish, Fionn) mac Cumhail (Finn McCool), the hero of the Fenian cycle of romances, and leader of the warrior band, the Fenians, or *Fianna* in Irish.

l. 4. *Niamh.* The lady of the Sidhe who enticed Finn mac Cumhail's son Oisin (or Ossian) away to Tír na nÓg ('The Land of the Young', that is, of those who cannot die, the immortal Sidhe: thus, their abode, 'Faery' or 'Faeryland'. It is located beyond the western sea.) See notes to *The Wanderings of Oisin*, pp. 520–2 below.

The Host of the Air

28 l. 4. *Hart Lake.* In Co. Sligo.

29 *The Song of Wandering Aengus.* Aengus, one of the Sidhe, was described by Yeats in 1895 as 'the god of youth, beauty, and poetry' (*The Variorum Edition of the Poems of W. B. Yeats*, ed. Peter Allt and Russel K. Alspach (New York, 1957; rev. 1966), 794.

l. 1. *hazel.* In Celtic tradition, the hazel tree was regarded as beneficently magical.

32 *The Valley of the Black Pig.* See Yeats's note (p. 479), in which he refers this poem to a widespread Irish legend to the effect that the defeat of Ireland's enemies will occur in this valley, and then goes on to make it clear that he regards the legend as having ancient roots in vegetative myths about the battle between winter and summer.

The Secret Rose

33 l. 3. *Holy Sepulchre.* The tomb of Christ.

l. 9. *Magi.* Persian wise men and magicians. Traditionally the three wise men from the East who visited the infant Jesus are supposed to have been Magi.

l. 10. *Rood.* The cross of Christ.

ll. 12–13. *and him | Who met Fand* . . . Cuchulain fell in love with Fand, a woman of the Sidhe and wife of the god of the sea, Manannán mac Lir. As a result his love for his wife Emer was temporarily overshadowed, according to the ancient tale 'The Wasting Sickness of Cuchulain and The Only Jealousy of Emer'. Yeats later devised his own more tragic version of this story, in which Emer loses Cuchulain's love for ever: see his play *The Only Jealousy of Emer* (pp. 270–81) and the notes to it below.

33 l. 16. *him who drove*. Caoilte, companion of Finn mac Cumhail.   *liss*. (Irish *lios*.) A small mound, often a barrow, popularly believed to be inhabited by the Sidhe, the ancient gods.

l. 19. *proud dreaming king*. Fergus: see note to p. 13, 'Fergus and the Druid'.

l. 22. *him who sold tillage*. Based on a character in a story called 'The Red Pony' from William Larminie's *West Irish Folk Tales*.

The Poet Pleads with the Elemental Powers

34 l. 3. *Seven Lights*. Constellation of the Great Bear.

l. 4. *Polar Dragon*. Constellation of Draco, or the Dragon, which seems half to surround the Pole Star.

35 *He Thinks of his Past Greatness when a Part of the Constellations of Heaven*. Compare Blake in his address to the Jews prefatory to ch. 2 of his long poem, *Jerusalem*: 'You have a tradition, that Man anciently contain'd in his mighty limbs all things in Heaven & Earth: this you received from the Druids. "But now the Starry Heavens are fled from the mighty limbs of Albion." ' The former title of Yeats's poem was 'Mongan Thinks of his Past Greatness'. Mongan was, as Yeats pointed out in his original note when the poem was published in the *Dome* (Oct. 1898), 'a famous wizard and king who remembers his past lives'. But he was best known for having been no other than Finn mac Cumhail, the hero of the Fenian cycle of romance tales. There may be a suggestion, then, that the heroic spirit of old Ireland, while it does persist, has grown weary, or at least that the poet has wearied of it.

l. 1. *Country of the Young*. In Irish, Tír na nÓg. See note to p. 26, l. 4.

l. 3. *hazel-tree*. A magical tree in Celtic tradition.

l. 4. *The Pilot Star and the Crooked Plough*. The Pole Star and the Plough (or Great Bear), the one at the zenith of the sky, the other near it. Thus, the Tree of Life reaches to heaven.

The Fiddler of Dooney. Dooney Rock, on the shores of Lough Gill.

ll. 3–4. *Kilvarnet . . . Mocharabuiee*. Refer to places in Co. Sligo.

In the Seven Woods

37 *Adam's Curse*. Adam was expelled from the Garden of Eden because of disobedience to God (Gen. 3: 14–24). The curse is that of having to work once outside the garden (Gen. 3: 17–19).

38 *Red Hanrahan's Song about Ireland* . Red Hanrahan is a character invented by Yeats, though partly modelled on a notable Gaelic poet, Eoghan Rua Ó Súilleabháin (Owen O'Sullivan the Red, 1748–84). Red Hanrahan is the

hero of a number of short stories by Yeats. Owen O'Sullivan appears in the original titles of a few poems from *The Wind among the Reeds*. He was himself the author of a fine poem, 'Ag Taisdiol na Bláirne' ('Strolling through Blarney') in which, as in this, Ireland is personified as a beautiful woman.

l. 1. *Cummen Strand*. Cummeen Strand, west of Sligo, not far from Knocknarea.

l. 5. *Cathleen, the daughter of Houlihan*. Cathleen ni Houlihan. Traditional female personification of Ireland also used by Yeats in his play *Cathleen ni Houlihan* (1902).

l. 6–7. *Knocknarea . . . Maeve*. See notes to p. 26, 'The Hosting of the Sidhe'.

39 l. 11. *Clooth-na-Bare*. As for previous note.

l. 15. *Holy Rood*. The cross of Christ.

The Happy Townland

40 ll. 41, 45. *Michael . . . Gabriel*. Archangels.

The Green Helmet and Other Poems

41 *A Woman Homer Sung*. The woman is Helen of Troy, whose abduction by the Trojan prince, Paris, caused the Greeks to lay siege to Troy, eventually sacking and burning it. This siege provides the subject-matter for Homer's epic, *The Iliad*.

42 *No Second Troy*. See note to 'A Woman Homer Sung', above.

The Fascination of What's Difficult

43 l. 4. *colt*. Pegasus, a Greek mythological winged horse associated with artistic inspiration. Dwelt on Mount Olympus (see note to l. 6).

l. 6. *Olympus*. Highest mountain in Greece. In Greek mythology its summit is the home of the gods. Pegasus (see note to l. 4) dwelt there, and carried the thunderbolts of Zeus, king of the gods.

On Hearing that the Students of our New University . . . University College, Dublin. Founded as the Catholic University of Ireland in 1851, it became University College, Dublin, in 1881 and a constituent college of the new National University of Ireland in 1908. This is the 'New University' to which Yeats refers.

Upon a House Shaken by the Land Agitation

44 l. 1. *this house*. Coole Park, Co. Galway, the home of his friend and patron, Lady Augusta Gregory (1852–1932); she helped to found the Irish Literary Theatre and the Abbey Theatre, Dublin, and herself wrote a number of plays as well as translating some of the Irish sagas. Yeats had just learned that, as a result of the agitation to which he refers, the rents of some of her tenants had been reduced by the courts.

At the Abbey Theatre. The Abbey Theatre was founded in Dublin in 1904.

(*Imitated from Ronsard*). A free translation of Pierre de Ronsard's sonnet, 'Tyard, on me blasmoit, à mon commencement' ('Tyard, they used to blame me when I started out').

44 l. 1. *Craoibhin Aoibhin*. (Irish, 'The Little Pleasant Branch', pron. 'kreevin eevin'). The pen-name of Yeats's friend, Douglas Hyde (1860–1949), folk-lorist, translator, co-founder of the Gaelic League, Professor of Modern Irish at University College, Dublin, and, though of Protestant stock, first President of Eire on the abolition of the Irish Free State in 1937. (Note that the Irish Republic was not established until 1949.)

45 l. 11. *Proteus*. In Greek mythology, a minor sea-god adept at changing his shape.

Responsibilities

46 Epigraph: '*In dreams begins responsibility*'. The 'Old Play' Yeats claims as the source has not yet been identified. Perhaps he wrote the line himself.

Epigraph: '*How am I fallen from myself, for a long time now | I have not seen the Prince of Chang in my dreams.*' | KHOUNG-FOU-TSEU. Khoung-fou-tseu is Confucius (*c*.551–*c*.479 BC), and the quotation is from his *Analects* (collected literary fragments), Book VII, ch. 5. The Prince of Chang is Châu-kung (d. 1105 BC), Chinese author and statesman.

[*Introductory Rhymes*]

l. 3. *Old Dublin merchant*. Benjamin Yeats (1750–95), Yeats's great-great-grandfather, a wholesale linen merchant.   '*free of the ten and four*'. Exempt from certain customs' duties of 10 per cent and 4 per cent. But Yeats has got the figures wrong, as he himself discovered: see his own note at p. 479.

l. 5. *Old country scholar*. John Yeats (1774–1846), Yeats's great-grandfather, Rector of Drumcliff in Co. Sligo.   *Robert Emmet*. (1778–1803), leader of a small uprising in Dublin in 1803. It failed and he was hanged.

l. 10. *A Butler or an Armstrong*. Benjamin Yeats married Mary Butler (1751–1834), a member of the great Ormonde family which had been in Ireland since the twelfth century. They converted to Protestantism. Grace Armstrong (1774–1864) was Yeats's great-grandmother.

ll. 11–12. *waters of the Boyne | James and his Irish when the Dutchman crossed*. In 1690, at the Battle of the Boyne (a river north of Dublin), the Catholic king James II (1633–1701), a Stuart, was defeated by the Dutch Protestant duke, William of Orange, who was subsequently crowned William III (1650–1702).

l. 13. *Old merchant skipper*. William Middleton (*c*.1770–1832), Yeats's maternal great-grandfather.

l. 15. *silent and fierce old man*. William Pollexfen (1811–92), Yeats's maternal grandfather, also a merchant.

47 *The Grey Rock*. Near Killaloe in Co. Clare. According to Irish folklore, it is the home of Aoibheall (pron. 'eevul'), a queen among the Sidhe, or fairies.

She is supposed to have offered Dubhlaing O'Hartagan 200 years with her if he refused to join his friend, Murchadh, son of King Brian Boru, in the Battle of Clontarf (1014). In this battle, the Irish forces of King Brian won a decisive victory. O'Hartagan refused the offer, and died in the battle. Yeats changes 'Aoibheall' to 'Aoife', which is the name of a mistress of Cuchulain who bore him his only son: it is not clear what, if anything, he intended by this change.

l. 2. *the Cheshire Cheese*. A chop-house in Fleet Street, London, where the poets of the Rhymers' Club used to meet in the 1890s.

l. 10. *Goban*. Goibniu the Smith, a Celtic god, one of the Sidhe, who made an ale which conferred immortality.

l. 15. *Slievenamon*. Mountain in Co. Tipperary inhabited by the gods or Sidhe.

48 l. 62. *Dowson and Johnson*. Ernest Dowson (1867–1900) and Lionel Johnson (1867–1902), poets who were members of the Rhymers' Club.

l. 71. *Murrough*. Anglicized spelling of Murchadh (see note on the poem's title).

49 l. 88. *Aoife*. See note on the poem's title.

50 *To a Wealthy Man* . . . Sir Hugh Lane (1874–1915), nephew of Lady Gregory, offered his collection of French paintings to the Dublin Municipal Gallery on condition that the Dublin Corporation raised the money to house them properly. The reaction, so far from being grateful, was hostile, and in disgust Lane gave the pictures to the National Gallery in London.

ll. 2, 3. *Paudeen's . . . Biddy's*. 'Paudeen' is an Anglicized spelling of Irish *Páidín*, 'Paddy'; 'Biddy' is a diminutive of Bridget. The names thus constitute, in context, a contemptuous reference to the Irish people.

l. 9. *Duke Ercole*. Ercole d'Este (1431–1505), Duke of Ferrara, a patron of the arts, praised in a Renaissance treatise on aristocratic manners, *The Courtier* of Baldassare Castiglione (1478–1529).

l. 12. *Plautus*. Roman comic playwright (*c*.254–184 BC) admired by the duke of Ferrara.

l. 14. *Guidobaldo*. Guidobaldo di Montefeltro (1472–1508), duke of Urbino, also praised by Castiglione (see note to l. 9).

51 l. 20. *Cosimo*. Cosimo de' Medici (1389–1464), the first of the great Medici family to be ruler of Florence, was a notable patron of the arts.

ll. 23–4. *Michelozzo . . . San Marco Library* . Michelozzo de Bartolommeo (1396–1472), court architect to Cosimo de Medici, designed the San Marco library in Florence.

September 1913. The month in which the poem was written. When read in relation to the poem as a whole, it conveys Yeats's sense that he is living through a period during which Ireland's aspiration to build a new national culture is being overwhelmed by petty materialism.

51 l. 8. *O'Leary*. John O'Leary (1830–1907), Irish patriot sentenced to twenty years' penal servitude in 1865. As part of an amnesty he was freed four years later on condition that he did not return to Ireland for fifteen years. He lived in Paris, returning to Dublin in 1885. Learned in Irish literature, he lent Yeats books and was something of a mentor. For Yeats's account of his friendship with him, see pp. 453–5.

l. 17. *wild geese*. Irish exiles who served in continental Catholic armies after the Treaty of Limerick (1691) and during the period when the Penal Laws were in force.

52 l. 20. *Edward Fitzgerald*. Lord Edward Fitzgerald (1763–98), one of the leaders of the 1798 Rebellion, who died while resisting arrest.

l. 21. *Robert Emmet and Wolfe Tone*. For Emmet, see note to p. 46, l. 5. Theobald Wolfe Tone (1763–98) attempted to bring French assistance to the Irish insurgents in 1798. He was captured when a French fleet he was with was defeated. Sentenced to be hanged, he committed suicide.

To a Friend . . . The friend is Lady Gregory.

Paudeen. See note to p. 50, l. 2.

53 *To a Shade*. The shade is that of Charles Stewart Parnell (1846–91), a brilliantly effective leader of the Irish Parliamentary Party, a post which they voted him out of when his adulterous affair with Mrs Kitty O'Shea was made public.

l. 9. *man*. Sir Hugh Lane, and ll. 10–19 refer to the controversy described in the note to p. 50, 'To a Wealthy Man'.

l. 17. *an old foul mouth*. William Martin Murphy (1844–1919), a newspaper owner who had supported attacks upon Parnell and opposed the Lane Gallery scheme.

l. 19. *Glasnevin*. Glasnevin Cemetery, where Parnell is buried.

54 *On Those that Hated* . . . A production at the Abbey Theatre, Dublin, of *The Playboy of the Western World*, by John Millington Synge (1871–1909) was greeted with hostility from the audience, apparently on the grounds of its disrespect for Irish life, and in the end with a riot, when reference was made to women standing in their 'shifts' (petticoats).

l. 4. *Juan*. Don Juan, legendary philanderer whose activities doomed him to hell.

The Mountain Tomb

55 l. 4. *Rosicross*. Christian Rosenkreuz, the legendary medieval founder of the Fraternity of the Rosy Cross: i.e. of Rosicrucianism, upon which the doctrines of the Order of the Golden Dawn were based.

Fallen Majesty

56 l. 1. *she*. Maud Gonne.

Friends

l. 2. *Three women.* In order of appearance in the poem they are Olivia Shakespear (1867–1938), Lady Gregory, and Maud Gonne.

58 *The Magi.* See note to 'The Secret Rose', p. 33, l. 9.

60 *The Wild Swans at Coole.* Coole Park, Co. Galway, was the home of Lady Gregory (see note to p. 44).

61 *In Memory of Major Robert Gregory.* Robert Gregory (1881–1918), Lady Gregory's only child, and a member of the Royal Flying Corps, was killed in action in Italy in 1918.

l. 17. *Lionel Johnson.* See note to p. 48, l. 62.

l. 25. *John Synge.* Irish playwright, John Millington Synge (1871–1909), author of *The Playboy of the Western World, Riders to the Sea,* and *Deirdre of the Sorrows.*

62 l. 33. *George Pollexfen.* (1839–1910), a maternal uncle of Yeats.

l. 34. *Mayo.* County in the western Irish province of Connacht.

l. 39. *opposition, square and trine.* Astrological terms for the relationships of stars or planets when their observed positions are at angles of 180°, 90°, and 120° to each other respectively.

l. 47. *Sidney.* Sir Philip Sidney (1554–86), the Elizabethan courtier and poet, author of the pastoral romance, *Arcadia* (1590).

l. 58. *Castle Taylor to the Roxborough side.* Both in Co. Galway, the latter being the childhood home of Lady Gregory.

l. 59. *Esserkelly.* In Co. Galway.

l. 60. *Mooneen.* Moneen, near Esserkelly in Co. Galway.

63 l. 66. *Clare.* A western county of Ireland, south of Galway, the border of which is not far from the places in Galway mentioned in the poem.

An Irish Airman Foresees his Death

64 l. 5. *Kiltartan Cross.* The crossroads in the barony of Kiltartan, near Coole.

Men Improve with the Years

l. 2. *triton.* In Greek mythology, tritons were minor sea-deities with the body of a man and the tail of a fish.

65 *Solomon to Sheba.* The Old Testament (1 Kgs. 10: 1–13; 2 Chron. 9: 1–12) describes how the queen of Sheba, in south-western Arabia, hearing of the legendary wisdom of Solomon, king of Israel and son of King David, visited his court and tested him with riddles.

The Scholars

67 l. 12. *Catullus.* Gaius Valerius Catullus (*c*.84–*c*.54 BC), Roman poet, author of passionate love poems addressed to a woman he calls 'Lesbia'.

On Woman

67 ll. 11–12. *Solomon . . . queens*. See note to p. 65, 'Solomon to Sheba'.

68 ll. 30–2. *The Pestle of the moon . . . birth again*. Yeats uses the traditional symbolism of the moon, which sees it as representing the principle of change, birth, and death, and extends it to encompass the idea of reincarnation. Written in 1914, the poem pre-dates the development of the lunar symbolism of *A Vision*.

The Fisherman

l. 4. *Connemara*. Sparsely populated area in the west of Co. Galway, some of it mountainous, some of it dotted with small lakes. Still largely Irish-speaking in Yeats's day.

70 *A Thought from Propertius*. Sextus Propertius (54 or 48–*c*.16 BC), a Roman elegiac and love poet. This poem is loosely based on part of his second book of Elegies.

l. 6. *Pallas Athena*. Pallas Athene, the Greek goddess of wisdom, and of many arts, including that of warfare.

72 *To a Squirrel at Kyle-na-No*. One of the seven woods at Coole.

Ego Dominus Tuus. Latin: 'I [am] your master.' The phrase comes from *La vita nuova* by Dante Alighieri (1265–1321), author of *The Divine Comedy*. It is spoken by 'the lord of terrible aspect'.

ll. 1, 7, and throughout. *Hic . . . Ille*. Latin for 'this' and 'that': thus, the given self, and that in the self which seeks the anti-self: this last point is expounded at ll. 67–76. (See note to p. 410, *Anima Hominis*). The use of speakers called '*Hic*' and '*Ille*' is derived from William Morris's poem, 'Hapless Love'.

l. 2. *old wind-beaten tower*. Ballylee Castle, Co. Galway, the Norman keep which Yeats bought, and to which he subsequently gave the name 'Thoor Ballylee', *Thoor* being an English transliteration of the Irish word *Túr*, meaning 'tower'.

l. 4. *Michael Robartes*. Fictional character who appears in some of Yeats's short stories and poems. His is a temperament which has a natural affinity with occult learning.

73 l. 26. *Lapo . . . Guido*. Lapo Gianni (*c*.1270–*c*.1330) and Guido Cavalcanti (*c*.1230–1300), poets, and friends of Dante.

l. 37. *The most exalted lady*. Beatrice, Dante's beloved, who in *The Divine Comedy* becomes for him a means of understanding a higher love, divine love.

74 l. 52. *Keats*. John Keats (1795–1821), the Romantic poet, admired for the sensuous detail of his work.

75 *The Phases of the Moon*. A reference to the system of Yeats's *A Vision* (1925): see note to p. 422.

l. 4. *Connemara*. Area of Co. Galway.

l. 8. *Aherne*. Owen Aherne, fictional character from Yeats's short stories, in which he is an associate of Michael Robartes.   *Robartes*. See note to p. 72, l. 4.

l. 15. *Milton's Platonist*. A reference to Milton's poem 'Il Penseroso' in which he refers to reading Plato by night in a 'lonely tower'.

l. 16. *visionary prince*. Shelley's Prince Athanase, from the poem of that name, whose soul was set apart 'as in a lonely tower'.

l. 17. *The lonely light that Samuel Palmer engraved*. 'The Lonely Tower' is an illustration to 'Il Penseroso' by Samuel Palmer (1805–81).

l. 27. *Pater*. Walter Pater (1839–94), critic of art and literature known for the preciosity of his prose style, which influenced both Wilde and Yeats.

l. 28. *Said I was dead*. Yeats mentions the death of Robartes in 'The Adoration of the Magi' (1896).

76 l. 45. *Athena*. See note to p. 70, l. 6.   *Achilles*. In Homer's *Iliad*, a hero of the Greeks in the Trojan War.

l. 46. *Hector*. Trojan prince, eldest son of King Priam, killed by the Greek hero Achilles.   *Nietzsche*. Friedrich Nietzsche (1844–1900), German philosopher, celebrator of 'the will to power'.

l. 67. *Sinai's top*. On the summit of Mount Sinai, which is in the Sinai peninsula between the Mediterranean and the Red Sea, Moses received the Ten Commandments.

79 *The Double Vision of Michael Robartes*. For Robartes, see note to p. 72, l. 4.

l. 1. *rock of Cashel*. St Patrick's Rock, at Cashel, Co. Tipperary, a hill fortified by the kings of Munster and containing several ecclesiastical ruins, including that of the twelfth-century Romanesque cathedral built by Cormac MacCarthy.

81 l. 56. *Homer's Paragon*. Helen of Troy.

l. 68. *Cormac's ruined house*. See note to l. 1.

Michael Robartes and the Dancer. For Robartes see note to p. 72, l. 4.

82 l. 19. *Athena*. See note to p. 70, l. 6.

l. 26. *Paul Veronese*. Paolo Veronese (*c.*1528–88), an Italian painter.

l. 29. *the lagoon*. The Venetian lagoon.

ll. 32–3. *Michael Angelo . . . 'Night'*. Michelangelo Buonarotti (1475–1564), Italian artist, sculptor, and architect who painted the ceiling, and the area behind the altar, of the Sistine Chapel in Rome with fresco designs of sacred themes from the Bible. *Morning* (usually called *The Dawn*) and *Night* are statues in the Medici Chapel, Florence.

83 *Solomon and the Witch*. See note to p. 65, 'Solomon to Sheba'.

84 *Under Saturn*. The Titan Saturn (in Greek, Kronos) was in classical mythology associated with the melancholy (and thus morose, gloomy, or 'saturnine') temperament. Yeats's title carries an astrological implication.

To be 'under Saturn' is to be under the influence of that planet and thus to suffer melancholy.

84 ll. 7–9. *an old cross Pollexfen . . . a Middleton . . . a red-haired Yeats.* William Pollexfen (1811–92), Yeats's maternal grandfather; probably William Middleton (1820–82), Yeats's great-uncle; the Revd William Butler Yeats (1806–62), Rector of Tullylish, Co. Down.

85 *Easter, 1916.* The Easter Rising of April 1916, in which combined republican forces of the Irish Volunteers and the Irish Citizen Army proclaimed an Irish Republic and occupied the centre of Dublin for five days against fierce opposition from the British Army. Fifteen of the leaders were executed.

l. 17. *That woman's.* Constance, Countess Markievicz (née Gore-Booth; 1868–1927), whom Yeats had known since she was a young woman.

ll. 24–5. *This man . . . wingèd horse.* Patrick Pearse (1879–1916), founder of St Enda's school and a leader in the Irish Volunteers. Thus also a leader of the Easter Rising. He was a poet: hence 'wingèd horse', i.e. Pegasus (see note to p. 43, l. 4.)

l. 26. *This other.* Thomas MacDonagh (1878–1916), an Irish poet.

86 l. 31. *This other man.* Major John MacBride (1865–1916), Irish patriot and separated husband of Maud Gonne.

87 l. 68. *For England may keep faith.* A Home Rule for Ireland Bill passed into law in September 1914, with the proviso that its operation be suspended for the duration of World War I and that it should be enacted when the war was over.

l. 76. *Connolly.* James Connolly (1868–1916) was born in Ulster and spent his youth in Glasgow. He was a socialist and trade unionist, and leader of the Irish Citizen Army.

Sixteen Dead Men. Fifteen leaders of the Easter Rising were executed by the British. The sixteenth is presumably Sir Roger Casement (1864–1916), executed in August 1916 for attempting to smuggle German weapons into Ireland.

ll. 7–8. *You say that we should still . . . overcome.* See note to 'Easter, 1916', l. 68.

l. 10. *Pearse.* See note to 'Easter, 1916', ll. 24–5.

l. 12. *MacDonagh's.* See note to 'Easter, 1916', l. 26.

l. 16. *Lord Edward and Wolfe Tone.* Lord Edward Fitzgerald (1763–98) and Theobald Wolfe Tone (1763–98), two leaders of the 1798 Rising.

The Rose Tree

88 l. 2. *Said Pearse to Connolly.* See notes to 'Easter 1916', p. 85, ll. 24–5, and p. 87, l. 76.

On a Political Prisoner. Countess Markievicz. See note to 'Easter, 1916', p. 85, l. 17.

l. 14. *Ben Bulben*. Mountain in Co. Sligo, not far from from the Gore-Booth family home at Lissadell. Countess Markievicz was born Constance Gore-Booth.

Towards Break of Day

89 l. 6. *Ben Bulben*. See note to 'On a Political Prisoner', l. 14.

l. 23. *The marvellous stag of Arthur*. White stags, and the hunting of stags, occur in a number of Arthurian tales.

Demon and Beast

90 l. 10. *Luke Wadding's portrait*. Portrait of Father Luke Wadding (1588–1657), an Irish Franciscan and Professor of Theology at the Irish College in Salamanca, by the Spanish painter, José Ribera (1588–1652).

l. 11. *Ormondes*. Family of the dukes of Ormonde, whose surname was Butler.

l. 13. *Strafford*. Lord Deputy Strafford: that is, Sir Thomas Wentworth (1593–1641), first earl of Strafford, and Lord Deputy of Ireland 1632–40.

l. 17. *the Gallery*. The National Gallery in Dublin, where the above portraits are to be seen.

l. 23. *the little lake*. The lake in St Stephen's Green, Dublin, not far from the National Gallery.

l. 26. *gyring and perning*. Both words refer to the system of gyres in *A Vision*. For 'gyre', see note to p. 152 below, 'The Gyres'; for 'perne' see note to 'Sailing to Byzantium', p. 95, l. 19, below.

91 l. 44. *Thebaid*. Desert country near Thebes in Upper Egypt known for the flourishing of early Christian monasticism.

l. 45. *Mareotic sea*. A lake south of Alexandria in Egypt in a region known for the flourishing of early Christian monasticism.

l. 46. *Anthony*. St Anthony of Egypt (?251–*c*.350), an ascetic monk who dwelt in the desert near Thebes.

The Second Coming. The poem alludes to the idea of the Second Coming of Christ foretold by Christ himself (Matt. 24: 27–31), but also, in its second verse-paragraph, to the Beast of Apocalypse in Rev. 17: 3–14.

l. 1. *the widening gyre*. A reference to the system of gyres in *A Vision* (1925): see note to p. 422 below.

l. 12. *Spiritus Mundi*. Latin: 'the spirit of the world'. An alternative name for *Anima Mundi*, 'the soul of the world': see note to p. 410, *Per Amica Silentia Lunae*.

92 *A Prayer for my Daughter*. Anne Butler Yeats was born on 26 Feb. 1919, and Yeats began this poem soon afterwards.

l. 4. *Gregory's wood*. The wood on Lady Gregory's estate, near Ballylee Castle, where the poem is set.

92 l. 25. *Helen.* Helen of Troy.

l. 26. *much trouble from a fool.* Paris, prince of Troy, abducted Helen, thereby causing the Trojan War.

l. 27. *that great Queen, that rose out of the spray.* Aphrodite, goddess of Love in Greek mythology, was supposed to have been born out of the sea.

l. 29. *bandy-leggèd smith.* Aphrodite's husband, Hephaestus, smith of the gods, was lame.

l. 32. *the Horn of Plenty.* In Greek mythology the horns of the she-goat Amalthea flowed with nectar and ambrosia. She suckled Zeus, the king of the gods, and when one of her horns broke off, she gave it to him.

93 l. 59. *the loveliest woman born.* Maud Gonne.

To be Carved on a Stone at Thoor Ballylee

94 l. 3. *Gort.* A neighbouring village in Co. Galway.

l. 4. *my wife George.* Yeats married Bertha Georgie Hyde-Lees (1894–1968) on 20 Oct. 1917.

The Tower

Sailing to Byzantium. Byzantium was the ancient Greek city chosen as his capital by the Roman emperor Constantine (AD 306–37), who rebuilt it and renamed it Constantinople. Centre of Graeco-Roman civilization after the demise of the Western Roman empire in 476. In a BBC broadcast on 8 September 1927, Yeats said that 'it is right for an old man to make his soul, and some of my thoughts upon that subject I have put into a poem called "Sailing to Byzantium". When Irishmen were illuminating the Book of Kells and making the jewelled croziers in the National Museum, Byzantium was the centre of European civilisation and the source of its spiritual philosophy, so I symbolise the search for the spiritual life by a journey to that city.' Yeats might have read in Benedict Fitzpatrick's *Ireland and the Making of Britain* (New York, 1922) about how 'Irish scholars, missionaries and pilgrims' formed 'literary colonies' in 'Constantinople' (pp. 10–11). Early drafts of the poem are explicit in evoking a medieval context and speaker (see Jon Stallworthy, *Between the Lines* (London, 1963), 102–3).

   A Vision, both in the 1925 and the 1937 edn., offers further insight (see pp. 441–2). But the reference there to the reign of the Emperor Justinian I (AD 527–65) does not entirely tally with the remarks in the broadcast quoted above, for the Book of Kells, as Yeats was well aware, was illuminated in the eighth century.

l. 1. *That . . . country.* Ireland. Yeats is repudiating a Gaelic tradition of poetic praise of Ireland in terms of her beauty and fecundity. Sir Samuel Ferguson's 'The Fair Hills of Ireland', for instance, is the translation of an anonymous poem in this tradition. It refers to plenteousness and the song of birds, expresses the speaker's desire to travel to Ireland, and mentions 'captains' who are 'sailing' there.

95 l. 11. *Soul clap its hands.* May recall Blake's story of his brother Robert's death, when the soul emerged from the body clapping its hands.

l. 18. *gold mosaic.* In 1907 Yeats had seen the mosaics of saints in the church of S. Apollinare Nuova, Ravenna. Ravenna had been the Byzantine emperor Justinian's capital in Italy after his reconquest of parts of the old Western empire.

l. 19. *perne.* Dialect: as a noun meaning 'spool' the word used to be common in Scotland and the north of Ireland. In this case it is used as a verb meaning 'to wind (as thread is wound on a spool)'. Yeats liked to use images of the spindle in relation to his system of gyres (for which see note to p. 152 below). Compare 'Hades' bobbin' in 'Byzantium', l. 11 (p. 131).

ll. 27–30. *But such a form . . . to sing.* Yeats's own note says that he had 'read somewhere that in the Emperor's palace at Byzantium was a tree made of gold and silver, and artificial birds that sang'. That somewhere is most likely to have been *Count Robert of Paris*, by Sir Walter Scott, with whose works Yeats had possessed a detailed familiarity since childhood. In this novel an Anglo-Saxon visitor to Byzantium figures prominently. The emperor's palace is described as containing a golden tree, with singing birds 'of various kinds curiously wrought and enamelled'.

The Tower

96 l. 9. *Ben Bulben's back.* Ben Bulben is a mountain in Co. Sligo.

l. 12. *Plotinus.* (AD 205–70), a Neoplatonic philosopher.

97 l. 48. *bog of Cloone.* In Co. Galway near Gort and not far from the tower at Ballylee, where the poem is set.

l. 49. *the man who made the song was blind.* Yeats has been describing a song by the blind Gaelic folk-poet, Anthony Raftery (*c.*1784–1835).

l. 52. *Homer that was a blind man.* By tradition Homer was blind, like Raftery (see note to l. 49).

l. 53. *Helen.* Helen of Troy, whose abduction instigated the Trojan War, subject of Homer's epic poem *The Iliad*.

l. 57. *Hanrahan.* See note to p. 38, 'Red Hanrahan's Song about Ireland'.

98 l. 85. *Great Memory.* A storehouse of archetypal images described in 'Anima Mundi' (see pp. 416–22).

99 l. 132. *of Burke and of Grattan.* Edmund Burke (1729–97), political theorist and orator; Henry Grattan (1746–1820), political leader and orator. Both were members of the Anglo-Irish Protestant Ascendancy; both were sympathetic to the plight of Irish Catholics.

101 *Meditations in Time of Civil War.* The Irish Civil War (1922–3) was bitterly fought between the newly formed government of the Irish Free State and those who rejected the Anglo-Irish Treaty (1922) which founded that state. The treaty stipulated the partition of Ireland, with the six counties of Northern Ireland remaining within the United Kingdom. Those who

rejected the treaty refused to accept partition, wishing for an Irish Republic of the whole island. They may be seen as ancestors of the Provisional IRA.

Ancestral Houses

102   l. 27. *Juno*. Queen of the gods of Rome, wife of Jupiter.

My House

l. 14. *Il Penseroso's Platonist*. See note to 'The Phases of the Moon', p. 75, l. 15.

My Table

103   l. 2. *Sato's gift*. Gift to Yeats of a ceremonial Japanese sword from Junzo Sato, Japanese Consul at Portland, Oregon.

My Descendants

104   l. 17. *Primum Mobile*. Latin, 'First Moving'. In the system of Ptolemaic astronomy, which was accepted in the Middle Ages, the cosmos consists of concentric spheres, most containing the planets, with the earth motionless at the centre. The spheres, however, revolve. The Primum Mobile is the outermost revolving sphere, driving the others.

The Road at my Door

l. 1. *Irregular*. An Irregular was a member of the IRA, or, to be more precise, those members of it who, rejecting the treaty and the resultant partition of Ireland, fought on rather than form the nucleus of the new Free State Army.

l. 2. *Falstaffian*. Large, bluff, jocose, and irreverent, like the comic character Falstaff in several of Shakespeare plays.

105   ll. 6–7. *A brown Lieutenant . . . national uniform*. Members of the Free State Army.

The Stare's Nest by My Window. 'Stare' is another word for starling.

I See Phantoms of Hatred . . .

106   l. 10. *Vengeance for Jacques Molay*. Jacques de Molay (1244–1314), Grand Master of the Order of Knights Templar, who was burned for heresy. Yeats's own note (see pp. 482–3) observes that the cry was said to have been incorporated 'in the ritual of certain Masonic societies of the eighteenth century, and to have fed class-hatred'. In view of the Masonic connections of Yeats's family and of the Golden Dawn, the references in 'Meditations in Time of Civil War' to 'cracked masonry' and 'loosening masonry', in the context of a rejection of hatred, suggest an element of self-criticism.

l. 20 *Babylonian almanacs*. Handbooks of astrological predictions which might be presumed to have existed in Babylon because of the association of that city, in ancient times, with astrology.

107 *Nineteen Hundred and Nineteen*. A year of heavy fighting in the Irish War of Independence.

l. 7. *Phidias'*. Phidias (*c*.490–*c*.423 BC) was an Athenian sculptor.

l. 8. *golden grasshoppers and bees*. Thucydides (*c*.455–*c*.399 BC), the Greek historian, refers to the Athenians' use of golden grasshopper brooches to fasten the hair. It is not known for certain where Yeats may have discovered an association of Athens with bees, golden or otherwise, but the symbolism, in 'Meditations in Time of Civil War', of honey as emotional sweetness may be relevant.

108 l. 46. *Acropolis*. The elevated part of the citadel of ancient Athens. The temple of Athene, or Parthenon, is its most imposing building.

l. 49. *Loie Fuller's Chinese dancers*. Loie Fuller (1862–1928), an American dancer, had a troupe of Japanese dancers, and with them performed undulating dances with whirling draperies startlingly lit.

l. 54. *Platonic Year*. Or 'the Great Year'. A major cycle of time, at the end of which the stars are supposed to return to the positions they occupied at the creation. An idea, expounded in Plato's *Timaeus*, which contributed to the cyclical theory of history in *A Vision* (see pp. 438–42 below).

109 l. 72. *Some Platonist*. Possibly a reference to the English Platonist, Thomas Taylor (1758–1835), who, in the commentary to his translation of a Neoplatonic work, Porphyry's *De antro nympharum* ('On the Cave of the Nymphs'), explains that the souls of the dead remember earthly forms even when they have forgotten their individual lives.

110 l. 118. *Herodias' daughters*. See Yeats's note on 'The Hosting of the Sidhe' at p. 476.

111 l. 128. *Robert Artisson*. See Yeats's note at p. 483.

A Prayer for my Son. Michael Butler Yeats, born 22 Aug. 1922.

ll. 10–12. *Some there are . . . Who have planned his murder*. In *A Vision* Yeats recounts how his ghostly Instructors informed him that evil spirits would attempt to undermine his health and that of his children.

112 l. 17. *You*. Christ.

ll. 25–32. *And when . . . With human love*. This stanza refers to the Flight into Egypt. When King Herod the Great of Judaea was informed by the Three Wise Men that the Messiah was to be born, and by his own priests and teachers that the birthplace would be in Bethlehem, fearing a threat to his supremacy, he ordered all male children dwelling there, of 2 years and younger, to be killed. But an angel warned Joseph and Mary, and they fled with the infant Jesus to Egypt for a while. See Matt. 2: 1–21.

Leda and the Swan. In Greek mythology Leda was raped by Zeus, the king of the gods, in the form of a swan. The egg which resulted contained Helen of Troy and Castor and Pollux. Thus the Trojan War resulted from this event. Yeats sees a parallel between this sexual intervention in history of a god disguised as a bird, and the conception of Christ, traditionally figured as fathered by the Holy Spirit in the form of a dove. But there is a contrast between the resulting eras, for Zeus's intervention gave rise to an age which revelled in power and conflict, whereas that of the Holy Spirit gave rise to one which, at least in theory, prized peace and mercy. For a fuller sense of what is involved for Yeats, see the sections of *A Vision* (1937) called 'The Great Year of the Ancients' and 'Dove or Swan', of which extracts can be found on pp. 438-42.

112 l. 11. *Agamemnon dead*. King Agamemnon was leader of the confederate Greek armies at Troy. On his return from the sack of Troy he was murdered by his wife Clytemnestra, because on the way to the war he himself had sacrificed their daughter, Iphigenia, to the gods. It must also be in Yeats's mind that Clytemnestra was herself a daughter of Leda by her husband Tyndareus.

113 *On a Picture of a Black Centaur by Edmund Dulac*. Dulac (1882-1953) was an artist and illustrator and a friend of Yeats.

l. 7. *mummy wheat*. Refers to the idea of wheat growing out of Egyptian tombs, and therefore mummies. Hence, figuratively, wisdom with ancient roots, or even roots in the wisdom of the dead.

l. 11. *seven Ephesian topers*. The Seven Sleepers; that is, seven Christians who were sealed in a cave near Ephesus during the persecutions of the pagan emperor Decius (AD 200-51) and, according to legend, were miraculously preserved, sleeping for two centuries, after which they awoke and were brought before the Christian emperor Theodosius II (401-50), whose faith was confirmed by the miracle.

l. 12. *Alexander's empire*. Alexander the Great (356-323 BC) who captured Ephesus in 334 BC, and whose empire was short-lived.

l. 13. *Saturnian sleep*. The ancient Roman god Saturn (identified with the Greek Kronos) was supposed to have ruled over a period of peace, tranquillity, and plenty known as the Golden Age.

Among School Children. The poem arises out of Yeats's visit to St Otteran's School, Waterford, in February 1926. See Senate Speech on 'The State of School Education', pp. 451-2.

ll. 5-6. *be neat in everything* | *In the best modern way*. The school was run on Montessori principles, those, that is, of Maria Montessori (1870-1952), who recommended the encouragement of both creativity and neatness.

l. 8. *public man*. Yeats was by now a Senator of the Irish Free State.

l. 9. *a Ledaean body*. A body like that of Leda (see note to p. 112, 'Leda and the Swan'), or by extension like that of Leda's daughter, Helen of Troy, to whom Yeats often compares Maud Gonne.

114 l. 15. *Plato's parable*. In Plato's *Symposium*, Aristophanes, one of the contributors to the discussion, asserts that humanity was originally spherical and possessed the attributes of both sexes, until Zeus divided it in two. Yeats 'alters' the tale so that the sphere becomes an egg, and the two sexes the yolk and white respectively (l. 16).

l. 26. *Quattrocento finger*. 'Quattrocento': 400. Name given in Italy to the 1400s, i.e. the fifteenth century. The finger is that of an artist of this period, and an earlier version of the poem makes it clear that Yeats was thinking of Leonardo da Vinci (1452–1519).

l. 34. *Honey of generation*. See Yeats's own note at p. 483.

l. 41. *Plato*. Greek philosopher (*c*.429–347 BC) who held that the physical universe was an inferior copy of the true world of Forms or Ideas.

l. 43. *Aristotle*. Greek philosopher (384–322 BC), student of Plato, but according importance to the observation of the physical world: thus, he was 'Solider'. He was tutor to Alexander the Great.   *taws*. A leather strap, divided into strips at the end, used to discipline children in Scottish, and some English, schools.

l. 44. *king of kings*. Alexander the Great (see note to l. 43).

115 l. 45. *Pythagoras*. Greek philosopher and mathematician (fl. *c*.530 BC) who discovered the mathematical regularity of the musical intervals of the octaves.

Colonus' Praise. A chorus from Yeats's translation of the *Oedipus at Colonus* of Sophocles (*c*.496–406 BC), the Greek tragic playwright. Colonus is an area north of Athens, associated with horses because also a site of the cult of Poseidon, god of the sea and giver of horses to man.

l. 8. *Semele's lad*. Dionysus, son of Zeus and Semele, god of wine and fertility.

ll. 9–16. *gymnasts' garden . . . stares thereon*. Refers to a park and gymnasium at the edge of Athens near Colonus, later the site of the Academy of Plato, in which an olive tree is said to have miraculously grown through the power of the goddess Athene, tutelary goddess of Athens.

116 l. 19. *the Great Mother*. Demeter, Greek goddess of crops and fertility.

l. 23. *Cephisus*. A river near Athens.

l. 28. *Poseidon gave it bit and oar*. Poseidon taught men both to ride and to row.

A Man Young and Old

117 *All Souls' Night*. All Souls' Day is the feast on which the Catholic Church prays for the souls of the faithful departed who are still suffering in Purgatory. This poem provides an epilogue to *A Vision* in both its versions.

l. 1. *the great Christ Church Bell*. Great Tom, the bell in the tower of Christ Church College, Oxford. Yeats was living in Broad Street, Oxford, at the time he wrote this poem.

118 l. 21. *Horton*. W. T. Horton (1864–1919), a mystical painter.

119 l. 41. *Florence Emery*. (1869–1917), an English actress.

ll. 46–50. *Preferred to teach . . . the unnoticed end*. Florence Emery left England to teach in a school in Ceylon in 1912, and there died of cancer in 1917.

119 l. 61. *MacGregor Mathers*. MacGregor Mathers (1854–1918), formerly Samuel Liddell Mathers, occultist and founder member of the Hermetic Order of the Golden Dawn. Yeats and he quarrelled and fell out in 1900.

120 *The Winding Stair and Other Poems*. Refers to the winding stair inside the tower at Ballylee Castle.

  In Memory of Eva Gore-Booth and Con Markiewicz. The sisters Eva Gore-Booth (1870–1926) and Constance, Countess Markievicz, née Gore-Booth (1868–1927), whom Yeats had known since 1894. Markievicz took part in the 1916 Easter Rising.

  l. 1. *Lissadell*. The Gore-Booth family home in Co. Sligo.

121 l. 30. *gazebo*. A summer-house or pavilion located so as to provide a view. But in Hiberno-English to make a gazebo of oneself means to make oneself look ridiculous.

  Death

  l. 7. *A great man in his pride*. Yeats was thinking of Kevin O'Higgins, Vice-President and Minister of Justice of the Irish Free State, who was assassinated on 10 July 1927.

  A Dialogue of Self and Soul

122 l. 10. *Sato's ancient blade*. See note to 'My Table', p. 103, l. 2.

  l. 25. *Montashigi*. Bishu Osafune Motoshige, a craftsman of the Oei period (1394–1428).

124 *Blood and the Moon*. See Yeats's note to *The Winding Stair and Other Poems*, pp. 485–6.

  ll. 13–14. *Alexandria's . . . the moon's*. The Pharos, or lighthouse, at Alexandria was one of the 'Seven Wonders' of the ancient world. The ancient Babylonians are supposed to have been adept in the art of astrology, and their towers or ziggurats to have facilitated observation of the heavens. The biblical Tower of Babel, referred to here, is thought to reflect Hebrew knowledge of Babylonian towers.

  l. 15. *And Shelley . . . thought's crowned powers he called them once*. Shelley, in *Prometheus Unbound* (iv. 103), refers to towers as 'Thought's crowned powers'.

  l. 18. *That Goldsmith and the Dean, Berkeley and Burke have travelled there*. Irish Protestant authors. Oliver Goldsmith (1728–74), playwright and poet; Jonathan Swift (1667–1745), satirist, poet, and author of *Gulliver's Travels*, who became dean of St Patrick's cathedral in Dublin in 1713; George Berkeley (1685–1753), philosopher; Edmund Burke (1729–97), orator and political writer.

125 l. 25. *Berkeley that proved all things a dream*. Berkeley argued that nothing can be known except the experiences of mind: physical qualities reduce to impressions. These exist only in mind: they originate in the mind of God, and matter does not exist.

l. 28. *Saeva Indignatio*. Latin: 'fierce' or 'savage indignation', from Swift's epitaph in St Patrick's cathedral, Dublin. Yeats uses the latter translation in 'Swift's Epitaph', p. 129, l. 2.

126 *Coole Park, 1929*. Coole Park was Lady Gregory's estate in Co. Galway.

l. 9. *Hyde*. Douglas Hyde. See note to 'At the Abbey Theatre', p. 44, l. 1.

l. 13. *John Synge*. See notes to 'In Memory of Major Robert Gregory', p. 61, l. 25.

l. 14. *Shaw Taylor and Hugh Lane*. Capt. John Shawe-Taylor (1866–1911) called a reforming landowners' conference in 1903, and his cousin Sir Hugh Lane (1875–1915) was an art collector (see notes to p. 50, 'To a Wealthy Man . . .'). They were nephews of Lady Gregory.

127 *Coole and Ballylee, 1931*. Lady Gregory's demesne at Coole Park, Co. Galway, was close to Yeats's home at Ballylee Castle ('Thoor Ballylee').

l. 4. *'dark' Raftery's 'cellar'*. The Gaelic poet Anthony Raftery (1784–1835) frequented Co. Galway as well as his native Mayo. In 'Dust hath Closed Helen's Eye' we learn that the 'cellar' was the name given by Raftery to 'the great hole where the river sank underground' (see p. 402). Raftery was blind ('dark'). See also Yeats's note to 'The Tower' at pp. 481–2.

128 *For Anne Gregory*. (b. 1911), Lady Gregory's grandchild.

129 *Swift's Epitaph*. A reasonably faithful translation of Jonathan Swift's epitaph in St Patrick's cathedral, Dublin, although the first and the fifth lines introduce ideas that are alien to the original.

At Algeciras—A Meditation upon Death. Algeciras is a city in southern Spain.

l. 11. *Newton's metaphor*. Sir Isaac Newton (1642–1727) once compared himself as a scientific discoverer to a boy looking for pebbles and pretty shells on the seashore.

l. 12. *Rosses' level shore*. The beach near the village of Rosses Point, Co. Sligo.

l. 16. *the Great Questioner*. God in judgement.

130 *Mohini Chatterjee*. An Indian Brahmin and sage (1858–1936) whom Yeats met in Dublin in 1885–6.

131 *Byzantium*. For this city, and for Yeats's thoughts about it, see notes to 'Sailing to Byzantium', p. 94.

l. 4. *great cathedral*. Hagia Sophia ('Holy Wisdom'), the cathedral built in 532–7 by the Emperor Justinian.

l. 5. *dome*. Hagia Sophia (see note to l. 4) possesses a large dome.

ll. 11–12. *Hades' bobbin . . . May unwind the winding path*. In Greek mythology, Hades was ruler of the Underworld. The name was also given to his realm. The unwinding is that whereby, according to Yeats, the spirit after death runs through all the events of its life in order to detach itself from them. This is explained in *A Vision* (1937): 'In the *Return . . . the Spirit* must live through past events in the order of their occurrence. . . . All that keeps the *Spirit* from its freedom may be compared to a knot that has to be untied . . .' (p. 226).

132 ll. 33–4. *Astraddle on the dolphin's mire and blood,* | *Spirit after spirit!* In classical mythology dolphins carried the souls of the dead to the Islands of the Blessed.

Vacillation

l. 11. *A tree there is.* Yeats found this tree in the collection of medieval Welsh romances, the *Mabinogion.* He would have interpreted it as a symbol of the cosmic Tree of Life, which in the Jewish mystical writings, the cabbala, has two aspects: one of wrath and one of mercy. Thus he is referring to the fundamental 'antinomies' of existence (see l. 5).

l. 16. *Attis' image.* Attis was a vegetation god, whose cult included a spring festival of death and resurrection. One of the stories about him has him castrating himself.

133 l. 27. *Lethean.* Referring to Lethe, in Greek mythology the river of oblivion in the Underworld.

134 l. 59. *the great lord of Chou.* Possibly Chou Kung, a twelfth-century Chinese statesman.

l. 63. *Babylon or Nineveh.* Babylon, capital of the Mesopotamian empire of Babylonia (fl. *c.*1728–*c.*1130 BC, and 625–539 BC); Nineveh, capital of the 'new' Assyrian empire, also in Mesopotamia, *c.*701–612 BC.

l. 74. *Isaiah's coal.* In Isa. 6: 6–7 one of the seraphim purifies Isaiah by applying a live coal to his lips.

l. 78. *Von Hügel.* Baron Friedrich von Hügel (1852–1925) was a Catholic philosopher of religion.

l. 80. *Saint Teresa.* St Teresa of Avila (1515–82), a Spanish Carmelite nun whose body was supposed to have remained undecayed in the tomb.

135 l. 88. *The lion and the honeycomb.* In the Bible (Judg. 14: 5–14), Samson kills a lion with his bare hands, and later discovers that the carcass has become home for a swarm of bees with their honey. He declares that 'out of the strong came forth sweetness'.

Gratitude to the Unknown Instructors. The instructors are the spirit-guides who instigated the automatic writing and other communications which in the end bore fruit in *A Vision.*

Words for Music Perhaps

Crazy Jane Reproved

136 l. 5. *Great Europa.* In Greek mythology Zeus, king of the gods, carried away Europa, daughter of the king of Tyre, to Crete, where she bore him sons.

Mad as the Mist and Snow

141 l. 7. *Horace*. Quintus Horatius Flaccus (65–8 BC), the Roman poet, author, among other things, of the *Odes*.

l. 9. *Tully's*. Tully is an alternative name for Marcus Tullius Cicero (106–43 BC), the Roman orator and politician.

l. 16. *Cicero*. See note to l. 9.

142 *'I am of Ireland'*. This title comes from a fragment of medieval English song, 'Icham of Irlande', upon which Yeats's refrain is also loosely based.

143 *The Delphic Oracle upon Plotinus*. The Delphic Oracle, so called because located at Delphi, was the most important oracle in ancient Greece. Its presiding God was Apollo. Plotinus (AD 205–70) was a Neoplatonic philosopher. After his death a follower consulted the oracle to find out where his soul had gone. Yeats was able to read the supposed pronouncement in a translation of a life of Plotinus by Porphyry (232–*c*.305) which was included in the preliminary matter of the translation of Plotinus by his friend Stephen MacKenna (1872–1935). This poem contains elements from the 'oracle'.

l. 3. *Rhadamanthus*. In Greek mythology, the son of Zeus and Europa (see note to 'Crazy Jane Reproved', p. 136, l. 5), brother of Minos of Crete and one of the judges of the dead in the Underworld.

l. 4. *the Golden Race*. In MacKenna's translation of Porphyry's life of Zeus Rhadamanthus and Minos (see note to l. 8) are referred to as 'great brethren of the golden race of Zeus'. By extension, the immortals.

l. 8. *Minos*. An early king of Crete, son of Zeus and Europa (see note to 'Crazy Jane Reproved', p. 136, l. 5). With Rhadamanthus and Aeacus, one of the three judges of the Underworld.

l. 9. *Pythagoras*. See note to 'Among School Children', p. 115, l. 45.

A Woman Young and Old

Her Vision in the Wood

145 l. 19. *Quattrocento*. Italian. Way of referring to the fifteenth century.

l. 20. *Mantegna's*. The Italian painter Andrea Mantegna (1431–1506).

147 *From the 'Antigone'*. This poem is Yeats's translation of a chorus from *Antigone* by the Greek tragic playwright, Sophocles (*c*.496–406 BC).

l. 6. *Parnassus*. In Greek mythology, Mount Parnassus is sacred not only to the Muses but also to the gods Apollo and Dionysus.

l. 7. *the Empyrean*. The highest heaven.

l. 10. *Brother and brother*. Antigone's brothers, Eteocles and Polynices, kill each other.

ll. 15–16. *Oedipus' child | Descends into the loveless dust*. Antigone, daughter of Oedipus, is condemned to be buried alive, but circumvents her fate by committing suicide.

A Full Moon in March

147 *Parnell's Funeral.* For Parnell, see note to p. 53, 'To a Shade'. He was buried in Glasnevin Cemetery in Dublin on 11 Oct. 1891.

l. 1. *the Great Comedian.* Daniel O'Connell (1775–1847), 'the Liberator', champion of Catholic Emancipation and the greatest Irish leader of the nineteenth century. Yeats sees him as a comedian, in contrast to Parnell as tragedian.

l. 4. *a brighter star shoots down.* Maud Gonne had informed Yeats that, as Parnell's coffin was lowered into the grave, a star 'fell in broad daylight'.

148 ll. 7–15. *the Cretan barb . . . Sicilian coin.* Yeats tells how he had a dream of a woman standing on a pedestal, shooting an arrow at a star. He interpreted this dream in the light of an ancient Cretan ritual whereby a priestess of the mother goddess ('the Great Mother', l. 13) shot an arrow at a child, whose death symbolized the death and resurrection of the tree-spirit, or Apollo.

l. 17. *Emmet, Fitzgerald, Tone.* See notes to 'September 1913', p. 52, ll. 20–1.

l. 20. *Hysterica passio.* Latin: 'hysteria'. See Shakespeare's *King Lear*, II. iv. 56: 'Hysterica passio, down, thou climbing sorrow.'

l. 33. *de Valera.* Eamonn de Valera (1882–1975), one of the leaders of the Easter Rising, became leader of the Fianna Fáil party and subsequently 'President of the Executive Council' and prime minister of the Irish Free State in 1932. He remained in this post for the rest of Yeats's life (though the Free State was reconstituted and renamed 'Ireland' in 1937).

l. 36. *Cosgrave.* William T. Cosgrave (1880–1965), prime minister of the Irish Free State, 1922–32.

l. 39. *O'Higgins.* See note to 'Death', p. 121, l. 7.

l. 40. *O'Duffy.* Eoin O'Duffy (1892–1944) was the founder of the Irish Fascist 'Blueshirts'.

l. 42. *Jonathan Swift's.* Jonathan Swift (1677–1745), satirist and Dean of St Patrick's Cathedral, Dublin.

149 *Supernatural Songs. I. Ribh at the Tomb of Baile and Aillinn.* In the Preface to *A Full Moon in March*, Yeats describes Ribh as 'an imaginary critic of St Patrick. His Christianity, come perhaps from Egypt like much early Irish Christianity, echoes pre-Christian thought.' For Baile and Aillinn, see the 'Argument' to that poem at p. 201.

151 *Meru.* A mountain in Tibet, sacred in both the Hindu and Buddhist traditions, and supposed to be the centre of the world.

New Poems

152 *The Gyres.* The gyres are the most fundamental component of Yeats's

occult system, expounded in *A Vision*. They are two moving cones or vortices which penetrate each other, the point of one being at the base of the other. They rotate in opposite directions. This opposition represents the contrary principles of existence: the objective (or 'primary', as Yeats calls it) and the subjective (or 'antithetical'). For more information, see the note on *The Great Wheel*, para. 4 (p. 548 below).

l. 1. *Old Rocky Face.* It is not certainly known to whom or what Yeats is referring. The manuscript drafts refer to 'Old cavern man, old rocky face'. There have been many suggestions as to the identity of this being, the most authoritative being Mrs Yeats's marginal gloss, 'Delphic Oracle'. This identification is not, however, seen as ruling out other allusions. (See Jon Stallworthy, *Vision and Revision in Yeats's* Last Poems (Oxford, 1969), 36–7.) A possible contender is Nietzsche's Zarathustra (in *Thus Spoke Zarathustra*), who lives in a cave in the mountains and whose philosophy of tragic affirmation was a growing influence on Yeats's thought in this period.

l. 6. *Empedocles.* (*c.*493–*c.*433 BC), a Greek philosopher from Sicily who saw the elements as being in a state of continual change occasioned by love and strife.

l. 7. *Hector is dead and there's a light in Troy.* In Greek legend Hector, son of King Priam of Troy, is killed by the Greek hero Achilles during the Trojan War. Subsequently the Greeks sack and burn the city.

Lapis Lazuli | (*For Harry Clifton*). Yeats had received the present of a Chinese lapis lazuli carving from his friend Henry de Vere Clifton.

153 l. 6. *Zeppelin.* A type of airship used by the Germans to bomb London during World War I.

l. 7. *King Billy.* 'King Billy' is in Ireland a common colloquial way of referring to William of Orange (William III), whose predominantly Protestant forces were victorious against the Catholic James II at the Battle of the Boyne (1690).

l. 22. *drop scenes.* Painted curtains lowered in front of the stage between the acts and at the end of a play.

l. 29. *Callimachus.* A Greek sculptor of the fifth century BC whose works included a bronze lamp shaped like a palm-tree.

l. 33. *His long lamp chimney.* See note to l. 29.

154 *Imitated from the Japanese.* The source is not known for certain.

An Acre of Grass

156 l. 15. *Timon.* Tragic hero of Shakespeare's *Timon of Athens* (1623), who is driven to misanthropic rage.

l. 16. *William Blake.* The poet, visionary, engraver, and painter (1757–1827).

157 l. 19. *Michael Angelo.* Michelangelo Buonarotti (1475–1564), the Italian sculptor and painter.

What Then?

157 l. 5. *Plato's.* See note to 'Among School Children', p. 114, l. 41.

Beautiful Lofty Things

l. 1. *O'Leary's.* John O'Leary: see note to 'September 1913', p. 51, l. 8.

l. 2. *My father . . . a raging crowd.* In a debate held at the Abbey Theatre on 4 Feb. 1907, Yeats's father, John Butler Yeats (1839–1922), defended Synge's *The Playboy of the Western World*, a play which had provoked riots in its first performances.

158 l. 5. *Standish O'Grady.* Standish James O'Grady (1846–1928), Irish historian and novelist.

ll. 7–10. *Augusta Gregory . . . The blinds drawn up.* Lady Gregory (1852–1932), Yeats's friend and patron, was threatened in 1922 by one of her tenants, who proposed to take some of her land in Coole Park by force. She responded by indicating how easy it would be for him to shoot her if he wanted to through the window where she sat every evening.   *Maud Gonne at Howth station.* Maud Gonne (1866–1953), Yeats's beloved. Howth is a fishing village on a headland north of Dublin, Howth Head, where Yeats and Maud Gonne spent a day walking after his first unsuccessful proposal in 1891.

l. 11. *Pallas Athene.* The Greek goddess of wisdom, of warfare, and of many arts and crafts.

l. 12. *Olympians.* The gods and goddesses of Greek mythology, who dwell upon Mount Olympus.

The Curse of Cromwell. Oliver Cromwell (1599–1658) in 1649–50 led a parliamentarian army to Ireland, most of which had been royalist, after the Puritans' victory in the Civil War in England. His nine-month visit was marked by massacres and barbaric cruelty, and, after the defeat of the Irish, by comprehensive confiscation of land.

l. 3. *The lovers and the dancers are beaten into the clay.* An allusion to a translation by Frank O'Connor (Michael O'Donovan, 1903–66) of an anonymous Irish poem of defeat known as 'Kilcash'. The second stanza of this translation ends 'The earls, the lady, the people | Beaten into the clay.'

159 l. 6. *His fathers served their fathers before Christ was crucified.* An allusion to the last line of a poem in Irish by Egan O'Rahilly (Aogán Ó Rathaille, 1670–1726) about the dispossession of the old Irish order. Yeats knew the poem as 'Last Lines' in a translation by Frank O'Connor (see note to l. 3), the final two lines of which run: 'I shall go after the heroes, ay, into the clay— | My fathers followed theirs before Christ was crucified.'

l. 18. *As the fox . . . destroyed the Spartan boy's.* Story told by Plutarch of how a Spartan boy stole a fox and, hiding it under his tunic, let it gnaw him to death rather than admit the theft.

l. 25. *a great house.* 'Big House' was a familiar way in Ireland of referring to a domicile of the gentry or nobility. It is a translation of a phrase in Irish, in which it would originally have applied to a house of the native Gaelic upper class.

The Ghost of Roger Casement. Sir Roger Casement (1864–1916) was executed for treason: he had been smuggling weapons from Germany to Ireland.

160 l. 4. *John Bull*. Popular personification of England.

l. 21. *John Bull has gone to India*. Reference to the incorporation of India in the British empire.

161 *Come Gather Round Me Parnellites*. Parnellites are followers of Charles Stewart Parnell (see note to p. 53, 'To a Shade').

l. 27. *A husband that had sold his wife*. Yeats believed that Mrs O'Shea's husband, before he brought divorce proceedings, knew of her adulterous liaison with Parnell and tolerated it because financial and other advantages were to be gained from it.

162 *Parnell*. See note to p. 53, 'To a Shade'.

Those Images

ll. 9–16. *Seek those images . . . That make the Muses sing*. At the end of 'An Introduction for my Plays', Yeats recalls the question asked of an Indian sage: 'Who are your Masters?' To which he replied, 'The wind and the harlot, the virgin and the child, the lion and the eagle.' Yeats's 'five' (l. 15) omit the wind.

163 *The Municipal Gallery Re-visited*. The Municipal Gallery of Modern Art in Dublin, which contains the portraits of the people to whom the poem refers.

l. 3. *Casement*. Sir Roger Casement (see note to p. 159, 'The Ghost of Roger Casement').

l. 4. *Griffith*. Arthur Griffith (1871–1922), a leader of Sinn Fein and a member of the Irish delegation to Downing Street which negotiated the Anglo-Irish Treaty in the latter half of 1921 (ratified 1922).

l. 5. *Kevin O'Higgins*. See note to 'Death', p. 121, l. 7.

l. 21. *Augusta Gregory's son*. Robert Gregory: see note to p. 61, 'In Memory of Major Robert Gregory'.

l. 22. *Hugh Lane*. See note to p. 50, 'To a Wealthy Man . . .'.

l. 23. *Hazel Lavery*. The American wife (d. 1935) of the Irish artist Sir John Lavery (1856–1941).

l. 25. *Mancini's portrait of Augusta Gregory*. Antonio Mancini (1852–1930) painted a portrait of Yeats's friend and patron Lady Gregory (1852–1932) which hangs in the Gallery.

l. 26. *John Synge*. See notes to 'In Memory of Major Robert Gregory', p. 61, l. 25.

164 ll. 39–40. *No fox can foul . . . An image out of Spenser*. Spenser, 'The Ruines

of Time', ll. 216–17: 'He now is gone, the whiles the foxe is crept | Into the hole, the which the Badger swept.'

164 l. 44. *Antaeus-like*. In Greek mythology, Antaeus is a giant who grows stronger when in contact with the earth. (His mother was Earth—*Gé*.)

On the Boiler

Why should not Old Men be Mad

165 l. 5. *Dante*. See note to p. 72, 'Ego Dominus Tuus'.

l. 7. *A Helen*. Figurative reference to Helen of Troy.

Crazy Jane on the Mountain

l. 1. *Bishop*. For Crazy Jane and the Bishop, see the poem with that title at p. 135.

l. 15. *Great bladdered Emer*. Emer was the wife of Cuchulain, the heroic champion of the court of Ulster at Emain Macha, near Armagh. There are a number of stories indicating that in ancient Ireland a woman might be prized for the strength of her bladder.

l. 17. *Cuchulain*. See note to l. 15.

Last Poems and Two Plays

166 *Under Ben Bulben*. Ben Bulben is a mountain north of Sligo, and not far from Drumcliff.

l. 2. *Mareotic Lake*. See note to 'Demon and Beast', p. 91, l. 45.

l. 3. *That the Witch of Atlas knew*. The witch in Shelley's 'The Witch of Atlas' (composed 1820), stanza 58, passes by the Mareotic Lake.

ll. 5–6. *by those horsemen, by those women . . . superhuman*. The Sidhe. See note to p. 26, 'The Hosting of the Sidhe'.

167 ll. 25–6. *Mitchel's prayer . . . 'Send war in our time, O Lord!'* John Mitchel (1815–75), an Irish nationalist, gave vent to this prayer in his *Jail Journal* (1854).

l. 44. *Phidias*. Greek sculptor (*c*.490–*c*.432 BC).

ll. 45–7. *Michaelangelo . . . half-awakened Adam*. Michelangelo Buonarotti (1475–1564) painted the ceiling of the Sistine Chapel. Central to the design is the depiction of God creating Adam.

l. 53. *Quattro-cento*. Fifteenth-century Italian painters.

168 l. 64. *Calvert and Wilson, Blake and Claude*. Edward Calvert (1799–1883), English artist and engraver, whose works include 'A Primitive City' and 'Ideal Pastoral Life'; Richard Wilson (1714–82); William Blake (1757–1827); and Claude Lorrain (1600–82).

l. 66. *Palmer's*. Samuel Palmer (1805–81), an English artist, associate of Blake and Calvert.

l. 85. *In Drumcliffe churchyard Yeats is laid.* Yeats was finally reinterred, according to his wishes, in Drumcliff churchyard in September 1948. His tombstone bears the epitaph which forms the last three lines of this poem (ll. 92–4).

l. 86. *An ancestor was rector there.* Yeats's great-grandfather, the Revd John Yeats (1774–1846).

The Black Tower

169 l. 7. *There in the tomb stand the dead upright.* According to T. R. Henn, in *The Lonely Tower* (London, 1950), 338, this refers to the way in which the ancient warrior Eoghan Bel was buried on Knocknarea, Co. Sligo.

170 *Cuchulain Comforted.* Cuchulain is the chief hero of the Ulster cycle of heroic sagas.

l. 1. *A man that had six mortal wounds.* Yeats's play, *The Death of Cuchulain*, recounts how Cuchulain receives six mortal wounds (pp. 324–33).

171 *In Tara's Halls.* Tara, Co. Meath, seat of the High Kings of Ireland.

The Statues

l. 1. *Pythagoras.* See note to 'Among School Children', p. 115, l. 45.

172 l. 14. *Salamis.* The Athenians defeated the Persians at the naval battle of Salamis (480 BC).

l. 15. *Phidias.* Athenian sculptor (*c*.490–*c*.432 BC).

l. 24. *Grimalkin.* Traditional English name for a cat.

l. 25. *Pearse summoned Cuchulain.* For Patrick Pearse see note to 'Easter 1916', p. 85, ll. 24–5.

l. 26. *the Post Office.* During the Easter Rising of 1916 the insurgent Irish forces made their headquarters in the General Post Office in Dublin.

News for the Delphic Oracle. The most celebrated of the ancient Greek oracles was that of Apollo at Delphi.

l. 1. *There.* In Elysium, realm of the fortunate dead in classical mythology.

ll. 5–6. *Niamh . . . by Oisin.* A woman of the Sidhe who entices Oisin to the Land of the Young, as recounted in *The Wanderings of Oisin*, pp. 185–201.

l. 8. *Pythagoras.* See note to 'Among School Children', p. 115, l. 45.

l. 9. *Plotinus.* Greek Neoplatonic philosopher (AD 205–70).

173 l. 13. *Straddling each a dolphin's back.* In classical mythology, dolphins carry the dead to paradise.

l. 26. *Peleus on Thetis stares.* In Greek mythology, Peleus, son of Aeacus, king of Aegina, marries Thetis, a nereid (i.e. a sea-nymph).

l. 31. *Pan's.* In Greek mythology, a fertility god who is also the patron of shepherds and herdsmen. He is generally depicted as having goat's horns, ears, and legs.

Long-legged Fly

l. 5. *Caesar*. Julius Caesar (*c*.100–44 BC). Roman general and statesman whose *De bello gallico* gives an account of his conquest of Gaul, including some idea of the careful planning and tactical shrewdness which facilitated it.

174   l. 11. *the topless towers*. Allusion to *Dr Faustus* (v. i. 94–5) by Christopher Marlowe (1564–93): 'Was this the face that launched a thousand ships | And burnt the topless towers of Ilium?' Ilium is Troy. Yeats's stanza presumably refers to Helen of Troy.

ll. 22–6. *The first Adam . . . Michael Angelo*. See note to 'Under Ben Bulben', p. 167, ll. 45–7.

A Bronze Head. A plaster cast head of Maud Gonne, painted bronze, in the Municipal Gallery of Modern Art, Dublin.

l. 7. *Hysterico-passio*. Yeats's misspelling; properly *hysterica passio*. Latin: hysteria.

175   l. 13. *McTaggart*. J. M. E. McTaggart (1866–1925), who in his *The Nature of Existence* (1921) argued that 'all substances are compound'.

176   *John Kinsella's Lament for Mrs Mary Moore*. Invented characters.

ll. 21–2. *she put a skin | On everything she said*. Hiberno-English: 'to put a skin on a story' means to polish it and make it more interesting.

Man and the Echo

178   l. 1. *a cleft that's christened Alt*. A glen on the side of Knocknarea in Co. Sligo.

179   ll. 11–12. *that play of mine*. Refers to *Cathleen ni Houlihan* (pp. 211–20), first produced in 1902. Set in the context of the 1798 Rising, the play seemed inflammatory to some of those who saw it.

l. 14. *that woman's reeling brain*. Margot Ruddock (1907–51), poet and actress, who suffered from a nervous breakdown.

l. 16. *a house lay wrecked*. Coole Park. After the death of Lady Gregory in 1932, the estate was sold to the Department of Forestry, who allowed the house to fall into disrepair. (It was finally demolished in 1942.)

The Circus Animals' Desertion

180   ll. 10–16. *that sea-rider Oisin led by the nose . . . fairy bride*. Yeats's poem *The Wanderings of Oisin* (1889) is his own version of the traditional tale of how Oisin (Usheen) was enticed away to realms of Faery by the lady Niamh, one of the Sidhe. In Yeats's version those realms comprise three islands, described in the first edition as of 'the Living', 'of Victories', and 'of Forgetfulness'.

ll. 18–20. *'The Countess Cathleen' . . . intervened to save it*. In Yeats's play *The Countess Cathleen* (first produced in 1899), the countess sells her soul to rescue the people from starvation, but is saved at the end. Maud Gonne took the title role in the first performance.

l. 21. *my dear*. Maud Gonne.

181 ll. 25–6. *when the Fool and Blind Man stole the bread | Cuchulain fought the ungovernable sea*. In Yeats's play *On Baile's Strand* (first produced in 1904), Cuchulain, having unwittingly killed his only son, goes off to fight the waves in rage and pain. Meanwhile, the Fool and the Blind Man steal bread from the ovens.

Politics. Epigraph: '*In our time the destiny of man . . .*' Quoted from the German novelist, Thomas Mann (1875–1955) by Archibald MacLeish (1892–1982) in his 'Public Speech and Private Speech in Poetry', *Yale Review* (Mar. 1938).

LONG POEMS

185 *The Wanderings of Oisin*. Original subtitle: 'and *How a Demon Trapped Him*'. See Yeats's note at p. 485 for a good, brief account of the background to this narrative. The choice of this subject-matter may be seen as significant. Ever since the Scottish author James Macpherson (1736–96) had published his tales of Ossian (Anglicization of Oisin) in the 1760s, Ossianic lore had come to signify the essentially Celtic. Stories of Oisin and the Fenians were common both in Ireland and Gaelic Scotland in the Middle Ages and later. The Irish felt that they had a stronger right to the material than the Scots, since even the Scottish versions were for the most part set in Ireland. Yeats can be seen as asserting his right to offer his own version of this quintessentially Celtic matter, and at the same time as asserting Ireland's prior possession of it.

Book I

l. 1. *S. Patrick*. (*c*.385–*c*.461). Traditionally responsible for the introduction of Christianity to Ireland from Britain (Patrick derives from a Romano-British name, 'Patricius').

l. 13. *Caoilte and Conan, and Finn were there* . Caoilte and Conan were members of the warrior band called the Fenians, followers of Finn mac Cumhail: see note to 'The Hosting of the Sidhe', p. 26, l. 3.

l. 15. *Bran, Sceolan, and Lomair*. Hounds of Finn.

l. 16. *Firbolgs*. One of the traditional races of Ireland.

ll. 17–18. *the cairn-heaped grassy hill | Where passionate Maeve is stony-still*. Queen Maeve is reputed to be buried under a cairn at the summit of Knocknarea, Co. Sligo.

l. 21. *findrinny*. From the Irish for 'white bronze': a gleaming alloy of some kind, perhaps of copper and silver.

186 ll. 41–3. *Oscar's pencilled urn . . . On Gabhra's raven-covered plain*. Oscar, the son of Finn, was killed at the battle of Gabhra.

186 l. 47. *Aengus and Edain*. In the Old Irish story *The Wooing of Étaín*, Aengus, the god of love and poetry, is one of the wooers of the mortal Étaín (or Edain).

l. 48. *Niamh*. Oisin's abductor identifies herself as Niamh.

l. 53. *the birds of Aengus*. The kisses of Aengus turned into birds.

l. 63. *Danaan*. Of or pertaining to the Tuatha Dé Danaan (the people of the goddess Danu), that is, the Sidhe.

Book III

192 l. 53. *bell-branch*. A legendary branch that induces sleep when shaken. *Sennachies*. Story-tellers, from Irish *seanchaí*.

194 l. 89. *Blanid*. Tragic heroine of Irish saga who is carried away as a spoil of battle, kills her taker, and is herself killed in revenge. *Mac Nessa*. King Conchobar mac Nessa of Ulster. *Fergus*. See note to p. 13, 'Fergus and the Druid'.

l. 90. *Barach*. Treacherously entices Fergus away from Deirdre and the sons of Usna so that they may be killed.

l. 91. *Balor*. One of the leaders of the Fomorians, or the hosts of darkness.

l. 94. *Grania*. Grainne, heroine of the tale of 'Diarmuid and Grainne'. She flees with her young lover Diarmuid from the amorous attentions of the aged Finn mac Cumhail. But he pursues them all over Ireland, and Diarmuid is finally killed on Ben Bulben in Co. Sligo.

195 l. 117. *Meridian isle*. Imaginary island at the equator.

198 l. 160. *Rachlin to Bera*. Rathlin Island off Co. Antrim in the north, and Beare in Co. Cork in the south—thus, at the extremities of the island of Ireland. The reference, then, is to the whole island.

l. 163. *rath*. Ancient Irish fort or fortified homestead.

199 l. 179. *Crevroe or broad Knockfefin*. Neither has been identified for sure, though Crevroe may be *Craobh Ruadh*, 'red branch', referring to the emblem of the kings of Ulster.

l. 184. *where Maeve lies sleeping*. i.e. her grave, supposedly marked by a cairn at the summit of Knocknarea in Co. Sligo.

Baile and Aillinn

201 ARGUMENT. *Aengus*. One of the Sidhe. See note to p. 29, 'The Song of Wandering Aengus'.

l. 4. *Ulad*. Ulster. *Buan's son*. Buan was a goddess of Ulster and Baile her son.

202 l. 7. *Lugaid*. King of Munster.

l. 14. *long wars*. The subject of the epic saga *Táin Bó Cuailgne*, 'The Cattle Raid of Cooley'.

l. 18. *Emain*. Emain Macha, near Armagh, seat of the kings of Ulster in the heroic period.

l. 21. *Muirthemne*. Cuchulain's home country in Co. Louth.

203 l. 73. *the Hound of Ulad*. Cuchulain, i.e. Cú Chulain, 'the hound of Culan', and champion of Ulad (Ulster).

204 l. 117. *Ogham*. Ancient Irish alphabet.

l. 118. *Rury's seed*. Baile was of the Ulster pedigree of Rudraige (modern Irish Ruadhraighe, or Ruaraí), to which many of the heroes belonged.

205 l. 130. *Leighin*. Laighin, that is, the eastern province of Leinster.

l. 142. *Edain, Midhir's wife*. Edain, or Etain, was a queen who was enticed away to the Otherworld by Midhir, who, like Aengus, was one of the Sidhe.

206 ll. 161–3. *Gorias . . . Murias*. Legendary cities from which the Tuatha Dé Danaan were supposed to have come to Ireland.

l. 165. *Cauldron and spear and stone and sword*. The four talismans of the Tuatha, which they brought with them from the legendary cities (see previous notes).

l. 194. *that long fighting at the ford*. The fight at the ford between Cuchulain and his dearest friend Ferdiad, which ended in the death of the latter, is described in the *Táin*.

PLAYS

211 *Cathleen ni Houlihan*. Play first performed in Dublin in 1902, with Maud Gonne in the title role. 'Cathleen ni Houlihan' is one of a number of traditional female personifications of Ireland. Another one that influenced Yeats is 'Mo Róisín Dubh', translated by James Clarence Mangan (1803–49) as 'My Dark Rosaleen'. This figure influenced his handling of the symbol of the Rose (see note to p. 12, *The Rose* (1893)). Mangan himself translated a traditional poem as 'Kathaleen-Ny-Houlahan'. Such personifications gained increased popular currency in the penal era (in which this play is set) as they permitted disguised patriotic utterance. Yeats's play stirred deep nationalistic feelings.

[SD]. *Interior of a cottage close to Killala, in 1798*. Killala is a village on the western shore of Killala Bay, Co. Mayo. A French expeditionary force under General Humbert landed here in 1798 in the hope of lending aid to the rising against the British authorities of that year. The enterprise was a complete failure.

212 l. 54. *Ballina*. Town in the north-east of Co. Mayo.

213 l. 83. *Enniscrone*. Town in Co. Sligo.

215 l. 140. *Too many strangers in the house*. Much of what the Old Woman (representing Ireland) says must be interpreted as an allegory about colonization and dispossession. Thus the 'strangers' here are the English and Lowland Scots settlers in Ireland.

215 l. 146. *My four beautiful green fields*. The four ancient provinces of Ireland—Ulster, Connacht, Leinster, and Munster—were often described as four green fields in nationalist imagery.

l. 148. *Kilglass*. A village near Killala.

216 ll. 155–6. *I will go cry with the woman | For yellow-haired Donough is dead*. Loosely based on a Gaelic lyric poem from the penal era.

ll. 181–4. *a red man of the O'Donnells from the north, and a man of the O'Sullivans from the south, and there was one Brian that lost his life at Clontarf*. Red Hugh O'Donnell, from Donegal, Gaelic lord and opponent of the Tudor campaign in Ireland; Donal O'Sullivan Beare (1560–1618), who resisted the English with Spanish assistance in 1607; Brian Boru, high king of Ireland, defeated the Norsemen of Dublin at the Battle of Clontarf (1016) in which, however, he lost his own life.

218 l. 238. *Some call me the Poor Old Woman*. 'Poor Old Woman' is a translation of the Irish *Sean Bhean Bhocht* (pronounced 'Shan Van Vocht'): another traditional personification of Ireland.

l. 246. *Do not make a great keening*. 'Keening', from the Irish *caoine*, means ritual lamentation at a funeral.

l. 248. *the white-scarfed riders*. Priests, who wore white stoles.

219 l. 274. *the touch*. Infection.

221 *Deirdre*. The story of Deirdre is one of the great tragic stories of Ireland. Indeed, traditionally it was known as one of 'the three sorrows of storytelling'. The name of the original Irish tale is 'The Exile of the Sons of Usnach'. It is one of the cycle of tales about the court of Emain Macha in Ulster in the days of king Conchubar and his champion Cuchulain. The most famous of these tales is the epic saga of *Táin Bó Cúailgne*, 'The Cattle Raid of Cooley'. For a brief account of the story of Deirdre and the sons of Usnach, see note to 'The Rose of the World', p. 17, l. 5.

Epigraph: *To Mrs Patrick Campbell . . . In Memory of Robert Gregory*. Mrs Patrick Campbell (1865–1940) was a leading actress of her day. For Robert Gregory, Lady Gregory's son, see note to 'In Memory of Major Robert Gregory', p. 61.

Persons in the Play: *Fergus*. For Fergus see note to p. 13, 'Fergus and the Druid'.   *Uladh*. Ulster.

225 l. 119. *Lugaidh Redstripe*. Another hero from the Ulster cycle of tales.

l. 121. *Queen Edain*. For Edain, see note to *The Wanderings of Oisin*, p. 186, l. 47.

226 l. 154. *raddle*. Rouge.

l. 161. *Surracha*. From *Sorcha*, the Gaelic Otherworld.

230 ll. 269–70. *The hot Istain stone, | And the cold stone of Fanes*. It is not clear what legend or myth Yeats may be referring to here.

234 l. 415. *the reaping-hooks*. The farmers of the area.

l. 419. *The crib*. A wicker bird-trap.

240 ll. 593–4. *the stones | That make all sure*. The 'hot Istain stone' and 'the cold stone of Fanes', which Conchubar has used for magical purposes (see p. 224, ll. 92–4).

l. 613. *the King of Leodas*. Invented Scottish king: the exile of Deirdre and the sons of Usnach (Usna)—Ainle, Ardan, and Naoise, her lover—had been in Scotland.

l. 618. *Scottish kings*. Encountered during their stay in Scotland: see previous note.

246 *On Baile's Strand*. Baile's Strand is a beach near Dundalk (Dundealgan).

Dedication: *William Fay*. Actor and director, friend of Yeats.

Persons in the Play: *Muirthemne*. Near Dundalk.   *Ulad*. Ulster.

[SD]. *Dundealgan*. Dundalk.

247 l. 19. *Boann*. Goddess. The Boyne is named after her.

l. 20. *Fand*. Goddess, wife of Manannán mac Lir, god of the sea, who loved Cuchulain: she appears as the Woman of the Sidhe in *The Only Jealousy of Emer* (pp. 270–81).

248 ll. 80–1. *that young man*. Cuchulain's son by Aoife, the woman warrior who had taught him the art of warfare.

l. 82. *Aoife's country*. Scotland.

l. 89. *Banachas and Bonachas*. Types of goblin.

l. 92. *Fomor*. Evil gods (in the Christian era, evil fairies).

252 l. 193. *Maeve of Cruachan*. Queen Maeve of Connacht had her capital at Cruachan.

l. 194. *Sorcha*. Inhabitant of the Celtic Otherworld.

253 ll. 255–6. *hawk . . . That, as men say, begot this body of mine*. Alludes to one of the stories about Cuchulain's begetting.

254 l. 267. *Country-under-Wave*. One of the realms of the Sidhe, that is, of the Celtic gods, later called fairies.

257 l. 364. *Shape-Changers*. Irish myth and legend is full of beings who can change their shape, including the Druids themselves.

260 l. 465. *he that's in the sun*. The god Lugh.

262 l. 541. *Laegaire*. One of the warriors of Ulster.

264 l. 587. *The Ever-living*. The Sidhe: the ancient gods, later called fairies.

265 l. 633. *crubeen*. A pig's foot.

267 l. 677. *Scathach*. A warrior woman from Skye who taught warfare to Cuchulain.

l. 680. *Uathach*. Daughter of Scathach.

l. 688. *Alba*. Name for Scotland in both Irish and Scottish Gaelic.

268 ll. 712–13. *Dubthach the Chafer?* | *He'd an old grudge.* From Ulster, but joined Maeve of Connacht after Conchobar's murder of the sons of Usna (see *Deirdre*, pp. 221–45).

270 *The Only Jealousy of Emer.* First performed 1922. Emer is Cuchulain's wife. The play is based on the Old Irish tale, 'The Wasting Sickness of Cú Chulain and the Only Jealousy of Emer'. The play, like the tale, is a continuation from the story of *On Baile's Strand* (pp. 246–69). Cuchulain's sickness is occasioned by his grief at having slain his only son.

Persons in the Play: *faces made up to resemble masks . . . wearing a mask.* This play shows the influence of the Japanese Noh theatre, which involves the use of masks and musicians.   *Eithne Inguba.* Cuchulain's mistress.

ll. 7–14. *How many centuries . . . That loveliness.* In Yeats's system in *A Vision*, which was in gestation during the period when this play was composed, reincarnation is a central concept. Humans are reborn in a cycle corresponding to the phases of the moon. The initial phases are characterized by an objective temperament, associated with truth; the middle phases are subjective, and associated with beauty both of desire and of the physical body. Therefore it would take many centuries for the beauty of a woman to be produced.

272 ll. 64–75. *Towards noon . . . He fought the deathless sea.* The story which provides the basis of *On Baile's Strand* (pp. 246–69).

273 l. 89. *Manannan, Son of the Sea.* Manannán mac Lir, god of the sea.

l. 111. *Old Manannan's unbridled horses.* The waves of the sea.

275 l. 146. *Sidhe.* The old gods, the fairies.

l. 148. *Bricriu.* A sower of discord.

278 l. 225. *the fifteenth night.* The central phase of the lunar cycle, that of the full moon, which represents perfect beauty. The idea derives from the system in *A Vision*. See notes to p. 270, ll. 7–14, above, and to *The Great Wheel* on p. 548 below.

l. 242. *A woman danced and a hawk flew.* Refers to an incident in Yeats's play, *At the Hawk's Well*, in which Cuchulain as a young man encounters Fand in the form of a hawk.

Calvary

282 l. 5. *God has not died for the white heron.* Yeats associated this bird with subjectivity. The subjective temperament does not require the moral salvation offered by Christianity.

ll. 11–14. *But that . . . soon.* The heron, being subjective, is associated with moonlight. Although Christ himself is also subjective, he initiates the objective Christian era. The heron's only recourse is to immerse itself in subjectivity.

283 l. 42 [SD]. *Lazarus.* Raised from the dead by Christ. See John 11: 1–45.

285 l. 84. *Martha, and those three Marys*. Martha and Mary Magdalene, Christ's friends and sisters of Lazarus; the Blessed Virgin Mary; and her sister.

ll. 90–6. *Take but His love away . . . moon at the full*. The crowd, lacking the strength and energy of the subjective temperament, relies on those of Christ. Without him their love is fragmented and weak.

The Cat and the Moon

289 [SD]. *Saint Colman's Well*. In Galway, not far from Coole.

292 l. 97. *the holy man in the big house at Laban*. Edward Martyn (1859–1923), one of the founders, with Yeats, of the Irish National Theatre. Yeats explained that this local reference (and that in the following note) could be omitted if it were thought that the audience would not gather its significance.

l. 100. *lecher from the county of Mayo*. George Moore (1852–1933). See also previous note.

297 *The Resurrection*. Refers to Christ's resurrection.

Dedication: *To Junzo Sato*. See note to 'My Table', p. 103, l. 2.

Headnote: *the Peacock Theatre*. A small theatre in the Abbey Theatre, Dublin.

ll. 1–2. *a staring virgin . . . holy Dionysus*. Pallas Athene, the Greek virgin goddess, snatched the heart from the body of Dionysus, when he was killed by the Titans. She took the heart to Zeus, who was the father of Dionysus. He ate it and subsequently begat Dionysus once again upon the nymph Semele.

ll. 7–8. *Magnus Annus . . . God's death were but a play*. Latin, 'The Great Year'. A lengthy period of time after which the sun returns to the same place among the constellations that it had occupied at the beginning of the universe: for Plato this was a period of 36,000 years, but Yeats, though he entertained belief in some such immense cycle, also thought that this period was subdivided into lesser cycles. Particularly significant to him was the subdivision of 2,000 years: roughly the length of time from the period of the destruction of Troy to the birth of Christ, and from the birth of Christ to his own era. These two periods are seen by Yeats as two large opposing *gyres*, or vortices, the first subjective, the second objective. But each period of 2,000 years is in itself divided into two such opposing gyres. (For the concept of the *gyre*, see note to p. 422, 'The Great Wheel'.) History is structured around this kind of alternation. But both subjective and objective eras claim origin in divine intervention. Thus God's death is a play; for both Dionysus (representing paganism and subjectivity) and Christ (representing objectivity, morality, and self-denial) will always rise again.

297–8 ll. 9–12. *Another Troy . . . Drive to a flashier bauble yet*. Influenced by Virgil's *Eclogues*, iv, which refers to the recurrence of the Trojan War and the voyage of the Argonauts.

298 l. 15. *that fierce virgin and her Star*. The Virgin Mary and the Star of

Bethlehem: Christ was born in the Roman empire. The lines assert a parallel, as well as a contrast, between the two virgins—Pallas Athene and Mary—in line with the last note but one.

298 l. 35. *the Eleven*. The disciples, excluding Judas Iscariot.

ll. 44–5. *James . . . Nathanael*. Disciples.

299 l. 49. *They were thirteen then*. The twelve disciples (then including Judas) plus Jesus.

302 ll. 160–1. *the god and the Titans that murdered him*. Dionysus, who was murdered by the Titans.

l. 176. *Astrea's holy child!* Astraea, daughter of Zeus, and patroness of the Golden Age, which was regarded in ancient times as the beginning of history. This 'beginning' will, of course, return, according to Yeats.

303 ll. 201–2. *When the goddess came to Achilles in the battle*. Pallas Athene visited Achilles in the battle around Troy: the divine can intervene in the natural world.

l. 203. *Lucretius*. Titus Lucretius Carus, *c*.95–*c*.55 BC, Roman poet, author of the long poem *De rerum natura* ('On the Nature of Things'), which expounds the philosophy of Epicurus. Yeats is thinking of the anti-religious and materialist aspects of Epicurean thought.

305 ll. 267–8. *a great stone over the mouth*. The stone over the door of the sepulchre which according to the Gospels was rolled back at the resurrection.

l. 280. *another Argo . . . another Troy*. See note to pp. 297–8, ll. 9–12.

307 l. 344. *Thomas has put his hand into the wound*. Thomas, the disciple ('Doubting Thomas'). The risen Christ invites him to feel his wounds to prove that he is the same person as died on the cross (see John 20: 25–9).

307 ll. 348–9. *O Heraclitus . . . live each other's death*. Heraclitus, philosopher of Ephesus (fl. *c*.500 BC), who believed that the universe was driven by the conflict of opposing principles.

ll. 352–7. *Galilean turbulence . . . Doric discipline*. The advent of Christ, foretold by the astrology of the Three Wise Men of Babylon, ushers in a religion with roots among the common people of Galilee, the region of Palestine from which he came. In its original impulse it is an undisciplined, but also intolerant, religion, opposed to the principles which motivate the late classical world.

309 *The Words upon the Window-Pane. In Memory of Lady Gregory in whose house it was written*. Lady Augusta Gregory (1852–1932) whose home was at Coole Park, Co. Galway. Yeats wrote the play there in 1930.

l. 2. *Ballymoney*. There are a number of townlands or villages with this name in Ireland.

310 l. 22. *Myers' Human Personality*. Book (2 vols., 1903) by F. W. H. Myers (1843–1901).

l. 23. *a wild book by Conan Doyle*. Sir Arthur Conan Doyle (1859–1930) was a believer in spiritualism and wrote on the subject.

l. 25. *Lord Dunraven*. This peerage is not fictional.

l. 26. *David Home*. Probably a mistake for Daniel D. Home (1833–86), a Scottish spiritualist.

l. 44. *Emanuel Swedenborg*. (1688–1772), a celebrated Swedish scientist who claimed that his spiritual eyes were opened at the age of 57. He claimed to have explored heaven and hell in vision, to have conversed with spirits, and to have witnessed the Last Judgement. His works influenced those of William Blake.

l. 49. *Harold's Cross*. A South Dublin suburb where the Yeatses lived from 1885 to 1887.

311 l. 54. *Grattan*. See note to 'The Tower', p. 99, l. 132.

l. 55. *Curran*. John Philpot Curran (1750–1817), Irish barrister and MP, an opponent of the Union with Great Britain.

l. 57. *Jonathan Swift*. (1677–1745), satirist and dean of St Patrick's cathedral, Dublin.

l. 58. *Stella . . . Journal to Stella*. Swift's name for Hester Johnson (1687–1728) to whom he wrote a number of poems, and also the letters which comprise this *Journal*.

l. 60. *Vanessa*. Swift's name for Esther (or Hester) Vanhomrigh (1690–1723), who fell in love with him when they met in London in 1708. The relationship was tense and unhappy.

ll. 62–3. *lines . . . upon the window-pane*. The poem is 'Stella to Dr Swift on his birth-day November 30, 1721'.

l. 81. *a poem Stella wrote for Swift's fifty-fourth birthday*. See note to ll. 62–3 above.

l. 85. *Donne*. John Donne (1572–1631), dean of St Paul's, and one of the finest exponents of the 'metaphysical' style in poetry.

l. 85. *Crashaw*. Richard Crashaw (?1612–49), Roman Catholic author of devotional poems in an intense, highly mannered, 'metaphysical' style.

311–12 ll. 86–9. '*You taught . . . fading eyes.*' Lines from the poem by 'Stella' referred above.

l. 104. *Bolingbroke, Harley, Ormonde*. Henry St John Bolingbroke (1678–1751), first Viscount; Robert Harley (1661–1724), first earl of Oxford; James Butler (1665–1746), second duke of Ormonde, from an ancient Anglo-Irish family. All were ministers, and all fell into disfavour.

l. 108. *Brutus and Cato*. Marcus Julius Brutus (85–42 BC), one of the leaders of the conspiracy against Julius Caesar, which he was prompted to join through fear that Caesar's dominance would erode republican liberties and end in restoration of the monarchy. Cato is either 'Cato the Elder'

(234–149 BC), a stern proponent of traditional Roman duty and austerity, or Marcus Porcius Cato Uticensis (95–46 BC), a stoic.

311–12 l. 110. *Rousseau*. Jean-Jacques Rousseau (1712–78), philosopher and author whose *Du contrat social* ('The Social Contract', 1762) was influential in preparing the way for the French Revolution.

l. 115. *saeva indignatio*. Latin: 'fierce' or 'savage indignation'. Quotation from Swift's epitaph in St Patrick's cathedral, Dublin. See Yeats's own version, 'Swift's Epitaph', on p. 129.

313 l. 159. *Some spirits are earth-bound*. The life of spirits after death is dealt with in Book III of *A Vision*, 'The Soul in Judgment'. For the particular case referred to here, see *A Vision* (1937), 224.

314 l. 168. *Sometimes a spirit relives*. See previous note and *A Vision* (1937), 226.

l. 169. *Swedenborg*. See note to p. 310, l. 44.

315 l. 199. *I feel like Job—you know the quotation*. Job 4: 15, 'Then a spirit passed before my face; the hair of my flesh stood up.'

l. 223 [SD]. *Hymn 564*. By John Keble (1792–1866).

317 l. 274 . *the Lord Treasurer*. Robert Harley, earl of Oxford (1661–1724).

l. 275. *Plutarch*. (*c.* AD 46–120) Greek biographer.

l. 280. *Hester Vanhomrigh*. See note to 'Vanessa', p. 311, l. 60.

l. 281. *Cato or Brutus*. See note to p. 312, l. 108.

318 l. 302. *constant attacks of dizziness*. Swift suffered from Ménière's disease, which affects the labyrinth of the middle ear, causing giddiness, nausea, tinnitus, and deafness.

l. 304. *Dr Arbuthnot*. John Arbuthnot (1667–1735), royal physician and friend of Swift and Pope.

l. 306. *a line of Dryden's*. John Dryden (1631–1700), a poet much admired in Swift's circle, wrote the line quoted in his mock-heroic satire, *Absalom and Achitophel* (1681), at i. 163.

319 l. 348. *'If some poor wandering child'*. Another verse of Hymn 564, *Dublin Church Hymnal*, first quoted on p. 315.

320 ll. 371–2. *'with no adornment but a face—'*. This line comes just before the couplet quoted next, in 'Stella to Dr Swift on his birth-day November 30, 1721'.

l. 375. *Chrysostom*. St John Chrysostom (*c.* AD 345–407), one of the Fathers of the Church.

l. 383. *'You taught how I might youth prolong.'* Another section of the poem 'Stella to Dr Swift'.

323 ll. 472–3. *Perish the day on which I was born!* Compare Job 3: 3, 'Let the day perish wherein I was born.'

324 *The Death of Cuchulain*. Finished in Dec. 1938, with some revisions in Jan. 1939. First performed Abbey Theatre, Dublin, 2 Dec. 1945. The dramatis

personae are Cuchulain, the warrior champion of Ulster; Emer his wife; Eithne Inguba, his mistress; Aoife, a female warrior by whom Cuchulain had his only son (see notes to *On Baile's Strand*, pp. 246 ff.); The Morrigu (sometimes called The Morrigan), a goddess embodying all things horrific, who sometimes takes the shape of a crow.

l. 2. *the last of a series*. The series of Cuchulain plays.

l. 7. *Talma*. François Joseph Talma (1763–1826), a French actor famous in his day.

ll. 14–15. *first performance of Milton's Comus*. A masque, performed for a small audience at Ludlow Castle, Shropshire, on 29 Sept. 1634.

old epics. The Irish epics, especially those from which Yeats derives the tales of Cuchulain, chiefly *The Táin*.

325 l. 37. *Degas*. Hilaire Germaine Edgar Degas (1834–1917). The painting may be the well-known *Ballet Girls*, which is in the National Gallery, Dublin.

l. 40. *Rameses the Great*. Pharaoh of Egypt (1311–1245 BC).

l. 46. *Emain Macha*. Capital, near Armagh, of the Red Branch kings of Ulster, who include Conchubar, Cuchulain's lord.

l. 47. *Muirthemne*. Cuchulain's home country in Co. Louth.

326 l. 62. *Conall Caernach*. An Ulster warrior.

327 l. 93. *When I went mad at my son's death*. As recounted towards the end of *On Baile's Strand* (pp. 246–69).

ll. 94–5. *it was my wife | That brought me back*. See *The Only Jealousy of Emer*, pp. 270–81, in which Emer renounces the love of Cuchulain in order to save him from Fand, the Woman of the Sidhe, who wishes to entice him away.

328 ll. 148–9. *At the Hawk's Well . . . Baile's Strand*. Yeats's play, *At the Hawk's Well* (first performed 1916, published 1917) tells the story of the encounter of Cuchulain and Aoife, *On Baile's Strand* of his killing his only son, conceived as a result of that encounter, unwittingly.

l. 153. *the grey of Macha*. A chariot horse with supernatural powers.

332 l. 239. *Usna's boys*. Naoise, who ran away to Scotland with Deirdre, and his brothers Ardan and Ainle: see Yeats's play, *Deirdre*, pp. 221–45.

l. 244. *No grip upon their thighs*. They are dead spirits.

ll. 245–6. *I meet those long pale faces | Hear their great horses*. The Sidhe, who are also spirits.

l. 255. *the Post Office*. The General Post Office in Dublin was the headquarters of the insurgents of Easter 1916.

l. 256. *Pearse and Connolly*. See notes to 'Easter 1916', p. 85, ll. 24–5, p. 87, l. 76.

333 l. 266. *Oliver Sheppard*. Irish sculptor (RHA) who executed a sculpture of the *Death of Cuchulain* placed in the Post Office as a memorial to the 1916 Rising.

334 *Purgatory*. First performance, 10 Aug. 1938, Abbey Theatre, Dublin.

335 l. 50. *the Curragh*. Area of Co. Kildare associated with the breeding and training of racehorses.

336 l. 64. *Aughrim and the Boyne*. The Battle of Aughrim, July 1691, and the Battle of the Boyne, July 1690, in which Irish forces were defeated by Williamite forces.

l. 94. *At the Puck Fair*. An annual fair, held 9–11 Aug. at Killorglin, Co. Kerry.

338 l. 154. *Tertullian*. Quintus Septimus Florens Tertullian (*c.* AD 160–220). F. A. C. Wilson suggests that Yeats is thinking of Tertullian's view that the soul could feel pleasure and remorse after death (*Yeats and Tradition* (London, 1958), 265 n. 70).

PROSE

343 *The First Book of Urizen*. A book by William Blake, the poet, visionary, engraver, and painter (1757–1827) printed by his own method of relief engraving with added colour. It is to some extent modelled on Genesis and John 1, and describes the separation from the other 'Eternals' of an invented being called Urizen, who, in his pride, thinks of himself as God, and creates a universe of limits and measure. His name is partly derived from a Greek verb, meaning 'to set bounds, limits', from which we also get the word 'horizon'. Urizen has negative connotations in Blake's invented mythology. This commentary is chiefly a paraphrase of Blake's words, combined with an explanation of some elements of his system.

moods. An important concept in Yeats's early work. See his poem, 'The Moods' (p. 27) and his essay of the same title (pp. 378–9).

the region of selfishness, of personality, of experience, the North . . . brotherhood. The reference to the points of the compass is reminiscent of *A Vision*, except that the associations are reversed. In *A Vision* the North is associated with complete objectivity, with impersonality, with 'the bosom of God', and the South with subjectivity. An interesting point to note, however, is that the tyrant god of Blake's mythology is associated by Yeats and Ellis with qualities Yeats prizes (subjectivity and personality) or comes to prize (measure).

'*Milton*'. The long poem, *Milton* (*c.*1804–*c.*1815), by William Blake.

344 *I believe in . . . magic*. Yeats joined the Order of the Golden Dawn on 7 Mar. 1890. This order was dedicated to the theory and practice of ritual magic.

346 *the Tree of Life*. In the medieval Jewish mystical writings known as the cabbala, the central symbol is the Tree of Life, which in its totality represents both God and the created universe.

The Book of Concealed Mystery. A book of cabbalistic writings (see above). For Mathers, in Yeats's footnote, see note to 'All Souls' Night', p. 119, on 'MacGregor', l. 61.

347   *Brigit, the goddess.* Brigit was a goddess of the pagan Celts, and thus of the pagan Irish.

Carmina Gadelica. Latin title (meaning 'Gaelic Songs') of a collection of Highland songs published in 1900 by Alexander Carmichael (1832–1912).

Finn mac Cool. i.e. Finn (modern Irish 'Fionn') mac Cumhail, legendary leader of the medieval warrior band known as the Fianna, or Fenians.

Paracelsus. Poetic drama of 1835 by Robert Browning.

prophetic books of William Blake. William Blake referred to some of his long poems as 'prophecies'.

Los's Hall. Los is a character in Blake's invented mythology. He represents the poet and imagination.

348   *the Hammer of Thor.* Thor was one of the gods of the pagan Germanic nations, including the Anglo-Saxons. He wields thunder and lightning and the sound of his hammer is the clap of the thunderbolt. His hammer is drawn in the shape of two triangular blades, with their apexes pointing inwards and attached to opposite sides of the haft.

The Society for Psychical Research. Body which sought to encourage the scientific study of psychic phenomena. Yeats was an associate member between 1913 and 1928.

349   *great memory.* The *Anima Mundi*, or 'Soul of the World': a repository of archetypal images constituting the memory of humanity. See note to p. 410, below, 'Anima Mundi'.

350   *Aran Islands.* Islands off the coast of Galway which were still, at the time of writing, a redoubt of traditional Gaelic lore and culture.

Shelley. Percy Bysshe Shelley (1792–1822), author, among other things, of 'Prince Athanase: A Fragment' (1817), and *Laon and Cythna; or, The Revolution of the Golden City: A Vision of the Nineteenth Century* (1817, but dated 1818), which was later slightly revised and published as *The Revolt of Islam* (1818). These are the works to which Yeats refers. Prince Athanase is a young idealistic solitary, who pursues ardent enquiries into the secrets of nature and existence.

Cythna's lover. Cythna is the heroine of *Laon and Cythna*, Laon her lover. See above.

351   *Lionel.* Lover of Helen in Shelley's 'Rosalind and Helen', the writing of which is contemporaneous with that of *Laon and Cythna*.

Prince Athanase. See above.

Maeterlinck. Maurice Maeterlinck (1862–1949), Belgian symbolist dramatist and poet.

352   *Shelley . . . Count Tolstoy.* For Shelley, see note to p. 350. The others are William Wordsworth (1770–1850), poet, author (among other things) of *The Prelude* (1850); Johann Wolfgang von Goethe (1749–1832), author of *Faust* (Part I, 1808; Part II, completed 1832); Honoré de Balzac (1799–1850), a great favourite of Yeats's, author of the many novels which make up the

Comédie humaine, including *Eugénie Grandet* (1833) and *Le Père Goriot* (1834); Gustave Flaubert (1821–80), author of *Madame Bovary* (1856–7); and Count Leo Tolstoy (1828–1910), author of *War and Peace* (1863–9).

352 *Mr Whistler's pictures*. James McNeill Whistler (1834–1903), 'aesthetic' painter.

Browning said in his one prose essay. Robert Browning (1812–89), the poet. The essay is the 'Introductory Essay [Essay on Shelley]' (1852).

William Blake. See note to *The First Book of Urizen*, p. 343.

Jacob Boehme. (1575–1624), German mystical writer who influenced Blake.

353 *Vala*. Blake's long poem, *Vala* or *The Four Zoas* (*c.*1797–*c.*1803). Either title may be used, and it is not clear which of them Blake intended to take precedence. The poem was never completed nor published in his lifetime.

Tennyson. Alfred Tennyson (1809–92), author of *In Memoriam* (1850) and *Idylls of the King* (1859). Appointed Poet Laureate, 1850; raised to the peerage, 1883.

Wordsworth. See notes to p. 352 above.

Songs of Innocence. (1789). A Series of lyric poems about innocence.

'The Ideas of Good and Evil'. 'Ideas of Good & Evil' is the title Blake gives in his Notebook to a series of sketches of emblems with verse mottoes.

'Prophetic Works'. By Blake. See notes to p. 343.

Axël of the symbolist Villiers de l'Isle-Adam. P. H. Villiers de l'Isle-Adam (1840–89), a French poet, was author of the visionary drama *Axël* (1890), a work of decadent tendency, which is influenced by the occult.

354 *Dante's*. Dante Alighieri (1265–1321), Italian poet, author of *The Divine Comedy*.

Wagner . . . Norse mythology. Richard Wagner (1813–83), German composer and poet, whose *Ring* cycle of operas (completed 1876) is based on the Germanic mythology held in common by the Norse and the pagan Germans, but for which the chief extant sources are Norse.

Professor Rhys. Professor Sir John Rhys (1840–1915), principal of Jesus College, Oxford, whose *Lectures on the Origin and Growth of Religion as Illustrated by Celtic Heathendom* (1888) was read by Yeats.

Enitharmon . . . Danu. Enitharmon is a female character in Blake's invented mythology; Freia (Freyja) is a female goddess in the Germanic mythology, Gwydeon (Gwydion) in the Welsh, and Danu, or Dana, in the Irish.

Vala. See note to p. 353.

Johnson's Dictionary. Samuel Johnson's *A Dictionary of the English Language* (1755).

355 *the Emerald Tablet of Hermes*. A medieval Latin work on alchemy attributed to Hermes Trismegistus, a mythical figure who was also supposed to have written the diverse collection of writings known as the *Hermetica*, most of which come from Egypt in the first to third centuries AD.

The Faerie Queene and The Pilgrim's Progress. Edmund Spenser (1552?–1599) wrote *The Faerie Queene* (1590–6) and John Bunyan (1628–88) *The Pilgrim's Progress* (1678). Both are allegorical works.

Vision of Blood-thirstiness. William Blake's engraving 'The Ghost of a Flea'.

Rossetti's . . . Virgin. Dante Gabriel Rossetti (1828–82), the poet and painter, whose paintings these two are.

356 *Michelangelo's 'Moses'.* Moses, a sculpture by Michelangelo Buonarotti (1475–1564).

Tintoretto's 'Origin of the Milky Way'. Tintoretto (Jacopo Robusti, 1518–94), Italian Mannerist painter.

Wagner's dramas . . . Giotto. For Wagner see notes to p. 354 above; John Keats (1795–1821), the poet, is celebrated for his odes; for Blake see notes to p. 343 above; for Calvert see notes to 'Under Ben Bulben', p. 168, l. 64; for Rossetti see note to p. 355; for Villiers de l'Isle-Adam see note to p. 353; Beardsley is Aubrey Beardsley (1872–98), decadent illustrator and author; Ricketts is Charles de Sousy Ricketts (1866–1931), book designer; Shannon is Charles Hazlewood Shannon RA (1863–1937), book designer and lithographer; for Whistler see notes to p. 352; for Maeterlinck see notes to p. 351; Verlaine is Paul Verlaine (1844–96), French symbolist poet; Giotto di Bondone (1266–1337), Italian painter and fresco designer.

Fra Angelico. (1387–1455), Florentine painter.

357 *Blake.* See notes to p. 343.

Vittoria Colonna. (1490–1547), an Italian poetess to whom Michelangelo addressed some verses.

William Blake. The quotations are from his ['A Vision of the Last Judgment'].

358 *Symons.* Arthur Symons (1865–1945), 'Decadent' poet and critic, and friend of Yeats. His *The Symbolist Movement in Literature* was published in 1899.

359 *Wagner.* See notes to p. 354.

Giovanni Bardi. (1534–1612), count of Vernio, Florentine patron of music and the arts.

Pleiade. Group of seven sixteenth-century French poets, including Pierre de Ronsard (1524–85) and Joachim du Bellay (1522–60), who sought to improve the standards of French verse.

Goethe. See notes to p. 352.

360 *The white moon . . . with me, O!* What Burns really wrote, in 'Open the Door to Me, O', was 'The wan moon sets behind the white wave, | And Time is setting with me, O'.

The gay fishes . . . the dew. From Blake's *Europe: A Prophecy* (1794), Plate 14, l. 3: 'Like the gay fishes on the wave, when the cold moon drinks the dew.'

360 *Brightness falls . . . Helen's eye.* Thomas Nashe (1567–1601), from his 'In
Plague Time: Adieu, farewell earth's bliss . . .', from *Summer's Last Will and
Testament* (1600).

Timon hath made . . . surge shall cover. Shakespeare, *Timon of Athens*,
v. iv. 220–3.

361 *Arthur O'Shaughnessy.* (1844–81). Yeats is referring to lines from his
famous 'Ode', 'We are the music-makers . . .'.

362 *Nine Hierarchies.* The hierarchies of angels: in the system of Dionysius the
Areopagite, there were three divisions of angels, each comprising three
orders.

'*the eye altering alters all.*' From Blake's poem, 'The Mental Traveller'
(*c.*1803).

Our towns are copied fragments . . . heart. The last three lines of a poem, 'The
Heart', consisting of two sonnets, by Francis Thompson (1859–1907).

363 *Demeter.* Greek goddess of corn and the harvest.

364 *Gérard de Nerval.* (1808–55), French poet.

Maeterlinck . . . Villiers de l'Isle Adam in Axël. For the former, see notes to
p. 351, for the latter, notes to p. 353.

365 *Songs of Innocence and Experience.* (1794), series of poems by William Blake.

Rossetti's. Dante Gabriel Rossetti (1828–82), poet and painter.

Rodin's. Auguste Rodin (1840–1917), the French sculptor.

Ibsen. Henrik Ibsen (1828–1906), the Norwegian dramatist, the strongest
note in whose work is that of realism.

366 *Irish Literary Theatre.* Name given in 1898 to the organization, promoted
by Yeats, Lady Gregory, and Edward Martyn, for the encouragement and
performance of Irish drama. This initiative led up to the founding of the
Abbey Theatre in 1904.

Mr Binyon. Laurence Binyon (1869–1943), poet.

Sophocles. (*c.*496–406 BC), Greek tragic dramatist.

Calderon. Pedro Calderón de la Barca (1600–81), Spanish dramatist.

Tir nan Oge. Irish, *Tír na nÓg*, 'Land of the Young'. The paradisal Irish
Otherworld, beyond the western sea, home of the immortal Sidhe.

Mr Bridges' Return of Ulysses. Robert Bridges (1844–1930), Poet Laureate.

Aran Islands. See notes to p. 350.

Gaelic League. Founded in 1893 for the promotion of Irish language and
culture by Douglas Hyde (see notes to 'At the Abbey Theatre', p. 44, l. 1).

Blake has said . . . Golden Age. The reference is to Blake's ['A Vision of the
Last Judgment'].

367 *William Morris.* (1834–96), poet, painter, craftsman, designer, and writer of
romances.

Mr Swinburne's Locrine. Verse drama by Algernon Charles Swinburne (1837–1909), the poet, first performed in 1899.

Colonus. See note to 'Colonus' Praise', p. 115.

Duncan. A mistake for Banquo, who, however, is conversing with Duncan when he utters the lines referred to (*Macbeth* I. vi. 3–10).

368 *Madox Brown.* Ford Madox Brown (1821–93), one of the first Pre-Raphaelite painters (for whom see note to p. 378 below).

n. 1. *Charles Ricketts.* (1866–1931), book designer.

n. 2. *J. F. Taylor.* John F. Taylor (1850–1902), barrister, journalist, and orator.

Dionysius, the Areopagite. An Athenian nobleman converted to Christianity in the first century AD. Mystical writings of the fifth century were long incorrectly attributed to him (the works of 'pseudo-Dionysius').

369 *Euripides.* (*c.*480–406 BC), the Athenian tragic dramatist.

Blake . . . 'every time . . . artery.' From William Blake's *Milton*, Book I, plates 28–9.

The Celtic Element in Literature

Ernest Renan . . . The Poetry of the Celtic Races. Renan (1823–92) was author of the essay 'La Poésie des races celtiques' (1859), translated by William S. Hutchison in 1896.

370 *Matthew Arnold, in The Study of Celtic Literature.* Matthew Arnold (1822–88) delivered lectures on 'The Study of Celtic Literature' in Oxford in 1865 and 1866. They were published in 1867.

Faust or Werther. Goethe's *Faust* (see notes to p. 352); and *Die Leiden des jungen Werthers* ('The Sorrows of Young Werther', 1774).

Kalevala. Finnish national epic compiled from a large number of traditional folk-songs by Elias Lönnrot (1802–84), first published in 1835, enlarged in 1849.

371 *Mabinogion.* Collection of medieval Welsh romances.

'Flower Aspect.' Gwydion and Math made her. In the story 'Math, Son of Mathonwy', from the *Mabinogion* (see above), Math, lord of Gwynedd, and Gwydion, his cunning counsellor, conjure a woman called Blodeuwedd ('Flower-face') from the flowers of oak, broom, and meadowsweet.

the burning Tree. From the *Mabinogion* tale of 'Gereint, Son of Erbin'. Compare 'Vacillation: II', p. 132, l. 11.

Keats's 'magic casements . . . forlorn.' From Keats's 'Ode to a Nightingale'.

'moving waters . . . human shore.' From Keats's sonnet, 'Bright star'— 'shores' in the original.

Shakespeare's . . . Carthage'. The references are all to *The Merchant of Venice*, V. i.

372 *Olwen.* Heroine of the love story 'Culhwch and Olwen' from the *Mabinogion* (see above).

Meet we . . . margent of the sea. From *A Midsummer Night's Dream*, II. i. 83–5. 'Met we . . .', etc.

What little town. From the 'Ode to a Grecian Urn'.

I know a bank. A Midsummer Night's Dream, II. i. 249–50.

Muscosi fontes . . . anethi. Virgil, *Eclogues*, vii. 45 and ii. 47.

373 *Song of Roland.* i.e. *Le Chanson de Roland*, eleventh-century epic poem in Old French concerning the deeds of Roland, one of Charlemagne's champions, against the Saracens.

Oisin. See note to p. 185, *The Wanderings of Oisin*.

The Songs of Connacht. i.e. Douglas Hyde's collection, *The Love Songs of Connacht* (1893). For Hyde see note to 'At the Abbey Theatre', p. 44, l. 1.

374 *O'Sullivan Bere.* Gaelic lord in Munster in the late sixteenth and early seventeenth centuries.

'A.E.' . . . of thee.' A.E. is the pen-name of George William Russell (1867–1935), author of the poem 'Illusion', the last two lines of which are 'A vast desire awakes and grows | Unto forgetfulness of thee.'

n. 1. *William Sharp.* (1855–1905), prolific author, sometimes under the pseudonym 'Fiona Macleod', in which guise he wrote 'Celtic' poems and tales.

375 *Llywarch Hen.* Welsh poet of the sixth to seventh centuries. The copy-text and all earlier printings have 'Leyrach', but this must be an uncorrected printer's error, since the translation of the poem has otherwise been accurately transcribed from Matthew Arnold.

376 *Samuel Palmer.* English artist (1805–81) and associate of Blake.

377 *visions of Purgatory . . . Lough Derg.* St Patrick's Purgatory, an island in Lough Derg; place of penitential pigrimage from the early Middle Ages onwards.

divine comedy. The Divine Comedy of Dante Alighieri (1265–1321).

Holy Grail, once it seems the cauldron. Referring to the theory that the legend of the Holy Grail is derived from that of a cauldron appearing in ancient Celtic myths. The Cauldron of Plenty, belonging in Irish mythology to the Dagda (the Good God), is taken to be a survival from such myths.

Mab . . . Puck. Queen Mab, identified as queen of the fairies in *Romeo and Juliet*, I. iv. 53 ff. Puck, a sprite in *A Midsummer Night's Dream*.

Sir Walter Scott. (1771–1832), the historical novelist, many of whose most important works concern the history of Scotland.

Richard Wagner and of William Morris. For former, see note to p. 354; for latter, note to p. 367.

Deirdre. See note to p. 221.

Sons of Tuireann. An ancient Irish quest tale.

Cuchulain . . . in the end. Cuchulain falls in love with Fand, a woman of the *Sidhe*, but in the end returns to Emer, his wife. This is the story which forms the basis of Yeats's play, *The Only Jealousy of Emer*, pp. 270–81.

Grainne with Diarmuid. The chief characters in the story of Diarmuid and Grainne, a love story from the Fenian cycle (the tales of Finn mac Cumhail and his warrior band).

Oisin. See Yeats's note at p. 485.

378 *Pre-Raphaelites*. Artistic movement, at first centred on the Pre-Raphaelite Brotherhood (1848–53), which prized the clarity and distinctness of Italian painting before Raphael. Among those associated with the movement were Rossetti, William Holman Hunt (1827–1910), and John Everett Millais (1829–96).

Villiers de l'Isle-Adam. See note to p. 353.

Mallarmé. Stéphane Mallarmé (1842–98), French symbolist poet.

Maeterlinck. See note to p. 351.

Ibsen. See note to p. 365.

D'Annunzio. Gabriele D'Annunzio (1863–1938), Italian poet, dramatist, and novelist.

Verhaeren. Émile Verhaeren (1855–1916).

Cuchulain of Muirthemne. Tales of Cuchulain retold by Lady Gregory and published in 1902.

Morte d'Arthur. The story of King Arthur, as told by Sir Thomas Malory (d. 1471).

379 *A General Introduction for my Work*. Completed in 1937 for a planned Definitive Edition of Yeats's works which was to have been published by Scribner of New York, but never appeared. For reasons of copyright I am relying on the text still widely available in *Essays and Introductions* (1961 and later printings), but it is conceivable that a more reliable text would emerge from a scrutiny of the Scribner Archive.

Tiresias. Theban seer who appears in Homer's *Odyssey* and in Sophocles' *King Oedipus*. He had experienced life both as a woman and as a man, and Hera (the Greek equivalent of Juno, queen of the gods) blinded him when, contrary to her claim, he asserted that women had more pleasure in sex than did men. In compensation, Zeus, king of the gods, gave him the gifts of long life and of prophecy.

Rosalind. Heroine of Shakespeare's comedy, *As You Like It*.

Cleopatra. (*c.*70–30 BC), queen of Egypt and heroine of Shakespeare's *Antony and Cleopatra*.

379 *The Dark Lady*. Name given to the presumed addressee or subject of some of Shakespeare's more melancholy and bitter sonnets.

Prashna Upanishad . . . Chandogya Upanishad. The Upanishads are a series of Indian spiritual treatises, written in Sanskrit between 800 and 400 BC. From 1935 to 1936 Yeats worked on translations of these with Shri Purohit Swami, published as *The Ten Principal Upanishads* (London, 1937).

Fenian leader John O'Leary. See note to 'September 1913', p. 51, l. 8.

380 *The Faerie Queene and The Sad Shepherd*. The former a long allegorical poem by Edmund Spenser (1552?–1599), the latter a late, unfinished play by Ben Jonson.

Shelley's Prometheus Unbound. Verse drama composed 1818–19, published 1820.

Thomas Davis. (1814–45), leader of Young Ireland, poet, and co-editor of the nationalist journal, *The Nation*.

The Nation. See above.

Standish O'Grady. Standish James O'Grady (1846–1928), writer on Irish history and mythology, whose works include the two-volume *History of Ireland* (1878, 1880). Not to be confused with his cousin Standish Hayes O'Grady (see below).

O'Curry. Eugene O'Curry (1796–1862), antiquarian and expert on the texts contained in old Irish manuscripts.

Mitchel. John Mitchel (1815–75), Irish nationalist.

O'Donovan. John O'Donovan (1806–66), Irish scholar from Co. Waterford.

381 *Slieve-na-mon*. Mountain in Co. Tipperary which appears in many old Irish romances.

Hayes O'Grady. Standish Hayes O'Grady (1832–1915), editor of *Silva Gadelica* (1892), a collection of tales from old Irish manuscripts, with notes and translation.

Lady Gregory . . . Cuchulain of Muirthemne. *Gods and Fighting Men* (1904) and *Cuchulain of Muirthemne* (1902) were Lady Gregory's retelling of the tales of Finn mac Cumhail and Cuchulain respectively.

Lady Charlotte Guest's Mabinogion. Lady Charlotte Guest's translation of the *Mabinogion*, a collection of medieval Welsh romances, appeared in 1838.

Carlyle. Thomas Carlyle (1795–1881), Victorian thinker and social and cultural critic.

Rosses Point. Coastal village in Co. Sligo not far from Drumcliff.

Queen Maeve . . . the bay. Legendary queen of Connacht, whose grave is reputed to be marked by a cairn at the summit of Knocknarea, Co. Sligo.

Visions and Beliefs. Lady Gregory's collection of folklore and tales, *Visions and Beliefs in the West of Ireland* (1920).

382 *Professor Burkitt.* Francis Crawford Burkitt (1864–1935), biblical scholar, Professor of Divinity and fellow of Trinity College in the University of Cambridge.

Dionysus. Greek fertility god.

The Golden Bough. Great anthropological work by Sir James Frazer (1854–1941).

Human Personality. F. W. H. Myers (1843–1901), *Human Personality and its Survival of Bodily Death*, 2 vols. (1903).

Neoplatonism. Philosophical followers of Plato and developers of his thought in the Roman period.

'tetragrammaton agla'. Magical invocation.

Doneraile. Town in Co. Cork, north of Mallow.

Synge of The Well of the Saints. The Well of the Saints (first produced and published 1905) by John Millington Synge (1871–1909).

James Stephens. (1824–1901), founder of the Irish Republican Brotherhood.

George Russell. Poet (1867–1935) who wrote under the pen-name of AE.

Pearse. See note to 'Easter 1916', p. 85, ll. 24–5.

Red Branch. Name for the dynasty of kings of Ulster to which Conchobar, Cuchulain's legendary lord, belonged.

Fall, Hercules . . . this world. From George Chapman, Σκια νυκτος. *The Shadow of Night: Cantaining* [sic] *Two Poeticall Hymnes* (1594), 'Hymnus in Noctem', ll. 255 6.

383 *Jesse.* Father of King David, thus 'the origin of the true lineage'.

MacDonagh. See note to 'Easter 1916', p. 85, l. 26.

Arnold Toynbee . . . The Study of History. Arnold Toynbee (1889–1975), historian, author of *A Study of History*, 12 vols. (1934–61).

Lord Edward. Lord Edward FitzGerald (1763–98), son of the duke of Leinster, and one of the leaders of the 1798 uprising.

384 *Visions and Beliefs.* See notes to p. 381, above.

Swedenborg. Emanuel Swedenborg (1688–1772), Swedish scientist and visionary.

Creed of St Patrick. Prayer attributed to St Patrick which suggests the union of man with all creation.

Unity of Being . . . human body. It is clear from *A Vision* (1925 version, p. 18), that Yeats is thinking of a passage in the unfinished *Convito* or *Convivio* of Dante Alighieri (1265–1321), author of *The Divine Comedy*.

Lecky . . . Eighteenth Century. William E. H. Lecky (1838–1903), historian, was the author of *Ireland in the Eighteenth Century* (1892).

385 *Swift . . . his tomb.* For Swift see notes to 'Blood and the Moon', p. 124, l. 18,

and for his epitaph see Yeats's version on p. 129. *Gulliver's Travels* was published anonymously in 1726.

385 *famous sonnet . . . That will forget thee.* Wordsworth's sonnet, composed 1802, 'To Toussaint L'Ouverture', i.e. François Dominique Toussaint L'Ouverture (1743–1803), son of a Haitian slave, who became governor in 1801, but led a revolt against Napoleon's decision to reintroduce slavery, and died in prison. The lines quoted are from Wordsworth's sonnet.

Emmet. Robert Emmet (1778–1803), hanged after leading a small-scale insurrection in Dublin.

386 *The Stream's Secret, Dolores.* Poems by Rossetti and Swinburne respectively.

Burns . . . Thomson and Cowper. The poets Robert Burns (1759–96); James Thomson (1700–48), author of *The Seasons*; and William Cowper (1731–1800), author of *The Task* (1785).

Ezra Pound, Turner, Lawrence. Ezra Pound (1885–1972), American poet and friend of Yeats; W. J. Turner (1889–1946), Australian poet, another friend of Yeats; D. H. Lawrence (1885–1930), English poet and novelist.

Sir Thomas Browne. (1605–82), author of *Religio Medici* (1642) and *Hydrotaphia: Urne Buriall* (1658).

George Moore. (1852–1933), Anglo-Irish novelist and friend of Yeats.

387 *Milton's . . . Palmer drew.* See notes to 'The Phases of the Moon', p. 75, ll. 15–17.

Countess Cathleen. Yeats's play, *The Countess Cathleen*, was his first stage-play. He completed a first version of it in 1892. A revised version was the basis for the first performance in 1899 at The Antient Concert Rooms, Dublin. It is a verse drama composed in iambic pentameters. For its plot, see notes to 'The Circus Animals' Desertion', p. 180, ll. 18–20.

The Green Helmet. Play about a challenge to Cuchulain. There had been a prose version, first performed in 1908 at the Abbey Theatre. The verse version, to which Yeats refers, was first performed in 1910 at the Abbey.

Paul Fort's ballad. Paul Fort (1872–1960) was a French poet, balladeer, and historian of poetry and ballads.

Robert Bridges. (1844–1930), Poet Laureate.

388 *Mallarmé.* Stéphane Mallarmé (1842–98), French symbolist poet.

389 *O'Connell Bridge.* Main bridge over the Liffey in Dublin.

On the Boiler. Intended to be the first of a series of occasional publications, this was written in 1938. The title refers to an eccentric old ship's carpenter he had heard tell of in Sligo who used to utter denunciations from an old boiler where he was seated on the quays. This explanation is contained in a preliminary section called 'The Name', which also includes the poem, 'Why should not old men be mad?' (see pp. 164–5). Other poems in the volume are 'Crazy Jane on the Mountain' (pp. 165–6) and 'The Statesman's Holiday'. The essays are 'Preliminaries', 'To-morrow's Revolution' (in this selection), 'Private Thoughts' (also selected), and 'Ireland after the Revolution'. The volume also included the play, *Purgatory* (pp. 334–40), which reflects the eugenicist preoccupations of 'To-morrow's Revolution'.

389 *Balzac*. See notes to p. 352.

Ruskin's Unto This Last. John Ruskin (1819–1900), theorist and critic of art, social thinker, whose *Unto This Last* (1860) was an eloquent criticism of *laissez-faire* economics and their social effect.

John Stuart Mill. (1806–73), liberal and rationalist social and economic thinker.

390 *Botticelli*. Sandro Botticelli (1445–1510), Florentine painter.

Ricketts. See notes to p. 368, n. 1.

Delacroix. Eugène Delacroix (1798–1863), French Romantic painter.

Talma. François Joseph Talma (1763–1826), French actor.

Anatomy of Melancholy. (1st edn. 1621) by Robert Burton (1577–1640).

Curtius. Quintus Curtius Rufus (fl. AD 41–54), biographer of Alexander the Great.

Hect. Boethius. Hector Boece, or Boethius (*c.* 1456–*c.*1536), author of a history of Scotland (Latin 1527; Scots translation, *c.*1536).

391 *Bluebeard*. Murderous husband 'Barbe-bleue' in Charles Perrault's *Contes de ma mère, l'oye* (1697) (*Tales of my Mother Goose*). Subsequently legendary.

St Augustine. St Augustine, bishop of Hippo (354–430), author of *The Confessions*.

Gray's 'Milton'. Thomas Gray (1716–1771), poet, author of 'Elegy Written in a Country Churchyard' (1751), in l. 59 of which he observes that 'Some mute inglorious Milton here may rest . . .'

n. 2. *Lewis M. Terman*. (1877–1956), American psychologist and IQ theorist.

392 n. 1. *Shephard Dawson*. (1880–?), psychologist and theorist of intelligence.
Cattell. James McKeen Cattell (1860–1944), psychologist.

393 *Lord Nuffield*. William Richard Morris, Viscount Nuffield (1877–1963), motor manufacturer and educational benefactor.

Mr Bernard Shaw. George Bernard Shaw (1856–1950), Irish playwright.

Lloyd George. David Lloyd George (1863–1945), leader of the Liberal Party, prime minister during the First World War, notable political orator.

Emperor Julian. (*c.* AD 331–63), a late Roman emperor.

n. 1. *Lord Horder*. Thomas Jeeves, Baron Horder (1871–1955), physician. *Leonard Darwin*. (1850–1943), author of *The Need for Eugenic Reform* (1926).

Karl Marx. (1818–83), author of *Das Kapital* ('Capital': vol. i, 1867).

393 *Macaulay*. Thomas Babington Macaulay (1800–59), Whig historian.

Plato's Republic. Plato (*c*.427–347 BC) in *The Republic* offered an account of an ideal state in which there would be wise rulers (Guardians) and a class of workers who would be kept under strict control.

394 *Major Douglas*. Major C. H. Douglas (1879–1952), British economist, critic of the heavy dependence on interest-taking of capitalist economies, and a strong influence on the economic ideas of Ezra Pound.

'A Vision'. See pp. 422–42 and notes below.

Michael Robartes. See note to 'Ego Dominus Tuus', p. 72, l. 4.

Thermopylae. Battle of 480 BC in a Greek mountain-pass of that name in which 300 Spartans, under their king, Leonidas, held out for two days against the armies of Persia under Xerxes. All perished, but their resistance allowed the Greek fleet to escape.

395 *Ninette de Valois*. (1898–   ), dancer and choreographer, born in Co. Wicklow.

396 *Vico*. Giambattista Vico (1668–1744), Italian philosopher who emphasized the importance of myth in the early history of humanity, and of imagination in the development of thought.

Hegel in his 'Philosophy of History'. Georg. Wilhelm Friedrich Hegel (1770–1831), philosopher. His lectures on the philosophy of history were collated by his students and published shortly after his death.

Balzac . . . Medici. See notes to p. 352.

n. 1. *Logic*. Treatise of that name by Hegel (see note to p. 396 above).

397 *Heraclitus*. (fl. 500 BC), philosopher of Ephesus.

Castiglione . . . Courtier. Baldassare Castiglione (1478–1529) wrote a treatise on aristocratic manners called *The Courtier*.

Titian. Tiziano Vecellio or Vecelli (*c*.1477–1576), Venetian painter.

Van Dyke. Sir Anthony Van Dyck (1599–1641), Flemish painter who, among other things, painted members of the English court.

Bishop Berkeley. George Berkeley (1685–1753), bishop of Cloyne, Co. Cork, philosopher.

Speaker Connolly's fine house at Celbridge. William Conolly (1662–1729), Speaker of the Irish House of Commons, had the house called Castletown built at Celbridge in Co. Kildare.

Sir William Temple . . . Bentley. Sir William Temple (1628–99) defended the classics by citing the 'Epistles of Phalaris'. These, however, were proved to be spurious by the great classical scholar Richard Bentley (1662–1742).

398 *Swift . . . Still cast it up and nauseate company*. Swift's 'Ode to the Honourable Sir William Temple' (composed 1689), strophe 3.

399 *Finn*. Finn mac Cumhail, the hero of Irish legend and romance.

Nietzsche's 'transvaluation of all values'. Friedrich Nietzsche (1844–1900), the philosopher, used this phrase to refer to the transformation of the dominant values of the late nineteenth century.

n. *Emer*. Wife of Cuchulain.

Poincaré. Henri Poincaré (1854–1912), French mathematician.

Henry Adams. Henry Brooks Adams (1838–1918), American historian and philosopher of history.

400 *Anima Mundi*. See notes to p. 410, *Per Amica Silentia Lunae*.

Henry More. (1614–87), fellow of Christ's College, Cambridge, and Platonic philosopher.

'mad as the mist and snow'. Refrain from Yeats's own poem, 'Mad as the Mist and Snow', pp. 140–1.

Jacob's dream threatening. In Gen. 28: 12–16, Jacob has a dream of a ladder stretching between earth and heaven, with angels ascending and descending it. The implication of Yeats's remark is not self-evident, but it may refer to the renunciation of a full humanity.

401 *Rosses Point*. Seaside village in Co. Sligo, near Drumcliff.

And she said . . . we shall part. From William Morris's poem, *Sigurd the Volsung*, ii. 65–8.

'Dust hath Closed Helen's Eye'

402 *Raftery*. Anthony Raftery or Antoine Ó Raifteirí (1784–1835), a blind poet born in Co. Mayo who also frequented Co. Galway.

403 *The friend that was with me*. Lady Gregory.

405 *Kilbecanty*. Kilbeacanty, Co. Galway.

Derrybrien. In the Slieve Aughty mountains on the borders of Co. Galway and Co. Clare.

Echtge hills. Slieve Aughty (see above).

Ardrahan. Town between Galway and Gort.

Kinvara. Village on the south-eastern shore of Galway Bay.

406 *Duras*. Hamlet on the southern shores of Galway Bay.

na mna Sidhe. Irish: 'the women of the Sidhe' (i.e. of the fairies).

'And Fair, Fierce Women'

408 *Knocknarea where Queen Maive is thought to be buried*. Knocknarea is a mountain near Sligo, and the iron-age queen of Connacht, Maeve, is reputed to be buried in a cairn at its summit.

Fergus son of Roy. See note to p. 13, 'Fergus and the Druid'.

409 *Burren Hills*. In Co. Clare, not very far from Galway.

Aristotle of the Books

409   *Goban*. The smith in Irish mythology, originally one of the Celtic gods.

410   *Per Amica Silentia Lunae*. From the Latin of Virgil's *Aeneid*, ii. 255: 'Through the friendly silences of the moon.'   *Anima Hominis*. Latin: 'the soul of man', contrasting with the second section, *Anima Mundi*, 'the soul of the world' (extracts from which begin at p. 416). In so far as it is possible to summarize this complex work, the famous assertion at the beginning of section V of *Anima Hominis* would be a good place from which to start: 'We make out of the quarrel with others, rhetoric, but of the quarrel with ourselves, poetry' (p. 411). It is poetry that wins Yeats's approval, the quarrel with ourselves that fascinates him. This quarrel may be formalized as the encounter between the self and 'the anti-self or the antithetical self' (p. 412). The idea of the anti-self is closely related to that of the Mask, which is the self's attempt to adopt the semblance of the anti-self. This anti-self is indeed what it sounds like: antagonistic to the given self, its opposite. The self is attracted by and desires an image of a being other than itself: 'He is of all things not impossible the most difficult' (p. 412). Another name for this being is 'the Daemon' (p. 414). The opposition and tension in this relationship is the source of the poet's creativity.

But not everyone is a poet, or even possessed of the subjective nature which Yeats saw as essentially poetic. The desire for this antithetical relationship is strongest in those who are of a subjective nature. In those whose nature is more objective the desire for the antithetical self is weaker. Yeats develops the theme of the contrast of the subjective and the objective character in *A Vision*.

If the soul of man (*Anima Hominis*) is internally divided, nevertheless it cannot subsist alone. For the image of the anti-self has to have an external source. While we may imagine that this source is in our experience of the world, the force that gives a unified form to the antithetical things we find and desire there comes from the supernatural, that is, from *Anima Mundi*. This is a repository of archetypal images, similar to Jung's 'collective unconscious'. But it is also the realm, akin to the occultists' 'astral plane', where spirits dwell. Spirits possess a subtle body composed of 'animal spirits' (p. 416). But so do the images that also dwell in *Anima Mundi*. It is important to grasp this conception, so alien to a contemporary reader: Yeats really does believe that spirits and images are composed of the same substance, and may merge with each other. The anti-self is not just an image of another being, but a spirit that haunts us. Hence Yeats's use of the word 'Daemon' (see p. 414), a term which takes on some importance in both versions of *A Vision*, where, however, it is spelt 'Daimon'. But, confusingly, not all of Yeats's formulations in that work allow one to feel confident that the term can simply be identified with 'anti-self'. Thus, in *A Vision* (1937), 84, Yeats explains that, before a soul enters a new life, 'The stage-manager, or *Daimon*, offers his actor an inherited scenario, the *Body of Fate*, and a *Mask* or rôle as unlike as possible to his natural ego or *Will* . . . ' This implies a controlling relationship to all the components of the self, and not just to the Mask that derives from the anti-self.

Yeats began to develop this concept of the anti-self chiefly as the result of a series of seances, occurring between 1909 and 1917, which seemed to indicate that his anti-self was the spirit of Leo Africanus (*c*.1485–*c*.1554), a Moor of Spain, educated in Morocco, who was forcibly converted to Catholicism in Rome, but escaped to Tunis and renounced the conversion. See Steve L. Adams and George Mills Harper (eds.), 'The Manuscript of "Leo Africanus" ', in Richard J. Finneran (ed.), *Yeats Annual No. 1* (London, 1982), 3–47.

Per Amica Silentia Lunae is structured as it is, then, because it expounds the mutually dependent relationship between the spirits dwelling in mortal beings and those that dwell in *Anima Mundi*. And mutually dependent it is. For just as we seek the Daemon, the Daemon, for its part, needs the desire of mortal beings to fulfil itself.

William Morris. (1834–96), craftsman, designer, poet, and author of prose romances.

Savage Landor . . . Imaginary Conversations. Walter Savage Landor (1775–1864), poet. His *Imaginary Conversations of Literary Men and Statesmen* appeared in 1824 (Parts I and II) and 1828–9 (Parts III–V).

Beckford. William Beckford (1760–1844), author of travel books and of the exotic oriental tale, *Vathek* (1786).

Simeon Solomon. (1841–1905), poet and translator from the Hebrew.

411 *Shadwell*. Charles Lancelot Shadwell (1840–1919), who translated Dante's *Purgatorio* and *Paradiso*. The former translation appeared 1892–9, the latter in 1915.

Dante Rossetti. Dante Gabriel Rossetti (1828–82), poet and painter, published *The Early Italian Poets together with Dante's Vita Nuova* in 1861. It was republished in 1874 as *Dante and his Circle*.

the most pure lady. Beatrice, the woman Dante loved, and who is represented as guiding him through Paradise in *The Divine Comedy*.

Boccaccio. Giovanni Boccaccio (1313?–75), author of *The Decameron*.

Guido Cavalcanti. (1259?–1300), poet and friend of Dante.

Gino da Pistoia. Cino da Pistoia (*c*.1270–1336), Italian poet and jurist.

Giovanni Guirino. The surname should be Quirino. The ensuing quotation is from Dante's sonnet 'Lo Re che merta i suoi servi a ristoro' as translated by Rossetti (see above).

412 *Johnson and Dowson*. See note to 'The Grey Rock', p. 48, l. 62.

413 *Caesar Borgia*. Cesare Borgia (1475/6–1507), powerful in the papal states during the papacy of his father.

414 *Plutarch*. (*c*.46–*c*.126). Greek essayist and biographer.

Daemon. A Latin word deriving from the Greek, and meaning 'spirit'. Yeats implies 'attendant spirit'. See third paragraph of note to p. 410, *Per Amica Silentia Lunae*.

Wilhelm Meister. Goethe's *Wilhelm Meisters Lehrjahre* (*Wilhelm Meister's Apprenticeship*), 1795–6.

414 *Heraclitus*. Philosopher at Ephesus, *c*.500 BC.

415 *'Doom eager'*. Translating *dōmgeorne*, Old English for 'eager for renown', in the Anglo-Saxon poem, *The Wanderer*, l. 17, where, however, it is plural, thus referring to more than one warrior.

Slieve-na-mon. Mountain in Co. Tipperary. The story comes from *Silva Gadelica: A Collection of Tales in Irish*, ed. and trans. Standish Hayes O'Grady, 2 vols. (London and Edinburgh, 1892), ii. 110.

416 *Anima Mundi*. Latin: 'soul of the world'.

More. Henry More (1614–87), the Cambridge Platonist, fellow of Christ's College.

Hippocrates. Hippocrates of Cos (*c*.469–399 BC), the Greek physician.

417 *Cudworth*. Ralph Cudworth (1617–88), Platonist, friend of Henry More and like him a fellow of Christ's College, Cambridge.

Blake said . . . or men. From *The Marriage of Heaven and Hell*, plate 16.

418 *Spenser's Garden of Adonis*. In *The Faerie Queene*, III. vi. The lines quoted are from stanza 30.

419 *Swedenborg*. See note to p. 310, l. 44, 'Swedenborg'.

Cornelius Agrippa. Henry Cornelius Agrippa von Nettesheim (1486–1535), German student of occult philosophy, author of *De occulta philosophia* (1531).

Madame Blavatsky. Helena Petrovna Blavatsky (1831–91), co-founder of the Theosophical Society, author of *Isis Unveiled* (1877) and *The Secret Doctrine* (1888).

420 *Caesarion*. Cleopatra's son by Julius Caesar.

younger Pericles Aspasia bore. Aspasia, mistress of the great Athenian statesman Pericles, bore him a son, also called Pericles. Landor (see notes to p. 410) wrote a series of imaginary letters called *Pericles and Aspasia*.

n. 1. *Landor's play*. The play is *Antony and Octavius: Scenes for A Study* (1856).

421 *Zoroastrian*. Pertaining to Zoroaster, supposed founder of the ancient Persian religion, which involved magic.

422 *From A Vision 1925*. Extracts, that is, from the first version of *A Vision*. A revised version appeared in 1937, extracts from which are given (see pp. 430–42).

A Vision, as the 1937 version makes clear, is the distillation of many communications, chiefly in automatic writing, Yeats received from the spirit world through the medium of his wife. He married Georgie Hyde-Lees on 20 Oct. 1917. The communications began several days later. The rudiments of the system he and his wife deduced from the many, sometimes cryptic, messages are laid out in the following note on 'The Great Wheel'.

The Great Wheel. The wheel of the twenty-eight phases of the moon, which is structured around the idea of reincarnation. Every soul incarnated on

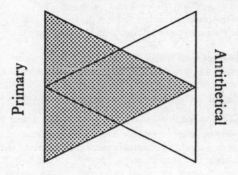

earth takes its character from one of the phases, or, to put it simply, is born into one of the phases, except that no soul is born into the phase of the full moon or the dark of the moon. Souls travel around the wheel, starting at Phase 2. The difference between the phases is a matter of the differing relative quantities of the subjective character on the one hand, and the objective on the other, to be found in each phase. (Yeats called the subjective *antithetical* and the objective *primary*.) In Yeats's diagram (above), the white colour represents moonlight, which stands for subjectivity. The dark, standing for objectivity, Yeats associated with the sun, or the solar quality. The more of moonlight (or the lunar quality), the greater the subjectivity of the person. The reason why no soul can be incarnated in either the full or the dark of the moon is that these two phases represent, respectively, perfect subjectivity and perfect objectivity, and there can be no perfection on earth.

But study of Yeats's diagram shows that the same relative quantities of subjectivity and objectivity will always occur in two of the phases, not one, except in the cases of the full moon and the dark of the moon, which occur only once each. Does this mean that one is reincarnated twice with the same quality thirteen times (remembering that there are twenty-six possible incarnations)? Not so. For there is also the direction in which the soul is heading to consider. Although Phase 14 (just before the full moon) has the same quantities of dark and light as Phase 16 (just after it), the former is travelling towards subjectivity, while the latter is already beginning its journey back towards the dark of the moon, and objectivity. This makes all the difference, and modifies the character of the soul.

But one should not conceive of the soul as a unity. It is composed of Four Faculties, which can be broadly compared with Blake's Four Zoas. They possess, however, their own specific functions in Yeats's system: they are Will, Mask, Creative Mind, and Body of Fate, which Yeats qualifies as 'the will and its object' and 'thought and its object' (*A Vision* (1937), 73). The number of the phase one is born into is the number taken by Will. But the other three Faculties take their qualities from different phases—see note to p. 425.

As well as the Great Wheel, Yeats had another image for the cyclic movement between rising and falling quantities of objectivity and subjectivity, solar and lunar, the dark of the moon and the light of the moon. This is the model of the *gyres*. He pictured the *primary* or objective quality as a dark vortex or gyre, and the *antithetical* or subjective quality as a white one, as in the diagram, taken from page 72 of the second version of *A Vision*. Here the *gyres* are shown as triangles, for ease of presentation. The soul travels around this diagram in an imaginary circle, starting from the left. Phase 1 is on the far left at the word *Primary*. Phase 8 is at the bottom middle of the diagram, where there are equal quantities of dark and light: this corresponds to the half moon. Phase 15 is at the far right, where the word *Antithetical* occurs. This is the full moon. The soul then travels back towards the left, over the top of the diagram. The middle of this journey is Phase 22, and the end, via Phase 28 (and back with *Primary*), Phase 1.

Just as a soul travels around the wheel, so does history. So a period of history can be said to belong to one of the phases. This means that, as with an individual soul, a phase of history will have, for instance, a Mask—that is, an image it adopts of what it desires to become. The movement of history can also be described by means of the interaction of *gyres*, and this is what Yeats does in the diagram of 'The Historical Cones' on p. 439—see the note to this, and the note to 'At the opening of Book V . . . ', p. 438. But when the cycle of twenty-eight historical phases is complete, the whole round starts all over again. This fact provides for a further complication: just as one half of the cycle is more subjective (*antithetical*) and one more objective (*primary*) so a complete cycle will itself be predominantly antithetical or primary, and its successor, the next cycle, will be predominantly of the opposed quality (or *Tincture*, as Yeats termed it). For the lengths of cycles, see note to 'Magnus Annus' in a song from *The Resurrection*, p. 297.

It should be added that Yeats has much to say, in both versions of *A Vision*, about the existence of souls between lives. But the second version has a far more developed account (Book II: 'The Completed Symbol', Book III: 'The Soul in Judgment'). Discarnate spirits at death are composed not of Four Faculties, but of *Four Principles*: Husk, Passionate Body, Spirit, and Celestial Body, corresponding to the faculties Will, Mask, Creative Mind, and Body of Fate. The first two are sense and its object, the second two mind and its object. There are stages in the life of the soul after death. In a stage called the *Return*, which comprises also a process called the *Dreaming Back*, the *Spirit* relives the events of its past life in order to separate itself from *Husk* and *Passionate Body* so that it may join with the *Celes-*

tial Body in a unity. But it subsequently goes through stages which lead to incarnation in a new earthly existence.

Antithetical and Primary. 'Antithetical' is subjective, 'primary' objective.

Arabic Mansions of the Moon. A reference to the importance of the different phases of the moon in Arabic astrology. See also Chaucer, *The Franklin's Tale*, which refers to a book which 'spak muchel of the operaciouns | Touchynge the eighte and twenty mansiouns | That longen to the moon' (1129–31). Yeats knew this passage.

423 *Murray's dictionary*. Sir James Murray was the first editor of the Oxford English Dictionary.

Tinctures. The word is derived from alchemy. It refers there to a spiritual character which can imprint itself on material things.

425 *A man whose Will is at Phase 17 ... at Phase 27*. It is helpful to consult Yeats's diagram. The Will is the given self. The Mask is its opposite, or anti-self. Therefore it is taken from the opposite phase of the moon on the wheel, i.e. Phase 3: one could demonstrate this graphically by drawing a line of diameter across the wheel. The Creative Mind, at Phase 13, is, however, in a mirror relationship with Phase 17: it possesses the same quantities of lunar and solar, dark and light, but from the opposite side of the wheel (still travelling towards subjectivity). The Body of Fate at Phase 27 is in a different kind of mirror relationship, possessing the same quantity of dark as the Will has of light, and vice versa.

426 *Dante in the Convito*. Or *Convivio* (1304–7). It is not clear what precise passage Yeats has in mind.

Commedia del Arte. Italian Renaissance comedy centred on Venice, and flourishing 1500–1750, in which stock characters wore masks.

The author of 'The Imitation of Christ'. Thomas à Kempis (1380–1471), a German monk who composed this devotional work.

427 *like Landor*. For Landor see notes to p. 410.

Robespierre. Maximilien-François-Marie-Isidore de Robespierre (1758–94), a leader of the Jacobins in the French Revolution.

428 *St Peter at his crucifixion reversed*. There is a tradition that St Peter's crucifixion was head downwards, because he did not wish to presume to adopt the position of the Saviour.

'Demon est Deus Inversus'. Latin: 'A Demon is a god inverted.' This was Yeats's secret Golden Dawn name.

Man's Daimon has therefore her energy. Note that the Daimon is now female. Yeats was to abandon this identification in the second version of *A Vision*. Here, the Daimon is reminiscent of a demonic fairy woman, of the kind Yeats was very familiar with from Irish mythology.

429 *Guido Cavalcanti*. See notes to p. 411.

Introduction to 'A Vision'

431   *Browning's Paracelsus.* (1835), poem by Robert Browning.

Wilhelm Meister. See notes to p. 414.

Ashdown Forest. In Kent.

Glendalough. In the Wicklow Mountains.

Rosses Point. Seaside village in Co. Sligo.

432   *Four Faculties.* i.e. Will, Mask, Creative Mind, and Body of Fate (see para. 3 of note to p. 422, 'The Great Wheel', and note to p. 425, 'A man whose Will . . .').

433   *Spengler's Decline of the West.* Oswald Spengler, *The Decline of the West*, trans. (London, 1926).

John Stuart Mill's attack upon Sir William Hamilton. John Stuart Mill (1806–73) disagreed with Sir William Hamilton (1788–1856). The former was a Utilitarian in ethics, the latter an Intuitionist who did not believe that morality could be reduced to calculation of benefits and relative benefits.

Swedenborg. See note to p. 310, l. 44.

Boehme. Jakob Boehme (1575–1624), sometimes called 'Behmen', German mystic who profoundly influenced William Blake. Contrary principles are essential to his system.

the 'Hermetic Students'. The Hermetic Order of the Golden Dawn.

Cabalistic imagery. Derived from the cabbala (to which Yeats refers later in the sentence), which are Jewish mystical writings of the Middle Ages.

435   *the Glastonbury thorn perhaps.* Flowering thorn, reputed to have been brought to Glastonbury by Joseph of Arimathea.

Rapallo . . . Ezra Pound. Between 1928 and 1934 Yeats and his wife used to stay occasionally in Rapallo, a town on the Ligurian coast of Italy. Ezra Pound had made his residence there.

437   *the English translation of Spengler's book.* See note to p. 433.

The elemental things that go | About my table to and fro. In 'To Ireland in the Coming Times', ll. 23–4 (p. 25), Yeats has, 'For the elemental creatures go | About my table to and fro'.

438   *Wyndham Lewis.* Percy Wyndham Lewis (1882–1957), novelist and Vorticist artist.

Constantin Brancusi. (1876–1957), modernist sculptor who worked with simplified organic shapes, especially ovoid ones.

At the opening of Book V . . . instructors. For the diagram, see note to p. 439. Book V is called 'Dove or Swan'. This title refers to Yeats's idea that historical eras are founded on the intervention in history of a combination of the divine and the bestial: that is to say, on a combination of the most intense experiences known to man. The ancient historical era of two thousand years (up until the birth of Christ) was founded when Zeus, in the form of a swan (the swan referred to here) raped Leda. Yeats prints the poem 'Leda and the Swan' (p. 112) after the diagram, at the beginning of Book V. See notes to this poem. The Christian era was founded when the Holy Spirit (traditionally represented in the form of a dove) made the Blessed Virgin conceive Christ. The contrast in the two birds is also significant: the violence of the swan is appropriate to a predominantly *antithetical* era (as Yeats believed the classical to be) which prizes subjectivity, heroism, and aristocracy. The dove is appropriate to the predominantly *primary* Christian era, which prizes peace, charity, truth, and innocence. The next era will be announced by a similar intervention: perhaps, Yeats thinks, something like the 'rough beast' of his poem 'The Second Coming' (p. 91), five lines of which he quotes (p. 441). For the coming era will again be predominantly *antithetical*.

black numbers. In the diagram on p. 439, the triangle with its apex pointing upwards is black, and so are the numbers of the phases and dates associated with its sides.

red letters. See note to p. 439, 'The Historical Cones'.

439 Figure: *The Historical Cones*. 'Cones' is another word for 'gyres' (see paras. 4-5 of the note to p. 422, 'The Great Wheel'). In the original diagram, the triangle pointing downwards, and the dates and phases associated with its sides, are coloured red, i.e. from 'o(1)' down the left-hand side to the apex at '(1)1050', and from there up the right-hand side to '(23-24-25)1927'.

440 *Blake's Mental Traveller*. Blake's poem 'The Mental Traveller' contains the line 'And She grows young as he grows old' (l. 20). Thus they move in opposite directions, like the two pairs of Faculties Yeats is discussing.

The Great Year. See note on 'Magnus Annus' in song from *The Resurrection*, p. 297.

441 *Thirteenth Cone*. The Absolute or God. The number derives from the idea of the twelve Apostles, plus one other: Christ. But the allusion to Christ is not to his incarnation, so much as to his status as part of the Godhead.

Somewhere in sands . . . desert birds. Quoted from 'The Second Coming' (p. 91). For their significance here, see note to p. 438.

Byzantine State. See notes to p. 94, 'Sailing to Byzantium'.

Justinian. As for above.

St Sophia. The great cathedral built by the Emperor Justinian.

the Academy of Plato. The academy founded by Plato in Athens where Platonic philosophy was still taught in Justinian's day until he closed it for its non-Christian associations.

Plotinus. (AD 205-70), Neoplatonic philosopher.

443 *The Adoration of the Magi*. Composed in 1896, first published in 1897 in *Rosa Alchemica, The Tables of the Law and The Adoration of the Magi*.

Aherne. Owen Aherne is a fictional character whom Yeats conceives of as a pious Irish Catholic.

443   *inquietude of the veil of the Temple, which M. Mallarmé considers a character-istic of our times.* In his essay 'Crise de vers' ('Crisis in verse'), in *Variations sur un sujet*, the French symbolist poet, Stéphane Mallarmé (1842–98), speaks of the changes coming over French literary taste: 'on assiste . . . à une inquiétude du voile dans le temple avec des plis significatifs et un peu sa déchirure.' ('We are present . . . at a disturbance of the veil of the temple by significant folds and to some extent its rending.')

444   *Michael Robartes.* This character represents the idealistic aspect of Yeats's personality: scholar, visionary, occult investigator, and at the same time drawn towards sensual beauty.

      St Brandan. i.e. St Brendan the navigator, the legendary Irish saint, who, some claim, discovered America.

      Islands of the Young. In Irish, *Tír na nÓg* ('Land of the Young'), the island homes of the immortal Sidhe, or fairies, in Irish mythology.

      Homer's Phæacians. The happy island of the Phaeacians is visited by Odysseus in Homer's *Odyssey*, Book VI.

      Fifth Eclogue of Virgil. The *Eclogues* of the Roman poet Virgil are pastoral poems.

      another Leda . . . another Achilles. For Leda, see notes to 'Leda and the Swan', p. 112. Achilles was the champion of the Greeks in the siege of Troy.

445   *Hermes the Shepherd of the Dead.* The Greek god, Hermes (by the Romans called Mercury) guided dead souls into the Underworld.

447   *The Order of the Alchemical Rose.* A fictional mystical order founded by Michael Robartes. For some of Yeats's occult associations with the Rose, see notes to *The Rose*, p. 12.

448   *Senate Speeches.* Yeats was a member of Seanad Éireann, the Senate of the newly formed Irish Free State, from 1922 until 1928.

      The Irish Language. The new Irish government was promoting the use of Irish in many contexts. The occasion of Yeats's outburst here was a motion in the Senate that its daily prayer be read in Irish as well as English.

      Debate on Divorce. The Irish government and Dáil (lower house of parliament) were effectively attempting to make divorce impossible by legislative changes. The Senate decided that a bill of divorce must receive a first reading in each house of parliament before it could be proceeded with in the Senate. While in theory this gave a right to divorce, the Catholic majority in both Dáil and Senate meant that a private bill of divorce would only be likely to succeed in the most exceptional circumstances.

449   *Milton.* John Milton published a work in favour of the liberty to divorce, *The Doctrine and Discipline of Divorce*, in 1643.

      An Cathaoirleach. Irish: literally 'Chairman', i.e. the Speaker.

      The monuments . . . Nelson. Referring to the monuments to Daniel O'Connell (1745–1833), Charles Stewart Parnell (1846–91), and Horatio, Lord Nelson (1758–1805).

450 *You never have any trouble about O'Connell.* The ensuing remarks make it clear that Yeats thinks that the private life of O'Connell, like those of Parnell and Nelson, did not always suggest respect for the institution of marriage. Yet no doubt is raised about O'Connell, because he was a Catholic, while the Protestants Parnell and Nelson suffer from the petty vindictiveness to which Yeats believes sections of Catholic Ireland to be prone.

There is a proposal to remove Nelson because he interferes with the traffic. Yeats believes the true reasons have nothing to do with the traffic, but with the vindictiveness referred to above.

people of Burke . . . people of Emmet. All are Anglo-Irish Protestants. For Burke and Grattan see notes to 'The Tower', p. 99, l. 132. For Swift see note to 'Blood and the Moon', p. 124, l. 18.

Robert Emmet (1778–1803), leader of a small uprising in Dublin in 1803, for which he was hanged.

Reveries over Childhood and Youth

453 *There was a large garden behind the house.* The house of his maternal grandparents, the Pollexfens, in Sligo, in which Yeats stayed for long periods as a child.

454 *Ellen O'Leary.* (1831–89).

John O'Leary. See notes to 'September 1913', p. 51, l. 8.

Davis and the Young Irelanders. Thomas Davis (1814–45), poet and leader of the Young Ireland movement.

Dowden's. Edward Dowden (1843–1913), Professor of English at Trinity College, Dublin.

455 *Inchedony.* i.e. Inchdoney, an island at the mouth of Clonakilty Bay, Co. Cork.

Callanan. Jeremiah Joseph Callanan (1795–1829), Irish poet and translator from the Irish.

Childe Harold. The long poem by Lord Byron, *Childe Harold's Pilgrimage* (Cantos I and II, 1812; Canto III, 1816; Canto IV, 1818), which was based on his travels in Europe and the Levant.

The Trembling of the Veil. See note to p. 443, *The Adoration of the Magi.*

Oscar Wilde. (1854–1900), the Anglo-Irish playwright.

Henley's. William Ernest Henley (1849–1903), poet.

456 *Walter Pater's . . . Renaissance.* Pater (1839–94). Yeats gives the title of the first edition (1873), which was later abbreviated to *The Renaissance.*

457 *Maud Gonne.* (1865–1953), the object of Yeats's unrequited love for many years.

withdrawal of the Irish Members. The policy of a boycott of the House of Commons by MPs of the Irish Party.

457 *Mr Birrell's university.* Augustine Birrell (1850–1933) was Minister for Education (1906) and Secretary for Ireland (1907–16). He was instrumental in the creation of the National University of Ireland, founded 1908.

458 *Scopas.* Greek sculptor of Paros, fourth century BC.

Artemisia's. Artemisia was the wife of Mausolus, who ruled Caria, in Asia Minor, in the fourth century BC. When he died, she erected the vast Mausoleum (from which we take the word), adorned with friezes by Scopas (see above).

How many centuries . . . That loveliness? From the first stanza of the First Musician's song at the beginning of *The Only Jealousy of Emer* (p. 270).

LETTERS

459 *To Ernest Rhys.* (1859–1946), poet and translator from the Welsh, of Welsh extraction, though brought up mainly in Newcastle.

Hendra. 'The House of Hendra' was a poem by Rhys. The House is haunted.

haunted. See above.

Blakes expression . . . golden bowl. Thel's Motto from the beginning of *The Book of Thel* (1789): 'Does the Eagle know what is in the pit? | Or wilt thou go ask the Mole: | Can Wisdom be put in a silver rod? | Or Love in a golden bowl?'

Katharine Tynan. (1859–1931), Irish poet and writer, friend of Yeats.

'Irish Love Songs'. Tynan was working on such a selection for the publisher, Fisher Unwin.

Davis. See note to 'To Ireland in the Coming Times', p. 25, l. 18.

460 *Walshes 'Irish Songs'.* Edward Walsh, *Irish Popular Songs* (Dublin, 1847).

Hyde. i.e. Douglas Hyde. See note to 'At the Abbey Theatre', p. 44, l. 1.

an 'old song resung'. Earlier title of 'Down by the Salley Gardens'.

'Rhymers Book'. The *Book of the Rhymers' Club* (1892).

When you are old. Yeats's final version is at p. 21.

461 *When you are sad.* Appeared in *The Countess Kathleen and Various Legends and Lyrics* (1892), but was not republished.

Davis, Fergusson, Allingham Mangan & Moore. Irish poets. For Davis, Mangan, and Ferguson (spelt thus), see note to 'To Ireland in the Coming Times', p. 25, l. 18. The other two are William Allingham (1824–89) and Thomas Moore (1779–1852).

George Russell (AE). See note to p. 374.

'Ideas of Good and Evil'. Yeats's collection of essays of that name.

462 *Dionysisic . . . Apollonic.* Nietzsche's categories of Dionysian and Apollonian, as expounded in *The Birth of Tragedy.* The Dionysian is sensual, pas-

sionate, and irrational, the Apollonian rational, dispassionate, and form-giving.

the transfiguration . . . and the incarnation. The transfiguration of Christ (see Matt. 17) and his incarnation.

your poems. Yeats was making a selection of AE's poems which came out as *The Nuts of Knowledge* (1903).

Dowson's. Ernest Dowson (1867–1900), poet and associate of Yeats's in The Rhymers' Club.

Byron in Manfred. Byron's *Manfred: A Dramatic Poem* (1817).

Forbes-Robertson. Johnston Forbes-Robertson, London actor-manager.

463 *The Dublin tragedy*. The Easter 1916 Uprising.

Cosgrave. W. T. Cosgrave (1880–1965), later prime minister of the Irish Free State.

Henry Dixon. A mistake by Yeats. Henry Dixon, a solicitor who took part in the Rising, was arrested but set free. Thomas Dickson, a journalist, who was disabled, was shot: he had no connection with the Rising, nor was he even a Sinn Fein sympathizer.

a poem. Yeats's poem, 'Easter 1916' (pp. 85–7).

to rescind the Home Rule Bill. The Home Rule Bill for Ireland had been passed by Parliament in 1913, but suspended when the First World War broke out in 1914.

464 *Player Queen*. i.e. Yeats's play, *The Player Queen* (first performed 1919).

H. J. C. Grierson. Sir Herbert Grierson. (1866–1946), Professor of English at Aberdeen University (1894–1915), and subsequently at Edinburgh (1915–35).

The Background of English Literature. Book by Grierson

'our life is a false nature' . . . 'couch the mind'. Byron, *Childe Harold*, Canto IV, stanzas 126–7. 'couch the mind' is a misprint in Grierson's work.

Haidée. In *Don Juan*, Canto II, Juan falls in love with Haidée. Her beauty and innocence are celebrated by Byron.

465 *'St Lucies Day'*. John Donne's poem, 'A nocturnall upon S. *Lucies* day, Being the shortest day'.

Blake illustration to Gray. William Blake executed a number of illustrations to the poems of Thomas Gray.

This time we had a packed theatre. Riots caused by the production of Sean O'Casey's *The Plough and the Stars* at the Abbey Theatre, 8 Feb. 1926.

466 *Olivia Shakespear*. Mrs Olivia Shakespear (1863–1938), with whom Yeats had an affair in 1895–7. They became lovers again for a while in the early years of the new century.

Carmichael. Probably Alexander Carmichael (1832–1912), the Scottish Celticist.

466 *'The Gates of Pluto'*. Book IV of *A Vision* (1925).

Harry Tucker. Mrs Shakespear's brother, Henry Tudor Tucker.

AE. See note on George Russell, p. 374.

Sean O'Casey. The playwright (1880–1964), author of *Juno and the Paycock* and *The Plough and the Stars*.

My dear Casey. Sean O'Casey was born John Casey, of a respectable middle-class Protestant family. He changed his name as a young man.

your play. The Silver Tassie.

468 *Swift, the Diary to Stella*. For Swift and the *Journal to Stella*, see notes to *The Words upon the Window-Pane*, pp. 309 ff.

Pope and Bolingbroke. Alexander Pope (1688–1744). For Bolingbroke see note to *The Words upon the Window-Pane*, p. 312, l. 104.

Masefield ... Siegfried Sassoon. The poets John Masefield (1878–1967) and Siegfried Sassoon (1886–1967).

469 *Riversdale*. House in Rathfarnham, near Dublin, to which the Yeatses moved in 1922.

De Valera. Eamonn De Valera was now prime minister of Ireland, having led Fianna Fáil to victory in the general election of 1932.

Swami's lectures. Shri Purohit Swami, the Indian mystic.

Cuala series. The Cuala Press, a small publishing firm owned and run by Yeats's sister Lollie.

My sister's books. See above.

essay on Louis Lambert. Yeats's essay on Balzac's novel can be read in *Essays and Introductions*.

Comte de Tilly. A translation into English, by Françoise Delisle, of the memoirs of the Comte de Tilly (1559–1632), appeared in 1932.

470 *Ethel Mannin*. (1900–84), friend and correspondent of Yeats.

You think it horrible ... into song? Yeats's poem 'The Spur' (p. 162).

Abyssinian war. The Italian fascist leader of Italy, Benito Mussolini, in pursuit of an East African empire, waged a war of conquest on Abyssinia (Ethiopia) in 1935–6. The Ethiopians surrendered in 1936.

471 *Dr McCartan*. Dr Patrick McCartan, whose role was as Yeats describes it.

Blake's lines. From 'The Everlasting Gospel'.

472 *Dorothy Wellesley*. Lady Dorothy Wellesley (1889–1956), duchess of Wellington.

Gogarty. Oliver St John Gogarty (1878–1957), Irish poet, novelist, and physician.

Wilfred Owen. (1893–1918), the war poet.

Casement poem. 'Roger Casement' is the poem she has seen, 'The Ghost of Roger Casement' (pp. 159–61) the one she has not. Sir Roger Casement

(1864–1916) sought armed assistance for Ireland in Germany in 1914, returning in a German U-boat in 1916. He was arrested, tried for High Treason, and hanged.

473 *your novel. Darkness my Bride* (1938).

Esther Waters. Novel (1894) by George Moore.

Rilke. Rainer Maria Rilke (1875–1926), poet born into the German-speaking community of Prague.

474 *Blake's design . . . for Blair's Grave*. Blake engraved a series of designs for Robert Blair's poem *The Grave* (1743). The particular design Yeats refers to is 'The Reunion of the Soul and Body'.

FURTHER READING

EDITIONS AND WORKS OF REFERENCE

Steve L. Adams and George Mills Harper (eds.), 'The Manuscript of "Leo Africanus"', in Richard J. Finneran, (ed.), *Yeats Annual No. 1* (London, 1982), 3–47.

Peter Allt and Russel K. Alspach (eds.), *The Variorum Edition of the Poems of W. B. Yeats* (New York, 1957; rev. 1966).

Russel K. Alspach (ed.), *The Variorum Edition of the Plays of W. B. Yeats* (London, 1966).

Edwin Ellis and William Butler Yeats (eds.), *The Works of William Blake*, 3 vols. (London, 1893).

John P. Frayne (ed.), *Uncollected Prose by W. B. Yeats*, i (London, 1970).

—— and Colton Johnson (eds.), *Uncollected Prose by W. B. Yeats*, ii (London, 1975).

George Mills Harper and Walter Kelly Hood (eds.), *A Critical Edition of Yeats's A Vision (1925)* (Basingstoke, 1978).

A. Norman Jeffares, *A New Commentary on the Poems of W. B. Yeats* (London, 1984).

John Kelly and Eric Domville (eds.), *The Collected Letters of W. B. Yeats*, i: *1865–1895* (Oxford, 1986).

Warwick Gould, John Kelly, and Deirdre Toomey (eds.), *The Collected Letters of W. B. Yeats*, ii: *1896–1900* (Oxford, 1997).

John Kelly, Eric Domville, and Ronald Schuchard (eds.), *The Collected Letters of W. B. Yeats*, iii: *1901–1904* (Oxford, 1994).

Philip L. Marcus, Warwick Gould, and Michael J. Sidnell (eds.), *The Secret Rose, Stories by W. B. Yeats: A Variorum Edition* (Ithaca, NY, 1981).

Allan Wade (ed.), *The Letters of W. B. Yeats* (London, 1954).

W. B. Yeats, *A Vision* (London, 1937).

—— *Autobiographies* (London, 1955, 1970 repr.).

—— *Mythologies* (London, 1959).

—— *Essays and Introductions* (London, 1961).

—— *Explorations*, selected by Mrs W. B. Yeats (London, 1962).

—— *Memoirs*, ed. Denis Donoghue (London, 1972).

—— *The Poems: A New Edition*, ed. Richard J. Finneran, 2nd edn. (London, 1989).

—— *Writings on Irish Folklore, Legend and Myth*, ed. Robert Welch (Harmondsworth, 1993).

CRITICISM

Hazard Adams, *The Book of Yeats's Poems* (Tallahaseee, Fla., 1990).

Joseph Adams, *Yeats and the Masks of Syntax* (London, 1984).

Harold Bloom, *Yeats* (New York, 1970).

Terence Brown, *The Life of W. B. Yeats: A Critical Biography* (Oxford, 1999).

Elizabeth Cullingford, *Gender and History in Yeats's Love Poetry* (Cambridge, 1993).

—— *Yeats, Ireland and Fascism* (London, 1981).

Seamus Deane, 'Yeats and the Idea of Revolution', *Celtic Revivals: Essays in Modern Irish Literature* (London, 1985), 38–50.

Denis Donoghue, *Yeats* (Glasgow, 1971).

Terry Eagleton, 'Yeats and Poetic Form', in his *Crazy John and the Bishop and Other Essays on Irish Culture* (Cork, 1998), 273–95.

Richard Ellmann, *Eminent Domain: Yeats Among Wilde, Joyce, Pound, Eliot and Auden* (London, 1970).

—— *The Identity of Yeats*, 2nd edn. (London, 1964).

—— *W. B. Yeats: The Man and the Masks*, 2nd edn. (London, 1979).

Richard J. Finneran, *Editing Yeats's Poems: A Reconsideration* (Basingstoke, 1990).

Ian Fletcher, *W. B. Yeats and His Contemporaries* (Brighton, 1987).

R. F. Foster, 'Protestant Magic: W. B. Yeats and the Spell of Irish History' (Chatterton Lecture, 1989), *Proceedings of the British Academy*, 75 (1989), 243–66 Rev. version pub. in *Paddy and Mr. Punch: Connections in Irish and English History* (London, 1993), 212–32.

—— *W. B. Yeats: A Life*, i: *The Apprentice Mage* (Oxford, 1997).

Daniel A. Harris, *Yeats, Coole Park and Ballylee* (Baltimore, 1974).

John Harwood, *Olivia Shakespear and W. B. Yeats: After Long Silence* (London, 1989).

Seamus Heaney, 'Yeats as an Example?', in his *Preoccupations: Selected Prose 1968–1978* (London, 1980), 98–114.

A. Norman Jeffares, *W. B. Yeats: A New Biography* (London, 1988).

Hugh Kenner, 'The Sacred Book of the Arts' (1955; repr. in Unterecker, *Yeats*, 10–22).

Frank Kermode, *Romantic Image* (London, 1957).

Declan Kiberd, 'Revolt into Style: Yeatsian Poetics', and 'The Last *Aisling: A Vision*', in his *Inventing Ireland: The Literature of the Modern Nation* (London, 1995), 305–15, 316–26.

Frank Kinahan, *Yeats, Folklore, and Occultism: Contexts of the Early Work and Thought* (Boston, 1988).

Edward Larrissy, *W. B. Yeats*, Writers and Their Work (Plymouth, 1998).

—— *Yeats the Poet: The Measures of Difference* (Hemel Hempstead, 1994).

David Lloyd, 'The Poetics of Politics: Yeats and the Founding of the State', in his *Anomalous States: Irish Writing and the Post-Colonial Moment* (Durham, 1993), 59–87.

Steven Matthews, *Yeats as Precursor: Readings in Irish, British and American Poetry* (Basingstoke, 2000).

W. J. McCormack, 'Yeats and the Invention of Tradition', in his *From Burke to Beckett: Ascendancy, Tradition and Betrayal in Literary History* (Cork, 1994), 302–40.

Conor Cruise O'Brien, 'Passion and Cunning: An Essay on the Politics of W. B. Yeats', in A. Norman Jeffares and K. G. W. Cross (eds.), *In Excited Reverie* (London, 1965), 207–78.

Marjorie Perloff, *Rhyme and Meaning in the Poetry of Yeats* (The Hague, 1970).

David Pierce, *Yeats's Worlds* (New Haven, 1995).

——, (ed.) *W. B. Yeats: Critical Assessments*, 4 vols (Mountfield, 2000).

Kathleen Raine, *Yeats the Initiate: Essays on Certain Themes in the Work of W. B. Yeats* (Dublin, 1986).

Jahan Ramazani, *Yeats and the Poetry of Death: Elegy, Self-elegy and the Sublime* (New Haven, 1990).

Edward Said, 'Yeats and Decolonization', *Culture and Imperialism* (London, 1994), 265–88.

Stan Smith, *W. B. Yeats: A Critical Introduction* (London, 1990).

Jon Stallworthy, *Between the Lines: W. B. Yeats's Poetry in the Making*, 2nd, corrected, impression (Oxford, 1965).

John Unterecker (ed.), *Yeats: A Collection of Critical Essays* (Englewood Cliffs, NJ, 1963).

THE GOLDEN DAWN

R. A. Gilbert (ed.), *The Magical Mason: Forgotten Hermetic Writings of W. W. Westcott* (Wellingborough, 1983).

George Mills Harper, *Yeats's Golden Dawn* (London, 1974).

Ellic Howe, *The Magicians of The Golden Dawn: A Documentary History of a Magical Order, 1887–1923* (London, 1972).

Israel Regardie, *The Golden Dawn: An Account of the Teachings, Rites and Ceremonies* (St Paul, Minn., 1978).

William Wynn Westcott, *In Memory of Robert Fludd* (London, 1907).

JOURNALS

There are two important journals devoted to the study of W. B. Yeats. One is *Yeats: An Annual of Critical and Textual Studies*, edited by Richard J. Finneran from 1983 onwards. The other is *Yeats Annual*, also founded by Richard J. Finneran, who edited the first two volumes (1982 and 1983). Since 1985 it has been edited by Warwick Gould.

INDEX OF TITLES OF POEMS

INDEX OF FIRST LINES OF POEMS